Yizkor Book of Our Birth Place: Bendery (Bender, Moldova)

Translation of
Kehilat Bendery; Sefer Zikaron

In the Original Yizkor Book
Yiddish and Hebrew Sections Edited by M. Tamari
English Section Editor: Dina Ginton

Originally published by
Bendery Societies in Israel and the United States 1975
(Hebrew, Yiddish, English, 488 pages)

Editor of the English Translation: Gloria (Schwartzman) Green

Published by JewishGen

An Affiliate of the Museum of Jewish Heritage - A Living Memorial to the Holocaust
New York

Bendery Community Yizkor Book - (Bender, Moldova)
Translation *of Kehilat Bendery; Sefer Zikaron*

Copyright © 2017 by JewishGen, Inc.
All rights reserved.
First Printing: October 2017, Tishrei 5778
Second Printing: March 2019, Adar II 5779

Translation Project Coordinator and Editor: Gloria (Schwartzman) Green
Translated from Hebrew by: Ala Gamulka
Translated from Yiddish by Ala Gamulka with assistance of Larry Gamulka
Layout: Sheldon Lipsky , Lynn Mercer and Joel Alpert
Cover Design: Rachel Kolokoff Hopper

This book may not be reproduced, in whole or in part, including illustrations in any form (beyond that copying permitted by Sections 107 and 108 of the U.S. Copyright Law and except by reviewers for public press), without written permission from the publisher.

Published by JewishGen, Inc.
An Affiliate of the Museum of Jewish Heritage
A Living Memorial to the Holocaust
36 Battery Place, New York, NY 10280

"JewishGen, Inc. is not responsible for inaccuracies or omissions in the original work and makes no representations regarding the accuracy of this translation. Digital images of the original book's contents can be seen online at the New York Public Library Web site."

The mission of the JewishGen organization is to produce a translation of the original work and we cannot verify the accuracy of statements or alter facts cited.

Printed in the United States of America by Lightning Source, Inc.

Library of Congress Control Number (LCCN): 2016944514
ISBN: 978-1-939561-60-2 (hard cover: 722 pages, alk. paper)

Cover photographs: from photographs of the original Yizkor book

JewishGen and the Yizkor-Books-in-Print Project

This book has been published by the **Yizkor-Books-in-Print Project,** as part of the **Yizkor Book Project** of **JewishGen, Inc**.

JewishGen, Inc. is a non-profit organization founded in 1987 as a resource for Jewish genealogy. Its website [www.jewishgen.org] serves as an international clearinghouse and resource center to assist individuals who are researching the history of their Jewish families and the places where they lived. JewishGen provides databases, facilitates discussion groups, and coordinates projects relating to Jewish genealogy and the history of the Jewish people. In 2003, JewishGen became an affiliate of the **Museum of Jewish Heritage - A Living Memorial to the Holocaust** in New York.

The **JewishGen Yizkor Book Project** was organized to make more widely known the existence of Yizkor (Memorial) Books written by survivors and former residents of various Jewish communities throughout the world. Later, volunteers connected to the different destroyed communities began cooperating to have these books translated from the original language—usually Hebrew or Yiddish—into English, thus enabling a wider audience to have access to the valuable information contained within them. As each chapter of these books was translated, it was posted on the JewishGen website and made available to the general public.

The **Yizkor-Books-in-Print Project** began in 2011 as an initiative to print and publish Yizkor Books that had been fully translated, so that hard copies would be available for purchase by the descendants of these communities and also by scholars, universities, synagogues, libraries, and museums.

These Yizkor books have been produced almost entirely through the volunteer effort of researchers from around the world, assisted by donations from private individuals. The books are printed and sold at near cost, so as to make them as affordable as possible. Our goal is to make this important genre of Jewish literature and history available in English in book form, so that people can have the personal histories of their ancestral towns on their bookshelves for themselves and for their children and grandchildren.

A list of all published translated Yizkor Books in the project with prices and ordering information can be found at:
http://www.jewishgen.org/Yizkor/ybip.html

Lance Ackerfeld, Yizkor Book Project Manager

Joel Alpert, Yizkor-Book-in-Print Project Coordinator

This book is presented by the
Yizkor Books in Print Project
Project Coordinator: Joel Alpert

Part of the
Yizkor Books Project of JewishGen, Inc.
Project Manager: Lance Ackerfeld

These books have been produced solely through volunteer effort of individuals from around the world. The books are printed and sold at near cost, so as to make them as affordable as possible.

Our goal is to make this history and important genre of Jewish literature available in English in book form so that people can have the near-personal histories of their ancestral towns on their bookshelves for themselves and for their children and grandchildren.

Any donations to the Yizkor Books Project are appreciated.

Please send donations to:
Yizkor Book Project
JewishGen
36 Battery Place
New York, NY 10280

JewishGen, Inc. is an affiliate of the
Museum of Jewish Heritage
A Living Memorial to the Holocaust

Acknowledgements for the Publication of the Translation

It is with great gratitude that I thank Ala Gamulka for her diligent efforts in completing this translation. Her husband, Larry, assisted with the Yiddish translations. My part in formatting, editing, scanning photos, etc., is minor in comparison. Thank you also to Shimon Joffe who translated the Table of Contents early on. Lance Ackerfeld, Yizkor Book Project Manager for JewishGen since 2009, gave me the encouragement needed to take on this project. He worked with me seamlessly, as I transferred material to him which ended up in HTML format, accessible to all on the JewishGen.org website. I only recently discovered that Lance is not at some office desk in the States – he lives with his family on a kibbutz in Northern Israel! Thank you also to Yefim Kogan, Coordinator of JG's Bessarabian SIG, for providing the Summary History of Bendery. As further proof of the value of JewishGen.org – it is through JewishGen projects that Ala Gamulka and Yefim Kogan discovered they are cousins!

Ala and I were delighted to get a heads up from Joel Alpert, Project Coordinator for Yizkor Books in Print, that the Bendery Yizkor Book was picked to be the next to go into print. Thank you so much, Joel, for broadening the accessibility of this book. It is thrilling to know that the once vibrant, caring, Bendery Jewish community will live on through these pages.

Special thanks to the National Yiddish Book Center in Amherst, Massachusetts and the New York Public Library for supplying the high resolution images used in this book.

Gloria (Schwartzman) Green

FOREWORD FOR THE TRANSLATION

Gloria Green, Translation Project Coordinator
Daughter of Jacob Moses Schwartzman
Granddaughter of Ephraim (Froim) and Hinda Schwartzman
Great granddaughter of Jacob Schwartzman and Tillie Spiwack Schwartzman

Count me among the legions who failed to ask a parent their family history while they were still living. I was only 22 when my father, the former Jacob Moses Schwartzman, died in 1966 – and of course too young to have thought to ask him in depth about his childhood before he came to America. My father had told us kids that he had walked from his home in Bendery, Bessarabia, to the port in Bremen, Germany to catch the ship to America when he was 18 years old. Beyond that, I knew virtually nothing about his life in Bendery. How does a young man with a third grade education have the drive to walk across Europe, then within three years bring his mother and three sisters to America, and then, as Giacomo Bernardi, become an opera singer and then impresario in Cleveland for nearly 40 years?

Ten years ago, nearing retirement, I began to seriously research my family history. The first thing I found was the ship manifest on EllisIsland.org for my father's arrival in 1906. The manifest indicated his passage to America was paid by "Uncle Leo Lerner." Googling Leo Lerner, I found that he was the Founder and President of the Federation of Bessarabian Jews in America. The Association's stated purpose was to establish an orphanage for homeless young Jewish orphan boys roaming the Lower East Side of New York City. I discovered Uncle Leo's wife was Rose Schwartz Lerner, and that they had married in Bendery. Aunt Rose was the direct family connection to my father, Jacob Schwartzman. From her death certificate, I learned her father was also named Jacob Schwartzman. The conclusion: Rose's father and my father's grandfather were one and the same.

My husband, in his eagerness to help me with my research, placed a request on eBay to be alerted when anything related to Bendery was listed for sale. A few months later, he got an alert about a book about Bendery. David paid the "Buy It Now" price and about six weeks later the book arrived in our mail, having been shipped from Israel! Unfortunately, only a few chapters of the book were in English. The rest were in Hebrew (or so I thought: actually, half were in Hebrew, half Yiddish).

Eugenia, a dear friend able to read but not understand Hebrew, kindly offered to look through the book for any references to "Schwartzman." There were plenty – but all related to the illustrious founder of the Hebrew High School in Bendery, Zvi Schwartzman, who arrived in Bendery some years after my father and the rest of his family departed. Eugenia informed me that *Bendery* was a "Yizkor" – Memorial book – and that other such books could be found on the Jewishgen.org's website.

Curious about what more the book had to say about life in Bendery, I reached out to the Jewish genealogists and researchers listed on the JewishGen Family Finder (JGFF) tool who were looking for family surnames in Bendery, to see if any would be willing/able to translate the book. After sending out inquiries to about a dozen of those listed, I got a bite!

July 19, 2009, was my lucky day when Ala Gamulka (Alexandra Tulchinsky Gamulka) wrote back her interest in taking on the translation of the Bendery Yizkor book. She also said "If you have other volunteers, let them begin towards the middle." Little did she know that she alone (with the assistance of her husband, Larry, in the Yiddish portions) would end up translating "the whole Megillah" – and, that it would take years to complete the task. As Ala wrote to me, "The interesting part about Bendery is that my maternal grandmother was born there while my father from Tiraspol across the river) attended high school there as well. My parents did not meet and marry till many years later in Bucharest. One of my cousins was on the editorial board of the (Bendery) Yizkor book." Over the past 8 years, Ala has generously given of her time to translate many additional projects for JewishGen, including *Rokitno Yizkor Book*, the Tarutino portion of the *Akkerman Yizkor Book*, and 34 articles from *Encyclopedia of Jewish Communities in Romania*.

While my father's family was nowhere to be found in the original book (till now, hooray – see the heading to the Preface!), from the descriptions of the vibrant culture of the Jewish residents of Bendery, I was able to gain an understanding of where he derived his passion for music and farm fresh food. Bendery was a close, loyal and caring, agriculturally rich community which held together through thick and thin through the decades. I learned about the many prominent citizens who went on to make Aliyah and lead successful lives in Israel. From the amusing anecdotes – the annually muddy streets after the winter snows melted when you could pay a man to carry you across the street – to the diary of the Rabbi who writes of the tragic progression of the Holocaust horrors as played out in Bendery, there is much to be savored and learned about Jewish life in the community.

In 2013, I had the privilege of being able to visit Bendery through the kindness of a friend whose mother had kept her apartment in Kishinev, the Capital of Moldova, and invited me to visit. Travelling by taxi from Kishinev to Odessa, Ukraine, then through Tiraspol to Bendery by streetcar, it was possible to compare the disparate cultures of those four cities under the starkly different current political climate for each.

While in Odessa, I visited the Holocaust Museum, where one of the displays explained the horrors that befell Jews who had not fled from Bendery by the 1940s. By stark contrast, in Bendery, at the Natural and

History Museum of Bendery, there was no trace to be found of the Jewish culture that once thrived in Bendery, and no mention of the fate of Bendery Jews at the hands of the locals, the Romanians, Germans and Russians. The Jewish population in 2013 was under 1,000, mostly elderly women who had not made Aliyah, down from over 10,000 Jews when my father left in 1906. Having made that trip, I realized how important the Bendery Yizkor book is, both to revive the names of many of the Jewish people who had once lived there, and to bring back to life their culture and way of life.

History of Jews in Bendery

A port city on the Dniester River, Bendery's name changed depending on what government ruled the region. While Russians called it Bendery and Romanians called it Tighina, the Jews always called it Bender.

Bendery was a vassal of the Ottoman Empire in the Principality of Moldavia from 1538 to 1812. From 1812 to 1917, it was under the Russian Empire as part of the Bessarabia Governorate, and from 1918 to 1940, it was part of the Kingdom of Romania. From 1940-1941 and from 1944-1991, it was part of the Moldova Soviet Socialist Republic. In between those years, from 1941-1944 during World War II, it was under German-Romanian occupation. Since 1992, it is located in a buffer zone of the self-proclaimed Transnistria Republic, which broke away from the Republic of Moldova.

Jews settled in Bendery its surrounding district in the 18th century or before. First records about a Jewish presence in Bendery are from 1769. In 1770 the first synagogue was built within the town fortress. During the Soviet time, the army battalion located in that fortress.

1808	101 Jewish families	
1816	500 families, 6.4% of total population	
1847	553 families	
1857	3,929 Jews	
1897	10,644 Jews from total population of 31,797	
1910	9,937 Jews, 34.5% of total	11 synagogues
1930	8,294 Jews from total of 31,384	31 synagogues
1959	5,986 Jews	1 synagogue
1989	4,595 Jews	1 synagogue
1997	919 Jews	1 synagogue
2004	383 Jews	1 synagogue

There are several small communities not far from Bendery with significant Jewish presence:

Tiraspol (9 miles), 8659 Jews in 1897, 6398 Jews in 1930
Causeni (13 miles), 1675 Jews in 1897, 1870 Jews in 1930
Petrovka (20 miles), 611 Jews in 1897

A Jewish hospital with a pharmacy, and a residence for the elderly opened in Bendery 1884. In 1912, there were two Talmud Torahs, 20 heders, a government secondary school for boys and a private secondary school for girls. Zionist parties had a strong following in Bendery, and many Jews left town for Palestine.

During the Romanian period from 1918-1940, the Romanians launched a policy of Romanization, and Russian language was restricted. Many Jews were communists and socialists. They were organized in groups to promote leftist literature from the Soviet Union. At the end of the 1930s, fascists were coming to power in Romania. On June 28, 1940 the Soviet army entered Bessarabia. Most Jews were glad at first that the Soviets had arrived and welcomed the Soviet Army. But there were many wealthy Jews, merchants and property owners, large gardens, etc., who were taken away by NKVD and sent to Siberia or to the far North. Most of them died – never to return.

June 22, 1941, Nazi Germany invaded the Soviet Union under the codename Operation "Barbarossa." In July of 1941 Romanian and German troops retook Bendery. Jews who had not been evacuated to the East of the USSR were killed in their own towns (often with the assistance of locals), or when relocated to Transnistria.

Bendery is now part of the non-recognized Republic of Transnistria. Some suburbs of Bendery are under Moldovan control, others are in Transnistria. According to the census of 2004, there are 383 Jews living in Bendery. There is a Sunday Jewish School, a youth club, library, a synagogue, and a charity center "Hesed Yosef."

See more at the following articles:
http://www.yivoencyclopedia.org/article.aspx/Tighina and
https://en.wikipedia.org/wiki/Bender,_Moldova and also at Bendery

KehilaLinks website:
http://kehilalinks.jewishgen.org/bender/bendery.html

Jewish Genealogy

Bendery is very fortunate that a variety of different records are available for the Jewish population in the 19th and 20th centuries.

Birth Records:*

Year	Number of records
1866	156
1871	167
1874	167
1876	174
1877	102
1877	59
1878	189
1879	20
1880	414
1881	264
1883	240
1899	54
1902	90
1908	22
1911	20

Marriages:

Year	Number of Records
1873	65
1874	30
1887	15

Divorces:

Year	Number of Records
1890	30

Revision Lists (Individuals Subject to Taxation):

Year	Estate/Class	Number of Records	Number of Families
1848	Middle Class	2,509	421
1848	Merchants	390	27
1848	Middle Class, Merchants/Additional	193	46
1854	Merchants	736	56
1854	Middle Class	388	47
1854	Middle Class/ continue from 2373291	2,353	379
1855-1857, 1869, 1873-75	Middle Class/ Additional	65	13
1850-1852	Additional, Military	133	44

Business Records:

1901 – 32 Jewish businesses. Source: 1901 *Klyachkin All Russia Business Directory*

1924 – 569 Jewish businesses. In the Bendery district – 1220. *Bessarabia Business Directory*, 1924-1925

To search and find records for the residents of Bendery, go to www.JewishGen.org. The many Family Stories, Family Trees, Travel Reports and more related to Bendery can also be found at the Bessarabia SIG website: www.jewishgen.org/bessarabia.

*Some records have yet to be translated, but most are translated and available at JewishGen.org.

Jewish Cemeteries in Bendery

The Old Jewish Cemetery in Bendery "Caucasus" was destroyed in the 1960s and garages were built over it. There is a monument in the existing Jewish cemetery where some remains from the old cemetery were reburied.

The existing Jewish Cemetery is one of the better preserved cemeteries in the whole Bessarabia/Moldova region. Bessarabia SIG completed photographing and indexing the cemetery, and now the index and photos are part of JOWBR with 5,110 burial records and 4,530 photos. In addition, there are 872 photos of Unknown Graves at Bendery cemetery. The Bendery Cemetery Report includes an exact location, maps of sections of the cemetery, 872 photos of all Unknown Graves, and a number of overview photos from the cemetery, including the beautiful gates. There are also a number of monuments commemorating mass killings of Jews: 714 Jews brutally killed April 5, 1917, and Jews killed by German fascists July-September 1941. The Bendery Cemetery report is available at Bessarabia SIG website or directly at

https://www.jewishgen.org/Bessarabia/files/cemetery/Bendery/BenderyCemeteryReport.pdf.

My Personal Story
By Yefim Kogan

Before World War II, my parents and many relatives used to live not far from Bendery (13 miles to the south), in a place they called Kaushany, and now known as Causeni. Some relatives who lost their jobs moved to Bendery in the beginning of the 20th century, others moved to Bendery after returning from fronts of World War II or from evacuation. I also know from the stories of my mother, Khinka Kogan (Spivak), that Bendery was a place where many women from smaller places would go to get a new dress before the Fall Jewish holidays, including my grandmother Elka Kogan. Many named her a "Modern Woman" for her wonderful new dresses. Some Jews would go to Bendery to attend a concert of a well-known Jewish theater group, or performer, like Sidi Tal, or others. Read more stories from 1930-1940s at the KehilaLinks Kaushany website: https://kehilalinks.jewishgen.org/Causeni/Kaushany.htm.

My father, Abram Kogan, after graduating from gymnasium in Kaushany, went to Bendery Commercial School to continue his education.

Yefim Kogan

JewishGen.Org Bessarabia SIG Leader and Coordinator

Notes to the Reader:

Within the text the reader will note "{34}" standing ahead of a paragraph. This indicates that the material translated below was on page 34 of the original book. However, when a paragraph was split between two pages in the original book, the marker is placed in this book after the end of the paragraph for ease of reading.

Also please note that all references within the text of the book to page numbers, refer to the page numbers of the original Yizkor Book.

The original book can be seen online at the Yiddish Book Center web site:

http://www.yiddishbookcenter.org/collections/yizkor-books/yzk-nybc313687/kehilat-benderi-sefer-zikaron

In order to obtain a list of all Shoah victims from Bender, the reader should access the Yad Vashem web site listed below; one can also search for specific family names using family name option. These lists are continually updated by Yad Vashem, so it is worthwhile to periodically search these lists.

There is much valuable information available on this web site, including the Pages of Testimony, etc.

http://yvng.yadvashem.org

A list of this book and all books available in the Yizkor-Book-In-Print Project along with prices is available at:

http://www.jewishgen.org/Yizkor/ybip.html

Geopolitical Information:

Bender, Moldova: 46°50' North Latitude, 29°27' East Longitude

Alternate names: Bendery [Russian], Bender [Yiddish, German, Turkish], Tighina [Romanian], Benderî, Tehinia, Tigina, Tiginia

Region: Bessarabia

	Town	District	Province	Country
Before WWI (c. 1900):	Bendery	Bendery	Bessarabia	Russian Empire
Between the wars (c. 1930):	Tighina	Tighina	Basarabia	Romania
After WWII (c. 1950):	Bender			Soviet Union

Jewish Population in 1900: 10,654 (in 1897), 8,294 (1930)

Russian: Бендеры.
Moldovan: Тигина.
Ukrainian: Бендери.
Yiddish: טיגינא, בענדער

In SE Moldova, on the Dniester, 31 miles ESE of Chişinău (Kishinev), 9 miles W of Tiraspol.

Nearby Jewish Communities:
- Tiraspol 9 miles E
- Copanca 11 miles SE
- Căuşeni 13 miles S
- Slobozia 14 miles ESE
- Petrovca 20 miles WNW
- Corjova 23 miles NW
- Grigoriopol 23 miles NNW
- Velyka Mykhaylivka, Ukraine 26 miles NE
- Lisne, Ukraine 26 miles S
- Răzeni 26 miles W
- Rozdilna, Ukraine 30 miles E
- Criuleni 30 miles NNW

Map of Bender in Moldova

By Jan Fine

Hebrew Title Page of Original Yizkor Book

קְהִלַת בֶּנְדֶרִי

סֵפֶר זִכָּרוֹן

ערך :

מ. תמרי

הוצאת ועד יוצאי בנדרי בישראל
בהשתתפות יוצאי בנדרי בארצות־הברית
ה׳תשל״ה — תל־אביב — 1975

Translation of the Title Page of Original Yizkor Book

Bendery Community Yizkor Book
(Bender, Moldova)

Editor:
M. Tamari

Published by Bendery Societies in Israel and the United States

Tel Aviv, 1975

BENDERY COMMUNITY YIZKOR BOOK

Editor: M. Tamari

**Published by the Committee of Bendery Immigrants in Israel
With the participation of the Bendery immigrants in the USA, Tel Aviv -1975**

Editorial Committee
(in alphabetical order)

In Israel: Pinchas Bendersky; Attorney Meir Greenberg, z"l; Zalman Drowetzky; Chanania Walowetz; Abraham Hayat; Mordechai Sever; Yitzchak Sverdlik; Yoseph Raviv (Rabinowitz)
*
In the USA; Leon Gurfel; David Carmel; Yakov Fein.
*

The Israeli committee, meeting on the 26 December, 1974, expressed its appreciation and thanks to PINCHAS BENDERSKY for his devoted work connected with the publication of this book.
*

The material in the book-photos, documents and lists, were collected from archives, libraries, science and remembrance institutes, and from individuals in Israel and abroad by Mordechai Sever. The map at the beginning of the book was redrawn from an old version by Mordechai Sever.

Table of Contents

Translated by Shimon Joffe

M. Tamari: The Book	1
Pinchas Bendersky: Generation to Generation speaks	4

HISTORY OF THE CITY (from the encyclopedia) — 61

Fortress and County Seat	61
At the end of the previous century	62
In the Margins of "Hamelitz"	72
Greeting cards	74

BETWEEN TWO WORLD WARS

Bella Shreibman-Rab: Jews between the citadel and the bridge	77
Nachman Lavonsky: Days gone by	80
Shevach (Sioma) Blei: Days of war and revolution	86
Michael Landau: Gone, my beloved brothers	89
Arieh Shreibman: In a sailing boat on a stormy sea	93
Shmuel Giboa: My life in Bendery	96

HASSIDISM IN BENDERY

N. Huberman: Bendery in Hassidic literature	111
Yonah Balaban (Hulda): Rabbi Moishele and His Hassidim	114

THE SECOND ALIYAH

Rivka Machneimy (Cholodenko): In the days of the Second Aliyah	116

THE SHWARTZMAN HIGH SCHOOL

Batia Steiner-Faigenbaum: The Kindergarten in the Schwartzman High School	136
Leah Steiner: The High School day by day and in moments of spiritual uplift	139
Nachman Levonsky: The Tarbut School, which did not survive long	143

YOUTH MOVEMENTS

Sonia Etlis: The Maccabi League	144
Yitzhak Sverdlik: Years of Expansion	146
Baruch Kaushansky: Preparation for Aliyah to Eretz Israel	149

Meri Horodetzky: Hashomer Hatzair	151
Pinchas Ben Shaul (Pinko): Hashomer Hatzair Among the First Movements	157
Yonah Balaban: Gordonia Movement	160
Moshe Horovitz And Mordechai Frank: The Beitar Youth Movement	165

THE CITY AND ITS INHABITANTS

Haim Raday: A Branch to Two Trunks	170
Leah Steiner: The Last Survivor of the Holy Man's Family	179
Mordechai Sever: Reminiscences of My Father's House	182
Leah Bat Chaya and Bezalel: A Childhood Affront	195
Leah Bat Chaya and Bezalel: My Father Reb Bezalel, the Cantor and the Talner Synagogue	197
Katya Shay (Fein): Memory Fragments of Days Gone By	200
Abba Sapir (Shaposnick): My Father's House – Open To All	203
Yehiel Efrati: Ordinary Folk Caught in Reality	204
Leah Steiner: Road of Suffering	207
Leah Steiner: My Bendery	209
Leah Steiner: Yehiel the Cobbler Teaches Me Zionism	211
Leah Bat Haya: The Intellectual Gentleman (on D.A.Natanzon)	214

IN THE FUROR OF THE SHOAH

Rabbi Shimon Efrati: From The Diary of a Wanderer	216
Zvi (Gersh) Sobol: Testament	234
Mira Geva: The Valley of The Slaughter Near The Fortress	236
Dr. T. Lavi–Levinstein: The Tighina Agreement and the Expulsion to Transnistria	237
Meir Grinberg: Bendery after the destruction	241
Rabbi Shmuel Bronfman: After the Shoah	246
Shmuel Delmetzky: Upon the Graves of Our Ancestors	254

PERSONAE

I.L. Toibman [Yonatan]: The Wertheim Dynasty	257
I.L. Toibman [Yonatan]: Reb Yossele Wertheim	269
Dr. Shlomo Bendersky	272
David Abramovich Natanzon	274
Dr. Baruch Nissenboim	276
Rabbi Efraim Drebrimdiker	278
Avraham Alexandrov	280
Baruch Holodenko	281
Dr. Alexander Khain	284
David Prozhansky	287
Hersh Kogan [Zvi Cohen]	290
Dr. Zvi Schwartzman	292
Zelig Sofer	295

Yaakov Shveidky	299
Avraham Wertheim	301
David Wertheim	303
Aryeh–Leib and Nadia Blank	305
Israel Blank	307
Noah Lifshitz	307
Hanina Krachevsky	311
Haya Glass	314
Yitzhak Reznikov	317
Dr. P. Yaroslavsky	319

THE THIRD ALIYAH

Yoseph Raviv: Bendery in the Past and Under the Soviet Regime	320
David Weiser: Signposts to Eretz Israel	326
Leah Shteiner: On a New Road	332
Leah Shteiner: The Saga of the Shrybmans–Sweetness out of Bitterness	335
David Carmel: Miracles at Sea	338

ROOTS IN THE HOMELAND

Rivka Davidit: Crabgrass	341
Eitan Haber: An Old Fighter in a New Role	345
Mordehai Sever: Echo Sounds	347
D. Ben Yehiel: Our Aunt Leah	348

LANDSCAPE AND BEING

Yaakov Fichman: Bessarabia (poem)	351
Mordehai (ben Moshe) Sever: Figures and Shadows Which Have Disappeared	352
A. Bauch: The Little Boy from the Ghetto	360
Rivka (Riva) Terer–Drobetsky: Recollections From Jerusalem of the 1920s	371
I. Gabbai: Simcha Tzehovel	375
Israel Gur: Tzehovel and His Roles	377
Y. Manik: Deep in Autumn Nights (poem)	379
Dr. Yosef Kruk: The Wertheim Family in the Real World	381
Yosef Shapira: Big Hearted David Wertheim	385
Mordehai Sever: Rabbi Eli the Ritual Slaughterer, Z"L – A Scholar and a Genius	387
Moshe Sever (Sverdlik): The Influence of the Synagogues	393
Moshe Sever (Sverdlik): A Proposal to Fund a Pension Fund Fifty Years Ago	396
The Activities of ORT and OZE	398

CONTENTS
(in Yiddish)

REMINISCENCES AND HISTORIC REFLECTIONS

Avraham Hayat: Bendery – My Hometown	400
David Carmel: Our Town	412
Itzik Manger: At The Dniester	427
Leon Garfield: Bendery as Seen in History	428

RELIGIOUS, SOCIAL AND CULTURAL LIFE

Prof. Yitzhak Fein: A City of Belief and Conspiracies	433
Leon (Yehuda–Leib) Garfield: In Changing Times	441
Yitzhak Abramovitch: Poem	458
Rabbi Dr. Aaron Wertheim: Memoirs from the Bendery Rabbinate	460
I.L. Yonatan: Bessarabian Zionist Activists Crusade	466
Hanania Volovetz: Ezrat Ani'im Charity	468
I.Manik (Lederman) z"l: The Teachers Street	470
I.Manik (Lederman) z"l: Diarde's Pay (poem)	472
Leon (Yehuda–Leib) Garfield: Poalei Zion in Bendery	473
Leon (Yehuda–Leib) Garfield: The Cultural League	478
Shmaria Hrushtesh: We Acted In The Theatre?	481
David Carmel: The Writer Rivka Davidit, z"l	484
I.Manik (Lederman) z"l: Now It Happens (poem)	485
Yosef Schwartzman z"l: Hazamir	486
Yaakov Fein: The Founding and the Activities of Maccabi	488
Yekhezkel Bronstein: The Poet Yehoshua Manik (Lederman)	490
I.Manik (Lederman) z"l: Ben Zion Shochat (poem)	495
I.Manik (Lederman) z"l: Father Sings a Folk Tune	496
Israel Rabinovitch: Thoughts For the Fifteenth of Shvat	498
Abraham Hayat: Mother	500
I.Manik (Lederman) z"l: Rabbi Moshe Sever	501
Mordechai Sever: Hear, Brother, Hear…	504
Two Generations in Public Life	505

FROM THE JEWISH PRESS

News From Bendery	507
In the Predicament of Need …	513
Memorial Service for the Riot Victims in Eretz Israel	518

OCCUPATION AND HOLOCAUST

David Wertheim, Z"L	523
Avraham Wertheim, Z"L	524
Women's Organizations in Bendery	525
"Women's Association" Bendery (Tighina) – 1931	526
Rabbi Israel Bronfman: Bendery After the Shoah	528
B. Levi: In Those Dark Days…	532
Miller David: Testimony of a Witness	533
Y. Manik (Lederman): Deep in the Autumn Night	538
Yehuda–Leib Garfield: In Your Blood Shall You Live	539
Yehuda–Leib, son of David, Halevi: The Bendery Society	543
Bessarabian Jews Intensively Construct a Building in Israel	544
The Progressive Bendery Benevolent Society	546
P.Bendersky: Afterword	547

English Section

David Carmel: Bendery	550
Memorial Candles	570
Errata	681

Family Notes

[Page 5]

The Book
M. Tamari
Translated by Ala Gamulka

The catastrophe which descended on European Jewry destroyed thousands of established Jewish communities. Some of them were of over a thousand years standing. The Jewish residents were uprooted and sent to exile or annihilation. A unique literature was the outgrowth of the upheaval. It is unparalleled in any other nation or language. I refer to memoirs, memorials and mourning scrolls in the form of Yizkor books. This is the way in which over four hundred Jewish communities sought solace by describing their past, especially that of the past two decades, by erecting monuments to their fellow citizens and their family. They wanted to ensure that they would not be forgotten and that future generations will be told about their predecessors and their history.

These enormous projects were prepared by collecting, verifying, selecting and publishing with unimagined diligence and dedication. They contain documents and descriptions amassed for thirty years. They are important not only for the continuity of the People of Israel, but also for the rest of mankind.

The time came for the Community of Bendery – maybe one of the last ones- to bear witness and to add to this magnificent and tragic story.

Bendery was situated on the right bank of the Dniester River, across from Tiraspol in Podolia, in the Province of Bessarabia (Moldova). For several hundred years, Bessarabia changed hands (Turkey, Russia, Romania, Nazi occupation, Soviet annexation). The Province lies between the Dniester and the Prot Rivers. It was called Tighina during the Romanian occupation and Bender or Tighin in ancient documents. It lies northwest of Odessa and close to Kishinev, the capital. Until the end of World War I Bendery was part of Tsarist Russia. It was then annexed by Romania. Its fate was decided and its image formed during the twenties and the thirties of the Twentieth century. During the Holocaust the community was destroyed and its Jewish citizens were among those exiled to the other side of the Dniester.

According to research (done by Dr. T. Lavi-Levinstein and M.Karp in the "Black Book"- written in Romanian and stored in Yad Vashem) a pact was signed on August 30 1941 in Bendery. This was the infamous "Tighina Pact" dealing with ethnic cleansing, exile and transfer of population for so-called economic reasons to camps in Ukraine, on the other side of the Dniester. This is how the term Transnistra was coined. (Proof that this pact could not have been achieved without the active involvement of Romania can be seen in the speech of the Vice Prime Minister, Mihai Antonescu, given on July 3, 1941).

The image of Bendery was forged by its topography, the ethnic make-up of its population, the friendly neighbourly relations and mutual cultural influences, its extraordinary benevolence, strong Zionist beliefs and love of the Land of Israel, Russification and the terrible tragedies culminating in the Holocaust. Bendery was influenced by Kishinev and Odessa during its blossoming period and it deteriorated under the Romanian occupation between the two wars. These characteristics were preserved during the Soviet period and during the Holocaust. The reasons for this can be found –although there are not many-in documents and testimonies, descriptions and images of outstanding personalities and ordinary folk, public institutions, Heders, synagogues and academies, schools and libraries, youth movements and sports clubs, choirs and drama groups. They all contributed a great love for Jewish culture and tradition, the Land of Israel, Renaissance and pre-revolutionary Russian literature and culture.

Although there were cordial relations with the Christian community, the Jewish community of Bendery knew how to preserve its unique ethno-cultural entity. The survivors, whether they found their way to Israel or whether they remained in the Diaspora (mainly the United States), are those who bear witness by their activities in many public arenas. Their wounds have not healed yet and they present their memoirs in these pages.

In this book we planned to present a wide and colourful panorama of the scenery of Bendery, its daily life and customs, its Rabbis and community leaders and educators. These are authentic images of those who fulfilled their debt to society, sometimes in wealth, but mostly in poverty. They were genuinely happy, but they also suffered. The natives of Bendery filled an important part in the Aliyah movement, beginning with the second and third ones, in illegal immigration and in settling the land. They played important and useful roles in making the country flourish and in its defence. Even those who were scattered in the Diaspora, mainly the United States, held pivotal positions and keep in touch, to this day, with their former fellow townspeople. It is with their help that this book could be published.

The natives of Bendery felt a deep commitment to bequeath their tradition to future generations. Those who follow will know their roots and will learn about the personal courage in the daily life of ordinary people who put the welfare of others above their own needs. Poverty and lack of funds did not stop these souls from giving to others and from believing better times would come, until they were cut down by cruel deeds.

There are two sad sections in the book- the Holocaust and the Necrology of family members as described by the survivors. This is an unparalleled and unconditional duty. Charity towards a living human being can always be reciprocated. However, it cannot be done with those who are no longer alive, especially when it comes to a whole community. It has been thirty years since the terrible events and memories may have dimmed. It was necessary to concentrate and strain to collect details and descriptions and to sketch personalities in order not to forget.

There was a great deal of diverse material about normal life in the town. Unfortunately, much less remains of the period of the Holocaust- except for one authentic testimony and a description of the Concentration Camp in Transnistria. This is due to the fact that Romanian archives could not be easily researched. Some documents were lost in bombardments and others were deliberately destroyed by the Romanian Secret Service. Ironically, it is only in the German Archives that one can discover more information. The only authentic material can be found in the words of Dr. T. Lavi-Levinstein and in the "Black Book" by Matityahu Karp deposited in Yad Vashem. All other searches and inquiries in Yad Vashem proved fruitless except for the section "In the Furor of the Shoah" in this book. The representatives of the book met with Dr. T. Lavi-Levinstein in Yad Vashem and were guided by him as to what should be included. One must also pay special attention to the section 'From the Diary of a Wanderer'(written in Central Asia) brought to us by Rabbi Shimon Efrati. It is a detailed and profound document describing the Soviet occupation of Bendery.

This book is published with sincere thanks and emotion, a sense of responsibility and absolute knowledge that it is incomplete. Under normal circumstances the manuscript would have been properly rechecked. However, the sense of responsibility of the natives of Bendery propelled them not to delay any longer. They felt compelled to salvage what could be saved and they knew the importance of this project for them and for future generations. It is hoped that, another time, others will add and complete and perhaps find additional documentation. It is published thirty years after the Holocaust and is one of over four hundred such books- perhaps one of the last. Structurally, many destroyed communities may be similar, but there is always something in each book to differentiate it from the others. Its publication is thus justified. We believe that the community of Bendery – for reasons previously mentioned- was a special one. Even if the book is published later than the others, it describes what was unique about Bendery. If not in its entirety, then at least in some sections, it not only emphasises and strengthens those who preceded us, but it also contributes information.

M. TAMARI
January 1974
5 Tevet 5735

[Page 7]

Generation to Generation Speaks...
Pinhas Bendersky (Tel Aviv)
Translated by Ala Gamulka

A writer once said: our nation has a wonderful custom of visiting the graves of our dearly departed so that we may remember them and continue our traditions. This is referred to in Deuteronomy 32:7 as "Remember the days of yore, understand the years of generation after generation". That is why, perhaps, we are more inclined personally and publicly to have special memorial days, to write testimonials and to hold commemorative assemblies. After the Holocaust that befell our nation, our need to erect memorials to the now extinct communities intensified. We must preserve the values of previous generations lest we forget. We want to continue the connection between our ancestors and their spiritual and historic descendants. There must never be a break in the link. Truthfully, all the Jewish communities of Eastern Europe have disappeared and there are remnants of only a few of them. It is the sacred duty of the former residents of Bendery, Bessarabia, the few witnesses salvaged from the ashes, to build a permanent memorial to our town.

Bendery was a colourful and deeply-rooted community. It had both Yiddishkeit and assimilation. The atmosphere in our town at the end of the nineteenth century and beginning of the twentieth century permeated our childhood and youth. It shaped our generation. Our life was full of longing for perfection and lofty ideals, belief in creativity and in the genius of mankind.

It is not easy after so many tempestuous years to relive that atmosphere and to include in it the images of our parents, teachers, brothers and sisters. I will do my utmost to recollect our town and our community. In addition to the geographic description I found in the encyclopaedia, I will give personal memoirs and experiences.

*

The history of Bendery begins in the sixteenth century- as I discovered in various documents. At first it was called Tighini in the District of Moldavia, Province of Bessarabia. The name Bendery originates in the Turkish language and means "gate". It signifies the right bank of the Dniester River which springs in the Carpathian Mountains and flows into the Black Sea.

A fortress stood in the northern part of town. It was built in the fifteenth century by the Genovese people and was later conquered by the Moldavians. At the end of the sixteenth century the fortress was taken by the Turks. They extended the town in the seventeenth century, changed some structures and called it "Ben Dura". In 1709 King Karl XII of Sweden visited Bendery. After the Battle of Poltava and the Russo-Turkish War the town again belonged to the Turks. It was conquered three times by the Russians and was finally annexed by them in 1812.

In 1818 Bendery became the capital of the district. The fortress was renovated in a superb manner.

Tsar Alexander I- known in history as "Alexander the Good"- was a liberal-minded person. He tried to bring to Bendery a large number of Jews because he felt they were the only ones who could develop the area. He also believed them to be good material for Russification. Thus he granted them rights, special preferences and many discounts. They did not have to pay taxes or serve in the army. It is clear that this was a drawing card for Jews from other parts of Russia, Wallachia and Romania.

The census of 1918, supervised by the Zamstva-pre October 1917 local government- showed that there were 32, 000 residents in Bendery, including nearby Borisovka and Giska. (As a young man I participated in the census with my then- girlfriend, Yeva Tiomkin.) There were 10, 600 Jews (about one third of the total) and the rest were Katzaps (descendants of the Ruriks from White Russia- the founders of Russia), Malorussians, Moluccas (Russian Orthodox sect in Tsarist Russia), Armenians, Moldovans and Germans.

Schools for Boys and Girls

In Bendery there were two elementary schools for boys and two for girls. Some schools were mixed (Jewish and Christian) and some were for Christian students only. There were also a municipal post-elementary school and a four-year technical school. The technical school prepared workers and clerks for the railroad company. They were all run by the government.

In addition, there were high schools for girls. One was run by the government while two were private (Mrs. Boyko's and Mrs. Grassimenko's). Later a high school for boys was opened. It was named after Tsar Alexander I. There was also a science high school.

The leading Jews, fervently committed to Zionism, wanted to give their children a Jewish Zionist education. In 1909 they invited to Bendery one of the top Jewish pedagogues of the era- Zvi Ben Yaakov Schwartzman. He was famous for his devotion to the Zionist cause and was given the task of opening a Hebrew four-year high school. It included secular studies in Russian. Thus, Jewish children did not have to attend secular schools. Those schools adhered to "Numerus causus" (limited number of Jews accepted). This experiment opened a new window for the younger generation and united it with the Zionist movement.

Schwartzman belonged to the left wing of the Zionist movement and he tried to instill in the youngsters the ideals of the labor movement. He always chose as assistants those teachers who thought like him.

Among the teachers I particularly remember is Yonah Yakovlevitch Gogol. He was one of the leaders of Poalei Zion (Workers of Zion) within the Zionist movement in Russia. He reached Bendery as a soldier in the Podolian Regiment which camped in our town. While serving in the army he helped organize Poalei Zion in Bendery (in secret, of course). He was completely dedicated to the movement and he brought in many members. He left our town in 1910. During the 1917 Revolution he joined Ravotsky who was a member of the Ukrainian committee. It was headed by Skorepedsky who was an under-secretary for Jewish affairs in Ukraine. Gogol was imbued with idea of defence against the wave of disturbances and rioters. He managed to form a

Jewish brigade from among the Jewish soldiers serving in the Russian army. His fervent wish was for self-defence. Even while he was teaching at the school he explained the idea of self-defence. He felt Jews must accept it as one of the ideals of Zionism.

The Fortress

Indeed Gogol and the brigade he formed succeeded in teaching a lesson to the gangs of Ukrainian rioters running wild in those days. Until members of the committee decided to eliminate him and this is how our beloved teacher's life ended.

In 1918, after Bessarabia was separated from Russia and annexed by Romania*, evening classes for students and young adults were officially sanctioned by the government. This was in addition to the high schools available in town. These classes were open to those who were unable to attend regular schools and were held in Russian. The curriculum was similar to that of the regular schools. The evening classes were administered by Nikolai Fyodorovitch Boldir. The teachers were academics and among them we should remember Maria Ivanovna Ivanova who taught history. Her students greatly enjoyed her classes. She was one of the Revolutionary Progressives and included overtones of actual politics in her lessons. She thus created great interest.

After they completed these evening classes, many of the students were accepted in Romanian universities and were able to obtain their degrees.

Heders and "Talmud Torahs"

There were many heders for young children, followed by the teaching of Gmara. In town there were also two "Talmud Torahs"- elementary religious schools. The "Jewish" Talmud Torah was meant for the children of the poor who could not afford to pay tuition. They were taught Bible and some Gmara. The other- the "Russian" Talmud Torah included secular education in addition to prayers and Bible. The rest of the curriculum was the same as that of the government elementary schools and was under its supervision. Teachers had to be licensed by the government after attending a Teachers' College.

The philanthropist Velvel Rabinovitch donated these two schools to the Jewish community at the end of the nineteenth century.

The second Talmud Torah was administered by Yehoshua (son of Issar) Tiomkin. He was born in Lithuania and was a graduate of the Volozhin Yeshiva and the Russian government Teachers' College. He was also a dentist and practised for some years. Tiomkin was one of the first in town to be well-versed in Hebrew studies: Talmud, Bible and Religious subjects.

It was rare for people to speak Hebrew in those days. Although he was not fluent he was able to express himself, as we would today. His reputation preceded him and he was invited to Bendery by the government inspector and on recommendation by the intellectuals in town. Before he arrived in Bendery he worked closely with the late educator Avraham Avronin, the famous Hebrew linguist. Together they had opened a Hebrew high school in Priluki, Poltava. He was a devoted Jew, but he was quite involved in Russian culture in those days. He did not join the Zionist movement in spite of his fervent dream in later years to leave the Diaspora and to go to Eretz Israel. Unfortunately, for reasons out of his control, he could not achieve his dream and he died in Galatz. He was a proud Jew who never felt inferior to the non-Jews. He often quarrelled with the authorities or the inspectors. His home was conducted in the spirit of Russian culture, but there was much Jewish content.

On staff was Mr. Landris who taught Russian. He also came from Lithuania and had graduated from the government Teachers' College. Hebrew was taught by Mr. Lev- a great scholar. He left Bendery, moved to Odessa and was replaced by the late Noah Lifshitz- the first Hebrew teacher in town. Mr.

Tiomkin's dedication produced many students who continued their studies in institutions of higher learning. He selected the most talented students and tutored them during vacations. He did this because he was devoted to them and not for commendation. He also interceded on their behalf with the authorities. He worked hard to get them into these institutions. In those days teachers were true idealists.

The Jewish community became the guardians of this Talmud Torah. These were the intellectuals as well as the Russificators who believed in assimilation. One person who stands out was the pharmacist Vineshneker. These people leaned towards the Russian language and its influence, but Tiomkin opposed this radicalism. He would not allow the removal of the Jewish spirit from the school. Another was Yitzhak Nissenboim who was well-known for his kindness. He donated funds for a Jewish hospital for the poor. He also sponsored a department in the Talmud Torah to teach Jewish children a trade. He introduced machinery and tools in the school. Special teachers were hired. It was the first step in the formation of a trade school for Jewish children in Bendery.

Houses of Worship

There were twelve synagogues in our town. Five of them were small (Kloiz), the Sadigura, Talne, New, the Butchers' and that of the town Rabbi. There were also those of Rabbi Yosef Shaposnick, of the grocers and the tailors and the shoemakers. There also existed shtieblach (tiny synagogues) that had a nice atmosphere. One was run by Leyzer-Yonah Prakansky and served the Jews who lived near the auditorium and the prison. Another was housed in the Jewish Talmud Torah.

Itzik Nissenboim from Bendery

A class from the Russian Talmud Torah headed by Mr. Yehoshua - son of Isser- Tiomkin with teachers and students 1923

The Study of Torah in the Houses of Worship

The minyans at Mincha and Maariv were full of congregants. They came to pray, but also to study a page of Gmara or a chapter of Mishna. Jews would shut their stores or would otherwise free themselves for several hours in order to learn Torah. They would do so between Mincha and Maariv or after Maariv. They sat around a long table by candlelight and studied together or argued vigorously many Halachic issues. Each person wanted to prove his point and his depth of knowledge.

I well remember the Talne small synagogue at dusk. The leader was Haim, the son of Rabbi Levi-Yitzhak, the son of Itele the Rebbetzin. He was the grandson of Rabbi Levi-Yitzhak from Berdichev. He was a gifted scholar and it was said of him that he had completed the study of the Mishna three times. If he would have stayed away from the bottle he could have become a famous genius. He was the final authority on all matters and was closely followed by the beadle, Rabbi Yosef. He knew every page and could easily find any page and any required verse.

On the eves of the new month or the blessing of the moon, after studying a chapter of Mishna, they would sit down to eat herring and drink liquor accompanied by dancing and the singing of lively Hassidic tunes.

*Bessarabia was conquered by the Romanian army in January-March 1918. From "Jewish Bessarabia" by David Vinitsky, Part A, page 35.

[Page 11]

The Auditorium

The auditorium

The auditorium served as the cultural center of town, be it for Russian or Jewish intellectuals. There were numerous lectures and theatre productions. I recall the excitement when famous performers appeared. They were Mormatzov, Feydotova, Vialtzova, Samrin, Yarmdova and others of their stature. I particularly remember the performance of Tchesovitz from Davideyev* who sang classic, popular and operatic songs. These were unforgettable experiences as were the lectures by the Priest Petrov- a popular Russian lecturer on philosophy. He was an important thinker and I never tired of listening to him.

There was once a heated debate between him and Misha Pustan during a lecture about the Belgian poet and playwright Maurice Maeterlinck in the auditorium. We should not forget the parties and masquerade balls on Christmas and New Year's.

I once appeared on stage, by accident, during the celebration of the three hundredth anniversary of the House of Romanov in 1913. I was assigned by the school the recitation of the poem "Who Is He?" by Apollon Nikolayevich Maykov. Afterwards, our Russian literature teacher, Fyodor Nikolayevich

Vlikov, approached me, kissed my forehead and awarded me a book by Pushkin. I was so proud, since I was the only Jew, that I was the one won a prize for reciting a poem by one of the greatest Russian poets.

The auditorium stage was used in winter only. In the summer months the Balanovy theatre was used for various cultural events. Famous circuses such as the Dorov and others were frequent visitors in Bendery. They found the location ideal. In addition, Jewish troupes – such as those of Avraham Fishezon and Peppi Litman – performed in Yiddish. They brought operas by Goldfaden, "Hassia the Orphan" and "King Lear". We considered ourselves theatre aficionados and were quite impressed by Adler's group. We performed in amateur productions directed by the Ashkenazy brothers (M. And V.). We also presented Russian plays to the students and other theatre lovers – "Cherry Orchard", "Uncle Vanya" by Anton Chekhov and plays by Ostrovsky.

The Four Seasons
Spring

This is the most beautiful season in a person's life since it makes one enjoy the awakening of nature and the renewal of life. In Bessarabia, as in all other parts of southern Russia, spring begins in the month of Adar. We felt the saying "When Adar enters, happiness increases" was especially true of this season. When spring began we came out of the end of winter and escaped the frigid air and the mud. It was already possible to open windows to air the house. It was as if the sun smiled and caressed us gently. Icicles melted from rooftops and dripped down. The sidewalks and the edges of the road where there were no sidewalks were covered with spongy earth since the mud was covered with a dry layer. Tree buds were visible and swallows were flying in the air announcing the coming of spring. It felt like an awakening from deep slumber. The "Song of Songs" was recited in Heder accompanied by a special tune.

The signs of spring were also evident in the preparation for the holidays. Purim followed by Passover. On Purim eve all Jewish businesses closed early and craftsmen put down their tools. Jews rushed to synagogues to hear the reading of the Megillah. On the following day stores were closed at noon. Everyday attire was replaced by holiday clothes and preparations were begun for the Purim meal to be eaten at dusk. The housewives were excitedly busy preparing fluden (a concoction of nuts and honey), and Hammentashen for their family and for the Mishloah Manot sent to friends and family. Every housewife worked hard to outdo her friends with her Mishloah Manot.

During the day people hurried carrying trays covered with white linen napkins. The trays had bottles of wine, fluden, and Hammentashen. The meal was rich with different dishes particular to the holiday.

The members of the household sat around tables together with all other members of the family. The head of the household sat at the top of the table that was laden with food and drink. There was joy and happiness in every Jewish home.

As soon as Purim was over, preparations for Passover would begin. Matzos were baked and borsht (beet soup) was prepared weeks in advance. This is how the borsht was prepared: the beets were placed in special pots to sour. A room was cleansed of all hametz and no one was allowed to enter it wearing non-Passover clothes after the pots were put there. The house was whitewashed and the books were dusted. The house was turned upside down.

The Matzos were baked in the only Jewish bakery specially prepared for this task. It was owned by Pinny Beker (Dubossarsky). Every housewife booked a day with him so she could supervise the baking of Matzos for her family. After they were baked, the Matzos were wrapped in white sheets and hung on a stick to be carried home by two porters. The Matzos were also placed in the special room to await the Seder.

I adored my town in that season. I loved to roam the streets and to enjoy its beauty and the smell of spring. The town was covered in green. There were acacia trees on both sides of the sidewalk dressed in green. This was especially evident on Pushkinskaya and Nikolayevskaya streets. They both led to the Boulevard. Bundles of branches hung from the trees emitting their fresh sweet scent. This scent, as well as that of the lilacs, is still in my nostrils.

The residents used to take walks on the "old Boulevard" to take fresh air. The Jews came every Shabbat afternoon and the others on Sundays. The change from winter to spring and the summer that followed was really felt there. The grass even felt renewed. The icicles floated down the Dniester. We, the children, spent hours watching them and never tired of this experience.

However, the good never comes without the bad. The month of May, at the height of spring, is also a "month of dreading". The student body had to pass exams in order to continue to the next grade. In those days, it was not sufficient to know the material which had been taught all year in the grade. It was also necessary to pass exams. This took place during such a beautiful season when everything in nature was inviting and caressing. Students had to stand in front of a group of teachers and unsmiling inspectors.

An atmosphere of gloom and embarrassment was prevalent until the students succeeded in their exams. Only then did their spirits lift and they could enjoy the summer vacation beginning in May.

The Boulevard

Summer

This season also had its own charm. The town and its suburbs had many vineyards, fruit orchards and vegetable fields. The area farmers (from Frakan to Gisska) would bring into town fresh red radishes, green scallions and cucumbers, and fresh tomatoes. They were coveted by urban residents after the long harsh winter. The Antoneyev apples and plums were still covered with dew. Who could resist these goodies!

The bathing season in the swimming huts on the river began. Bathing in the river was one of the pleasures in town. Many guests would come from the surrounding towns- even from Kishinev. They wanted to escape the noise and the dust of the city in the hot summer. They found peace and enjoyment bathing in the Dniester and the clean air of the suburb of Borisovka. They rented rooms in houses which stood between the fields and near the Borisovka forest. This forest was the pride of our town. It served as a site for summer trips for the youth as well as for illegal meetings of the young Zionists. We met for political discussions and sing-songs of popular and Hebrew tunes. Our leader was the Hebrew teacher, Prozhansky, who was a member of Poalei Zion. It was so pleasant to enjoy nature and it left us with wonderful memories. As previously mentioned, the Boulevard held an important place in the hearts of the residents of town, especially the youth. It was a place for boys and girls to meet.

City Hall authorities did their utmost to allow the residents to enjoy themselves on the Boulevard. On Saturdays and early Sunday evenings an army band of wind instruments played there. They played marches, waltzes, and Russian compositions, classical and popular tunes. Unfortunately, the Jewish children always had clashes with the local youths. They would come on purpose on Saturday afternoons to fight Jewish children and to prevent them from enjoying Shabbat walks on the Boulevard. There were intense battles using stones, sticks and ropes. The Jews always arrived in groups since no Jewish child would dare walk there alone.

The leading citizens of town – wealthy merchants and army officers- established their own club in the Boulevard. It had a cafeteria and a games room. It must be noted that some of the wealthy Jews and the aristocrats were also part of this Christian crowd. Our Golden youths did not give up on joining this club. They usually played cards or billiards. In the summer, they brought in female gypsy singers.

The first movie house was also built in the Boulevard. Called "Science and Life", it was erected in 1907. In a wooden hut I saw- for the first time in my life – a silent movie. For the price of ten kopeks we saw "The Three Musketeers" by Alexandre Dumas Sr. In addition there was also a film by Max Linder, a popular comedian of the times.

Sometimes later, Hatzkelevitch moved the cinema to his yard on Haruzina Street. Over the years, two additional cinemas were opened- "Record" and "Dakdenas". Pictures were accompanied on the piano by Haim Shakhnovski, the son-in-law of Cantor Tuvia and also by Mrs. Bon-Miller

Fall

If Passover announces spring then Succoth is the time for our rejoicing, especially when it includes Simchat Torah – a very happy holiday. On the eve of Simchat Torah the synagogues were filled with men, women, boys and girls. Everyone stood together. It was the only time in the year the audience was mixed. Women and girls came to kiss the Torah and to bless those who circled the synagogue saying: "May you live to do it again next year". The reply was "you too!"

Long before the hour for circling with the Torah, boys and girls occupied the benches in the synagogue. The boys raised their flags topped by an apple and a lit candle.

Cantor Tzalel began with "You have been shown to know...". The leaders of the community were honoured by the first Hakafot, followed by those who sat by the Eastern wall. The rest of the crowd came after them each according to his social status.

The real celebration began on the following day when the congregants accompanied each Gabbai to his own synagogue. The entire town was dancing. (Even our Christian neighbours behaved well towards the dancers.) The Gabbai was surrounded on all sides by the crowd, slightly drunk, dancing around him holding wine bottles and accompanying him with pomp and circumstance. The streets were filled with celebrants, each synagogue with its own chief Gabbai. The true Jew could thus be discovered. Why should he worry about exile, earning a living, the authorities? The Jew is happy with his Torah, his belief in G-d and the totality of the Jewish people. This is how the Diaspora Jew could celebrate his people and his G-d.

Every season has its magic. In Southern Russia the differences in seasons are deeply felt. Only people indifferent to nature or lacking inspiration could not sense these changes.

The fall in Bendery would sometimes cause us to shiver. On rainy days the dampness touched our bones. Fall also brought with it to the city dwellers the need for special preparations for winter.

The signs announcing fall were the falling leaves and shorter days. There were also some light breezes.

During our walks in the fall on our Old Boulevard, I loved to look at the bare trees and to listen to their whispers.

We must remember the special sadness in Jewish hearts that comes with the fall season. In addition to the worries it brought, the mood also matched the look of nature.

According to the poet Al Harizi, the month of Heshvan is "good and beautiful, fertile and wet". However, the skies were cloudy, dark, and gray and the Jews had their worries. This was the time for conscription. We remember well the groaning of the Jews during conversations on the streets and in the synagogues.

The order to serve in the army frightened parents of sons all year, but as the date for reporting for duty neared they could not sleep at night. Anything was worthy in avoiding the trouble of serving in the army. They would search for places where the Provincial ministers and military doctors were "good" or known to be "kind". They could then be persuaded to help. Fathers would travel for weeks, far away from their families to obtain a special document to free their sons from active military service. (They would remain in the reserves). Sometimes they searched for a location where they could inscribe their son as an only child. They would then receive a "white ticket". This was a great accomplishment and they would have a celebration worthy of a wedding. If all else failed they would pretend the son had an illness that could free him from military service. Sadly, there were incidents where the results were maiming and sometimes death ensued.

The villagers would congregate in Bendery for that purpose. Since Bendery was a District capital, it served as a center for reporting to the army. The boys, nicknamed "Beasts", would petrify the Jews. They were drunk, screamed and rioted in the streets. Jewish parents were afraid to allow their daughters to go out on those fall evenings.

Winter

Winter arrived in its fill bloom after the muddy ground froze. The mud of Bendery was well-known in the area. It had a special charm in winter and to this day it brings back pleasant memories of frost and snow.

This was a time for school vacation since it was Christmas. It was fun to go on sleds and to ice skate in every canal. On our way home we had fun in the canals, especially the largest one. In the summer the local drunks would fall asleep on their banks. We used them in winter to have a good time.

In winter the Auditorium was used for balls starting at Christmas. There were also lectures and performances by top talent existing in Russia at the time. Our province was not forgotten because there was a cultured audience that appreciated good artists. In this way the Auditorium had a great influence on the local intelligentsia and the student body who sought cultural experiences.

*He was a rabbi's son and had converted when he was accepted at the Tsarist Opera in Petersburg. Shalom Aleichem remembers him as a friend in "From the Market". Return

[Page 15]

The Jewish Scene in our Town

We switch the discussion from nature to the people of our town, especially the Jews. The purpose is to commemorate our parents, siblings and friends in the time we lived there. It is a life which ended and will not be experienced again. We will describe personalities of our town as I remember them- from the sublime to the ridiculous, their culture, customs, character and aspirations.

When did the first Jews appear in Bendery? How many were there? When did they strike roots in a growing community? This is not a matter of statistics – it will be discussed further in the book. These are reminiscences and memoirs.

The Wertheim Dynasty

The ancient cemetery in Bendery does not contain a single marker detailing the exact date of the arrival of the first Jews- except for the grave of the "Old Tzadik". It was built like a small house with a sloping roof on two sides. The Tzadik was an ancestor of our main clergy, Rabbi Shloimke Wertheim. The legend was that thanks to blessings by the Tzadik there were no pogroms in our town, unlike other cities, especially Kishinev. I believe that it was due to the cordial relations between Jews and Christians as they were involved in commerce and social life. This was true until the Holocaust engulfed us. Even our community was destroyed.

In order to portray, in a simple way, the Jews of Bendery, we must begin with the distinguished Rabbi Shimon Shlomo Wertheim. He was a gifted scholar and he and his family served as the focal point of the community. He was the offspring of a lineage of rabbis existing in Bendery for one hundred and forty years. The father of this dynasty was the "Old Tzadik" Rabbi Aryeh-Leib, the brother of Rabbi Moshe from Sovran and the son-in-law of the Maggid Nahum from Chernobyl, Ukraine.

How did the Old Rabbi, the father of the dynasty, arrive in Bendery?

There are two versions of the answer. One says that the Old Rabbi was sent to Bendery by order of the Rabbi of Sovran. The second proclaims that he was brought by a wealthy Jew who found him in a small town in Podolia during his travels. Either way, he was the seedling that grew and produced magnificent fruit for our town.

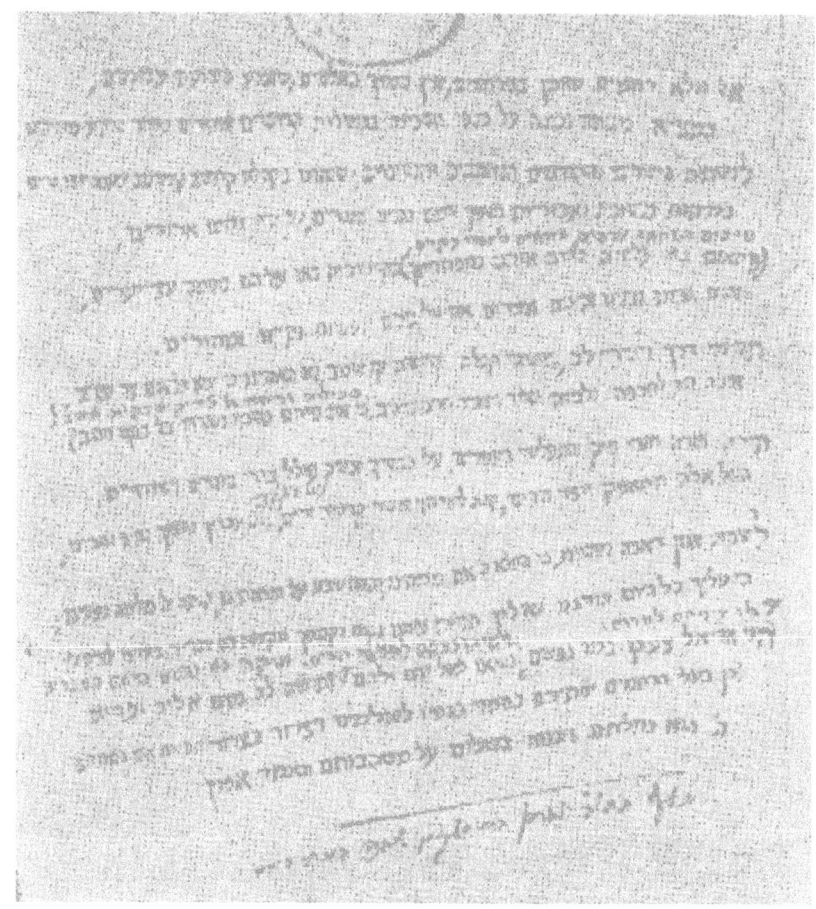

Prayer in memory of those who perished in the Kishinev pogroms in 1903. It is handwritten by Yosele Wertheim.

Rabbi Shloimke was much like his father, Rabbi Yitzhakl. He was a charming and impressive personality who was respected by Jews and Christians alike. His blue eyes projected the beauty of the Torah. His presence proclaimed tradition and lore of past generations. He stood out among other rabbis in Bessarabia by the fact that he merged the present with the scholarship he inherited from his parents. He saw our future in the building of Zion as our homeland.

After the Kishinev pogrom he traveled to Paris to negotiate with Baron de Hirsch the settlement of agricultural families from Bessarabia in Eretz Israel. Even Max Nordau was enthralled by the Late Rabbi Shloimke. In 1907 Rabbi Shlomo Wertheim, together with Rabbi Y.L. Fishman from Ongany, published a religious Zionist periodical called "The Dove". They were both leaders in Mizrahi.

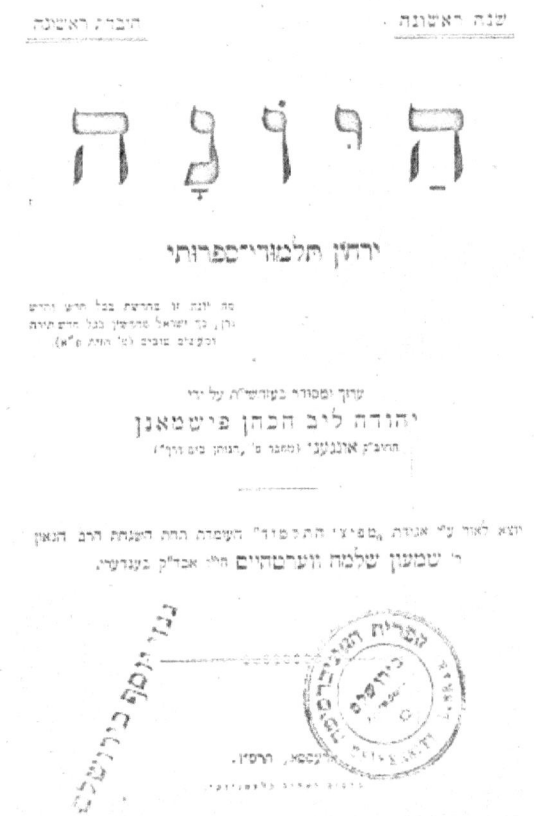

The Dove – A Literary – Talmudic Periodical

Edited by Yehuda-Leib Hacohen Fishman

Published by The Union of Distributors of Talmud under the supervision of Shimon Shlomo Wertheim

Rabbi Shloimke steeped his children in Zionism. His eldest son was much like his father both externally and internally. He was invited to serve as chief Rabbi in many communities in Russia and in Poland. Even before Mizrahi was founded he formed an association of religious Zionists. Later in his life he made Aliyah, and was buried in Jerusalem after his death.

In 1914, at the start of World War I, the late Rabbi Wertheim arrived in Eretz Israel via Turkey. His letters, read aloud to a small group of followers, were full of love for the country and sadness for those who lived in exile.

The Rabbi's family was the pride of our town. Each member was a jewel and had an important part in building our people and our land. Except for three of his children- David, Haya and Srulke- all made Aliyah. They continued their activities in building the land in various arenas. The three who did not go were always in contact with Eretz Israel and with Zionism. They contributed to the Zionist movement.

I remember the honor and respect given to the Jews of Bendery due to the stature of the Rabbi. He was chosen by the Tsarist authorities to be president of the electoral committee for the eighth Duma (legislature) in Bessarabia.

The "lions" of the group were the judges who poured water on the Rabbi's hands. Pinhas Dayan was a patrician Jew and a Torah scholar. Parents who wanted their sons to learn Torah would send them to him. Even Rabbi Wertheim sent his son Srulik to study with him.

Avraham (Avremel son of Yehiel and Brucha) was an honest and simple man. He never stopped learning Torah and Gmara and was also the mohel in town.

The ritual slaughterers were similar. Foremost was Leib Brodsky. He was a tall, handsome man and a scholar. He wrote a book about the connection between Adam and the present. He was also an expert in Astronomy. It was said that he knew all the sayings of the sages about Zion by heart. He was followed by Zeidl Yotam. He was a bright and honourable man, helpful and knowledgeable.

Next was Leib Hunis Chaplik- a religious man. He was highly intelligent and a good judge. In addition to ritual slaughtering, he was also a cantor. His voice was pleasant and he wrote and published a book called "Light unto the Jews".

Rabbi Ben-Zion Berdichevsky was absent-minded and a dreamer, but honest and straight-forward.

Last, but not least, was Moshe Sverdik (he changed his name to Sever in Eretz Israel). His nickname was Rav Moshele. He was charming and respected. We can say he was a scholar, deep-thinker, G-d fearing and kind. In addition to dealing with Torah matters (he was known to be a Mishna expert), he was also involved in charitable affairs. Even prior to the founding of the Jewish bank in town, he made certain there were funds available for the poor and for dowries. He was also an active and energetic man and was involved in every institution meant to help the "little man".

Over the years he collected sayings of the sages. They were published in three volumes by the Rav Kook Institute ((to be discussed further in the book). He was a Zionist, made Aliyah and settled in Zichron Yaakov. His late father had made Aliyah years earlier and lived there. His father was also well-versed in Torah. An intelligent and dignified man, he served as the Rabbi of the settlement. Many people would ask for his counsel and sought his guidance.

These were our ritual slaughterers. They were scholars and community leaders in addition to their professional duties.

Fathers paved the way for their sons. Mordehai Sever, the son of Moshe Sever, was talented in many fields: painting, music and poetry. He was an excellent translator of poetry from Yiddish and Russian. In Eretz Israel he worked in several fields. He began by working on the railroad and then he was employed in the office of the Hadassah Hospital in Safed. He was also a correspondent for "Al Hamishmar" (On guard). He now edits biographies of personalities active in the labor movement on behalf of the Central Committee of the Histadrut.

The Jews of Bendery

Bendery and its residents were different from other Jews in Bessarabia. In order to understand this statement it is necessary to stress the great difference between the Jews of Northern and Southern Bessarabia. Their culture and customs were influenced by their ethnic surroundings and forged their separate images.

Influence of Odessa and Wallachia

It is well-known that Bessarabia lay between the Prut River and the Dniester River. The Jews of Northern Bessarabia, on the banks of the Prut, absorbed the culture and character of the Jews of Romania and Wallachia. Their speech and language had a different intonation- the "R" and "A" were sharper in Yiddish. The Southern Jews in Bendery and Ackermann pronounced them more softly.

The Jews of Bendery did not resemble the simple, natural and hard-working Jew of Bessarabia. In contrast to Jews from other villages in Bessarabia, the Jews of Bendery craved an urban existence. They wanted to be like the Jews of Odessa, which was not far away. Bendery was situated on the banks of the Dniester, facing north towards the District of Kherson with Odessa as its main city. As well, the people of Bendery were different. As a result, the town was nourished by two cultures- Russian and the mysticism of Wallachia. Odessa, where the best intelligentsia, Russian culture and the arts were concentrated, influenced Bendery to a great extent. However, Bendery was also influenced by Wallachia. There were there many Hassidim and scholars (even Russian ones) as well as groups of activists in all movements and trends which existed in that time in Russia.

Not all the residents of Bendery had been born there. Our ancestors came to settle from many parts of the Russian Empire. They came mostly from Ukraine, but also from Lithuania, Poland and Russia.

A Tale About a Store Open on Shabbat

In spite of different origins the Jews of Bendery lived in peace and harmony among themselves. I do not recall any sectarian controversies except, perhaps, one. It occurred when Kaiser, owner of a book and stationery store on Haruzina corner Alexandrova, broke the tradition which had existed for many generations. He was the first who dared to open his store on Shabbat. I do not know if he did it to "anger" or because the authorities demanded that at least one stationery store stay open on Shabbat. (The Russian girls' high school, the science high school and all other schools held classes on Shabbat). The teachers and students complained that when they needed textbooks and writing utensils on Shabbat they could not obtain them. The trade was only operated by Jews and therefore there was a demand to open such a store on Shabbat. The controversy was huge and the town was buzzing. "Have you ever heard such a thing? To dare open a store in Bendery on Shabbat!" Although it was a mixed town- Jews and Christians- on Shabbat it was a typical Jewish town. The marketplace was empty even of non-Jews. All the stores were closed and the Jews hurried to their synagogues. The town was dressed for Shabbat. "Here comes this evil man – a brother to Dotan and Aviram – and he desecrates the holy day." The town erupted. Avigdor Shreibman, old man Hatzkelevitch and my late grandfather were the leaders. These observant Jews made a lot of noise and delayed the Reading of the Torah on Shabbat. They railed even against Rabbi Shloimke who never argued on Shabbat. Slowly, the storm subsided. This was the first controversy.

Election of the Official Rabbi

The second controversy- as I recall- was about the election of the official Rabbi. The position had been occupied for many years by Mr. Kolpekoshi – an educated and noble Jew from a respected family and well-loved by the town scholars. He was himself a Jewish scholar as well and was full of love for his people. The year the election was to be held, by law, for the position, a new candidate appeared. He was a poor Jewish student, Efraim Darbrimediker, a scion of the family of Rabbi Levi Yitzhak from Berdichev. Although he was a grandson of respected rabbis he could not be compared to Kolpekoshi. The town was divided into two camps: the intellectuals on the side of Kolpekoshi and ordinary folk led by Zalman, the chimney sweep, on the side of Darbrimediker. It must be said that the fact that Zalman was a chimney sweep did not prevent him from being involved in community issues. Never quiet, he would scream and curse. He was even capable of attacking the person reading the Torah on Shabbat by announcing his opinions. Issues could be the community or the Korovka*, or elections of committees and their chairmen. He was involved in everything. He was simple and crude and even rumoured to be a denouncer to the authorities. He was feared because no one wanted to be the subject of his rude attacks and they often gave in. He held the Jewish community hostage. It seems like a paradox that the poor and the craftsmen supported him. When the election came Zalman found a cause and made a great deal of noise. In a loud voice he forced the choice of Darbrimediker as the official rabbi. The townspeople were quite ashamed. Zalman the chimney sweep was assisted by Bondarov who came from a good and well-respected family

Era of Hassidism in our Town
The Rizhiner Dynasty

This was a period of great Hassidism in sections of the Jewry of Eastern Europe. Bendery was also involved in the movement. Hassidism in Bendery was influenced by rabbis from Wallachia and Moldova, in particular the

Rizhiner dynasty. It was multi-branched. Rabbi Itzik'l, the father of Rabbi Shloimke, was the leading follower and did not allow other Hassidic sects to come. At one time, no leader of any other sect was able to visit – as long as he lived in town. He considered himself to be the continuity of the Baal Shem Tov and therefore only he could be the leader. In spite of that he did not leave behind any followers.

On the other hand, the Hassidim of Bendery had great respect for Rabbi Israel from Rizhin and his sons. They had great influence on their followers in Bendery who were very different from Hassidim in Podolia, Volyn and Poland. They followed the customs of the Rizhin court by wearing clean clothes, being well-groomed and being more restrained than Hassidim in other parts of Eastern Europe. This was evident mainly in the influence of Rabbi Israel the Rizhiner and his sons. They did not look like other Hassidim and there was certain nobility about them. They were generous and carried themselves in an imposing manner. The father of this dynasty settled his sons in many parts of Ukraine, Romania and Wallachia. They were in the towns of Pashkan, Bahush and Ajuta on one side and Sadigura on the other. They built their center in Bendery. We must add that in addition to the Rizhiner Hassidim there were also some Lubavitch and other groups such as Talne, Elsky and Karlin. However, they were few in number and did not stand out.

The Pashkan Hassidim included Yossel Shaposnick and Haim Immes. His father, Velvel, was one of the wealthy and great men of Bendery. It is interesting to note that Haim's two step-brothers, Manny and Yasha Immes, as they were called, were most supportive of their father's Hassidism. They were not followers themselves and were considered to be aristocrats. The Rabbis were regular visitors in Bendery. Each time they came to town they would be received in public with pomp and circumstance. They usually stayed at the home of Yossel Shaposnick, a highly-religious man. He was wealthy and had a welcoming, spacious home. He built his own synagogue with a mikve and a bath house. He was charitable and had great influence in town.

Other important Hassidim worth mentioning for their influence in the community were also Rizhiners. Shmuel-Abba Sudit, "the lion", was beloved and well-liked for his intellect and intelligent comportment with all people. His sayings were famous among the Jews of Bendery. He was a scholar and gave wise counsel. He never missed an opportunity to do a good deed and would overcome any obstacle to do it. His nobility affected his surroundings. Sudit was an enthusiastic follower of the Rebbe from Pashkan and was their representative in town. He respected everyone without exception, even if it was a secular person he did not like or agree with. In spite of being a Hassid and religious, he did not disqualify the assimilated. He loved to argue with them and they loved to argue with him. They always parted on good terms. As a religious man he would not shake a woman's hand, but if there women who did not know the custom he would say "I believe what you tell me."

Shmuel- Abba Sudit

Another important Hassid was Levi Hochberg (Levi the Bricklayer as he was called because he owned a brick factory). He too was religious and well-liked by people. For many years he served as the collector of Meir Baal Haness charity boxes and he also transferred the money to Eretz Israel. He made Aliyah with his two sons. He died and was buried in Eretz Israel, as per his instructions.

There were also Israel Chulak and his sons- enthusiastic followers and Buya Abramovitch. It was said of him that he represented Torah and greatness. He was wealthy and donated to all causes. Haim Volovetz was a religious man and a kind one and was viewed by the town leaders as honest and affable. These were the people closest to the Rabbi.

Lubavitch Hassidim

In addition to those already mentioned there were other Hassidim-followers of Lubavitch. The leader was Shebt'l Berman. He was a scholar and a strong personality. He was chosen often to the religious committee as the representative of the Ultra-Orthodox. He ruled the committee.

Among the Lubavitch, Aaron-Moshe Shneirson stood out. He was a scion of the Shneirson family of Rabbi Shneyer Zalman Shneirson from Liadi. Well-known for his kindness and scholarship, Aaron-Moshe Shneirson was considered, in our town, to be a deep thinker and a Torah student. He studied day and night. His sayings were like pearls and were spread in town as soon as he uttered them. I recall that once he was studying Gmara with Yossel, the Rabbi's son, in the synagogue. Suddenly, Aaron-Moshe stood up near the window between Mincha and Maariv and he saw a local drunk sprawled on the sidewalk. He turned to Yossel and said: "My friend, do you see this man? He is more decent than us!" "How?" asked Yossel. Aaron-Moshe replied: "This man follows in his father's footsteps. Are we also following in the footsteps of our fathers?"

Although he was a religious Jew he did not prevent his sons and daughters from studying secular subjects. He allowed them to obtain an excellent education. One of his daughters became a professor in a Russian university. His daughter, Bluma, lives in Eretz Israel and was one of the first kindergarten teachers in the Tarbut schools. She spoke Hebrew even then and educated Jewish children in a Zionist atmosphere. She was highly sought in Bessarabia as a director of Tarbut kindergartens. One son changed his family name to Yoeli and was a journalist with Davar.

Moishele Landman

The respected Moishele Landman arrived in Bendery from Poland in 1908/09. I do not recall his origins, but as soon as he arrived in town he settled and followed the customs of the Hassidim. He received donations and requests for blessings and was surrounded by followers who were ordinary craftsmen. These were Jews who barely eked out a living and performed hard physical labor. Moishele was their backbone and he revived their spirits. They were careful in following the commandments and listened to him when he taught the portion of the week.

He was pleasant, calm and was able to influence and lead his followers. He walked on the street with his head down. It seems he did not want to accidentally look at a woman. When he went to the ritual bath his secretary, Mordehai, followed behind him. They never walked side by side. One cannot imagine the singing and dancing around this rabbi's table on Shabbat during Seudah Shlishit, on holidays or on the New Month.

It was a special celebration. The faces of his followers would shine as if they had entered a wonderful world without any pain or worry.

The leader of the Hassidim was Mordehai Eli Cohen (brother-in-law of David Gurfel). (He was nicknamed Mordehai Eli the Blind One). He eked out an existence and lived in dire straits, but he was always content and served G-d happily. No one could compare to him when he was with his Rabbi. He was one of his closest followers.

After the war, Moishele arrived in Israel with other survivors. He settled in Jaffa and was surrounded by simple followers. They had come to Israel from Romania, some even from Bendery. In Jaffa he opened a small synagogue and followed the customs of the Hassidim. He died and was buried in Eretz Israel as any religious person would wish. He was survived by a son who worked for the government and by a married daughter.

*Korovka was a special tax levied by the Jewish community on Kashrut. The money was used to help the poor and for religious purposes. Return

[Page 19]

The Jewish Way of Life
Characteristics of Bendery Jews

As I previously mentioned, I see the Jews of Bendery as a unique part of the general Jewish population of Bessarabia. Our Jewish brethren came to settle in our town from many parts of Russia. They lived harmoniously with the locals, sometimes next door to them. The special image of Bendery was formed by its topography and scenery. The Dniester on one side with its characteristic scenery, the villages with their green fields, the fortress in the middle of a square, the army camp outside town. The 55th Podolian Regiment (Cossack Junta) was also located in town. All these, without doubt, left their imprint on the economic and social life in Bendery.

There were two streams within the Jewish community in Bendery- the Hassidim and the Enlightened. They were both valuable and influenced the development of Jewish society, especially the youths.

Even Hassidism in Bendery was different. There was no opposition to the intellectuals involved in developing national movements and European culture. There had been such opposition in other Jewish centers in Russia and Eastern Europe. At the end of the previous century there had been an inner crisis in the intellectual development of Jews in Russia. It did not touch the intellectuals in Bendery who sought ways to obtain secular knowledge without losing Jewish values. They wanted a modern life within Jewish tradition. In those days national revival, founding of a homeland and living productively had a great socialist meaning for people. These aspirations went hand in hand with the plans of the Russian intelligentsia and its best youths to renounce Tsarist oppression and to change the image of "Mother Russia". The agitation in the Russian intelligentsia greatly influenced the Jewish intellectuals and their youths.

Heders and Religious Teachers

Zionism was the mainstay of thought among the intelligentsia. Parents started to look for ways of integrating the prevalent secular education with Jewish national ideas. A Jewish child began his education in a Heder at the age of three. He continued until his Bar Mitzvah. Subjects taught were: Torah with Rashi and some Mishna and Gmara. In Kindergarten a Jewish child learned the Aleph-Bet, Torah and Rashi. He was educated in ways of the Torah and was taught to follow its commandments. He had to learn the morning prayer of Mode Ani by heart. For any negligence, forgetfulness or rudeness, the children were punished physically (at least a pinch on the cheek, if not a hit by a rod). A worse punishment – embarrassing and isolating- was being made to stand in the corner.

The Rabbi's Synagogue

The kindergarten teacher, Shmuel Krassilover, was an expert in pinching even though his forefinger was truncated. A child's cheek became red and swollen. This seemed to be the prevailing method of pedagogy in those days. The teachers either had not heard of modern methods or completely rejected them. These teachers themselves could only read rudimentary Hebrew and the Psalms.

Another early childhood educator in town was Shlomo the Melamed. He was short and good-hearted. His students were fortunate since he seldom used corporal punishment. His assistant brought lunch for the children from their homes. The children were in Heder from morning till evening. It was easier for their mothers. Of course, the assistant had to first sample the food. His other task was in winter to carry the younger children over the thick mud on the streets. He would accompany rows of children home after school. The teacher waited until the last child was carried across by the assistant.

A third teacher was Avraham the Tobacco Sniffer. It seems he liked to sniff a great deal of tobacco. He started as an assistant and was promoted to the position of teacher. His fees were low and poor families sent their children to him. His Heder also served as a dovecote and the children were entertained as well as educated.

Children attended Heder in the period between Succoth till Passover. After that the teachers spent their time chasing parents to convince them to entrust their children to them.

When a male child was born the teachers would bring the children to visit the mother (usually at home). They were taught to pray loudly the Shema wishing for the good health of the baby. On the eve of the Brit, as thanks, they would receive candies in paper bags. The children were very happy. Some were not too shy to ask for candy for their younger siblings who were at home.

From Kindergarten the child went to a teacher of Torah and Rashi. In town there were four such teachers. Baruch Kolker was a tall, skinny man, religious and kind; Yoel Dobserer was also kind and knowledgeable; Eli Gamburger was strict and dressed differently upon his return from America. His students had to work hard and in addition to Torah and Rashi also learned some Hebrew including grammar. Parents who wanted their children to try different approaches sent them to him. Yankel Linevsky was a scholar, somewhat enlightened, who taught reading of the Torah in addition to Hebrew and grammar.

In these Heders the children spent whole days from morning to night. In the winter they returned home carrying a container with a lit candle. As they walked on the street they created much noise and screamed constantly. Often a child would arrive home missing one boot stuck in the mud.

Hanukkah and Tu B'Shvat were special holidays for the Heder students. At Hanukkah there was playing with dreidls and anticipating Hanukkah gelt from parents, grandparents, aunts and uncles. The children spoke only of this during the eight days of the holiday. Every child wanted to boast that he was richer than his friends. This sometimes caused fights between good friends.

Tu B'Shvat was different. On that day all the children brought fruit growing in Eretz Israel. Usually it was carobs, sometimes figs and raisins and occasionally almonds. The teacher and students sat around the table and said "Shehecheyanu". He told them stories about Eretz Israel- as much as he knew.

It was proof that every Jewish heart yearned for Eretz Israel and that even fruit growing there would evoke longings for Zion and Jerusalem.

The teachers had a custom of visiting students' homes on Shabbat afternoon in order to test their knowledge and to show the parents how much the children had achieved. The student was warned on Friday afternoon about the impending visit. He had to study hard in order not to fail. Friday and Shabbat became two days of trepidation and unrest until the child overcame the ordeal.

When a student reached Bar Mitzvah age he would transfer to a special tutor who taught Gmara. There were two in town: Pinhas Dayan, a great scholar and Leib Sunis, the ritual slaughterer. Usually, the Hassidim and clergy sent their children to these two.

National Spirit in a Traditional Education

The awakening of national aspirations and Zionist activities began to affect the Jews in Bessarabia, especially in Bendery. They searched for modern education appropriate for the times. They wanted traditional Jewish knowledge integrated with national aspirations and modern scholarship.

There were two such Heders in town. Studies were conducted in Hebrew, including written grammar, in addition to the study of Torah and Prophets. This was still the mainstay of the new trend. The two teachers who began this new wave were themselves true lovers of Zion and quite active in Zionist circles. One teacher, Baruch Holdonka, was one of the principal orators of the movement. He was a wonderful person, well-versed in Torah. He was also an enthusiastic follower of Theodore Herzl and devoted to the Zionist movement. On Shabbat during prayers he was surrounded by Zionists and students from the Russian schools. He held discussions with them on current matters in the Jewish community. I remember how he concentrated on "At the Crossroads" by Ahad Haam. He brought to synagogue copies of the newspaper "Hatzfira" (The Siren) and other Hebrew publications. He read aloud, translated and explained important articles. His listeners enjoyed following the serial story "A Guest for Shabbat" by Nahum Sokolov in "Hatzfira". He was also a delegate to various Zionist congresses.

His students benefitted from Zionist teachings. Their parents wished to integrate basic traditional Jewish values with modern studies. No wonder that the students at the Science High School were the first to arrive at the Heder every afternoon as soon as they finished their secular studies.

The second teacher of this genre was Avremel Kreitzman. He also taught Hebrew language and grammar in addition to religious studies. In contrast to Holdonka, he continued the custom of visiting homes on Shabbat to show parents what their children had achieved. He also attracted many students from the Russian schools who wanted to learn Torah and Hebrew. He hired an assistant – Haim Glass. Glass came to Bendery from Poland where he was a Yeshiva student in his youth. He then became a Labor Zionist. Glass was adored by his students. His caring and worrying about educating the youths occupied him constantly and he believed in the new trend. I was one of his students in Kreitzman`s Heder. Our Hebrew texts were: "A New Path", "Language of Our People", works by Steinberg and "Young Plants" by A.Z. Rabinovitch.

"Reformed Heder" – Avremel Kreitzman, Baruch Kolker, Haim Glass and their Students

Zionist activity in town was concentrated in special groups of students, working youths, store clerks and craftsmen. At the center of activity one could find the Hebrew teachers who tutored privately. Noah Lifshitz, an excellent teacher must be remembered. Fluent in Hebrew, he instilled in his students a love of Zion. He liked to unearth the mysteries of our origins, the basis of our uniqueness. He had been a Yeshiva student in his youth until he became interested in scholarship and the Zionist movement. He came to Bendery from Kishinev where he had served as the secretary of Hovevei Zion (Lovers of Zion). Lifshitz then began his teaching career- particularly Hebrew language and grammar. He was a pleasant conversionalist and sprinkled his speech with clever sayings and remarks. His home became a meeting place for scholars and youths drawn to Zionism. He was the Godfather for these young people and drew them into the movement. He published articles in "The Exile" and "The Siren" (Hatzfira) as viewpoints of the Jewish Provinces.

There were also evening Hebrew classes for girls who studied in the Russian schools. They were administered by Projensky and Postelnik (from Poland). They were the first to open Hebrew kindergartens- Tarbut. There Jewish children first heard Hebrew songs and watched plays in Hebrew.

The first junior high school was opened in town by Mr. Rynewman, a scholarly Jewish teacher. It served as the first school for Jewish girls whose parents did not want them to study in Russian schools. The curriculum was based on that of the Russian schools run by the government. In addition, there was Yiddish reading and writing. The school was closed on Shabbat and this fact made it easier for parents to send their daughters. The girls acquired a general Russian education as well as Jewish knowledge. The girls who graduated from the school were accepted into the fifth and final grade of the government high schools.

The preparation in this school was so excellent that it earned a very good reputation within government pedagogic circles. (A small number of these girls are still with us to this day.) This junior high school run by Mr. Rynewman and his daughters was closed in 1908. The school must be remembered as one of the catalysts for the pursuit of education among the Jews of Bendery.

[Page 24]

The Libraries

Cultural activity in Bendery was mainly centered on the public libraries. They had a great deal of influence on cultural development, the youth and the intelligentsia. The Jewish public showed interest in reading secular books by avidly following novels by Shumer. The dressmaker, the undergarment seamstress, the hat maker were women who could read and write in Yiddish. The supplier of this literature was Berish the Parcel Carrier. In his basket, which served as a store, he carried religious articles such as fringes of prayers shawls, prayer books for daily use and High Holidays. He would walk the streets and spread his wares in the synagogues. He also had romance novels by Shumer. Shumer was the first Yiddish romance writer before the classicists- Peretz, Mendele, Shalom Aleichem- published their works. Berish would lend a book to his subscribers for one kopek. The romance novels, welcomed by the readers (especially the women) had titles such as "The Bride on the Tree", "The Runaway Bridegroom", "The Angry Mother-in-law". The stories were sentimental and tragic about brides, bridegrooms and mothers-in-law living in Eastern Europe. The readers shed tears as they read by dim candlelight. They would crack seeds and eat them as they read.

Administration of the Jewish Library standing in the doorway

Mihailov Street, also called the Teachers Street, was filled with these female readers. The first library in Bendery was thus founded by "The Parcel Carrier".

The influence of the libraries was felt in the general development of the town. The Municipal Library, situated in City Hall, was large and rich with Russian literature. The peaceful reading room was roomy and airy and became a meeting place in the mornings and in the evenings for students and the intelligentsia. They were interested in different topics in politics, cultural life and philosophy. We often met our teachers there. One could also find most of the Russian newspapers from all over the country. The librarian was Mr. Vanyushka. He was nice, educated and liberal-minded. He knew classic Russian literature and philosophy and was well-versed in other cultures. He could not be fooled. Whenever someone came to exchange a book he wanted proof that the book had been read seriously, questioned the readers and held discussions with them. Woe to the reader who did not know the book well. He would then advise the person: "It is better for you to take Nikrassov's grammar to read instead."

The Jewish library in Bendery was founded in 1907-08 by a group of students from the Chief Rabbi's synagogue. They were the Rabbi's son, David Wertheim, Yitzhak Fein, Vodoboz and me. The library consisted of only three shelves with small books in Hebrew published in those days. These were short stories by Yehuda Steinberg, A.Z. Rabinovitch, and Ben Ami (translated from Russian) and monthly youth journals "Shvalim" (Trails), etc. Subscribers were selected from among the youths who had already learned Hebrew and were close to the movement of the "Lovers of Hebrew". Membership dues were five kopeks per month. (Every subscriber was warned to speak Hebrew only and would be fined five kopeks if he did not do so. The fine money was used to purchase new books). Actually, even this library was illegal since in order to open a library a government permit was necessary. Otherwise, the authorities were suspicious of a conspiracy.

The Zionist teacher Noah Lifshitz and the General Zionists Hirsh Kogan, Moshe Haham and Israel Blank as well as the Zionist youths, founded a library called The Russian-Jewish Library. It was first located in the home of Noah Lifshitz and he was the first librarian. It then moved to the community building on Fidotov Haruzina. When the library was moved to its new location the librarian was Yasha (Yaakov) Bendersky, the son of Dr. Shlomo Bendersky, a well-known doctor and public figure.

The Russian-Jewish Library
(Librarians Yasha Bendersky and Y. Lifshitz lend books)

Another small library was the one in the Hebrew High School of Dr. Z. Schwartzman. There were no fees. Dr. Schwartzman was a top pedagogue and he supervised the library. He advised students as to their choice of suitable books and often questioned them to see if they understood and could analyze the content. These were the best classic literary works of Russian and Jewish authors. The teaching staff directed the student reading to topics about Jewish life and culture.

Lastly, the libraries in town served as a place for intellectual development among the Jewish population.

[Page 26]

Liberal Yiddish Journalism

Another source for education in town was the liberal Yiddish journalism evident in Russia and Poland at the time. The Yiddish newspaper, "The Friend", was published in Petersburg. It was informative and excellent especially when it spoke about Jewish life in Russia and the rest of the world.

A second Yiddish newspaper was "Today" – the most popular in Poland. The Hebrew newspapers "Hatzfira", "Hashachar", and "Hashiloah" were received in the homes of distinguished Zionists and scholars. Intellectuals who knew Russian obtained "Vozhod" "Razesviet" – Zionist journals and "Jewish Life"- a journal about Jewish life in general. Other important newspapers, in many homes, were "Odessa News" and "Life in Bessarabia" that disseminated scholarship among the Jews of Russia. Others were "Russian Word" from Moscow and "Russian Purpose" from Petersburg. They were liberal newspapers and influenced life in Russia in those days. The illustrated journal "Sky" was rich in content. It was beloved by students since there were contributions from the top leading Russian writers such as Andreyev, Artzivshov, Gorky, Chekhov, Block, Yassnin, Apokhatin and others.

Savings and Loan Bank in Bendery

(The Little Jewish Bank)

My late father subscribed to the journal and we were happy when it arrived. I waited impatiently for the monthly edition. All of these publications nourished the enlightened generation in the Jewish as well as the Russian worlds.

The Enlightened Group

As is the custom all over the world, there is one outstanding person in any group. In the enlightened group the leader was a fine, aristocratic and special person. He was David Abramovitch Natanzon. His parents were not among the wealthy traditional crowd. He reached cultural heights on his own. He was highly involved in Russian culture and was a acute writer on current affairs. He wrote for "Odessa News" – one of the largest liberal newspapers in South Russia. It was popular among the liberal intelligentsia. Many of the leading educated people wrote for this newspaper. D.A. Natanzon also wrote for "Life in Bessarabia" – one of the most popular and advanced newspapers in Bessarabia. It was published in Kishinev. Its editor was Zhakovskaya from the movement Volaya Naroda. In 1910 or so Natanzon established and edited the newspaper "Yuzhni Kray". He attracted the best Jewish correspondents who wrote in Russian. One of them was the dentist Hein who was an extraordinary columnist. The public avidly read his columns.

Natanzon, in addition to his newspaper and journalism, did not forget his Jewish people. He was always involved in establishing institutions for ordinary people and he took care of them. He was not involved in the Zionist movement since he believed that when a change of government came to Russia the life of the Jews would improve. In those days there was a contradiction between the two ideologies. He did not even participate in any other community activities.

Natanzon was one of the founders of the first fund to assist small Jewish merchants and craftsmen. All his life (too short, to our great sorrow) he headed the fund. His helpers were the ritual slaughterer Moshele Svredik (Sever), pharmacist Vineshneker, Alexandrov and others. All those who were involved in public Jewish life were warm-hearted Jews who worried about the needy. This fund was referred to as "The Little Jewish Bank".

The enlightened people in town were active on the managing board together with the Hassidim and the religious personnel. There was constant friction between the two groups. The enlightened wanted closer supervision of the Korovka and other departments. These were "clothing of the poor", "Food for the Poor", "weddings of Poor Brides" and "Caring for the Dead". Those among the liberals who were most active on the managing board (until the Zionists intervened) were the brothers I. and M. Immes, Vineshneker the pharmacist, Leib Blank from the flourmills, Alexandrov and Haim Fustman. Among the ultra Orthodox were the beadle from Agudat Israel, Shebt'l Berman, Avremel

Wertheim, Shmuel Immes and others. Of course, Zalman, the chimney sweep, always contributed.

Students at the Train Station 1920

The Managing Board of the Community

Community life was not run by the board only. There were some public figures who each concentrated on their special areas of interest and were devoted to it. We must mention Haim-Hirsh Weisman- a respected and educated merchant. He was involved with the people and gave his children both a traditional and secular education. He was a caring Jew and would not rest until he could be of help to others. Weisman came to Bendery from Proskarov, Ukraine. He was involved in activities dear to his heart. He was especially devoted to ordinary people and took care of the children attending the Talmud Torah.

First Jewish Locomotive Driver in Our Town

One of Weisman's sons, Pinhas, was my close friend. He was a young man with good looks, a good heart and loyal to his friends. He cared for his fellow human beings. He was blond and blue-eyed. I still see his smiling face in front of me. We both dreamed of publishing a youth journal in Hebrew. We forced ourselves to speak Hebrew only. It was a difficult task. In 1917-18 during the Kerensky upheaval he was the first Bendery Jew who wanted to do physical labor although he was unprepared for it. He chose to work as a mechanic on the train locomotive. Many of the youths envied him. He was an idealist and that's how we knew him. Unfortunately, to our great sorrow ,he died after a short illness at a young age. His death left a strong impression on his friends and everyone mourned him. May his memory be blessed.

Leaders of the Community at the End of the Nineteenth Century

The leaders of the Jewish community of Bendery- as much as I remember- according to tradition handed down by our parents, were those who founded the community and led it in the previous century. They were: Itzy Nissenboim, Velvel Immes, Mordehai Kalman Fenitch, Shimon Sultan and I. Perlman.

They were ultra Orthodox, wealthy and charitable merchants. They were the leaders and the spokesmen for the community. Itzy Nissenboim was at the head. I remember him, but I only heard about the others from my parents. He was a man of merit, kind and charitable. He cared for the poor as he would for his own children. When the water carrier`s horse fell he turned to Itzy for help. The same was true of the wagon owner, the driver, and the bride lacking a dowry. Where else could they go? A widow who could not afford tuition for her children also would come to him. No one came away empty-handed. When funds were collected for the poor he would say: "I will give double of what you collect from everyone else! " When he saw the need by any Jews, especially the poor, for hospitalization he built a new hospital. It was a magnificent building for those times. It was called the Jewish Hospital. He was a wealthy man and lived well. Every morning he went in his cart, pulled by two horses, to supervise the work in the hospital. If he found anything wrong he would rectify it.

Others I mentioned had wonderful qualities as well. When it came to distributing charity to the poor on the eve of holidays, to supporting the Talmud Torah and the guesthouse, they competed to see who could be the first. They were highly respected and well received in town.

In those days, there was a nice custom in our town – as in other communities. It actually continues to this day. On Friday nights the beadle of the synagogue would approach each man and offer him a guest for Shabbat. (The beadle already knew how to match people). These wealthy men fully accepted the offer. Thus, one could often find guests for Shabbat in many homes. At times, the guests were missionaries from Eretz Israel. The happiness at hosting was multiplied many times on that occasion. The neighbours could join the missionaries after dinner to hear stories about Eretz Israel and Jerusalem.

Seating by the Eastern Wall

I well remember the panorama of these Jews as they sat by the Eastern wall in the Sadigura and Talne synagogues. They were handsome and respected, well-mannered and revered. Among them were these families: Shreibman, Sirkis, Weiser, Shlomo Pagis, Shmuel Chaplik, Buya Abramovitch, Yehoshua Reznik, Moshele Levinstein and Avraham Kushner. In the Talne synagogue there were Sh. L. Boris, H. Immes, I. and M. Immes, Sh. A. Sudit, A. Pasternak and Hirsch Mandel. In the Sadigura synagogue the men were not only good-looking, but they also were of good character in their relations with G-d and man.

Even the beadles in the synagogues were well-versed in Jewish subjects. This was especially true of the beadle of the Talne synagogue, Yossel. He was a gifted scholar. I often observed that during study time in the synagogue, between Mincha and Maariv, when Levi (the Rebbetzin's son), was teaching, as a difficult problem arose, all would turn to Yossel for a solution. The same was true of Eli, the beadle of the Sadigurian synagogue and Leib, the beadle of the old synagogue. It was obvious that they were chosen not only because they could serve the synagogue, but also because they were learned and observant.

[Page 29]

Cantors

The cantors in our town were considered among the best and were well-known everywhere. In addition to being cantors they were of good character. The cantor in the Sadigura synagogue, Pinie Misonzshnik had a pleasant voice, could read music and was one of the most beloved cantors in town. He was a scholar and was well-received by the public not only in his synagogue, but also by many other people. On holidays and the High Holidays he would gather around him a choir made up of his sons and other youths. Krasiltzik conducted the choir. Several famous cantors arose from among the choir members – Yosef Schwartzman, son of the shoemaker Simcha Schwartzman and Muny Balaban, son of Moshe Balaban (now in Argentina).

Betzalel Steiner, known as Tzalel the Cantor, led the services in the Talne synagogue all his life. He was short, innocent and modest, observant and a

Hassid. His style was one of pleading to G-d. His lamentations on Tisha B'Av were unique. He was a Talne Hassid, but he learned a great custom from the late Meir'l Promishlianer, the Tzadik from Promishlian. Although he was very poor and depended on contributions from his followers, he still gave to anyone in need on the eve of Shabbat. It was his custom to delay his dinner on Thursday night until he distributed money to the poor folk- a tenth of his weekly income. In addition, he asked others to do the same. He visited the residences of the needy and secretly deposited their share under the tablecloth. These people were able to use the money for Shabbat. He followed this custom all his life until he made Aliyah to Eretz Israel.

Left; Betzalel Steiner (Tzalel the cantor)

Right: Buya Abramovitch – One of the best of Bendery

There were always such generous people in many Jewish communities – May their names be blessed.

Steiner was a religious man, but he gave his children a secular education. His daughter was one of the first kindergarten teachers in "Tarbut" and in the Schwartzman high school in Bendery. He sent his children ahead of him to Eretz Israel and he and his wife followed. After some years spent in Eretz Israel, they died and were both buried in Haifa.

Other cantors who stood out in synagogues were: Tuvia Shchanovsky in the Old synagogue, Shimon (Shimele) Greenberg (also called Genzil because he was skinny like a stick), in the synagogue of the Clerks.

Doctors and Medical Personnel

Among the best known people in town was Roitman the medic. He belonged to the most popular medical group in Bendery. It is hard to believe, but often the doctors in town would consult him in special cases. He was so knowledgeable in his field and saved many lives. He could prescribe medications. He had a strange appearance- walking with a cane under his arm. He was also famous for biting his lower lip. When he entered a house he would say: "What! You could not find anyone else to bother? The patient will live somehow."

There were many good doctors in Bendery. We must mention Dr. Bernstein who loved Russian culture, Borovsky who had a warm Jewish heart, Vanderberg who was strange, nervous and severe (he worked in Itzy Nissenboim's hospital), Rynewman- son of the teacher. Among the non-Jews were Dr. Dovagel, a military doctor and an expert in his field, but a drunkard and a Jew-hater, Dr. Petrov, from the Russian clinic, who was nice and kind.

Outstanding Jews

There were two outstanding Jews who worked for the Tsarist government. They formed an integral part of Bendery. The first was policeman Kahanovitch. In spite of being a Jew he was chosen for his position because he had served in the Nikolayev army (those who were taken into the army during the reign of Nikolai I). He spoke an excellent Russian and his Yiddish was Russian-accented. He stood out with his big beard, trousers tucked into boots and his sword on his side. He wore a uniform and would stride quickly holding a briefcase under his arm. His job in the police was to distribute proclamations to the residents. Sometimes he stood guard at the entrance to the Balanovy theatre and other times at the door of the Auditorium when plays were staged there.

The second person was Yaakov Liev who served as a Jewish government clerk. He did the weighing at the old train station and worked for the railroad. He wore a uniform including a hat with a visor. He was a quiet man, polite, easy-going, religious and well-respected. I do not know how he obtained this position. He gave his children a Jewish education as well as a secular one. One of his sons was a pioneer in Eretz Israel in the Third Aliyah. When the Romanians came to Bessarabia he left his job and went with some of his family to Eretz Israel. His daughter was married there as well as the son who preceded him. His wife came from a respectable family in our town. (Other families from our town who joined in the Third Aliyah are discussed further on.)

The Economic Situation of the Jewish Residents

The Jews of Bendery were merchants, grocers, brokers, agents, religious personnel, tailors, shoemakers, carpenters, barrel-makers, blacksmiths, hat makers and furriers. Most craftsmen in town were Jewish and thus the profession was referred to as "Jewish work". The merchants dealt in grain and wine. Many families lived off these businesses. In town there were large grain warehouses and wine cellars.

Among the businessmen we must mention Asher Kishinovsky who headed the grain merchants group. He was an honest and respected businessman who was of good character and true to his word. He was quite generous and loved to help those in need. His good reputation preceded him and his references were always helpful.

Another was Moshe Haham who was also a grain dealer. He was a scholar and was active in Zionist circles.

We must also mention the Shreibman and Sirkis families.

The leader of the wine merchants was Moshe Rabinovitch. He was a scholar and composed a journal in Hebrew. His wine was used for Passover – even by the ultra Orthodox.

Shlomo Pagis was religious, respected and charitable.

Among the flour merchants there were several scholars - one was Shmuel Abba Sudit. Hirsch Weiser (his daughter Aniuta Weiser-Boris was our first dentist) was inquisitive and involved in both cultures, Jewish and Russian. He was intelligent and wise and gave his children a secular education as well as a Hebrew one. His home was full of national spirit.

I can still see him leaning in the doorway of his shop watching and thinking. He loved to have deep discussions and was an original thinker and was quite broad-minded.

The lumber merchants were David and Shlomo Stoliar (on Krapostnaya Street), Laskin, and Goligorsky – behind the prison in Giska.

The grocers were the brothers I. and M. Immes who owned the largest store.

The fish-mongers were Moshele Saltonovitch and Moshele Levinstein.

The pharmacists were Mulman, Zaidman and Vineshneker.

All the people mentioned were of good character, involved in the community and respected. Some were religious; others were assimilated (except for Vineshneker who was active in Jewish affairs). Others were Russianizers who loved Russian culture. Among the ordinary people there were some important personalities. The tailor Latman was active in the Zionist movement. Meetings were held in his house to discuss Zionism, distribution of funds and dissemination of proclamations. Every meeting was hidden from the police. It was well-known that in Tsarist times, the Zionist movement was forbidden since it was too liberal. Many ruses were used to be secretive. His home was open for such events. On Shabbat people would meet around a table laden with refreshments (as pretence) and they would discuss items on the agenda. He himself would visit homes to distribute funds. He was the permanent Gabbai in the tailors' synagogue. As a committed Zionist he achieved his dream and went to Eretz Israel with the pioneers of the Third Aliyah. He and his wife died there and their sons and daughters followed them to Eretz Israel.

We must also mention Shlomo Buchbinder. Although he was not active in the Zionist movement he loved his fellow Jews. He was the assistant Gabbai in the same synagogue. In 1910 he went to Eretz Israel on the Second Aliyah. He became a member of a labor movement kibbutz. Now, in his old age, he resides in an Old Peoples' Home. His parents also came on the Third Aliyah and died in Eretz Israel.

Another wonderful Jew from among the craftsmen was the shoemaker Simcha Schwartzman. He was religious and loved to study Torah. His son Yosef studied with Pinie the cantor when he was a young boy. Yosef became a cantor in the United States. Simcha Schwartzman gave his children a good Jewish education.

Transporting goods in Bendery – grain, wine, flour- was done by the railroad or on jetties on the Dniester. Carts made of long boards were used to bring the goods to the depots.

The haulers worked in the warehouse and in the store. I still remember Mr. Sobel who lived in a little house on the banks of the Dniester. He kept a stable there. He was an honourable, religious Jew. He always kept his promises and watched what he said.

Well-liked and respected by others, he gave his children a secular education. One of his sons studied at the University of Kharkov and then moved to Kiev. Those Jews who continued their studies while doing hard physical labor for their livelihood brought honor to our town. Sobel was killed by a stray bullet during a battle between the Bolsheviks and the Romanians across the Dniester.

The Suburbs of Bendery

For this topic it seems necessary to divide the town according to its sections, suburbs and their residents. Each section had its own type of residents and its own character.

The surrounding area from Michaelovskaya Street (also called Teachers' Street) up to Kaushanskaya Street was unique. Most of the residents were the ritual slaughterers, teachers and ordinary folk. However, the area from Sovoronaya Street to the Auditorium was different. Its residents were well-known merchants, Hassidim such as the Shreibman family, headed by Shmuel, and the Stoliar family who were lumber merchants. They would congregate in the Talne synagogue located there.

The more privileged lived in the area from the Auditorium to Giska. It was an area almost completely self-enclosed where everyone knew each other's business. There were even marriages among the neighbours. The grain and lumber dealers resided there. The most respected people in town were: Azriel Shreibman, Leizer-Yona Farkonsky, Yehiel Boratnik, Hirsch Laski, and Alter Pasternak.

A totally different section was the one enclosing Harozinskaya Street (actually called Drivasovskaya Street until 1907), Nikolayevskaya, Pushkinskaya and Alexandrovskaya. As a rule, Jews lived there among non-Jews, especially the Moluccas. The elite Jews, highly respected in town lived there. There were important merchants, Asher Kishinovsky (previously mentioned), and Haim Volovetz – a dear and pious Jew, honest in his relations with G-d and man. He brought up a beautiful family. Mulman, the pharmacist, was the most assimilated of them all. He was polite, honest and highly intelligent. Other educated, well-liked Jews lived there as well. It was a quiet suburb where the Russian language flowed especially among the young. The Post Office and the Judicial Bureau dealing in agriculture and real estate were located there.

A different area was the one from the end of Kaushanskaya Street to Sergeyevnaya (including the Glinnes). Here resided scholars such as Moshe Sverdik, Aaron-Moshe Shneirson and wealthy, charitable people – the Blank family. They were quite active in the community. Their flour mill was located there as well. Moshe Stern and Goldenfeld were owners of a brewery. They were rich Jews and belonged to the elite of the town. These two families, Blank and Goldenfeld, had great influence in town. Nearby were the simple, hard-working folk- ordinary labourers. They were poor and their life was hard. Their homes were mainly in the Glinnes and the area extended from the valley. It was almost impossible to distinguish between the streets. The mud was very deep in the winter. This was also a mixed area of Jews and non-Jews who all lived on the banks of the Dniester and the jetty. Relations between them were cordial. Retired army officers resided there. However, their sons- the cadets- were Jew-haters. They often sent their dogs to attack Jewish children passing on the street. The children sometimes reacted by throwing stones. Both factions often ended up with injuries...

Political and Communal Life

Bendery saw itself as an integral part of the rising nationalistic movement in Russia in the previous century. It was not surprising that the Jewish national movement, together with the spirit of the Russian culture, influenced the development clearly seen at the end of the last century. It was strongly felt among the intelligentsia. There was opposition to assimilation- considered a false solution to the Jewish problem. It was coupled with disappointment with the liberal movement in the Russian intelligentsia which had given rise to pogroms in Kishinev and Odessa. The Jews understood that assimilation was not an answer. Another road to redemption had to be found- return to one`s roots and homeland.

Most of the activity took place in the institutions- trust cooperatives, public libraries, Heders and Zionist schools. In addition, practical deeds were seen in the distribution of funds to the poor and the collection of money for Jewish National Fund. There were groups composed of students and working youths- such as store clerks, office workers, tailors and seamstresses. The Hebrew teachers were at the centre of this activity and educated a whole generation of loyal Zionists. Many of them were among the first pioneers in the Second Aliyah. Hanina Kratchevsky became a music teacher at Herzliah High School in Tel Aviv. He brought with him members of the Zipstein family. He was followed by Kasp, one of the first "Young Workers" in Eretz Israel. He was a typesetter and organized a strike at the Shoshani Brothers plant protesting the exploitation of workers. He later became owner of a large printing plant on Avoda Street. It still exists and is run by his son and brother in Kiryat Mlacha in south Tel Aviv. Another was Buchbinder who was a member of Poalei Zion. (I remember the day they left Bendery for Eretz Israel.)

Zionism grew roots especially in two sectors of the Jewish community of Bendery: the intelligentsia which had already absorbed secular and Hebrew education and the group of small merchants and craftsmen. The pious opposed Zionism in those days.

Young people were mainly concentrated in "Zeirei Zion" and "Poalei Zion".

As in all Jewish communities in Eastern Europe, the Zionist movement in Bendery sprang from "Hovevei Zion" (Lovers of Zion). It was headed by Dr. Shlomo Bendersky who was the chief spokesman of Zionism in Bendery. He was kind, aristocratic and pure-hearted. He participated in the first Zionist congresses and was elected secretary of the Bessarabia wing of the Zionist movement before the arrival of Dr. Yaakov Bernstein-Cohen. He organized the Zionist mail and distributed circulars arriving from the Central Office of the Zionist movement. His warm demeanour lit a spark in the souls of the Jews and directed them to the national Zionist movement. Dr. Shlomo Bendersky did not only influence the educated masses, but also the workers who attended meetings of Poalei Zion. He was surrounded by the most active educated Jews in Bendery. One was Hirsch Kogan, an educated and scholarly Jew, a brilliant orator who had great influence on his listeners. His sayings became slogans in our town. Another was Baruch Holdonka and other students. Dr. Bendersky died in 1908.

That year there was a Typhus outbreak in Tiraspol, on the other side of the Dniester from Bendery. The doctors there were overwhelmed and they could not overcome the spread of the disease. Tiraspol was not part of Dr. Bendersky`s jurisdiction, but as a doctor who had sworn an oath he went to help his colleagues. The irony of fate is that among all the doctors, Dr. Bendersky was the only one to contract the disease and he died from it. When his passing was announced, everyone in town greatly mourned him. Even the non-Jewish residents had great respect for him as a man and as a physician. His funeral was quite large. There were delegations of Zionists from all districts in Bessarabia as well as representatives of the authorities and the non-Jewish community.

Haim Greenberg, a regular visitor in Bendery and active in Zionist circles, had close relations with him. Greenberg was quite talented and stood out as a brilliant speaker. He excited the youth and fought voraciously with those who opposed the Zionist idea. He was still young- a handsome man. He could be seen on the streets wearing boots, a round cap on his head and a cape on his shoulders. Every visit he made was a special event for the local Zionist youths.

After the demise of Dr. Shlomo Bendersky there was a reorganization of the Zionist groups in Bendery in order to continue his work. The new grouping included Hirsch Kogan, an intelligent man totally committed to Zionism and the teacher Noah Lifshitz who joined Hovevei Zion in Kishinev and was Dr. Bendersky`s assistant. Lifshitz and Hirsch (Zvi) Kogan were the leading spokesmen in the movement. Others were Israel Blank, Moshe Haham and Baruch Holdonka. They represented the general Zionists movement in town in those years.

Zeirei Zion in Bendery 1906

1) Shifra Immes 2) Leah Rabinovitch –Greenberg

3) Hanina Kratchevsky 4) Olya Rivlin 5) Haim Greenberg 6) Paulina Bendersky

7) Noah Lifshitz 8) Yonah Gogol 9) Esther Lifshitz-Kasp 10) David Natanzon

[Page 34]

Poalei Zion and Zeirei Zion

At the beginning of the century the first buds of the Zionist labor movement began to show. With this came a hope for renewal of life in Eretz Israel based on principles of labor and productivity in order to improve the condition of the Jewish people in its homeland.

The students were the pioneering leaders and others followed them. The teacher Gogol (previously mentioned) and Haim Greenberg of Zeirei Zion of Bessarabia were those who laid the foundation of the Zionist labor movement. Haim Greenberg was able to draw the best students in town to the organization. It was a good beginning, but the most intensive work really began after the Revolution in 1917, especially after the Balfour Declaration.

Group of Poalei Zion 1913

The years 1910-1917 were years of stalemate in Zionist activities in Russia in general and in Bendery in particular. Except for collection of funds for Jewish National Fund and distribution of money to the needy there was no daily Zionist activity. Only in 1917 when there was general activity in Russia was there an awakening among the Jews. Zeirei Zion began to function on a large scale. There had been cultural activity before, but now Zeirei Zion also performed publicly and politically. In the elections to the Russian Assembly, the Zionists trounced the Bund. From 1917 on the leaders of Zeirei Zion in Bendery were Muni Fustman, David Wertheim (the Rabbi`s son), and several students. The influence of their activities was felt in town especially among the students and young workers. We should also mention Seni Natanzon, son of Koppel, the beadle of the community. He was a cultured man who had special influence on the working youths in town. He was a Marxist, but he was devoted to Poalei Zion. He and his wife Esther'ke opened their home to the youths who would meet there for political and cultural discussions. He was killed by the Nazis in the village of Romanovka while she died in exile in Russia.

Pioneering members of the Third Aliyah from Bendery 1920

In 1919 the first Zionist conference after World War I was held in Kishinev. Among the central figures were Moni Postman, David Wertheim and Yosef Kushner. The general Zionists were represented by Hirsch Kogan (previously mentioned) and Israel Blank – an active public personality.

At that time a weekly magazine called "Value and Work" appeared in Kishinev. It was published by Zeirei Zion. Moni Postman founded the first Yiddish daily "The Jew" and two years later – "Our Time".

The members of this young movement took their place on the Community Board. They ran into opposition from the ultra Orthodox especially Shebt'l Berman who headed Agudat Israel. The strange fact was that David Wertheim, his in-law, led the other side.

In the public battle with the Bund the youths of Zeirei Zion concentrated on the prevailing issues. In a debate between the two groups I had to appear as a member of the Bund to defend Zeirei Zion and to eliminate the illusions of the masses.

Zeirei Zion did not only demand allegiance, but they also led by example. They were among the first pioneers with the Third Aliyah to Eretz Israel after World War I.

Third Aliyah Pioneers from Bendery

In 1920 the first group of seven members from Bendery made Aliyah. They were Pnina Wertheim (the Rabbi`s daughter), Pinhas Bendersky, two Tiomkin sisters, Hava (my partner in life) and Shoshanna (a dentist), Avraham Sirkis, Monia Lev and David Weisser.

When we arrived in Eretz Israel, we immediately went to Petach Tikva – the mother of settlements. We began to build our pioneering life by working hard. Two days after our arrival we went to the orange groves in the area carrying hoes on our shoulders. We were "intellectuals" with hands unused to labor, but we really wanted to work. Our hands hurt, but our spirits were high. This was our fervent desire and we knew it would be tough.

Pioneers of the Third Aliyah at Work in the Orange Groves in Petach Tikva
1921

Second row- standing (unidentified)

First row – seated: Pnina Wertheim, Hava Bendersky, Pinhas Bendersky, Meir Levi (Monia Lev)

Four Families that Preceded Us

As mentioned above, we believed to be the first group from Bendery to come on the Third Aliyah. However, when we arrived in Petach Tikva we there found four families from Bendery. They had come several months earlier and had somewhat settled by then. Reuven Kritzman, a wealthy Jew from Bendery, bought a flour mill in Petach Tikva and was quite successful. The Rampel family of seven was headed by a wealthy man. Motel Shreibman and his family of five worked in the orange groves although they had been wealthy grain merchants in Bendery. Weissman brought his family of three and worked in peeling almonds. He had been a grocer in Bendery, but managed to earn a living in Eretz Israel.

All of these people had not been members of the Zionist movement and did not participate in any of its activities. They were simply Jews who yearned for Zion and wanted to live in Eretz Israel. These families were our support group when we arrived and we became good friends. We, the seven youngsters, founded a mini commune. It was the first such commune and it had a reputation of hard-working and loyal members. We always had work and were sought out. The women- Pnina and my wife- ran the household and the men went to work. We were content for two years. We then dispersed to different locations and found our own niches.

Middle Class Immigrants and Groups of Hashomer Hatzair

More families from our town soon followed: Noah Lifshitz, the teacher, Latman, the tailor and Avraham Kushner. Avraham Kushner was a wealthy factory owner, a scholar and very bright. He was well-liked and highly respected. He was often quoted- "This is what Avraham Kushner said".

Latman, the tailor, was an active Zionist. He and Lifshitz were among the first middle class immigrants in the Third Aliyah.

In 1923 groups of Hashomer Hatzair began to make Aliyah. They were absorbed in kibbutzim.

The Hassidim and the Assimilated

Those who went on the Third Aliyah left their imprint on the town where life went on. The influence of Russian culture was felt in Bendery. All intellectual movements from Russia reached our town. On the other side were the Hassidim and the scholars. These were the town Rabbi and Levi Darbrimediker, Nahman Dayan and Pinhas Dayan, the ritual slaughterers. There were other religious personnel who had served with the merchants Avraham Kushner and Shmuel-Abba Sudit. Many people would spend nights learning Torah and they were indifferent to world events. In addition, there were the assimilated who spoke only Russian. There were some Zionist families who spoke Russian at home, but they kept their Judaism since the best weapon against assimilation was Zionism.

The chief assimilationists were Mulman the pharmacist, Zaidman and Dr. Bernstein. They had no major roles in the Jewish community. They believed in educating Jews in Russian. They followed a group centered in Petersburg which had as its goal the dissemination of secular education to the Jews of Russia.

Bund, Social Democrats and Socialist Workers

The second movement following the Zionists was the "Bund". The movement was independent since it had left the social democratic party in Russia after the pogroms in 1903. They believed that the best solution was a life within the revolutionary movement in Russia. The Bund encouraged socialist activities within the circles of workers and craftsmen. It was headed by Oshan, Krasiltchik and others from among the student movement. Debates between Zionists- especially Zeirei Zion – and Bundists were stormy. This was more so after the Kerensky Revolution in Russia. During elections to the Jewish Community Board and the Municipality there was a real party war. The Bund managed to elect Oshan to the Municipal Board. He was an excellent orator and appealed to the residents. Kesselman, the tailor, represented the craftsmen. When Bendery was annexed by Romania he left on Aliyah with his family. He lived in Eretz Israel for the rest of his life and continued to practice his profession.

In addition to the Bund there were other revolutionary Russian movements- the Social Democrats and the Socialist Workers.

One Friday, I believe in 1911, just before Shabbat, two young Jewish men shot at an officer from Kritzky on Haruzina Street. The shots were heard everywhere since it was usually quiet in town. When it became known what had happened there was great panic among the residents. That Friday night of the pogrom very few attended synagogue. Many people locked themselves in their homes that night. After a long search, the police found the guilty men hiding on the roof of locksmith Koonstein. The officer was not hurt. The two young men were transferred to the Petropavlovsk fortress in Petersburg and were exiled to Siberia.

I Particpate in a Conspiracy

The episode in which I participated occurred in 1912. That year a student by the name of Misha Sokolov was sent to Bendery by order of the Socialist Workers. He was Moluccan and rented a room from my grandparents who lived among the Moluccas on Nikolayev Street opposite the Old Post Office. It was intended that he use the room for a conspiracy – living with observant Jews among the Moluccas. Misha's cover was being a teacher's aide in the high school. I was one of his students as was my good friend Zioza Bronstein. Sokolov felt we were candidates to abet him in his task. He was capable and intelligent and we took to him. He gave us leaflets to distribute among the railroad workers in Bendery. He prepared us well and we swore to him that "we would not blab or reveal ourselves". He instructed us to meet Smirnov, one of the railroad workers, in the Old Station (Bendery One) and to give him the leaflets to hand out among his co-workers. We did this three times until one day Smirnov warned us that the police was suspicious of us. We had to tell Sokolov and to be careful ourselves. We immediately went to Sokolov and he disappeared from town without a trace. We saved ourselves and our parents from great unpleasantness.

Bendery was – like other towns – open to many revolutionary movements prevalent in Russia in those days.

Guests from Eretz Israel

Guests who arrived from Eretz Israel greatly impressed us, the youth. The sons of Avremel Kreitzman, the teacher, and Levi Fenitch were students at Herzliah High School in Tel Aviv. (Yitzhak Fein also studied there). We were surprised to see how they were dressed – shorts and high socks. It was the first time we saw grown boys dressed life that. Everyone talked about it. We were also in awe of the strange version of Hebrew they spoke. We had not heard it from our teachers and we did not understand it was the Sephardic pronunciation. Every young person wanted to shake their hands or to go for a walk with them. I remember how those who did so were envied. The sister of Kratchevsky, the teacher, also came and left a very good impression. She and her brother had lived in Bendery until they made Aliyah. She would walk on the street wearing an Arab headdress and spoke Hebrew. She was the topic of conversation among the women. Everyone wanted to spend time with her.

All the guests were very special to us.

Under Romanian Rule

Bendery after the conquest of Bessarabia by the Romanians

The annexation of Bessarabia by Romania in 1918 was an event that seriously shook our town. This terrible change affected the lives of the population in general and the Jews in particular.

As previously stated, from the start of the eighteenth century, Bessarabia was conquered several times by the Russian army. In turn, it was returned to the Turks. In 1812, according to the Bucharest Pact, it was annexed by Russia. Russification followed and the Russian rule over Bessarabia continued until World War I. From 1914 on Romania demanded from the countries in the pact to have the province returned to it. However, Tsarist Russia absolutely refused. It was only after the February 1917 Revolution and the Civil War in Russia that the United States and France agreed to the annexation of Bessarabia by Romania. However, Russia, now the Soviet Union, was against the annexation. Communist armies, camped on the other side of the Dniester, crossed the river in order to battle the Romanians. The Russians knew about ammunition depots in the Bendery fortress left by the Tsarist army. They intended to hit the target and accomplished their plan. The explosion in town was frightening and badly shook the people. It was the first time the residents ever had to seek shelter in cellars. There was exchange of fire between the two armies. Several residents were killed, among them Mr. Sobel (as previously mentioned). He lived on the western bank of the Dniester and was hit by a bullet shot from the Russian side during the exchange of fire. The Blank brothers' flour mill went up in smoke and the tumult and the rushing about cast a great fear. The Romanians behaved cruelly, riding their horses with red ribbons attached to their tails as if mocking the red flag of Communist Russia. They shot indiscriminately and killed passers-by in order to scare the residents and to vanquish them. Many people left town at that time. They abandoned their homes leaving everything behind and made their way to nearby villages. It was the first time the town residents, especially the Jews, felt what it was like to be a refugee. Those who did not leave their cellars in time were hunted down by the Romanian army. Many homes were ransacked and were emptied of belongings. The Romanians took two innocent Jews out of the cellars and shot them to death. They were Mr. Shousterman, a well-respected man and owner of a large fabric store and Melech "seller of coal, wood and plaster". The community mourned the two precious Jews.

Due to the separation from Russia cultural life was diminished and the new situation created havoc in the economic existence of the Jews.

Bendery had been the center of agricultural produce and sent its products all over greater Russia. Suddenly, its cornucopia was dried out. After the annexation by Romania everything changed. Since Romania was an agricultural country, it did not need the Bessarabian produce. This commerce, which was a good source of revenue, was in great difficulty. Many wealthy merchants found themselves in trouble. They rushed about trying to maintain their businesses. The Romanian government levied high taxes on commerce. Taxes were collected with strictness and in brutal conditions. The merchants suffered and many Jews who had been considered for years as respectable and proper were in need of sustenance. They had to dismiss many of their clerks. Craftsmen also lost much of their income under the new Romanian regime. Even independent workers hung by a thread since they did not speak Romanian. Those who suffered the most were lawyers and teachers (some had taught Russian). They did not want to pledge allegiance to the Romanian regime and to become citizens. The situation, of course, caused large emigration from Bendery as well as from the rest of Bessarabia. Some went to countries that would accept them, but the majority went to Eretz Israel. They had always longed to do it. The town was nearly emptied of well-known, public figures and intellectual youths. It was a sad event.

Under these conditions, the Zionist movement overcame all obstacles and grew. The cornerstone for the Hechalutz – pride and joy of the Zionist movement – was laid in spring 1919. At the Zionist conference in Kishinev the following represented Bendery: David Wertheim and Moni Fustman (Zeirei Zion), Israel Blank and Haim Fustman (General Zionists). This conference created an interest in all parts of Bessarabia. Many members of Zeirei Zion in Bendery went to Eretz Israel on the Third Aliyah. They led the way for those who followed. The realization of the dream was an important educational tool among the Jews and the influence of Zeirei Zion grew among the youth. The Aliyah of any member became an important event among the Zionist youths. This is why the Third Aliyah which began in 1920 is so essential.

In the years 1919-1920 there was a constant stream of Jewish refugees reaching our town. Many were pioneers from Ukraine. Bendery, already in Romanian hands, was a border town between Russia and Romania. The Soviet border town was Tiraspol on the other side of the river. It was enough to cross the Dniester, separating the two towns, to be in a safe haven in Bessarabia. Unfortunately, there were many who died in this dangerous transit. Muni Immes, one of the leading citizens of Bendery, was killed while escaping from the Communist regime.

This is the end of my story. In these lines I intended to remember those distant years from childhood and restless youth. These were years that moved smoothly until World War I in 1914. The stormy revolution of February 1917 stopped on the doorstep of Bessarabia after its annexation by Romania.

As the years grow distant it seems that these memoirs become clearer. They feel closer to each other and I see them in a new way. Every part becomes a link in a chain which preserves the atmosphere of those days. I honestly admit that I am a great patriot of Bendery. I unconditionally love the town, its scenery and its people. If these notes will help to add another stone to the monument to our town, among all other holy Jewish congregations, then they fulfill their mission. If, here and there, I omitted a name or an event it was not that they were not worthy of remembering. It was because there was not enough space. I beg forgiveness from all those whose names I did not mention.

Those who remained in town after I left in 1920 will fill in the blanks. We will light a memorial candle to our brethren and we will be joined by the generations to come so the chain will not be broken and the times that are gone will not be forgotten.

[Page 43]

History of the City

(From the encyclopaedia)

Fortress and County Seat
Translated by Ala Gamulka

Bendery was a fortress and county seat in Bessarabia on the banks of the Dniester. It was annexed by the Russians in 1812 and it became an administrative county seat. The town was still then surrounded by walls.

In 1770 the synagogue was built. When the town was moved to a new location, a kilometre away from the fortress, it was only possible to attend services on Yom Kippur. In the forties of the last century, the first local rabbi, the Righteous Rabbi Leib Wertheim, authorized the destruction of the synagogue. He was a grandson of Rabbi Shimshon Wertheim from Vienna. The building had been in poor shape and the bricks were used to build charitable edifices.

The elders told several anecdotes about the building. There were no gravestones found in the ancient cemetery. (The oldest gravestone seems to have been erected in 1781). Many Jews used to prostrate themselves at the grave of the Righteous Rabbi Wertheim in the old cemetery. They had erected a special tent so candles could be lit there. Visitors would drop notes into a special container. The notes would list their problems and difficulties due to poverty and they begged the Righteous Rabbi to plead on their behalf. In 1810 Rabbi Wertheim founded the "Hevra Kaddisha" (Burial Society). – as noted in their records.

According to the 1847 census there were 553 families in Bendery. In 1861 there were 2349 Jewish men and 2263 Jewish women. In 1897 the population reached 31797 of which 10654 were Jews.

In 1909 there were 11 Jewish Houses of Worship. (In 1861 there had only been 5 synagogues). They were the Sadigura, Talne, Ozrei Misshar (merchants), the Carpenters' and others.

The hospital was built in 1884. In 1904 "Help for the Poor" was established. There were also Savings and Loans Funds and two Talmud Torahs. The private one had four classrooms and one hundred and fifty students. The public one had a Trades class and one hundred students. There were twenty Heders and two private schools- one for boys and another for girls.

The "meat tax" brought in 9-9500 roubles. Most Jews were merchants or tailors.

In 1847 there were also other Jewish communities in the surrounding area.

Workers and apprentices gathered near the workshop of the Krassnolov brothers (The weapons needed for self-defence of the Jews of Bendery were concentrated here)

[Page 44]

At the end of the previous century
Translated by Ala Gamulka

Bendery as mirrored in "Hamelitz", 1882-1898

This is a selection of articles from "Hamelitz" (Hebrew language journal). The articles were written by correspondents from Bendery: Israel Bendersky, Yitzhak Miller, Ben Arye, "Righteous of his Generation", "Shemer", Mordehai Atchkover, and the most outstanding among them- Baruch Holodenko.

This rare material reflects upon life in this provincial town as it enfolded about one hundred years ago. It was a life full of good deeds and kindness as well as disagreements and unusual events.

The transcript is given as is in order to maintain the authenticity of the material and to preserve, as much as possible, the public atmosphere of those times.

Revenge using poison (1882)

Assuming guardianship (1882)

A good deed (1883)

Launching the construction of the new hospital (1883)

Pursuit and oppression of the teachers in Bendery (1883)

Anti-Semitism (1884)

Disagreement (1885)

Dedication of the new and enlarged hospital (1889)

A home for the Talmud Torah and Help for the Poor (1890)

Permission to study Gmara as instructed from above (1897)

Caring for Jewish soldiers (1898)

Revenge using poison

Bendery. One of the butchers, P.B., owed 100 roubles to the tax collector, L.A. The tax collector threatened that if P.B. did not pay up he would not be allowed to sell meat. The butcher was angry and he decided to take revenge. On the morning of May 9 he put poison in a samovar and brought it to L.A.'s house. When L.A., his wife, three children, his maid and a neighbour drank from it, they began to vomit and were unable to stand up. If not for Dr. Gorodensky (one of our own) who came to their aid, they would have all perished. The police and the detectives came to investigate and to find out who wished those seven people dead. L.A. told them that his neighbour is P.B. They searched the latter's house and found poison under the sink. When they asked his wife about it, she replied: "Taste and you will know!" The doctors knew that it was poison. The man and his wife were arrested and will be tried in court.

Mordehai Atchkover   Hamelitz June 8, 1882

Assuming guardianship

On 15.10.1882 a sales agent of Mr. Firshtenberg, the owner of the flour mill, was travelling by train. He received a load of wheat from the village of Saidak. When he was a distance of three kilometres away from the Zholtin station, the wagon driver killed him.

It is rumoured that Mr. Firshtenberg has undertaken to support the family of the slain man until his sons reach adulthood.

Hamelitz   21/9/1883

A Good Deed

"Shemer" (our correspondent) praises Yehoshua Shivel, Kalman Fanish and others who are collecting donations. The funds were intended to assist the poor by lowering the price of flour. Some of the others are: the wealthy man ---, in spite of losing profit, as well as, Zvi Firshtenberg who sells grain at cost and mills it for free.

Hamelitz (13)   1883

Launching the Construction of the New Hospital

The honourable wealthy man Yitzhak Nissenboim has donated to the building fund of the hospital by buying a large lot for 2450 roubles.

Hamelitz (31)   1883

Pursuit and Oppression of the Teachers in Bendery

The provincial minister has demanded from the appointed Rabbi a list of all the teachers who run Heders not sanctioned by the authorities. He threatens to prosecute the perpetrators and to severely punish them.

Hamelitz (61)   1883

Our Salvation depends on Education and Nationalism

Israel Bendersky, a medical student, published an article entitled "Our Salvation Depends on Education and Nationalism". He begins thus: The true intellectuals of our generation are those who actively engage in the rejuvenation of our nation and our future. It is thanks to them that our people have begun to discuss the resettlement of the Land of Israel while they sit with their families around the dinner tables or when visiting their friends on the Holidays.

The assimilationists, on one hand, want to throw away everything we (not they) have achieved with blood and sweat. They are prepared to caress the feet of those who trample us and to kiss the hands that oppress us. On the other hand, the intellectuals of our generation worry about our people. They ask: "How can we help the Jews?" Some say that only when civilization embraces us will the Jews be safe and Isaac and Ivan, Jacob and Johann or Jean will dwell together.

In every generation our persecutors are prepared to annihilate us. It does not matter if the reasons are religious, national or economic. There are cases of respected doctors who cannot obtain positions – even after they have cured famous Russian leaders. Professor Mandelstam- an ophthalmologist- was shunned by his colleagues because he was a Jew. This writer feels that knowledge and education will liberate us from difficulties. He ends by talking about an episode that happened on the fiftieth anniversary of the University of Kiev. Professor Benedict was elected as a Fellow at the university. The administration of the university was distraught when they discovered Benedict was a Jew.

Israel Bendersky

Hamelitz 81, page 1334 published 22.10.1884

Anti-Semitism

Yosef Immes writes from Bendery that on Monday, 30.7.1884, one of the citizens, an honest man, went to market to buy something. He stumbled and fell on one of the peasants. The peasant began shouting that the Jew wanted to steal his money. About two hundred peasants heard the shouting and attacked the poor Jew. They beat him severely and he is now close to death...

Signed: Righteous of his Generation

Hamelitz (1082/41)   1884

Disagreement

Hamelitz, Bendery. Avraham Rabinovitch writes in Hamelitz 5 of 18.1.85 about the rift between the Talne Rabbi and his followers and the local Rabbi who refuses to add a ritual slaughterer to the seven already employed. Those on the side of the ritual slaughterers informed on the Rabbi saying his house was built without a permit. The Rabbi was exonerated at the trial. Then they spread rumours that the Rabbi's house was a meeting place for criminals. A provincial representative investigated and the fighting and bad-mouthing increased.

Editorial comment: If this is true, then it would be necessary to mourn our brethren of this town. It could be considered a place for exiled idol worshippers – like Sodom and Gomorra.

Hamelitz 62, page 998   16.8.85

Dedication of the New Hospital

(B. Holodenko wrote on 6.11.89 in great detail about the dedication of the extension of this new hospital. It seems that the following article was also written by him).

Bendery (Bessarabia) 6.8.85. Today the Jewish community celebrated the dedication of the new hospital built thanks to the efforts of Y. Nissenboim. The funds used were left by his late father-in-law Blank as well as donated by community leaders.

At noon all the guests were assembled – fifty people including military personnel, doctors, pharmacists and other leaders. Everyone stood in a circle in the courtyard. The famous cantor Pinie Maherson (specially invited for this occasion) accompanied by a choir sang the "El Melech Natzor". It commemorates the death of Moshe Montefiore. They also sang a "Dedication Song" and toasted the Kaiser and the Director of the hospital. Everyone cheered and sat around a beautifully set table. The Rabbi praised all those who worked on behalf of the building of the hospital and all were elated.

Following my report about the dedication of the hospital, I cannot lie. Unfortunately, the in-fighting in our community has not stopped. What one builds another destroys. Even when it came to the building of the hospital, some wanted an accounting on all the funds collected and the expenses incurred. Who knows if the building will survive these fights?

Denials
Hamelitz 68, page 1103, 9.9.85

Ben Gershom denies the accusation. He claims Nissenboim bought the house and the lot in 1883. He then collected 2000 roubles from the town and 1800 roubles from the "meat tax". He used these funds to renovate the house. Dr. H. Gorodetzky (a doctor who did not receive a prize in his hospital) bought all the equipment. The community leaders were grateful to Nissenboim.

Hamelitz 104, 10.5.1887: B. Holodenko reacts to the article in "Hamelitz 92" in which the Talmud Torah of Bendery was praised together with other schools in Odessa. We were amazed because we knew that it is not praise-worthy since it is a dark, damaged house. Its windows cannot be opened. Every year 3000 roubles are spent on it. It is not economical. This is the seventh year of its founding, but how can it set an example to larger cities?

I wished to tell the author that it is improper to lie or to repeat rumours and to deceive the readers.

Dedication of the New Extended Hebrew Hospital

Bendery, Bessarabia, October 1830.

Yesterday, our town celebrated the dedication of the new Hebrew Hospital with great pomp and ceremony.

In 1884, our brethren, headed by Yitzhak Nissenboim, realized a hospital was needed in our town. They began the work and the new hospital was opened on August 6, 1885. I reported about it, at the time, in Hamelitz. As time went on, the directors saw that the hospital was too small and could not accommodate all the patients. Six more beds were needed in addition to the twenty permanent ones. They sent a letter to the provincial authorities. The amount of 21.111.18, collected as the "meat tax", was already in the coffers of the government. The directors wanted to use this money to build a second Hebrew hospital. The government agreed. Nissenboim donated the lot near the existing hospital for the second one. He worked hard to bring the project to fruition.

In a few months we will see a large, two-story building. I do not exaggerate when I say that this hospital will be equivalent to hospitals in bigger cities. In addition to its physical appearance it also will have wonderful facilities inside. Nothing is missing. Water from the Dniester is piped in to all parts of the building. Dirty water is removed.

This building, a tribute to its founder, Y. Nissenboim and the other directors, was dedicated on Sunday, October 29.

This is the agenda of the dedication:

10:00 am. The hospital was filled with people- Jews and gentiles alike. No one was absent from the spacious gathering place. The famous cantor, M. Shchanovsky, a native of our town, sang beautifully, accompanied by his choir. They chanted Psalm 118: 19-23 and a Psalm about dedicating a building. His wonderful voice pleased the crowd. This was followed by Dr. Bernstein's reading the history of the first hospital from its inception to this day. He then declared the official opening of the second hospital. Although the official name is Hospital for Hebrews, no one, Jew or Christian, will be refused medical attention.

The District representative read a telegram sent by the Provincial Minister. In it he expresses his congratulations and his thanks to the founders of the hospital. He apologizes for not being able to attend. Afterwards, the special guests congregated in one location and everyone else went to different rooms. There tables were set with food and drink.

Telegrams and letters from important government ministers from Odessa and other big cities were read. Everyone cheered and all were delighted. The founders were praised. One of the speakers was Dr. Bloomenfeld from Kishinev. Another was the Priest who said the gathering reminded him of what was found in Jerusalem- patients from many lands. He hoped peace would prevail among the healthy as well.

The mayor, V.A. Vlasenko added: "Let us drink to the ancient nation who is constantly wandering, but is still able to serve as a model to us. I do not wish to say one word against these wonderful people and their good deeds. They are always the first when it comes to performing charitable work, while, to our shame, we are the last to do it. Sometimes we even do nothing. Imagine this, my friends: we received a permit to build a hospital so many years ago. We even had the funds. Our Hebrew brethren managed to build, at their own expense, not one, but two hospitals. We are still thinking about it. Don't think this is the only reason I admire these people. As mayor I know our citizens and I know I speak the truth. Let us take the bathhouse as an example. We remember that last summer the Hebrew bathhouse burned down. The smoke had barely disappeared and we heard construction sounds. These people are great and their deeds are wonderful."

If an honourable Christian could utter these words without fear in front of important politicians, what can we add? May we have more people like him!

The celebration continued till evening. People came and went and Nissenboim ordered his workers to serve more wine. Everyone was very happy.

Nissenboim donated 100 roubles to provide shoes for the barefoot Talmud Torah students and 25 roubles to the Municipal school. All this was done in honour of the great event of the day- October 17, 1888. Everyone was grateful.

Finally here is the list of income and expenses and the number of patients in our hospital:

1885 – 67 patients (53 Jews, 14 Christians); 62 cured, 5 died. Expenses 5405 roubles

1886 – 201 patients (151 Jews, 50 Christians); 174 cured, 27 died. Expenses 6861 roubles

1887 – 282 patients (210 Jews, 72 Christians); 258 cured, 24 died. Expenses 5822 roubles

1888 – 302 patients (218 Jews, 84 Christians); 272 cured, 30 died. Expenses 6408 roubles

1889 – 306 patients (217 Jews, 89 Christians); 272 cured, 34 died. Expenses 5500 roubles

Regular income:
'meat tax' 4000 roubles each year.

Membership- 1300 roubles on the average

Patients paid 9 roubles per month.

Private donations

Income and expenses were almost equal.

B. Holodenko

Hamelitz number 241   6.10.1889

Building for the Talmud Torah and Help for the Poor

Reported by B. Holodenko 20.2

Changes in the administration of the Talmud Torah.: The elderly Zeev Rabinovitch donated a large spacious house on the outskirts of town to be used by the Talmud Torah. He will be only paid 200 roubles per year for the rest of his life. Upon his death, the sum will remain in the treasury of the school and will also be used for other needs. The price of the building has increased to 5000 roubles. It had been rented until now for 600 roubles annually.

Zeev Immes donated 200 roubles to the Talmud Torah and also added a trades workshop for the students for next year.

The cries of the miserable poor dying of hunger and cold have touched the hearts of our wealthy leaders. Last week they held a meeting where 500 roubles were collected. They are prepared to give more. The funds will be distributed among the poor. When spring arrives commerce will resume and the poor will find work.

(We are reminding our town leaders and our Rabbi to make proper arrangements for the distribution of Matzos and funds at Passover. Last year there were some problems).

B. Holodenko

Hamelitz 48   27.2.1890

Permission to study Gmara as Instructed from Above

Yitzhak Miller reports:

A government supervisor, in charge of the schools and the Heders, forbade the teaching of Gmara since it had not been included in the original permit. After some tumult and confusion, Rabbi Shimon Shlomo Wertheim, the school director, appealed to Rabbi Zvi Rabinovitch of Kovno. The latter sent Rabbi Sh. Sh. Wertheim the circular in the original Russian. It was shown to the government supervisor. He thanked Rabbi Sh. Sh. Wertheim for his input and he then apologized.

Yitzhak Miller

Hamelitz 22, page 3   27.1.1897

Worrying About Jewish Soldiers

Ben Arye reports that the town leader Mihel Immes looked after the Jewish soldiers stationed in our town (Kosher meat).

Bendery (Bessarabia). We give many thanks to our leader Mihel Immes. Out of the goodness of his heart he took care of the Jewish soldiers. He canvassed and received donations from everyone. The money will be used for Shabbat and Holiday meals. This year, at Passover, he worked diligently to find homes for the soldiers where they could eat and drink.

May he be rewarded by the Almighty and may the soldiers and the poor souls he helped be blessed.

Ben Arye

Hamelitz, number 110   29.5.1898

[Page 48]

In the Margins of "Hamelitz"
Translated by Ala Gamulka

A. "They love the Rebbetzin..."

Bendery (Bessarabia) August 10, 1887.

A new event – a woman fools the people!

Our readers were previously disgusted upon reading about the deception of our foolish brethren. They follow holy and righteous people who, in turn, use them. The more they are misused, the more they follow. We have also shown that our writers have attempted to point the correct road, but to no avail. Still, I find it necessary to inform the readers about the new affliction.

For some years, the daughter of the Talne Rabbi has been visiting Bessarabia. She is accompanied by a group of assistants and handlers who dance to her tune. She first went to Kishinev where she amassed 1500 roubles. She then came to our town where she stayed at the home of the wealthy widow M.B. for eight days. These were busy days for those of our locals who hate work and love the Rebbetzin. They spent their time eating, drinking and celebrating. They also held Shabbat services. Many people attended her as one would a righteous person. She dispensed food and drink. While she was here she travelled in a fancy carriage when visiting the homes of the rich. They gave her donations in order to obtain her blessings. Many followed her from house to house, singing and dancing. As she left she was accompanied to the train station by twelve carriages and many people on foot.

When I first saw this performance I consoled myself by saying that it was a unique event. I was astounded to discover I had been wrong. The Rebbetzin returned several times. It became a must for her to visit us.

In those days we had another visitor. It was the daughter-in-law of the same Rabbi, the mother of the Tzadik of Talne. She followed the same path as the first visitor. She collected 200 roubles here.

As the prophets said, our townspeople fell under the spell of these women. Shame on you, my brethren. You jump to give your money to these women without thinking. Know that I am aware of these events and I have fulfilled my duty by writing about them.

B. Magicians and Soothsayers

Yesterday, when our people came to visit the cemetery, as they usually do, they discovered the following:

A gravestone was toppled and broken. Among the broken stones a human hand was found. Everyone ran back to town to inform the Burial Society and the police. When they checked the burial plot it seemed that it had not been disturbed at all. When they dug out the body they found one hand missing and the other one tucked underneath. There was no doubt that a human being was involved in this event since no animal would have moved the heavy stones or would have come back to refill the grave.

Why would anyone perform this vile deed? No one knows. Some people think that thieves were involved. However, why did they take away some fingers and not the whole hand? Others believe that the bones were taken by magicians or soothsayers. Why was the hand outside while the grave had been refilled? Many people decided that it was a sign from G-d to point out a sin committed in town – as discussed in the Talmud. Since I am not involved in the investigation and I am not interested in mysteries, I will not decide on any of the choices. Let us leave it for now and I will inform the readers as soon as a decision is made.

B. Holodenko

Hamelitz 1887

[Pages 49-50]

Greeting Cards
Translated by Ala Gamulka

(Dr. T. Herzl, - Yitzhak Yaakov Raines – Shimon Shlomo Wertheim)

    Lydda, 17 Kislev 1903

    Yitzhak Yaakov Raines

    Mizrahi Office #2252

Our greetings to our famous, honoured, hard-working and devoted Rabbi Shimon Shlomo Wertheim and to all his followers,

His letter reached me and I was delighted to read his wise words. I am pleased he is reacting positively to our ideas. Not only is he happy about them, but he is truly working on behalf of those living in our Land. I am hopeful his effort will not be in vain and our thoughts will be blessed. Let us hope G-d will strengthen him and help him in all his deeds. May he be blessed for his holy work.

I wish to be informed about the results of his trip to Paris. He went there to intervene on behalf of fifty families wanting to settle in Eretz Israel. Was he successful? Did the Baron* listen to his suggestions? Does he hope to execute his plan? I really want to know the results.

I hope that when you return to your town you will work on establishing an organization of Orthodox Zionists and that you will continue to disseminate Zionism in the Province. I am waiting for your reply regarding the methods to use and the routes to follow in order to plant the seeds of Zionism in the hearts of the religious followers in Bessarabia and other places. I know you have an excellent reputation and you can achieve a great deal. I have also written to the Rabbi from Manzir.

While I await your kind words, I send you greetings from the depth of my heart.

Your friend in Jerusalem, who respects and cherishes you,

Yitzhak Yaakov Raines

Shimon Shlomo Wertheim

    Bendery, Bessarabia

    25 January, 1904

Dear and Respected Dr. Herzl, Great Jew, Spokesman for his People. May he be praised throughout the world!

I have a request on behalf of my people. Here, in Bendery, there are fifty families who must leave because they are being persecuted, even more so lately. They are mostly young, honest and capable of physical labor. They are prepared to do their share and to overcome any obstacles on their way to the Land of their Forefathers. Their hopes will be dashed if they do not receive help from any organization. I am afraid these precious souls will be lost in the plains of Argentina.

I undertook to go to Paris to plead on their behalf and ask the Baron* to help these families to settle in Eretz Israel. I was unsuccessful. I was promised that they would be allowed into Anatolia after the land in question will have been purchased. After all these promises I realized that all is in nought and they would only be able to reach Argentina.

After I consulted our friend, Rabbi Raines, the head of Mizrahi, we decided to turn to you. Dear Sir! Perhaps you can find a way to help these people. They are prepared to travel to Eretz Israel at their own expense. They will endeavour to obtain a permit for settling even if they have to become Turkish citizens. Between them they can come up with 10,000 roubles.

Please try to come up with a solution to save these young, fresh people we need so badly in our Land. You, dear sir, are the heart of Israel and you will surely solve this issue. We will follow your advice.

With great respect for you,

Shimon Shlomo Wertheim

Reply to Rabbi Shimon Shlomo Wertheim to his letter to Dr. Herzl.

    Mizrahi Office

    Lydda

    7 Nissan 1904

#3130

Dear and Respected Rabbi and Precious Friend,

We received your heartfelt letter and we are rushing to answer. Just before Shabbat, we received a reply from Dr. Herzl about the fifty young people from your town who wish to settle in the Land of our Forefathers. They have 50,000 roubles at their disposal. These are his words: "I will send my recommendation to the manager of the Treasury in Jaffa, Mr. Levontin. I will seek his opinion on how to satisfy their request. If it is possible, we will do all we can to bring them to their destination."

After this message we feel that if the bank in Jaffa can do anything for these dear people, it will. We know Mr. Levontin to be an enthusiastic Zionist who is keen on resettling our land. It would also be a good idea for you to address Levontin himself and to give him all the details so he can assist his brethren.

His address is:

    Direktor des Anglo-Palestina Compania

    Herrn M.D. Levontin, Jaffa, Palestina

We greet the Rabbi and praise his work. We wish him a Happy and Kosher Holiday.

With respect and honour,

Mizrahi Office

* Baron Edmond Benjamin James de Rothschild (August 19, 1845 – November 2, 1934) was a French member of the Rothschild banking family. A strong supporter of Zionism, his generous donations lent significant support to the movement during its early years which helped lead to the establishment of the State of Israel.

[Page 53]

Between Two World Wars

Jews Between the Citadel and the Bridge

Bella Shreibman-Rab (Kfar Saba)

Translated by Ala Gamulka

Childhood recollections are like coins embossed for many years in someone's memory. Lucky is the person whose coins shine and glow all his life.

The street in Bendery where I was born lay between the ancient citadel built by the Turks (when they conquered southern Russia) and the Russian Orthodox Church. The church was enclosed by a fence and was located in the busy marketplace.

The street was entirely populated by Jews and was nicknamed "Street of the Jews". At its end were located warehouses used to store grain from where they were exported to central parts of Russia. At dawn the doors of these warehouses – tightly locked at night- were opened. Merchants stood in the broad doorways and bought wheat brought in by farmers from the countryside. The wheat was piled high in these large warehouses. The merchants bargained and fingered the wheat. This was a daily morning routine.

The Jewish homes were lined up on both sides of the street. The white acacia trees grew along the whole street. The Jewish families had many children and many were inter-related.

The population of the Jewish street was like that of a small, close-knit community. The atmosphere was calm, without any bitterness or envy. Mutual help was constant in this street. The Jews of Bessarabia were well-known for their generosity, goodness and sense of humor. They knew how to overcome difficult situations. They would pronounce amusing and heart-felt sayings and they knew how to wait for better days.

The Dniester flowed- ½ kilometre in width- just behind the street. There was also a big bridge. The citadel stood on a higher hill on the steep bank of the river. This ancient citadel looked like all citadels described in fables. Turrets were shooting up in the four corners with very tall windowless stone walls. A deep canal separated it from its surroundings.

The Square in front of the Church (savor)

The regular army of southern Russia was stationed in this citadel. It had barracks for the soldiers and living quarters for the officers. Soldiers trained there all day. Among them were Cossacks from the Don area dressed in their colourful costumes. They were put up in special barracks. Every morning they would leave the citadel to go to the stables outside where they washed and brushed their horses.

Between this citadel and the Street of the Jews there was a spacious square used for military parades on festivals and special occasions. (During the Holocaust this square served as a killing ground for 700 Jews who did not manage to escape the Nazi murderers – Germans and Romanians alike).

We, the local children, used to watch these parades which were accompanied by a military band and acrobatics of the Cossacks on their horses. We did not feel any fear even though there were many non-Jews in the crowd.

These memories are forever etched in my mind!

A gray metal bridge connected both sides of the Dniester. On the other side there was a Bulgarian village – Farkani. Its inhabitants were ethnic, tall and industrious. They worked their fertile land. Every morning these farmers crossed the bridge to bring their excellent produce to sell in the markets of Bendery.

Men and women formed long convoys as they carried woven baskets brimming with vegetables, dairy products and live fish.

The convoy was somewhat long. The farmers carried scales and were prepared to stop on the Street of the Jews to sell their fresh produce.

The Street of the Jews also had a vineyard belonging to the family of Shmuel Shreibman. In the summer there were convoys of carts filled with large baskets of grapes for making wine. Large barrels were brought into the courtyard. The scent of wine could be felt far away. There were many stores selling groceries, notions and workshops of barrel-makers, carpenters, shoemakers, tailors, etc.

Shabbat brought absolute peace and quiet to the street. There was no commerce and no coming and going. Peaceful Jews were seen marching to synagogues accompanied by their offspring. They carried prayer books and prayer shawls. On Succoth we celebrated by building large succot- to be shared by several families. On Simchat Torah the synagogues were crowded inside and outside and the festivities were outstanding. This is how the street looked on Holidays.

In the hot summer days young and old rushed to bathe in the Dniester. Men and women bathed separately. On Friday mornings we used to see the Jewish and non-Jewish coachmen washing their horses in the river.

This happy life, full of hard work, was not common in other towns of Tsarist Russia.

The spoken language was Yiddish with some Russian words added.

Actually, the younger generation attended school and spoke Russian. At home the children were a\taught Yiddish since these were mainly traditional families. Zionism also came to this Street. The women belonged to various charitable organizations – "Help for the Sick", "Providing for Poor Brides", "Anonymous donations", etc. Most of the women were involved in these activities.

It is believed that at a distance of years gone by and with the perspective of time passed, everything seems rosy. However, these are my memories of a distant and happy childhood in a Bendery of fifty years ago. Since then, I made Aliyah, with my family, in 1920.

[Page 55]

Days Gone By

Nahum Lavonsky (Kibbutz Ayalon)

Translated by Ala Gamulka

I was born on the eve of WWI when our town was still part of Tsarist Russia. I was a child during the war and I can still remember the thunder of the cannons, the bombing of the bridge on the Dniester and running to hide in the cellars. Bessarabia, including Bendery, was conquered by the Romanians in 1918 with the help of the British and the French. It was thus separated from Russia after one hundred years. On the other side of the river there were gangs of rioters- the troops of Petlura, Mahno and others. They organized pogroms attacking the Jews of Ukraine. However, the Romanians wished to please the new population and could not allow attacks on their Jews. So, thanks to the Romanian conquest, the Jews of Bessarabia were spared.

Typhus was rampant in town and many people were felled by it. The hospitals could not accommodate all the patients and the authorities even set up temporary hospitals in several public locations- even in the "Auditorium". The patient care was quite poor and many of them escaped to their homes. This was a dangerous act because they could have been punished by the law.

After all the members of my family had recuperated from the illness, I fell ill myself. My parents hid me at home. If I remained alive, it is thanks to "Roitman Feldsher".

"Roitman Feldsher"- Roitman the medic- was not a medical doctor, but he had a great deal of experience in the medical field. He was considered by the population to be an excellent diagnostician. He was a good man, well-liked by everyone. Roitman would walk from house to house using his cane and he cured the sick – even if they could not pay. Many people sought his counsel and he was able to save many patients. He even invented a cure for headaches known as "Roitman's Powder". He was poor and he died at an old age before WWII.

My father, Avraham Lavonsky – known as Avraham the Teacher- made his living teaching Jewish children to read and write. He taught generations of students. At first, we lived on Michaelovskaya Street and then we moved to Lermontov Street. It was renamed "Street of the Teachers" because most of the teachers had their Heders on this street.

The New Market during Romanian Rule

Children would come to study with our father on a daily basis. The synagogue father attended was damaged in the war and the Torah scrolls had to be removed. Our house became a house of worship once a week. There were about twenty Jews who attended on Shabbat. Father was well-known as an excellent prayer leader. He had a beautiful, pleasant voice and we loved to listen to his heart-felt praying.

We were a large family, but we rented two small rooms from Itzel Fishman (Itzel the Glazier). There was no indoor plumbing.

After WWI hard times came upon us. It was difficult to earn a living, but the needs were still great. Many refugees, escaping the pogroms of Petlura, crossed the Dniester. They wandered from place to place and tried to reach America. The war separated many families who constantly tried to reunite. The refugees remained in Bendery in the meantime. They were received with open arms. In those days, my mother's sister and her two daughters stayed with us. She waited for six years to travel to her husband in America. After much trial and tribulation, she managed to reach him.

A few years later we moved from Itzel the Glazier's house to David Bock's. He was nicknamed David the Scratcher because he used to repair shoes. A simple Jew, he was healthy, tall and energetic. He was one of the storytellers who had served in the Tsarist army for fifteen years. He would tell amazing stories about his army service. Many times we, the children of this street, used to congregate to listen to his tales. In his old age he repaired the synagogue in his courtyard. It was called the Zionist Synagogue.

He died at an old age before WWII.

In the 1930s there were close to 17, 000 Jews in Bendery and surroundings. Some had come from small towns in Russia and Ukraine and they settled in Bendery where they could earn a living. These were good, honest, hard-working Jews. On weekdays they were busy earning a living, but on Shabbat and Holidays they rested and enjoyed themselves.

As is well-known, Rabbi Shloimke Wertheim was our chief Rabbi. Soon after his death, his grandson, Ahrale, son of Rabbi Yossele from Poland arrived.

Although I was a child, I well remember the eulogy of Rabbi Shloimke by his grandson Rabbi Ahrale. It was given at the big synagogue. He spoke about the fact that one of the sons, Leybele, was murdered by criminals on the road to Bendery after WWI. This was a secret hidden from Rabbi Shloimke.

Avraham Eliahu Hazin was the brother of the Rebbetzin Bobka. She was the daughter of Nahman Dayan. Hazin was an honest Jew, well-loved by people and active in public life. He died a tragic death. At the end of WWII he was on his way to Astrakhan in the Soviet Union where his daughter Doba and her husband lived. The rest of the family, including Rebbetzin Bobka, died there too.

In Bendery, as in other towns, many Jews earned their living by working at a trade. They were carpenters, tailors, glaziers, shoemakers and blacksmiths. It was the custom many years ago to nickname people according to their profession. I remember some of them: Shimon the Shoemaker (Fishman), Shmuel the Blacksmith (Nafah), Moshe and Haim the Glaziers (Gershkovitz), Shlomo the Cooper, Maltzik the Tailor, Zalman the Tinsmith, Simcha the Shoemaker and Zalman the Chimney Sweep. Some were named after their hometowns: Herschel Tulchiner (Tulchin); by their appearance- Idel the Blind Man or referring to an event in their lives-the Prisoner. Many of them were killed in the Holocaust. A few managed to escape into Russia and returned to Bendery after the war. Some of them arrived in Eretz Israel after the war.

It has been said previously that the separation of Bessarabia from Russia left an imprint on the economic life of Bendery. The town was stopped in its tracks and did not develop any more. Other towns also could not develop during the reign of the Romanian kings – Ferdinand and Karol II. There were no factories and other sources of income dried up. The youth grew up and could not accept the situation. Those who graduated from high school could not continue their studies. Even those who were apprentices in the trades did not foresee a good future. Their parents had owned stores or dealt in commerce and they did not wish to follow in their footsteps. They searched for something well-founded so they could better their lives. This is how Zionist groups flourished in Bendery as they did in other parts of Eastern or Western Europe (excluding the Soviet Union). A new generation arose that tied its future to the Zionist movement. Young men and women belonged to "Hashomer Hatzair". "Gordonia", "Young Pioneer", "Beitar", etc. Young people from good families left school- sometimes before graduation – and prepared themselves for Aliyah. They were in a rush and wanted to leave the country before they were called to serve in the army. Army service was a waste of time for them. However, the gates of Eretz Israel were locked because of the politics of the British Mandate - especially after the Riots of 1929.

The youth did not give up and they tried other means. Many came to Eretz Israel invited by family members living there; others arrived as tourists for the "Oriental Fair" and "Maccabia" and remained. Some travelled to other countries in Europe or America hoping they would eventually reach their hoped-for destination of Eretz Israel. This is why former residents of Bendery are scattered all over the world.

At the end of the 1920s the Communist Party had some influence on the Zionist movement, especially among the young. The Party was at the height of its popularity mainly due to the economic situation in Europe and America. Many young people joined the Party. Some ran away to the Soviet Union during the winter when the Dniester was frozen. The authorities did not approve and they persecuted the youth. The prisons and secret police headquarters were filled with them. The Romanians were afraid of the Bolsheviks and in their pursuits they did not distinguish between Zionist and non-Zionist youth. Everyone was a suspect in their eyes. There were mass arrests before every Worker's holiday. I recall one Friday afternoon in the Jewish library. The reading room was filled with young men and women reading newspapers or books. The Romanian detectives burst in and took everyone to secret police headquarters with great force and cruelty.

Bendery was not imbued with anti-Semitism as were other towns. Perhaps this was due to the good relations between Jews and non-Jews. Changes came at the end of the 1920s. Some Christian students from Romania came to visit our town with the purpose of popularizing the teachings of the anti-Semitic

Koza. The Jews of Bendery learned of this visit and prepared for it. They were ready for self-defence. Indeed, after several days it was obvious that the anti-Semitic students did not succeed in causing riots and they went back hanging their heads in shame.

In 1932 it was my turn to go to Hahshara (Preparatory Kibbutz) before making Aliyah. I went to Iasi to an agricultural ranch of Hashomer Hatzair. I returned home not knowing when I would make Aliyah. Luckily, I received an invitation from my brother Moshe, z"l who was residing in Eretz Israel. I managed to arrive in Eretz Israel on the eve of Passover 1933. (My sister had arrived a year earlier as a tourist visiting the exhibition).

My arrival in Eretz Israel made me intent on bringing the rest of my family. I was fortunate, after a short time, to bring my parents and my sister and her husband, the late Sioma Mironinsky. He was murdered in the 40s by the British Secret Service. It was during WWII. Sioma was an educated man who had been one of the pillars of the "Hashomer Hatzair" movement in Bendery. He was also active in public life in Eretz Israel. He gave his life for his ideals. He did not live to see the defeat of Nazi Germany or the establishment of the State of Israel.

After my parents arrived in the country they settled close to my brother, z"l, in Beit Haoved near Ness Ziona. Father was a traditional man who was used to attending synagogue daily. There was no synagogue yet in the settlement. Since he was an energetic man, full of initiative, he connected with different people in Ness Ziona. He founded the first synagogue in Beit Haoved with the help of Rabbi Haim Tepper of Ness Ziona. He even influenced the settlers to attend Shabbat services. It was his good deed to perform. He was 68 when he died. May his memory be blessed. He was a kind-hearted, smart and honest Jew. He understood reality and in his will he did not ask for anything that obligates his children. He was afraid they could not handle it.

My mother, Rachel Lavonsky, daughter of Nahman Rotfarb, was born in Proskarov, Ukraine. She grew up in Kishinev and was immersed in Jewish tradition. She was quite advanced for a woman of her time. She read many books and was well aware of her surroundings. She was easy to get along with and understood young people. She always found a common language with them. She never complained about her poor health and was always happy with her lot. She died at the age of 74, having had the fortune of seeing the establishment of the State of Israel. My parents were lucky to live and die in our country. They were both buried in the cemetery in Ness Ziona.

My brother Moshe, z"l, lived in Eretz Israel for close to forty years. He arrived there in a roundabout way in the early twenties. He worked building roads and the drying of the swamps. He was always a member of the work force. He contracted malaria and travelled to France to recuperate. He had a good life in France, but he missed Eretz Israel and returned after a year and a half. He worked as a labourer in the orchards of Ness Ziona. He built a house in Beit Haoved and was totally dedicated to the settlement. He was an active worker who loved books. He was an honest man who lived on his hard-earned income. In the fifties, when his economic situation had improved and he could dream about an easier life, he fell ill and died at the age of 58.

May his memory be blessed!

I cannot honestly write these memoirs of Bendery without mentioning my brother who is still abroad. He was the first in the family to join the Zionist movement – he was one of the pillars of "Hashomer Hatzair" in Bendery. He went to Hahshara twice, but he never managed to reach Eretz Israel. Aliyah was closed before he joined the army as well as when he was liberated. He could have gone, as did many others at the time, to South America. He did not wish to do so. Only Aliyah was acceptable to him and yet he never succeeded. He was one of the best students in Schwartzman high school and he was always ready to help anyone who wanted to learn. He studied and taught Hebrew. He became a teacher in Ismail and was a principal for many years. He is quite dedicated to education and taught many generations of students. When WWII broke out he was able to escape to the Soviet Union. After the war he returned to his hometown and continued to teach.

He was an excellent mathematician and was known in our town as Mathematics Champion.

After thirty three years of absence from my town I visited Bessarabia. I went to Tiraspol, Kishinev, Chernovtsy, Balatz, Orgeyev and Hotin. On my way to Kiev I passed many towns and villages. I even went to Moscow and I met Jews everywhere. They were hungry for news from the Jewish world. I met all members of my family still alive. Bendery, my hometown, remained unreachable. I saw it from far away, but I was unable to visit.

[Page 58]

Days of War and Revolution
Shevach (Sioma) Blei (Haifa)//
Translated by Ala Gamulka

Our town, Bendery, completely changed during the Holocaust years. There is no trace left of our atmosphere of the early days. The best times of our youth, our dreams and our yearnings disappeared forever.

Even today, fifty years later, I visualize the special beauty of our town that so captivated our hearts. I think of the suburb of Boriskova with its holiday cottages, the magnificent Dniester where we sat on the banks and dreamed or we crossed to the other side, the fruit orchards nearby emitting aromas in summer and autumn. I remember the summer holidays when the young people who studied out of town returned and always enriched our lives. On the other hand, in winter, the beautiful Dniester was covered in snow and ice. It became a "war zone" for snowball fights between our youth and the non-Jews.

It is especially important to mention the exciting times when the youth of Bendery were divided into various political groups. The Zionist pioneers included many of the eventual settlers and kibbutz founders in our land. The radical youth participated in the October Revolution. The personalities that even then formed the backbone of our town and contributed to our rich cultural life were: A. Postman, A. Alexandrov, Israel Blank, B.A. Natanzon, Hersh Boger and others.

I remember our town in times of war, revolution, changes of regime and occupation. A special event happened in 1910 (or 1912) when Tsar Nikolai II, himself, came to town. Our townspeople, I among them, ran to the fields. We were hungry for special occasions. When we reached our destination we discovered the train moving slowly with the Tsar standing on the steps dressed in magnificent attire.

I remember the declaration of war in 1914. The auditorium was full of mobilized men. I also remember the way the town looked when war broke out. Out town became a military centre and soldiers were billeted in all the houses. In our home there were soldiers from the Tatar division and we befriended them. They even wrote to us from the front.

When the war was over, the revolution began. It was followed by demonstrations by the railroad workers, riots by soldiers and mobs. The rioters poured wine in the cellars, robbed and destroyed everything in their way. At that time the local militia was founded. Our Jewish students were among its first members. It was led by the Georgian notary Zahankli.

The Romanians betrayed the Allied (countries against Germany) during WWI. When the Germans conquered half of Romania, the Romanians made a separate peace with them. As compensation, Romania was given a free hand to occupy Bessarabia. The Romanians crossed the border, took Kishinev and on November 27, 1917 (new calendar) bombed our town on the side of the citadel. There was a direct hit on the ammunitions depots in the citadel. As a result, a huge fire was burning. Pieces of ammunition flew noisily in the air accompanied by black smoke that covered the sky. The whole town was burning. I was not far away as I watched this frightening scene. I ran home and my worried parents decided to leave town with other residents. We began to run towards the military camp to hide there.

This day is etched in my memory because it was my Bar Mitzvah day. Tfilin had been prepared for me, but I was unable to put them on. It should have been the biggest celebration in the life of a Jewish young man.

The next day – a Friday- it was rumoured that the Romanians had occupied our town and Bendery became a border town. The German soldiers arrived by train and marched on Harozinskaya Street to the bridge in order to cross to Tiraspol in Ukraine. Soon a revolution broke out in Germany and as a result German soldiers began to go through our town, some singly and others in groups. They were dishevelled, in tatters and unarmed. This is how they returned to Germany.

The Civil War was raging in Russia. The Red Army occupied town after town. The White Army of Danikin hurriedly retreated from Ukraine crossing on our bridge on the Dniester.

I stood with others on the hill and we saw many trains coming back. When the last train approached the watching crowd was banished and the bridge was bombed by the Romanians. Again, it was a Friday. Soon the French army arrived to help the Romanians and they fortified themselves along the Russian border. Many of them were black soldiers from Senegal. The town was revived.

One Saturday night on a Romanian holiday, there was a big party. Almost everyone in town took part. They danced and celebrated late into the night. We returned home happy and excited and we had difficulty falling asleep. Suddenly, we heard noise, shots and screams of panic. We ran outside scared and we saw that those Romanians who had just shown us hospitality and celebrated with us were leaving town in haste. We learned that some members of the Red Army had succeeded in crossing the Dniester. They were joined by the Senegalese who betrayed the French and brought them to Ukraine. Soon the Russians were everywhere in town. The main French army was in Boriskova and they attacked the Russians. When the Russians escaped they were joined by some of our best youth- they had been in the underground. Only five or six young men remained who had not managed to run away and they hid in town. The agent of the Romanian Secret Service discovered their hiding place and denounced them to the Romanian police. Their fate was unknown.

The Bridge on the Dniester Destroyed in WWI

I was then working in the pharmacy of Lvovsky-Kogan-Kaushansky. Our clients were among the leadership of the regime and they discussed these events freely among themselves. Inadvertently, I discovered many bits of information. I had to listen, swallow and keep quiet. Soon everything calmed down and life was back to normal. "Hashomer Hatzair" was founded and I joined them. The best youth left town and moved to many parts of the world. I made Aliyah in 1925 with the first group of Hashomer Hatzair. I joined group C of the kibbutz section of the movement. It divided itself into Kibbutz Giva'at Haim and Maabarot in the Hefer Valley.

Good-bye Pushkin Boulevard and my hometown Bendery!

[Page 60]

Gone, My Beloved Brothers
Michael Landau (Tel Aviv)

Translated by Ala Gamulka

There was a chain of villages and towns all along the Dniester which separated Romania and Russia between the two world wars. The majority of the population there was Jewish and was concentrated on the banks of the river. The river had not served as a border before 1918. It had merely separated Ukraine from Bessarabia - they were both parts of Russia. In these villages and towns life was exemplary during the Romanian rule of 1914-18. This chain of villages- Hotin, Ataki, Soroka, Rezina, Rashkov, Bendery (Tighina), Akkerman, etc. - was the backbone of Jewish education, Zionist movements and community life (unknown before 1918). The Jewish population found itself in the spring of the Russian Revolution and was searching for its proper place in the unfamiliar whirlpool of foreign terms and ideologies. It concentrated on what was natural for it- the development of Jewish life.

Bessarabia was a province on the outskirts of the Tsarist Russian Empire. There were millions of Jews scattered in border towns in Ukraine and Poland. The number of Jews in these areas was considerable. The small number of Jews in Bessarabia could not develop an independent cultural life in those days - as was possible in Ukraine and Poland. In Odessa there were many Jewish intellectual powers who founded cultural institutions. These institutions nurtured a strong Jewish cultural community with outstanding social entities and a well-established Zionist movement. The close proximity of Odessa to Bessarabia allowed the latter to benefit from the larger and stronger influences in Odessa in particular and in Ukraine in general.

Jewish Bessarabia produced great Hebrew and Yiddish writers. The Jewish center in Ukraine influenced the Jewish population of Bessarabia then numbering not more than 300,000 people. The echoes of the national movement were felt in Bessarabia. Writers such as Yaakov Fichman, Sh. Ben Zion, Yehuda Steinberg and many others never forgot Bessarabia even though they had moved to Odessa, Kharkov or Yekaterinoslav. They never missed an opportunity to mention Bessarabia with love and admiration.

Suddenly, for political reasons, Bessarabia was separated from Ukraine and was closer to a different Jewish community. Bessarabia became part of Greater Romania. The Hebrew culture and Jewish national movement were quite different there.

At the end of World War I the Jewish population of Romania was composed of four streams of Jewish culture with different languages, diverse histories and new leaders. The osmosis among the Jews in the four streams- Old Romania, Transylvania, Bukovina and Bessarabia- was only possible along one path. It could only happen at the beginning of the growth of the Jewish population in Greater Romania.

Truthfully, the separation of these four areas- between the two World Wars- did not allow for agreement between the diverse Jewish groups. However, when it came to discussing Zionism, all disagreements disappeared. Thus, at the end of 1918, after the Romanian army entered Bessarabia, there was a Zionist convention in Iasi. A Zionist delegation came from Kishinev and there was great cooperation between the two groups.

In the 1920s there was a state of emergency in Bessarabia- a fear of irregular Communist forces sneaking across the Dniester. This caused tension between the military regime and the population. It stands to reason that the Jews of Bessarabia, like the Moldavians, could not cooperate with the Russians - especially since Russia, in spite of its state of upheaval at that time could have forced the cooperation. However, the Jews were shoved into a corner by the Romanian army as a safe bet. At the same time the other minorities (Ukrainians, Russians, and Germans) attracted the attention of the suspicious government. At the end of 1918 and later the Jews tried to publish newspapers in Yiddish or Russian in order to lure the 300,000 Jews along the new political path.

(I do not wish to assess the quality of the press in those times. It did exist, although some of its motives were materialistic).

The national development in Bessarabia began with a Bundist newspaper "Das Vort" (The Word) which did not last long. It was followed by a Zionist daily "Der Yid" (The Jew). It promoted mass education, improvement of spoken Yiddish and the establishment of Hebrew and Yiddish schools (elementary, secondary and professional). All this influenced the cultural life. Yiddish schools flourished in larger towns.

Jewish Life in Bendery

Bender (Tighina in Romanian) was a small provincial capital town. It had a population of around 20,000 people of whom three-quarters were Jews. There were craftsmen, small merchants and professionals such as doctors and lawyers. There was great cooperation within the Jewish community in all parts of public life. The community leaders knew that their work was directed along two paths: Zionism and Socialism (Bund). Here and there some Communists existed either underground or behind the Bund. The Bundists in Bendery were not as powerful as the Zionists. Community life was influenced by all events in Eretz Israel. There were Hebrew cultural activities, newspapers such as Der Yid and later Unzer Zeit (Our Time). It was felt that Jews had two choices:

Aliyah to Eretz Israel or emigration to America

Staying in Bendery and hoping the Soviet Union would conquer them (very few hoped for this...)

In the surrounding villages of the province (Soroka, Beltz, Orgeyev, Hotin, etc.) there were agricultural preparatory groups. The intensification of Jewish life meant Zionist and pioneer activities. Many emigrants from Bessarabia, especially those originally from Ukraine, planned to go to Eretz Israel. They settled in kibbutzim and Moshavim. Many people came from small towns in Bessarabia. 70,000 refugees arrived from Ukraine and sat on their suitcases waiting to continue their journey. Some were forced to go to America because the gates of Eretz Israel were shut to them. Future pioneers from Kherson were kept in detention camps in the villages of Bessarabia- e.g. Kotuiozny-Mare. There they waited for legal permits to make Aliyah. Many emissaries came from the labour movement in Eretz Israel in order to encourage, direct and prepare the young pioneers so desperate to begin a new life.

Bendery was similar to other towns and villages and the leaders competed in collecting funds to support Aliyah. The American Joint helped those who emigrated to America. The Zionists wanted to ensure that these young people who wanted to could reach Eretz Israel.

Among those who resided in Bendery I remember some whose homes served as centers for the Zionist movement. One of those was a Lithuanian Jew, highly intelligent and steeped in tradition - Haim Fustan. Everything he did was for the good of the Zionist movement. He owned a printing press. His wife was emotional and enthusiastic about the welfare of the local Jews. Haim

Fustan had deep Jewish roots while his wife was steeped in Russian culture and literature. She spoke neither Yiddish nor Hebrew and resembled the locals.

The Fustans brought up a son, a daughter and another son. The latter was a member of the London Philharmonic and fell in the Battle of Burma. Haim Fustan also had three children from his first marriage. His eldest son, Moshe, rose like a meteor after he completed university in Odessa. Although he was only twenty he breathed a new life into the Zeirei Zion (Young Zionists). A year after his return to Bessarabia from Ukraine he founded the daily 'Der Yid'. He was also elected to head the local delegation to the Zionist conference in Kishinev in April 1920. He and Dr. Yaakov M. Bernstein-Cohen represented Bendery in the annual Zionist convention in London. Soon, like all rising stars, he left Bessarabia and went to study at the London School of Economics. Upon completion of his studies he was appointed lecturer at the University of London. At the age of 38 he was made a full Professor of Political Economics of the Middle Ages at Cambridge. His step-brother led the Revisionist Party. He, together with attorney Rubashevsky and his dentist wife, led the younger generation in Bendery.

Many important leaders, such as Zvi Cohen, Israel Blank, etc., disappeared in the upheaval of war. (Perhaps they have descendants in Israel who could speak about their families). The educator Schwartzman made Aliyah and became the principal of a high school in Eretz Israel. Others were fortunate to live in Eretz Israel and to continue their activities there.

How can anyone evaluate the extent of the loss incurred in the destruction of a large part of Jews of Bessarabia? When we look back and see how much this community contributed to the Jewish people we feel the great pain even more. These people were cruelly cut down and Eretz Israel lost one of its main sources of Aliyah.

In commemoration of these Jews from Bendery we also remember the many other communities that were great examples of Jewish life. The Jewish community of Bessarabia sustained such a great loss, but it was still able to plant beautiful seeds in our homeland. They are a reminder of their tradition and their ancestors and the strong love they had for Eretz Israel.

[Page 63]

In A Sailing Boat On A Stormy Sea
(Our Aliyah inside a coal container in 1920)
Arieh Shreibman (Kfar Saba)

Translated by Ala Gamulka

Our father, Mordechai Shreibman, was born in 1879 and made Aliyah, illegally, in 1920, with his extensive family, on a sailboat. He was a veteran of the vineyards in Petach Tikva. When my father settled in Kfar Saba in 1927 he joined the working public in its struggles within the Hebrew movement and against the local authorities. He was a respected public personality and became one of nine people appointed by the British governor to the first local council. He was the chief Gabbai (sexton) in the Great Synagogue in Kfar Saba and was quite active on its behalf.

My father was one of six Shreibman brothers from Bendery. He was highly respected by the residents of Bendery and was constantly traveling on business. Our mother, Yocheved, was a lovely, bright woman. She ran the large household and brought up her only daughter, Bella and her four sons Meir, Arieh, Elisha and Avraham. We had a traditional home, but we were not overly strict in religious matters. We, the children, were taught Hebrew from Kindergarten on (it was the first Hebrew Kindergarten in Bendery). We were steeped in the strong connection to our distant homeland. We sang about the Jordan River, Mount Carmel, the Sharon Valley and Mount Hermon. We continued our studies in the same atmosphere in the newly established Hebrew high school of Dr. Zvi Schwartzman. My father and his friends were instrumental in its founding. Our home was open to all who loved the Hebrew language and to those who longed to see their homeland. We gratefully drank in any news from this distant, yet so near, land.

We went by boat on the Black Sea and reached Istanbul. However, we were unable to continue on our way because we lacked visas and a boat. Our father ran about, exchanged money, tried hard and finally obtained a travel permit to Beirut. After a two-week stay in a hotel we went down to the hold of a freighter just emptied of its cargo of coal. In this black and filthy storage place we stayed on the floor -father, mother, we the spoiled children, and a group of young students from Russia making Aliyah. From Beirut we continued by stagecoach - piled high with luggage. We were deep in thought about what awaited us on this unknown road and we wondered about our future. Where were we going?

In the meantime, the stagecoach came nearer to Sidon - a small port in Lebanon. The sun set and we were left in an alley near the fishing wharf. It was all strange to us and we were a big family. Father distributed the suitcases among the children, each one according to his ability. We were warned not to make a sound and we stole down in a row to the beach. We took off our outer clothing, entered the water and reached a sailboat. There were several fishing boats tied to poles in the water. The young students who had previously traveled with us joined the group. There was also a Jew from Jerusalem who was returning home. The captains were two Arabs wearing a red fez and wide pants. They told us to lower our heads deep in the boat so we would not be seen from shore. When we disobeyed they threw blankets on us so we would look like cargo.

It was a wonderful night and the sea was calm. The moon shone on the white sails of the fishing boats. Only the Jerusalemite did not agree to lower his head. He sat erect and mumbled the Travel Prayer (Birkat Haderech). The ropes were loosened and the boat sailed and floated on the high seas. The next day, before noon, the sea became stormy. Streams of white foam hit the sides of the boat and rocked it like a nutshell. The waves were high and then they were low. We all became seasick. We used up all the lemons we had prepared. Everyone hung on to the sides of the boat. Mother could not rest and worried about her children. Most of the travellers fainted and lay helpless. Even the Arabs who steered the boat had to fight the insubordinate sails. They had never seen such a storm. We were afraid the boat would turn over and we could drown. Those who believed in God prayed their last confession (Vidui) and the others shook with fear. We were still far away from our destination.

In the early hours before dawn the Arabs managed to direct the boat towards shore. We reached Atlit, near Haifa. There was a group of Jewish fishermen waiting there among the ruins of an ancient fort. They came into the water naked and carried us to safety on their shoulders. We were soaked and exhausted.

Thus we were reborn in a new homeland. From then on we took an active part in the resettlement, rebuilding and defence of our home in difficult times.

"The Tribunal"

[Page 65]

My life in Bendery
Shmuel Gilboa (Kiryat Haim)
(Formerly Mica Greenberg)

Translated by Ala Gamulka

My life in Bendery was filled with the sadness of childhood. It reflected the decaying existence of a Jewish village in Eastern Europe between the two wars. This was a dying village whose continuation depended on nearly nothing. It seemed to me that my life in Bendery was a typical example of the life of the youth of my generation.

1. Sadness of childhood
A. Early childhood - fear and terror

My earliest memories of "self" come from the feeling of dread during the Romanian conquest. I was three years old and my sister, Manya, was three weeks old. We sit on the shores of the Dniester clinging to our mother. Father is busy with arrangements to transport us to the opposite shore to Uncle Aaron in Tiraspol. A tortured return to Bendery follows. We run quickly to a damp and cold cellar to hide from the incessant shooting; darkness and a tremendous roar coming from the blowing up of the bridge on the Dniester; a lull and then a restarting of the shooting.

After the conquest there was a lack of confidence. A train from Kishinev was attacked by thugs. A Jewish passenger was killed and the city was teeming. At night there were robberies and break-ins. Before bedtime Father would carefully check the locks and bolts on the doors and the window shutters. During the night of the attack on the train we were awakened by a terrible noise. Someone on the outside was shaking our door and trying to break in. My parents and I yelled "Guards! Help!" The noise outside stopped, but it seemed to me that someone had managed to break in and was on his knees rattling the metal headboard on my bed. I was shivering and wondering when this dark figure would leave. I eventually fell asleep.

Soon the new authorities were in control. For around twenty years our lives moved along two paths typical of any Jewish village in the former Russian Empire: a struggle to survive and to preserve Jewish life.

B. Struggle to survive

What was the source of subsistence for the Jews of Bendery? How did my late father, Yitzhak, earn a living?

Bendery served as a commercial center for the surrounding countryside. Its Jews made their living from the Romanian peasants in the area. The peasants brought their agricultural produce into town: wheat, fruit, dairy, and, in winter, lumber for heating. They bought what they needed – groceries, notions, fabrics, work implements. They had their wagons repaired and their horses shod, etc. For all these needs the Jews also ran inns in spacious courtyards where there was room for the horses, bulls and the wagons in which they traveled to town. There were also taverns and tea houses, shops and workshops. Blacksmiths, belt makers, locksmiths and carpenters served the peasants. The Jews also made a living by running small corner groceries and they worked as painters, glaziers, electricians, owners of bathhouses and cinemas. Of course, there was also religious personnel- rabbis, judges, ritual slaughterers, cantors, etc.

My father's story is sad. For over three years he owned a clothing store in a booth in the church square. Those years were good. We had real electricity and our copper samovar hummed quietly for hours each day. On Friday night there was an aura of holiness with a white tablecloth on the table and a challah covered in a sparkling cloth. Mother blessed the candles in the silver candlesticks. Father would return from synagogue service. Our beautifully painted home was engulfed with the singing of "Shalom Aleichem, Angels of G-d" We would sit down to the specially set table and during the meal we sang Shabbat songs. I remember the melodies to this day.

When I turned five there was a celebration in our home to commemorate the fact that I was now ready to learn Torah. "At five a boy begins to learn Torah". Many guests came and there was festive atmosphere. Under the guidance my rabbi I read a portion from the Torah and I felt like I was "King of the Regiment".

However, these wonderful times did not last. For a reason I still do not know, my father closed his store and never reopened it. He was impoverished and he never recovered. After that our lives were difficult. We had to leave our beautiful apartment and move to a simpler one. We continued to move from one apartment to another.

Father remained unemployed. Eventually, he began to sell fabrics to peasants in a distant village. He was away from home for many days trying to earn a living in that village. We, at home, were in great need. When he would return we were not always happy because often he came back empty-handed.

In spite of this I have some good memories of our struggle for Jewish survival.

Kindergarten teacher Batya Shteiner with Grade One and Kindergarten students of the Schwartzman High School.
(In the center, Dr. Schwartzman and Kindergarten teacher Batya) 1922-23

C. Jewish survival

My mother, Pessia, z"l, was the one who kept up the struggle for my Jewish education. She did it along two paths- Hebrew High School and Heder (Talmud Torah).

i. Hebrew High School

The family of "Tzalel the Cantor" (nickname for Rabbi Betzalel Shteiner, the cantor) lived in our courtyard. Their oldest daughter, Batya, was the Kindergarten teacher in the Schwartzman High School. She influenced my mother to enroll me in this Kindergarten when I was four years old. For the next ten years I was a student of the Schwartzman Hebrew High School.

From an early age I absorbed the Hebrew language. The holy language of prayer and Torah was spoken by me. At home, on the street and among friends we used Yiddish and Russian, but in school only Hebrew was heard (Ashkenazi pronunciation). We did not study all subjects in Hebrew mainly due to the lack of textbooks or appropriate teachers. We had some non-Jewish teachers, but the atmosphere in the school was nationalistic and Hebrew. This formed the emotional basis of our Jewish existence. We celebrated every Jewish holiday. The sounds of "Hatikvah" were often heard in the school. We truly believed that "our hope to return to our homeland was not lost". No wonder that many of the students joined youth movements: Maccabi, Hashomer Hatzair, Gordonya, Beitar and other Zionist groups. Many of them made Aliyah.

The second path my mother put me into was the

ii. Heder and Talmud Torah.

Mother took care not only of my secular education, but also of my religious studies. In the same courtyard where Batya, the Kindergarten teacher lived, there was also a "Heder" and the home of the teacher A., the "redhead". Even prior to Kindergarten, when I was three and a half years old, my mother rushed to send me to him to learn some "Yiddishkeit". In a play on the words of Ecclesiastes (1: 18) I can say that "the beginning of learning is the beginning of pain". We sat in a long, narrow room in his home. Every child had a prayer book or Torah in front of him. The Rebbe sat at the head of the table. He would come to sit by each child for a few minutes in order to teach him. This is how I studied on a daily basis. After two weeks, I sat, as usual, and read "kamatz aleph –A" "Patach Beit –B". Everything moved smoothly, but suddenly, I stopped because I had forgotten how to pronounce "Kaf" with a dot underneath. The Rebbe glowered at me and I saw his pointer on my stumbling block in the open prayer book. Nothing helped. In order to shake my young memory he opened a drawer. Without saying a word, he showed me the thin whip lying there. I did not understand his hint and I was still stuck. I just could not remember. Suddenly he shot the whip at me with full force. I fell off the bench and found myself under the table on the clay floor. I was screaming "I am hungry! I want to eat!"

Still sobbing, I climbed back on the bench. The Rebbe did not reveal the secret I had forgotten. My heart was full of hatred and I returned to my seat on the other side of the table.

From this Rebbe I continued to others. I had many teachers even when I studied in the Hebrew High School, especially during the summer vacation. When we became poor, my mother sent me to the Talmud Torah. There were times when I studied in the Hebrew High School in the mornings and I went straight to the Talmud Torah on the other side of town. In the dark of night I would return home, on another side of town, on Sovoronaya Street.

From all these teachers, I best remember two in the Talmud Torah: Old R. Shimon and the stern Mr. Yankel Lonievsky.

Learning in Heder and Talmud Torah was dry and tedious. There was translation into Yiddish after each word followed by Rashi interpretation. In spite of poor teaching methods the "Heder" refined our senses. Reading prayers together, reciting Torah portions using incantation, the special feeling of blessings after the Haphtarah – all these awakened emotions and elevated our souls. My knowledge of the Hebrew language, learned in the Schwartzman Hebrew High School, brought life to the letters in the holy books in the Heder and the Talmud Torah.

In addition to the Hebrew High School and the Heder, there was another factor in my education in Bendery – youth movements.

iii. Youth movements

My mother directed me to the Hebrew High school and to the Heder, but I found my own way to the youth movement- Hashomer Hatzair. Father never interfered and mother did not stop me. I did not find any contradiction between the life of the Heder and the atmosphere of the Hashomer Hatzair clubhouse. I was eight years old and I came for a simple reason. I liked a girl my age that used to visit and play with her friend who lived next door to the clubhouse. There was a gap in the fence and I could see my beloved through it. I joined the Hashomer Hatzair to be there. I even went to the library in order to impress her. I began to read books in Hebrew in the library run by Mrs. Pistrova.

I soon forgot my original motive and I became an enthusiastic member of the movement. My heart was enthralled by the atmosphere in the clubhouse. I belonged to a group and I thoroughly enjoyed all the activities: singing and speaking together, camps, nature trips and exciting games in the forest. Communal life, education to be considerate of others, helping each other and looking after weaker people – all this fostered in us special values. I cannot describe how much we loved our counsellors Niunia Bendersky and David Stoliar. The movement awakened in us the spark for self improvement and encouraged us to aspire to self-perfection. I immersed myself in reading. I taught myself Yiddish and I was able to read serious literature at a young age.

The movement held district conferences in villages and in the forests. Special friendships were formed between different young people from other areas. They corresponded and visited each other.

I was immersed in daily life and did not understand the ideological side of Hashomer Hatzair. It can be heard in the Yiddish lullaby:

"Sleep my child, my dear one!

The big houses, beautiful palaces are built for the rich.

When you, my child, will get older,

You will understand the difference between rich and poor"

We sang rapturously.

"Our Father, our King, have mercy on us and answer us. Do a good deed and save us!"

However, someone actually watched and listened to the "socialist tripe" of Hashomer Hatzair. Two or three years later the clubhouse was closed by the Romanian security forces and we had to continue in secret. We no longer had our beautiful house in the large courtyard, but we met in small groups, in private homes. Eventually we moved to the Maccabi sports facilities. The Revisionist Beitar also had its headquarters there. We were all together – Beitar, Hashomer Hatzair and Maccabi.

My enthusiasm for Hashomer Hatzair decreased and I switched to Maccabi. There I began to play chess and it became more important for me than sports- the real purpose of Maccabi.

In spite of all my activities in school, Heder and the youth movement, our home situation overshadowed everything. The natural happiness of childhood was transformed into one of true sadness.

In the meantime, my childhood years were gone. I was already thirteen and I began to worry about my future. What would I do in life when I get older?

2. Aimless youth
A. Worse economic conditions

My few young years in Bendery were an expression of the worsening economic conditions for Jews and especially for their young people. There was an accelerating economic distress and the authorities severely punished Communists. Many young Jews were enthusiastically drawn to Communism.

Every so often someone would cross the Dniester to the Soviet Union. I well remember Misha Kaushansky, Yoske Lvovsky and others whose names I have forgotten. Every crossing of the river brought a tightening of security, persecutions and oppression. At nightfall there was police presence on every corner. You could be arrested for almost anything, at the will of the police officer. It was dangerous to have a book with socialist content. Once, on May 1, I went to the library with the book "The Hunger" by Fink. I was afraid I would be arrested. The lack of intelligence of the police officers can be seen from an incident that happened to me.

I was interested in Astronomy and I wanted to see the moon through a telescope. I could not find one so I decided to use the idea behind it. On a moonlit night I stood on the street with a friend holding two small mirrors and a magnifying glass. We were hoping to see an enlargement of the moon using these aids. A police officer appeared and began to question us because we looked suspicious to him. He asked us: "Are you signalling to the Communists?" Our explanation of our astronomy experiment was unacceptable to him and he took us to the police station. The officer on duty freed us with a smile.

Soon I left the Hebrew High School- before graduation.

B. Leaving the Hebrew High School and transferring to Ort

In the beginning of the school year in the fall of 1929 I left the Hebrew High school and transferred to the vocational school Ort. Why did I not graduate after so many years of study at the Hebrew High School? There were several reasons. One was definitely worries about my future. What will I do after graduation? A diploma from Schwartzman Hebrew High School could take me to university, but only outside the country. Could I possibly dream about such an event? On the other hand, I could learn a trade in Ort and perhaps that would help me in life?

I studied in Ort for three-and a-half-years. I took machine shop, engraving and galvanizing. The principal was always a Jewish engineer. There were three in my time- Finkelshtein, Flexer and Vasiliev and Finkelshtein again. The vocational teacher was always a non-Jew. No matter what, he swore in colourful Russian. He would begin in one workshop and finish in the blacksmith's shop 50 metres away.

My hands were not meant for this work. I was an excellent student in academic subjects, but I was only average in any handiwork. I had made a mistake. I was not meant to do this work. It was not the proper route for me. My teenage years should have been the best years of my life, but they turned out to be an inappropriate preparation for a trade. In addition, our life at home was full of poverty and our family still grew. We were four children: I and my three sisters Manya, Baila and Ethel, the baby.

C. Situation at home worsens

The poverty and neediness at home accompanied me constantly like evil shadows. Still, our spiritual and educational life did not stop. Our mother scrimped and saved from her meagre funds to pay for school supplies: books, notebooks and, later, drawing equipment for Ort.

ORT Vocational School
(Teachers and students)

In those days, I was interested in two things: playing chess and reading books. I often played in tournaments on an empty stomach or read by the poor lighting of a small gas lamp. Sometimes there was no glass cover, just a small wick, but I still continued my reading of many books in Yiddish, Russian and Romanian. I also went to Maccabi, especially after we succeeded in forming an active chess club.

In the meantime, I completed my studies at Ort. And then what would happen?

D. Graduating from Ort and becoming a tutor to young children

Truly, what could one do in Bendery without a trade that was in demand?

In 1932 I finished my courses at Ort, but I really did not have a trade and I could not find a position based on what I had learned. What will I do at the age of seventeen? Luck would have it and I was offered a teaching position in the village of Kitzakny. There were four Jewish families living there. They owned stores. I was hired for a season, winter or summer, to tutor their young children in Hebrew, prayers, Torah and mathematics, etc. I changed residence every week or two, moving from one family to another. Five or six children came for lessons for several hours each day. I was free the rest of the time.

Will I always be a tutor of young children? Perhaps I should complete high school? I spoke to Gregori Yakovlevitch Schwartzman and he agreed to let me write the final examinations every year on condition that I come to school at the beginning of the school year. I did so. In my ample free time in Kitzakny I studied the material of the Sixth Form which I had abandoned and I prepared myself for the finals.

However, events turned differently. I was swept up by the idea of Aliyah to Eretz Israel. How did this happen?

3. The solution : Aliyah to Eretz Israel
A. Preparation for leaving

I did not finish high school. The trades I learned in Ort were not useful. At home there was only abject poverty. I was only a tutor of young children in a village land I was living with different families. These were listless days, without a purpose. What will tomorrow bring? What will happen in a year? In two years?

These struggles brought out the idea of leaving Bendery and abandoning Romania.

Even during my childhood I was aware of relatives and friends leaving Bendery. When I was five my aunt Hannah and her husband left for the United States right after they were married. They settled in New York. At the same time, my good friend Myron Kleinman, his mother and sister made Aliyah. Two years later, Nahum Piker went as a pioneer. He left me as a souvenir a Hebrew book with colourful pictures. Another uncle, Nahum, immigrated to Argentina. Some people went to Canada and others to Brazil. Bendery made a contribution to the general trend of the immigration of Jews from Eastern Europe. My turn had come. When the final decision was to be made, my Hebrew education influenced the result. It had to be Eretz Israel. How was I to achieve this goal? There was one route: Hahshara through a Zionist youth movement. This is how I came to "Gordonya". I became a member. Instead of Aliyah being only a solution to my problems it became the purpose of my life. New horizons opened up. A new way of life was unveiled to me in"Gordonya". Now my life continued along two paths: the social and ideological life in "Gordonya" and Hahshara.

B. Social and ideological life in Gordonya

The social milieu was similar to that of the Hashomer Hatzair of my childhood (except for scouting activities which were not done in Gordonya). However, what united all youth movements at that time were the constant ideological discussions among us and with others from other movements. It was a true rainbow including Communism, Agudat Israel, Hashomer Hatzair and revisionist Beitar. We talked and argued about everything: the Soviet Union as the fulfilment of dreams, Birobidjian as a solution to the Jewish problem, the Internatzional Two and Three and Peace on Earth. Matters which troubled workers in Eretz Israel worried us as well: common union with Arab workers, Zionism, socialism, private and public finances, national and private settlements and the ideal settlements: Moshavim (cooperative settlements), Kvutzah (small agricultural collective settlement) or Kibbutz (larger collective settlement).

We had a clear stand on every issue. We truly believed in the ideology of our movement.

The late A.D. Gordon was our spiritual father and his writing guided us. We searched his books for solutions to issues in the world in general and in the Jewish world in particular.

The ideology was anchored not only in our spiritual life. It was also a guideline for our daily life. We knew we could turn our dreams to a true reality. We called it "Hagshama" (implementation).

Every movement had a special finite purpose. Of course, I believed the finite purpose of Gordonya was the correct one, the true one, the best of all! It was the implementation of the labor vision of A.D. Gordon, by merging man and nature. The road to implementation was so simple! One must make Aliyah to Eretz Israel and to live there in a Kvutzah like Degania and to belong to an association of Kvutzot (not, God forbid, the United Kibbutz movement). I adhered to this ideal of living in a Kvutzah in Eretz Israel. I did not see the purpose of studying trades in Ort or finishing high school. What use would it be for me in a Kvutzah in Eretz Israel when there I would work the land in the midst of nature? It would be better for me to reach my finite purpose faster.

It was the spring of 1933. Before going to Hahshara I went to see Gregori Yakovlevitch Schwartzman to thank him for giving me the opportunity to complete high school. I told him my plans. He shook my hand and wished me luck.

I went to Hahshara hoping I would soon be in my Kvutzah in Eretz Israel.

C. Hahshara

Many young men and women from Bendery believed the only road to Aliyah and to obtain a permit to go to Eretz Israel was to join the Hahshara. Very few were accepted and of those only a small number made Aliyah. The needs were great, but opportunities for Aliyah were minute. We spent several years in Hahshara. I spent four years there – from May 1933 to July 1937 when I finally made Aliyah.

The stops on my route to Eretz Israel were Hoshi, Oreshti, Sofaifka, Ripichani, Beltz, "Masada" and again Beltz.

In Hoshi we lived in a stable cleared of manure. Footstools joined to each other were placed in the space for the stalls. In Oreshti we worked in orchards from morning to night.

In Sofaifka we worked in beet fields. We were crowded in a small hut that barely accommodated us. We built a tent-like structure made out of bamboo shoots. On the first night there was torrential rain and the water came inside. We escaped back to the hut. However, in the beet fields of Sofaifka I met Soyba Bercovitch from Akkerman, my wife today.

In Ripichani we worked in a sugar factory on day and night shifts. In Beltz we were woodcutters. The congestion was great and there was not enough work. Only a few of us worked and supported the others. We were starving.

Once, when we wanted to see a play in the theatre of Bartov, we tried to fool our stomachs. We got up at noon and so we skipped breakfast. In the evening we went to the play and we returned close to midnight. Who eats dinner at such a late hour? We went to sleep and the next day we did the same "trick" and were able to save enough to see a second play.

In "Masada", near Beltz, we had more adequate accommodations and it was a true agricultural Hahshara. There was only one "Masada" and there was only enough room for a small number of participants.

Members of Gordonya from Bendery tilling land in Masada, Beltz August 1937

No wonder that under these conditions, with a small chance for making Aliyah, many members left us during this long road in the Hahshara. Some were deemed ineligible by the movement. We nicknamed the process "selection" because it was quite severe. Only those considered capable of living in a group were awarded a permit. I was fortunate to be among them. However, four years passed until I received the good news. It was April 1937. While I was in Hahshara in Beltz I was told to return home to wait for the date for my trip. I went home and waited impatiently for my coveted date for Aliyah.

D. Aliyah – 48 hours of fear

The day I left Bendery was a symbol for my miserable life there. I made Aliyah to Eretz Israel during the days that were full of fear before the war.

I finally received a cable from the "Hechalutz" center asking me to go to Bucharest where I would be given all the necessary papers. From there I was to go to Constanza – the embarkation port for Eretz Israel.

It was Saturday and I went to the train station with my father and mother. We bought a ticket for Bucharest and we went to the platform. Suddenly, someone approached me and asked me: "Where are you going?" When I innocently replied "Bucharest" two secret policemen suddenly appeared and took me to a room in the station. Only later did I find out that the Prime Minister of Poland and Colonel Beck, the Foreign Minister, were to visit Bucharest on the following day. One of the security measures taken by the Romanian authorities was not allowing travel to Bucharest to "suspicious characters" like me.

I discovered all this only later. In the meantime, I was kept in solitary confinement. Horrible thoughts engulfed me. Why was I arrested? I thought back to all my previous activities. Where did I sin? All this on the brink of my Aliyah? Is my arrest connected to my Aliyah? My army service had been postponed for one year. We are now in July and I am to present myself again in January. Perhaps they are trying to stop me from making Aliyah so I would not avoid army service? G-d in Heaven, what will be my fate? Will I really have to stay in this hellhole to serve additional time in the army? I was trembling and I was scared. The dark figure that stood near my bed in my childhood returned. I ran crazed back and forth.

After about half an hour- which seemed like an eternity- I heard the steam whistle from the outside. The Bucharest train left the station and I remained behind. Dear G-d, woe is me! A detective came and told me to go home. He warned me not to dare travel to Bucharest. I felt relieved and I understood there was no connection to my army service. What will happen to my trip to Eretz Israel? My papers are in Bucharest and the ship leaves from Constanza on the following Monday. What can I do?

My father and I went to the post office to send a telegram to the "Hechalutz" centre in Bucharest. I informed them that due to circumstances beyond my control I would go straight to Constanza. I requested that my papers be sent directly to Constanza.

At midnight I took the train to Galatz to begin my journey to Constanza. It was a moonlit night when I said good-bye to my parents. My little sisters Bailaleh and Etaleh were asleep. I kissed my beloved sister Manya- three years younger. We said good-bye with a kiss and a handshake. My sister and I innocently believed that we would soon meet again. She was to make Aliyah in, at most, a year. She, too, was a member of Gordonya.

Bendery (Tighina) train station

My mother, father and uncle accompanied me to the train station. My father had prepared money for bribing, if necessary. The station was nearly empty. Detectives stood in doorways. One approached my father to tell him that I was not allowed to leave Bendery. His opposition dissipated when he received money. I crossed the platform and boarded the train. I sat on a bench all alone. Suddenly, my mother, may she rest in peace, appeared. She was a skinny, pale and suffering woman. I asked her: "Mother, what happened?" She gently replied: "My son, I want to see you once more!" She looked at me lovingly and left – forever... She never saw me again. In 1942, during World War II, she died in Kazakhstan and was buried near my father and on the shores of the Caspian Sea. Her heart was full of longing for her son in Eretz Israel. I found this out later from my sister Manya.

I traveled one night and then another night changing trains until I reached Constanza. All along the trip, my heart was full of fear. Were my papers transferred from Bucharest on time? Will I reach the ship on time? Will I be arrested in the train station in Constanza? Did the secret police of Bendery instruct the secret police of Constanza to stop me from leaving the country?

When I finally reached Constanza after many trials and tribulations I saw a group of detectives at the exit from the station. What should I do? There was no choice. I took a chance. No one approached me and I was allowed to go through. I was free!

That afternoon I boarded the ship 'Romania'. Slowly the coastline disappeared and with it the misery of my life in Bendery.

How painful is it that I am the only one in my family to have survived. My dear parents and sisters were not so fortunate. My mother and father died of hunger during the war. My sisters remained alive and returned to Bendery. They raised families in this terrible hellhole!

[Page 75]

Hassidim in Bendery

Bendery in Hassidic Literature
by N. Huberman
Translated by Ala Gamulka

Kishinev is mentioned in Hassidic literature in the times of R. Leib –Sarah's son – (1729-1798). It was part of a fable about Kaiser Franz-Joseph.

Bendery is alluded to by R. Yaakov of Polanaa in a story written in 1769. This was related to me by an individual from Bendery. Apparently there was an old custom that a governor from one place was not allowed to enter a fort belonging to another one. However, this time one of them did do so. The governor had to pay a fine for allowing it to happen.

The late R. Leib Wertheim was the chief rabbi of Bendery. He was the grandson of R. Shimshon Wertheim from Vienna who was known in Hassidic literature as R. Shimshon, the Viennese. The nature of R. Leib and his methods were not known in detail. He is listed in the roster of Hassidim who died since the time of the Baal Shem Tov as having passed away around 1782. The Jews of Bendery would come to pray at his grave, to light memorial candles and to leave special notes- as was the custom among the Hassidim of Podolia since the days of the Baal Shem Tov.

Among the Bessarabian Hassidim the Sadigura and Chernobyl dynasties stand out. It is obvious from their names which are affixed to many synagogues. It is well-known that the split caused many controversies. Churches served as hotbeds for rioting, at times. However, the Bessarabian Hassidim did not wish to fight and soon cooler heads prevailed. Until 1847, there were, in Bendery, synagogues named after Hassidic Rabbis from Sadigura and Talne, as there were in other towns in Bessarabia. The descendants of Rav Schneerson's family – one of the founders of Chabad – settled in several towns in Bessarabia and named synagogues after him.

The Hassidim of Bessarabia had many beautiful customs. Among the wealthy there was always competition on who would distribute more food to the poor prior to the High Holidays, entertain more guests for meals at their table, support more Torah students, Yeshivas, Talmud Torahs, etc.

When Zionism arose, the Hassidim were its biggest opponents, whether in secret or openly. Their activities were full of hatred and animosity. In many homes there was disharmony in the family. Fights between fathers and sons reached a scandalous level. After Bessarabia was annexed by Romania in 1918, many Hassidim of the Sadigura and Chernobyl dynasties moved to Bessarabia. The number of Hassidim decreased.

Zionism captured the hearts of the people and replaced the Hassidic zeal.

(From an article by N. Huberman titled "Hassidism in Bessarabia", published in the book "In the Lands of Bessarabia", compilation A, 1959, edited by K.A. Bertini)

Hassidim in Bendery

The first Hassidic court in Bessarabia was established in the 1820s. R. Aryeh-Leib Wertheim, founder of the Wertheim dynasty, had his headquarters in Bendery. He was the son of R. Shimon-Shlomo of Sovran and the brother of R. Moshe-Dov. R. Aryeh-Leib was a member of one of the most important families in Ukraine and he was the grandson of the Maggid R. Nahum of Chernobyl. R. Nahum was the father of the Chernobyl dynasty (Twersky Hassidim), a brother-in-law of R. Shalom of Prohovitz. He, in turn, was the grandson of the Maggid of Mezerich and the father of R. Israel of Rozin.

In 1814, R. Aryeh-Leib became the chief Rabbi in Bendery. He served in that position for 41 years. He died at the age of 82 in 1854. His followers traveled to see him, to give him special notes. His influence was great not only in southern Bessarabia, but also in Odessa.

In the Pinkas of "Sayers of Psalms", the first signature is that of R. Aryeh-Leib Wertheim. The last entry is in the year 1881.

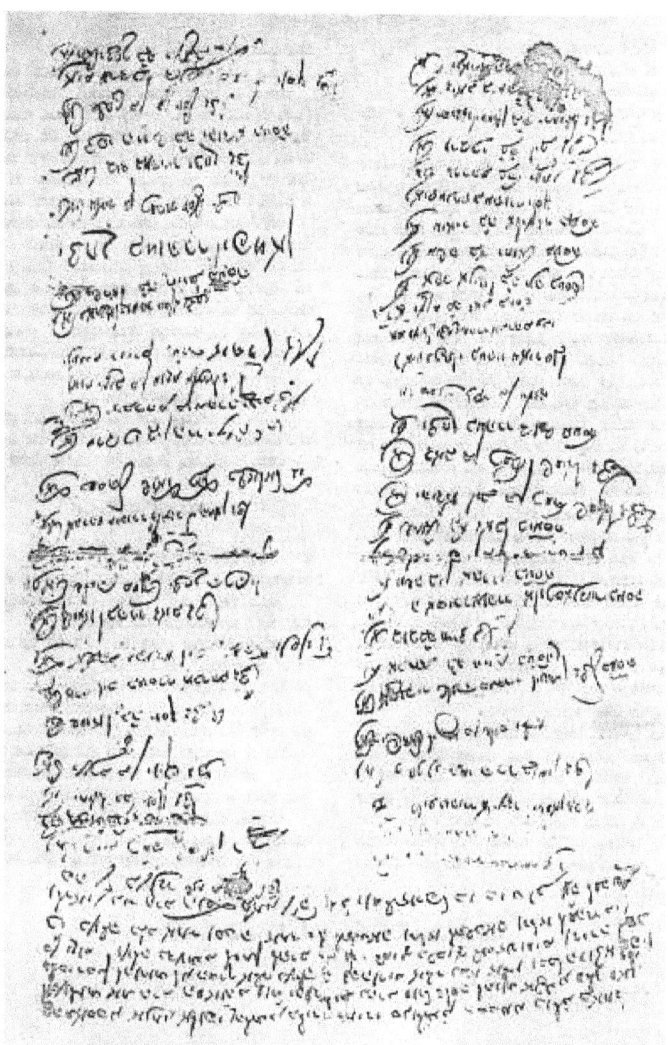

Appointment letter of R. Aryeh-Leib Wertheim, z"l

[Page 77]

Rabbi Moishele and His Hassidim
by Yonah Balaban (Hulda)
Translated by Ala Gamulka

I do not wish to write extensively on this topic, although I really should. I am certain greater and better people have already done so. I only wish to highlight and describe Hassidism in our town. As seen through the eyes of a young child.

My father, Pinhas Balaban, z"l, was close to Rabbi Moishele Landman and I was able to feel moments of sanctity and personal exultation. I absorbed the holy atmosphere around the much admired late Rabbi.

The first thing that left an indelible mark on me has to do with the purchase of a home and a house of worship for the Rabbi and his household. The Hassidim- my father, may he rest in peace, among them – decided to sell raffle tickets to the Jews in town. Their aim was to buy, with the proceeds, a large home for the Rabbi. There was one condition – the winner had to turn over his winnings to the Rabbi! The timing was not great: this was wartime. In spite of the hardships they proceeded with their plan. I avidly followed the plan conceived by my father and his fellow Hassidim. They did everything to ensure the success of the raffle. It took place on time. Their happiness when the house was purchased was indescribable.

In this way the gifts of a home and a house of worship were given to the Rabbi. My father did not stop with these gifts. He made certain the Rabbi would not lack for anything. Since my father was a fish monger he ensured that there was plenty of fresh fish for Shabbat and for every holiday. The Hassidim were served tasty gefilte fish during all three Shabbat meals. They were prepared by the Rebbetzin, may she rest in peace.

* * *

During World War I and the Bolshevik Revolution which followed, the population, on many occasions, had to hide from the bombardments in cellars. There were days when it was impossible to go outside since there were street battles between the Reds and the Whites. There were conquests and retreats and there was a great loss of life.

My father, the loyal and dedicated follower, was not afraid of the pitfalls and the dangers. He overcame all obstacles. Every Monday, he disappeared for several hours. At first, we did not understand how our father could leave us at such a difficult time. He would go, at great personal danger, into the tumultuous streets. Fires would erupt in destroyed houses and dead bodies lay in the streets. However, my mother, Feiga, may she rest in peace, calmed down by explaining that father tried very hard to reach the Rabbi's house to see how he and his family were managing and to try to help them...

I understood everything and I stopped asking questions.

* * *

Soon better days arrived. These were days full of light and happiness, Hassidic dancing and singing. In the center of this was the holy Rabbi. Many of our townsfolk probably remember Simchat Torah in Rabbi Moishele's synagogue. In addition to the regular Hassidim, many other Jews came to enjoy the Hassidic celebration. They were delighted to be honored with Hakafot. Some were even fortunate to eat Haloshkes (cabbage rolls filled with ground meat and rice) cooked by the Rebbetzin. The Master of Ceremonies would announce "such and such receives a haloshke and non-Jew receives a slap" (a play on words in Hebrew). Everyone would applaud happily and Hassidim danced. Their coats flew around and the sweat poured down their faces. Their voices were hoarse and everyone was very happy.

My father's devotion to and his admiration of the Rabbi were well-known. When he spoke the Rabbi's name he always added – May the Rabbi have a long life. It seems that the Rabbi reciprocated. Anything connected to Pinhas Balaban was important to him, e.g. special water for baking Shmura Matzo always came from the tap in our yard. Even if the distance between the two houses was great! A few weeks before Passover a "convoy" would arrive. It was led by the Rabbi's sexton, followed by Hassidim carrying pails to filled with water from our yard and to be used for baking their Matzo.

I was a young child then, but I remember how proud and honored we felt that of all the taps in town, ours was the one chosen. This custom continued for many years, even after my father's death.

When my devoted father died, the Rabbi honored him by following his coffin on foot to the old cemetery five kilometers out of town. Everyone talked about this event since it was unique.

This was our Rabbi- beloved by everyone, surrounded by loyal followers. May their memory be everlasting!

[Page 81]

The Second Aliyah
In the days of the Second Aliyah
by Rivka Machneimy (Holodenko), z"l
[daughter of Baruch Holodenko, a well-known educator, delegate to the Zionist Congress, correspondent of "Hamelitz"], Ein Harod

Translated by Ala Gamulka

1911
I Make Aliyah to the Galil

I came to Eretz Israel on the 7th day of Tishrei (1911), three days before Yom Kippur. I arrived with many others at the famous hotel owned by Haim Baruch in Jaffa. It was well-known for its filth and messiness. Before nightfall I went to the Laborers Club to meet people and to inquire about work. In my heart I had decided to go to the Galil. When I asked what kind of work I would find in the Galil. I heard the reply: "If you want to cook or do laundry you will certainly find a job there!" I could not accept these words. I had imagined that in Eretz Israel I would work in the fields like a simple Russian peasant.

I did not think I would come to Eretz Israel to be a servant. After a few minutes, I replied: "You can't frighten me!" I began to inquire about how to get to the Galil from Jaffa. I discovered that during Hol Hamoed of Succot there was a group of pioneers planning to go to the Galil. I went to meet them

We were thirteen people, mostly new arrivals and a few old-timers. The trip was difficult and exhausting, but the scenery was beautiful. We were so intent on seeing everything that we did not feel the tribulations.

On the fifth day we reached the Kineret where we met the members of the settlement. I cannot describe the beauty of Lake Kineret as we first saw it. It was peaceful, wide and deep.

In spite of my excitement I did not forget my main purpose – to find a job. I approached one of the members and asked him about work. At the same moment, someone from another settlement asked if I already had a job. He offered me a job on a new work farm on Mount Poriah. There were only five members there and they needed someone to cook and do other housework. I was delighted to accept the position and I went off with him.

Rivka Machneimy (Holodenko)

We reached the farm on Mount Kineret. Towards evening I found, in the fenced yard, a pile of stones and pieces of wooden building materials strewn about. I heard many languages spoken, especially Arabic. I believed these were Arab laborers who came to build homes. I later discovered that Sephardic Jews also spoke Arabic.

Suddenly I heard loud singing from the rickety dining hall. It actually resembled a shed. In the dark room one could barely see people, but one could hear singing and animated dancing. The people looked like shadows because the lighting was dim. Suddenly there was loud banging that scared me. It was a dinner bell. In the shadows one could barely notice tables made of boards and the sound of plates and cutlery, accompanied by talking. The noise grew and was impossible to take. Again one could hear the singing of "El Yvneh Hagalil" and again wild dancing erupted. I sat shocked and I wanted to escape from the din. I just did not know how to leave. The room was completely full and there was no space to move a limb. I finally came outside. I was upset and full of longing for home. I was on the verge of tears. I was full of inner doubt and I asked myself if I could really stay there. Didn't I want to escape from here and to go home? Then I thought to myself: "Wouldn't it be great to be able to consult with someone about work somewhere else?" As I was wandering alone, some people approached me and asked me: "Where are you from? What do you want to do? Will you stay here?" They begged me to remain there as a cook. They talked about the place and about their past, their work and their plans for the future. This was a desolate place.

I then found out about the farm in Migdal where there was someone from my hometown. I decided to reach him and consult with him about what I should do. In the morning I went there without informing the person in charge. The beautiful scenery enthralled me and I arrived very quickly.

In Migdal I met my friend. We spoke about home, mutual friends and Eretz Israel. He invited me to stay in Migdal. I refused remembering the miserable situation in Poriah. Suddenly, the person in charge from Poriah came looking for me. I spoke about my doubts. He then explained that it was a new farm and the members were young and inexperienced. I decided to return to Poriah and there I became a partner in the redemption of Eretz Israel.

Malaria
November 10, 1911

I have been working in the kitchen for the past few weeks. It was not as terrible as I thought. I was afraid that getting up early would be difficult. I realized it was good to be up before everyone and to do my work without any interference and with a clear head. Lately I try to get up at dawn and to read in bed. The library has not been organized yet and I cannot get books. The books I brought from home are dispersed among my friends. I wrote home asking for more books to be sent to me. I should have taken more with me.

Tomorrow there will be a meeting where work will be discussed. It is difficult for the members to work with the Arabs. I look at their lives: they eat their thin pita bread which they heat on the fire. Sometimes they prepare a black coffee which is impossible to drink. At night they sleep on the ground. Their lives are miserable, but they do not complain. Our members complain non-stop. At night they fall into their beds utterly exhausted.

How do Jews build a Homeland?
December 5

Today I received a letter from home. I was so happy. Father asked me what has been accomplished in Eretz Israel and what was happening there. He wanted to know how Jews work the land and build a homeland. As a seasoned Zionist he knew more about Eretz Israel than I did, but I was fortunate to be there. I could see everything with my own eyes. He only knew information from books and from his intense work in the Diaspora. How terrible! Father has not yet seen Eretz Israel and who knows if he will ever do so... It is only three months since I left home and I miss my family! I would be so happy to see my father in Eretz Israel. (My mother died when I was a baby). Father is dedicated to Zionism and he has not yet been able to see the first steps of the pioneers who came before me.

From time to time I re-read the letter and my longings become unbearable. A fear engulfs me. "Can I really pass this test?"...

The hour is late. It is a good thing no one came to my room. I need to be alone.

The kitchen in the beginning
December 12

Today I wrote a letter home and I included dried local flowers. I wrote about my work in the kitchen feeding fifty to sixty people. It is good they do not know how difficult my conditions at work are.

I put together the first kitchen on the farm. I hung up a few sacks to create a cooking area. I dug a trench, added some rocks and placed a pot on top of them. I am constantly worried that the pot will topple over or that the food will not be good. I gathered some wood from the building site and I also found some twigs and branches. I was wearing a dress with a tight skirt that I brought from home. I was unable to jump over the trench so I cut slits on the sides. My high heels also hindered my work.

My work hours are from 4:30 in the morning to 9:00 in the evening. After work I help my friends. I mend trousers and wash shirts. I am the only woman on the farm and the men are not used to doing this work.

1912

First General Meeting
January 5, 1912

Today I began to rearrange the kitchen. We now have a cooking stove and I will no longer get wet in the rain. Soon another woman will join us and my joy is unimaginable. It is difficult to be the only woman. In addition, there is no one to relieve me.

It is raining very hard and all the members stayed in and did not go to work today. This hampers my work. The wood is wet and the fire would not light. This made it difficult for me to prepare a meal.

After supper a few members came to the kitchen and helped with the dishes. They felt sorry for me and told me that on rainy days I should serve food that did not need to be cooked. I disagreed and I continued to cook even on rainy days.

Today was a good day. I heard that a family with children was coming. They also had grown children in Kineret and Yavneel.

Tomorrow there will be a meeting with a lengthy agenda. Only I realized I had made a mistake at home. I still do not know enough Hebrew. I had concentrated so much on learning Russian instead of Hebrew. I decided to speak Hebrew, but it is hard. My friends know more and to try to correct my mistakes. There is no way to learn the new language because there is no one to teach me and I have no free time. After work I have to look after friends sick with malaria.

Quinine for the members – to block Malaria
January 10

I wish the new kitchen would be built already. There will be a room for me and for the new female member who is due to arrive soon. I will be a better cook, too. Maybe on Shabbat I will go to Kineret to visit Hannah Meizel and I can get instruction from her on cooking with local products. In spite of all the difficulties in my work I believe that it is not so terrible. My main wish is for the members not to be sick. A week ago I was in Kineret where the malaria is worse even though they receive quinine on a regular basis. At our meeting we spoke about the need for a daily dose of quinine.

Working in the fields is not so easy now. The earth is being prepared for ploughing so almonds and olives can be grown. When will I leave my kitchen work and change to the fields? First, I want to fix my kitchen so the new woman will find it easier to do her work.

I have been writing and I did not realize the hour is late. I have to get up soon to go to work.

More Malaria patients
January 22

This week I read very little. I had to look after the new member who is already ill with malaria. He was very sick and had high temperature. I could not leave him. If he is still so sick tomorrow we will take him to the doctor in Yavneel. He lay in bed all day by himself. I went to him several times to bring him a drink. It is difficult to do it while I am working. D. Came back from work today with a high fever. It seems he, too, has malaria. There are many sick men and there is no place for them to lie down. This saddens me very much. When the kitchen is built there will also be rooms for the members. I went today to the Bedouin tents to get some milk for the patients, but I did not understand anything they said. I gave them a pail and showed them money. I also asked for some eggs. I paid them what they asked and I returned home happy. The first time I went there with Meir Hazanovich -He was [later] killed in Merhavia in 1913. Now I know the way to go by myself. There are more and more patients and I am worried...

Father lectures at Zeirei Zion assembly
January 28

Today I received a letter from some friends from home. They included reports of an assembly of Zeirei Zion. They write that there is much work to be done and that new members have joined. They write with enthusiasm about Father. (Rivka, the author, is the daughter of Baruch Holodenko, a well-known educator and a delegate to the Zionist Congress. He was also a correspondent of "Hamelitz").

They sent me a copy of a lecture he gave at a meeting. It is good that father is so devoted to this movement. They envy me that I am fortunate to be living in Eretz Israel. Would that one of them could also make Aliyah!

I am invited to Merhavia
February 5

I was invited to work in Merhavia. It was difficult to decide because I was used to my place. I had made friends and I was deeply involved in Poriah. Besides I really did not want to work in the kitchen again, although I was not as afraid as before.

On Friday night there is a party to celebrate the new planting and the members said they could not plan it without me. I undertook the decoration of the dining room and the preparation of the food. The director told me not to go to work in the fields and to start preparing. I did not want to lose a day of work since we are under contract for the job. Every member is important.

This week I received letters from home. Soon one of my good friends will arrive. Today some tourists from America visited and took some pictures. They will probably be shown in cinemas in America. Perhaps one of my relatives will recognize me. The news from home gave me the energy to do my work.

My pay is equal to that of the male laborers
February 8

It's a celebration- five girlfriends came to Poriah! Tonight we arranged a work schedule. We are planning a vegetable garden for our own use. Since the new female arrived I have been working in the laundry and in the fields. Now I work in stone removal. As of tomorrow I will be planting olive trees. The farm has a personal account for every worker. On the first day I was given 9 grush for the job while the men were allotted 2 francs (the equivalent of 11 1/2 Turkish grush). After a few days I was earning as much as the men. The work in the fields was hard – removing stones, pulling up roots of old plum trees, planting olive and almond trees. There were two supervisors who watched the laborers. In spite of all this I was very happy. I discovered a new world where fieldwork was valuable.

Now two women will work in the kitchen and I will be in the field. Another woman will do the laundry and the fifth will work in the vegetable garden.

From now on life here will be like in any settlement. We have two families now and we are more mature. We can now set an example.

I want to find my own way in life
February 11

Today I worked with a member who is expert in planting. He has been here for two years. I would like to be a veteran in Eretz Israel. I have not seen much –not even settlements nearby. On Shabbat I visited Kineret. It is so beautiful and I did not want to leave.

When I first came to Kineret I was asked to join a farm led by Hannah Meizel. I refused thinking that I wanted to find my own way in life. It probably would have been easier for me to learn, to work and to perfect my Hebrew. Here I have a purpose even if there are hardships. We are creating something new while in Kineret I would have come to something established. I would like to see the fruits of my labor, to see the place where I first began to develop and to grow.

At work we often have a supervisor. It is not pleasant. He does know all about work in the fields and he is almost native-born. He gets along with the laborers. Still...

We aspired to the sublime
February 12

I had a good day at work today. We sowed almonds and I worked in the olive grove. Field labor rejuvenates me physically and mentally. One can think, listen to birds chirping, and sing. All this is helpful in creating even if one is nervous and one wishes for more.

I miss my friends from home. We grew up together and we aspired for more.

When I came home from work I felt I had a temperature. Could it be malaria? I did not tell anyone because I wanted to go to work the next day. If I take quinine maybe my temperature will not rise.

I have become a wagon driver
March 4

Today I continued to work with R., a wagon driver. I am his assistant. The field was full of small and large stones. There is a wadi nearby and we have to fill it up with stones. I asked R. to let me have the reins, but he refused. I begged and begged and he finally agreed on condition that I carry the large stones while he brings the small ones. I, of course, was thrilled and took the reins. I did not care about the conditions that he gave me as a joke. I was not insulted. I drove the wagon all day and I was in a good mood. One thing made me laugh: whenever we came close to the wadi he got off because he was afraid we would turn over... In the evening, at the table, he spoke about our mutual work and the "condition." He was delighted and everyone laughed.

On the other hand, Sh. has promised to teach me how to drive a wagon without any conditions...

My worth increases within the group
April 14

Today I worked with Sh. He works well. In a few days we will begin to harvest the wheat. I will work with him hauling the wheat. How great! In Russia I envied the peasant women who worked in the fields. I dreamed about it. This will be my first harvest in Eretz Israel.

I was very tired. We connected watering pipes to a new line. Tomorrow I will continue to uproot the old plum trees. We have a contract for the job and I am part of it. I am so happy.

A night spent watching an ill patient
May 2

While supper was being served I noticed that one of the new members was missing. I was told he was ill. When I finished my work in the kitchen I took a lantern and I went to the barn where the patient lay burning with fever. I asked the person near him to put the patient in my bed and I began to look after him. I placed cold compresses on his forehead and I prepared quinine for him.

It was quiet in the dining room. Everyone was asleep and I sat writing in my notebook. At times the night watchman came over and asked about the patient. He asked: "When will you go to sleep? How can you work tomorrow if you do not sleep?" I teased him and I asked him: "How can I leave the patient all alone? I am healthy and I can mange without sleep…"

What will happen to the patient? What will happen to all of us? Malaria! That's what everyone says.

As I listened to the patient's breathing I heard, from far away, the singing of Meirke Hazanovich, the night watchman. The patient talked through his fever and sometimes I was scared. Suddenly he said: "Rivka, bring me a wagon with rubber wheels and take me home." I burst out laughing and I soothed him. His fever was now lower and I was thrilled. He began to perspire and I closed the window. I gave him two quinine pills.

The night watchman came to the window and told me that I have to go to work. I tiptoed quietly out of the room. I was so sorry to leave the patient alone. I was going to try to visit him during the day.

Wheat is brought to the threshing floor
May 6

This week we started to bring the wheat to the threshing floor. How can I describe how great was our satisfaction? We rise at 2:00 am and it is very quiet. Everyone is still asleep. We go to the fields where we pile the wagons high. We continue to the threshing floor. The moon lights our way and we do not even feel that it is night time. Dawn breaks slowly and we see our members setting out to work. At eleven we stop our work and we take a rest until 2:00 pm. We then return to work and stay till evening. We work a day and a half every day. The flies begin to pester us. After we bring in the wheat I will go to Merhavia. I will try working there and I may decide to stay.

I do not regret my decision
June 5

I remember when my father realized that he could not influence me not to make Aliyah at such a young age (I was only seventeen). He spoke to me and said: "How will you earn a living when you have never worked even one day?" I replied: "There must be other people like me and they are working…" I do not regret my decision. I have been here for ten months and I cannot honestly say I am happy with everything here, but I am here. There will be improvements in the future as the country develops. The people of Israel will flourish in this land.

Flowers for my birthday
June 11

Today was a hot day in the fields and it was difficult to work. We dug trenches for the planting of olives. I came back from work tired and in a bad mood. It has been two weeks since my last letter from home. My brother in Argentina invites me, "in all seriousness", to come to him. If I agree he would arrange the trip. He probably thinks I am in dire straits. I was shocked at receiving this letter and I will not reply.

We decided to arrange a meeting of the members to plan cultural events. It is a necessity in life.

When I came home from work, a surprise was waiting for me. In my room I found a bunch of wild flowers in a vase on the table. A note was attached. It said: "Shalom Rivka. Today is your birthday. I came to congratulate you, but you were not home. I could not stay. I remembered it was your birthday from two years ago and I decided to wish you a Happy Birthday. I gathered some flowers for you on the way." I completely forgot about my birthday, but D. (my father's student) remembered and was not too lazy to come from Migdal. I understood why he did it – he heard I was lonesome for home. Since he was older than I he wanted to help me...

Social life develops
August 22

Tonight a few members met in my room and talked about work. We read some foreign newspapers and sang Hebrew songs. It was very good. After everyone left I felt badly. It has been a year since I had seen anyone from my family. How I would love to see my father! I did not imagine that I would spend a whole year in Eretz Israel and I would not see my father. I hoped he would come because there was a plan he would be part of a mission. However, it has not yet happened.

In Merhavia

I have not written in my diary for some time. I have been in Merhavia for two months. I have a feeling that I will not stay here much longer. I have made some friends here and I have worked in different jobs. Now I am working in the kitchen with a friend. There are now about ninety members in the cooperative. The economy is quite similar to that of Poriah. People here are older and they seem to be quite knowledgeable. In the evenings, the veterans of Merhavia sit at the table in the dining room and sing beautifully in Hebrew, Russian and Yiddish. I do not know why it is so hard for me here and I want to return to Poriah.

An outing in the area
October 10

This is the first time a whole group of us went on an outing in the area. It is beautiful. The fields are covered with a carpet of flowers. A Bible expert described what was here in ancient times, how Merhavia was conquered and what its members dream about. We returned at nightfall. I was very tired, but I had to work in the kitchen because someone got sick. Even here people get sick.

I must read Hebrew
November 12

I have been lying in the hospital for a few days because I had a malaria attack. The hospital was located in an Arab hut built of straw and clay. The beds are covered with white sheets. The nurses look after everyone – it is a real hospital! When rain begins to fall, the white sheets are covered with pieces of clay falling from the ceiling. The mood of the patients and of the nurses changes. Still. Sometimes someone bursts out laughing.

My fever has not yet decreased. They give me quinine and I am almost deaf. My ears ring and I cannot hear what people are saying to me. I am very weak. I am embarrassed because I had been so strong. I have not worked for a week and I miss it. Y. Visited me. He sat with me for a long time. He read poems by Bialik to me. It is hard for me to understand poetry in Hebrew. He explained every word and promised to teach me Hebrew. Maybe I will be more successful here because the work hours are more regular. If they do not put me back in the kitchen, I could stay. I could also take part in reading programs being planned. Y. brought me a copy of "Anna Karenina" by L.Tolstoy translated into Hebrew. I still find reading difficult, but I must get used to reading in Hebrew.

1913

March 10

A friend from home has arrived here. She brought me regards from everyone and especially from my father. He was still lecturing at the Zeirei Zion club every week. He loves being among young people. It is well-known that my father wrote a will. In it he dictates how his estate is to be distributed after his death. Half of it would go to a Zionist group, a portion to his wife and the rest was designated to subsidize a young person going to Eretz Israel. Everyone was impressed. My longings for home overwhelmed me and I did not wish to see anyone. Tonight I felt what it meant to cry with happiness.

Can there be another plan for building our country?
March 18

I must decide, finally, that I will not stay here. What should I do? Should I return to Poriah? Will they take me back? I cannot find a place for myself here even though it is so beautiful. There are plans for future development. Perhaps the way of life will change, too. Cooperative living could be a new method for building the country. Many people will find it interesting. They are already talking about educating the children in a cooperative setting. Of course, this is still in the planning stage. If it succeeds, it will bring a big change in our lives.

Today at work I spoke to someone who has been here for a year and a half and he is unhappy. He would not leave because he is attached to Merhavia. It is his opinion that it should not be a decision based on personal needs. Degania presents the best example for the proper way to live. I believe he is correct and I enjoyed our conversation.

I learn to bake bread
April 4

I continue to work in the kitchen. We have just learned how to bake bread. Shifra Betzer, a veteran here, taught me many new tasks. Today we brought the wheat from the threshing floor to the yard. I am thrilled to meet veteran members and to be with older people.

We are four women sharing a nice room. We have interesting activities. Tonight we spent reading together.

I am back in Poriah
October 8

When I returned to Poriah I had a feeling that I had come home, in spite of liking my life in Merhavia. I want to live in a group. There are others here who want the same thing.

Happiness mixed with sadness
October 16

This is a new phase in my life. I am planning to create a family. I do not know why it is happening right now. I see all the problems in life. My happiness is mixed with sadness. I wrote a letter home announcing my happy news. The paper was wet with my tears.

I embroider a flag
October 21

Some members from Poriah together with others from other places are planning to establish a new settlement in the Galil. It will be located in Sharona (between Bayt Vagan and Sejera). They have begun their preparations. The director of Poriah will be in charge there as well. All night long I embroidered a flag for the ascent to the new place. On it is written: "May your hands be strengthened, the conquerors of Sharona. Go up and be successful". The whole camp is happy because a new settlement will be founded in the Galil. I am so thrilled because some of my friends from Kineret will join the group. I would like to go there, too.

Aleph returned from work today quite sick. He has a high fever. Sh. and I sat by his bedside all night. I was there till midnight and Sh. stayed till morning. The patient is so quiet and only at times does he ask for water. He is so nice, still a child! If his mother were here, he would feel better. We take good care of him. Everyone loves him. He calls me"my sister". The older women call me "the mother" of the children.

I am going to become a mother
December 10

Soon my secret will be out: I am going to become a mother. My heart is so full of happiness as well as sadness. Why? I am going to become a mother. What great happiness! I never felt a mother's love because my mother died when I was a year and a half. I do not even remember her. I do remember well my longing for a mother's love...When I was a child I envied every child who had a mother.

Now when I think of the child that will be born I know I will be happy that I am its mother. Although I did not benefit from a mother's love I will devote myself to loving my child. I will provide everything the child would need.

1914

I am going up to Sharona
January 10

It has been some time since I last held my notebook. I did not write about the move to Sharona even though I was very excited that day. It was a beautiful day. We walked from Poriah to Sharona singing and dancing. A wagon carried different necessary products. H. held the flag. At nightfall we reached the designated location. We entered one of the abandoned huts and began to clean and to prepare space for the members who were to stay there all night. This is the first time in my life that I was fortunate enough to found a new settlement on its first day.

They are waiting for news at home
January 18

I am waiting impatiently for the day of delivery to come. I am worried. How will I manage with a baby? Who will give me advice? Mrs. Abramson is my counselor and she teaches me everything. However, I am absorbed in thoughts about my baby. At home they are waiting impatiently for news from us.

I am expecting
February 4

Tonight, after work, I sewed clothes for the baby.

In Tiberias
March

I am all alone waiting for the birth, far from everyone. Around me are people who are strangers and are not really interesting. In spite of everything I want to overcome all problems. After all, I am not fifteen years old. I am a grown woman almost twenty years old. I have to be strong. I am ashamed of my weakness and my disquiet. I am staying in a hotel in Tiberias where I am waiting to give birth. There is no one in my room. I sit writing in my notebook and I walk around the room. In the dead of night the landlady comes to tell me that if I feel unwell I should call her. She will take me to the hospital. I was very excited. This old woman understood me and came at midnight to offer her help. I did not know how to thank her for her kindness.

The first baby girl in Poriah
April 6

My daughter, Geula (Redemption), is already one month old. She is a lovely, serene baby. She lies all day and no one even notices her. From the hospital we took a wagon home. The road was full of ups and downs and sharp turns. Our wagon drivers are real "experts". When we came home I made sure my daughter had not suffered any harm on the journey. I do not yet have a bed for her. Our own beds are wooden slats on top of boxes. I placed her on the floor in a copper tub. I put blankets and pillows all around her. Mrs Abramson, my counselor, says that my daughter is good and is developing beautifully. She calms me down whenever I get nervous and worry about the child's health. I do not want to wake her up from a deep sleep when it is feeding time. All the members come to see the baby. They do not leave her alone. Every time someone comes to see her, something new about her is discovered. She is an "only child" – there are no other girls. My little daughter has brought much happiness to our lives.

Geula (redemption) for the Jewish People
April 12

I received a letter from father. He says: "Let us hope the Jewish people will be redeemed in her lifetime. I hope I will be fortunate enough to meet my dear granddaughter". He is happy with the name we gave her- Geula (Redemption). This is a symbolic and uncommon name.

Sailing on the Kineret
May 4

Some of our members decided to go sailing on the Kineret. Of course, they would not go without me. I was afraid to take my daughter. However, my friends took the responsibility on themselves and we did join them. It was a wonderful trip. We went to the other bank of the Kineret where we visited Tabha. We also took a rest there. We then went to the synagogue in Kfar Nahum. A day like that gives you boost for a long time. My daughter benefited from this trip. It was a beautiful day and the lake was calm.

Tonight I will not spend time with my friends in the dining room because I have to get up early to go to work in the kitchen. I still have a lot to do for my little girl. I also have to do laundry. Y. brought me water to the room so I will not have to fetch it from far away.

In the almond orchard
July 25

Today I worked in the almond orchard. One of the members brought Geula to me at work. He was not working today so he had time to play with her. In the afternoon he took her for a walk. I was very happy with this visit and so was my baby. In general, she does not make it difficult for me to do my work. When I am in the kitchen she plays on a mat in the dining room.

War has begun
August 1

Today I received Geula's first picture. She is sitting on a chair. I will send it home. They will all be so happy. Father will be thrilled because he has not yet seen her in person. Father is getting older. Who knows if we will see each other again! Now the war has begun and who knows how long it will last. Our situation is already worse. We must continue our work more diligently, to produce more locally so we do not have to depend on imports.

In Beitanya
August 12

From Poriah we moved to Beitanya because we could receive some land there. Y. was really drawn to the offer. I had to move also for my young daughter, Geula. She needs to have some friends and to attend a nursery. There is a nursery teacher here. I do not really want to stay here because life here is not interesting. In addition, there is danger of malaria.

Last week we all had fever and there was no one to give us a sip of water. I planted a vegetable garden, but it is not enough work for me. I do not have friends or work here. Who will help me? Whom can I consult?

On Shabbat I went to Poriah. The place is developing beautifully. There are so many improvements and I really regret that we left Poriah. I thought of going to work in Kineret in the "Group of Twenty", but what will I do with my child? I cannot leave her with Y. because he works far away from home. No! I cannot leave her!

Very harsh living conditions
August 25

I was asked to work, on a short time basis, in a laborers' kitchen in Bayt Vagan and I agreed. Geula and her father stayed in Beitanya and I visit them. The laborers work here drying swamps. Some of them are from the "Group of Shepherds". The office in Tiberias arranged a workplace for laborers here as well as a union kitchen. The onus is on the kitchen staff (I and another woman). As part of their pay the laborers receive grain, vinegar, and beans, but no oil can be found. Petrol for cooking is also unavailable. We cut down trees and collected thorns nearby. It takes a long time to cook a soup on stones. We bake bread in the Arab village of Avodya. When there is no one else who can go there, I go by myself with a sack of grain placed on a donkey. On the way I have to go through Wadi Figes (this is where Yehezkel Nisanov was killed in 1911). The grain is not always ground in time so the bread is not always ready before the laborers leave for work. They often go to sleep hungry. There is no sugar and tea is drunk with plums or artificial honey made with carobs. We use it also for baking. Camardine (an Arab dish of dried apricots boiled and rolled) is smeared on bread.

Life is very difficult here. The laborers sleep in a barn or outside on rugs and mats. Today we nearly did not go to work. How can anyone work without food? In spite of everything I tried to bake the bread at night, but it was not ready by morning. There is nothing I can do to correct the situation. I wanted to speak to someone from the committee and to tell him it is difficult to live and work under these conditions. Today the taboon (Arab stove) broke. How will we bake the bread? I went to a few places to see if I could use their taboons, but I was not successful. They were in use. I will have to make a lot of noodles. I had great difficulty with my cooking today. I did not have enough wood for the cooking. I went out to gather twigs and I could not find any. I made a light meal. I feel that it is my fault that the food is so poor. It is my duty to report on conditions here. Perhaps something will be done.

I am alone on a dangerous road
August 26

I received a letter from Y. in Beitanya in which he tells me that our daughter, Geula, is sick and that I must return home. The letter reached me in the afternoon. Everyone was at work. What do I do? How can I leave my co-worker to work alone in the kitchen? She would not go alone to the flour mill and the laborers would be left without bread.

I gave her some instructions. I left a letter for the director asking him to get her help. I left on my journey. I had no choice. My worries about my little girl kept my mind off any thoughts about the dangers on this road. I had more pep and strength to walk faster.

I do not know how I reached the half-way mark. Suddenly, I saw A. I could not recognize him from a distance. He was angry that I was walking alone so late in the evening. He began to yell at me. "How dare you walk alone in the evening on this road?" I had never seen this quiet man so angry! It was difficult to prove to him that I had to come tonight to my sick child, Geula. When he calmed down he told me he had come from Yavneel with the intention of visiting me. On the way he wanted to see Geula to give me a report on her. When he reached Beitanya he found out Geula was sick. He then decided to ride his horse towards me to bring me to Beitanya. How happy I was to have met him because otherwise I would have come to Beitanya late at night.

I found Geula with very high fever. I began to speak to her, but she did not recognize me. I sat by her bedside all night. Only in the morning did Geula recognize me and she burst out crying: "Don't go away again. I don't want to stay here!" My heart was breaking and I cried with her.

L., the pharmacist, told me several times that if I wanted a healthy child, I must take her away from Beitanya. Here, malaria hits her often. I decided to take her to Bayt Vagan, in spite of the hard life there.

She is better today. She got out of bed and wanted to go for a walk. I fell near her bed. I thought I was just weak, but when I took my temperature I saw it was above 40 degrees Celsius. I had malaria again.

Today, Sh. Came from Bayt Vagan to see how Geula was doing. He told me the situation there was bad without me.

[Page 93]

The Schwartzman High School

The Kindergarten in the Schwartzman High School
by Batia Steiner-Faigenbaum, (Efaal – Kiryat Segal)
Translated by Ala Gamulka

In memory of Dr. Zvi Schwartzman, Principal

When I completed the courses offered by Yehiel Halperin, z"l, in Odessa, I returned to Bendery in order to be a Hebrew Kindergarten teacher of Jewish children. It was my dream and I was looking forward to fulfilling it. At first, I was upset. Days, weeks and months passed and no one offered me a job. I did not know to whom I should turn. My despair increased from day to day. It seemed as if a Kindergarten teacher was not needed in our town. I was waiting for a miracle.

One day, the principal of the Hebrew High school, Dr. Schwartzman, asked to me to come to see him. He greeted me with warmly and he explained his daring plan for the Hebrewcizing of the school. Until then studies were mainly done in Russian with only a little Hebrew used. He wanted me to be the teacher in the Kindergarten to be opened by the High school.

Kindergarten class of the Schwartzman High School 1928

To this day, I remember what he said to me on that occasion: "The children will absorb the language quickly. You will make sure of it. They will continue studying in Hebrew in the ensuing grades. Eventually, they will graduate in Hebrew. Even their diplomas will be written in Hebrew. This is how we will Hebrewcize the school completely." He was very excited. It was obvious this was his dream for the future. Of course, I eagerly accepted his offer.

It must be noted that his career as a principal of the Hebrew high school did not always run smoothly. When the Kindergarten was opened, the parents of the "intelligentsia" class were afraid that the children will lose their Russian. The more religious parents thought their offspring will become heretics. There were only some who were excited about the plan. Those were the ones who could not afford the tuition. We started without a budget, any equipment or assurance the plan will actually work out.

I was a new Kindergarten teacher and I had no experience. The thick notebooks filled with methodology of pedagogy writing – which I brought from my courses – were not helpful when it came to practice. I had to create something from nothing. Dr. Schwartzman had full confidence in my ability. We advanced step by step. I reached the point where my students spoke Hebrew. They even had little spats in Hebrew! I will never forget the Hanukah party in the school. The Kindergarten children went up on the stage, paraded holding blue and white flags and lit the candles. They sang the "Song of the Maccabees" and their eyes were shining.

It is a winter day. The skies are gray and the cold from outside can be felt in the Kindergarten. It was Tu B'Shvat. I told the children about the holiday of the trees as it is celebrated in our homeland and how their little brothers and sisters plant trees. They listened intently and their eyes shone. They said the blessing over the fruit – figs, carobs and raisins. They sang "In Eretz Israel the sun shines and the fig trees bloom..." The Kindergarten room was filled with light and warmth.

The seeds sown produced beautiful fruit. I was fortunate to see that many of these children graduated from the Hebrew High school. They made Aliyah and established their homes there. Today, they invest their talents, energies and love.

All of this happened because of the dream of a special person – Dr. Zvi Schwartzman

(Transcribed by the author's sister – L. Sh.)

The Schwartzman Hebrew High School

[Page 95]

The High School day by day and in moments of spiritual uplift
by Leah Steiner (Tel Aviv)
Translated by Ala Gamulka

In blessed memory of Dr. Zvi Schwartzman

Students of the High School 1912

I was accepted at the Schwartzman High School after it became coeducational. The curriculum was the same for boys and girls. This was the biggest day of my life until then. Why? There had not been a Jewish school in our town before that. My father, a great Hassid, refused to send me to a public school. He did not want his daughter to desecrate the Sabbath. I stayed home and I envied every other child passing by with a school bag. My parents could not afford to hire private tutors. Occasionally, I had tutors who charged very little or nothing. I was not satisfied with what I had learned and I did not feel the bliss of attending school regularly. This is why the school is so dear to my heart. I know that the school's existence was a true miracle. The unfriendly authorities were always after the school's administration. Also, there were never sufficient funds to run it properly. The worry that this wonderful school would no longer exist occupied my mind. There was good reason to worry.

One winter morning I was on my way to school. The streets were blanketed with fresh snow. Everything around me looked festive. Alas! When I came into the classroom I found it nearly empty. There were whispers that there would not be any classes that day because the teachers were on strike. The classroom felt very cold because the furnaces had not been lit.

Several times time I had heard conversations from the principal's office _ Gregori Yankelevich was speaking. He told parents that he could not go on any longer. The debts were too high and there was no money. The store owners complained that the winter was too hard and the peasants did not want to come to town to buy. "Wait till the holidays" However, the clergy could not even promise that much. They just said "We will pay, with God's help". The craftsmen were home, cold, sick and hungry. Who can pay tuition? I felt miserable. Outside a flock of blackbirds landed on the snow covered acacia trees. They announced: "It's bad, it's bad…".

A miracle happened. Our principal- the captain once again _managed to free his ship _our school-from obstacles. We not only continue, but we are preparing for a Hanukah party. We have all become artists. We build sets, paint backgrounds and prepare programs. The choir and the orchestra practice. The night of the party the hall is decorated with carpets and greenery. There are two pictures in gilded frames hanging on the main wall. One is of Tsar Nicolai Alexandrovich and the other is of Queen Maria Feodorovna.

In the meantime we continue with the program, the candle lighting, a play about Hannah and her seven sons, one-act plays by Chekhov, Y.L. Peretz, Shalom Aleichem, etc. Then come the comedians _ our students Simcha Tzehovel, Selig Sofer, Weiser. (The first two continued performing in Eretz Israel while the third worked in security). They were also in charge of the dancing. Our students were the dancers: boys who look like leading men and lovely, slim girls. It is their first dance with boys and they blush. Confetti rains down and everyone is happy.

In the wee hours of the morning the students congregate around our principal. He sings Hassidic melodies with his eyes closed. I especially recall the song: "Why is the soul descending?" He seems to be in another world, far away from everything around him and his job. Some students take advantage of these moments and lift him on their shoulders, shouting "Bravo" "Hurray".

The regimes changed and the decrees came and went. Our principal, Dr. Schwartzman confidently steered his ship- the Hebrew High School in Bendery.

Teachers and students of the High School 1915-16

High school orchestra 1917

Grade seven in the High school with teacher S. Y. Gorin

Row 1: (seated) Tinkelman, Gendelman, Yehuda Lonievsky, teacher Gorin, Shalom Hayat, Pessach Gurfel.

Row 2: (Standing) Zissia Shaposnick, David Pisterov, Shalom Barshadski, Zechariah Kleiman, Y. Rotman, Rosen Zweit (Vardi)

First graduating class of the Schwartzman High School

[Page 98]

The Tarbut School, which did not survive long
by Nahman Lavonsky
Translated by Ala Gamulka

After World War I, when Bendery was conquered by the Romanians, the authorities opened more public schools. The Jews were obliged to send their children to these schools. This forced the closure of the private heders. The Jews of Bendery did not want to send their children to the public schools because they were open on Saturdays. On the other hand, Dr. Schwartzman's Hebrew High School could not absorb all the Jewish children. The high school had high academic standards, but it did not receive any government funds. In spite of the high standing, the authorities did not recognize the Schwartzman diplomas as university pre-requisites. The graduates had to travel to France, Belgium and other countries where the diplomas were accepted, to continue their studies.

In the early nineteen twenties, a Tarbut school was founded on the Poteshtovnaya Street. This school could not exist without government funds. The low tuition paid by the parents and the small subsidies given by the Jewish institutions were not enough. In spite of these pitfalls, the founders were able to bring the school to good standards with the help of excellent teachers. They were Bentzion Postelnik, David Projensky, Haim Glass and Israel Wertheim. Romanian was taught by Greenberg, Shuster and others.

The authorities did not think highly of this school. After a few years without funds Tarbut School closed. Its students were dispersed to other schools. Some went to the Schwartzman Hebrew High school and others attended the municipal high school.

Teacher Haim Glass with class in Schwartzman Hebrew High School 1920s

[Page 101]

Youth Movements

The Maccabi League

by Sonia Etlis, Yitschak Sverdlik, Baruch Kaushensky

Translated by Ala Gamulka

Insignia of Maccabi Bendery (Tighina)
– handwork of Leibl Bendersky, z"l

First Steps

Maccabi's first activities in Bendery in 1916 were begun by Gutov Vasiatzky. He assembled a small group of children in a vacant lot. A Russian sports coach, a retired soldier, was brought in to give us physical education training. A special fund was used to buy equipment. During the 1917–1919 revolution, Bertensky (just returned from Belgium) and the late Avraham Zigberman decided to renew the Maccabi activities. These activities followed the Czech system. New members joined and the total reached 200 young people aged 8–18. The committee in charge included Yasha Fein, Yakir

Kleitman, Benno Duborsky, Abramovitch and Etlis. We then spent two years working in the Maccabi Kishinev branch. It supplied us with materials. A special trainer, by the name of Trinchka, was brought in from Czechoslovakia. All those who were active, except for Zigberman, went to Kishinev for a special course. Upon completion they all returned as counselors.

We used to plan successful sports evenings in town and nearby. The income was used to finance other branch activities and the number of members doubled. Maccabi grew in importance and we had additional help with the formation of a new committee headed by the dentist Dr. Yaroslavsky. Two years later Dr. Gurfinkel was elected chairman.

As the branch developed, groups were organized with different counselors. Zonia Bitensky was in charge of gymnastics; light athletics was headed by Abramovitch; women's athletics and equipment were under Etlis and football was supervised by Granovsky.

Maccabi Bendery

[Page 102]

After the death of Zonia Bitensky, his assistant, Yakir Kleitman took over.

Liova Schwartzman organized a special orchestra of 20 young men. It subsequently was expanded into an orchestra of wind instruments and it played at all Maccabi functions.

Those active in the group were Yasha Lederman, Polya Berman, Nadia Ruvinsky, Marussia Duborsky, Zina Etlis, the Kogan sisters and others.

In 1925 Zeev Zhabotinsky visited Bendery and Maccabi organized a reception, In spite of the honor guard, Zhabotinsky showed his appreciation for the fact that young Jews were undertaking the security of visiting lecturers. This became a permanent event whenever the Iron Guard was in town; community leaders invited Maccabi to organize defence groups. (At one time, a group of butchers was organized to help).

Maccabi was also recognized by the authorities: when the Romanians planned military parades, they invited Maccabi to include their young members. These marchers were praised for their organized walking.

Maccabi Bendery Football Team

Years of Expansion
by Yitzhak Sverdlik, (Tel Aviv)
Translated by Ala Gamulka

I joined Maccabi of Bendery when it had 150 members. The committee at the time consisted of A. Zigberman, Fustan, Asher Kishinevsky, Mrs. Manus, and Attorney Fisher. Upon a recommendation by the committee I was sent with a group of others for training in sports. Later I became the treasurer of the Maccabi committee. In 1931–1934 I served as chairman of the counselors committee. Aaron Alter and I were appointed as supervisors of the training locations of Maccabi in Romania. I was also in charge of the drama group of Maccabi in our town.

I was very close to the instructors committee whose members included Yitzhak Abramovitch, Yakir Kleitman, Leibl and Haim Bendersky, Haim Shaposnick, Grisha Schwartz and Sioma Buckstein. They were all devoted to the organization and to the planning of special evenings and plays every month in our town.

[Page 103]

As the anti–Semitic activities of the Iron Guard in Romania increased, our Jewish young people organized themselves for self–defence. A group of Romanian students arrived by train and began to attack the Jewish senator, Moshe Zipstein, z"l. He avoided being murdered with the help of the local police. As a result, I organized a group of friends– Moshe Pravis, Lionya Bronfman, David Flavish and Yosef Spiegel –to go to the train station number 1. We began to dismantle the tracks so that the train with the anti–Semites would be derailed. Our luck did not hold out and the secret Romanian police discovered us and placed us in jail. It was only through the intervention of our parents and Senator M. Zipstein that we were released after 48 hours.

Maccabi 1934

(When Yitzhak Sverdlik made Aliyah)

In the middle are seated (from right to left) Attorney Rubashky, Yitzhak Sverdlik, Misha Fustman

A second incident: The authorities invited us, as was their annual custom, to participate in the Romanian Independence Day festivities. I was approached by the officer in charge of the festivities. He, very politely, asked me to fold our national flag. I replied, just as politely, that `we will remain here with our national flag or we will leave`. When a negative answer was given I gave the order to our group to leave and go to our building.

After we dismantled our flags and dispersed the participants, Senator M. Zipstein arrived accompanied by the mayor. They asked us return with our flags. We did not return to the festivities.

Maccabi Counselors

[Page 104]

Preparation for Aliyah to Eretz Israel
by Baruch Kaushansky (Pardes–Hanna)
Translated by Ala Gamulka

Soonya Bitensky, z"l – Founder of Maccabi in Bendery

Funeral of Soonya Bitensky, z"l, near the Great Synagogue of Bendery

In 1932 the emissaries of Hechalutz visited our branch with the intention of organizing members to attend a preparatory kibbutz. It was expected that after this preparatory time there would be certificates for Aliyah awarded to the pioneers in the program.

About ten members were sent in 1933 to Leoneti (near Bendery) to work in vineyards. There were 80 members in total from other Maccabi branches in Romania.

The work was exhausting and the living accommodations were poor. We were not really used to field work. The overseers dealt with us in a cruel manner. They brandished pistols while pretending to maintain order. These conditions were impossible and one by one we returned home.

The preparatory kibbutz in Leoneti eventually was dispersed a few months after its formation. However, the members of Maccabi did not give up and attended other preparatory kibbutzim. In this manner they were able to fulfill their dream of Aliyah.

[Page 105]

Hashomer Hatzair
by Meri Horodetzky (Netanya)
Translated by Ala Gamulka

Hashomer Hatzair was one of the first Zionist youth organizations in our town. Some years earlier, Maccabi had been established and it was active along with Zeirei Zion. However, Maccabi's purpose was the development of sports among the Zionist youth. In 1921/22 a General Scouts group was founded by Lionya Kreisin, a young, idealistic Russian, and a student in the public high school. He was joined by a group of young Russians, some of them Jews. They followed the precepts of Baden Powell which advocated sayings, trips, the Ten Commandments of the scouts, common uniform and most important the symbol of scouting on our shirts.

Within the Jewish student body of Bessarabia, there was the formation of the following groups: Hatalmid (the student), Hahaver (the friend), etc. These were academic groups and did not have Aliyah as a goal in contrast to the Hechalutz who had Ukrainian refugees as members and who saw Bessarabia as a transit place on their way to Eretz Israel.

Ways were sought to accomplish the aims of Hechalutz, Hahaver and Hatalmid and some members, students in the Schwartzman Hebrew High School, decided to establish a branch of Hashomer Hatzair in Bendery. It was founded along the lines of other branches in Bessarabia– Kishinev, Balti, etc. The model for the Hashomer Hatzair branch was the mother organization in Eretz Israel. There Hashomer Hatzair was involved in guarding Jewish settlements, especially those near the borders. A description was given in different articles in "Yizkor" and "Our communities". Everyone bemoaned the death of Yosef Trumpeldor and his comrades during their defence of Tel Hai. The event became a legend and the Jewish youth all wished to emulate them and to come to Eretz Israel.

Those who were instrumental in the establishment of the Hashomer Hatzair branch in Bendery included Mussia Sverdlik (today called Mordehai Sever), Niunia(Natan) Bendersky, Yasha (Yaakov) Shvidkey, z"l, Munia Poronchik (now called Menahem Efroni), Bibik Frank (Dov Ben-Shaul), Sioma

(Shevach) Bley, Sioma(Zalman) Etlis, Yitzhak Shaposnick(Shefi), Buzia Bernstein, and others.

The first "house" of Hashomer Hatzair was leased from H. Hatzkelevitz in his courtyard on the main street (Harozinskaya Ulitza). It was next to the cinema theatre "Nauka Zhizen". Hashomer Hatzair presented theatre productions in a hall decorated with flags. In the middle was hung a picture of Yosef Trumpeldor (drawn by M. Sverdlik). Underneath was the slogan "It is good to Die for Your Country" in addition to other sayings. There were also announcements of activities, excursions, etc. (The first troop of Hashomer Hatzair in Bendery was named after Trumpeldor).

[Page 106]

The news about the establishment of the branch of Hashomer Hatzair spread quickly in town and many young men and women began to attend meetings. They listened eagerly to the speeches of the young counselors. The activities were interesting: scouting trips, games, Morse Code, discussions on Zionist topics, news of the kibbutzim in Eretz Israel (Merhavia, Beit Alfa, Degania, Mishmar Haemek, etc.). Every discussion was, usually, accompanied by the singing of well-known songs- "Kadru, Kadru, Pnei Hashamayim", "Lo Bayom Velo Balayla", "El Hatzipor" by H.N.Bialik, "Sahki", by Tchernikhovsky, etc. As the branch grew activities were transferred to a larger location near the area called Steppe and close to the town citadel ("Karpost").

In those days the branch of Hashomer Hatzair in Bendery reached its highest growth and development and it had a few hundred members. We had closer contact with branches of Hashomer Hatzair in Bessarabia and Romania (Kishinev, Iasi and Bucharest). We took part in country-wide activities by attending conferences and demonstrations in various locations. These activities were always dedicated to topics important in the Jewish world. At the beginning of 1923 our first two members to make Aliyah were Shlomo Klavenski (now Shlomo Levni) and Mordehai Sverdlik (Sever). The latter used to send letters and even books to the Bendery branch. Some of these were "Hakevutza", "Bnei Krinitza" which discussed issues relevant to the group. This maintained a real contact with Eretz Israel.

As our members grew older there was a new issue- that of personal fulfilment. There were stormy discussions as to whether we should continue our studies or make Aliyah. In addition there were internal struggles with parents and teachers who did not agree that we should stop our education as it would result in the interruption of our future careers. Around 1925 there was a preparatory kibbutz established in Iasi. Many of our members attended this preparation for pioneering. Among them were Yehiel Eidelman (Efrati), Bibik Frank (Dov Ben Shaul), Yitzhak Shaposnick (Shefi), Shlomo Zeidel, z"l, the brothers Krassik, Hannah Shvidkey, Zhenia Zaik, etc.

The first contact made by Mordehai Sever–already in Eretz Israel–had many results. The next group of pioneers were the family of Efraim Veinman (Carmi) and the Reznik family whose two daughters were members of Hashomer Hatzair. They were followed by other members and our connections were even closer. In the meantime, those members who were not yet ready, for personal or family reasons, to go to the preparatory kibbutz in Iasi or Balti, established a local preparatory kibbutz in the garden of Rabbi Efraim Drabmridiker (the Rabiner) located in a suburb near the old railway station. There existed already a permanent group of adults and we, the young ones, joined them. We had come during holidays to help them in the garden. This group was also hired in town to cut trees and to work in factories.

Soon there were clouds in our existence. There were sad reports about blood riots in Eretz Israel and Aliyah stopped. The economic situation in Bessarabia worsened as a result of the depression and the tightening of the political regime. In Romania, many anti–Semitic leaders were in charge and the Jews were the first to suffer from dire restrictions. All this influenced the general well–being of our youths and created personal breakdowns. They did not see any future for themselves in their place of residence, but they had no hope of making Aliyah. There were restrictions on numbers made by the British mandate. As a result, some of our members had to immigrate to North and South America. Among them were close friends such as our beloved counselor Niunia (Natan) Bendersky, Sioma (Zalman) Etlis, Yaakov Tilis, Auerbach and others.

Hashomer Hatzair in Bendery – a group of members

Center – Pinko ben Shaul (member of kibbutz Maabarot);

Second row from left – Ilusha Zaik (leaning on a stick); last on the right– Lionya Kaushansky;

Top row – Meir Horodetzky (from Netanya);

Center of top row – Yonah Shvidkey, z"l, (was member of kibbutz Ein Hamifratz)

[Page 107]

Hashomer Hatzair in Bendery – a group of members

Center – Pinko ben Shaul (member of kibbutz Maabarot);

Second row from left – Ilusha Zaik (leaning on a stick); last on the right– Lionya Kaushansky;

Top row – Meir Horodetzky (from Netanya);

Center of top row – Yonah Shvidkey, z"l, (was member of kibbutz Ein Hamifratz)

Hashomer Hatzair in Bendery (Tighina) – the first group from Aryeh Division who made Aliyah in 1932.

It must be noted that in this time of depression inside and outside, when our youth was in bad shape, there were some Communist instigators that influenced them and they managed to entice some of our best members. They believed that the Communists would solve the problems of our people. This interruption passed after help was received from Hashomer Hatzair in Kishinev. Again there was a reawakening among our youth and activities were resumed. There was a drama group which presented the play "Mentchen" by Shalom Aleichem. This left a lasting impression.

In 1928/29 the signs for a new world war and anti–Semitic actions were evident. The leaders of the haters of our people were Goga and Koza and their followers. They managed to stop the growth of Jews with political and economic means. The authorities were harder on the Jews of Bessarabia and accused them of being more loyal to the Soviet Union across the Dniester than to Romania. In particular, Jewish youth suffered since they were not permitted to study in Romanian universities. The secret police, the infamous Sigurantza, constantly arrested these young people accusing them of belonging to the Communist party.

[Page 108]

The Romanian authorities followed all activities of Hashomer Hatzair. There were arrests and searches for forbidden literature or anything else they found objectionable. We were forced to pretend to join forces with Maccabi. Soon the authorities began to bother Maccabi as well. We tried to change our location from the residence of the Shvidkey family or our house. It is obvious that due to the persecutions by the authorities, the Hashomer Hatzair branch suffered and its influence on the youth of Bendery lessened. The golden age was over and only remained a memory in the minds and hearts of its members.

The first world Maccabia took place in Tel Aviv and members of Maccabi were permitted to participate. The illegal Aliyah by some of our members gave us hope. The door opened, if only slightly, for our own Aliyah.

After many years of suffering and sorrow in our Bendery community, when we reflect within a historical perspective, we realize that we were so right. We, young and inexperienced, saw a solution for our persecuted people. The only way was to go as pioneers to Eretz Israel and to pave the way for our co-religionists to come to our homeland.

Hashomer Hatzair Among the First Movements
by Pinchas Ben Shaul (Pinko) (Kibbutz Maabarot)
Translated by Ala Gamulka

I was unable to be one of the founders of Hashomer Hatzair in Bendery since I was too young at the time.

Hashomer Hatzair was among one of the first Zionist youth organizations in Bendery. It had three principles: Zionism, pioneering and kibbutz life and thus it became a prime Zionist youth group.

Everyone who joined had to personally identify with these principles by becoming educated along national lines, preparing for physical work (pioneering), making Aliyah and joining a kibbutz in Eretz Israel.

We lived in turbulent times of national and social reawakening. There was a fresh breath of life among the youth of our town. They were ready for action and learning. Hashomer Hatzair tried to find a solution for their national and social needs.

In the late 1920s, on the other side of the Dniester, the Soviet Union attracted the youth. It was soon after the great October Revolution. The names of Lenin, Trotsky, Bukharin and Alexandra Kolontaya were enveloped in fables and charmed the Jewish intelligentsia in our town. Many of them were caught up in Communist ideas.

The intended land, Eretz Israel, was far away and was tightly closed. Aliyah was stopped and rumors of blood baths reached us. These rumors caused a depression in our older members who were on the cusp of making Aliyah. Some of them immigrated to Latin America as a temporary refuge until the gates of Eretz Israel would reopen.

I was young when I joined the movement and I was fortunate enough that my "leader" was Niunia (Natan) Bendersky. He was a charming and talented educator. It was not only his ideology and teaching that were wonderful, but especially his approach. He held personal discussions with each young member. He organized night trips and evenings by the fire. He managed to instill in us a desire for a better world, different from our daily existence. He also taught us values of purity, justice and belief in people. The atmosphere in all the groups, even in the older ones, was similar.

Our branch of Hashomer Hatzair– as was the case in other towns– was an island of Hebrew in the ocean of alienation, "Red assimilation" and the decrepit life of the "Golden youth".

We spoke Hebrew within our "house" and outside it as well in addition to fulfilling all Zionist goals.

[Page 109]

Every member of Hashomer Hatzair saw himself or herself as a temporary resident in the Diaspora until Aliyah would be fulfilled and kibbutz life achieved. The counselors were personal models and influenced the young members. They, in turn, served as ideals for the non–organized youth who did not necessarily agree with our ideas. They treated us with respect and honor.

Hashomer Hatzair Group with its Flag

Our Hashomer Hatzair branch reached its heights at the end of the 1920s. There were hundreds of young boys and girls of all ages active in it. The education instruction followed a plan and was on a high level. We participated in seminars in Kishinev, in meetings, trips on Lag Baomer to the forests nearby and at public evenings at the Schwartzman Hebrew High School that brought in many people. Our Hashomer Hatzair also collaborated with other Zionist organizations such as Zeirei Zion, General Zionists and Gordonia.

The common activities were: donations to Jewish National Fund, public meetings to discuss events in Eretz Israel, elections to Zionist congresses and anything in the general framework of "Workers of Eretz Israel". We ran into some problems, as well. The Zionist pioneering youth movement which had a radical Socialist ideology was suspect by the Romanian secret police (Sigurantza). We were followed for a long time and they watched us constantly. Many times, in the mornings, we found a lock with the wax stamp of the secret police on our door. It was accompanied by a "polite" invitation to present ourselves in their headquarters.

The best Jewish youth of our town belonged to Hashomer Hatzair and our educational activities continued in spite of all difficulties until the Soviet conquest and the annexation of Bessarabia by the Soviet Union. After that the axe fell on all national–Zionist activities since the Soviet authorities believed them to be against the regime.

The Soviet conquest brought about the end of a beautiful and eventful time within the Jewish youth in our town. The hopes of hundreds of young men and women were dashed and they were unable to fulfill their dreams.

Still, several hundred Hashomer Hatzair trainees from our town were fortunate to make Aliyah and to live in kibbutzim, settlements and towns. Everyone did it his own way.

[Page 110]

They all contributed to building the country and helping in its development. Many of them were members of the Workers Union (Histadrut) and socialist Zionist parties. I will always cherish the wonderful counselors who provided us with all that is good and beautiful and who brought us to this day.

[Page 110]

Gordonia Movement
by Yonah Balaban (Kvutzat Hulda)
Translated by Ala Gamulka

The Gordonia branch in our town stemmed from the Young Hechalutz founded by M. Malamud.

In the spring of 1927 I was invited, by chance, to the "Hall" (this is how it was called by everyone in town). I was allowed to participate, on the sidelines, in a discussion being held among the senior members. It was led by M. Malamud and the topic was "Sects and Groups in Judaism". The main emphasis that evening was on the Karaites. I listened with a gaping mouth to the discussion and I was totally charmed by the fact that people my age were arguing about a serious matter instead of having a good time. I immediately asked to be allowed to join the group.

In autumn 1928 there was a unification of four groups of Young Hechalutz with Gordonia.

The main patron of this unification was the well-known and enthusiastic Zionist, Shimshon Schechter, z"l .from Hechalutz central. After unification we saw ourselves as part of a large pioneering movement that had centers in many parts of the Diaspora. It had goals proposed by a global leadership.

***

The main purpose of Gordonia was the education of youth towards the establishment of a working people in Eretz Israel– our ancient and new homeland. It fostered equality, social justice, Hebrew culture and communal life. We planned all our activities along these lines.

Gordonia Group Prior to Preparatory Kibbutz
(in the center Eretz Israel emissary Meshi, November, 1929)

The young people were divided into sections according to ages[1]: 12 years olds were scouts; 14 year olds were Reawakeners; 16–17 year olds were seniors and the 18 year old were the Implementers. The latter were to go to a preparatory kibbutz. Every section was divided into groups.

The actual activities were as follows: the younger groups studied Hebrew, songs of the homeland, Yiddish and Hebrew literature, Zionism, geography of Eretz Israel, Jewish history, etc. The older groups learned about workers movements–Jewish and general–, socialist theory and the Kibbutz movement.

Sabbath nights were dedicated to singing and at the end of the next day there were activities such as discussions, dances and simply fun.

In order to pay the expenses of the hall and other costs there were membership fees. We made certain that our budget was supplemented by income from theatrical presentations and parties open to the general public.

[Page 111]

We fondly remember Umansky from Zeirei Zion who was our theatrical director.

The members of the branch also participated in general Zionist activities such as Jewish National Fund and elections to the Zionist Congress, pro-Zionist meetings, etc.

We took part in sports activities as well. Lag Baomer was one of the most exciting times for our young members. That day we would leave at sunrise and we paraded on the streets carrying our blue and white flag[2]. We sang lustily and continued on to the forests near our suburbs (Borisovka, Giska, etc.) When we reached our destination we found tents housing the pioneers who had come the previous night. During the day we had communal meals, games, dancing, athletic competitions and a festive parade at the end.

Many Jews came to watch us and the celebration was thus enhanced.

***

It was clear to us that although we were learning Hebrew and the history of Zionism we also needed to learn to work and to get used to communal life. For that purpose Hechalutz established several preparatory kibbutzim which the 18 years olds attended prior to making Aliyah.

Near Balti there was a farm called Masada which had 120 hectares of choice soil, a small barn and a chicken coop – all for self provision. This is where members of Gordonia prepared themselves.

Hechalutz (with the help of Zionist friends) maintained this farm and those who worked there strove to be self-sufficient.

There were other preparatory kibbutzim, such as Ripichani (sugar factory) and Aresht (large vineyard) which also were inhabited by hundreds of young people who wished to make Aliyah.

After completion of the preparation– 6–8 months–candidates for Aliyah were approved.

Members of Gordonia in Bendery in 1932

***

The crisis began. The Mandate government assigned very few Aliyah certificates and there were many candidates for each one. Aliyah became as difficult as the parting of the Red Sea.

Many young people waited for many years to make Aliyah. Some gave up and immigrated to other countries hoping to find another way to fulfill their dreams.

However, for various reasons and mainly because of these difficulties, Gordonia of Bendery did not have hordes of pioneers making Aliyah. Even those who were not successful in making Aliyah were fortunate to have a strong Jewish, Zionist and socialist education.

[Page 112]

I am certain that these people followed the precepts they learned all their lives.

Translator's Footnotes:

When I served as secretary of the branch there were many 9–10 year olds who wished to join Gordonia. Unfortunately I had to refuse them since we only accepted those 12 and older. A few days later these children returned and teased us by saying "We do not need you anymore. Mizrahi has also opened a

Gordonia! They accepted us gladly." (At that time a branch of Bnei Akiva was founded under the religious Zionist party, Mizrahi). Return

When we passed through the streets on Lag Baomer– or at any other parade– the women who peeked from the windows would say:" Here comes the Hall". The children always said I am going to the Hall, meaning the branch and this is how the parents referred to us.

The Beitar Youth Movement
By Moshe Horovitz And Mordechai Frank (Netanya)
Translated by Ala Gamulka

The blood baths of 1929 in Eretz Israel left an imprint on the Jews of the Diaspora and resulted in a reawakening among the youth of our town.

In September 1929 Avraham Zingerman, z"l, and some students from the Hebrew High School organized a youth group which became the Trumpeldor Covenant in Bendery –Beitar.

At certain times the Beitar group was considered the largest youth movement in town as well as the one with the most outstanding Zionist activities.

:

Founders of the branch

Among the founders of the branch were Neta Blank, Moshe Yatom (Rabbi's son), Zvi Sverdlik, Shmuel Spooner, Micah Polsky, Avraham Kapusta, and others. Within three months the number of members reached 70–80 young people, most of them high school students. The first activities were held in the Maccabi house. As the branch grew we moved to the Hebrew High School building.

A few months later Yosef Visliv, z"l, joined it. He was one of the first Maccabi counselors. Under his leadership the group grew to 250 members of all ages.

:

Activities

The main activities of the branch were educational and Zionist such as the study of the Hebrew language, athletic, military and agricultural training.

The educational activities were supervised by students of the Hebrew High School and leaders of the Revisionist party in town. These were attorney Kh. Rovshavsky, Misha Fustan, Shalom Hayat, Israel Pasternak, David Dorfman, and others.

The members of the branch participated in all activities of the Zionist movement, Jewish National Fund, Tel Hai Fund, Hechalutz of Beitar. They also distributed Zionist and Revisionist literature among the residents.

Until 1932 only boys belonged to the branch. After that, girls were permitted to join.

Two days a week were dedicated to the study of the Hebrew language. Everyone was obligated to speak Hebrew within the branch. They all wore a patch with the first Hebrew letter designating the Hebrew language. These activities were supervised by the high school students.

The branch published a weekly bulletin in Yiddish and Hebrew. Its editor was Dr. I. Lederman–Yardor who also organized a drama club. Plays by Peretz, Ansky, Shalom Aleichem as well as some written by the director were performed.

Mr. Kogan, the main cantor of the synagogue, established a choir of 40 members. They performed together with the drama club.

There was also an orchestra of strings and wind instruments. It was directed by Shmuel Kogan (son of the cantor). It accompanied the drama club and it also performed at various celebrations in town. These performances by the orchestra produced a good income for the branch.

:

Ceremonial and athletic activities

The first military–athletic activities were run by Haim Shaposnick, Avraham Sautzky and other Maccabi counselors who joined them.

In 1932, a course for counselors in defense activities was held under the direction of Yosef Dukler, the Beitar emissary of Etzel from Eretz Israel.

The course went on for six weeks and produced a team of counselors who later were active not only in town, but in other parts of Romania as well. Among them were: Yaakov Oshan, Fima Brodsky, Miriam Borsotzky, Shuka Grebet, Buma Grebet, Moshe Horvitz, Malka Vodoboz, Haim Tomshopolsky, Malka Sverdlik, Mordehai Frank, David Flavish, Fima Friedman, Haim Kishinovsky, Haim Reznik and others.

[Page 113]

Within the athletic activities, a football team was formed. It played against non–Jewish teams and did well against them. This was a source of pride to everyone in town.

One of the central events in the life of Jewish community was the parade of all youth movements on Lag Baomer. Beitar stood out with its neat appearance, nice uniform and good marching.

Seniors group and agricultural work

Connected to the branch was a group of army veterans, called "Covenant of the Soldiers". It was under the direction of A. Sautzky and Yoske Kamelis. There were about 100 members and they all belonged to the Revisionist Party in town.

Some of the members went to do agricultural work, under the auspices of the pioneering Beitar. About 70 of them were in Balti, Zestevna and other places. They were preparing themselves for actual work in Eretz Israel.

In the summer of 1934 the branch, under the direction of Moshe Horvitz, established a local preparatory kibbutz in the vineyard of Eli Abramovich.

The members of the branch served as counselors and leaders in other preparatory kibbutzim in Romania.

Beitar Branch in Borisovska Forest, Summer 1932

Illegal Aliyah

The number of available certificates diminished and the members began to prepare themselves to perform illegal Aliyah.

The first attempt at illegal Aliyah was done in 1934 by Moshe Horvitz on a cattle boat. He failed because he was discovered by the Mandate authorities in Haifa and was sent back.

The ship called "In spite" had the following members of Beitar: Mordehai Bronfman, Mendel Goldmacher, the sisters Esther and Shoshanna Grebet,

Yosef Gutskozek, Pessach Hochman, Haim Tomshopolsky, Yitzhak Mitelman, Moshe Friedgidler, Arieh Gödel, Arieh Slatnovitz, Moshe Klein, Moshe Kaushansky, Haim Reznik, Riva Reznik, Natan Schultz and others from town who were not members of Beitar.

Changing of the Guard

After Yosef Visliv, z"l, made Aliyah, the leadership was taken over by Dr. I. Lederman–Yardor. The branch flourished under his direction and the range of activities was broadened.

The highlight of the activities of Dr. Lederman–Yardor was the organization of the illegal Aliyah in the entire country, In order to fulfill this mission he moved to Bucharest where he did serious work for the Jews of Romania together with Yosef Klarman and Yosef Katzenleson.

Closure of the branch

When the Russians entered town the branch was closed. Its last commander, Buma Grebet and his assistant, Buma Eidelman were arrested and sent to Siberia. When World War II broke out all the members were dispersed throughout Russia together with the rest of the Jews. Many of them perished during the war.

After many years of exile in Siberia, Buma Eidelman and his family were able to make Aliyah before the Six Day War. Other members who reached Eretz Israel were Avraham Persis, Malka and Ziska Kamelis.

During the 11 years of the existence of the branch in town its leaders were Avraham Zigberman, z"l, Danny Reifman, Yosef Visliv, z"l, Dr. Lederman–Yardor, Micah Polsky, z"l, Buma Grebet, z"l.

***

This is a shortened version of the story. It serves only to touch on the Zionist activities of the branch and the Jewish community. It is not a full history. If any names have been omitted due to time passed and forgetfulness, we ask for forgiveness.

Beitar Leaders, Bendery 1932

[Page 118]

The City And Its Inhabitants

A Branch to Two Trunks
by Haim Raday (Jerusalem)

(I am a native of Bendery and I belong to two families. One is the Shabtai Berman family and the other is that of Rabbi Shimon Shlomo Wertheim. Both families are worthy of entire books, but this is a shorter version.)

Translated by Ala Gamulka

The two families were quite different with opposing approaches and views about everything– particular and in general. They were even different when it came to Zionism. However, both families were dedicated to the town and contributed to its growth. One gave money and wisdom and the other its intelligence and goodness.

It is difficult to describe Bendery in those days without these two central figures– R. Shabtai Berman (I am his grandson, the son of Moshe) and R. Shloimke Wertheim. The former was an enthusiastic follower of Chabad, wealthy, extremely pious and definite in his Judaism. He would fight for his people even with the authorities. He reminded you of a character in the literature of Mendel Mocher Seforim. This was my grandfather Shabtai Berman. He lived his entire life in Bendery and was an opponent of Zionism. He sent his sons to a Lubavitch yeshiva. He was fortunate to make Aliyah and died in Jerusalem at the age of 96 and was buried in Sanhedria.

On the other hand, my other grandfather, Shloimke, was a scholar and well–versed in world affairs. He was a Torah expert and an authority on all Jewish texts, but he was also worldly. He had five sons. The first, R. Yosele became a Rabbi while the second, R. Leibl was a businessman. The three younger ones – Avremel, Duvid and Srulik were active in Zionist affairs. They graduated from high school and traveled to Odessa to continue their studies. On the way they cut off their ear locks, their beards and "lost" their black hats. The father understood that he could not win and he accepted the new winds of progress in the world.

There is a story about Avremel who was studying in Odessa. He came home to Bendery for Passover and was visited by a friend from Odessa. The latter did not look Jewish since he wore a Russian-type hat. When he knocked on the door, my grandfather opened it. The guest asked "Is this the home of Avraham Solomonovich?". Grandfather, with his beard and curly ear locks, wearing a long black coat and a fur hat, told him in poor Russian:"Okay, if you call Avremel Avraham, I can understand that. However, since when am I Solomonovich? What's wrong with you? What kind of Solomonovich am I ? Pheh! Since you have already come, you may enter and I will call your Avraham Solomonovich."

His answer demonstrated his opposition to modernity and a reluctance to accept new terms and trends. However, he tacitly agreed with them. My grandfather, the chief Rabbi, was excited by Zionism and dreamed of Eretz Israel. He organized groups of supporters in Bendery and surrounding area- about 100 families. In spring 1913, on the eve of World War I, he went, on their behalf, to Eretz Israel. He spent a few months there and negotiated with the Sheikh of Ramle (an Arab village then) to purchase some of his land. He then went to Baron de Rothschild in Paris to obtain his support for the settlement of these 100 families. War broke out suddenly and he was obliged to return in a roundabout way home. He had to go through Scandinavia in the north to reach Bendery. He did not complete the negotiations.

On this voyage he was accompanied by a beloved Bendery resident- Shimon Kharker. Upon his return there was a beautiful reception in my grandfather's synagogue. During his speech and his stories about the Holy Land, there was much emphasis, as was customary of all the Jews of Bendery, on food. This is what he said in his colorful Bessarabia Yiddish:"Eretz Israel is a strange land where the poor eat oranges, figs and pomegranates while the rich are obese because they eat too many potatoes". It must be noted that in those days, potatoes where not easily available in Eretz Israel.

My grandfather Wertheim's house stood in the center of town on Komandantskaya Street (not far from the central church square). It served as a meeting place for brilliant students, emissaries and the grandchildren of this large rabbinic family. In 1910, a huge fire eliminated the house, synagogue, warehouses and a new "modern" building was erected in place. There were also stores attached. During the short period of time until World War I broke out the story was told that not a night would pass without guests there. My grandfather always welcomed strangers with open arms saying:"You can eat as much as you want, but the sleeping arrangements are by a schedule".

Grandfather was widowed at a relatively young age. My grandmother, Miriam-Rivka, died in childbirth with her umpteenth child. He was left with ten children. He remarried, but it was unsuccessful. He married again, the daughter of the judge of Bendery and this time it worked. She was known as Auntie Bobka. As was true of all rabbinic homes, there was great poverty. The children slept two to a bed and some even on benches or chairs brought in from the synagogue. His salary was paid by the community on a weekly basis every Thursday night. This was the day for slaughtering cattle for the Sabbath. If there was not enough income to pay the taxes and the judges, Auntie Bobka would find a private loan. In her dining room there were many charity boxes (Meir Haness, Modiin Yeshiva, Bridal Fund, and Help for the Needy) which she would fill every week. However, when there was no salary payment she would open these charity boxes and borrow from them. She used to place notes inside acknowledging receipt of a specific sum. When she had money she would repay these loans, even adding to them. R. Meir would receive a dividend.

In contrast to Grandfather Shabtai, grandfather Shloimke did not have succah built. At the end of Yom Kippur he would place a stake in the yard for the succah that leaned on the stairs to the women's auxiliary of the synagogue.

The person who built the succah every year was Zalman Hanger. He was a stout man, very pious who worked as a day laborer all day. One day he injured his finger badly with an axe. He tore off part of his shirt, bandaged his finger, and continued working. Grandfather came out and ordered him to stop working and to go to the hospital. He did not wish to do it since he was a daily laborer and if he stopped working, how would he feed his family? The argument continued, but finally he listened to Grandfather and went to the medic. He had to miss a few days of work and upon his return he refused payment for time missed. Grandfather threatened him that he would take him to the Jewish court. For the sake of peace and to honor the Rabbi, he accepted the money.

It was built in 1886 by the late sainted Rabbi Itzikel and was renovated in 1936 (50th anniversary). Financial support was given by the Bendery Society of Brooklyn, New York.

The Rabbi's Synagogue The "Rabbi's" Synagogue

There was an elderly woman who lived in my grandfather Shimon–Shlomo's house. No one knew how old she was and why she was there or how she came to Bendery. She became an essential part of the household, but no one knew what she was doing there. After some years, a legend grew about her– that she was widowed and arrived at the Rabbi's house in Bendery. Her surname was unknown and probably not even those close to the rabbi knew it. She was known as Auntie Etel.

[Page 119]

There was a Jewish man in Bendery by the name of Saltonovitch. He was a widower who owned a store selling dishes and other household goods. His store was the first one in the circle at the entrance to town. There were others in town by the name of Saltonovitch and to distinguish him from them he was referred to as "the one from the church square". One day, Auntie Etel entered the store to buy a glass bowl. She chose one and began to bargain with him. It was a late spring afternoon and Saltonovitch asked her:"Auntie Etel, why do you need this bowl?" She replied:"To eat from it". Said the man:"Why don't you buy a larger bowl and we will from it together."

It was a good match.

*

Grandfather Shabtai was very wealthy. It was said that he was not like other millionaires who have thousands of rubles. He really had 1 million rubles in Moscow.

Truthfully, he had many properties. He had a leasing contract good for many years of the Gerbovitzi forest and a large part of the swamps of the Dniester where reeds would grow. When the swamps froze in the winter, the locals would cut down the reeds. The crop was given over to the military and also sold to the residents for use in lighting furnaces.

At the onset of World War I, on a Friday night, there was an exchange of fire between the Romanians trying to conquer Bendery and the retreating Russian army. Bombs fell in the swamps and in the warehouses containing the reeds that had been cut. Everything was burned in the ensuing fire. The town was covered in soot and ashes. When R. Shabtai came back from synagogue he brought some guests home for Kiddush. It turned out that he no longer had to worry about his properties and could spend his time learning Torah and doing good deeds.

Grandmother Charna died in spring 1924 on a Shabbat morning. Grandfather still went to synagogue and made Kiddush upon his return. He ordered the table to be set as always, but forbade singing.

All that day no one, especially the grandchildren, was allowed to shed any tears or even to be sad since it was Shabbat. As soon as Havdalah was completed the wailing and mourning began. The youngest daughter began to sob and to scream: "What shall we do? What shall we do?" Grandfather approached her, slapped her and said: "Why are you asking? If something could have been done, wouldn't I have done it? Everything is in God's hands! God gives and God takes away. May his name be sanctified."

Grandfather Shimon–Shlomo went to Eretz Israel to establish a new settlement of Bessarabian Jews. He returned to Bendery close to Purim. His impressions of the Holy Land and his enthusiasm for religious Zionism are shown in some of the letters he sent his family and that have been preserved.

When he returned from Eretz Israel there was a reception in his honor in the synagogue. Hundreds of Jews crowded the synagogue while thousands remained outside due to lack of space. My grandfather said the Gomel blessing and praised Eretz Israel.

On this trip to Eretz Israel, grandfather was accompanied by his youngest son, Srulik, who stayed to study at the Herzliah High School. When Russian citizens were evacuated he returned to Bendery through Egypt and the Balkans. After his stay in Eretz Israel he spoke Hebrew well and remained a loyal Zionist. He was killed during the Holocaust.

*

In the house of my grandfather R. Shimon–Shlomo there was a Gabbai, not of the synagogue, but only for the Rabbi. His name was R. Nahman and he served as sort of a rabbi. The Wertheim family had been rabbis for generations and only my great-grandfather, R. Itzikel, did not want to serve as a rabbi. He worked as a judge in the Jewish court of our town. My grandfather, R. Shimon–Shlomo continued along this road.

R. Nahman Gabbai was already an old man during my childhood. It is said that he worked for seven years serving three generations. Tradition tells us that he liked a drink. He would pass a keg and would taste from it. He enjoyed life. When the Rabbi discovered the truth he sadly expelled him. After that, R. Itzikel took his place.

R. Nahman was a short and rotund man with a hawk nose and thick eye brows. He had a beard and long ear locks. He was a healthy man and a good-hearted one. He was always happy and liked the old and the young. Unfortunately, he liked his liquor, but he did not know how to control it. Once, at a Purim meal, when the food was tasty and drinks were plentiful, all the wine at the table was finished. Grandfather hinted to R. Nahman to go to the cellar and refill the jugs. R. Nahman took the two jugs and left. Time passed and he did not return.

[Page 120]

Grandfather sent the sexton to see where R. Nahman had gone. A few minutes later, the sexton returned with the jugs and reported that he found R. Nahman lying on top of the barrel sleeping with the hose in his mouth! He obviously had decided to sample the wine and fell asleep.

R. Nahman Gabbai – In the Synagogue of the Wertheim Dynasty

Another time Grandfather sent him to Kaushany to buy two barrels of wine– the best in the area. R. Nahman came to the village, went to the kosher vineyard and went down to the large cellar. With a goblet in his hand he tasted from every barrel. He was enjoying life. After his tour he turned to the vineyard owner and praised his product. He believed that the wine in barrel number 16 was the best. He wanted to assure himself by pouring another goblet. It was rumored that there were 120 barrels in the wine cellar.

In his old age, when he was over eighty years old, closer to ninety- R. Nahman became ill and quite weak. He was admitted to the Jewish hospital where he drove everyone crazy. He wanted to know what was wrong with him and they would not tell him. Finally, the doctor told him was suffering from Pleurisy. When he asked what it meant the doctor told him he had water inside his chest. "I have water!" yelled R. Nahman. "May those who pour, headed by Hershel Kunitzer, die! Such scoundrels, criminals, liars! It is their fault that I am sick. It is because they mixed water with their wine!"

There is another story connected to the hospital. As is well-known, Grandfather Shabtai was one of the founders of the hospital and was always involved in its management. He was very pious and impatient and was a tough supervisor. On the other hand, R. Shimon-Shlomo, the town rabbi, was peace-loving and kind. He got along well with people.

In the early 1920s there were many refugees from Russia who arrived in Romania. Among them was Leibl Glantz, the famous cantor (he died in Israel a few years ago). He was young, handsome and single, but he was already well-known as an excellent cantor. Grandfather, influenced by his sons who were members of Zeirei Zion, wanted to invite him to lead services on Shabbat. He needed the income. However, R. Shabtai, his in-law objected to allowing this young beardless fellow to lead the services. Grandfather Shimon -Shlomo replied:"Let's marry him off to Dora Markovna! He will have a wife and a beard". Dora was the head nurse in the hospital, but she was an old maid and had a beard...

In spite of his hard headedness, R. Shabtai could not help but burst out in laughter upon hearing this original idea. He agreed to allow Leibl Glantz to lead the services that Shabbat. This performance paved the way to his being offered a position as the chief cantor in Kishinev and eventually in America. He made Aliyah after Israel became a state.

There was another man who was nicknamed the Innards Guy, because he dealt in innards. He spent many years enjoying the hospitality of my grandfather, the rabbi. Some say it was twenty years and others think it was thirty and maybe even more. He arrived in Bendery from a village in Volyn where he left a wife and children. He searched for a religious home where he could serve. No one knew how he came to the house of R. Itzikel.

[Page 121]

In any event, he was important in our lives since he was considered part of the family even though he did not have an official position. He lived in a small windowless room near the synagogue. He kept his wares there too. He was sickly and had a deep cough, but he would always appear when help was needed. His talent was to be the tenth man for a minyan. This was always a special honor. Perhaps he did it because he was close to the synagogue entrance.

One day the man disappeared and no one knew what had happened to him. It was rumored that he died in Kishinev and was buried there.

*

There was also Zalman who was a tiny man. He had jet black hair, a thick beard and unusual eyebrows. He was near-sighted, almost blind. He had been born in Bendery, a member of a family that had been there for generations. He was not a successful man and even when he was young he could not even work as a laborer.

At last Zalman was appointed as the sexton in my grandfather's synagogue...

The Last Survivor of the Holy Man's Family
By Leah Steiner (Tel Aviv)
Translated by Ala Gamulka

(To this day, I mourn the loss of my Feigale!)

It happened on the morning of Tisha B'Av 1926: a young woman, slim and pale with coal black eyes, entered the secret police headquarters (Sigurantza). Our town had been previously conquered by the Romanians. She seemed scared and begged the police officer to "arrest me because I killed by aunt"…

However, the police officer did not understand what she was saying and threw her out of the station. She subsequently went to the shore of the Dniester and jumped in the water. Thus ended her short life–it was full of suffering.

*

It was Feigale, the granddaughter of Rabbi Levi Darbrimediker and a great-granddaughter of the Tzadik of Bendery. The elders in town always told wonderful magical tales about the latter. Feigale was born in a Ukrainian village in the house of her maternal grandfather the Rabbi from Tzitzilnik. Her mother died young and Feigale was brought to our town at the age of seven. She lived with her paternal grandfather, Rabbi Levi. I first met her at a Kiddush prepared by her grandmother, Itele the Rebbetzin, in her honor. I recall tables laden with food. The women who were invited, among them my mother, were charmed by this intelligent and knowledgeable young girl. We, the other young girls, were drawn to her because she was attractive, sociable and a lover of games.

When Feigale arrived, her grandfather's "shtiebl" [a small synagogue located in a home] was no longer in fashion. R. Levi was quite elderly and weak and all accommodations in the courtyard meant for visitors were falling apart. They contained broken down furniture and moth-eaten clothing. We played in these areas– hide-and-go-seek, hopscotch, mock weddings, etc. The spiders spun their webs, the geckos climbed the walls and the ceilings, rats peeked through the floors. It seemed as if they all took part in our games.

In the front of the yard was Rabbi Levi's tiny synagogue whose ceiling was sloping and falling. On holidays and Shabbat one could still hear the sounds of prayer and the singing of the followers and their rabbi. On week days we would lock ourselves inside hoping we would not be discovered. There we read the first books translated into Russian – The Prince and the Pauper, Uncle Tom's Cabin, and the works of Tolstoy, Pushkin, Gorky, Dostoyevsky and others. Feigale identified herself with the orphaned and miserable protagonists. She was kind-hearted and would share her last penny and her simple food with the poor. She also prayed and kept fast days.

I remember that on Yom Kippur she was the only girl in the Women's Auxiliary. She fasted and prayed fervently all day. She seemed to be hovering in a pious and pure world. During the Third Meal in the shtiebl she stood near her grandfather. He blessed the wine with reverence and she held the Havdalah candle with her face shining.

Not too long afterwards her grandfather, the beloved rabbi Levi, died. Soon, her grandmother Itele also died and Feigale remained alone with her aunt Sarale, a bed-ridden invalid.

[Page 122]

These two souls earned their livelihood by selling all valuables and jewelry in the house. Feigale graduated from high school and was considered gifted. However, in our town it was not the custom to encourage talent and to award scholarships. She hoped to attend university, but she did not succeed.

Every winter the winds and snow did more damage to the house and they lived among the debris. The invalid was affected by this terrible existence and her piety made her lose her mind. Feigale was a victim of tantrums even though she was loved. The invalid imagined that Feigale was sewing on Rosh Hodesh– when it is forbidden or that she made some dish treif. Perhaps the meat was not soaked long enough or Feigale sold items without telling her. Everything was accompanied by hysterics with Feigale trying to calm her down.

What actually happened on that fateful morning of Tisha B'Av? Who knows? It can be surmised that on this fast day the invalid had a hysterical attack and accused Feigale of all kinds of things. Feigale, on her part, tried to calm her down, as usual. Even now I can almost hear her voice begging: "Stop. Stop. I will lose my mind because of you". Sometimes I can see her hugging and kissing her aunt and asking her to calm down. All was in vain. Suddenly she saw an item in her hand and she was tempted to scare her by showing it to her. If the aunt would stop her yelling, Feigale could go back to her books.

Her gentle hand that always comforted the invalid now became a weapon. Afterwards there was no one left to hug and to kiss and from whom to beg forgiveness.

[Page 123]

Reminiscences of My Father's House
By Mordechai Sever (Tel Aviv)
Translated by Ala Gamulka

"When I reminisce about the good times, I must mention, the ritual slaughterer, Rabbi Moshe Sever, who is still with us. He collected the sayings of our sages of blessed memory and published them. We still use this literature and I thank him in the name of all those who read his words."

(From a speech made by the third president of the State of Israel, Sh. Z. Shazar on the 23rd day of Av in 1963 in Zichron Yaakov, on his "Voyage of Reminiscences".

Bendery– capital on the Dniester

Our town on the Dniester was beautiful. It had a Turkish name– Bendery. It was a capital district town in Bessarabia, Russia. The town was surrounded by mountains and hills and had many fruit orchards, vineyards and forests. During harvest time there was much work, bustle and hustle, selling of produce and its transport. However, in times of blight and drought many Jewish residents were in dire economic conditions. They even suffered from the cold in the winter. Originally, the tsarist authorities did not allow them to live a healthy and economic life. In addition, during the rainy season there were unbelievable puddles and swamps in the streets. People would earn their living by transporting passers–by from one side of the street to the other. They used carts or carried them on their backs.

Nearly half the population of the town was Jewish. The community was independent in nature and was well organized. There were 14 synagogues and there were many members of the clergy and public leaders, Hassidim and Mitnagdim, many educational and cultural institutions, a Hebrew–Yiddish–Russian library and even a Hebrew High School. The school was one of the first to exist in the Diaspora and was founded in 1912 by the late Dr. Schwartzman. The school held many activities of the youth movements, sports groups and drama clubs (in Yiddish and Russian). There was also the Hazamir choir that was founded during World War I. It performed in Jewish communities on the other side of the Dniester. There were also presentations to collect money for charities such as "Help for the Sick", "Clothes for the Poor", etc. and for any people who were in need.

With the help of R. Yitzhak Nissenboim, a wealthy man in town, and others, a hospital and Seniors Residence were erected. There were also Jewish bath houses. Due to this foresight there was a strong Jewish community. Russian newspapers, edited by Jews, were published and they wrote about the community. They were even read in the rest of the world. The newspapers also attracted talented writers and poets who gave their opinions about ongoing events. Commerce, small industry, flour mills, printing houses, tea houses and saloons were all in the hands of Jewish residents. They mostly served the farmers in the area.

The Dniester River

[Page 124]

This was Bendery on the eve of World War I. My father was born there and received his education for most of his young years. He established a family when he married my mother Rachel who was always a big help to him.

David had a Violin…

My father served as a ritual slaughterer although he was ordained as a rabbi. It turns out that he even served as a rabbi and ritual slaughterer in Bolgrod two years earlier. My paternal grandfather, R. Israel, the ritual slaughterer in Bendery, became ill and was told by doctors to quickly change climates. He made Aliyah in 1907 and his position became available. He recommended that my father take his place and that he would send my grandfather some money to help him in Eretz Israel. From that time on everyone gave my father the nickname, Rav Moshele Shohet. I was thus referred to as Motel, the son of Moshele the shohet.

I remember that my father was upset about the fact that because his father had many children he, my father, did not receive the best education. He had to acquire his education on his own and he became a teacher. He married my mother, Rachel, the daughter of Rabbi Matityahu Morgenstern, president of the Beit Din in Bolgrod. Together they reached a ripe old age and had many children, grandchildren and great-grandchildren. His greatest success was the publication of his book "A Collection of Sayings". He reached great heights with its success. The book contained 100, 000 sayings of our sages. My mother created a wonderful, peaceful home in our modest residence in Zichron Yaakov. I will add some reminiscences about my father's life as I remember them from my childhood.

I can see my late father studying Gmara late at night, bent over his desk with a dim gaslight and chanting. I used to wake up in my crib, listen to his pleasant chanting and fall asleep again.

When I grew up I understood in a deeper way certain Psalms such as "I will thank you at midnight" and the wonderful fable about the "violin that hung over King David's bed and which the midnight wind would play by itself. David would then study Torah until dawn". I noticed again my father's tunes and I thought of him as blended in with the King David as it they were one.

Father – for me legend and reality

My father was determined to give me, his oldest son, whatever he missed in his childhood. He taught me Torah and good deeds and all the tradition acquired from his father. I do not remember being taught the letters by any rabbi. When I entered Heder I already knew the Hebrew alphabet. In addition, my father told me many stories and legends from our ancient culture. The characters of Adam, Eve and the snake; Nimrod, Noah and his Ark; our patriarchs and matriarchs; the selling of Joseph; Exodus from Egypt; heroes of Israel and its Kings; the Temple and its destruction; the Maccabees; the exile and the prophecy of the resurrection and the coming of the Messiah – all these were etched in my young brain. Later, I knew about the lives of important figures in Jewish tradition such as Rabbi Akiva, Hillel, and Rabbi Hanania Ben Dossa. I also learned all the legends about them.

My father also raised me to follow practical mitzvoth– to join him in synagogue, to bless the food, to pray Shema in the evenings, to wear tzitzit, etc. In spite of all this he did not hesitate to bring home Hebrew school texts which included simple drawings. They were edited by Yaakov Fichman and Luboshitzky. I also remember grammar books, parts A and B by Shatzky.

One time my father surprised me by singing songs in Hebrew which had a definite nationalistic hue. I understood their content. I remember words from the song "Once There Was a King" which saddened me:"My lover has left me". This was a reference to God and the Jewish people who were likened to a groom and a bride. Another song was the well-known lullaby "Lie down and sleep, my dear son" by Luboshitzky.*

[Page 125]

This is how my father introduced me to the "familial tragedy" of God and the people of Israel. I suffered greatly from this discord. I listened carefully to all the prophecies and speeches by our sages.

It is possible that my father heard these songs when he visited Zionist circles in our town. The Hazamir choir would perform often and sang in Yiddish, Hebrew and Russian. One time my father made me very happy by sending me his own illustrations of birds and other animals, houses and trees. I was lying in hospital inflicted with Scarlet Fever.

Moshe Sever – Teaching Torah to his son Shabtai

*I am grateful to the musicologist and folklorist, R. Moshe Bik. He provided me with the lyrics of these songs. I discovered that the words "My lover has left me" come from the poem "Noisy Dove" by Meir Halevy. Here are three of them:

"Oh, how I fly!

I only wander,

From rock to rock,

Oh I descend…

My lover has left me

When he was angry at me

Where will he lead me

I feel so dejected…

Have pity on me– the deserted one,

Bring back my lover,

Return my rock

And I will go under your wings!

Embarrassing questions, imagined deprivations and "inventions of childhood"

At the age for attending Heder my father first sent me to a private tutor by the name of Shalom Tsap. To this day I do not know if it was his real name or if it was nickname because of his goatee (Tsap in Yiddish means goat). In his Heder there were also girls. His assistant would carry us home on his back during the rainy season and over the puddles.

While I was absorbing legends and folk stories from my father I also became aware over time of other issues. How is it possible for everyone, while reciting the Shema, to say "Michael is on my right and Gabriel on my left". There could only be one Michael and one Gabriel in the world! How can it be that they stand next to all of us?

[Page 126]

Another question related to the legend that all the Egyptians drowned in Red Sea and no one was left behind. However, another legend speaks of Pharaoh who remained alive to see the miracles performed by God.

I used to ask my father these questions, but I was afraid to ask them of my teachers. They would consider me a heretic and would punish me. Another classmate did ask how it was possible that the waters parted for the Israelites when they left Egypt and he was told by the angry rabbi:"Don't you see!" When I began to study Gmara I was given additional material to study by myself.

When I asked the teacher the meaning of the word "seducing", he banged on the table and yelled: "You always ask things you do not need to know". When he did not want to answer embarrassing questions posed by his pupils he would rage against them saying:"You are just stubborn". In this way we created an atmosphere of, games, jokes and word games. I still remember one of them following the order of the Hebrew alphabet in a mixture of Yiddish, Hebrew and Russian.

My father had democratic views and he chose to send me to Talmud Torah where needy pupils attended. Many of them would come to school hungry. I remember that my good friend was Skolnik. He was an orphan and lived with his grandfather, the bath attendant in the steam bath. Sometimes he would join us for a meal in our house. Once, when warm clothes and winter boots were distributed, I was passed over. I was angry about this exclusion. It was only as I became older that I understood that I had been wrong since I did not need those items, but other children did.

My father allowed me to draw, to write, to construct, to play with the insides of old watches and to listen to and imitate singing on the gramophone. I recall one trick I played when I "built", in our courtyard, a sort-of gramophone. I hid under a crate and placed a kettle on top of it. I then instructed my younger brother to throw a stone inside and then I would begin to sing. The neighbors and the non-Jewish water carrier were amazed to hear singing coming from the "gramophone crate". It was the lullaby "Quietly fall asleep my dear child..."

*A Luboshitzky poem speaks about the same topic in allegorical way. Here are a few stanzas from his lullaby:

> Lie down, fall asleep, my dear son,
>
> Listen to the poem;
>
> In days gone by in faraway places
>
> There was a city
>
> Your ancestors
>
> Lived there once
>
> They lived a happy life–
>
> In those places.

But, the ancestors, because of their good life

Left the teachings of God

And the sunshine of their success

Became thick shadows.

When God was angry with them

He exiled them from the city

Lie down, fall asleep, my dear son

Listen to the poem.

[Page 127]

Father speaks about H.N. Bialik and our relationships

I created a magic place on the tall wooden fence and used a hammer to hang an old clock, barrel rings, used kettles and pots, horseshoes, torn boots, etc. Suddenly, a torrent of rain threatened my "kingdom". I stood in front of it not knowing what to do. My father called to me urgently: "Motele, come quickly to see what beautiful books I received from Bialik in Odessa." I thought there would be illustrations in these books, but I was disappointed. I found two books beautifully bound in black. It was Haagadah (the fable) by H.N. Bialik and Kh. Rebnitzky. The books did not appeal to me at all. Later my father told me who the writers were. He added that Bialik writes beautiful poetry and that he even gets paid for them…

I asked my father how much he paid for these books. My father replied that he paid nothing since the books were gifts from the authors.

I discovered that my father found an error in the commentary on the topic "Tzedaka collectors" in the book. He wrote to them and, in return, the authors sent him a thank you letter indicating that they would correct the matter in the next edition. This story is told in I. Kh. Rebnitzky's book "David and his writers" which was published by "Dvir" in Eretz Israel.

My father's attitude to the descendants of Yeshayahu Halevy Horvitz who wrote the book "Holy Tables of the Decalogue" did not leave an impression on me. When I arrived in Eretz Israel in 1923 my paternal grandmother Mindel told me that she had been born in Tiberias. Her father was R. Shabtai–Shepsil Horvitz who had been the town rabbi there. He eventually moved to Russia and was a rabbi in Kilia in Bessarabia. Shabtai–Shepsil was one of the sons of Yeshayahu Halevy (he lived 300 years ago). It is not known whether my grandfather was the last in this dynasty of Tiberias or not. What we do know is that most of those in the Horvitz family revere his descendants as saints. His book dealt in 613 mitzvoth according to their order of mention in the Torah and as seen in the Kabala. It had a great influence on the religious Jews. Many researchers tried to verify the family tree of this rabbi, but there are gaps in our knowledge.

My father wants an improved world

My father was a philanthropist and was ready to help others. He was follower of the Rabbi from Sadigura and of Hillel. He knew how to respect every person and was careful not to insult anyone, young or old. He believed that one should honor one's friends. He always looked to make life easier for the unfortunate and the sick. He also published articles in Hebrew and Russian press in other countries. He would explain, using diagrams and statistics, the importance of his proposals to rebuild our people by establishing funds, e.g. to help poor brides or pensions for the elderly. His proposal was mentioned in an article in the publication "Pensions" in July 1965. My father's words are cited in the advice to members to think ahead of the time when they can no longer work. They would have a regular pension legally and would not have to depend on donations. He also dedicated himself to Welcoming Visitors, Talmud Torah and other loan funds. In Zichron Yaakov he worked hard to establish proper records in the cemetery while still looking after old gravestones of farmers and laborers from Aliyah B who died of old age or from malaria. Often their relatives in their original country did not know where they were buried.

He was demanding, but he was also an achiever. In my childhood, I remember that he would be the last to leave the synagogue after Friday night services in case there was a visitor who did not have a place to eat. He dedicated himself to host Jewish soldiers who passed through our town with the Russian army. He also cared for Jewish refugees from Ukraine after the revolution and the riots. I was a young child still when I helped him to distribute food to a hundred guests sitting at tables in our old synagogue.

One Shabbat he cried bitterly when he went to the courtyard of the Sadigura followers with a letter from Ukraine in his hand. One of the refugees read the letter. In it there was a description of the horrible deeds performed by the rioters from the armies of Danikin, Petlura, Makhano and others. May their memory be erased! They cruelly murdered men, women, old people and even children and babies.

Signs of the times and events in the war

It is most likely that my father hoped to see me as a qualified teacher like him and he always praised me as "one with a good head on his shoulders". He insisted that I stay with a class learning Talmud with top teachers who came from Poland or Lithuania. However, the times intervened. We received newspapers and books in Yiddish and Hebrew – Hatzfira, Hamodia, Hafsaga, Our Time and Jewish Library published by I. L. Peretz, etc.

[Page 128]

The Hebrew High School opened and my childhood friend entered it. Father did not want to separate us and even my mother wanted me to study in the Hebrew High School. It was a difficult decision to place the son of the ritual slaughterer in the school. Eventually, my friend's father influenced my father to enroll me in the Jewish school where there were no classes on Shabbat. There was even teaching in Bible and Hebrew in addition to secular studies.

After a long deliberation, my father allowed me to enter under certain conditions. My friend and I would have to continue religious studies after school, to pray in the synagogue on a daily basis and to follow all mitzvoth. We agreed and managed to keep the bargain at the beginning...

One winter night, before dawn, when I was 10–11 years old, I went to the first Minyan at the synagogue. The dark skies were strewn with shining stars and I was a mere small dot in the field of snow covering the street. Suddenly I thought I saw a tall devil with horns on each side of the head. He approached me and I was frozen in place out of fear... I then realized it was only a tall and robust woman carrying two milk jugs and a yoke on her shoulders. When I recovered, I heard her asking me, in Russian, of course, "Where are you going, little boy?" I was able to reply: "To synagogue, to pray." The woman was impressed and said upon leaving: "Very nice, little boy, pray to God!"

I must admit my transgressions. I did not always keep my promise. My father was of two opinions: he was happy that I was receiving a general education in a Jewish, not Russian, high school, but he was afraid–and for good reason–that I would be further away from religious studies and the following of practices as I had been taught at home. It was true, my studies occupied more of my time and I did not have the opportunity to learn Mishna on a daily basis. My father would teach me Talmud and sometimes I studied by myself. However, my head did not enjoy the different topics discussed. Eventually, due to lack of time, I prayed by myself at home before I went to school. The agreement was not fulfilled. My father suffered as a result. He was a patient and gentle person and he tried to influence me with kindness. Once when we were walking on the street he asked me:"Tell me, Motele, when I die, will you go to synagogue every day to say Kaddish?" I was shocked by this question and since I wished to make him feel better I replied:"Yes". His response was:"Why do you care if I am alive?" He was smiling in triumph and I could add nothing.

Another collision took place when I prepared "business cards" and stamped all my books with my name in Romanian (during the conquest of Bessarabia by the Romanians in 1918). Instead of Mordehai Sverdlik I put Max Sverdlik... My father once opened one of these books and, with sarcasm, asked "Who is this Max Sverdlik?" I will hit this Max". We both laughed and the incident was over.

My father's work and reputation in Eretz Israel

Many years have passed since 1923 when my father made Aliyah with his family following the wishes of his father. I came six months earlier as a "licensed electrician". This occupation gave me a permit to make Aliyah according to the regulations of the Mandate. I was still under age then. My father took the position of ritual slaughterer in Zichron Yaakov from my grandfather. The latter continued to sit as chairman of the judicial courts in Zichron Yaakov and its vicinity. After a few months of working in the construction of a children's institute in Shfeya and in the paving of the road there, I went to Haifa to seek another position. There was much unemployment in those days. There was not enough work and the laborers suffered the shame of hunger and the need to receive charity. Many people left the country and some workers committed suicide. There were many articles written begging people not to give up. I began to work on the railroad. There were a few Jews among a multitude of Arabs and Egyptians.

We were five children at home, but only three sons remained. We doubled and tripled the number of descendants and our parents enjoyed grandchildren and great–grandchildren. The happiest was my father who had lived a hard life. He continued to do charitable work, helping the needy, receiving visitors, adding to the library in the synagogue and even rebinding the prayer books, writing a log at the Hevra Kaddisha and even in writing articles. He wrote about topics such "The synagogue as a community building", "The need to draft girls in the army" etc.

[Page 129]

I must admit that in the 1920s I never imagined that my father collected sayings by marking them in his texts. Suddenly, I heard rumors that something important was taking place in my father's lab and that he collected many sayings. He had not yet finished his mission. Dr. Yomtov Levinsky and G. Kersel were preparing their first publication called "Folk Lore", and they invited my father to send articles to "Folk Lore" and "Words of the Week". They said that my father's collection was greater than that of Bialik and Rebnitzky who had about 2,500 articles. He even had more items than K.A. Perla (7000) and Rabbi Aaron Hayman in London (30 000). Rabbi Hayman visited my father's house in Zichron Yaakov in 1937. After two weeks he was quite impressed that my father had a collection of 100,000 articles and sayings. Rabbi Hayman was prepared to help him to publish this collection. Unfortunately, 12 days after his visit with my father, Rabbi Hayman passed away. The dreams aroused by him in my father did not come to fruition.

Rabbi I.L. Maimon encourages publication

In the course of time my father's work became known by sages, rabbis and writers who began to visit him in his house in Zichron Yaakov, These were Rabbi. I. L. Fishman (Maimon), chief rabbi A.A. Herzog, Rabbi Amiel, Rabbi Prof. Simcha Assaf, minister David Remez and Sh. Z. Shazar, our former president, author David Zakai, the linguist Yitzhak Avineri, and others. All the visitors saw the great work my father had done and were quite impressed. They began to publicize his work in various articles. My father also received letters from within the country and outside it from rabbis, authors, scholars, linguists and others who would consult him on the origins of sayings. My father replied to all quickly and with pleasure.

Rabbi I. L. Maimon suggested my father copy his collection on cards so that a book could be published by topic, not in alphabetical order. The Rav Kook institute negotiated with my father (I took part in it). It felt that my father, due to his advanced age, would not be able to prepare his book for publication. A qualified editor was hired– A. Darom. This was done with the help of Yitzhak Raphael.

In 1961–62 three volumes of my father's book were published, In addition, dozens of articles full of praise could be read in the press. The book was well received not only in our country, but also in America and Europe. It became a best seller and was recommended by professors to their students as a text. When I visited the Soviet Union in 1966 I presented myself to Chief Rabbi Levin in Moscow. He recognized me as the son of the author of the collection and told me he had a copy of this important book. My father began to organize the book alphabetically according to the beginning of each part and he succeeded in achieving two thirds of the job. He did not complete it and died on 9 Sivan 1967 at the age of 86. This is what we put on his gravestone:

> **Rabbi Moshe, son of Israel, Sever (Sverdlik), Ritual slaughterer**
> **May his name be inscribed in the**
> **Book of Life**
> **A man of Torah, he was honest and a servant of God and a lover of his creatures.**
> **Author of "The Collections of Sayings"**

Municipality of Petach Tikva memorializes his life's work in its library

A year after my father's death, my friend (who was like a brother to me), Eliezer Roey, the director of the municipal library in Petach Tikva, began to speak to me. He told me that in the library there will be a section named after the late Reuven Katz and he wanted our family to donate to it our father's book collection. It would be called the "Section for the Sages of Our People" named after Rabbi Moshe Sever, z"l.

[Page 130]

There was no equivalent library in Zichron Yaakov that could house his collection. In the Petach Tikva area there are numerous Yeshivas and Bar Ilan University and we felt it was logical that such a collection would be used by their students. This would have pleased my father. So it came to be and the "Section for the Sages of Our People" named after my father, was established.

With the placement of his collection at the municipal library in Petach Tikva the adage "Torah returns to its home" was achieved.

A Childhood Affront
By Leah Bat Chaya and Bezalel
Translated by Ala Gamulka

In memory of my mother, may she rest in peace.

My mother was a righteous woman and followed all the commandments, whether big or small. There was no Eruv* in our town so she was not in the habit of carrying on Shabbat on her way to synagogue. It was my responsibility to carry since I was still little. I especially enjoyed the task in the winters.

We used to leave the house in the morning when there was a blanket of white, pure snow on the streets. Every miserable shack, every misshapen fence, every muddy pile and every stinking trench disappeared as if by magic when covered in white. There were no footsteps coming from the marketplace and drunks did not lie in front of the saloons. The business owners were dressed in white garments and were on their way to services. The calm of Shabbat was felt everywhere. Sparrows jumped over chimneys singing happily. I held my mother's soft and warm hand and I was happy.

When we came close to the synagogue we would meet the wives of the wealthy members of the community. They sat in the women's auxiliary covered in magnificent shawls. These shawls were made of black quilted velvet and decorated with expensive fur. I often put my hand on the velvet and carefully touched it so that its owner would not notice. I was thrilled to my fingers and I wished my mother would have such a shawl. My heart ached looking at her bald fur, but my dream never came true. This was true of many childhood dreams.

One Shabbat, as we were leaving synagogue, my mother turned to me and said:" Leah'le, I promised Tzirel, the wife of Shlomo Gabbai, to send you to her tomorrow. She wants to give us some pickles." I was uncomfortable with this task and I thought to myself:"Why take pickles? We have our own." I did not dare say no to mother.

The next afternoon my mother dressed me in my coat–its sleeves were too short– and her scarf was wrapped on my head. She placed a large clay pot in my hands. I did not need to look in the mirror to know that I looked ridiculous in my outfit. I reluctantly made my way to the house of Shlomo Gabbai. Upon arrival, I stood for a long time in front of the glass door. I peeked in hoping I would not run into any of the children. My hopes were dashed. As soon as I rang the door bell I heard wild skipping from the upper floor. In front of me stood "the red –headed one", the only son of R.Shlomo. He did not open the door, but he looked me over from top to bottom through the glass. His green eyes were mocking and he burst out in wild laughter. The dog near him also began to bark loudly. I was afraid he would send the dog to attack me. I saw myself fighting him off, my clothes in shreds and my arms bitten and scratched. I wanted to run for my life. At that moment, the maid, a kind old woman, appeared and let me inside. She told the boy off. She did cross herself several times and moved her head to and fro. I saw pity in her eyes. She gave me the pickles and sent me home.

When I left home there was still light outside, but when I returned there were stars in the sky and lights could be seen in windows. I walked alone on the snowy path and snowflakes were swirling around me.

[Page 131]

This time they did not amuse me. I was sad and I felt the mocking green eyes all the way home.

I blamed the round clay pot with the pickles for all of this. I was almost ready to get rid of it and telling my mother that it fell and broke. I thought better of it by telling myself that I could not fool my mother and cause her grief. She did send me, but she probably had no choice as she could not refuse the wife of Shlomo Gabbai. She is probably now worried about me. I rushed home.

When I went to bed that night, after the Shema prayer recited nightly– I added my own "When I grow up I do not wish to be a cantor, to wear a poor fur like my mother. When I am a mother myself I will not send my child to Gabbai's wife to get pickles or anything else."

* Eruv– a rabbinic rule that allows people to carry on Shabbat further than 90 paces from their home.

My Father Reb Bezalel, the Cantor and the Talner Synagogue
By Leah Bat Chaya and Bezalel
Translated by Ala Gamulka

In memory of my father, z"l

The ancient house of learning of the Talner Hassidim has disappeared from our town Bendery and is no longer there, as happened to all the other houses of worship. My father toiled there for thirty five years as the leader of services. For me it was part of my childhood memories. There are many memories that I have from those days. I visualize the old building with its thick walls. It was a fort for the Talner Hassidim and my father was one of them. There was a long glass enclosed entrance way and it was cooler there in the summers because it was surrounded by nut trees. On Shabbat and Holidays young boys would climb the trees, collect nuts and put them in their pockets. R. Yosele, the old sexton, would come out dressed in his faded Talit and yell at them:"You are defiling Shabbat!" His goatee would shake and his eyes were full of fire, but the boys would just scatter.

I was always anxious for the Holy Ark to be opened for the Torah to be read. I loved to look at the Torah scrolls covered in colorful silk and velvet. The covers were embroidered and had silver crowns. Where are these scrolls? Where are the people? Where is our community?

*

I recall the eve of Tisha B'Av when people sat on the floor mourning and without shoes. They would read the Scroll of Lamentations in candlelight. I still hear my father's voice:"How did the city sit so alone…" His keening had all the emotions of the fear of the annihilation. I was a young child and I could imagine our temple going up in flames. I mourned with all the others. I also remember Yom Kippur: the congregation was wearing white kitels and prayer shawls. The fear of the day of judgement was seen on their faces. The memorial candles and the light fixtures cast a shadow on them. In the quiet my father begged God:"Forgive the sins of these people", "Forgive us, absolve us, and pardon us". You could hear sobbing from the women's auxiliary.

*

My father knew how to mourn the destruction of the temple, to ask for forgiveness on Yom Kippur, the day of judgement. However, he also knew how to rejoice on Simchat Torah and to infect the crowd with his joy. "Please God, Help Us!"– His voice would envelop us while he held the Torah scroll. His face would shine and the congregants joined him in encircling the synagogue. Even we, the children, danced and sang holding flags topped with apples and lit candles.

*

On summer mornings my father would stand deep in prayer with his Talit covering him. I was a little girl and I tried to catch the sun rays coming through the trees in the yard. A visitor arrived in the synagogue and sat down to rest. Father finished his praying, folded his Talit and turned to the visitor: "How do you do? Where are you from?" He would invite the visitor to his home and sometimes the guest would stay for weeks. Mother would take care of all his needs. The guest would go with him to Friday night services. You would hear "Shalom Aleichem" and happy chants. The house was full light and happiness as we welcomed the Shabbat...

[Page 132]

*

One winter day you could see, through the windows of the synagogue, the garden deep in snow. Ahrale the eccentric, assistant to Yosele the sexton, brought in a bundle of firewood donated by a congregant. My father is surrounded by the congregants ready for evening prayers. Each one has a tale of woe. One says that the wind blew out his roof during the night while another tells about the snow that broke his ceiling. The milkman's cow is ailing while the wagon driver's horse died. The porter's house is full of insects and there is no bread or firewood. Young boys are not attending classes because they do not have any shoes to wear. As they are telling their sad stories a woman burst in asking R. Betzalel to pray for her daughter who is giving birth. Another woman, dressed in black, brought her young child and asks my father to teach him to say Kaddish for his father. A widow comes in tears because her only son who was providing for her was taken into the army instead of the son of a wealthy man who bribed the authorities. "Where is justice?"

*

It is no wonder that my father continues to pray and to worry about his congregants. I see him sitting among his people, pale and skinny and trying to strengthen them. He is so burdened by these needs and is almost ready to give up. Soon he goes out again to visit the wealthy congregants and to ask them to help the less fortunate.

*

There were many joyous events in which he participated. Some congregants had many children and he often was the Godfather at their Brit. He organized wedding ceremonies for young couples who could not afford them. One would hear his melodious voice officiating at the ceremony. Everyone recognized his lovely voice.

[Page 133]

Memory Fragments of Days Gone By
By Katya Shay (Fein) Haifa
Translated by Ala Gamulka

A. A gallery of families

I often recall the streets of my town: Harozinskaya (many stores), Constantinovskaya, Nikolayevskaya, Alexandrovskaya, Sergeyevskaya, Pavlovskaya and Kaushanskaya. I think of the people, members of families, who are no longer with us– either dead or scattered in many countries.

I shall describe a gallery of families – a socio-economic slice of our town: Dubossarsky (bakeries), Yanishevsky (tailor), Yanishevsky (store owner), Lvovsky (owner of the cinema and the perfume store), Immes, Rabinovitch, Shaposnick, Gutov, Goldberg, Sirota, Tilis, Berman, Dr. Kipnis, Lavonsky, Kamelis, Poronchik, Sverdlik, Burs, Figler, Shitman, Kleitman and Kreimerman –(clothing stores),the Nissenboim family whose son became the director of Hadassah hospital in Haifa, Krasnov (pharmacy owner), Fishbein, Dr. Petrov, Drahelis, Avraham Zigberman (Zhabotinsky's body guard when he visited Bendery), his father, the teacher, Seltzer, Feffer, Fein, Shneirson, Goldfarb, Krassnolov, Hersh Kogan, Israel Blank, Kh. Fustman, Rivlin, Natanzon, Mulman (pharmacy owner), Makhelis, Doliner and Piny the cantor (Misonzshnik).

My parents were supporters of the school and were also active in helping the needy. They helped to establish the community kitchen. Our home was always open and everyone who came was cordially received.

I remember with reverence Dr. Zvi Schwartzman, the principal of the Hebrew High School. He was a dear man with a dynamic personality. He knew how to instill knowledge and how to inspire us. His sons, Dr. Yaakov and Boris inherited the aristocratic traits of Dr. Schwartzman and his dear wife.

B. Collections for Eretz Israel

There were many good and generous Jews in our town. They volunteered for every good cause be it the synagogue or the Hebrew High School. Dr.

Vilensky and Haim Greenberg came to town as emissaries from Eretz Israel and my mother collected gold jewelry as donations.

C. The Rich Poet

Mr. Bentzion Pastelnikov, a Hebrew teacher composed poetry in Yiddish on sad topics. The poetry was mostly about Jewish life, pogroms and the suffering of ordinary people. Avraham, the tailor, would recite the poems with excitement and even Zina Pastelnikov joined in.

D. The New Synagogue is opened with a gold key

I remember the inauguration of the new synagogue on Mikhailovsky Street. It was a gala occasion and all residents came to watch the opening with a gold key.

E. A War of Ideologies

Much has been said about the youth movements in my time. I will only recall the constant war of ideologies between Hashomer Hatzair and Zeirei Zion. I was a counselor in Maccabi having been trained by Monia Feldman from Kishinev. We had many activities for Eretz Israel, among them balls where money was collected.

F. Bendery Residents in Public Life

Bendery was, indeed, a small town, but it produced many highly educated people. They were creative and motivated and were successful in many fields of activities. In spite of all the differences of opinion and approaches, our community was united. We were very proud of this fact.

It is necessary to mention our residents who had important positions in Eretz Israel and in the Diaspora. These are Attorney Yosef Kushner (he was also a member of the Knesset);

[Page 134]

Shlomo Klavenski– secretary of the Dental Technicians; Pinhas Bendersky – a director of the post office; David Pisterov– active in the union in Petach Tikva; the members of the family of the late David Wertheim who was also active in the Histadrut and in Zeirei Zion in Russia and the United States.;

Avraham Wertheim who was head of labor relations in the Histadrut ; the late Rabbi Yosef Wertheim; Pnina Wertheim, z"l, head nurse in Hadassah; Yentel the Kindergarten teacher; Haya, my brother, Dr. Fein's wife; Reuven Schrybman (Shariv) active in Histadrut; Haim Radi of the Berman family, secretary general in the Foreign Ministry; Ruth (Rassia)Berman, an officer in the army; Batya Shteiner, a Kindergarten teacher while still in Bendery and who continued her work in Eretz Israel; Sh. Zahoval, z"l, an actor in the Ohel theatre; my brothers Dr. Yitzhak Fein and Yasha Fein (secretary of the organization of Bendery Residents in the United States); Yosef Fein in Argentina; my sister Donya Fein, married to Professor Orlinsky; Pola Berman in Uruguay; Dubossarsky and Lerner in France. We, the women, worked diligently in all aspects of public life– Organization of Working Mothers, WIZO, etc.

G. I Made Aliyah

I left Bendery at a young age. I lived in Czernowitz for two years and after much effort I succeeded in being accepted at the university. I was refused at first because I was Jewish and I had to pass complicated tests. My pride in my people propelled me to prove that we, too, could succeed. I am proud that I was able to prove myself to the non-Jews. At the first opportunity I made Aliyah when I received a visa.

Many years have passed since, but I remember with longing and appreciation all those people. I only mentioned some of them above. I will never forget those wonderful days...

My Father's House – Open To All
By Abba Sapir (Shaposnick) Tel Aviv
Translated by Ala Gamulka

R. Abba Shaposnick (Sapir) was born in Bendery in 1897. He was the son of R. Yosef and Sima–the youngest of 10 children.

Interviewed by I. Haviv

I studied in the private house of learning founded, by my late father, on Sergeyevskaya Street. I was in a group of students and among them were Leibl, son of Haim, Immes, the sons of Shmuel–Abba Sudit, Pinhas Shaposnick and others.

Our teacher, Rabbi Hershel Tulchiner, came from Poland. He taught many students, some even were ordained as Rabbis– R. Avremel Kunitzer, Rabbi Mordehai Yatom, son of Zeidel the ritual slaughterer. Prior to that class I had studied with Rabbi Baruch Kolker.

When I grew up I dealt in business. In 1921 I moved to Galatz. I married my good wife, the daughter of Rabbi Shimon Halevy Gottesman. I was the director of the Jewish community in Galatz for over 20 years and I was one of the founders of Mizrahi and Hapoel Hamizrahi. We made Aliyah in 1944.

Until my move to Galatz I had been involved in all aspects of Jewish life in Bendery:

1. Help for the Sick. Its chairman was the pharmacist Isaac Mulman. The members of the committee were Dr. Khain, Shmishelevitz, Moshe Doliner and others. The purpose of this institution was to provide medical help to all who needed it. The doctors attached were: Ranoman, Vunderbar, Bondarov, etc. Those who were sick also received financial help for buying medications and for living expenses.

2. Clothing for the Needy. This institution provided clothing and shoes for children who attended the Talmud Torah. Funds were organized by the committee whose members were Yoel Vodoboz, Shimon Averbuch, David Wertheim and I. Before the formation of this institution there was a similar group and its members were Immes, Fustan, Israel Blank, Hirsh Kogan and I.

*

My father's house was always open to visiting rabbis. They would come from Rakhamistriovka, Talne, Feshken, Bahush, Agut, etc.

[Page 135]

My late father was the chairman of the Mishna society. Every Hanukah there was a siyum (ending) for those studying Mishna. There was always a meal involved. All the rabbis and scholars in Bendery took part.

Leybele Blank (from the family of Alter Blank)– owner of the flour mill and one who considered himself "Free", wanted to become a member of the Mishna society. He was not accepted. One time when the Rabbi from Rakhamistriovka was visiting us, Leybele asked him for a recommendation to the Mishna society since his own father was a member of that dynasty. Leybele was thus accepted as a member of the Mishna society and always took part in these annual events.

In Bendery there was an owner of a modern flour mill by the name of Hershke Firshtenberg. He was once told that one of his guards allowed flour to be removed without an official permission from the office. When the guard was caught, he was brought to the office. He was a Jewish man with a large family and he was petrified. He was certain that he would lose his job.

As he entered the office he was quite surprised that instead of being reprimanded, the owner–Firshtenberg– asked about his family and how much he was earning. When the owner heard that his salary was quite low he told him:"From now on you will receive a raise and you will not need to repeat your deeds".

Ordinary Folk Caught in Reality
By Yehiel Efrati (Haifa)
Translated by Ala Gamulka

My father, Yosef Mendel Eidelman, (nicknamed Yehiel, son of Berel the Hazan) was a wine merchant on Harozinskaya Street. Since he dealt in wholesale he was not permitted to sell to individuals. In spite of this prohibition, we did sell to individuals in the saloon. Often, Jews would come in to drink a glass of wine. In this fashion I was able to meet several people that I wish to mention.

A. Skaymaka

I do not remember his name, but he was nicknamed Skaymaka (chair in Russian). Whenever he heard this nickname he would be very angry with those who used it.

He earned his living by selling animal skins. He used to leave his house early in the morning and travel to the villages where he bought animal skins from the farmers. He sold the skins to leather merchants in town. He wandered daily in the villages, dressed as one of the farmers. He did return home in the evenings.

When he came home he would wear his Shabbat clothes, put on a tie (he did not have a beard) and buy a fresh loaf of bread and a salami. He came in to the saloon and ordered a litre of red wine and enjoyed his meal. Since he had no teeth he could not chew the crust. When he finished his meal he would pack away the crust and leave.

He was not a scholar and perhaps he did not even know how to read a newspaper, but he was keen on politics and loved to discuss it. Since he had to rise early he was worried that perhaps he put on his Tfilin earlier than permissible. (He obviously was unaware of the law in Shulchan Aruch, 10, 2 which states the proper rules). He was honest, simple and earned his own living.

B. The Righteous Convert – the chimney cleaner

In our town there was a righteous convert, a chimney cleaner. He was called Avraham, the chimney cleaner. He would come to our saloon between jobs and would drink a litre of wine. He was interested in philosophy and the world. He listened to my opinions even though I was only a high school student.

He was a simple man who always had a smile on his face. He worshipped scholars and listened carefully to what they were saying. He was impressed by everything new. He could neither read nor write and always needed other people in order to learn. He discovered new things on a daily basis and was always enthusiastic about everything he learned.

C. Dreaming about Aliyah

On Sergeyevskaya Street, near our house, there was a shoemaker whose name I do not remember. Everyone called him "the old shoemaker". He owned his house and he saw himself as one of the town leaders. However, in spite of his wishes, he still remained a craftsman and not a town leader.*

[Page 136]

I was still a young boy when I would sit in his shop where he worked with his son. I admired the quickness of his work. He, too, was interested in politics, especially anything connected to the Jewish people in their wanderings and Eretz Israel. He truly aspired to make Aliyah, but he did not achieve the dream since he was afraid to travel by boat and thought he could reach his destination by land.

*Leader in Bendery– see remark 15 at end of article by P. Bendersky

Road of Suffering
By Leah Steiner (Tel Aviv)
Translated by Ala Gamulka

...this is what my friend told me: I grew up in my grandmother's house in a Ukrainian village called Cherny. When I was six, she died and my maternal uncle in Bendery took me in. My aunt and uncle had a nice house and a large grocery store, but they were unkind and miserly. I came to them in the winter. When they left for work in the morning they would lock me in and I had to sit most days looking out the window like a prisoner. I finally had the courage to ask my uncle to send me to a Heder (I had attended a Heder in my village for two semesters). My uncle did not even lift his eyes from his filthy ledger and replied angrily:"In our town girls do not study in a Heder and it is too late to send you to a public school". A few days later I begged him:"I really want to learn! I want to get out of the house!"

One morning when he left for work he took me with him without saying a word. We trudged through snow for a long time and my limbs froze. When we reached the church square I saw the crosses on the golden domes sparkling in the sun. I shut my eyes in order not to sin. Suddenly, my uncle pulled me into the yard from which was heard a school bell. Children, accompanied by their teachers, were coming out of the school next to the church. I was scared about where he was taking me. My uncle called out to a teacher who was his customer – "Vasily Vasilevich!" He handed me over to the teacher together with a gift of a large cone of sugar (this is how sugar was produced). I did not know any Russian and I could not understand the lessons. I was truly afraid. I returned to the store, full of customers, after a few classes.

Inside the store there were peasants wearing their large furs and the women covered in colorful sweaters. My aunt, behind the counter, was busy serving the customers. My uncle watched the customers' bags to make certain they did not steal. I went down to the cellar and I sat in a corner. I was so upset. This was my first day in school. I did learn, but I was insulted many times. During recess the other children would encircle me and mock me mercilessly. I was like a small and helpless animal caught in a trap. I began to advance in my studies and the other children discovered that I could help them. They stopped their mocking and approached me for help in math, to copy my homework and to whisper the answer to them when they were called up to the blackboard.

I was a young child, but much of the household work was given to me by my aunt. I could do my homework or read a book only in the evenings when I had to use the weak street light in front of the house – to save on kerosene. The lack of love and warmth at home caused me to seek them in school. I wanted to be close to my non–Jewish schoolmates and to be like them. To receive attention from the nice priest I attended his religion classes even though I was not obliged to do so. The crosses and the church bells no longer scared me and my longing for my wonderful grandmother and the Heder of Moshe–Kalman subsided. I distanced myself a little from my origins.

An incident occurred which brought my back to my past. This is what happened: our teacher, the daughter of the priest, was a young woman that I really liked. She prepared us for the end of year party. Since I was an excellent student I was asked to recite the poem "Road of Suffering" which describes the crucifying of Jesus.

[Page 137]

I identified with his suffering and I recited the poem with great emotion – my tears were flowing. I saw myself on stage – the audience applauding and everyone praising me. I could not wait for this great moment in my life. The evening of the party an inspector came to the school and he cancelled my performance. He shouted to my teacher"Nadezhda Petrovna. What is with you? She is Jewish!" This is after he looked me up and down with evil eyes.

For many days I remembered his voice saying "She is Jewish!" Then I found the answer – "I am Jewish and so I will remain!"

*

My friend succeeded in her studies and she graduated from university with distinction. She worked hard for her livelihood. She continued her Hebrew studies and eventually she became an excellent teacher in Hebrew schools in the Diaspora. She continued to do so in Eretz Israel and was quite beloved by her pupils. She also taught Braille and was able to help her students on their "Road of Suffering".

My Bendery
By Leah Steiner (Tel Aviv)
Translated by Ala Gamulka

When I say "my Bendery" I do not mean the Russian capital city or the Jewish community in it. I refer to my childhood home, the streets and laneways called "the Jewish streets". In the center was the street named after the ancient Turkish fort and at its end the square with the Russian Orthodox Church. My earliest memories are of the many fires around our home that would be lit on warm summer nights. I remember being taken outside in my father's arms and watching the fires. There were flames and much smoke and Jews carrying pails of water and women and children crying. The usual reason for these fires was that one of the owners wanted to improve the look of our street by setting his humble abode on fire. He used the insurance money to build a new home...

When spring came and the snow melted the streets were full of black mud. It was difficult to walk there even with good boots. In summer every wagon would send a cloud of dust. Our yards were plain without any sign of greenery. We would sneak a look into the yards of our non-Jewish neighbors where there were fruit trees growing. No one could touch these fruit!

In our neighborhood we had the owners of saloons, small groceries, craftsmen and religious personnel. We had many houses of worship and study. These would be filled to capacity on Shabbat and Holidays. On Yom Kippur the voices of those praying were so loud that I imagined that their voices and the sound of the shofar would reach the homes of the wealthy members of the community.

There were many Heders in our neighborhood and one could hear the sound of the young pupils as they repeated their lessons and the older ones translating Torah pages into Yiddish. On the other hand, we also had many saloons in the area. Many Jews earned their living from them.

The drunkenness caused many fights which sometimes brought the police. One could hear their whistles and screams and the store owners would quickly close their shops. The mothers would collect their children from the yard and lock the gates. We had to be very quiet – not to make any sound. We would think to ourselves–what is the purpose? We were also uninvited guests at many Jewish and non-Jewish weddings. We loved the Klezmer music, especially Avremel the fiddler. He was short, but an expert musician.

[Page 138]

When he placed his fiddle under his unkempt beard and brought down his bow the sounds were sad and happy and touched our hearts.

Another source of enjoyment was the Dniester. In the heat of summer mothers would go to the river with their children. We loved to splash in the cool water, to watch the women doing laundry on the stones and singing Ukrainian melodies.

Wagon drivers and water carriers would come inside the river with their animals. Some would swim and others would float on the water. We were jealous of the good swimmers and we followed them. At times it seemed that they would disappear and perhaps drown, but soon we would see them come up again. At times there was a riverboat carrying children like us (for us it was but a dream).

One harsh winter day when the street was covered with snow shining in the sun, the coming of Christmas was felt in town. The villagers arrived in hordes to attend church services and they carried crosses. They were led by the fat priest wearing a golden tunic with his long braid trailing on his back.

I recall that in spite of the fear of looking at the crosses, how could we not sneak a peek? Sometimes it was also Hanukah time and our holiday took second place. Our shutters would be closed and the door bolted with an iron stick. They were in their church, but we were fearful and tense. The church bells rang at midnight as if to warn us of a massacre. Our household was prepared and even, I, a young child, would not fall asleep until my eyes closed on their own. I had frightening nightmares. In the morning I would wake up and all was well– our house stood and we were all alive. The night passed quietly and the peasants returned home without touching us. We then relit our candles and talked of the miracles of the Maccabees...

The End of Michaelovsky Street Near The Dniester

[Page 139]

Yehiel the Cobbler Teaches Me Zionism
By Leah Steiner (Tel Aviv)
Translated by Ala Gamulka

Hilikel (Yehiel) the cobbler – that was his nickname because he was short. His workshop was located near our house in a broken down shack with a leaky roof. Inside there was a low table with his tools, two stools and a few wooden cases used for sitting. A rusty iron furnace stood there winter and summer. The walls were covered with faded posters depicting gentlemen, fancy ladies and smiling children showing off their elegant shoes. Yehiel hung up these posters, not as a decoration, but as protection from rain and wind that would come in through the boards. There was a pile of old shoes and faded boots near the main wall. On that wall he hung a picture of Dr. Herzl surrounded by a collection of old "shekels" that he was able to afford with his few pennies.

His shoe shop served as a sort of club for all craftsmen who could neither read nor write. When one of them entered, Yehiel would stop his work. In the winter he would feed the furnace with some of these old shoes to make it warmer for his guest. He would then take out a batch of crumpled newspapers, read and explain the politics of those days. He would even add a dose of Zionism.

The shoe shop drew us, the children, although the blacksmith's shop was more enticing. However, the blacksmith, black with ashes, did not allow us to come nearer and we could only watch, from afar, the magical bellows which went up and down and heated the embers. It had black edges with white eyes which beat down on the heated iron pieces. They seemed to be imaginary creatures.

On the other hand, Yehiel welcomed us as beloved guests. As he worked he would tell us stories about wars, robbers and princes. The stories engaged our imagination. We were also thankful that he repaired our old shoes and sewed new ones for the holidays.

On a nasty day it was pleasant to sit in Yehiel's shoe shop with the furnace blazing and he, bent on his work table, making holes in the sole and quickly putting in the nails he had kept in his mouth. His anvil would jump in his sinewy hand. When the work was completed he would polish the sole with his crooked and blackened thumb and would hum: "Let us return to our homeland…"

One day he asked me, pointing to the picture on the wall, "Do you know who this man is?" He did not wait for my reply and he said:"It is Dr. Theodore Herzl!" and he continued:"He is like Moshe Rabenu for the Jews. He is prepared to remove us from among these cursed people who attack us. He wanted to bring us to our homeland. However, like Moshe, he was unable to complete his mission and he died". He then added: "He said 'If you wish it, it is not a legend.' If the Jews will wish it we can make it on our own." I asked, "How will we reach Eretz Israel and the Messiah has not yet come?" Yehiel smiled and replied kindly: "We will get there without the Messiah. We can rent ships and go on the high seas from Odessa to Constantinople and from there we will come to Jaffa a few days later".

I imagined these huge ships with all residents of the Jewish streets, young and old, my family and I. I shivered with happiness. Yehiel continued his story of the wonderful land where oranges, figs, dates, almonds, raisins and other fruit that we only taste on Tu B'Shvat are grown. The children of Israel are brave; they are heroes like the Maccabees. They know no fear!

As I am sitting enthralled with his words, the door opened and his spouse, Feiga-Etel, came in wrapped up in her thin sweater. She was shivering with the cold.

Yehiel stopped his tale, took a faded boot from the pile and hit it with his hammer as if angry because his wife interrupted his dream…

She sat quietly for some time and then she opened her toothless mouth and turned to me with a sneer:"He is telling you the story of his Palestine where the herds are fed dates, figs and oranges. He wastes his time on nonsense and does not worry about earning a living." I left the shack remembering her words. I was embarrassed.

It is evening. We can see, through the frosted windows of our saloon, the drunks on the street with smoke surrounding them. You can also smell sweat, vomit and spirits. Someone is playing a harmonica and singing in a drunken voice. Yehiel is sitting in a corner and continues to build his dreams about Basel where the World Zionist Congress was held, about halls decorated with crystal chandeliers, Herzl speaking, his face shining. The Messiah! King of Israel!

[Page 140]

Maybe we are already in our promised land, far from the Diaspora, far from this low life, far from the bitter Feiga–Etel, far from this cursed saloon. He then sings:"we will return to our homeland…"

Unfortunately, Yehiel, as others of our residents, did not reach the Promised Land. They all believed in redemption and loved Israel with all their hearts. They were all massacred or lost on route. Yehiel died as he was fleeing.

May their memory be among all the sainted members of our town.

In the Bendery Train Station– saying goodbye to those making Aliyah
(Lieder family)

[Page 141]

The Intellectual Gentleman
(On D.A. Natanzon)
By Leah Bat Haya
Translated by Ala Gamulka

My late father was a pious man. He seriously followed the saying: "Anyone who teaches his daughter Torah it is as if he taught her prayers" (Sota, c, d). A tutor taught me to read Hebrew and how to pray. I learned to read Russian later, in secret. I used to borrow books from my friends who attended school and could get library books in the Pushkinskaya.

I loved reading and I longed to go to the library by myself. However, one had to give a deposit of two rubles and I did not have them. I found a solution. Our neighbor, a simple and poor tailor had a son who attended public high school. He was very proud of his son. I also saw him as an intellectual. I sought his advice. He told me about David Abramovich Natanzon, the editor of the newspaper "Southern Corner" published in Russian in our town. He was also a member of the board of the Pushkinskaya library. It was possible to obtain books from the library with his signature, without a deposit. The boys also told me that he and others had used this signature and he said he would recommend me to Natanzon.

The next day I put on my Shabbat clothes and I went out. I was quite shy and it was not easy to go on streets I had never been on before and to present myself to a stranger. I was petrified, but when I got there I was enthralled by the beautiful houses which seemed to me like palaces. At first I saw tiled stairs and a lot of greenery. It was a beautiful spring day. The acacia trees were flowering and their scent almost drugged me. It was so quiet there. I compared it to our area, the Jewish streets where there were only miserable houses. I stood in front of a two-story house and I counted the stairs, but I did not dare go up. My courage deserted me and I was ready to run back home. At that moment I saw the library. There was a large sign with gold letters. It said: PUSHKINSKAYA. I forced myself to go up the stairs and to enter the building.

A street in Bendery in the shade of the Acacia trees

[Page 142]

Natanzon was sitting at a large desk and reading some papers. He did not seem to feel my entrance. I waited for some time and then he turned to me and gave me a warm smile through his gold-rimmed glasses. It was as if he had been waiting for me. His smile encouraged and embarrassed me at the same time. I could only greet him in Russian. All the words I had rehearsed on the way deserted me. He understood why I was there. He invited me to sit down, asked my name, signed the request and wished me good luck.

Since that day the rich library became my source of treasures of the greatest Russian writers: Pushkin, Lermontov, Tolstoy, Dostoyevsky, etc. I was thus propelled to continue my studies in order to progress.

This is what I know about my benefactor: he was one of the most beautiful personalities in our town. In addition to editing the newspaper, he was also a leading member of the Jewish community. Sadly, he was young when he died – only thirty-nine years old.

This article is a memorial to our intellectual town resident, a special person who wished to light the way for others, especially for us, the needy children. He did a lot for us.

May his memory be blessed!

[Page 145]

In The Furor of The Shoah

From The Diary of a Wanderer
by Rabbi Shimon Efrati (Jerusalem)

Translated by Ala Gamulka

I found this diary in the belongings of a rabbi from Bessarabia who died in eastern Asia. He bequeathed the diary to us and I am publishing it without any changes.

(As requested by Rabbi Efrati, the article is published as it was written, especially words that would end with the letters that also signify the name of G–d)

It was Thursday evening and I was praying the evening prayers when Motti Finkelshtein came to the synagogue and announced: I just heard on the radio that the Soviet Union gave an ultimatum to the Romanian minister Gafenka that Romania must vacate Bessarabia within 24 hours. This is to be done without harming any government property in Bessarabia. I finished my praying and I went home. There, my friend, Berel Abelman, son of Rabbi Yonatan Abelman of Bialystok, was waiting for me. He was a clever and energetic Torah scholar and we began to consult about our next step. I said that he should go, on the following day, to Iasi. He had deposited all his money in the bank there. However, he refused to do so saying that he could not abandon me, the rabbi. He would remain with me no matter where I went. At midnight we heard the first shots on the Dniester– the border between Russia and Romania to this day.

On Friday, the eve of the holy Sabbath, there was much activity in town. Men and women ran from store to store carrying their purchases. Some had shoes and others clothes; some had sugar and others – flour. There was great preparation for the arrival of the Red Messiah in our town. The people did not forget their rabbi. Some brought wine and others came with different products. No one wanted the rabbi to suffer during the first days.

At noon we heard the sound of trumpets – the Red Army crossed the Dniester and was approaching our town. Many people, even those on the right, wore red ties and went to greet the Red Army. I stood at the window with old Arky – the Chazzan in grandfather's synagogue and we looked at the army troops marching erect on the street and singing victory songs. They enchanted everyone with their victorious singing. In my heart I felt that it was an end of an era and the beginning of a new one. I was saddened to hear the song My Moscow. Moscow was happy and taking giant steps on the Don River, the central waterway of Europe. I was deep in thought when I suddenly heard the elderly voice of Arky saying: "Rabbi, let us go to the mikve in honor of the special guest that is coming– the Sabbath". I agree and I go down the steps in front of the Holy Ark on which I was standing. We go outside in the direction of the mikve. The streets are full with men, women and children all dressed in holiday clothes. Isaac Finkelshtein comes towards me and says: " Rabbi, this is the day we were waiting for. We will no longer see the black ones who were the followers of Koza and Goga and who made our lives miserable". I nod as if saying let us hope you are not disappointed, you and all those who believe in the coming of their Messiah.

I returned from the mikve and I put on Sabbath clothes. I even wore my shtreiml in spite of the fact that Abelman was against it. I told him that I did not wish to show anyone that the rabbi was defeated. I went to the synagogue and I prayed.

[Page 146]

Week One

Saturday evening

Shabbat was a strange day. Many of the regulars did not come fearing that they will be accused of being obsolete. At the same time there were many newcomers from the Shaarey Zion synagogue. Their synagogue was one of the first to be closed because they did not want to be shown to be Zionists and haters of the people. I must also mention another event that happened. In the morning, when I arose early, I went to the gate to see if anyone was coming to recite Psalms, as was done every Shabbat. As I stood there a car passed full of Jewish youth. One of them, I believe the smallest one, when he saw me, yelled for the driver to go on. We then noticed a young woman who had worked as a clerk in a store. She was with her mother, dressed in Shabbat clothes. She told her mother in a loud voice – look how they envy us. Later, during the war, I saw this young woman in eastern Asia. When I reminded her of that Shabbat she agreed that she believed then that justice and honor were coming to us, but she was disappointed.

On Shabbat members of Shaarey Zion approached me and asked me to look after the Torah scrolls and the Holy Ark from their synagogue. If the authorities saw that no one was taking care of these items they would confiscate everything. I agreed to their request and I promised to transfer everything from their synagogue to ours. In spite of it being Shabbat, stores were open and the residents brought them food and clothing.

Day One

The stores were open again. The authorities decreed that anyone who had Romanian money had to exchange it in the federal bank. The rate was forty Lei for one ruble. People hurried to the bank and stood in line to exchange their savings. It was rumored that the previous night there was a search made at the residence of Attorney R., former leader of the Revisionists. The search produced diamonds and other precious stones hidden in the cellar. He was arrested. Today, many of the wealthy residents came by themselves to the bank with money to be exchanged. They were prepared to donate their property to the state treasury. The offer was accepted. Today I had a visit from the former community leader, Mr. B., who told me he wished to cancel the communal property. This was the building of the Hebrew high school– one of the most beautiful edifices in town and the Talmud Torah as well. There was also a rehabilitation center in one of the suburbs. He wanted to deed these buildings to the temporary municipal committee. This committee supervises all properties in town and expects our properties to be given over. He was disbanding the community and had already let go all office workers. The ritual slaughterers would continue their work as feather collectors in the cooperative of those who collect rags and other old items. The authorities are interested in the collection of feathers and allow slaughtering in the abattoir under the supervision of the cooperative. Anyone who comes to slaughter pays not for that task, but for the feather plucking that the ritual slaughterer usually does. The ritual slaughterer receives a membership card as a laborer and his salary is commensurate with this position. He is allowed to take Shabbat off as a day of rest. All the ritual slaughterers belonged to this cooperative since they could not enter the abattoir. There would be no more ritual slaughtering and no kosher meat. The schools were closed and only the cemetery remained in the hands of the community. He asked me if I wanted to take the responsibility for the running of the Hevra Kaddisha since there was no other member of the community who would do it. I have no other way of earning a living right now. I agreed to present myself on the following day in the community office when it would be disbanded and the Hevra Kaddisha would come under my jurisdiction.

He still did not know what would become of the building where the community office and the certified matzos bakery were situated. It could be that the building, too, would be confiscated or I would be given a job there. The cooperative of the disabled was interested in taking over the bakery, but that it was possible I would be allowed to use the office.

We will see tomorrow what will happen.

[Page 147]

Day Two

Today I transferred all belongings of Shaarey Zion and its Torah scrolls to our synagogue. I gave the keys to Tshizikov, the supervisor of all municipal property. From there I went to the community building where Mr. B., the former president, and Mr. M. were waiting for me. Soon, Mr. Krishtzenka, head of the disabled cooperative, arrived and informed us that he was taking over the machinery in the bakery as well as part of the office. He left me a small room for the running of the Hevra Kaddisha. The community books were housed there. I had to agree to these arrangements and so I became the director of the Hevra Kaddisha as well as its registrar. I had two workers who cleansed the bodies as well as a guard for the cemetery. In the middle of the discussion, Mr. Tshizikov came and informed us that according to the law the cemetery belonged to the town, but we were permitted to look after it –this was my responsibility. I agreed to these conditions. Mr. Schmaltz, the former chairman of the cemetery, agreed to work with me as a member of the committee. I am satisfied with this result.

I went home. On the way I saw the soldiers of the Red Army going from store to store and buying everything. The shop owners had been ordered to sell all their merchandise and to put the money in the federal bank. Many shop owners brought keys from their stores and warehouses to the municipality saying they did not want to deal in foreign goods. The merchants walked with their heads down– very unhappy with the big trade. They knew they would have to pay twice as much as they would take in.

Day Three

Today I had a visit from the head of the N.K.V.D, i.e., the secret service. I was sitting in a room in my synagogue and he entered. He introduced himself and wanted to know who I was and what my position was. I replied that I was a Rabbi. When he asked me if I was a believer I said that I believed completely that there was a leader in the world and that it would not function without one. A ship needs a captain. He then asked me about dialectic materialism and I replied positively. He further asked why I did not follow their beliefs and after I explained he left angry and disappointed.

Today I began my new position as director of the Hevra Kaddisha. I prepared a budget with Mr. Schmaltz and I will be receiving 200 rubles per month. Still, I sold my watch today. The soldiers grab any watch as a real bargain. Nothing is as important in town as a watch and Jews are selling theirs. They get the equivalent in rubles (a rate of 40 Romanian Lei to one ruble). Everyone thinks they made 200 percent on the sale since they had bought the watch in lei. This may change soon, but in the meantime the Jews are selling and the soldiers are buying.

The cemetery guard came next. He is a simple Russian who has been in this position for 13 years. When I asked him "How are you, Comrade Marco?" He innocently replied: "I don't know what the term Comrade means. You are the Rabbi and I am Marco". His sons already addressed me as Comrade Rabbi and I replied accordingly.

Day Four

Today the shops were eliminated. The owners had to transfer to the municipal committee all goods still in their possession as well as the money collected in the sales since the Red Army entered town. They thus began to "use" the wealthy. The few factories in town were taken over by the workers. Committees were formed and each committee had to get approval from the secretariat of the party. The secretariat was located in the fancy building of the former governor. There is talk of nationalizing large private homes, i.e., those with more than 700 sq.m in area. Many owners of large homes are searching for smaller ones in the suburbs and there is much bargaining over any house with two rooms.

There are three-person committees going around town and listing all tenants. The main questions on these printed forms are: What is your occupation? How large is your apartment (how many rooms)? Where are you from (What did your father do)? Do you belong to the Party (an active member)? They also announced today that as of next Sunday every citizen will be given an Identity Card. Every citizen must bring any documents he has and they will be exchanged for Soviet citizenship.

[Page 148]

Everyone wants to receive the new documents and to be inscribed in group 1– as a worker. It was explained to me by a Jew from the other side of the Dniester that there were three groups: the first group were workers – the ideal; the second group were clerks who were considered loyal to the regime; the third group was the lowest – merchants, factory owners and estate owners. In their document the description was "kulak" which means "a user". These people were to be exiled to a different country. I trusted in G-d and knew my fate was determined by him. I cannot say that I was maltreated, but I was still not treated well. I was dressed in rabbinic garb using a cane and people looked at me as if I was a deformed creature that had to be allowed to live and earn my living. They were certain they would defeat me. In city hall, where I have to go often to deal with the chairman of municipal property, I am not viewed as an "enemy of the people". It is because there are many young Jews working as clerks there who have not been turned against me yet. Some are afraid to ask how I am and to speak with me in public. For example, attorney B, a friend, now crosses the street when he sees me. I am not angry with him. There is a saying that explains this gesture – "he, too, is in dire straits". Soon, lawyers will also be purged and he is afraid for his life.

Day Five

Today, the department of lodging began its work. It was headed by the crude Jew named Shpigel. The first victim was Z.K., a gentle Jew. He was a cattle merchant with an aristocratic appearance and a generous soul. He was so distraught when he was evicted from his home that he suffered a heart attack and died. I had to arrange the funeral. All participants, laborers among them, walked with their heads down, bent with sorrow; even the Chassidim mourned his death. They said that man must control his soul in order to reach redemption. If there are victims, we must accept the fact. After the funeral I was approached by K.I. who had worked for him as a clerk. He cried bitter tears and said: "They came to free me from Z.K. Who asked them to do it?" I continued my work in the name of G–d.

I was so happy when Shabbat came! I arrived in the synagogue, rested, in the morning before prayers began. My friends were waiting, ready to chit–chat. There was much comfort in this prayer service. After services I went for Kiddush to my mother's house and then to visit my brothers and sisters. Shabbat was ours to enjoy. I am still afraid that things will change.

M.L. came during my sermon and announced that A., owner of the soap factory, committed suicide. He was an honorable man and a generous one. He was one of the first to give money to anyone who came to ask. He never refused a request on behalf of public institutions or funds. Although he was not among the richest, he was still important. He, himself, worked in the factory and had five laborers who adored him. He left a letter for his wife asking forgiveness for his act. He said he had no other choice since he could not continue to live in this hateful atmosphere.

I was the director of the Hevra Kaddisha and it was my duty to go to the cemetery to prepare a new row for those who commit suicide. I did it, but I was fearful. Jacob was afraid of two things: the first was when he was almost killed during his circumcision and the second when Esau brought him food. He did not know which was worse. For me it was life under Bratianu, the Romanian Prime Minster and fear of Koza Goga or the present situation. Only G–d knew the answer to the question.

[Page 149]

Day Six

Today the purge of the lawyers began. The biggest and most important were eliminated. Every candidate was investigated and if anything objectionable was discovered, he was disbarred. Lawyers were not allowed to have private offices where they would receive their clients. There was only to be a general office. Every lawyer who was approved had to serve in this group. The group was headed by A. and he was trusted. The only cases accepted were those that dealt with crimes against government regulations. There were no commercial cases since there was no private business. For instance, on the first day in court a man was accused of selling eggs to a bakery. He had bought these eggs from farmers and resold them at a small profit. This was a crime called "speculation". The man was not earning a living through his own labor. The fact that the man was feeble and could not do labor and was poor did not interest anyone. He was arrested. His wife came to the general lawyers' office and paid a sum of money to the chairman so that a lawyer would be sent to court. The lawyer could not do much since he was a government employee. He could only ask the judges for forgiveness. These judges were called "Peoples' judges". There were three of them: the chairman was a qualified judge and the other two were chosen by the municipal committee from among its laborers. They all wanted to show their loyalty to the regime and judged accordingly. They did not consider the truth. This poor man who realised a small profit by reselling eggs was sentenced to 8 years. There was a popular saying that when a man went to work his wife would say to him: "my Husband: go in peace and come back in peace, but don't get any 'years'".

Thus it was not important that the lawyer be someone well-versed in the law. It was only necessary for him to be acceptable. An old deaf man was accepted. He had no longer practiced as an attorney during the Romanian period. He only wrote appeals. His sons were members of the Party and he was allowed to continue as a lawyer. His brother who was a brilliant and experienced lawyer was not accepted because he had been president of the Jewish community. The lawyers group was headed by a loyal Party member. I once had to go in front of the committee and the deaf lawyer stood up and gave me his seat. I still received a negative answer. The deaf lawyer subsequently spoke to me and told me he had been told off by the chairman for giving a seat to the rabbi since he was an "enemy of the people". They hated religion. However, the week passed and another Shabbat was coming. The Mikve was shut down and there was a rumor that they wanted to destroy it and to build a new bathhouse. It was no longer acceptable for our use.

Week Two

Saturday evening

The second Shabbat under the Russians passed. The synagogue was half full, but there are now two Holy Arks containing Torah scrolls: one on the east wall and the other brought from the Shaarey Zion synagogue and placed on the west wall. We put there all the spoiled scrolls. We had more benches, but fewer worshippers. Our hearts were full of sadness. What will happen if the remaining synagogues are also eliminated? Where would we put our Torah scrolls and other religious items? There were already four synagogues that were shuttered and I had to move the Torah scrolls to us.

The butchers' synagogue, a magnificent building, is to be given over to the municipality. The town secretary requested a letter signed by all worshippers attesting that they are ceding the building. The municipality is planning to establish a community centre there. Everyone will sign because they are afraid not to do so. There is a magnificent holy ark there and we need to arrange to obtain it with all the books.

Last night, during the Shabbat meal, a representative of the municipality came with an invitation to visit the town treasurer. I visualize the large building that was founded by my sainted ancestors being destroyed. I know there is a plan to eliminate all synagogues in town, but G–d is my witness that I will not hand over our synagogue. It was built and founded by my late grandfather. I will refuse to do so as long as there is a breath in my body.

[Page 150]

Day One

Today, after prayer services, I was obliged to go to the police to hand over my identity card. I had to request the protection of the Soviet government. I stood in line with my co–religionists even though some offered to give me their place. I refused since I did not wish for them to suffer because of me. They could have been denounced to the authorities as followers of the Rabbi. I waited for my turn and I entered the director's office. He saw that I had been a Polish citizen and informed me I would be awarded Soviet citizenship. He was certain I would be delighted. I was to return in a few days to receive the documents.

There was a group of Jews standing outside and arguing about who would be given a proper document and who would receive a blemished one. Among them stood Yankel the wagon driver. He was broad–shouldered and taller than the rest. When he saw me he said: "No! Our rabbi would not be given a blemished document. He is the rabbi of the poor. I went to see him when my horse died. The rabbi and Dov Abelman gave me their own money and I was able to buy a new horse. Not one of the wealthy members of the community would even give a penny." From the police I continued to city hall to see the secretary. He asked me to prepare a list of all synagogue treasurers. I did not agree and I told him that these names were available in the archives of the community and I would not know the answer. There obviously was an inquiry as to who was loyal to the regime. In the corridor I met a Pravoslavian priest. He, too, was probably summoned for the same purpose. The priests, too, walked with their heads down. Today was the first Sunday they were not allowed to ring their church bells.

Day Two

Today, the confiscation of houses began. Committees of three people, accompanied by the party secretary and holding nationalization documents came to confiscate houses. Already, 80% of the houses in town had been confiscated. This included every house that had more than 2 rooms and affected all craftsmen and businessmen. It was so dire that almost every house that had a store or if the owner even lived somewhere else, was confiscated. The margin was anything over 700 sq.m, but they did not pay attention to this rule. One clerk was in charge of several houses and was to supervise the homes and the tenants who were to pay the rent and look after any repairs. Sometimes the tenant was able to reach the department for approval for repairs. Our house, too, was confiscated in spite of the fact that there were many heirs involved. I tried to appeal to the department director, but it was of no use since it was the rabbi's house.

Today he invited me to his office to discuss other synagogues in town. I discovered that the house next to our synagogue was confiscated and would be used as a hospital for the sailors on the Dniester. They wanted to invest a great deal of money and would probably need our synagogue building in order to enlarge the hospital. I told the director to forget his idea. I would not give up our synagogue building and they had no hope of enlarging the hospital.

Day Three

Today I went to the small office in the old community building and I found many people waiting there wishing to erect stones on the gravestones of their ancestors. They knew that at this moment I still had the cement and stones needed. Most likely if I were to ask the authorities for this material later I would be refused. There was a great demand for gravestones and the bakery manager, in the same courtyard, was upset that there were so many people passing through there. I told him that he took the bakery by force. He threatened me saying he would push for my removal from there. I decided to transfer my office to a room in my synagogue, but I wanted first to receive permission from the director of municipal property. I went to him accompanied by Mr. Schmaltz. We were upset about what was happening to us.

[Page 151]

Was it not enough that property of the community, worth millions, was confiscated? The beautiful building of the Hebrew high school, the Talmud Torah facilities, recently refurbished, the sanatorium in the suburbs and our matzo bakery– a large building with machines, all were taken away. The offices of the Jewish community became an apartment for the bakery manager and we were given a small room for 5 people. Schmaltz and I waited for the arrival of the director, but suddenly, Schmaltz became ill and he died on the spot. Everyone congregated and the entire town heard about his death. We transferred the body to his apartment. This is how we lost a loyal and honest member of the community.

Day Four

The whole town was affected by the sudden passing of Schmaltz. He came from a poor home and always like to tell us that he learned to save from childhood. He put penny to penny and was finally able to save enough to go to Odessa. He worked there as a laborer in the port. At the same time he learned how to be a locksmith and he returned to Bendery as a master of his trade. He got married and opened a locksmith shop. He managed to save money and eventually erected the first factory in Bessarabia dedicated to woodwork. He treated his workers as if they were his children and they loved and respected him – Jews and non–Jews alike. He taught them to follow his example and not to cheat on their wives or to get drunk. He became an important member of the community and always contributed to all institutions. He did not close the locksmith shop located in his home and he loved to putter about in it when he came home from work or from the community. He was a pioneer of industry in Bessarabia and aspired to make Aliyah. When the Soviets entered Bendery his factory and homes were confiscated. He expected to be evicted from his apartment and just could not handle the situation. His funeral was well attended. He was also eulogized by one of his workers, a Russian non–Jew who loved him. I, too, added my comments. May he rest in Peace! The Hevra Kaddisha absorbed the cost of the funeral since he was a dedicated worker in it.

Day Five

Our lives followed a new path and many people were able to adapt. Many people became night watchmen and they received the salary of a laborer since every institution needed them. During the Romanian period there were two watchmen on the main streets with all the large stores, but now every store and institute needed a watchman. This was a result of the revolution when "counter–revolutionaries" tried to harm government property and thus watchmen were required. This profession was good for Jews who kept Shabbat since they did not have to work on that day. Even our R. Berel Abelman became a watchman for the office in his house. Every night he entered the office, turned on the electricity in his former dining room and studied his books. In this way he "watched" government property. Even those who had money saved from before or had something to sell looked for some work. They looked at the unemployed as "parasites". One of Stalin's tenets was "The one who does not work, does not eat". Even B. Abelman who sold his belongings on a daily basis tried to find a decent job. He was not young and not strong and so a "watchman" position was appropriate. He really could not live on his meagre earnings. When asked what he lived on he replied that he ate benches, watches, tables and household goods. This is how one became accustomed to a new life, a life without money or respect.

R. Dov (Berl) Abelman

[Page 152]

Day Six

We saw new faces today. In Kishinev, the capital city of the Republic, there were many people who were not trusted to be loyal to the new regime. These were previously wealthy and leaders of various political parties. Among them, of course, were the Zionists. Young or old, healthy or sick, they were taken out of their homes and sent to Bendery. Some were mentally ill, such as the industrialist B. How could he be an enemy of the Soviet regime? We did our best to find lodging for them. We knew it was only a beginning and that more were to come. After inquests, some– over a million people– would be sent to the interior of the country. In Kishinev, Zionist leaders were arrested. Among them was the leader of Mizrahi – Rabbi Levi Sternberg. He was accused of having contact with foreign governments. Editor Rozenhaft and D. Vinitsky were also arrested. In Bendery, the former mayor, a gentle person, was arrested. He had also been arrested during the Koza regime having been accused of being a Shabbat Goy. He was good to our community and helped to refurbish the Talmud Torah building. As I write these words I found out that he committed suicide. Thus, one of the righteous among the nations has died.

Today, I. Blank, a Zionist leader in town, came to see me. A wonderful man, he opened his heart and told me he felt our destiny will be the same as that of the Jews of Kishinev. The persecution was being done slowly. G–d will have to protect us.

Week Three

Saturday Night

New worshippers came to our synagogue from other places that had been closed. They came from the Butchers' synagogue and other houses of worship. There is great pressure to stop worshipping, but sometimes we have among us Red Army officers who outwardly seemed to be only observing the prayer services. However, if one looked into their eyes, one would see them awed by being in a house of worship. It was evident that their souls were craving prayer just as did the secret Jews under the Spanish Inquisition.

Today, during services there was discussion of the rumor that the municipality is planning to levy heavy taxes on synagogues thus forcing the treasurers to shut down. Almost all synagogue treasurers have resigned by now and only the very elderly are willing to undertake the position. However, if it turns out that the treasurers are responsible for the high sums being levied, even they will resign because they would become personally liable. I would then be obliged to call a meeting of all treasurers. It is still too early to go to the tax office to find out the actual sum and who is responsible. Today, new refugees arrived from Romania who came to live under Soviet jurisdiction. They were born in Bessarabia, but had lived in other parts of Romania. They now had the opportunity to return. They had left properties in Romania when they escaped.

[Page 153]

First Day

Today a new rumor was circulated and it frightened us. That which we fought against whole–heartedly has come. Mixed marriages have occurred in our community. Old Sh.'s granddaughter married a mean, dark–haired non–Jew. There is also talk of another Jewish girl who is to wed an army officer. We had kept the barrier, but now there is a break in it. There are no more Jewish schools for our children. There is no mikve and no keeping of Shabbat. Now mixed marriages – where are we now?

Today I transferred my office from the former community building to my room in the synagogue. I will stay here and not venture out. I know people who pretend they do not know me – "the enemy". There are others who are still connected to me, but when I walk outside I do not recognize them and I avoid them as they avoid me.

On the corner of the main street there is a cellar of the coal maker. He is an observant Jew who keeps Shabbat. Every time I passed his cellar he would greet me with: "Good morning, Rabbi!" However, today, in order to avoid his greeting, I crossed the street so he would not see me. Officers who passed by looked at me to see if I am the one called "Rabbi". This is why I moved my office and I stayed there. Today the Old People's Home was closed. It had been a good place for the elderly who had no family. The atmosphere was caring and Jewish. Those who had relatives were ordered to go to them and the others were sent to another Home where there were non–Jews. No one wanted to agree to this, but these elderly people are either in relatives' houses or in non–Jewish Homes.

Day Two

Today I went to Kishinev to visit Rabbi Tsirelson– the chief Rabbi of Bessarabia who was eventually killed. I was confronted by a horrible scene. Even this elderly man was not spared and he was moved from his large apartment. The Beit Din building was confiscated. Rabbi Tsirelson was left with one room where he placed his large library. He was all alone. His wife had died two weeks earlier and he had no children. There is no one who could take care of him. A few congregants managed to find an old woman who came to cook his meals. The Rabbi did not complain about all this. He was only worried that he had written a book which had not been published yet. He asked me, if I were to be freed, to publish it. It is his last book and he put much of himself into it. Of course, I promised I would and even asked him to come to me in Bendery where I could look after him. He replied that he was already old and ready to die and wanted to be buried next to his wife. She had always made sure he could do his work in peace and to study Torah. His tears were flowing as he spoke. I, too, cried when I remembered his reputation as a great Jewish leader.

I spoke to the remnants of the Jewish community in Kishinev and asked them why they did not visit the old Rabbi. They replied that they were afraid of the authorities since "Rabbi Tsirelson was considered to be Enemy #1". I noted that their conditions were even worse than were ours in Bendery. Kishinev is the capital and everyone is being watched. I returned home depressed and angry.

Day Three

Today I received, in the mail, the newspaper "Red Star" written in Yiddish. The content was all proletarian and only the language was Jewish. Every article came from Russian newspapers. Topics were discussion about the Kolkhoz and how those working there can take care of their families. All the news items were about events in the Soviet world and compliments to Papa Joseph (Stalin).

[Page 154]

What concerned me most was the rave review of the film "Khmelnitsky". Bogdan Khmelnitsky had killed many Jews in 1648–1649, but now he was described as a hero who fought for his people. I asked myself: how low have conditions reached that this evil man who murdered so many Jews is now a hero. There was no mention of his deeds against our people. His cruelty was legendary. He would cut open bellies of Jews and place cats in them. He then sewed the cut so they could not even die in peace. Where was this newspaper printed? Not in Honolulu, but in Kiev, the capital of Ukraine. This is the Ukraine where every village has a cemetery dedicated to those who were murdered at that time. There were many brides and grooms who were murdered by Khmelnitsky's soldiers. Now the government was interested in this propaganda to show a close relationship between Russia and Ukraine. Supposedly, Khmelnitsky wanted these close relations between the two states. We have reached a terrible stage in our lives if Khmelnitsky is being lauded for his horrible deeds. [The writers of these articles were Jews who, no doubt, had heard about these atrocities in their childhood.]

Day Four

Today I went to the police to obtain my identity card. I managed to get it based on section 38 of the citizenship law. Others were judged on section 39 which was far worse. These people could only reside in small towns and not in capital cities. They also could not get employment in government offices and could be exiled to Siberia. I felt for them since among them were many fine people, observant and kind. Their only crime was to have owned stores. The new authorities did not wish to hear that these shop owners had been under the Romanian regime. They could not work in government offices and had no choice but to open a business. Communists always said: "Moscow does not believe these tears and these words". Moscow was suspicious of them that they would be against their regime.

I went to the tax department to be informed about taxes levied against synagogues. I saw there the son of our formerly wealthy townsman who had all his property confiscated. He was now obliged to pay 100,000 rubles to the treasury. This son stood with tears running down his face and begged saying that their entire wealth consisted of real estate and it was no longer theirs. Where could he find the money requested? Besides, if the property now belongs to you then you are now liable for the taxes. The clerk, unmoved, replied: "You have to pay and if you don't the court will send you to prison". The son was sobbing, but it was no use. "They do not believe me in Moscow..." My turn came and I gave the clerk my name. He said, with a sneer: "I can see that you do not want to leave your position as a rabbi. You know that you will have to pay 40% of your salary while other clerks and workers only need to contribute 2%". I told him I no longer was employed as a rabbi, but worked for the Hevra Kaddisha as a clerk. He then said: "The Hevra Kaddisha is not a government institute and you must pay 40%". He added that he wanted to assess the synagogue with an insurance fee since the edifices belonged to the government and they need to be insured. It is up to us to pay the fee. I did not reply. When I left he said: One way that can help you is if we obtain more synagogues in town, your fee would be smaller." I told him that I could never arrange for them to get the synagogues in which our ancestors prayed. I walked out deep in thought. Was it possible that after the destruction of the Jews of Poland the Bessarabian community would also disappear? I then met the elderly R. Zvi Goldis who understood my mood. He told me: "Rabbi, don't give up hope. It is written that you will be not destroyed for bad deeds– this is G–d's promise".

Front cover of the Hevra Kaddisha of Bendery ledger
(National Library, Hebrew University, Jerusalem)

[Page 155]

Day Five

A typhus epidemic broke out in town and there were many victims. Among them was my Beit Din colleague, the late Rabbi Avraham Haim Ashkenazy. He was a descendant of a famous rabbinic family. I had to take care of the burials. There were occasions when the hospital refused to send us the bodies for a Jewish burial. I did not rest until I was able to succeed by pleading with the municipal director of the department. There was even a case of the suicide of H. K., one of the most important merchants in our town. He was traveling by train to a nearby village and fell out. They did not want to give us his body, but I forced the issue and managed to bury him in a special row for suicides. I had prepared this row when the Red Army came to town. Our custodian, Marco, told me that the day before workers from the municipality came and took the wooden boards I had piled up. I planned to use them to build coffins for the dead.

I had also prepared stones obtained from private people to be used for the graves. I complained to the director about the removal of the boards. He replied that they were needed for building roads for the army. I warned my custodian not to allow anything to be removed without my presence. I would make them sign for anything they take. This was in case they asked for a report on items bought with funds from the institute. I felt my life was now in danger.

Overturned stones in the cemetery of Bendery
(collection of Rabbi Efrati)

[Page 156]

Testament
by Zvi (Gersh) Sobol (Hadera)
Translated by Ala Gamulka

In 1936, the Romanian Foreign Minister, Titulescu, had close ties with the Soviet Union and as a result, the bridge across the Dniester was rebuilt. It had been destroyed when Bendery was conquered by the Romanians. A train without passengers travelled back and forth in the direction of Bendery–Tiraspol.

Four years later, on June 28, 1940, the Russians conquered Bendery as they took Bessarabia and Bukovina. Six months later members of the NKVD arrived in Bendery, accompanied by soldiers. They arrested the citizens they considered "disloyal elements" and "kulaks" (Jews and Christians). They ordered them to prepare food for two days, pack their belongings and they then sent them, with their families, in convoys to exile in Siberia. Among the exiles were Israel Blank, the important Zionist leader and his wife Sonia, Moshe Prokopetz, Tuvia Avergun, Yaakov Otoshansky All Zionist organizations were eliminated – Maccabi, Hashomer Hatzair, Gordonya, etc. Those Jews who were not yet touched managed to find jobs in public institutions and in government owned shops.

On June 22, 1941, when the Germans attacked Russia, more Jews from Bendery were exiled as "disloyal elements".

On July 4, 1941 the Germans entered Bendery and conscripted the youth for military tasks. The recruitment office was located in the former Schwartzman High School building. During the battles the fortress (Karpost) was destroyed and the town was burning. Flames could be seen in Tiraspol across the Dniester.

Before the German conquest the Soviets announced on the radio: "Anyone wishing to leave Bendery could join the convoy set for this purpose". Most Jewish residents were spared from the Germans by escaping on these Soviet trains. Sick people were transferred on gurneys and wagons to the train. Among the escapees was R. Eliezer Sobol who was ill with cancer. He died on the road near Dnieperpetrovsk and was buried there by his sons.

The pier on the Dniester

(In the background is the bridge on which an empty train passed daily from Bendery to Tiraspol)

In July 1945 I was discharged from the army and I returned to Bendery. I found it in ruins since the Russians had been shooting at the Germans and Romanians. I found about 100 Jews and a few more who came from Abkhazia.

[Page 157]

In 1958 many Jews were forced to leave Bendery because food did not reach them. It was directed to Moscow. Whatever food did come their way was extremely expensive. Others returned to their hometowns.

Bendery became a rehabilitation resort again.

Today there are a few miserable Jews left in Bendery.

The Valley of The Slaughter Near The Fortress
by Mira Geva (Mira Geva is the granddaughter of Haike Kogan (nee Immes))
Translated by Ala Gamulka

The Romanians entered Bendery on June 22, 1941.

Grandmother Haike Kogan (nee Immes), the wife of Hersh Kogan, together with her grandson Liova and his wife were preparing themselves–as were most of the residents of the town– to board a train taking all those who wanted to do so to Abkhazia, in central Russia. When they arrived at the convoy, to join the large group waiting for the train, Liova's wife remembered that she had forgotten some item at home. She estimated that there was enough time for her to go back home, take the said item and return to the train. Grandmother said that she would not go alone and would wait for Liova and his wife. Unfortunately, the train left before they returned and they remained under the Romanians. The Nazis were then entering Bendery.

The German Fascists at first gathered all the elderly Jews in town and took them to the fortress. Grandmother was among them. She walked shoeless for a distance of six kilometers. When they reached the fortress the elderly, among them Shmuel Immes, were shot and buried in a mass grave. Then the remainder of the Jews were gathered and killed. They were buried nearby.

This valley of slaughter near the fortress was the Babi Yar of Bendery.

The ruins of the old cemetery of Bendery

[Page 158]

The Tighina Agreement and the Expulsion to Transnistria
by Dr. T. Lavi–Levinstein
Translated by Ala Gamulka

"The Romanian army crossed the Prut River on July 2, 1941 and the whole of Bessarabia was conquered only on July 26. On July 5 there was a slaughter in Yeditz – 500 Jews; July 6 – 60 dead in Novoselitsa; July 7– 10 in Parlitza, Balti region; July 6 – Bricheni and Lipkany. The list is endless… In Balti the first massacre took place on July 11", so continue the chronicles of the events.

The expulsion of the Jews of Bessarabia happened in one action in September 1941. During the first months of the war over half the Jewish population was eliminated or were expelled from Transnistria. This was a new title for the areas between The Dniester and the Bug.

On August 30 an agreement was signed in Tighina (Bendery) between the Germans and the Romanians on the subject of Transnistria. The Romanian representative was Brigadier–General Tatrianu and the German one was Major–General Haufi. The agreement was between two military commands and not between two states. This is emphasized by Brust.

The first section of the agreement established that Romania is responsible for security, administration and economics in Transnistria. Transportation, according to section 3, is under the German command. This is not all. According to section 4: "A Romanian will be the administrator of Transnistria. However, in the common interest of the warring parties, he will be dependent on decisions of the senior military command…An advisor from the German command will be attached to the top Romanian administrator."

As to the Jews: "It is not yet possible to transfer the Jews east across the Bug. Therefore, they should be kept in detention camps and they are to be used for labor until their transfer will be possible".

Max MIntz had written a doctoral thesis in law. He claims that the Tighina agreement forced the Romanians to transfer the Jews to detention camps. It is odd that there are still those who ask who invented the expulsion of the Jews to Transnistria. Brust is convinced that the plan to expel the Jews to

Transnistria under terrible conditions was hatched by the Romanians. In fact, the German influence could not be found there.

There is one fact that Brust admits: the Germans liked these plans. He had the chance to research a handwritten note by General Hansen, chief of the German military delegation in Romania. On August 17, 1942 Hansen reports on a meeting with Marshall Antonescu. The Romanian leader gave him news that will certainly please Hitler and will result in his goodwill towards Romania. In addition to the news of the constant efforts made by Romania in military and economic fields for the common goal, Bessarabia and Bukovina are now completely clean of Jews. He adds that he knew it was not exactly true.

As is well known, the "Final Solution" was decided upon at the famous Wansee conference on January 20, 1942.

Truthfully, the Romanian army and the civilians took part in all pogroms. These pogroms took place on the actual battle fields. It is easy to reach an additional conclusion: It was not only the low life of the civilian population and the peasants, but also the Romanian soldiers who decided that it would make sense to eliminate the Jews since they were doomed already. They thus fulfilled the intentions of their German masters, but they also enjoyed everything they stole from the Jews.

Still, the Romanians wished to shirk responsibility for the extermination of the Jews. In section 3 of the second part written in August 1941 it is said:

[Page 159]

"The Romanians expelled thousands of handicapped people, including children and those who were unable to do hard labor from Bessarabia to areas under German command. As a result, 27,500 Jews were sent back to Sventia, Mogilev–Podolsk and Yampol. Looking at a map tells us that Yampol and Mogilev are situated on the eastern side of the Dniester, across from the district of Soroki, at the entrance to Transnistria, north of Bessarabia.

In section 7 of the Tighina agreement it is said: "the transfer of the Jews eastward across the Bug is not possible at this time". This sentence indicates that there was readiness on the part of the Romanians to give over the Jews to the Germans. One of the reasons was that the Romanians wanted to have local residents on their side in Bessarabia and in Transnistria.

It is no wonder that in spite of the fact that there was a Romanian governor in Transnistria as of August 19, 1941 and the fact that there was an agreement signed on August 30 with Romania, the Einzatzgruppe continued to report about exterminations performed by the Germans.

(From "In the Land of Bessarabia". Tome 1, pages 151–157)

Auerel Marculescu

In the Detention Camp of Transnistria (1943)

"On 30.8.1941 the Tighina agreement was signed in which we were to be "ethnically cleansed". The Jews were to be expelled to the new territory under Romanian administration and German command – Transnistria."

(The Jews of Bessarabia, page 482)

...the Tighina agreement about Transnistria was only signed on August 30, 1941. The Romanian authorities demonstrated their plans clearly. On July 3, 1941 Mikhai Antonescu, Deputy Prime Minster, spoke to the Romanian delegation sent to Bessarabia and Bukovina, including the administrative managers. He said: "The ethnic cleansing will be done by expelling or isolating in labor camps. These will be places where it will not be possible to change the situation as far as Jews and other nationalities are concerned. These are people whose loyalty is in doubt. In order to complete the "cleansing" it may be necessary to do forced expulsion of Jewish elements in Bessarabia or Bukovina. They have no place there".

(M. Karp, "The Black Book", vol.3, page 91)

(Ion Antonescu also made a declaration about this topic on July 8, 1941)

"On 1.9.1941, the general commander of the police informed the gendarmerie in Tighina, by telegram, that as of September 6 expulsions of Jews will begin. This will be done in groups of 1000. He asked him to prepare units of gendarmes as escorts as well as wagons for luggage".

(M. Karp, "The Black Book", vol.3, page 85. Also document #73, pages 116–17)

In report #88 of 19.9.1941 there is a discussion about the condition of the Jews of Tighina. They were gathered in camps and were given work. Some were to be exterminated. In general, the Romanian population was quite anti-Jewish.

(The Jews of Bessarabia, Diaspora Encyclopedia. Page 474)

[Page 160]

Bendery after the Destruction
By Meir Grinberg z"l, Attorney (Tel Aviv)
Translated by Ala Gamulka

Two cycles denoted the annihilation of the Jewish Community of Bender. The first one was begun by the Fascist Rumanian regime which arose after Hitler came to power in Germany in 1933. It broadened its influence during five-six years until 1938. In general, the persecution of Jews grew during that regime and in particular, the Jews of Bender suffered even more. This was due to the fact that during their reign they considered the Jews as Bolsheviks as the city was close to the Dniester. The Soviet town of Tiraspol was situated on the other side of the river. Although the Jews of Bender were considered loyal citizens of Rumania, they were occasionally summoned to the office of the "Siguranza" to answer questions or to explain leftist actions of which they were totally innocent. This situation deteriorated so much that Jews were afraid to venture out in the evenings. They anticipated terrorist attacks of the "right" who acted in the name of the notorious "Iron Guard" under Romulus Bertianu(?). The Jewish youth organized itself for self-defence purposes.

These persecutions reached a peak when the Jewish lawyers were thrown out of the Law Society. Among them were the well-known Yefim Borisovich Rovshavsky(?), Ziska Zmora, Pincus Grinberg, Boris Titiner and others. After they lost their privileges they did not dare enter the court house.

This cycle of persecution had not yet closed when a second one began for the Jews of Bender. This happened when Bessarabia and Bucovina were conquered by the Soviet Union on June 28, 1940. The tragedy was that the Jews of Bender were considered Bolsheviks by the Fascists, but were seen by the Soviets as untrustworthy Trotskyites. This did not only happen to the "bourgeois" Jews- the businessmen. Even those Jews who identified themselves with the Communist faction within the Jewish Community were not received any better. These were people like Radiboim(?), Isaac Kofman, Yoske Galperin, Berel Spivak from Kaushan.

The Soviets did not only reject the Jews. They would not accept other local Communists like the brothers Bichkov and Ivan Kopofnanko. To everyone's surprise, many others found themselves in a very difficult situation. They were terribly disappointed by these "saviours" with whom they had always identified.

In one year- from June 28, 1940 to June 22, 1941—(when Germany suddenly attacked its ally, the Soviet Union) - the Jewish Community of Bender was destroyed. Friends and acquaintances of long standing became strangers to each other. One was suspicious of the other due to their insecurity in the work-place under Communist rule.

The NKVD did its work. Every so often one Jew or another would disappear. When the bad news came no one dared approach the authorities to question or to help those considered innocent until proven guilty. Any inquiry was interpreted as a political action. Those who were still free stayed away in order not to incriminate themselves. They were obliged to turn their backs on their friends in spite of their pain and sorrow. They had to pretend that everything was clear to them and that they should not question anything.

The first to disappear were Yosef Halperin, Attorney Yefim Rubashky, Moshe Zufshteyn, Misha Kishinovsky, Fishel Bendersky (from the iron goods store In Kripostnoy) and others.

The abuse of the Jewish Community reached its heights on the unforgettable terrible day – June 13, 1941. On that day, at dawn, the NKVD squad attacked like a pack of hungry wolves (as they did in all towns in Bessarabia and Bucovina). They arrested, brutally and without cause, many innocent people.

At the same time there was a conference of lawyers of the Republic of Moldavia in Kishinev. Those from Bender who participated were Grinberg, Kroscon and others. When they returned home at the end of the sessions they heard about many arrests among the Jews of Bender. Those arrested were exiled in cattle cars, separated from their families. The men were in one car while the rest were in another one. It was clear to everyone that this was sadistic cruelty planned by the twisted inhumane minds. Among those arrested were: Ilya Abramovich, Shebtel Merisis(?), Sara Sheinfeld, Gendelman, Pincus Grinberg and others.

I do not have the strength to describe the suffering of our members and their inconceivable conditions. We saw the inhumane separation of families and wondered how long man can suffer. We will bring out some details and we will leave the rest for the reader so he can reach his own conclusions.

Fathers heard the screams of their wives and children from the second car (attached to their car) and could not help them. They suffered horrible emotional and physical hardship for many days. Adults had to relieve themselves in front of children due to the crowding. The cattle cars were closed on all sides. The oppressive heat that June forced men, women and children to be semi-naked. As if all that was not enough, these people were forced to stay in the train station for three days so cargo from Bender Provaia could be loaded. Hundreds of Bender residents came to say good-bye to their relatives. They did not know where their families were being sent and whether they would ever see them again. They did not know if this was a one-time event or if it was part of a plan. There was no one to give them answers. The Jews of Bender did not yet know that this was only the beginning and that the next step would be the emptying of the city of its Jews and the annihilation of the community.

Mobilization of the Youth at the Beginning of the War

When the war broke out all the young people were mobilized immediately. The draft meeting place was the Boys Federal High School. We spent eight hours there. Through the windows we could see German aircraft bombing the railroad tracks between Bender and Tiraspol. At the same time, all the families were ordered to present themselves to the railway station in order to be sent out of town. This was the first train to leave Bender. There were others later. It is difficult to describe our situation as we thought all our dear ones were exterminated. Some people grabbed bicycles and rode to see what was happening. They returned to tell us all were still alive.

After about 250 people had gathered in the school we were transferred to the Schwartzman Gymnasia. More people joined us there. We reached a total of 500 and since there was not enough room we were taken back to the Boys Federal High School (Kazionaya Gymnasia). As we arrived, a bomb hit the Schwartzman Gymnasia and destroyed the building. We breathed a sigh of relief since had we stayed there no one would have remained alive. The total darkness did not stop the Germans from finding Jewish institutions and locations where there were mobilized men. It is important to note that few in the population were interested in designating specific locations to the Germans. As a result all the synagogues were bombed.

A month later, the Central Headquarters of the Soviet Army ordered the release of all soldiers from the conquered territories. They were transferred to work in military industry. This showed a lack of trust in the population of the territories annexed by the Soviet Union after the Ribbentrop-Molotov Pact. There were many deserters from the army.

My family had reached Odessa and I continued to search for them. I arrived at the train station and I found myself in a crowd of more than 50 000 people. Many refugees had come to Odessa before the Germans had bombed the railroad station.

Bender was emptied in one night.

It was impossible to cross the bridge to Tiraspol without permit (Komendirovka). Since I was the regional chairman of one of the Law Societies, I tried to give permits to everyone in spite of regulations. Many people were saved this way. Attorney Balatzianu- formerly Minister of Industry- helped me a great deal. He worked with us in a department located in Rudshavsky's store.

Many family tragedies occurred during these passages. For instance, Yosef-Haim Levitt left Bender and his family remained. Many families were separated and heard nothing of each other. Of those who escaped, some were saved, but others were killed by the Nazis. Among them were Abelman and his wife who were buried in the middle of the street (according to testimony of the locals).

The Jews of Bender had two options. They could go to Stalingrad or to Petrovskaya. However, the Germans advanced rapidly and by the end of October 1941 the Jews had to flee from these places.

In the port of Makhachkala on the Caspian Sea there were 300 000 Jewish refugees and there I found my mother and my sister. From there we went to Sami-Platinsk.

The tragedy was the length of the trip. After a month and a half, we reached the last stop with great difficulty. We had travelled continuously without washing or changing our clothes. We lived on bread and water we obtained in stations on the way. Lice pestered the people and practically ate their flesh. Due to the lack of minimal sanitary conditions Typhus spread and killed many people.

When we reached Sami-Platinsk people were being sent to kolhozes. I was appointed regional director of the Law Society and so we tried to survive. I stayed there with my family until September 1944 when I received a telegram from the Minister of Justice of the Soviet Union to return to Moldavia. I was to appear in front of the Minister of Justice of Moldavia. The road to Kishinev was difficult. Usually, one would move only a few kilometres per day. However, due to the telegram from the Minister of Justice we had no trouble and we reached Bender in good time. I disembarked and my family continued on to Kishinev.

It was difficult to recognize the city we had left behind. The central section (Horovinskaya) was destroyed except for the Weissman house. The first person I met was Manya Tomshpolsky who used to sell bread in the building. Next came Shtopelmn's brother-in-law who used to sell medications prepared with boiling red wine. Our house was gone except for a few steps.

Then I met Mrs. Gingis and I gave her regards from her son who was with me in Sami-Platinsk. She had believed that he was no longer alive.

I met little Imes, Zifshteyn's son and Levinson. They told me that I had relatives in Bender who were living in a railway car and were starving. I met with them and I decided to leave Bender. I went with them to Kishinev to join my family.

July 1941 was the month when the Jews of Bender were dispersed. September 1944 was their time of return from all parts of Russia. Unfortunately, only a few returned.

(Dictated by Attorney Meir Grinberg z"l to Y. Raviv, April 1970)

[Page 162]

After the Shoah
by Rabbi Shmuel Bronfman (Jerusalem)
Rabbi in Bendery 1945–60

Translated by Ala Gamulka

Prior to WWII there were about 5,000 Jewish families (18,000 souls) in Bendery, on the Dniester, near the ancient Turkish fortress. The town had 18 synagogues, a Jewish hospital, a seniors' residence, several schools, kindergartens, a Talmud Torah and a Hebrew high school. There were also many public institutions in the fields of culture, economics and social assistance.

As a rule, life in the Jewish community was similar to that of other such places in the rest of Czarist Russia. In 1918 the Romanians conquered Bessarabia and took over.

Jews dealt in commerce, small industry and crafts, free trades or they were synagogue employees, etc. Many worried about making a living and were quite poor. In addition, there was the constant fear of the authorities (during Czarist Russia) and the Romanian commissars). The authorities always watched the earning sources of the Jews and managed to take money from them.

I was born in 1915 and I can serve as an eye witness to the condition of the Jews of Bendery during the Czarist Russia times and the Romanian occupation. I studied in a Beit Midrash until the arrival of the Red Army. I heard from many residents that they "prayed" for the arrival of the Soviets. G-d listened to them and the Soviets conquered Bessarabia. For awhile, the Jews of Bendery could rest after the frightening pursuits by the Romanians.

In 1941, when the German–Russian war broke out, hordes of Jews began to escape the Nazis going towards Soviet Russia. The Soviet authorities enabled the "escape" and thousands of Jewish and non–Jewish residents used the opportunity to go into Russia. It was especially easy for the Jews of Bendery to go into Russia since they were on the banks of the Dniester. This was a natural border between Romania and Russia. Thanks to this advantage many Jews were able to escape the Nazis. In comparison to other Jewish settlements, the Jews of Bendery were more fortunate, but there were still several hundred victims of Nazi persecution.

[Page 163]

Among them were the elderly and the young. May G-d avenge their murders!

******

When the war was over the refugees and the remnants began to return to their former homes from exile.

In November 1945, I was liberated from the labor force and I returned to Kalarash, my home town. I found it in ruins. I had no opportunity to settle there and I agreed to the proposal of Rabbi Yosef Apelboim- from Kishinev- to move to Bendery. The community needed a spiritual leader.

What was the situation in the Bendery community at the time? When the survivors returned to Bendery they first went to the cemetery where they prostrated themselves on the graves of their dear ones and sobbed and screamed. As they recuperated somewhat the Hevra Kaddisha was reorganized and Shabbat services were put in place. There was only one synagogue building left intact- the Sadigura. The Nazis had used the building to house their horses.

The Jews immediately began to refurbish the synagogue building by cleaning it and preparing it for suitable use. There was a women's section as well. Mr. Shuster, a veteran of the war, was invited to be the cantor during the High Holidays. For the first time since WWII the Jews of Bendery were able to conduct services on Rosh Hashanah and Yom Kippur 1945 in the sole synagogue in town.

Soon the Jewish leadership was organized. Among the leaders were: Yaakov Kochuk, Haim-Moshe Fishov, Yosef-Moshe Goldmacher, Meir Hochman, Yehuda-Leib Alter, Alter Itzkovich, Efraim Sudit, Avraham Finkelshtein (Chirelis). In addition, several young handicapped people returned from the war and pitched in. The chairperson was Yaakov Kochuk who had been the bookkeeper in Zeidel Katzap's business. He was a fine person, generous and nationalistic. It is thanks to his devoted service and with help from others that the Jewish community was reorganized.

After Succot, Yaakov Kochuk was invited to the municipal committee where he was told to register the community in the Interior Ministry of the

Moldovan Republic in Kishinev. He was also ordered to appoint a spiritual leader according to Soviet law. I was officially installed as spiritual leader of the Bendery community on 15.11.45.

In those days the leaders of the community were: Yaakov Kochuk–chairman (he died in 1949); Yosef– Moshe Goldmacher– first treasurer (he made Aliyah in 1956 and died there in 1967); Shlomo Burstein, and Yehuda-Leib Alter (moved to Riga in 1958 and died there). The steering committee consisted of: Alter Itzkovich (left Bendery later); Avraham David Giterman – a good person (lived in Bendery for many years) and Noichovitz.

Yaakov Kochuk–chairman of the community executive committee of Bendery, who worked tirelessly and loyally to rehabilitate the Jewish community after the Shoah.

He died of a heart attack.

After the synagogue building was refurbished the community undertook the organization of the two cemeteries– the old one in the lower section of town, near the Dniester and the new one, in the upper section. The old cemetery had been ruined by the Nazis and the Romanians and the Russians completed the job. During my service as chairman of the community (1947–1957) the Soviet authorities came many times and demanded from me to willingly sign over the old cemetery to the authorities. They intended to annihilate it. I categorically refused . The authorities did not pay attention to my refusal and confiscated the cemetery. It became a location for pigs, without our knowledge or agreement.

[Page 164]

One day a disease struck the pigs. Hundreds of them perished and the remainder were evacuated from there. When we saw that the old cemetery was completely ruined we announced, in the synagogue that anyone who had relatives buried there would be able to transfer the bodies to the new cemetery. The community moved the graves of our sainted members of the Wertheim family to the new location and built a tent over the new graves. It still exists to this day. The Christian neighbors used the gravestones to build houses. The authorities erected a fence from some of these stones around the municipal sports field. They later apologized saying it was the Romanians who had done it in 1943.

Rabbi Israel Bronfman with his family (Rabbi, ritual slaughterer 1945–1960), in his backyard on Potshtovaya Street, corner Michaelovsky

During the Stalin regime the authorities were quite strict and mean to the Jewish community. Several times members of the community were called in and given new instructions about the administration of the synagogue, the cemetery, baking of Matzo and even inviting cantors to lead services.

In 1948, after the founding of the State of Israel, the authorities conducted a thorough search in the synagogue. They looked everywhere and at everything. I did not know the purpose of the search. However, the results were positive and nothing forbidden was found. Sometime later I discovered that there were such searches in many other Jewish communities on the same day. It seems that it was connected to the arrival of Golda Meir in Moscow. She was the first Ambassador from Israel to the Soviet Union. Many Jews then decided to apply for immigration visas to Israel and the NKVD was suspicious that the Jewish communities were behind these requests.

During Stalin's reign the NKVD did not interfere with the inner working of the communities and allowed them to elect their officials without any special permit. On the other hand, there were "characters" (special agents) that frequented the synagogues and reported on all happenings. On the High

Holidays it was possible to even find Christians among the worshippers– NKVD clerks dressed as civilians. There was no special pressure at the time and no interference in religious matters such as circumcision, Jewish wedding ceremony and kosher slaughtering. I, as a rabbi and ritual slaughterer, had to pay very steep taxes. The members of the congregation helped me and contributed funds for these taxes. In general, my congregants took care of me and I was careful there should not be any reason for the authorities to find fault with me. G–d really protected us.

The situation changed with the death of Stalin. During the reign of Khrushchev the NKVD became the KGB. We no longer had agents in the synagogue, but the candidates for leadership had to be approved by the Ministry for Religious Affairs. This fact interfered with the autonomy of the community. The subsequent leaders were affiliates of the KGB.

[Page 165]

Rabbi Bronfman (second from left), chairman of the community Monblit (second from right) Bendery 1957

In 1957, I was ordered by the Ministry for Religious Affairs to resign my position as chairman of the community. In 1960, I was forbidden from serving as rabbi of the community. I left Bendery and moved to Odessa.

A Conversation with Rabbi Israel Bronfman (30.4.72)

In spite of great interest, it was not possible to prepare a list of the victims in Bendery who were murdered by the Nazis and buried in a common grave on that terrible day. Many of their relatives did not return to town and although everyone knew whom they had lost, a list was not available.

After some Jews –about 300 families (800 people) – returned to Bendery, Rabbi Bronfman tried to get permission from the authorities to erect a memorial on the common burial place. The engineer–architect, H. Bronfman, even designed a plan for the gravestone – 18 meters in size. However, Mayor Isayev who actually went with the plan to Kishinev was unable to receive permission. When the Rabbi approached him he rudely replied: "Don't bother me!"

It seems that D.B. Abelman was one of the last to be murdered in the murder pit between the fortress and the Dniester because when the Soviet authorities returned to Bendery, his nephew, close to them, tried to find his body. He found it wrapped in his vest and his Talit Katan and even his identity card. It was then possible to transfer his body to the new cemetery and to bury him.

On Abelman's grave it was written:

"During the horrors of Hitler you, too, were murdered. Your friends will never forget you".

*****

When the decision was made by the authorities to destroy the old Jewish cemetery, Rabbi Bronfman was unable to sleep. Even when he walked on the street he saw the images of the broken gravestone of the rabbis and good people of Bendery. It was only after he transferred the tombs of Yehuda–Leib Wertheim, R. Itzikel, R. Shloimke and R. Levi Darbrimediker to the new cemetery that he stopped seeing these images. He still could not sleep. It was only after the special tent was erected over these tombs and an eternal light placed there that he could rest.

[Page 166]

The Jewish hospital and the attached seniors' residence were transformed by the authorities into a nursing school.

The Sadigura synagogue became a sports club.

The butchers' synagogue was now a dairy producing milk and butter.

The grand synagogue was connected along the basement to the Shaposnick synagogue and it became School #3.

The Talmud Torah– a large building– became a music school.

Schwartzman's Hebrew high school was now a factory manufacturing shoes.

The Sadigurian Synagogue (Collection of Rabbi Sh. Efrati)

****

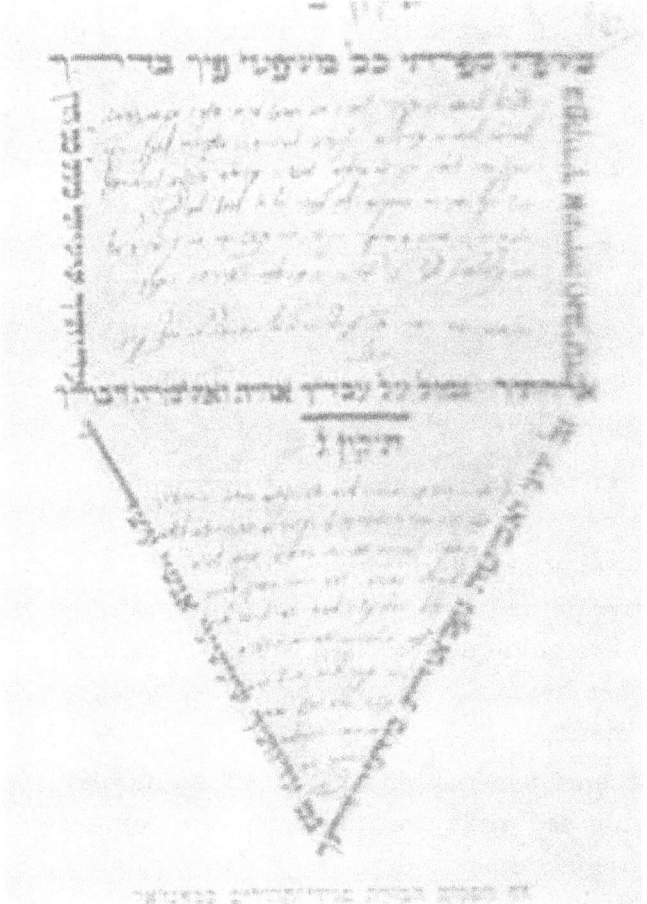

A Page from The Ledger of Psalm Sayers of Bendery (1844)

[Page 167]

Upon the Graves of Our Ancestors
by Shmuel Delmetzky (Haifa)
(Impressions from a quick visit to Bendery in 1966)
Translated by Ala Gamulka

"Anyone who ever visited Bendery must return for a second time. There is something unexplainable that draws a visitor to this town. The southern sun caresses you, the streets are long, straight and endless, and the white houses are surrounded by green gardens. Our hearts are pulled by a special force and we become enchanted with this town on the banks of the Dniester."

These enthusiastic lines we read in a nice pamphlet written in Russian and dedicated to Bendery. It was published by the tourist department Intertours from Kishinev.

It is a wonder that in spite of the publicity and campaign to encourage tourism, foreign tourists are not permitted to enter Bendery. However, we, the Israelis, who are based in Kishinev during our tour of the Soviet Union– only an hour's drive from Bendery– refused to give up. We wanted to visit our birth town where we had taken our first steps.

We decided to request permission to visit Bender even if only for a few hours. We were allowed to come after we explained that we wished to go to the cemetery to visit the graves of our ancestors.

****

In a car that was assigned to us three Israelis started out accompanied by a top representative of the tourism office, in addition to the driver. The tourism person was meant to guide us, but he apologized saying he could not be with us all the time since he had to go to Tiraspol. We soothed him saying we were certain we could manage.

It was a hot summer day in 1966. All along the road we looked at everything we could see while the Russian guide pointed out, with pride, the green fields and the factories.

The guide found that his Israeli companions were interested because they had their own story of green fields on desert land and the building of a nation. Our conditions had been slightly different.

We looked ahead, but we remembered the distant past of Jewish Bendery: the Hebrew high school with its teachers and students (where are they now?), the youth movements full of life where young people dreamed of Aliyah, active Zionist parties, synagogues, especially the Die Naye Shul (Great Synagogue) where famous cantors performed (from Roitman to Leybele Glantz), the town parks where we spent wonderful times.

I recall how we used to congregate as youths in the "new" park in the center of town armed with sticks and stones. We were ready for the arrival of the members of the Iron Guard who were rumored to be coming. They did not appear because foreign visitors were not welcome at the time.

Memories engulf me of the infamous Romanian security services that left their mark on the Jewish youth. The gendarmerie where Jewish youth were taken and beaten for belonging to the youth movements– they were accused of being Bolsheviks.

What awaits us in town? We are not expecting any surprises since we know how things are, more or less. All we want is to meet some friends and acquaintances that have survived.

****

One of us (I believe it was our friend Mordehai Sever) asked our guide to allow us to see the "Babi Yar" of Bendery– the place between the bridge and fortress, where about 700 Jews, men, women, the elderly and the young, were cruelly murdered.

We have now reached the entrance of the town. We see the famous "Borisovka" and we pass the fortress. An armed guard stands at its gate – a reminder of old times.

In the wide field between the bridge and the fortress there is no sign of the cruel massacre that was inflicted on hundreds of our brethren. When we continued the rest of our visit to the Soviet Union we did not find any signs of such massacres even in Babi Yar in Kiev…

We drove on the bridge spanning the Dniester (half of it was under water after the Russians bombed the bridge as they were retreating during the civil war) and look at the river banks. We recall those days when the bridge separated warring states and its frozen waters served as a route. Young men went towards the revolution while hungry Ukrainian peasants came the other way to escape forced collectivism.

Much water has flowed on the Dniester since that time and now the river separates two friendly towns. Its waters are used for bathing by both populations as if nothing has happened since we left Bendery. Today we have come to honor those who are no longer with us.

We reach the center of town and we say goodbye to our guide agreeing to meet again at a designated hour in order to return to Kishinev.

****

True to our promise, we turn towards the cemetery. Indeed, if you wish to refresh your memory of the past you should visit the cemetery. There, the Hebrew letters on the gravestones will remind us of all the people who represented the town in their lifetime. The gravestones– some truly magnificent– stand as a reminder of a beautiful Jewish community that is no longer.

We return to the center of town and each one of us is interested in what matters to him. After all, the purpose of our visit is to touch base with our friends who are still there. We easily find them and the happiness is indescribable. These friends that we knew before "the flood" are the last generation that still "knew Yosef". They belong to the past that is gone and will not return. Our social atmosphere that we knew so well some years ago has disappeared. There is no institution that symbolises Jewish existence...

The town has changed and even the famous trenches filled with water and mud have disappeared. Here and there one finds large apartment buildings that resemble our public housing. The main street, named after Lenin – originally Harozinskaya – is clean and wide and there are many buildings on it.

After a warm reception in Jewish homes, quick conversations and heart-wrenching goodbyes we leave Bendery full of memories of our friends. They remain with us to this day.

In the meantime, our guide has returned to take us back to Kishinev. On the way he asks us innocently: "Isn't it wonderful to visit again with friends and relatives?"

We politely reply: "Yes, it is nice."

[Page 169]

Personae

[Page 171]

The Wertheim Dynasty
(The history of the rabbinic seat in Bendery)
by I. L. Toibman [Yonatan]
Translated by Ala Gamulka

A tree with many branches!

The story would be incomplete if it did not include the tale about grandfather's daughter. He was the Hassidic Rabbi from Brone in Volyn. Much was said about her beauty and intelligence. She was ordered to hide when the Polish doctor Leiman would come. She also knew the laws in the Shulchan Aruch without having learned Torah. She was unschooled, but was quite intelligent.

Miriam-Rivkale came to Bessarabia and raised outstanding sons and daughters.

If truth be told, the word "Bessarabia" frightened grandfather since no one from our village in Volyn had ever gone there. No one really knew where Bessarabia was located in Russia. It was only known that it was further than Odessa, somewhere in Wallachia.

My grandfather was keen on joining the dynasty of the "elder rabbi" from Bendery– that was R. Arieh Leib, brother of R. Moshe-Zvi from Saravan. However, he was hesitant because of the great distance. Bessarabia! He sought advice, but eventually he agreed to the match. He knew that the father of this family, R. Arieh Leib, was the son-in-law of the Maggid R. Nahum from Chernobyl of his own dynasty.

For years there were stories about the fancy wedding that went on for a month and involved many villages and towns from near and far. It was nicknamed "the great wedding".

The owner of the estate gave the two families two carriages drawn by four horses in order to greet the groom and his family. They waited in the inn owned by R. Shaya. Several drivers who resembled Cossacks with their hair styles rode to meet the guests and brought them to the town gates. Grandfather and others came in the carriages to greet them. They went around the marketplace and the Red House seven times. The groom's family were housed in the homes of the wealthier members of the community.

No one knows how many turkeys and fattened geese were brought by the followers from the villages. They were served at many meals where the guessing continued as to the number of guests that had come to the big meal after the ceremony. The numbers varied between a 101 and 150.

The groom's family brought with them two melodies. One was that of Adon Olam which is quite sad at the beginning and at the end. The second melody began with sadness and crying, but ended with happiness.

The two tunes were absorbed in the community and could be heard throughout Volyn. They were sung by the followers of Stolin-Karlin and by those from Trisk- each in its own way. Klezmer bands played them at many happy occasions in Volyn.

After the Seven Blessings the guests left and returned to their homes. It is reported that saying good-bye to the bride was akin to that of our matriarch Rebecca. There were no camels and the nanny stayed home. She did cry a great deal because she was going so far away – to distant Bendery in Bessarabia.

Grandfather was quite emotional at this moment and worried about his daughter. It may be that this was just a father who would miss his beloved daughter. It may also be that his heart told him that she would die at a young age and he would only know about it in his old age. In any case saying good-bye was difficult.

She stood in the doorway with tears in her eyes and put her hand on the mezuzah. Grandfather blessed her and wished her to be happy. She left and went to Bendery.

[Page 172]

Bendery

According to many, Bessarabia is likened in its scenery, temperament and climate to Eretz Israel since it located in the area between the Dniester and the Prut. Thus, Bendery can be compared to Yaffo.

As you enter Bendery you stand on a hill and see the ruined fortress. It is as if you see all of Bessarabia.

This land is part of a brown prairie, watered by the rivers and dew. Most of the year the land is laden with produce, wheat, vines and fields full of sheep and cattle.

It is morning time. The marketplace is filled with farmers and their heavy baskets. You can find all types of plums still covered in frost, citrus fruit, red apples whose seeds are sonorous. The large square is strewn with cloth bags filled with grapes of different kinds. They are to be sent to distant places. These bags are emptied into warehouses owned by Jews who will export the grapes. High piles of watermelons and pumpkins are everywhere. No one fears that they will be stolen.

In one of the lanes one sees a skinny Jew with his talit under his arm. He is probably one of the idlers in town who can be found in the marketplace. They go from table to table, handle the poultry and the newly-caught fish, squeeze the watermelons with all their might and sniff the fragrant yellow watermelons. They select the best and return home with heavy bags.

You can hear sounds of happiness from the saloons. These are farmers who are now drunk. They are happy to have sold their produce. They sing to Russia and Moldova, Volga, Doyna. These tunes touch the Jewish soul. They have been around since the days of the Baal Shem Tov who used to wander in these areas. The cantors sang them and also the Chassidim in Shtipenshti and Hosh. They were brought to the "big wedding" by the in-laws to grandfather's house.

Heinich the cantor, a sickly Jew, also chanted the tune and adapted it to different prayers from the High Holidays.

*

The Rabbi's court and the magnificent synagogue are located in the busy marketplace. All visitors look at this building which reminds them of those edifices depicted on silken challah covers received from yeshivas in Jerusalem. There are two towers on both sides of the Western Wall with polished cornices and tips and protuberances reminding us of the Tower of David. There is beautiful Jerusalem stone. The interior of the synagogue is different from any others. An artist was brought from Odessa and he painted some of the walls and towers of Eretz Israel, the Western Wall and the Old city gate. The painting almost calls out:"if I forget thee, Jerusalem…"

*

Rabbi Itzikel and his son Rabbi Shloimenu – he is so young that his silver talit still has its original folds – are planning to make Aliyah. They have a few followers among the wealthy members in the synagogue. Among them is R. Leib Brodsky, an aristocratic Jew who is extremely knowledgeable in sacred texts such as "moreh nevuchim", "Kuzari" and others.

The whole synagogue is ready to go to the Holy city of Jerusalem.

Rabbi Itzikel and his followers were true lovers of Zion even before religious Zionists appeared on the scene. They were all well-versed in ancient sayings praising Eretz Israel. This aristocratic rabbinic family also spoke of Sinai and the Mount Moria even though the former was secular and the latter religious in meaning.

[Page 173]

For generations the longing for Zion did not have a name. From time to time an emissary from the Holy Land would visit. He came from the Meir Baal Haness yeshiva and had the scent of the beloved land. Everyone congregated around him because he had been fortunate enough to step on the Holy Land. There was always an atmosphere of festivity when the emissary came.

Six generations had lived in this court. The time spanned about 140 years in this home attached to the synagogue and its women's section.

*

How did the father of this dynasty of Rabbi Aryeh-Leib from Ukraine reach Bendery in Bessarabia?

The story is that he was brought to Bendery by a businessman who had visited him in his village in Podolia. The new transplant grew roots and produced fruit.

The front of the synagogue of Rabbi Itzikel, *z"l*

What did this businessman from Bendery see in the young man to bring him to the new place? He did it on his own, without consultation.

There is a family record, written in 1774 that says that the appointed rabbi was a 'king in Bendery'. He was allotted a salary of two rubles per week.

There is a basis for the conclusion that the new rabbi filled the role of leader of the Chassidim and had many followers. He was also a teacher and a judge and served as a model for his generation and those to come.

In the second family record, given to the son of Rabbi Aryeh-Leib, it is written that Shimon-Shlomo would be appointed his successor. This was decided by his followers, of which there were many.

In the ledger of the Hevra Kaddisha of 1844 we find several sections that give information about the daily life of the Jews of Bendery. These Jews were generous to those less fortunate and led a kosher life. They were true Chassidim. Even those who could not read were encouraged to recite Psalms since the Rabbi believed that it was good for the soul.

In winter, on Friday night after midnight, the old beadle dressed in furs and a leather belt around his waist, walks outside and bangs on the windows and wakes everyone. They are being summoned to come to the synagogue to recite Psalms.

[Page 174]

The hour is early, the town clock has struck three, but most of the Psalm reciters have already slept 7 hours after the meal. One can hear the doors creaking and young people meeting their friends on the dark street and walking together. They walk in the frozen mud. Jokers say that this walk is mentioned in the Psalms– we tread timorously in the House of God.

Rabbi Itzikel Wertheim, z"l

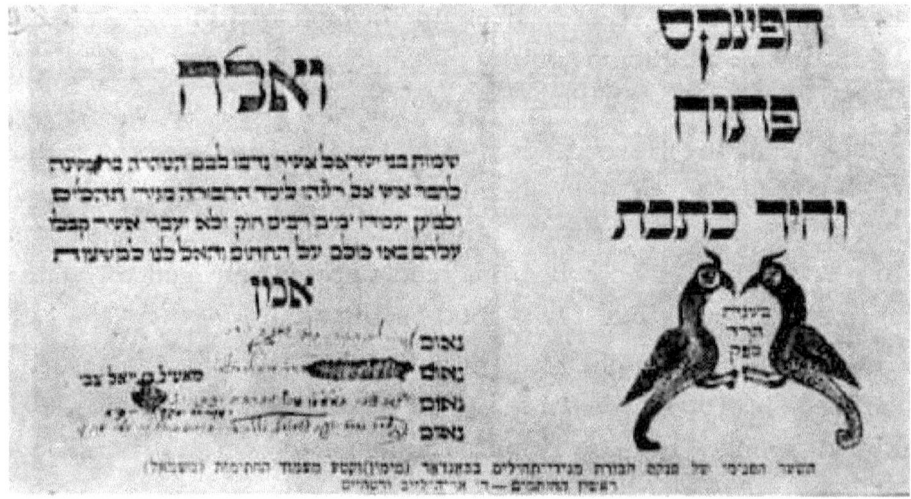

Ledger of the Psalm Society in Bendery showing some signatures [1844]

In summertime there were people who went to the Dniester to immerse themselves in the fresh and clear water. They would return with their robes and towels to the synagogue. They did so in spite of the fact that there is a prohibition against inappropriate dress when seeing the king even if it is only to chant psalms.

The black soil of Bessarabia was plowed by many true believers and the seeds of popular Chassidism and real belief were sown.

The daughter in the house

The daughter of the Rabbi from Volyn came as a bride to the home of her in-laws in Bendery, Bessarabia.

Her letters to her grandfather speak of her strong feelings of homesickness and her observations of life in Bendery. In spite of the fact that there was a rumor that there was an abundance of fruit and vegetables in Bendery – unavailable in Volyn– it was not so. There were grapes on the Shabbat table for the "shecheyanyu" blessing on the second day of Rosh Hashanah, but there were only four or five per person. Even those few disappeared immediately. On Succot there were baskets of the grapes brought into the house and wine was plentiful. The people here are so different and one has to get used to them.

These thoughts were written to her father in her letters. Her father replied with love and was thrilled to hear news of new grandchildren. He would send congratulations, give a list of names and enclose gifts of money.

Some years passed and she died. Five sons and five daughters followed her coffin. The house had burned down.

[Page 175]

A spark from the candles lit for Shavuot fell in the courtyard and all the buildings were burned. Rabbi Itzikel died three days later. It was a hint that there was a new order in the dynasty. Everything was burned and only the chair at the head of the table was saved. On the chair was a sign with the inscription: this is the chair of the sainted holy man.

The new leader is Rabbi Shimon-Shlomo Wertheim. He resembled his father Rabbi Itzikel. His face reflected intelligence and knowledge.

If Rabbi Itzikel was one who looked into the past, then Rabbi Shimon-Shlomo always faced the future – to the coming generations of rabbis. Again there were three generations in the courtyard that had now been rebuilt.

Rabbi Shimon–Shlomo Wertheim, z"l

The three generations were: the father, called Rabbi Shloimenu by our townspeople, his son, Ben Porat Yosef – Rabbi Yossele with the golden curls and the grandson Ahrale. These were the three parts of the dynasty.

The courtyard was filled with new melodies, sons and daughters and many friends.

One son, very handsome and sporting a beard, was brought up in a strict way. He gave speeches in excellent Hebrew at Lovers of Zion meetings and was a delegate to the Congress. The father watched him with love and trepidation that he should not change too much.

Another Rabbi had expressed concern over the behavior of the sons and the father explained that his way was that of Jacob: 'I will move along slowly at the tempo of the flock and the pace of the children' [Genesis 33:14]. He added the interpretation of Avrabanel: Go children and heed my words. It does not say come children. The younger generation has a heavy load on its back and they do not need to be taught morals. One must understand their ways that are strewn with obstacles and to go with them step by step and to teach them love of God.

Another son who is clean-shaven ended up in America and there he was one of the great leaders of Zeirei Zion. He travelled everywhere and encouraged the youth to build Eretz Israel.

The Rabbi's daughters followed many paths– Kiev, Odessa, courses for kindergarten teachers, nursing school, preparation for Eretz Israel. They loved their father who encouraged them. They always returned home to celebrate holidays and then they left again.

The oldest son served as a rabbi in many important cities and, before Mizrahi, he founded the 'Ultra-religious Zionist Organization.'

Father and son, together with Rabbi Fishman from nearby Ungani, planned Zionist programs for rabbis to encourage them to endorse the movement.

The rabbi's courtyard consisted of the four sections of the Shulchan Aruch on one side and an unconditional love for Zion on the other side.

This partnership of the two rabbis– questions and answers about what is permitted and what is not, special "tables" for the followers, rabbinic decisions– was outstanding. There is a story told about our rabbi that shows that he was even greater than the "old rabbi": the latter, when a woman was brought before him that the dibbuk [evil spirit] entered her– banished the dibbuk. However, the former when confronted with the same issue, banished both the woman and the dibbuk.

In the rabbi's study there is a green desk with a telephone. The Beit Din meets regularly and there is activity all day.

At home, on the eastern wall there is a picture – Panorama of the Holy Land. During Kiddush and Havdalah on Shabbat and Holidays all eyes are focused on it.

In 1903, after the Kishinev pogroms, Rabbi Shimon-Shlomo traveled to Paris where he negotiated with the representatives of the Baron about settling 50 agricultural families from Bessarabia in Eretz Israel. He encouraged them to leave and make Aliyah. He understood full well that he was undertaking a great responsibility for the lives of many people.

In Paris the Rabbi held a meeting of Jews from Eastern Europe and Dr. Max Nordau highly regarded the "grand rabbi" from Bendery.

[Page 176]

Nordau offered his assistance and promised that the Rabbi's request will be looked at most carefully. However, a telegram arrived with the following words:"Palestine impossible, we agree to Anatolia".

On his way back from Paris, the Rabbi visited his grandfather–in–law and this represented the strengthening of family relations. Everyone was impressed that he was going to Paris– so far away. The Rabbi spoke about the magnificent city and its chief rabbi, R. Tzadok Hacohen. He described him as an outstanding rabbi and a most observant man. They spoke about Rashi and other sages of Paris.

The visit represented the first time that electric light was seen in grandfather's village. The guest ordered the closing of doors and took out a small utensil from his pocket. He pushed a button and there was light!

The guest also had a copy of the newspaper "Hatzfira" and grandfather looked at the headline which said:"The Jews of Russia do not yet have equal rights".

Grandfather asked:" Firstly, what does this mean? Secondly, we are sworn in and are careful not to harm the honor of the state…"

When WWI broke out, the Rabbi was in Eretz Israel. When he stepped on the holy terrain he felt a yearning. Have passed Lydda, Ramle, Beitar and said "each name excites my soul". He is unable to contain his emotions in these special moments of his life. He occasionally asks himself:"How did I earn this privilege? I did not see any sheaves of wheat. The one who sees sheaves of wheat in his dreams can achieve redemption". He finds an answer in his letter:"I was privileged because of my ancestors who came from the tribe of Judah–Kalev Ben Yefuneh. My ancestors and I are absolved from any blame from the sin of the spies".

He arrives at the Western Wall and he writes:"We wish to see the goodness of God if he so desires. We should no longer spill our blood on foreign lands. I will respond if called upon".

He finally returned to Bendery after a lengthy round–about route. He gladdened hearts in describing the Holy Land…

The sons and daughters are scattered in various countries. They all desire to be in Eretz Israel to bask in the light of Zion.

His daughter Pnina is the first to make Aliyah. Her soft hands are used for working the land in Ein Ganim. She then was a nurse in hospitals in Safed and Jerusalem where she also cared for her patients with words of encouragement and comfort. She never had her own family, but spent her life inside white walls. After her comes the second daughter and then a son who filled a role as a mediator, almost like a rabbi. He was followed by the third daughter.

The father imbued in his children an unconditional love of Eretz Israel. The rabbi died knowing his children were in the Holy Land.

The special chair stands near the table as if it is urging continuity. It represents generations of those who used it for so many years.

The oldest son, Yosef, served as a rabbi in a large community in Poland. There were two communities who fought over who should get him and they went to a Beit Din over the issue. The community of Ostro felt the rabbi could not refuse to serve them. However, the community of Khrovshov maintained that his grandfather had served them in the past.

The decision by a Rabbi from Rovno was in favor of Khrovshov.

Rabbi Yosef had many sons and daughters. His followers were from Beltz and Gur, but he was a Zionist and a member of Mizrahi. He was the eldest son and he saw himself as responsible for filling the empty place in Bendery. He sent his son, R. Ahrale, to take his place for awhile.

Soon the branch came back to the trunk. The son came back to his father's house, but he wanted to sail to Eretz Israel from a Romanian port. Bendery was closer to Eretz Israel.

On the first day of Tevet, 1940, the Russians entered Bessarabia. From Tiraspol, on the other side of the Dniester, one hears:"we will be with you in the spring". It was obvious that under this regime there will no longer be a rabbinic tradition. R. Yosef appointed his son-in-law as the keeper of the seal and he himself made Aliyah.

On his last winter morning in the Diaspora he went to the graves of the five generations, said good-bye to the Zionists in the cemetery and recited Psalms. He announced: 'Dear grandfather. I was fortunate to sit in your seat and my father's seat for six years. I did my best not to shame you. The time has come for me to make Aliyah with my family. I am going to the land you wanted to reach. I am certain I am following your orders...''

[Page 177]

It seems that of all the Zionists in the "tent" the saddest grave is that of the mother – the daughter of the Volyn grandfather.

The newcomers came to Jerusalem and the inherited seat moved together with the painting.

The dynasty continued...

[From Nof vegeza – scenery and trunk]

Shimon–Shlomo Wertheim and his family

[Page 178]

R. Yosele Wertheim
by I.L. Toibman [Yonatan] Z"L
Translated by Ala Gamulka

The diminutive of the name, assigned to children in the courtyards of the Tzadikim, was typical of the bearer. It evokes sweetness and goodness deeply rooted in love for other Jews and it always emanated from his countenance – from his first steps until his last day in Hadassah Hospital in Jerusalem.

The Rabbi's Synagogue

Built in 1886 by Rabbi Itzikel, z"l and renovated in 1936–7

His image and personality were formed in his father, Rabbi Shlomo-Shimon's house and during the lifetime of his grandfather R. Itzikel. They had both been the town rabbis and taught Rabbi Yosele Torah and wisdom. His father encouraged in him love of Zion while his grandfather was an example of a scholar and a Chassid. Although Yosele admired his grandfather and thought him to be a Chasid, he, himself, was also one.

Rabbi Yosele used to tell a childhood story that occurred during Succot while he was involved in a game of nuts. He suddenly looked up and saw his grandfather sitting alone in the succah and after gazing at him, he could no longer return to his game. The memory of this event stayed with him forever.

During those days, when the father and grandfather were still alive, the handsome young Jew followed a life of Torah and work. He would not enjoy the love, loyalty and goodness without blessing God. He was eager to perform deeds for Eretz Israel.

Some years before the formation of Mizrahi, Yosele founded the "Ultra Orthodox party for Eretz Israel. He spoke in many synagogues and had many followers who loved Zion like him.

In the Wertheim house it was not enough to love Zion– it was time to make Aliyah. The son was as avid as the father to disseminate the idea of Aliyah to everyone around them.

Yosele received his rabbinic smicha (ordination) from one of the greatest rabbis and by then he already had a family. He served the community of Ostilo. His wife came from there. He was only 24 years old at the time. He was the rabbi of a Chassidic Polish village where there were many factions and dynasties interested in gaining his favor.

The young rabbi, a Zionist and the scion of rabbis found himself in a difficult situation. He tried to be independent without giving up crucial ideals.

[Page 179]

These were not easy times, but his people loved him unconditionally and encouraged him constantly.

Mizrahi was founded and a framework was established. He was one of the first to join. He traveled to many towns, spoke to the congregants and participated in many conferences. He was also a member of the executive committee of Mizrahi and his reputation preceded him. He was a well-educated rabbi who had a love of Zion.

His village became too small for his activities and he looked for a larger forum. He was interested in the position of rabbi in Ostro – a large and important community in Volyn.

These were times of pogroms and the Jews in Russia suffered greatly.

Ostro now became a border town – near the Russian border. He served as the rabbi of Ostro for some years and was highly respected and loved.

He took a chance in helping to hide people in his attic and subsequently providing them with proper documents so that they would be saved. The chief rabbi of Tel Aviv, the late Rabbi Aronson, was one of those saved. Others were journalists, writers, famous or not so famous cantors and simply Jews who came to his door wearing summer clothes in the dead of winter. His home emitted warmth and gave them refuge.

These refugees were able to convalesce in his home and were encouraged to rebuild their lives. It was not in vain that these people blessed him as Ben Porat Yosef.

Years went by and the Jews of Poland were struggling with the new regime. The rabbi was concerned about his congregants, but he always smiled and comforted others.

His father, Rabbi Shimon-Shlomo, died and his seat was now available. It called Rabbi Yosele to return home. He knew it would not be an easy job after his years in Poland, but he knew it was his duty to continue the dynasty. Bendery will be his last stop in the Diaspora- it is closer to Eretz Israel.

Rabbi Yosele spent six years as the rabbi of Bendery. The Jews of Bessarabia suffered much in those years and Rabbi Yosele took care of his flock. His Shabbat sermons in his synagogue were inspirational and lasted the full week. He encouraged everyone to make Aliyah.

Thunder announcing the coming war was already heard and he was fortunate to be able to save himself in time.

On the first day of Tevet, 1940, Rabbi Yosele went to the cemetery and visited the graves of five generations, said goodbye and made Aliyah.

It was amazing to see how ready he was to go to Eretz Israel and to accept whatever awaited him there. "I am ready to just be a beadle in any synagogue in the holy city of Jerusalem. I do not need anything else"- so he said.

Rabbi Yosele was fortunate to have his own synagogue with his followers who came to hear him speak and teach. He was very happy. He said:"How much luckier am I than my ancestors who dreamed of making Aliyah until their last moment!" He felt this way to his last day. This was a terrible day for all of us.

He was on his death-bed in "Hadassah" and looked towards the Mount of Olives where he would be buried.

He told the writer of these lines: "I cannot dictate where I should be buried. Any place in this holy city will do."

May dear Rabbi Yosele rest comfortably in his humble grave in the land of his dreams, on Mount of Olives. May his memory be blessed.

[Hatzofe- 3.5.1946]

[Page 180]

Dr. Shlomo Bendersky
Translated by Ala Gamulka

Dr. Shlomo Bendersky

He was born in Kishinev in 1866. When he was young he founded, with Meir Dizengoff, the first group of Hovevei Zion [Lovers of Zion] and he was a member of the group of university students called Nes Ziona in Odessa. He was studying science at the university there [together with Zvi Belkovsky and Shimshon Rozenboim]. He then studied medicine in Budapest and after graduation he lectured at the university there. In 1897 he came to the Bendery area to serve as a doctor.

He was a dedicated Zionist and was a delegate to the Third Zionist Congress in Basel in 1899. He was elected to the steering committee of Bessarabia–Volyn. He was also a community leader in charitable organizations.

He contracted Typhus while looking after patients and died on the 18 day of Cheshvan, 1908.

[From the book "Pa'amei Hage'ula" by A. Tzantziper [Refa'eli], Page 102]

Circular sent by Dr. Shlomo Bendersky

[Written in Hebrew in his capacity as a Zionist leader in Bessarabia–Volyn]

Dear Friend!

The Hebrew Colonial Bank informs us, via the Vienna Executive committee, that you are representing the bank. I am addressing you, dear sir, not as a bank representative, but, moreover, as someone who is dealing with the new movement of rebuilding the land in Eretz Israel, Our unadulterated love for our people and our strong belief in our hopes for the future have given us the strength to fight hatred and to create a treasure that will be unparalleled,

We do not want to lose time due to politics and our hopes must not be postponed. We see in this bank something that would help us in fulfilling our aspirations and reaching our goals. Our wish is to resurrect life in the land of our ancestors. We do not want to miss the opportunity at this time.

For all these reasons I am asking you, dear friend, not to lose any time and to continue to work on our behalf by distributing bonds and collecting the funds thus generated.

We know you are on our side and that your love for our cause has propelled you to found the bank last year. Your help will allow us to perfect our work and will encourage our brethren to devote themselves to our cause. God willing, we will succeed in our plans...

Bender,

12 Nissan, 1900

[Page 181]

David Abramovich Natanzon
Translated by Ala Gamulka

David Abramovich Natanzon was born in Tiraspol [Podolia] in 1877. At age 9, he moved with his family to Bendery. He attended high school there and prepared himself for matriculation three years later. He had to interrupt his studies due to the death of his father and took upon himself to provide for his family, He established a printing house in the Russian language and next to it a stationery store. The store was managed by his wife, Atalia [from the Bendersky family in Dubossary, Podolia].

His lack of formal education did not stop him from many varied activities in town. He founded the Russian language newspaper Yuzhni Krai and served as its editor-in-chief. He was also a columnist in the famous democratic newspaper in southern Russia- Odessky Novostie. He was well-known to his readers and all intellectuals of the era read his works with interest.

Atalia Natanzon

He was also an honorary member of the municipal Russian library – Pushkinskaya as well as one of the founders of the Russian-Yiddish library. He was a member of the Red Cross, "Help for the Poor", "Clothes for the Needy", "Help for the Sick", etc. He was involved with the cooperative Savings Bank [The Jewish Little Bank]. This bank looked after small merchants who could not carry loans at high interest. He was also active among the railroad workers and many other community groups.

David Natanzon

He was at the forefront of intellectual activity in town and he stood out, in particular. He dedicated himself to all public programs and always fulfilled his tasks. He was well regarded by both Jews and Russians and served as an example of honesty and dedication to public works. Anyone who came to him found him to be a good listener with an open heart and a ready hand to offer help.

He died on 26.09.1916 in Odessa, after surgery.

His death caused great pain and sorrow and all the town residents mourned him deeply. He died young, in the midst of his charitable good deeds.

[Page 182]

The press in southern Russia and the Jewish newspapers were filled with obituaries describing his important activities.

His wife, Atalia, an excellent person in her own right, always stood next to her husband and encouraged all his activities. She was well regarded by the town intelligentsia. Their daughter, Susie, was very young when he died and did not really know her father. She made Aliyah and works in the Communications Department.

May his memory be blessed.

Pinhas Bendersky

Dr. Baruch Nissenboim
Translated by Ala Gamulka

He was born on 30.04.1886 in Bendery. His father died when he was very young. His widowed mother had five children, but she made certain each one of them obtained a higher education. After the pogrom in Kishinev, in 1903, she decided to make Aliyah. She died there at the age of 90.

His brothers also made Aliyah and became farmers, among the founders of Yavneel. Dr. Baruch Nissenboim first visited his brothers in 1911. He finished his medical studies in Strasbourg [then in Germany] and took his government exams in Russia in 1914. He was sent to the front as a doctor during WWI and spent 3 years as an assistant doctor in the Finnish regiment. He earned 4 medals. After the war he served as a doctor in a workers area in Odessa as well as in private practice. He made Aliyah on the ship Ruslan [the last to leave the Soviet Union] and worked at "Hadassah". He was active in the Bukhara House and Mea She'arim in Jerusalem. A year later he was appointed director of the Internal Medicine department in the hospital.

He was one of the pioneers of medicine in the country and worked diligently in promoting good health. He became the medical director of the Haganah and founded Magen David Adom [he was its vice-president].

A year later he was transferred to "Hadassah" in Haifa when the new hospital was opened. He ran several departments there. He was also the director of the hospital and had a private practice in Haifa for many years.

During the events of August 1929 the residents of the old Jewish neighborhood, Arad Al-Yahud, escaped to Hadar Hacarmel. Dr. Nissenboim undertook the task of finding accommodations for them in the Reali School and the Technion. He also supplied them with foods and other needs. Naturally, he also took care of the health of the women and children.

During that time he heard about the pogrom in Safed. He immediately sent an ambulance with a doctor from Haifa. He then made certain all 60 injured were transferred to Haifa. He managed, within 24 hours, to turn an entire floor of the Technion into a hospital ward. He received beds and blankets from the representative of the Jewish Agency, Eliezer Dory [Dostrovsky]. For taking care of the injured from Safed he received high praise from the British High Commissioner. He was also sent a letter of commendation from the Minister for the Colonies, Lord Pasfield.

Founding of the Magen David Station

In 1931 the Haganah asked Dr. Nissenboim to open a Magen David Station in town. He was actually the chief physician of the Haganah in Haifa and area. He did this until the establishment of the State.

Dr. Baruch Nissenboim

During WWII he was appointed as the medical emergency doctor. When battles broke out in December 1947 Dr. Nissenboim, with the help of Kupat Holim, refitted the Borochov Rehabilitation center into a military hospital. Over 1000 injured residents of Haifa were cared for in this hospital. The injured fighters of the Haganah were brought there from other areas.

Dr. Nissenboim went into private practice for various reasons still in 1932, except for one year as a district doctor of the Ministry of Health, after the establishment of the state. He was mainly in private practice, but he always volunteered for Magen David Adom.

[Page 183]

After the establishment of the state Dr. Nissenboim continued to serve as a district doctor in Haifa and area. He was, in fact, an officer. At the age of 75 he retired from this position.

He was fortunate to be recognized for his extensive medical activities and was chosen as an Honorary Citizen of Haifa.

He died in Haifa on 8 Kislev 1971 at the age of 84.

Rabbi Efraim Drebrimdiker
Translated by Ala Gamulka

Rabbi Efraim Drebrimdiker [a rabbi in Bendery]

Rabbi Efraim [son of Shneyer Zalman] Drebrimdiker is a descendant of Rabbi Levi Yitzhak of Berdichev [his family name was also Drebrimdiker]. He was born in the village of Ladizin, Russia in 1886 and died on 12.3.1958.

He was orphaned at a young age and after his Bar Mitzvah he lived with his grandfather [a grandson of Rabbi Levi Yitzhak of Berdichev]. He studied hard and received smicha (ordination). He decided to take secular studies to obtain a high school diploma, but his family objected and withdrew their support. He had to leave home and subsisted on private tutoring.

After obtaining his diploma at the age of 20 he studied for three years in the Commerce Faculty in Kiev. He lived in dire straits and again gave private lessons. In 1912 he was chosen by Bendery as their rabbi. He held this position until 1940.

Rabbi Efraim was a kind hearted Jew and he excelled in public activities within the community in Bendery in general and in Zionist circles in particular. He listened to every request that came his way and always tried to help everyone. In the 1920s he was also a Bible teacher in Russian in the Public Girls High School. He helped establish the Schwartzman Hebrew High School in Bendery.

In 1925 the Hebrew High school building, privately owned, was to be sold. Rabbi Efraim volunteered to travel to London with Dr. Schwartzman and there they obtained funds to buy the building. In this way this important educational institution continued its work. It provided Jewish and general studies for a generation of young people who continued in the Zionist and pioneering spirits until it was closed by the authorities in 1936.

After WWII and the evacuation he lived in Czernowitz and served there as a rabbi until he died.

His warm personality was beloved by everyone and added to the wonderful history of Bendery.

Avraham Alexandrov
Translated by Ala Gamulka

Avraham Alexandrov was an energetic and educated Jew and was appointed by Yitzhak Nissenboim to run all his businesses, especially his estate in Bendery. When anyone approached the "old man" he would direct them to Alexandrov:"Go to him and tell him to help you. You will receive what I promised".

Alexandrov was a native of Novgorod.

After he left his job with Nissenboim he was the manager of the Loan Bank – Creditny Bank. He then bought and ran the best printing press in Bendery.

Alexandrov entertained all the important people in town in his house. He was fortunate to have hosted Haim Nahman Bialik at one time. His close friends included Dr. Zvi Schwartzman whom he had helped to complete his academic studies.

[Page 184]

He was respected by the Jewish community because he was dedicated to them and to Zionist causes.

Sonia Kahanov

Avraham Alexandrov

Baruch Holodenko
The First Hebrew Journalist in Bendery
Translated by Ala Gamulka

He was born in 1850 and died on 24.6.1925.

Baruch Holodenko had a special place among the important personalities in Bendery. He worked diligently in all public institutions and had special qualities.

He was the first journalist among the Jews of Bendery who wrote, in Hebrew, at the end of the 19th century about the Jewish community of Bendery. He was published in Hamagid, Hamelitz, etc.

Special attention must be paid to his article in Hamelitz published in this book about the dedication of the Jewish hospital in Bendery. It was an unforgettable national holiday within the Jewish community. The mayor drank a toast in honor of the Jewish community and the Jewish people.

Since he was a distinguished representative of the community he was chosen as a delegate to the seventh Zionist Congress and to many Zionist committees in Russia. He met many important people and corresponded with the greats of Russian Jewry.

He educated several generations of students who carried the national flag with enthusiasm. Many of them even made Aliyah encouraged by his loving image.

His descendants were part of the Second and Third Aliyah and settled in many places, even in a distant border kibbutz in the Negev.

It is so sad that in spite of his wish to make Aliyah and his dedication to the cause he was unable to fulfill the dream and to see Eretz Israel.

The memory of Baruch Holodenko will remain among the great dreamers and fighter for the rejuvenation of our people and our land.

Baruch Holodenko

Inscription on his grave:

> This was an honest and outstanding man
>
> Who worked hard all his life
>
> His name will be a blessing
>
> In the words of his admirers and those who honor him
>
> He was industrious and knowledgeable
>
> He was full of literary information
>
> R. Baruch Holodenko
>
> Died at the age of 75
>
> B. Tammuz, 1925
>
> May his memory be a blessing!

[Page 185]

The elderly teacher, Baruch Holodenko, stands out within the scenery of Bendery. He wears a black hat and wrinkled clothes. His feet are moving– they drag mud –from morning to night.

What does R. Baruch do all day? First, he visits three to four houses to prepare teams for soliciting funds for Jewish National Fund at that evening's wedding in the large hall. He then tutors Hebrew for a couple of hours. He then goes to the medical store of Hersh Kogan where he participates in a discussion about inviting a Zionist speaker from Odessa to a debate about the Bund. He follows this with two more tutorials and so on until sundown.

R. Baruch has a special interest in this debate since his daughter Rivka* made Aliyah in 1911 at the age of 17. She went to work the land, but WWI had put a stop to all correspondence between them.

It is clearly understood that in addition to his technical and practical assistance all year he is also invited to lecture. At Hanukah he spoke about the Hasmoneans. His topic was "Victory of spirit over army and might". In the month of Adar he will speak again as well as before Succot.

His home was poor and needy, but his wife did not complain about her lot because she admired his work and his activities.

His wish is to make Aliyah, but he does not dare dream. His dark eyes shine with tears when he hears news from Eretz Israel and he is thrilled to listen to a new Hebrew song. Ish"i Adler, a teacher at Herzliah High School in Tel Aviv, visited Bendery. For Holodenko his visit was like a Sabbath because he enjoyed it so much.

This is how Baruch Holodenko lived– in an atmosphere of Eretz Israel– in Bendery. He trudged on his weak legs through the mud in the winter and was barely to breathe in the summer. He never stopped his holy work.

He continued to educate a generation of students to love Hebrew, Zion and pioneering until he was confined to his deathbed in the Community Hospital.

I.L. Yonatan

[From "Chapters about the Jews of Bessarabia", Nissan 1958]

* Rivka Machneimy, z"l, lived her whole life in Kibbutz Ein Harod. Her diary is published in this book.

Dr. Alexander Khain
Translated by Ala Gamulka

The dentist, Dr. Alexander Mikhailovich Khain, stands out among the many wonderful, progressive and pioneering personalities of Bendery. He was well-known as a public figure, journalist and editor in the Russian language about Jewish topics. As a regular journalist he signed his articles with the pseudonym "Odos".

Dr. Alexander Khain

He had an aristocratic look and he dedicated his life to others. He especially was active in helping the poor and in social agencies in Bendery such as "Help for the Sick," "Clothing for the Poor," etc.

He was also involved in developing cultural activities in the population and he looked after the amateur drama group which performed from time to time. He even managed to encourage people to attend.

[Page 186]

The story of his life is told by his daughters and his son:

Alexander Mikhailovich Khain was born in the Mozilov District and was among the most developed and cultured people in those times. He graduated from high school in Moscow, having been invited by his brother who was an important merchant with privileges in the capital. In Moscow he learned Russian well. His children were educated in Central Russia in a Russian high school. However, at home, Dr. Khain taught his children to love Judaism, the Jewish people and its traditions and the Promised Land. He was an ardent Zionist and he applied it in all aspects of public life. All his life his deeds were directed towards the public good and to collecting funds to finance them. His spouse helped him constantly in his charitable work and encouraged his actions in spite of the fact that he traveled a great deal.

He was an unbelievably honest and hard-working person. He taught us to follow in his footsteps. He influenced his children and just a look from him would ensure that we followed the proper route.

He was a tireless worker and he worked in the hospital's dental clinic until his last days. He would not give up going to work in winter and in summer and in old age.

He lived in Bendery during two periods of time: the first as a young boy and the second when he returned in 1912-13 and stayed there for many years. His public work in Bendery was varied and wide. He was one of the organizers of "Clothing for the Poor" and he was a supporter of the Schwartzman Hebrew High School. [Once he gave the school two rooms in our home for two classes which could not be accommodated in the school building].

He wrote many articles in local newspapers as well as in the Odessa press. [Unfortunately, all the articles we had saved have been lost].

In Bendery he was active in "Hazamir" where there was a choir and a drama club. There were plays presented and I took part in one of them as "Injured Palestine". There was with me a young man by the name of Kaushansky who made Aliyah and changed his name to Agadati. I believe he opened the first folk dance school in Eretz Israel. There was also Zina Pistrova who became an opera singer in Bucharest.

Anyone who needed help knew that Dr. Khain would not refuse him. He did it for its own sake and not to be recognized.

It is sad that this man, who worked so hard for his people and his country, did not reach Eretz Israel. We, his children, live and work in the land he loved so much.

Father and mother were killed on the way to camps, not far from Rodalnia, and were probably buried there in a mass grave.

We trust that his friends and acquaintances will always speak well of him.

David Prozhansky
Translated by Ala Gamulka

David Prozhansky

He arrived in Bendery from White Russia in 1908 since he had been exiled from there by the Tsarist government for his "revolutionary sins". It was well-known that about 100 years ago Bessarabia served as an exile destination for "elements unwanted by Tsar Nikolai I". Even Pushkin was sent there. Obviously, the Russian secret service considered Bessarabia a distant unwelcome place in those days and sent their political prisoners there instead of Siberia. For David Prozhansky, Bendery did not seem like a place of exile since he felt very welcome there.

When he arrived in Bendery he served as a private Hebrew tutor and he soon became known as a talented teacher. He was friendly and was well-liked by everyone. He became close to the liberal Russian youth and especially the Jewish ones in Bendery. He was well educated and knew general and Jewish literature well. His lectures were filled with nationalistic ideas in a Zionist-socialist vein. He especially believed in the Autoemancipation of I.L. Pinsker.

[Page 187]

After he managed to attract a circle of young people, he organized "Poalei Zion" [I was one of the participants]. In spite of the fact that it was not permissible to have gatherings, we used to meet every Shabbat afternoon –in different homes– for political discussions, hearing literary lectures and chess matches.

David Prozhansky was our leader and usually the lecturer. There were some visitors from the outside such as the theatre group of Esther-Rachel Kaminska. There was much enthusiasm with her appearance and Prozhansky presented her with an album, signed by all young people in town. She thanked us profusely.

When he observed that the local library lacked the Jewish and general classics, he did not rest until he established a fund to purchase Yiddish copies of them. All the books were ordered from Warsaw. He was a warm man and an intellectual and he understood all the social problems. He was loved by the youth.

When Bessarabia was conquered by the Romanians it was discovered that he secretly was an agent of the Soviet regime. After WWI I visited Bendery and I found him as the leader of a group of "Poalei Zion" that was true to the October revolution... After WWII it became obvious in his letters that he was quite disappointed in Soviet Communism. He was still friendly to them, but he was a Zionist and he cared deeply about his people.

I was an emissary from the United States on this visit and I cooperated with him in the organization of a branch of the "Culture League" in Bendery. I saw how he was beloved by the youth and how hard he worked.

He died in 1970.

L.G. Brooklyn, N.Y

*

Professor Yitzhak Fein [Baltimore, United States] visited the Soviet Union and met with David Prozhansky. These are his remarks:

...Parents are still allowed to teach their children the Hebrew alphabet, but how many of them do so? Officially, there is no prohibition against performing a Bris, celebrating a Bar Mitzvah, visiting a synagogue, but... it is preferable not to do so if one values his life.

What happens when an older Jew wants to learn? It is done in secret since it is illegal to learn "dangerous" subjects. I met one of them, a Jew of 80 years old– David Prozhansky. I remembered him from fifty years earlier, before the flood. We were so happy to meet.

He spoke to me about what happened to him. What is he doing now? He is a pensioner and in his old age he became an artist. I told him that it is quite common in America– many people do it. It seems that I did not quite understand what he meant. Even now, in his old age, he teaches Torah, in spite of the fact that it is quite dangerous to do so. He has two young Jews who come and if they can take a chance, so can he. He does not have any textbooks so he draws letters for them and this is how they study. What devotion!

[Yiddisher Kemfer", New York]

*

In 1966 I visited Bendery for 7 hours and I met my friend David Prozhansky. He was quite old, skinny, but his Jewish sad eyes shone in his face. He tried to speak only Hebrew and complained that he could not obtain books in Hebrew. I was so sorry that I had not brought one for him.

I found out later that he had been a Hebrew teacher all his life– until the end.

I brought him new clothes as a gift and he was thrilled with the attention I paid him. When we said good–bye he kissed me warmly. I asked him to describe Bendery in the past thirty years– the Holocaust and the return of the Jews. He was unable to talk about it.

M.T.

Hersh Kogan [Zvi Cohen]
The Zionist Center at Hersh Kogan's in Bendery
Translated by Ala Gamulka

The pharmaceutical warehouse of Hersh Kogan served as the Zionist Center for many years. It was used as a meeting place by Zionist leaders in Bendery.

Hersh Kogan was tall and slim. His brown beard had a sharp end, his eyes shone with intellect and his tongue was used to argue with opponents. He always had useful sayings. His talents were evident.

[Page 188]

His well scrubbed store was used daily, between the hours of 12 and two in the afternoon, for Zionist affairs. Active members, friends and veterans of the Zionist scene met there daily. There was a Mr. Alexandrov, a wealthy Jew who had great influence in the community; next to him sat Mr. Kh, Fustan, the owner of a printing press. Another was Solomon Pavlovich Rivlin who spoke Russian and cited verses about "Altalena" to Jabotinsky. Of course, a special place within this group was kept for the old teacher B. Holodenko who came to bring money and receipts.

Hersh Kogan – Zvi Cohen

Leader of the General Zionists in Bendery

Later on R. Shabtai Berman, nicknamed R. Shepsil, also visited the store. He was ultra–Orthodox, but loved Israel in his own way.

When R. Shabtai Berman arrived, a sharp argument developed between him and the Zionists. They made stinging remarks that turned into bickering and angry words, but ended in peaceful statements so that there would be time on the next day to continue the discussion.

[In any case, the store owner would on occasion leave the dispute in order to serve a customer–a bar of soap, perfume, or a magic potion for regenerating hair.]

The pharmaceutical warehouse served as a Zionist center for many years. A stranger who would come in during those hours would have reached the conclusion that these Jews and the Zionist issue were more important than earning a living.

Bendery was not unusual. There were many towns and villages in Bessarabia where the Jews had similar set-ups which were the center for Zionism and lovers of Israel– adults and many young people. Many such groups were involved in the dream of redemption and the existence of the Jewish people.

Let these paragraphs serve as a small remembrance to those few saints who helped us to establish our State of Israel.

I.L. Yonatan

[From "Chapters about the Jews of Bessarabia", Nisan, 1958]

*

Hersh Kogan's granddaughter, who grew up in his home, says the following:

He was an intelligent and welcoming man and many people came to him for advice and help. Even priests arrived to discuss Biblical subjects as well as religious faith.

All through the Soviet regime he was afraid that he would be exiled to Siberia for his Zionist "sins". Many of his Christian friends stood by his side in bad times and saved him from persecution. Still, he suffered greatly because one of his granddaughters converted and married a Christian. He died at the age of 72 on 31.5.1941, about three weeks before the Romanians entered Bessarabia with the help of the Germans.

His granddaughter remembers well two episodes:

Once R. Hersh Kogan went to meet Bialik who was arriving in Bendery by train. They walked on the main street and Bialik, as was his habit, talked constantly. When they reached Kogan's home, Hersh invited him in saying:"This is my house where we can continue our conversation". However, as soon as they entered the home, Bialik stopped talking and did not say anything else. H. Kogan was sorry about this all his life.

He was very honest and served as a model to others. His granddaughter, as she recalls, wanted to make Aliyah with her boyfriend and Hersh Kogan was head of the Israeli office in Kishinev. However, he clearly informed his granddaughter that he would not give them certificates out of order and they could not influence him to change his mind.

[Page 189]

During that time Mr. Berger came from Kishinev and while he was visiting Yitzhak Grinboim he related that Hersh Kogan refused to award a certificate to his granddaughter and her boyfriend. Y. Grinboim wrote a special letter to the Israeli office in Kishinev and recommended the certificates be given. At the meeting when the certificates were discussed, Hersh Kogan, who was the chairman, announced: "This evening I am not chairing the meeting since you are discussing the awarding of certificates to my granddaughter and her husband". He promptly walked out.

Dr. Zvi Schwartzman
(Teacher of important people)
Translated by Ala Gamulka

The thousands of students of Dr. Zvi Schwartzman remember with deep admiration, to this day, the time they spent learning in his High School. He laid the cornerstone of the Hebrew High School in Bendery in 1912. It became a famous institution far and wide and many students from nearby villages came to acquire an education – an advanced Hebrew–national education.

It is no wonder that to this day Dr. Schwartzman is considered a pioneer in Hebrew education in southern Russia. He "did" before he "heard" before WWI. The leaders of Bendery, V. Weisser and his friends, representing a group of parents, turned to him and asked him to undertake the job. He gave up his own career in medicine and accepted their request. He was studying in Berlin after completion of a degree in Physics and Mathematics in the University of Odessa. He came to help his people by establishing a Hebrew High School in Bendery. He worked hard without any government financing. He first established the middle school [4 grades] and then he continued with the senior grades. It was a difficult task to formulate curriculum from nothing. The school was successful and produced thousands of graduates who were all well versed in Hebrew studies and were Lovers of Zion. Many of these students became famous in cultural, artistic and public fields. We mention some of them: "Ha'ohel" Theater actor Sh. Tsakhoval, z"l and Avraham Ben Yosef of the Kameri, the poet Zrubavel Gilead, the Zionist leader David Wertheim, z"l [he was a student and later a teacher in the school] and Prof. Yitzhak Fein, now in the United States. Among his students are members of the Knesset, famous doctors and other professionals.

Dr. Zvi Schwartzman

Dr. Schwartzman knew how to attract outstanding teachers who even produced textbooks in Hebrew. They became well known even outside of Russia. Dr. Schwartzman's illustrated Hebrew geography book appeared in the 1920s, Yitzhak Reznikov's mathematics book in Hebrew and Shmuel Gorin's history text are examples. These books were used in our country for many years.

Dr. Schwartzman suffered greatly throughout the different regimes– the Tsar, the Bolsheviks and the Romanian conquest. He held on with all his might to preserve the school in spite of all difficulties. That is why he was so beloved by his students and admirers. When he made Aliyah in the mid 1930s a big party was planned in his honor and many of his former students attended.

[Page 190]

Here in Eretz Israel he dreamed of creating his own school, but for many reasons it was not to happen, He worked as an organizer of the teachers section of the workers union. Even in this task his aristocratic personality came through. This is evidenced by the words of the educator Menahem Rodnitsky [Adir] [Hed Hakhinukh, Elul 1952] – to the bright personality of Dr. Zvi Schwartzman"– right after he died at the age of 82.

In spite of all his troubles, physical and mental, in the various cruel regimes, Dr. Schwartzman always knew how to foster personal relations with his students and to counsel them in their development and learning. Even today – 25 years after his death, the memory of Dr. Schwartzman still shines brightly. He was a dear man and has stayed in the hearts and minds of his students and his friends. This is the way it will always be for us.

Mordehai Sever

["Hed Hakhinukh", vol. 42, Page 10, 20 Cheshvan, 1968]

Special Reception in our Land for a Distinguished Educator

When Dr. Schwartzman made Aliyah, for the second time, in 1937, he immediately encountered the tough reality and the unpleasant treatment of the Education department dealing with immigrant teachers. They would have preferred a young recent graduate to a seasoned teacher of his age. The doors of the schools were closed to immigrant teachers and they could not find other employment to earn their keep. In Tel Aviv itself there were more than 50 unemployed teachers who were abandoned and who did not have enough food. They walked around like shadows showing depressed faces. The Teachers Federation did not rush to assist them, but other teachers felt their despair and pressured the Federation to help their unemployed brethren who would have died of hunger. The Federation, at the insistence of these teachers, decided to collect two days salary from employed teachers in order to help the newcomers. The branch in Tel Aviv chose a special committee to look after the unemployed and it opened an employment office.

Dr. Schwartzman was unemployed and he was asked to run this office. He was the right person in the proper place. He was a true friend and felt the despair of his colleagues. He looked after them and never stopped caring. He collected the two-day salary contributions and walked from school to school to do it.

Many times he heard unpleasant remarks from those teachers who tried not to pay in and he was insulted by the unemployed who almost lost their minds due to the despair they felt. However, Dr. Schwartzman kept his cool and did not care about his personal honor. He undertook a heavy burden for a small salary which was less than that of a new teacher. In the last year his health weakened, but he continued his work diligently.

He hid his pain until he collapsed on the job, during a meeting with members of the committee of the unemployed. Even in his last moments he did not want to bother anyone and he apologized for disturbing them.

It is only due to the dedication of Dr. Schwartzman that the employment office gained the respect and trust of others and succeeded in finding work for the unemployed teachers.

His students, friends and admirers keep his memory in their crying hearts. He died too early.

Menahem Adir

("Hed Hakhinukh", vol.42, Page 10, 20 Cheshvan, 1968)

Zelig Sofer
Translated by Ala Gamulka

I first met him when I was 8 as I was preparing for entrance exams to the Schwartzman Hebrew High School in Bendery. My tutor was a student in the high school – Donya Rivlin. During one of the lessons, Zelig, a friend of Donya, appeared and offered, of his own good will, to help me in Russian pronunciation according to grammatical rules. I felt his warmth and willingness to help from that first moment. He wanted to help me, a Jewish child who had difficulties with this foreign language– the language of the country at that time. When I discovered that he was good in art, his worth grew since I loved art.

Some years later, Zelig appeared on amateur Russian theater stages in our town. He appeared together with Senya [Simcha] Tsakhoval who usually had more serious parts. Zelig was very comfortable on the Russian stage and even introduced some Yiddishism in his performance. For this introduction of Yiddish terms he was nicknamed Zatz and this name stuck to him for the rest of his life.

In the mid 1920s I met Zelig when he was the first administrator of "Kumkum" [kettle] and later Matate [broom] – the early satiric theatres in our country. He was involved in running the theatre. He was tall and skinny and sometimes hunger showed in his eyes. He used to speak to me warmly about the poet Avigdor Hameiri, founder of the Kumkum, about his new creation, the song about Jerusalem seen from Mount Scopus. He would say:"If someone could make sure Avigdor Hameiri would be fed daily, it would be very important." He did not say one word about his own needs.

[Page 191]

Dr. Schwartzman, the principal of the high school in Bendery, arrived in 1936. I was among his first students, perhaps the first, to visit him in his school in Givat Hamoreh near Afula. A group of us decided to prepare an evening for him and we sent a note to all former students in our country. On 1 Adar 1936 we held a banquet which remains unforgettable in our memories. Zelig was the Master of Ceremonies of the party. Several former students gave speeches and there were skits and songs by S. Tsakhoval and David Weisser, z"l; these were reminiscent of evenings held in the high school in Bendery in the past.

In those years, 1936–1937, there were bloody attacks in the country. Gangs of unruly Arabs escalated the terror against the Jews by burning crops in the fields, destroying property, attacking settlements and murdering Jews of all ages only because they were Jews. The Mandate government decided to erect a fence in the North-Taggart Wall, along tens of kilometres.

The security situation worsened daily, especially near the open and wild borders of Syria and Lebanon. Gangs of terrorists and arms smugglers came through these parts. This was a wire fence 2 meters tall and measuring 6m in width over 4 iron columns.

There was serious unemployment in the country and thus there were many who were available for this work. It was decided, in spite of directives of the Mandate, to establish a row of Jewish settlements along the borders and in strategic points in the country.

On the night of 21.3.38 a large group of fence makers went to the north of the country. It was a time when the Arab gangs were attacking Jewish settlements and guards. The press reported daily about fires and shooting near Tiberias, in the fields, shots against the border police, murders on the roads, etc.

The camp in Hanita consisted of tents in the heart of a menacing Arab population, in areas far from other Jewish settlements. It was open to the bullets of the murderers. Many times the members of the camp had to go to the aid of the settlements being attacked. There were also victims among the members of the camp.

I was a reporter for "Davar" in the Upper Galilee and I came to the camp in Hanita. Among the hundreds of people I knew, Zelig Sofer suddenly appeared almost naked, quite tanned and wearing shorts on his long legs. Zelig was involved in carrying stones, gravel, building material, etc. He was one of the first to volunteer for this work.

"Shalom, Zelig!", "Shalom, Shalom, how are you?" It was a hurried conversation because time was short and the work was heavy. It was only during mealtime that we were to speak. Zelig, in his lovable simplicity, his eyes dark and burning, said: "There is a need and I volunteered!"

Many years have passed since then, I am in the north of the country and in Jerusalem and he is in the south. It was only sometimes that we meet hurriedly. Everyone is in a rush, but we speak of meeting more often. When I moved to Tel Aviv I discovered that Zelig was working at the airport in Lydda and later in the Zionist Organization of America building. Zelig still dreamed of the theatre because it was in his blood. Zelig then disappeared.

One morning the newspaper announced his death.

Zelig was good and did good deeds for others. He was a pioneer, a dreamer, a man of the theatre and our eternal fighter...

Our Zelig!

Mordehai Sever

Memories of Zelig Sofer

I met Zelig in 1926/7. I do not remember exactly how we met, but after a few minutes I felt as if I had known him a long time. He, like me, was crazy about the theatre and we became close immediately.

In 1927 the Kumkum theatre was founded by Avigdor Hameiri and Eliezer Donat and I was fortunate to be among the first actors. The troupe had 5 actors [among them– Rafael Klatchkin], the painter Ir–Shay and a stage hand. Our purpose was to present a literary cabaret with political satire on a small stage. We worked without an administrator at first, but soon Zelig undertook this role. We worked as a team and we barely earned our keep, but we were young and enthusiastic and nothing stood in our way. Zelig was always full of energy, but he was unable to use it because our horizons were quite narrow. We traveled the entire country in two months and soon we needed a new presentation.

[Page 192]

A year later there was a dispute within Kumkum between its director, the poet A. Hameiri, and its members [Zelig among them]. They left Hameiri and in 1928 founded the satirical theatre the Matate. The new artistic director was I.M. Daniel. Naturally, Zelig was the administrator of the Matate.

In addition to his energy, Zelig also was a graphic artist. He designed the first posters for the theatre. There were some really beautiful ones at the beginning.

When Zelig left Matate he opened an office for the selling of tickets to Habima when the troupe came to our land– at the end of the 1920s.

I did not see him for a long time after he began to work in the airport in Lydda, but then the artistic sense touched him again. I met him at the Zionist Organization of Americas house at different functions which he had planned. We met again just before he died.

He had a wonderful sense of humor and was a good friend –always ready to help those in need. It is too bad he died at a time which was so difficult, but was full of friendship and simplicity. Unfortunately, this is not true of present times…

Yaakov Timan, Actor

Yaakov Shveidky
Translated by Ala Gamulka

In those days, early in the 20th century, Yaakov immersed himself, together with some friends, in the establishment of a network of branches of Hashomer Hatzair in Bessarabia and Romania. He dedicated himself to preparing the youth for a life in Eretz Israel. We were fortunate to have him and we saw in him a wonderful counselor and educator. He knew how to prepare himself and to imbue the youth with his knowledge and strength. His friends and acquaintances loved him, especially the young children who were constantly involved with him.

The Jewish youth of that time were right in the middle of the ideological trends that existed in the general public as well as in the Jewish community. They would strive constantly –without being directed from above [there was no such above yet] – to acquire political knowledge, movement education and awareness of nation and socialism in addition to the needs of their Jewish background. Yaakov was well informed in these fields and had great instinct and he found himself attracting the youth to the Hashomer Hatzair movement.

Yaakov was one of the first in this arena and eventually he was among the leaders of the movement. In spite of his being younger than other leaders he showed great depth of knowledge in ancient and new Jewish culture. He also had a good background in general culture. This, in addition to his personal abilities, placed in the forefront of the movement.

Several of his friends and family members made Aliyah – some to kibbutzim, some to work on the roads, railroad or be security guards. However, Yaakov remained to look after the movement in the Diaspora. When he tried to make Aliyah the doors were closed and many like him, leaders of the movement, were forced to leave the semi–Fascist regime and to go to Argentina, France and other countries.

In France, Yaakov completed studies in Chemical Engineering and established a family. His dream was still in his heart and when he visited Israel a few years ago he even promised to send his surviving son and daughter [his oldest daughter died in the Holocaust] to come there. After this visit his daughter remained in Gan Shmuel for 6 months and decided to remain. However, Yaakov himself did not live to see this happen as he died of a heart attack.

Three years have passed since then and we are still mourning our loss.

Friends and Members of the Family
[Al Hamishmar, 6.9.1965]

Avraham Wertheim
Translated by Ala Gamulka

Avraham Wertheim

He was the son of Rabbi Shimon–Shlomo, the 8th generation after the Baal Shem Tov. He, too, had a good reputation. At the beginning of his activities he helped those who were less fortunate. When the Joint came to the aid of the Jewish victims after WWI, he was one of its representatives and was situated in Brisk, Lithuania.

[Page 193]

He had a warm approach and a natural love for other human beings and these attributes led the way for all those who were in need in those terrible times. He contributed greatly to the success of ORT in his area and later in Brisk. He eventually made his way to Warsaw after the Civil War, wandering through Ukraine. From there he made Aliyah and settled well. He established a family and continued his public activities. He first cooperated with the late Dr. Bernstein–Cohen in redemption of land, but he then joined the Jewish Agency at the request of Yitzhak Grinboim. In his new position Wertheim successfully struggled with the prohibitions of the Mandate.

When the state was founded he transferred to government work and became head of the labour relations department. He brought with him a background of seeking justice and wishing to establish truth in all matters. He was fortunate to serve the State of Israel and our country was lucky to have such a man to be one of its founders. His legacy continues to this day.

Haim Radi

[Davar 14.11.1968]

David Wertheim
Translated by Ala Gamulka

He was a son of Rabbi Shimon–Shlomo and was born in Bendery in 1896, the offspring of a veteran rabbinic family that had served in Bendery for 7 generations. The family members were descendants of the Baal Shem Tov and many greats in the Hassidic movement. He absorbed the religious–nationalistic atmosphere in his father's house– Judaism and popular Hassidism. He studied in heders and in the Hebrew Gymnasia of Rabbi Azriel Hildesheimer in Berlin. He served in the Russian army in WWI.

At the age of 17 he founded a Zionist youth group in Bendery. The elite of the Jewish students joined and they established a Hebrew library in Bendery. He had an excellent background in Judaism and in general education and spent 20 years as an outstanding pedagogue in Bessarabia and later in the United States where he taught Hebrew. He had a great influence on the youth and brought them closer to popular Zionism and to the Zeirei Zion movement. He also taught them the excitement of Hassidism, love of Israel and Zion.

David Wertheim

In 1923 he arrived in the United States and took an active part in popularizing the Zeirei Zion movement among American youth. Haim Greenberg, z"l, and Dr. David Rabalsky came to the United States and together they led the movement until it amalgamated with Poalei Zion in 1930. The new union was called "Zeirei Zion–Poalei Zion." In 1931, one year later, he was chosen as the general secretary of the new movement and he remained in the position for the next 13 years. He contributed his energies to the Zionist

Labor movement in the United States, to Keren Kayemet, United Jewish Appeal, Histadrut Campaign, Zionist congresses and the Zionist Council. He was involved in all Zionist activities in the United States. He was also active in Labor Zionist [Farband] and the World Union. An outstanding speaker, he ably brought Zionism, for many years, to the United States and many countries in Latin America to many Jews. His speeches, in Hebrew and Yiddish, were full of Biblical references, folklore, Hassidism, pioneer life in Eretz Israel. He had many followers who listened to him as they did to Zvi Maslyansky and Dr. Shmariyahu Levin and his influence was deeply felt by Jews in United States. He took part in all Zionist Congresses beginning with the 15th in 1927 and ending with the 23rd in 1951. He was a member of the Zionist Executive Committee from 1935. From 1945 and until his death [with a recess of two years] he was the director of the Histadrut Appeal in the United States and he brought the message of the Histadrut to all parts of the United States and Latin America.

[Page 194]

When the State of Israel was founded he tried to live in Israel and served as the head of HIAS for two years. For family reasons he was forced to return to his public positions in the Diaspora.

The constant travelling and the difficult work with the Histadrut Appeal, for many years in Latin America, weakened him physically and caused heart disease. He died in Havana, Cuba on 10.4.53 while he was visiting there as part of his job.

He died while on national duty for the Zionist cause and he was only 57. He was buried in New York. He left a wife [Hebrew teacher] and a daughter.

His memory will remain as one of the greatest pioneers that emerged from Bendery in this century.

Aryeh–Leib and Nadia Blank
Translated by Ala Gamulka

Nadia Blank   Aryeh–Leib Blank

It is impossible to write about life in our town and the people in it without mentioning the names of two patrons of its institutions – Aryeh–Leib and Nadia Blank.

Aryeh–Leib Blank owned a large flour mill and a sawmill in the district. He was born in 1874 to his father Alter and his mother Mirel Blank. He was raised in a traditional observant Jewish home, but he later became more progressive. This was the prevailing mood in the Jewish world in Russia at the time. The Blanks conducted their home in this atmosphere.

The traditional Jewish education Aryeh–Leib had received in his childhood left its stamp on his character. As all other heretics, R. Leib knew the needs of his people. He was close to the authorities and many Jews used his protection when they needed help. This was especially evident in 1914. Since he was close to the governor of the district he was able to free many Jews from military service. He served on the board of directors of the high school and the Girls' school. He helped many students who could not afford the tuition. Also he was active on the Executive Committee of the Jewish community together with the pharmacist Vineshneker, in spite of their having a difference of opinion.

[Page 195]

Many times he was asked by R. Shloimke to donate to Jewish institutions in town and he never refused. Anyone in need – a poor craftsman, a wagon driver, a widow, a poor bride – knew that he would never refuse them. He was involved with his businesses, but when he turned 30 he hired a tutor to teach him Talmud and Mishna. He chose R. Avraham Dayan who came on a daily basis to learn Gmara with him. It eventually became too hard for him physically and he had to interrupt his studies.

He died peacefully in 1920 and was buried in Kishinev. Since he was a great philanthropist, the Hevra Kaddisha refused to take money for his interment.

His wife, Nadia, was a great help to him and was very active in various Jewish and Russian institutions in the disbursement of funds to the poor.

When a stream of Jewish refugees arrived from Russia and as a Typhus epidemic came, Nadia erected special shacks for the sick. She dedicated herself to their well being, but became ill herself. When she recuperated she moved to Paris with some of her daughters. She died there.

P. Bendersky

Israel Blank

Israel Blank A leader of the General Zionists in Bendery

Noah Lifshitz
Translated by Ala Gamulka

Noah Lifshitz was among the early educators and molders of the Zionist generation in Bendery. He was considered to be the mainstay of Zionism and the young generation leaned on him.

Noah Lifshitz was born in Kishinev at the end of the 1870s.

He spent his young years in the yeshiva of R. Shalom Perlmutter in Kishinev where he was known as a gifted Talmud and Torah student. In his youth he was also interested in general education. After much travel he arrived in Odessa where he studied pedagogy. At the same time he joined Hovevei Zion under the leadership of M. Dizengoff and he became its secretary.

Noah Lifshitz

In 1890 –together with the Hovevei Zion group from Kishinev–he was chosen as a delegate to the first convention of Hovevei Zion in Odessa under the chairmanship of Dr. Pinsker. Together with Dr. Bernstein–Cohen he took an active part in the conference. Upon his return he was elected secretary of the movement in Kishinev and he undertook, with M. Dizengoff, to spread the national dream among the Jews of Bessarabia.

[Page 196]

After many years of public and Zionist activity in his town, Noah arrived in Bendery in early 1920s. His career as a private Hebrew tutor began here. He taught children of Jewish merchants who wished to give their children a Jewish education in addition to the secular studies they followed in government schools. He made his living giving these private lessons. He served as the general secretary of the Zionist movement in town. Together with Dr. Shlomo Bendersky, he was in charge of the postal agency of the Bendery district. This had been decided after the First Congress. Noah Lifshitz did most of the work and he fulfilled his task with dedication. The elite of the Jewish and the Russo–Jewish intelligentsia always surrounded him. He was admired for his modesty and gentle demeanor, his extensive knowledge in Jewish culture and the classical Russian one.

Since he wanted to draw the youth, especially the students, to the Zionist movement, he opened a library where it was possible to acquire knowledge of Torah and Jewish culture. He collected about 300 books which served as a basis for the library.

The first librarian in this library was his oldest daughter, Esther. She came on the Second Aliyah with the first pioneers. The library was at first in a room of the Zionist club. However, the Tsarist police came and locked it [there was probably a denunciation]. Such institutions were illegal during Tsarist times. Lifshitz was sent to court. After much effort –including those who believed in secular culture for the Jews in Russia – the case was dismissed and a permit arrived from Peterburg (St. Petersburg) allowing the reopening of the library.

At first the books were brought to the home of Lifshitz as if it were his own private collection. Once the permit arrived, two rooms were rented in the courtyard of Yefifanov and this was extended with the help of certain people in town. It was then known as the Russian–Jewish Library and contained several thousand new books. The library also had progressive and liberal Russian newspapers. In addition there were political meetings where many arguments ensued. It was like a club for the Jewish intelligentsia in town. The second librarian was the third daughter of Lifshitz, Rachel, She, in turn, gave the position over to Yasha Bendersky [son of Dr. Bendersky].

Zvi Kasp and his family

Noah Lifshitz was highly involved in the life of the Jewish community and was very well liked. He organized the Jewish Bank which gave loans with convenient conditions to the poorer elements in town. He was chosen as the chief bookkeeper of the bank and he remained there until it was closed when Bessarabia was conquered by the Romanians.

After the bank was closed Noah Lifshitz went back to teaching and was accepted as a Jewish Studies teacher in the Russian Talmud Torah supervised by I. Tiomkin.

In 1921 he made Aliyah with the rest of his family. He earned his living by serving as the primary secretary in a school in Tel Aviv.

In Tel Aviv he found his son Yosef whom he had sent in 1910 to study at the Herzliah High School and his daughter Esther who arrived in 1911 and married a fellow townsman, a member of Poalei Zion, Kasp – owner of a large printing press; his second daughter Malka who made Aliyah a year after her older sister and worked in the workers kitchen of "Achdut" on Nahalat Binyamin Street.

Noah Lifshitz died at an old age on 15 Elul 1935 and was buried in Nahalat Yitzhak in Tele Aviv.

P. Bendersky

Hanina Krachevsky
Translated by Ala Gamulka

Hanina, son of Yitzhak, Krachevsky was born in 1877 in the village of Petrovka [Yehupets] in Bessarabia. During his youth his parents moved to Bendery and he studied at the Talmud Torah. Even as a young child he stood out for his singing voice and his fine musical ear. Whenever he heard a song he was able to repeat it exactly, to the great delight of his family. They were all musical. In school his clear sweet voice was heard above the voice of the other children. He got the attention of Mr.Shkhanovsky, a teacher in the Talmud Torah, who was also a cantor. He gently looked after the child and taught him musical notes and to play the piano. The child wished to sing in a choir of one of the cantors, but his parents were vehemently against it.

[Page 197]

Hanina Krachevsky

By chance, the famous cantor Zeidel Rovner came to Bendery and he convinced Hanina's parents to allow the boy to join his choir. Finally, the parents agreed and the young boy moved to Kishinev, Zeidel Rovner's home town. The fame of this young singer spread quickly and the synagogue always had a large crowd that came to listen to his lovely voice. The news even reached the government offices and the governor, a lover of music, came with other high officials to hear the young boy as he sang solo. His beautiful voice sounded like silver bells and the governor was enchanted and praised him profusely. Hanina only stayed a short time at Zeidel Rovner's. The boy's fame with his beautiful soprano voice spread to other cities. A man came to

Kishinev from Kherson and convinced the boy to come to the Choral Synagogue in Kherson. Hanina remained there for many years and learned music from the choir leader.

When he was 22 years old, Hanina Krachevsky went to Warsaw where he passed a test and became the conductor of an orchestra and a choir. He spent some time as conductor of a military band. He felt the need for musical creation and he did not want to sing holy prayers in the Diaspora. He left his job and made Aliyah. This is where his creative work really began. Eighteen years ago every teacher was able to create something from nothing. Our Late friend was one of the first to pave the way among other educators here. He arrived full of love and the creative spirit and his mouth and heart were full of song. Soon after he arrived he began to teach singing in the Girls School and in Gymnasia Herzliah. From the first moment his colleagues felt his creative strength. Before he came on the scene singing in school was dull and forced. Noah was the first to teach children solfege and he organized choirs with two or four different voices. His choirs were well organized, harmonious and in good taste. He often chose folk songs or synagogue prayers that he loved. In addition he also taught classical European singing. He was the first to establish orchestras, wind and string, in the Gymnasia. He also taught in the Teachers College where the students learned to play the Concertina. The Hanukah parties in the Gymnasia were always a special event in Tel Aviv. The songs he taught, his own creation or that of others, were sung throughout the country and even outside it. When he did not have prepared songs he worked hard day and night to write new ones. He was an enthusiastic person and he knew how to excite others and to encourage them to work in his favorite field. When he found students, or just other youth, who were musically talented, he would teach them privately.

[Hanina Krachevsky (Top Centre Choir Conductor) speaking to M. Dizengoff and Haim Weitzman]

[Page 198]

Many of those who had been his students established choirs and taught music in many parts of the country. His crowning glory was the large choir of close to 200 people that gave concerts in Jerusalem and Tel Aviv. When the Hebrew University was officially opened he was the conductor of this large choir. It left an indelible mark on many spectators.

His road was not always paved with roses. He had much sorrow in his work. He was always afraid that he could not succeed in all he had planned. All this in spite of the many compliments he received from his colleagues and students. He was always fearful that he had not done enough. He wished for perfection. Perhaps this is why he appealed to listeners with his songs. This is why so many people are mourning the first Hebrew music teacher in the schools of Eretz Israel.

I. Dushman

Reception for Lord Balfour in the Tel Aviv City Hall

Haya Glass
Translated by Ala Gamulka

We carry silently the burden of our life

Like camels walking in the desert

With gloom we sprawl on the earth

While the storm is strengthening

When the caravan stops

Because our burden is too heavy

Your look from the clearing brightens my way

I will now be able to carry the burden...

Zrubavel 1932

Haya Glass

The poet Zrubavel was the son of Haya Glass, z"l.

She was born on 8 Elul 1887 and died on 26 Tevet 1964

Haya was born in Anayev in south Russia to a working family– the Bierbrier Family. She moved to Bendery in her childhood.

Haya, the oldest daughter, graduated from a girls' professional school and began to bring earnings home in her youth. She was a master seamstress. She also joined the Zionist youth movement – Halutzei Zion – later Zeirei Zion and was very active in it. She met her life's partner in the movement. Together with Haim Glass she prepared herself for Aliyah. Their first child, Zrubavel was born on the eve of WWI and their move to Eretz Israel was delayed.

The war and additional years of travel and trouble delayed the Aliyah of the young family until 1923. Mother and child arrived and went to Ein Harod, but the father came only two years later. In Ein Harod their second son Yuval was born.

Haya was one of the oldest women in Ein Harod when she arrived. However, her energy, life experience and capability helped her integrate into this young and active society.

[Page 199]

She did everything other women did– cooking, taking care of the children, laundry and sewing. In season she worked in the fields and the orchards. Most of her time was spent in her profession of seamstress. Later when there was a need for orthopedic belts she learned how to sew them and helped others as well.

She was pleased with all the achievements of Ein Harod and the movement and she felt their pain when there were divisions among the members.

In her last years she suffered greatly, but she always liked to speak about Ein Harod, of the early days when she walked without shoes near Mount Gilboa until the present time when the settlement had grown.

She was the first member of Ein Harod to have a great-grandchild. She was the first of the dynasty in the kibbutz.

The House of the Glass Family

I met Haya in 1910, if I remember correctly, at a meeting of friends held in Bendery. The purpose of the meeting was to establish Halutzei Zion and people came from all over Bessarabia. Many of them were students, children of middle class families. Haya was one of the few members from the proletariat among us. She had been a seamstress from early youth and that was definitely a working profession.

We wished to bring to the movement working youth and we were quite happy when we were able to convert the few members of the proletariat into active Zionist socialists. This is what Haya was. She learned Hebrew from the man who became her husband – Hebrew teacher Haim Glass. He made Aliyah in 1909, but he became ill with a serious case of malaria and was forced to return to Russia for treatments. On his way back to Eretz Israel he stopped in Bendery. He became involved in Zionist activities and encouraged the youth to dream of Aliyah. He married Haya and their first born was called Zrubavel.

Their home became our center. All activities were held there and it became a home full of warm hospitality, always open to our group of Zionists.

The home of the Glass family forever remains in the memory of all the members and especially in those who made Aliyah.

Rafael Shufman

(Kfar Yekhezkel)

Yitzhak Reznikov
Translated by Ala Gamulka

Yitzhak Reznikov

Our unforgettable master teacher Yitzhak, son of Baruch-Moshe Reznikov, was born on 18.10.1886 in Ukraine and he died on 23.12.1843 in Jerusalem.

Issar Borisovitch, as we always called him, was a model figure as a great teacher and educator, a counselor and a good friend to his students. He was a scholar, well educated with a good sense of humor. He was loved and admired by everyone who met him. He was a close loyal friend of the principal of the Hebrew High School in Bendery- Dr. Zvi Schwartzman- and he helped him in many events that befell this important institution. He left his stamp on his students for the rest of their lives. He was close to them in age and was their friend in addition to being their teacher. He helped his outstanding students to perform on stage in all school parties.

In spite of all this he was quite modest and at times he was even an introvert. Everyone knew he had a wonderful personality, and that he was an outstanding teacher and a gentle soul. He was involved in his people's culture and had been a student of a famous Yeshiva in Odessa directed by Mendele Moss and a young Rabbi. They were both authors of texts in history and mathematics in the 1920s in Bessarabia. These textbooks were even used in Eretz Israel.

After 7 years of teaching in the High School in Bendery he became a principal of a Hebrew school in Kishinev. He subsequently travelled to Germany to complete university studies and to teach Hebrew. In Breslau he organized "intensive courses" in Hebrew. The courses were famous and among his students one could find spiritual and political leaders of German Jewry. He published the Hebrew newspaper [with vowels] "Hagesher". It preceded "Hegue" and "Omer" in our country. He also edited a Hebrew–German dictionary, workbooks for learning Hebrew and a "Small popular library" that had easy to read literature. He also translated, in the 1930s, the book "Ofir",

[Page 200]

by Meder, into Hebrew. It was published by "Amanut" in Tel Aviv.

When he made Aliyah he suffered, at first, absorption problems and difficulty in integration into the work force. However, he organized a series of lectures in Beit Haam and in the Workers Seminar in Jerusalem. He was eventually offered a position as a teacher of Bible, Hebrew language and literature in the senior grades of 'Rehavia' in Jerusalem. He was well liked by his students and colleagues. He died while he was still trying to instill knowledge in his students. He is mourned by all his students, friends and acquaintances.

His shining memory will always accompany us.

Mordehai Sever

Dr. P. Yaroslavsky
Translated by Ala Gamulka

Dr. P. Yaroslavsky

Dr. P. Yaroslavsky who is now a senior citizen resides with us in Eretz Israel. He lived in Bendery from 1918 to the end of 1922. He was a dentist and also was quite active in public and Zionist circles.

His main activities were:

1. He organized the branch of Zeirei Zion in Bendery. The branch had had ups and downs previously and he served as its chairman.

2. He founded, with a group of young workers, Maccabi in Bendery. In addition to sports activities the group also took part in national projects, such as different funds.

He also helped in the development of ORT in Bendery.

[Page 202]

The Third Aliyah

[Page 203]

Bendery in the Past and Under the Soviet Regime
by Yoseph Raviv (Rehovot)
Translated by Ala Gamulka

"Numerous Clausus"

Bendery, the city of my birth, stays in my imagination from the day I began to study in the Heder of my noble teacher, Yaakov Lonievsky. I particularly remember the important task I was given. The water carrier used to bring a barrel of water twice a week and the Rabbi trusted me with the job of counting how many times he went back and forth from the wagon to the container which stood at the entrance. Why was I given this job? Probably because he thought I knew arithmetic. This fact also influenced my future career because I was accepted at the Schwartzman Hebrew High School.

From Lonievsky's Heder I went to Eli Gamburd's Heder and I studied there every afternoon. (In the mornings I attended – as did all boys my age – the public school "prihodskaya").

When I completed my studies with good marks, I applied to the municipal high school (Gorodskaya). On the first day of school, I came with my father only to find out that although I was eligible for entrance, they were not accepting any Jews this year. There was a "flood" of Russian students. Of course, I could not fight this decision, but I started to cry. My father took pity on me and suddenly said: "Let's go to the Schwartzman High School". At the Schwartzman High School – studies were just beginning – I was received by Gregory Yaakovitz himself. When my father related my story he said: "True, the deadline for accepting students has passed, but I will test you in arithmetic and we will see!" I passed the test successfully and I heard him tell my father: "I do not want to give up on such a student". And so I became a High School student.

I spent eight years of my life in the Schwartzman High School. They were full of wonderful experiences and events together with other Jewish students. This came after spending three years of studying with Russian students. I was involved in Jewish life and I studied Hebrew and Bible with Israeli teachers, such as Naphtali Zigelboim, Moshe Epstein and others. They instilled in us a love of Eretz Israel.

Zionist activities and an argument with the "Bund"

After the 1917 revolution, as Zionist activity grew in Bendery, my love for Eretz Israel became even greater. I was still very young, but I remember the Zionist gathering in Bendery in the Dakdenas cinema hall, soon after the revolution. The "bund" wanted to us to fail, but the Zionists like H. Pustan, Hersh Kogan, Israel Blank and others stood their ground. To this day I remember Pustan's words to the "Bund" members: "You will not dare stop the redemption of Eretz Israel. The dream of Eretz Israel is stronger than all of you!" In essence, from that day on I saw myself as a partner in the realization of the dream of the redemption of the people of Israel in their own land.

I was involved with Hashomer Hatzair and Zeirei Zion. I participated in the selling of shekels, the emptying of Jewish National Fund boxes, the selling of fruits from Eretz Israel on Tu B'Shvat, in discussions about life in Eretz Israel and I read Hebrew books. When Hechalutz came to Bendery we saw our way to fulfilling the dream of the redemption of Eretz Israel.

The chapter of Zeirei Zion grew seriously and we moved from the home of Sonia and David Pisterov to the Goldfarb Hall. There we even had lecturers from the central office in Kishinev, such as Leib Glantz, David Wertheim and Haver Skvirsky. The latter knew how to excite the youth with the idea of settling Eretz Israel. From that time on we strove to bring to fruition the dream of working in the Land, to take part in the establishment of settlements and in defending them. These youth groups were also influenced by the Aliyah of several families from Bendery. Among them were friends and relatives such as the Goldmans, Sverdlik (Moshele Shoichet) and the family of Moshe Holodenko.

Some to the university and some to Hachshara and Eretz Israel

When I graduated from the Schwartzman high school in 1923, I saw that many of my classmates dispersed to universities in Prague, Ghent, Brussels, etc. I was prepared to go to Ghent, but it seems that my wish to make Aliyah postponed that trip and brought me to the Hechalutz on Benderskaya Street in Kishinev. I remember being asked by many good Jews in Bendery – who feared my going to Eretz would influence their children – "Do you really think that you will bring redemption? Would you really exchange the University for hewing of wood and hard labor?"

[Page 204]

Zeirei Zion in Bendery in the 1920s

I decided to fulfill my dream. Hundreds and thousands of youth in Bessarabia would forgo – like me – higher education and employment. They burned bridges behind them and went to Hechalutz. They went for preparation in Hahshara so they could fit in to their new lives in Eretz Israel. I was in the first group in the Hechalutz branch in Iasi in Romania. I remember well the wonderful reception by the Romanian Jews. They opened the doors of their factories to us and helped in every way possible. The location of the Hechalutz center in Iasi was in Pakurer and it became the social center for Jewish youth in town.

I left home with great sadness, but I believed that eventually I would bring my family to Eretz. Indeed, after the 1929 events my sister and her husband came. They were followed by our parents.

The pioneers had great strength and courage during these hard times and they were ready to do anything for their country. They formed the basis for the founding of the State of Israel.

Work and Defence

We lived in the valley for many years and we then moved to the centre of the country. My wife was Shulamit, daughter of the famous educator, Baruch Holodenko. Our three children were born in Moshav Ga'aton near Rehovot. We were under fire in those days and we learned to defend ourselves with guns. We knew no one else would help us. "If I am not for myself, who is for me?"

Our life on the border taught my wife to protect the children during shootings and to help me, in free times, to defend our home.

And so we worked hard in our fields in daytime and stood guard with a gun at night. Together with our three children we lived to see the founding of our state. Two of our children live in border settlements.

Still, with all this, we did not forget our hometown of Bendery and we dreamed of seeing it again. Indeed, when the Soviet Union permitted Israelis to visit their relatives in the old country we decided to fulfill our dream and to visit the remnants of the Holodenko family in Kishinev and to go to Bendery.

[Page 205]

Visit to Bendery after 40 years

In 1964 i went to Kishinev with my wife Shulamit and we also obtained a permit to visit Bendery. We happily drove to Kishinev (accompanied, of course by a "guide"). This was after an absence of over 40 years. As we passed through the streets I did not know which way to look – at the many changes in town, at the Jewish guide who was pretending not to notice and was speaking quickly about Bendery – as if we had never been there before. I wanted to ask him: "Dear comrade! When will we go to the Sadigura Synagogue where I prayed with my parents all those years? What about Schwartzman's Hebrew High School where I spent my wonderful youth? Where are all the Jewish institutions and the various youth movements?" However, I could only think about these questions–and to mourn in secret. We came to the house of relatives. The woman did not look at us first, but at the person behind us. It was only when the door was closed that she opened her heart. We felt the longing for the times when the family was together: father making Kiddush over wine, mother blessing the candles and the house full of Shabbat warmth. All this had disappeared from Bendery and had been replaced by a cold and foreign atmosphere all around us. The desire not to show feelings and not to cause suspicion, the connection between relatives and visitors only existed in looks exchanged secretly.

The Jewish atmosphere no longer exists in Bendery. We found there Jews estranged from their Judaism, afraid to be seen with a relative from Israel. They were almost hanging in the air as if any light breeze could topple them. The question that was felt was: what will be our future?

This is a quick summary of the Soviet Union 50 years after the revolution. Everything seen through a Jewish prism was painful and desperate. The energy and knowledge of the Jews has been lost and we really need them to help build our homeland.

I have reached the conclusion that there is no hope for the continuity of the Jews there and that they will be lost if they do not find a way out.

Ruins from the past

Our big dream to see our home city turned into a sad and strange reality. We left Bendery without finding even a thin thread that would connect the rich Jewish past of Bendery with the dour present. One no longer hears the Yiddish language – neither in the street nor in the home. Anyone who does not speak Russian had difficulty in communicating even with those closest to him. Only the elderly still remember the language, but it is strange to speak to them in Yiddish because they switch to Russian. Not one Bendery Jew is willing to speak about the past either due to fear or because they wish to forget what cannot be helped. Most of the residents of Bendery, whether Jewish or not, seemed like strangers in my eyes. No one remembered the previous names of the streets. It was difficult to be objective and to look at the progress of the city in some areas. We knew the Jews were not part of all this and are only tolerated there. It hurt to see the constant fear in the eyes of our relatives and the question: "What are doing for us?"

It is difficult to explain to them that there is not much we can do in spite of our strong desires to do so. They long for our homeland, but they only hear about it in closed rooms, in whispers and with lowered heads. Their eyes are filled with worry about young and old. What will happen to us? In spite of the freedom and absence of Jewish life, they still want their children to be among Jews. They do not want them to forget their heritage. There is comparison between the vibrant Jewish life in Bendery of 50 years ago and the weak and strange existence at present. The only hope is that a day will come when these good Jews will join us in our free homeland.

We left Bendery with a breaking heart saying: Let us meet again in our land!

Water Carrier

[Page 206]

Signposts to Eretz Israel
by David Weiser, z"l (Petach Tikva)
Translated by Ala Gamulka

Painful childhood among the non-Jewish children

I was brought to Bendery from Ukraine at the age of five. We lived there in an unfriendly atmosphere among Christians, the people of the "Black century" who considered all Jews as thorns in their sides. Obviously, as a young Jewish boy, my life was not easy among these people. I was beaten often for no reason. I did not accept this treatment silently and I repaid them.

One day, when I was nine years old, I had to leave home and hide for about one month. The reason for this was as follows: I returned the beatings on one of my torturers to the point that he was crippled for the rest of his life. I returned home and I was fortunate that my parents reached an agreement with the injured party. I lost all contact with the non-Jewish children, but I did not have any Jewish ones either. I was quite lonely.

For two years I moved from one Heder to another and from one Rabbi to another. The last one I studied with was R. Avremele, "the Redhead". He was proficient in slapping and other children suffered along with me.

My father–Velvel (Zeev) Weiser, z"l–was a community leader, well versed in Jewish topics. He was also proficient in Russian and knew the ways of the land. He was known as a well-educated man and he was quite active in Zionist affairs in those days.

My mother, Sheindl Veinshteyn, came from a family of judges. She was intelligent, smart and beautiful. She made sure there was an income in the household. We had many guests from the elite of the Christian community. They respected her and called her "Beautiful, smart Sheindl".

David Weiser, Z"L, Speaking at an Evening in Memory of Dr. Tzvi Schwartzman

(Evening took place in Tel Aviv to commemorate the 25th anniversary of the death of Dr. Schwartzman)

My father takes care of my education

My father did his utmost to make me independent and to have me acquire an education in Hebrew and in Russian. My first steps in Hebrew were taken in the school of the teacher, Ben–Tzion Gratzenberg.

[Page 207]

He taught Hebrew in Hebrew, in contrast with the Heders of those days. I am grateful to this teacher for awakening in me my love for our holy language. In this school, for the first time, a Hebrew play was staged. I had a part in "On the banks of the Jordan River". Afterwards, my father sent me to the Tarbut School which was run by the talented teacher and proud Jew–Mr. Shlomo Ben Tzvi Leandres.

A year later, I passed the entrance exams and was accepted in the municipal high school. I found there a highly anti–Semitic atmosphere. My father was worried and said: "What will become of my son?" My father did not only worry about me, he also cared about the social and cultural conditions encountered by other Jewish children. These children were unable to enter public schools. He then came up with an idea–to open a Hebrew high school in our town. Together with his friends, Moshe Haham, z"l and Israel Batzman, z"l, he obtained a permit to open such a school. They invited Dr. Tzvi Ben Yaakov Schwartzman, from Balta, Ukraine, to be the principal of the school. He was a brilliant man, well educated in the sciences and also a very gentle and warm hearted man. He was an outstanding educator.[1] (I spoke about him at the memorial evening on 22.11.1967–25 years after his death)

What did the Schwartzman Hebrew High School mean to us?

When the school first opened with 4 classes it was a pre–high school. There was great happiness in the Jewish community. Jewish children no longer needed the charity of the non–Jews. Four years later there were 8 classes and the title High School was proudly posted on the gates.

Young Jews came in hordes from surrounding towns and villages to be nurtured in the school. I, too, transferred to the school and I entered the fifth level. I encountered a pure Jewish atmosphere and I could now breathe it in. Soon I made new friends. Our school was well known throughout Russia and even outside it. This was due to the high academic level. Dr. Schwartzman managed to hire a staff of outstanding teachers. Among them were Itzhak Borisovitz Reznikov, David Wertheim (the rabbi's son), Nafatli Zigelboim as well as other cultured Jewish educators. We acquired our knowledge through love for the language and our homeland. It is also important to mention the non–Jewish teachers who always took part in our celebrations at Purim and Chanukah: Dimitri Yeforovich Nikolai, drama teacher and critic, who directed our plays and Dimitri Soveiletch Pirlik who conducted our string orchestra. They both loved us in spite of their being observant Christians. May their memory be a blessing eternally.

We must remember that the school also educated some famous people. These were Professor Yitzhak Fein, now in America, and my childhood pal Simcha (Senya) Tzahoval, z"l, an excellent actor in Israel. His name became well known in the Diaspora when the "Ohel" troupe made a tour. I must also mention here Yitzhak Natani (Natanzon), a lawyer and an important figure in the Mapam in England, Yosef Kushnir, a lawyer in Haifa and a former member of the Knesset and Eliahu Shaposhnik, a doctor in the Dizengoff clinic in Tel Aviv. There were others who were active in cultural and artistic circles in our country.

Schwartzman Hebrew High School Teachers and Students (1915–1916)

[Page 208]

A tale about a deserter from the Passover Fund

Our town was blessed with the publication of two newspapers that honestly reflected life in our community and in the Jewish Diaspora. These were: Bessarabski Telegraph (Bessarabia Telegraph) and Yuzni Krai (Southern Corner). There was a reporter who wrote under the name of "Yurick". He was a sharp guy, a good listener with penetrating eyes. He was aware of all that was near and far and knew about different peoples and various languages. Nothing escaped his attention and we tell a story about him:

On the eve of Passover the community leaders levied a tax on the wealthier members to help needier members. It was Maot Hitin (kamkha depaskha).

One of the influential members of our town, Anonymous (I deliberately do not mention his name since he passed away many years ago), refused to donate saying: "The amount I was ordered to pay is slightly exaggerated". These words reached Yurick and he wrote a scathing article denouncing Anonymous. At the end he added "It is easier to put Mr. Kradonsky, owner of the cinema "Decadence" through the eye of a needle than to receive a donation from him".

The matter was settled in a positive way. Kradonsky complained that he was not as heavy and large as described by Yurick. He said he only weighed about 150 kgs.

Bendery helps its brethren

In 1918 the town changed its appearance when hundreds of Jews, refugees from wars and pogroms, came to us from Ukraine. The community grew and the Jews of Bendery opened their warm hearts to help their brethren. Many of the refugees were housed by relatives, but the rest were looked after by the community leaders. Everyone was promised honest earnings.

In 1919, the students of the graduating class were organized to teach courses to the Jewish population in general and the working class in particular. We prepared them for imminent Aliyah to Eretz Israel. We received special funds from the community and from individuals to cover expenses.

Pioneers of the Third Aliyah

Hava and Pinhas Bendersky, Roza Tiomkina and Penina Wertheim

We, the pioneers of the Third Aliyah

In 1920, I graduated from the Schwartzman Hebrew High School and that August we sailed as a group of four from the port in Galatz, Romania to Turkey. We were on the way to our homeland–Eretz Israel. In Turkey we were joined by Pinhas Bendersky and his wife Yeva (Hava), her sister Roza Tiomkin and Penina Wertheim. Penina later became one of the first registered nurses graduating from Hadassah. Together we reached the port of Jaffa in the "Mahmudia" on 14.11.1920. We then lost contact with Bendery.

In 1936 an evening was organized in Tel Aviv by Zelig Sofer and other students of the Hebrew High School. It was held in honor of Gregory

Yakovlevich Schwartzman and his wife Esfira Borisovna. They had just made Aliyah and there were many friends attending. Everyone reminisced with sketches from previously staged plays in the school.

The grand past of our young years in Bendery will never be forgotten.

Footnote

The late author was chairman of the event and conducted it with humor and talent. Hundreds of participants–students and friends of the Schwartzman Hebrew High School appreciated his work. Return

[Page 209]

On a New Road
by Leah Shteiner (Tel Aviv)
Translated by Ala Gamulka

When Bessarabia was conquered by the Romanians in 1918 the Jews did not lose their national freedom and their lot was not like that of their poor brothers in Russia. How should one celebrate this freedom? Our town–Bendery–had always moved slowly. After WWI, when it was separated from Russia, it was left poorer and emptier. There were no factories to provide employment and no post high school institutions. There was no challenge for the youth. This situation sent many of them towards Communism and thus the Romanian authorities became suspicious of all residents. This led to denouncements and arrests.

In those days I was a student in the Sixth Form at the Schwartzman Hebrew High School. All the students in my class had to carry their Identity cards at all times and they were to present themselves monthly at the offices of the Secret Police. We suffered many indignities and our principal, Dr. Schwartzman, would scurry from clerk to clerk trying to free his students from prison. We did not learn much of the Romanian language because we saw no purpose in staying home reading books and owning a graduation certificate. Did we really need another language? In the universities the anti–Semitic leaders beat and exiled Jewish students. There was no prospect for a place to study or for a job.

No wonder, then, that being a pioneer and being prepared for Aliyah were our lifeline –a fresh breeze and a beacon. The authorities did not stop us. The preparatory kibbutzim were not easy and the work was back–breaking, living conditions were terrible. We ate mamaliga (corn pudding) waiting for our certificates for Aliyah.

In 1925, I made Aliyah with a group of pioneers from our town. For safety reasons we left home secretly. We travelled in dirty train cars to the port of Constanza. The train would stop at times either due to lack of coal or an obstacle on the tracks and we then were forced to disembark and to wait for the next train. We were afraid that we had been denounced and we would be brought back and imprisoned. It was only when we reached Constanza that we heaved a sigh of relief. We boarded the ship where we were surprised to find a group of prisoners of Zion from Russia. They had served in Siberia and somehow made it to a safe haven. We heard from them about the terrible conditions they had experienced and about friends they had left behind. When we heard their story we realized there was no comparison with our suffering.

We slept on a moldy floor in the depths of the ship. Our meals were inadequate, but the exiles from Russia inspired us with their enthusiasm-greater even than ours. There were conversations, songs and endless dancing all through the voyage.

On our sixth day, at dawn, we saw Haifa in all its glory and beauty. Mount Carmel was enveloped in a blue mist and the rays of the sun cut through. Our hearts were pounding and we burst out singing Hatikva with trepidation and strength.

As we were disembarking from the ship we were surrounded by a horde of large Arab sailors wearing wide pants. Their kefyehs (scarves) covered their menacing eyes. We did not understand one word in their language, but they screamed at us and pushed us into rickety boats. They seemed like pirates. In those days, ships could not come closer to the shore or to drop anchor at the pier. These sailors brought us to our desired shore–of course, not without being paid–and they also did not miss any opportunity to steal from us whatever they could.

In the absorption center we received useless inoculations and some local currency to cover our immediate needs. This was a loan from the Jewish Agency.

From here we were dispersed. Some went to southern settlements to work as farm laborers and others came to the Galilee and Samaria to join kibbutzim. Some of us arrived in Afula and joined a group of kibbutz 3 of the Hashomer Hatzair.

In those days Afula was a field full of thorns stretching from horizon to horizon and reaching the mountains of Nazareth. Here and there one could find a skeleton of a small house being built by pioneers dressed in torn clothes and shoes, wracked by malaria. On their backs they carried bricks and bags of cement. They built and sang songs, in particular the newly written anthem of Afula.

[Page 210]

Our friends joined the builders. They were drunk with happiness and returned from work covered in whitewash and their hands bleeding. Still, they sang. Hordes of local tiny flies, stinging and irritating, greeted them. There was no relief from them and they infiltrated eyes, ears and noses. Locals advised the workers to smear gasoline on their bodies as protection and one could smell them coming. Malaria and other diseases attacked us, but the enthusiasm was great and the purpose for being there helped to overcome all obstacles. Eventually, the children of storekeepers, merchants and religious personnel became laborers. They learned to work hard and cooperate with others. These were days of youthful and bubbling existence.

After a week of work we rested. We lit campfires that lit the entire area and we danced a hora around it–until dawn. There were many circles of dancers–Hashomer Hatzair, members of work teams and single laborers who danced until their breath gave out. People were happy for having achieved their dreams and because they were missing their families and, in spite of difficulty, were adjusting to new conditions.

Afula was built and became a city in Israel. Many kibbutzim were built throughout the land. The original small group of dreamers–3–established three magnificent settlements: Givat Haim Ichud, Givat Haim Hame'uchad and kibbutz Ma'abarot of the Hashomer Hatzair.

The youth from our town who came with us in 1925 and those who came later were the builders of our country and its defenders. They settled in Moshavim, moshavot and in the city and they brought up a generation of children who worked, fought and defended.

Many of our friends are no longer alive. This article is a memorial to them. May their memory always be with us.

The Saga of the Shrybmans–Sweetness out of Bitterness

by Leah Shteiner (Tel Aviv)

Translated by Ala Gamulka

As is well known, the Romanians entered Bessarabia and there were many battles in Bendery between them and the Russian Army. Our town went from hand to hand. One early morning the sound of buzzing bullets and exploding ammunition stopped and there was quiet. Some people were daring and peeked outside. They informed us that the Romanian army was passing through our street–Krapostnaya. They also told us that Motel (Mordechai) Shrybman, one of our neighbors, went out to greet them with bread and salt. We did not know whether to rejoice or cry. Jewish hearts, used to disturbances, were full of fear. The same day, Shrybman was warned by a higher authority that he was seen and that "the Soviets would return shortly". He would then be punished accordingly. The Soviets did return, but it was only 25 years later. In theory, Motel could have waited for them, but he did not. He abandoned his home and left town with his family. A long time later a letter from him was received by his relatives. In the letter Shrybman described their dangerous flight and travels across the seas in freighters. It took several months. Thanks G-d they reached Eretz Israel–their dream fulfilled. They were now in Petach Tikva and he and his wife were working in local groves.

The story of the bread and salt, the mysterious disappearance of the Shrybmans and their reappearance in the Holy Land made headlines among us. The Jews were touched by the story, especially the fact that they were day laborers. How could it be that Motel Shrybman, a wealthy Jew, Gabbai in the Talner synagogue with a seat at the eastern wall, owning a beautiful house and living a comfortable life was now a day laborer in Eretz Israel? Even his wife and daughter are suffering with him because of his terrible lot. This was a topic of conversation on the street, in the marketplace, in the steam room and the house of learning. Eventually all was forgotten.

Another letter arrived from Motel where he announced that after many trials he managed to get some land. He now had a farm in Balfuria, named after Lord Balfur. He now had fields and a vineyard. Some Jews rejoiced in the news and compared him to the biblical Boaz while others remarked that it is not so easy to work the land. More letters came and they were distributed among the population. Every reader added details from his own imagination and so the Saga of the Shrybmans was invented in the Jewish areas of Bendery.

[Page 211]

I made Aliyah in 1925 and I joined kibbutz 3 in Afula. One hot summer day I went to nearby Balfuria to visit the Shrybmans. I was interested in seeing a Hebrew village in our homeland. I had dreamed about it for many years in the Diaspora. Here it was in front of me–farm houses among the trees. Green lawns greeted me. The cows mooed and a donkey brayed, chickens peeped and doves cooed. There was a taboon–a rural Arab oven–and a woman was baking bread in it. She wore a kerchief on her head and her tanned face was shining from the heat of the oven. I thought to myself: "This is Yocheved Shrybman!" I remembered that on a cold winter day she passed our house wearing a fancy fur coat with her facing reflecting the snow covering everything. I was still a young child and I was awed by her appearance. She sensed me and recognized me immediately. She greeted me warmly and said: "Leah'le, Leah'le, Haya's daughter" with tears in her eyes. It was as if she was hugging her old friend by holding me. She was remembering her former life of calm and good fortune. She invited me in and we spoke of our town, about home. I looked at Yocheved the farmer, my elderly travel companion.

Towards evening Motel and his boys came home. They were covered in dust and sweat, but the scent of the fields accompanied them. I remembered them as pale spoiled children, but now they looked fit, tall and as if they had been farmers all their lives.

Motel was a farmer in the homeland and loved working the land. He was attached to his farm and invested hard work in it. He was proud of his sons who became farmers like him. Some years later, after Yocheved, his wife, died and he could no longer work on the farm, he moved to Kfar Saba. The sons continued to work hard and became leaders in Kfar Saba. The family grew and spread. Motel was fortunate to have grandchildren and great-grandchildren and he lived to a ripe old age. When he died he left a good name and reputation. Motel and Yocheved will always remain in our hearts.

Pioneers of the Third Aliyah in Bendery in the 1920s

[Page 212]

Miracles at Sea
by David Carmel (New York)
Translated by Ala Gamulka

The State of Israel announced that 1964 was the year of honoring illegal immigration. This was in commemoration of the first ship of immigrants that reached shore thirty years earlier. From that time on a story of courage and dedication began and there is no equal to it in history. At first there were refugees from Nazi Germany, Poland and Hungary. These were countries where Jews were persecuted by cruel governments. These pioneers wanted to come to Eretz Israel, but they were unable to do so since the British mandate did not allow them in.

Israeli citizens who came after the founding of the state and the youth that were born since then know about the heroism of Aliyah Bet only from stories they learned in school. This year they will learn in school and view exhibits of the ships and boats. They will hear about the frightening story of the "Patria", the ship that exploded in the port of Haifa. Many people were killed in that explosion. They will also hear about "Exodus," a large ship that was forcibly returned to Germany.

The illegal immigrants used many ruses to break down the British closure. Some came in the middle of the night while others used false certificates or came without any papers. My story is dedicated to the Year of Illegal Immigration.

*

It happened in the 1930s during the reign of the Nazis in Germany. Thousands of Jewish refugees wandered across Europe in those days. They went from country to country and struggled to reach Eretz Israel. The Zionist institutions began to organize illegal immigration (Aliyah Bet) with the intention to bring to Eretz Israel those Jews who did not obtain certificates from the Mandate government. The newspapers in America published reports that the British arrested Jews found on a Greek ship without any identification papers. These Jews were held for 84 days in dire circumstances and without proper nourishment. They were then exiled to an unknown location. Another time the British caught a small boat of illegal immigrants with 60 men and 5 women near the port of Jaffa. They were sentenced to a few years in prison.

*

During Hanukah of 1934 I left New York for a visit to Eretz Israel. I embarked on a ship going from Trieste to Jaffa. It was an Italian ship full of immigrants, pioneers and some elderly people. I wanted to get to know the pioneers and I went down to Third Class. A young man and a young woman approached me and asked if I came from America. We discussed the difficult situation in Europe and problems besetting the Jews. They told me a secret— there were 23 young men from Poland and Hungary on the ship without any documents. I promised them I would do what I could. I was introduced to these young men who were quite nervous and afraid of being discovered.

I decided to do something for these young men. I knew some members of the crew–Italian sailors. I only knew a few words in Italian, but we found a common language. We reached an understanding. A few sailors would help these illegal immigrants to disembark for the payment of five pounds sterling per person. The total came to $575 which was a considerable amount in those days.

The captain allowed us to hold a Hanukah party on deck. It was a concert for Jewish National Fund. Before the concert we went from cabin to cabin in First and Second classes and we collected money. One of the passengers was Dr. Nahum Goldman who donated 10 pounds sterling. The rest of the passengers were quite generous, as well.

The concert was very successful and we collected almost the entire amount of money needed. We gave it to the sailors and they fulfilled their promise. When the ship docked in the port of Jaffa, the illegal group was brought to shore with the use of many ruses. From the deck we saw Yitzhak Ben Tzvi. He was then chairman of the National Council and represented the Jewish community in front of the British. He, together with the British representatives, checked the passports and certificates of the newcomers.

In Jaffa I later met the young men. It is difficult to describe how thrilled they were that they had rrived in peace. It was, for me, the happiest day in my life– that I was able to help my brethren who were in trouble.

I recalled the words of Isaiah: "Those redeemed will return to Zion with happiness and song" (Isaiah, 35:10, 51, 11)

(Printed in "The Family", 13 Nissan 1964, New York)

[Page 213]

Roots In The Homeland

[Page 215]

The author Rivka Davidit,
from the House of Davidovich, z"l
Translated by Ala Gamulka

Rivka Davidit

She was born in Bendery on 17.2.1908. She made Aliyah with her parents in 1921 and was educated in Tel Aviv. She taught for two years in a kibbutz. Rivka published, as of 1930, poems, stories, articles in magazines as well as children's songs (mainly in "Davaar" and "Davaar for Children"). For many years she had a regular column, in Davaar, reviewing cinema and theater. This was written under the pen name of "Atalef" (bat) and "Daughter of Levi". Her books for children were: Ziftinok, "Hartzit habar hak'tana"(Small wild chrysanthemum), "Mi Ohev ma"(who likes what), "Dagey zahav" (goldfish),

"Asara Mekhozot leyaladim" (ten plays for children). She also published translations.

(From "Lexicon of Hebrew Literature in the last generations", G. Karsel, Volume 1)

Marking a year since her death

Crabgrass

It occurred to me to make a small garden near the house. However, to do that I had to get rid of crabgrass–that wild growth that comes up in every place where it was not planted. It sends its roots into every new plant and kills it.

It was a pleasure to dig deep into the ground to reach the hidden roots–the "bad roots" in my imagination–and to pull them with all my strength. Some of the roots curled up like dry and evil snakes as if there was no sign of life in them. Do not believe it because it was a pretended death. Every little part of the roots is waiting for the first opportunity to send its tentacles right and left.

I pulled out the evil crabgrass as quickly as I could. I did not leave even the slightest of remnants. There was a pile of pulled out grass and I was going to burn it. I was told that even the smallest leftover could spread and grow again. However, all this hard work tired me out and I postponed the burning to the following day.

That night I had a strange dream. I found myself in a courthouse with judges sitting at special desks along the walls. There was a great crowd of onlookers in the hall.

The door opens and a guard is leading a small woman with her hands cuffed.

–There she is! – says the guard.

–Who is she? – I ask.

–The criminal! – he answers.

I look at the small woman and to my amazement her face is quite ordinary without any signs of her being a criminal. She is neither ugly nor beautiful, neither smart nor stupid. One can see this woman does not love or hate anything, but she is depressed and is cowering like a pursued animal.

I go to the woman with good intentions, but when I look at her strange ears which are pointed to the sides, I hesitate. This is only a miserable woman and one should pity her.

The woman seems to understand what is happening inside of me and she says:

[Page 216]

–It is impossible to love me. I am not good looking or smart. I have no special abilities. Everyone hates me and you are like all the others.

–I do not hate you–I tell her– I feel sorry for you.

–No! You do not pity me. I am a thief. No one likes a character like me. No one loves for nothing. Everyone needs a repayment for their love.

I was shocked by her words, but I found them to be logical and honest. I approached her and said: I love you, but tell me why you steal.

She looked at me with scorn and replied:

–No one gives me anything of their own volition. That is why I steal. You are lying. You do not love me.

I asked the guard in a whisper: Who is this woman and what is her name?

–Her name is "zero"– he said.

–Zero?

–Yes. I wanted to say Crabgrass!

I woke up with an uncomfortable feeling. It was before dawn and I could think about my dream. "No one loves for nothing", said the small woman. Is that really so? Is it only reciprocal relations that exist between people? Everyone, then, only likes what is beautiful, rich, whole and certain. If someone is rich our love could be given to someone who could get along without it. However, the poor, ugly and weak are really those who need our love and we cannot do it.

What is the wisdom and courage to love the special ones? We enjoy them. However, try to love the "crabgrass" if not only because it is miserable and no one else will pay any attention to it.

Dava'ar for Female workers 2.71[(107)55]

"You should love your friend as you love yourself". This is what a former president, Zalman Shazar, z"l, said. He meant it to refer to those weaker and needier of help and encouragement.

An Old Fighter in a New Role
by Eitan Haber, Military reporter
Translated by Ala Gamulka

Major–general Aharon Davidi is the son of Rivka Davidit, z"l

Major-General Aharon Davidi was appointed as the chief officer in the Parachute corps in the Israel Defence Forces. Thus a young officer came out of anonymity and into the public limelight.

Major-General David is the second generation of high command in the IDF. He is one of the future generations in the army and we expect much from him.

Commendation

Anyone who served in the IDF before the Sinai Campaign, during the Fedayeen (terrorist gangs) attacks or someone who was interested in defence does not need to be introduced to Major-General Davidi He was born in Tel Aviv and is 38 years old. He is an inseparable part of the retaliation activities and is always in the first line of those who plan and participate in these activities. He is modest, cool-minded and considerate in speech and deed. His exemplary behavior and his bravery in one of the retaliation activities brought him a commendation from the chief of the army, General Moshe Dayan. In one of the first such activities, in a battle near Gaza, a platoon mistakenly attacked a water plant instead of the army camp nearby. The commander of the platoon was killed – Sargeant Sa'adia Elkayam. For a few minutes there was despair in the platoon, either because its commander was killed or because they lost their way.

Aharon Davidi (only a sergeant-major in those days) immediately took command. He organized the platoon and attacked in the correct direction–the army camp.

Davidi was not originally meant to command the platoon, but he continued to do so until the end of battle.

[Page 217]

The Sinai Campaign

Until he joined the Parachute corps, Davidi was a communications officer in the Hagana. Later he was one of those who took an officers' course in the Hagana in Shefya.

In the War of Independence he served as an officer in the Negev contingent– usually in communications. He spent time in Kfar Darom just before it was conquered by the Egyptians.

Before he joined the Parachute Corps he was an instructor in the school for officers. In the Parachute Corps he was a unit leader, assistant commander of a platoon and a commander. During the Sinai Campaign he was among the fighter in the Mitla Pass. At the end of the war he was sent to study in the Ecole Superiere in Paris – a military academy.

(Yediot Aharonot, 3.10.65)

Echo Sounds
by Mordehai Sever
Translated by Ala Gamulka

Where are the brothers,

The sisters.

Who wandered

In convoys?

Did the voice of

The people disappear?

Did their forever

Stop?

Where is the song

That woke me

From a dream

Early in the morning?

Is the song

Lost forever?

Is it lost

And nothing left?

Alone I walk

In the fields

And I gather

Echo sounds.

The loud echo

Of the people

That like the sea

Brings their sound.

[Page 218]

Our Aunt Leah
by D. Ben Yehiel
Translated by Ala Gamulka

Leah Rachman (nee Ehrlich) "Aunt Leah"

We were told that she is an unusual person and that everything we write about her would not suffice. People tried to find beautiful words to define her exactly, to describe her in one sentence–but they were unsuccessful.

There was something so humane and comforting about her. If you mentioned her in the bases and offices of the Air Force you would get a warm reaction. This feeling superseded the uniforms, the positions and her officers' status.

We heard about it from her co-workers and from her, too. As for myself–I did not imagine that Aunt Leah was actually such a "true one".

We first were told about Leah by the education officer in the Air Force: "On the day I assumed my position, I heard mention of Aunt Leah several times. At first I thought that she was someone's aunt. Later I had a formal introduction to her and she was presented as the representative of the Committee for Soldiers. However, my true feelings about her came as a result of working with her. I saw her less as an official representative and more as a good mother who takes care of her children and makes sure they are dressed properly, eat well, etc."

Aunt Leah describes how she found her way to our Air Force:

"During the Mandate there were many British soldiers here. I thought to myself that one day, when we will have our own soldiers, I would be prepared to do everything possible for them. In fact, the day came and we had our own soldiers. Here, in Pardes Hannah, a small club was organized and we had many soldiers from the entire area. In spite of the fact that I had small children at home, we managed. It can be said that have accompanied the IDF from the first moment". Aunt Leah smiles: she uses the term "we" not because her Hebrew is not good enough, but due to her true modesty.

Yes, I truly love our soldiers and they are the dearest and most wonderful people for me. Truthfully, I did not expect things to reach so far. At first I intended to do whatever I could in my area and I helped on a specific base. The commander was transferred to a different location and he begged me not to abandon his new unit. I adopted these soldiers, too and thus my activities grew. We are the kernel that began the whole story.

My grandmother is...the aunt

My activities slowly expanded and there were more locations and adoptions by the Committee for Soldiers – everywhere in our country. We hold meetings with the soldiers and we help them whenever possible. The Committee gives me all the assistance I require. Of course, the work is not as easy and simple as it was in the past, but I still have my strength. I will not abandon the work. My children are very proud of me. Even my grandchildren call me Aunt instead of Grandma.

"What we are doing now is: I am the aunt of the Air Force, Nahal (army youth group), and border patrol. When I come to an Air Force base I help to furnish the clubhouses, to put curtains in the rooms and provide special articles not usually distributed by the army. We arrange the rooms occupied by the pilots and place a toaster and a refrigerator in the clubhouse. In general, we try to make the life of the soldiers and pilots as pleasant as possible. There are also day cares and playing fields for the children of the soldiers, family clubhouses and an advanced medical clinic. I do whatever I can for them. We also purchase musical instruments and we organize the distribution of board games and newspapers.

"Sometimes I get tired", says Leah, "But I do not break down. I never considered leaving this position. I cannot live without it. Even when I am resting here, at home, my phone rings. They always need me. Everyone thinks I only exist for them. In essence, I exist for so many..."

(From the "Air Force Bulletin", year 20, No. 76, May 1968)

[Page 221]

Landscape and Being

Yaakov Fichman
Translated by Ala Gamulka

Yaakov Fichman was born in Balti (Bessarabia) on 25.11.1881 to a veteran Bessarabian family that was active in commerce and agriculture. (His father was a merchant, leaser of fields and a breeder of sheep).

He studied sacred Jewish subjects and was a diligent reader, but he was avidly interested in nature and scenery. This interest followed him all his life and continued during his years spent in Eretz Israel.

He died in Tel Aviv on 18.5.1958.

In the poem below Fichman expresses his love of his origins and the bitter lot of the residents in the Jewish communities in Bessarabia.

(Biographical details taken from "Lexicon of Hebrew Literature in recent generations, Part 2, page 602)

Bessarabia

The scenery of my origins where animals roam

The earth in the fields is warm and shallow

The wheat there is abandoned in the sun

The yellow grain moves slowly.

Such clear scenery; in the vineyards an almond tree

Throws its shadow on a brown plain;

In the depth of the fields is a mournful rampart

Inside the valley there are dreams and music.

There simple Jews, quiet like clods of earth,

Crush the grapes and produce cheese with vigor

In the summers they wind their way.

Where are they now? A night wind carries their ashes

And spreads them in cold, foreign places

Their blood streams through the sands.

[Page 222]

Figures and Shadows Which Have Disappeared
by Mordehai (ben Moshe) Sever (Tel Aviv)
Translated by Ala Gamulka

Is it only with the ascending waves that there will be a song for the sea? Will we not hear the songs with the descending waves?...
Rabindranath Tagore

There are many, many figures from the past which accompany me in my lifetime. It seems as if I continue my conversation with them to this day.

This time I will not discuss those who stood out as leading lights in our town, but I will write about ordinary people in Bendery. They struggled daily for their existence and disappeared quietly.

Clearly, it is not possible to describe the lives of all my teachers, relatives, friends and acquaintances from those days. Still, I will attempt to discuss, even if only a little, some memories of them as they are reflected in the prism of my childhood and youthful dreams in Bendery.

These figures of the past stand out in my memory as if I were seeing them at present. It is like a movie.

Here are Rabbi Herschel, the teacher and Rabbi Mordehai the redheaded Bible instructor continuing to complain to the board of the Talmud Torah of Bendery about the lack of salary raises.

I can see my most admired teacher –the elderly Rabbi Mordehai. He is short in stature and sports a white beard and a velvet kippa on his head. He is the only one of all my teachers that taught me, in addition to Gemara and Commentaries, French and Logic. He did not ask my parents for permission.

Now I see my beautiful and graceful teacher– Clara Schrybman. She prepared me for entrance examinations to the Hebrew High School. She had perfect diction when reading out loud.

I recall that one day, the young and promising poet Milya Leandres came to my father. He had written "Exit from Egypt" which was published in the Russian language newspaper in our town called Yuzhni Krai (southern corner). To this day I can hear and remember the sentence about the "Egyptian oppressor that left his mark on the back of the Jewish slave".

I will never forget the first Morning Prayer before the school day began in the Hebrew High School. It opened with the famous national tune of "Cry Israel". It was played by the violinist Y. Reidiboim, my classmate. Reidiboim was orphaned when he was in First Form when his father, a well respected lawyer, died. My friend soon lost his hearing for no reason. He was dealt a cruel blow at a young age and could not take part in normal youthful activities. He disappeared from view.

I remember with great sorrow my friend, younger than I, –Meir Dikler. He was killed defending Stalingrad against the Nazis and he left behind a young widow.

In my early youth I would pray with my father in the Sadigura Synagogue. I was taught musical notes by Pinny, the Cantor, to prepare me for participation in his choir at the end of the High Holidays. His son, Shmarya, opposed including me among the singers since I was so young. I tried to convince him to allow me to sing by offering him a few coins I received from my mother, but I was unsuccessful.

In that same synagogue I was once told by Leibel the Sexton the story of his life. He arrived alone in Bendery from Lutsk to look for work. He spoke about his life with a sad smile and while washing the floors and dusting the benches.

I remember the carrier Meishel(Moshe) laden with packages. He did not speak much and toted his suffering in silence. Even then I thought of him as exemplifying the saying: "You will eat bread by the sweat of your work".

[Page 223]

After Meishel the carrier, I turn to the blind beggar who sat in the mud near a shack in the fish market. I would hand him a penny I had received at home in order to buy a bagel on my way to Heder. Near the beggar were the fish mongers, vegetable and chicken sellers trying to warm their frozen hands over glowing embers.

In my memory I see the Sabbath and Holiday eves and the market days when our town was filled with Jews. Among them were agents, matchmakers, collectors – not like established merchants and vintners. Also the craftsmen who were a little more certain of their income as well as "luftmenchen" (wind people) who were always struggling to earn their keep.

Two figures in our town stand out. One is Idel, the Blind one, who was loyal to the Russian Duma and joked about his condition by saying that he would love to "see" the famous minister Gutshkov who was passing through our town. Another was a revolutionary who sold notions in the row of stores near the church. When the October Revolution broke out I saw him riding a horse adorned with a red flag and blowing a trumpet. As he progressed along the main street he announced: "Redemption has come!"

The line of figures of men, women, the elderly and the young continues as we saw and heard them in our youth. It was in front of the synagogue during Torah reading on Shabbat or holidays, in the Hebrew–Russian library, in the movie theatres and municipal auditorium near the park, on the main street, in the stock exchange and in the market, in gatherings and youth movement parades and even at the train station. These were moments of saying good–bye to those leaving– either going to Eretz Israel or to other countries. Then we received news of terrible events during WWII and the Holocaust that followed. The beautiful people of Bendery were sent to Transnistria, Caucasus, Central Asia, Siberia, etc. Those who remained were eliminated in a cruel way.

My article is dedicated to all those mentioned above, explicitly and implicitly, who were members of the Bendery community and died as Jews sacrificing themselves. To everyone that filled our lives with meaning in happy and sad times. They are gone forever now.

I lower my head in respect and in memory of these people.

A socialism lesson in the synagogue

"About Moses it is written: a prayer for Moses, a God–fearing man. About the poor it is written: a prayer for the poor who will speak in front of God. They are both prayers – to tell you that everyone is even in prayer"

(Exodus Raba, 21)

"A prayer of a poor man comes first in front of the Almighty…"

(Zohar, 8–1, 168)

"There is nothing closer to the heavens and more desired than the prayer of the oppressed."

(Emanuel the Roman)

When I was very young my father, of blessed memory, made a deal with me. He agreed to allow me to study in the Hebrew High School in our town as long as I continued to do the morning prayers in the synagogue and I studied religious subjects at home. Indeed, daily, early in the morning, I prayed with the first minyan in the synagogue named for Rahman in Bendery.

As a rule, those who had a yahrtzeit (Memorial Day for their departed) for family members would be given the honor of leading services. One morning a short Jew came to the praying stand. He looked down trodden and was dressed in torn clothes– his occupation was collecting rags in town. When one of the sextons saw the rag collector at the praying stand he scolded him and shouted that he would not allow him to lead services because he was so badly dressed... A tumult arose and whatever the poor man said about his yahrtzeit for his dearly departed family did not convince the rude sexton.

I was very young, before my Bar Mitzvah, but I was horrified by this event and I told the sexton off. I reminded him that according to Jewish tradition all people are equal in the eyes of God. I even quoted Raba, a famous Gemara scholar. He used to wear rags on purpose to pray to God as a poor and humble person. I even said that it is a sin to stop a Jew from leading the service on the day of his yahrtzeit.

[Page 224]

The sexton peered at me wondering who could be this upstart youngster in his synagogue. He was ready to eat me alive. However, when he was told I was the son of Moshele the Shohet he left me alone. The rag collector now had the courage to threaten to take him to the Rabbi for arbitration. After other congregants defended him, he was finally allowed to lead the services. He prayed with great meaning as if to prove that one had to seem poor to pray to God.

This was my first lesson in democracy and socialism.

The Hanging

One day when I was on my way to Heder in the morning I saw a large crowd in the gate to the courtyard on the corner of Kishinievskaya and Harozinskaya streets, near Velvel Chulak's grocery store.

I went into the courtyard and there, near the wooden structure containing the storage units and outhouses of the tenants, I saw a well-known teacher,

Mr. Leandres. He was reading, in a Litvak accent, from a sheet in front of him. As I came nearer I saw an old man hanging by a rope. He was dead.

It turned out that the old man had committed suicide and had left a letter as his will. In it he said that no one was to blame for his death and that he had killed himself because he was all alone and could not support himself.

This event happened more than 50 years ago, but I still remember the mournful reading of the letter by Mr. Leandres. He also spoke of the lot of a lonely and down-trodden person.

In Bendery there were several such lonely people and only because some kind souls helped them did they survive. However, not everyone benefitted from a helping hand.

The day I was born will be cursed...

(Job, 3, 3)

I was a sensitive and alert young child, but I was not studious and successful in school. However, many events in our history, described in the Bible and fables, left their stamp on me for the rest of my life. For example, to this day I remember how I was shaken when I learned the story of the death of Moses. He was not allowed to enter the Promised Land after all the travels and suffering in the desert. Moses was the person who carried his thankless people with their complaints throughout their wanderings.

In addition, I was deeply touched by the story of Job. He was a good and honest man, God-fearing and the father of seven sons and three daughters. He also had sheep and camels, cattle and she-asses. He was quite wealthy and an important person in the community. When Satan had discussions and struggles with God, Job was the victim. He lost his children and his animals were struck by terminal illness. He never turned away from God, but cursed himself: "The day I was born will be cursed..."

I was quite impressed with such stories and when one evening, I returned from Heder, I saw a young man wearing torn clothing. He was sitting near the wood shed of Moshe Terer with his hands on his arms. There was a crowd of children near him. As I came closer I heard him say, in Yiddish,–the day I was born will be cursed!

This was quite a depressing scene and I was shaken by the fact that what I learned in Heder about Job was being applied in real life. I felt God was testing me...

I was a young child and I was upset that I was unable to help the poor soul. I came home depressed.

For me this was an allegorical comparison between what I had learned and what I saw. However, for this unknown young man this was the tragedy of a lonely person who had no roof over his head and was hungry. No one could help him.

I will never forget this event in our town.

The anonymous Jewish soldier

Some events and sounds follow a human being all his life. This is in addition to personal experiences. This is how I remember an event from my childhood.

[Page 225]

One morning I found myself on Pavelavkaya Street near the Butchers' synagogue and I heard women howling from inside the apartment of a dressmaker. As I came closer I saw a large crowd around the keeners and inside there was a wooden coffin. It seems that there was a Jewish soldier in it. He fell in a battle in WWI and the authorities brought the body to his family as per their request. The soldier was the fiancÃ© of the young dressmaker who was crying by his side.

The war inspired Jews to create sad folk songs that were often sung by the dressmakers, tailors and other craftsmen. I clearly remember verses describing how family members say good–bye to a soldier (in Yiddish):

Let us say good–bye, Yasha (Yaakov) is leaving us.

And the reply: 'Stay well, my dear sisters

You were the best and the most attractive'

There were many folk songs that accompanied the Jewish soldiers who served in the Tsar's army. Many died in foreign lands without knowing why this war was fought. There were also Jews in the opposing armies.

To this day I bow my head in memory of these soldiers who were sacrificed.

Let these words be a memorial to our dear town members and family who left us too early.

The Beloved and Loved in Life and Death

We were two young dark-haired boys dressed in school uniform with shiny buttons when we sat together in class in the Hebrew High School of Bendery. My friend, Yitzhak Bauch, was a good-looking young man, alert and smiling. He often sang folk songs and prayers. Even after he transferred to the municipal high school, I remembered him for his aristocratic behavior.

After I finished doing my homework I would play with my eight-year old neighbor – Zina. She had platinum hair and clear eyes. I remember her dressed in a white Ukrainian dress embroidered by her mother Massya. When she grew up, Zina was a beautiful high school girl. She was active in Maccabi as was her brother – well-known coach and trainer – Soonya Etlis. Our family moved to a different area of town and I was busy with Hashomer Hatzair (Young Guard). I lost touch with Zina and we would only meet occasionally.

Years passed and our youth were dispersed to many countries. At the age of 17, I made Aliyah with the first members of Hashomer Hatzair in 1923. Those who remained were integrated into life in Bendery with all the changes in regimes.

One day I heard, in Eretz Israel, that Zina married Yitzhak Bauch who was then a law student. They even had a child. I was happy since both of them were very dear to me.

After WWII and the Holocaust I found out that Yitzhak, an officer in the Red Army, had been critically injured in the battle for Stalingrad. Zina and her mother and young child had wandered to eastern Asia. They were 'fortunate' to see Yitzhak who was brought to them. He died in front of the wife, her mother and the young child. They had to bury him there. Zina was in mourning, but was consoled by an older Jewish refugee. This man helped her, her mother and her son Efraim and she married him. She kept her former name– Zina Bauch.

After 44 years of absence, I visited Bendery in 1966. I had been given a special permit in Kishinev. I first went to Zina's house, near the Dniester – my childhood home. When I banged the gate, Zina came out towards me and we immediately recognized each other. In spite of the years, I saw in Zina's face the beauty and charm of former years. In the house I found her elderly mother and her 29 year-old son, Efraim. He already had a son, worked as a geologist and his hobby was poetry. The old mother and Zina received me like a long lost relative with warmth and tears of joy. Efraim gave me, as a memento of my visit, a book, in Russian, of his poetry, dedicated to me. The book was called "Electrifying Night". I translated and published, in this book, the touching poem "The Little Boy from the Ghetto".

[Page 226]

The Little Boy from the Ghetto
by A. Bauch
Translated by Ala Gamulka

He made bread from sand at mealtime

On a hot summer's day in the scorching sun

The sad dwarf with huge eyes–

The little boy from the ghetto.

Without knowing the urgency of the times

He suddenly laughed

But he realized he was wrong to laugh

The little boy from the ghetto.

At night, bent over him with his tangled beard

With intelligent and sad eyes

His grandfather Baruch prayed for him

His face yellow and lined

Afterwards the elderly men wrapped in white

Swept the floor with their hands–

They sat like immobile hillocks,

Murmuring prayers with their lips.

It is not that it is difficult to appease God

So many tears were shed

He was tiny, but understood so much

The little boy from the ghetto.

The sad dwarf who saw much

He did not live there alone

He had friends – the twinkling stars

They were not yellow, the ones in the night

These were white stars, so clearly visible

He waited for them as it became dark

He knew: when they redden in the sky

Everything will be good and happy

May I see in the clouds so I can come closer to the stars!

I am a little boy and my life is bad

My father and mother, grandmother and grandfather

Why were they the first?

They said–it will be better there–different

The chimney is large and emits

Beautiful black clouds.

Why is my old man crying?

Did he not know?

You are lucky; soon you will become a cloud

My little boy from the ghetto.

There will be peace and children

Will roll hoops on a hot summer day

Above them will hover a cloud in the heavens

My little boy from the ghetto.

Translated from Russian into Hebrew by Mordehai Sever

[Page 227]

Before I left Kishinev, Zina and her husband came from Bendery, by train, to say good–bye. We talked for hours and reminisced. Zina's eyes told me more than her words. They begged me: "Take me with you to Israel!" When we stood face to face she whispered, as if excusing herself: "...I was alone and helpless with my elderly mother and my child in eastern Asia. This man (her husband) saved us from a bitter end!"

On the way to the train station in Kishinev I said goodbye to her and her husband with warm hugs and kisses. When I returned home I stayed in touch by corresponding with Zina. Three years ago I found out that Zina died of a heart attack.

The images of Zina and Yitzhak Bauch, beloved and loved in life and death, with their bitter end in a foreign land, will never leave me.

Death Games….

Simcha the shoemaker was a simple, but respected personality. When he was dressed up for Shabbat and Holidays he reminded us of Theodore Herzl with his black beard. He served as the sexton of the Tailors' synagogue and other synagogues for about 18 years. On Shabbat and holidays he would lead services. He was devoted to the needs of the observant and I would compare him to people like Yohanan the Shoemaker and Yitzhak Nafha.

His wife, Henya, was an outstanding homemaker. Together, she and Simcha brought up their 3 daughters and 5 sons in good Jewish tradition. She supervised her household and even baked her own bread. On Shabbat and holidays she would read prayers and sayings to the women in the synagogue from the Korban Minha – the holiday prayer book. The women around her stood when she stood and sat down when she did. When she cried, they followed her example. It is not surprising that she was dubbed "The Leader".

We were neighbors in one courtyard and I was a very close friend of her sons Yossel and Moshe who were born after her daughters Rosa and Hannah. Yossel stood out from an early age with his beautiful voice. His brother Moshe, a year older than me, was my childhood playmate.

Once Moshe scared me when he took out his father's siddur from the cupboard and told me he would pray to God that I would die if I do not follow his instructions in our games. I remember, with a smile, this innocent playfulness and I often wondered why Moshe had to threaten me with death when I was only five years old? It was only 60 years later, when Moshe died in the battle for Sevastopol during WWII, that I became sad when I recalled how we, the children, played games of life and death. We did not know how tragic could be the lot of man upon this earth. Death shortened many lives and this childhood game became a bitter reality for him, his family, his relatives and friends.

Yosele Schwartzman– the cantor

(26.1.1902 – 25.2.1969)

He was known from childhood as an honest and refined person. He charmed everyone with his pleasant voice as a soloist in the choirs of the "New" and "Sadigura" synagogues. He performed with the cantors Gedalya Gurman and Piny the Cantor – Pinhas Misonzshnik. After studies in Heder and Yeshiva he went to New York at the age of 18. There he studied music with Prof. Olaf of the Metropolitan Opera and others. He soon became an accomplished cantor and joined the company of other greats – David Roitman, D.M. Shteinberg, Leybele Glantz, etc. He served for thirty years in the Ahavat Achim congregation in Atlanta. He earned the love and respect of the congregants. He also received an honorary degree from the Jewish Theological Seminary of America. In addition, he was elected as a board member of the Association of Cantors in United States and Canada.

I came to Eretz Israel in the 1920s and I heard that Yosele Schwartzman was located in the United States. I had great affection for him and I tried for many years to write to him. I was unsuccessful. It is only recently, in the 1960s, that I reconnected with him through our mutual friend David Carmel. From then on our friendship flourished through constant correspondence. Once, when I did not respond to his letter within a week, I received an urgent telegram from him because he was worried.

In his lengthy letters to me, Yosele recalled events from the time of Hazamir in Bendery. The choir traveled to give concerts in other locations in the area. When the choir traveled by boat on the Dniester it would give concerts and the singing could be heard on both banks of the river. He also remembered his participation in theatrical productions in town in plays by Goldfaden, Gordin, etc. He listed the names of all synagogues, cantors, sextons and teachers. He even promised to send me a special article about the development of cantorial music in Bendery. In the picture of Hazamir that I received there was a dedication in Russian to the soloist alto Yosef Schwartzman dated 25.8.1913

[Page 228]

Right to left: Ahrale Gelfand, Kipnis (folk songs) and Moshe Koussevitzky

Pinhas Misonzshnik (Piny the cantor)
Cantor in the synagogue of the followers of Sadigura in Bendery

[Page 229]

Cantor Yosef Schwartzman with his singers in the Butchers' Synagogue in Bendery

In the many letters I received from him he told me about his life and his development as a cantor. His lot was cruel as his father and brother were killed in the Holocaust and the war and his two sisters died young. His youngest brother survived in Bendery, but when he visited Yosele in Atlanta he was afraid to open his mouth since he feared the authorities when he returned home. His oldest sister in the United States was widowed, as was he. This is what he wrote about his father: "the Nazis murdered my father and I keep his yahrtzeit on Yom Kippur".

He found it difficult to accept that we had lost touch for so many years and he wanted to come to Israel to visit. In his letter dated 6.10.68 Yosele wrote, in Hebrew: "...my soul is tied up with your soul. I am your true friend...". I was angry when he wrote to me in a letter dated 6.1.69: "...Motele, when you go to the Western Wall, pray to God on my behalf..I am Yosef, son of Simcha and Henya..." In the next letter from 20.2.69, he said: "If God wills it I will come to Israel to see you. However, if we are not successful, you must feel my true friendship. This is especially so since I am alone and have been so for many years." This was his last letter to me from the United States. Five days later, on 25.2.69, my unforgettable friend, my Yosele, died of a stroke in his house in Atlanta.

A short time after his death, his daughter brought me, from the United States, a pack of letters, pictures and handwritten notes which she found on his desk. Among them was a letter he started to write two days before he died, on 23.2.69, but which he did not complete. In this letter he described in colorful language how we stood together as children watching the big fire in the synagogue and the rabbi's house. It was rumored that during the fire many "names" of siddurs and mahzors flew in the wind directly to the old cemetery. A few days earlier Rabbi Itzikel Wertheim, from the famous dynasty, had been buried there.

Letters flying on wings of the winds...childhood memories that are gone...dreams that remained unsolved...The beloved image of Yosele comes from them and remains part of my being.

[Page 230]

My friend Israel

When I studied in the Heder of Rabbi Shmuel Krassilover, z"l, my friend, Israel, was a year older than I. He was a redhead, freckled, and imaginative. He was good-hearted and loved to help others. I believe he was very young when his mother died and he sought warmth in others. He used to tell confusing stories.

I recall that he was the one first told me about the wonderful atmosphere in the Schwartzman Hebrew High School. He described, with excitement, the unforgettable Isaac Borisovitch (Yitzhak Reznikov, z"l), the great Hebrew teacher who became a true friend to his students. I fell in love with this teacher even before I had met him.

What really excited my friend Israel was the high school uniform with its shiny buttons and the hat encircled by blue tubing. He was especially keen on the silver insignia of our school.

He worshipped those who wore uniforms, in particular, the soldiers and officers. He was fixated on this and he could not find a solution. Every once in a while I would see him run, with other children, after a group of soldiers passing in the streets singing.

Eventually, my friend Israel dropped out of the high school (perhaps even during the first year). To my great sorrow I found out that he was deficient in a social and intellectual sense. I worried about what would become of my friend.

It is more than 50 years since we said good-bye in the Diaspora. I, along with many friends, made Aliyah. From time to time friends and acquaintances came from Bendery and I would always ask them about my childhood friend.

"Oh, him"–I would be answered immediately –"He works as a firefighter in Bendery and wears his colorful uniform with pride..." Some years later, one of my friends who made Aliyah informed me that he saw Israel wearing the uniform of a ticket collector on the train.

Since the end of WWII and the Holocaust I have not heard anything about him. As I was writing these lines, my friend B. told me that he heard that Israel had not survived.

The Teacher Yosef Rivkin–a resident of Bendery

One winter morning our principal entered at the beginning of class and said the following: a refugee, a teacher, has just arrived in town and his name is Yosef Rivkin. He gives private lessons in Hebrew language, Bible, Mathematics, etc. I recommend him to the students and their parents since he could help them with their studies and he could also prepare them for examinations. Anyone interested should contact me.

That week teacher Rivkin was invited to our house to teach my younger brother Hebrew, Bible and Mathematics. This took place after my brother's regular Heder studies. Slowly Yosef Rivkin became a part of our household.

One cold and snowy winter day, the teacher came to our house. Here was a Litvak (Lithuanian) Jew, wearing glasses, skinny and dressed in wrinkled summer clothes. He was shivering from the cold and was coughing often. Instead of a warm winter coat he had an old women's scarf around his chest.

My mother received him nicely and served him hot tea. She even invited him to come every morning to drink hot tea. He now joined our other regular guests for breakfast: the sexton of the nearby synagogue Issachar Diarde and a Jewish soldier named Meir–Leib who was serving with his unit in our town. The new teacher and the other guests would go to the large samovar and drink tea. He felt comfortable in our home and even had conversations about different topics. However, when we tried to find out if he had a family or any relatives anywhere we failed. Yosef Rivkin stubbornly refused to answer our questions and would change the topic.

As we got to know him we discovered an interesting and cultured man, a Litvak who was knowledgeable in many fields. "A Litvak always knows everything". Truly, Yosef Rivkin was a Misnaged (opposer) and he would scorn the Hassidim who depended on their Rabbi to save them from all troubles… He also made fun of the boors who pretended to give a sermon on biblical topics of which they were quite ignorant. Once on a Friday night in our home he told us that a neighbor asked him if he had already welcomed the Sabbath saying: "…did you already degrade the Sabbath." Instead of asking if he had celebrated Shabbat.

[Page 231]

Rivklin would ask those who pretended to be Torah students: "Tell me, when you do not understand a word or a phrase in the Gemara, why do you hum endless tunes?"

I do not remember if he had many students after the recommendation by Dr. Schwartzman and if he ever got a proper winter coat. On my last visit in his cold and miserable room I saw a new small table and some books my father had given him. This was just before we made Aliyah.

Some years later some of my friends made Aliyah and when I asked about Yosef Rivkin they told me he remained alone in Bendery for the rest of his life. No one ever knew if he had any family.

He took his secret to his grave.

Rabbi Shmuel Krassilover– my Rabbi

Each one of us carries memories of his distant childhood and the images of those beloved at that time. These were authorities to be trusted at all times and they are engraved in our hearts.

One of these authorities whose image is with me since childhood was my Gemara teacher– Rabbi Shmuel Krassilover (of the house of Horowitz). The name Krassilover probably came from the village where he or his parents had lived– Krassilov or Krassilivka.

In Bendery, Rabbi Shmuel was well-versed Jew and a wise man. He had a great sense of humor and would tell good jokes. He had a nice appearance – a white beard and hypnotic eyes that would see right through people. His students were more afraid of his stare than of his crop made out of several layers of leather.

If truth be told, his students were more afraid of the thumb in his right hand. It was rumored that it had been cut off on purpose so he would not have to serve in the Tsar's army. This unseen thumb would be used to pinch the students in a certain place. The students would really suffer.

I personally do not remember that he either hit or pinched me. Perhaps it was because I was usually quiet. However, I know he really disliked it when I would burst out in loud laughter for no reason. There was a reason because my relative, Itzik, sat next to me and when we looked at each other we would burst out laughing... In order to control myself I put my fingers in my nostrils, but then I would laugh even louder. Everyone in class heard me and this angered the Rabbi even more: "To laugh without reason in the middle of class?" Since he was smart and kind he would forgive our childhood nonsense and would joke: "Do you see how idiocy gets them?"

To this day many of his students recall his jokes as if they had just happened. I remember that I once came to Heder with a swollen eye. R. Shmuel greeted me: "Look at him. He sinned in the eye"– a play on words. This was based on something we had learned the previous week about Jacob's mourning the death of Rachel.

R. Shmuel Krassilover (Horowitz) – the famous teacher in Bendery

[Page 232]

If a student hesitated a moment prior to reading the Rabbi would hurry him up by saying: "Read, read…I am the water carrier…". Another instance was when Jacob is dying and he gathers his sons to his bedside saying: "Come on guys (in Russian)". When a student had difficulty with a portion of the Gemara where different opinions were offered, the Rabbi said "the ducks are walking shoeless".

I am not sure it was so good for him to be joking so much, but I remember a patrician man in front of me. In my childish mind he seemed to be like Abraham and his wife Rachel was similar to Sarah. His daughters Malka and Sarah looked to me like our biblical mothers Leah and Rachel.

One day when I was 8 years old, Rabbi Shmuel paired me with Khilik, my classmate, and told us: "You are beginning to learn Gemara with me. This is a secret and you must not tell anyone at home". He opened a large tome of Gemara and on the first page was written in large letters –Baba Metz'ia. He began to chant the first Mishna: "Two people are holding a talit and each one says I found it, I found it". He pointed to me and my friend Khilik and in my imagination I saw us holding such a talit and each one claiming it to be his. We walked home with pride that we were now learning Gemara. We hummed the song of Shalom Aleichem in his story "Hey, Hey, it is nothing". The song said: "We are not afraid of anyone, only of God".

We are already learning Baba Metz'ia! When we came home we could not contain ourselves and we told our parents and neighbours the "secret"– that we are learning Gemara. The next day when the Rabbi asked us if we had kept the secret as we promised, I burst out crying. The Rabbi comforted me and even made me laugh out loud when he deliberately mispronounced some words.

We learned material that would make us afraid of spirits and ghosts, snakes, scorpions and beasts. The Rabbi would scare us by saying we should not think of these things at night.

I liked all his explanations and my imagination was stirred so much that I began to draw on paper images of what we had learned and he had described. My first drawing was that of the ten tribes as described in the Torah as well as other biblical figures. Rabbi Shmuel Krassilover and his wife Rachel looked at my drawings and murmured: "Beautiful, beautiful".

More than 50 years have passed since I had last seen Rabbi Shmuel Krassilover. His wife Rachel died before him and he, too, passed away. His eldest daughter Malka is gone and only the younger daughter, Sarah was left (in the United States). There are many grandchildren here in Israel and outside it and they remember with pride their ancestor. The special blessing is the fact that so many of his students are with us here and in the Diaspora and they all remember with love the image of their wonderful and exceptional teacher. We often repeat his many jokes as he paraphrased important phrases. His puns were amusing and legendary.

[Page 233]

Rabbi Shmuel Krassilover educated several generations of students. They remember him with love and kindness for the fun they had in his classes during those bad times when there were no civil, cultural, social and economic rights. He probably never imagined that after so many years his students would remember him with so much appreciation and gratitude.

Recollections From Jerusalem of the 1920s
by Rivka (Riva) Terer–Drobetsky
Translated by Ala Gamulka

Riva Drobetsky, the first wife of Z. Drobetsky and daughter of Rabbi Moshe Terer, z"l, was a beloved, kind and aristocratic woman. She stood out in her gentleness and was quite modest. She walked through life with purpose and sweetness. She never looked for honor, even if she deserved it. In addition to all these qualities one should add the fact that she had a keen eye and could write about all events. She had a great literary talent, in an excellent Russian style. The reader always read eagerly everything she published. It is incumbent upon us to include two articles in remembrance of her good reputation– for all who cherish her.

These two articles were sent to the Diaspora while she lived in Eretz Israel and they were published in various newspapers in Bessarabia, in Russian.

This is the first letter about Jerusalem and her impressions of the city (Published 21. 12. 1923 in Yuzhnaya Bessarabia)

A. A letter from Jerusalem

"Up to now you know very little about Jerusalem. The European press is not very interested in this corner of the globe. Our capital is above all other capitals in the world. She is in the thoughts and feelings of all Jews.

I will begin with the road to Jerusalem from Jaffa.

I went with a group in public transport, even though there is a train to Jerusalem. The trip by train is quite tiring and uncomfortable and takes two hours. The ride by car is only one and a half hours. The scenery is unbelievably beautiful. It is difficult to paint it, even for the best artist. When you leave Jaffa you do not, at first, feel anything different since you see a flat plain. Here and there you can glimpse orange trees and sometimes even groves. When you reach half–way the scenery changes completely. Suddenly the colorful mountains appear. Jerusalem is 800 meters above sea level and the air is cooler and clearer than Jaffa's.

In the summer Jerusalem serves as a resort for people from the south and the seacoast who escape the heat. In the winter it is extremely cold and sometimes there is even snow – up to 36 inches. The hills around Jerusalem stand out in their beauty.

[Page 234]

The road from Jaffa to Jerusalem snakes its way through the hills. The car we were in seemed like a fly climbing a wall and constantly in danger of falling into the valley. There are places where the road is actually on the verge of deep valley. On one side the hills reach the sky, so to speak, and on the other side there is a deep crevasse and the trees in it look like tufts of grass. The path loops like a snake with dangerous sections. Your breath stops when you look down. It is difficult to understand how one passes this edge of the crevasse, but the car continues as if nothing matters and nothing would stop it. It seems as if the driver steers it by feel only.

Riva Terer–Drobetsky

The air is sharp like needles and the fear leaves you when you observe the beauty of nature around. You almost do not notice the precipice. You want to fly like a bird, but when you reach the outskirts of Jerusalem you wake up as if from a sweet dream. How sad that the dream is over!

Jerusalem leaves a mixed impression on you. If you expect a European city you are quickly disappointed, but it does not look like a typical oriental town – large and full of people. Some buildings were erected hundreds of years ago and others are very modern. The city does not have a homogeneous look. It is so beautiful that it is difficult to describe it. What caught my eye and I want to tell you about it is the feeling that you are on holy ground. This is where our prophets walked.

I want to discuss some symbols this holy city represents. It is a historical city, full of rich memories that touch the Jewish heart. I will begin with the

Western Wall, the remnant of our temple that was destroyed. This remnant brings people to pray by it. There are always people praying there and asking the almighty to help them.

Not far from the Western Wall, on a higher hill, is the Dome of the Rock– a beautiful building.

It was built about 1000 years ago by a Turkish Sultan on the site where our temple had stood. The interior and the structure were kept as originally built so many years ago. When you enter the Dome of the Rock you cannot even see all the richness inside. It is difficult to express this. The roof of the Dome is covered with precious stones. The inside is covered in expensive carpets and there is a rock in the middle. It is as if the rock is growing out of the ground and is surrounded by a banister. It is believed that it is the altar to which the Kohanim would bring the sacrifices. (It is believed, according to tradition, that it is the rock from which water was extracted.) You feel an inner tremor as you come nearer to this place. You begin to think about our history since the destruction and the exile. You whisper so as not to wake previous generations. In the wall there are two stone thrones and according to legend this is where the kings would sit on their visits to the temple.

In the fort nearby you can find the stables of King Solomon, under the floor of the building. They look as if they have been built recently.

From there I went to visit the grave of our matriarch Rachel. It is located in Bethlehem. It is only during the month of Elul that the Arabs allow the Jews to visit this holy place.

It is very difficult for me to forget this rare experience and that is why I am writing about it.

[Page 235]

B. Recollections from the Fourth Aliyah

A second letter from Riva T. sent to the editor of Nashy Vremya on 16.9.1924.

Editor's note: I just received this letter from Eretz Israel. Its author wrote it without an angle – as someone looking at both sides. The author describes in simple and sincere words how he sees the new Eretz Israel. I find that it is proper to bring a few sections for our readers who hold the country close to their hearts:

There is no tendency here to immigrate to the United States. No one is leaving. On the contrary, lately there is an increase in emigration from Poland.

The newcomers are not only laborers, but some wealthy people running away from the Polish authorities. There are also some from Russia, victims of the revolution, but they are penniless. There is great hope placed on the emigrants from Poland. There are plans for them to establish factories and plants. It is clear that Tel Aviv benefits the most from these plans since it is in the center of the country. Tel Aviv is becoming an industrial and commercial center. Since it is a new city it draws the attention of many with its modern architecture and colorful ambience. There is much culture there. The women coming from Poland are impressed with the modernity of the city since they were prepared for a primitive and wild Asian town. They see here many things Europe does not yet have especially clothing, furniture. All these are produced within the country. In addition there is much grown in our farming communities by our brethren – fruit, vegetables, animals. The women wonder and ask: "Are these the Jews who are considered as parasites in the Diaspora? Wonder of wonders."

I bring all this to you to awaken your interest in our country.   R.D.

Translated from the Russian by P.B.

When we read these letters we see how sharp the eyes of R.D. were as she saw much and she was alert to all problems – be they public or national.

Riva Drobetsky lived in the country from 1921 to 1927. She returned to Bendery for health reasons and died there in 1930. She was only 30 years old.

Picture taken before he made Aliyah. Right to left: Senya Tzehoval, Zelig Sofer, (Yosef P. in the middle) Avraham Zoberman? and Kleyman

Some handwriting is unclear.

(Goes with the article about Simcha Zehoval on Page 236)

[Page 236]

Simcha Tzehovel
by I. Gabbai
Translated by Ala Gamulka

Simcha (Senya) Tzehovel

It is customary in all theatre schools in the world to include in the curriculum talks and discussions about important actors from the past. It is important from a professional and an ethical point of view to do it. However, we do not have it yet here. We have a short history and we do not teach about it. It is to be hoped that this attitude will change in the future, but in the meantime, we owe a great deal to our important actors who founded the Hebrew theatre in Israel.

I am dedicating this article to my friend, like a brother to me, Simcha Tzehovel, z"l. We sat next to each other putting on makeup for thirty years. We were also close friends.

Simcha Tzehovel was a great actor who was quite creative, but he had a strong temperament. He knew how to excite his fellow actors with his deep and powerful voice. He was reserved and quiet in his daily life and was dedicated to the theatre. He spoke clearly and slowly whether in conversation with a friend or a general discussion. We would joke with him: "Senka, say something concrete…" He would smile in a good natured way even if we did not accept what he said. On the stage he spoke well.

His "Olympian calm" when roles were distributed for a new play was an example to all of us. He did not compare roles. Tzehovel believed in Stanislavsky's classical saying – "There are no small roles, there are only small actors." He believed in it until the end of his days. The roles of the butcher and the policeman in The Witch, the bath attendant in The Travels of Binyamin III, the elderly general Krotitzky in The Wise Man and many others were turned by Tzehovel into brilliant performances. He portrayed these roles with love and happiness. He performed them as he had done his unforgettable starring roles in "Jacob and Rachel", "Jeremiah", "King Lear", "King Solomon and the Shoemaker," "The Forest" and others. It seems to me that when he performed he did not do it for the audience, but for his friends in the cast. It was as if he wished to demonstrate what one should do in the theater.

The theater was his home and his colleagues were his family. He was one of the few who were always happy with the success of a friend and he knew how to encourage others. He distanced himself from any publicity that did not directly have anything to do with his craft. He used to say: "No cafe, not even an artists' cafe, ever produced a good actor…" He never boasted and never talked about himself in the third person. He never bragged about his successes.

[Page 237]

Tzehovel managed to perform eighty–five roles on the stage of our "Ohel" theater. Very few others managed to be so versatile – tragic and comic, leading and character roles. These were quite different, but he always undertook each assignment with a full heart.

Ten years have passed since his amazing voice was silenced. The number of actors has increased since then and new theater groups have been formed. The greatness of one of the first actors on the Hebrew stage– Simcha Tzehovel, z"l, must be told to all the new actors.

Tzehovel and His Roles
by Israel Gur
Translated by Ala Gamulka

Simcha Tzehovel – Mendel in "Fishke the Cripple"
by Mendele Mocher Seforim

The wonderful harmony between his clear voice and his body movements comes from deep within his early biography. Tzehovel grew up in the Russian village of Tiraspol on the banks of the Dniester and he then lived in Bendery, Bessarabia. He was always interested in performing on stage. His maternal grandfather was a cantor and a ritual slaughterer. Tzehovel was influenced by his grandfather in spite of the fact that he had a Russian education. The grandfather's tunes soon were heard in the grandson's pleasant voice and everyone predicted he would become a cantor. Tzehovel always said that this is where he first thought of performing. Another nurturing place was the fact that the family resided right across from the municipal summer theater. It was mainly used for circus events. Many of the performers rented rooms from the Tzehovel family. The young boy was delighted to have such close contact with them. He was enthralled by the circus and soon joined them. Morning and evening he would train on the trapeze. A few months before he died, Tzehovel told me that to this day he feels sentimental about the circus and cantorial music. (We all felt this when he performed on stage. Do you remember his leap as Joe Dunmore in Priestley's "The City of Tomorrow" or Mack the Knife in Three Penny Opera? Or as Kurt in "The Pure Race" by Kedelburg? We cannot forget his energetic dancing in the wedding scene in Fishke the Cripple.)

In high school he was one of the regular performers in many holiday productions. Even then he stood out in his dramatic abilities. The drama teacher recognized his talents and recommended him to a well-known theater school. However, the revolution of 1917 put a stop to these plans. Only his ambitions remained.

Many Jewish theater groups came to town and many of us joined them. These performers exaggerated their naturalism and lived a poverty-stricken life.

From the book: "Those who played kings and the poor" 1957.

[Page 238]

The Poet Y. Manic (Lederman), z"l
by Y. Manic
Translated by Ala Gamulka

Y. Manic

Manic was born in Bendery. In his youth he studied in Heders and dedicated himself to acquiring a general education. He went to America and studied at the University of Chicago.

In 1935 he made Aliyah as a pioneer and continued his literary work.

He published, in Yiddish, five books: poems, proverbs, satires and sometimes children's books.

His works have been translated into Hebrew and English.

He had positive reviews in Israel and in the Diaspora.

Deep in Autumn Nights

Deep in autumn nights
I wander through destroyed villages
A stream of blood snakes
And follows me and blocks my way.
It is not long ago that life was gone from here
There is no more evening tune
I knew well the surrounding sounds
From the forest and the area
It is here, not long ago, that my childhood was spent...
Now, one can hear an owl keening
The windmill hovers like a ghost
That has lost its wings...
It seems that God himself
Is moving about in forsaken alleys
He is pursued by angry shouts
That hit like stones and make him cry.
A small synagogue– a memorial to the destruction
The sound of prayers is silent forever
An orphaned Torah scroll
No one is left to rejoice with it
An old Menorah
Is flickering and dying
All the Sabbaths are gone...

Translated from Yiddish by Mordehai Sever

[Page 239]

The Wertheim Family in the Real World
by Dr. Yosef Kruk
Translated by Ala Gamulka
We All Have But One Rabbi – Rabbi Avraham Wertheim

The Russian intelligentsia stood out along its own special lines. Their status gave them additional rights, but it was a burden for them. Their hearts identified with the down-trodden, those with little or no rights. The slogan "Go with the people" was part of their identity for many years.

"Going with the People" was well received by the Jewish intelligentsia as well. They and their nation stood at the head of the list of the down-trodden and persecuted. For many years, the youth, the university students and even the high school ones, believed in the theme of "go to the Jewish street." Avraham Wertheim, z"l, belonged to the latter group.

He was a scion of a large rabbinic family which consisted of many geniuses, righteous ones (Baal Shem Tov, the Chernobyl rabbi, the Maharasha and Shore the grain merchant). His mother came from Volyn and was the daughter of the chief rabbi of Brezhne. Avraham Wertheim stood out from an early age as someone with a keen mind and everyone predicted for him a great future in the rabbinic world. He was an outstanding student, but he did not use Torah as a tool.

There were many Jewish intellectuals who became famous later on and who made their way from Yeshiva to Russian culture. There were many reasons for their turning their backs on the Yeshiva. They saw their personal success in Russian culture (later in the Polish one, too). Avraham Wertheim devoted himself quite energetically to Russian culture. Truth must be said that he never really left the Yeshiva in order to cross to the other side. He always searched for integration of the secular and the Jewish cultures – the union of national Jewish redemption with the universal one.

World War I

During WWI Avraham Wertheim's activities truly stood out. The Tsarist authorities, under terrible conditions, exiled the Jewish population from the cities and sometimes even from entire districts. This is when the young Jewish intelligentsia showed a wonderful spirit of volunteerism. There were people who had never done physical labor – writers, scientists, students and Yeshiva boys — who left their homes and went to save Jews during this horrible time. Avraham Wertheim was one of these good people – representatives of Jewish institutions helping the refugees.

When WWI was over, the problems for the Jews did not disappear. There were pogroms – attacks on Jews – in Ukraine and southern Russia. Entire towns and villages were destroyed and it was dangerous to offer help. Avraham Wertheim stood out with his tremendous energy, great love for his people and his wisdom. He found solutions in the most complicated predicaments.

He often traveled to dangerous locations where there were pogroms expected. He sometimes even arrived in the middle of the pogrom, or right after in order to try to save whatever possible. In 1919 Wertheim was a representative of the Red Cross and offered help in the name of this neutral organization. He ran the department of "Victims of Pogroms" of the Red Cross and organized help.

Many times I asked Wertheim to write his memoirs from those days (perhaps he left some notes in his will). There was great importance to his activities as he often placed himself in great danger in order to save Jews – his brothers in trouble and in prison.

In Poland

It proved later on, for many Jews in Russia and Ukraine that their only salvation was in escaping this hell by immigrating. Avraham Wertheim moved to Poland.

[Page 240]

his time he did not come as a private person – in order to save himself — but in order to continue helping and organizing. He joined the American Jewish Joint Committee, in particular the department for the homeless and those in need of repatriation. He organized a section for charitable banks and supervised them. He was not an official, just a good person who loved his people and saw their needs. He traveled to many parts of Congress Poland, Galicia, Lithuania and Volyn.

In Eretz Israel

He made Aliyah in 1933 and began to work in the labor department of the Jewish Agency. When Israel was declared a state, he was in charge of the department dealing with disputes under the Labor department.

This was not an easy job. The State was young and its future depended on successful economic development. There was a great need to have a country that was run intelligently, with foresight and still give rights to its workers. In addition, it was necessary to make certain that there was room for industrial and technical development and that it was done with efficiency and innovation. It was not easy to organize relations between employers and workers. After all, we are speaking of the capricious Jewish temperament... Wertheim helped a great deal with small and large disputes with his tact, professional acumen and his insistence on solving issues. There is no doubt that he wrote an important chapter in the difficult work of the Labor Department.

We all have but one Rabbi

Avraham Wertheim was a Zionist and a socialist from his early days. He stood out with his true love of the Jewish people and his grasp of the socialist–humanist world. He was inspired by his desire to establish a new society, following socialist tenets. He was a member of the party and he understood the need for unity of workers. In the last years he helped to found the "Socialist Unaffiliated Club" in Jerusalem in order to allow for free discussion within all streams of the labor movement and to establish true unity. Typical of his point of view was his speech in 1953 to the first conference of government employees. The prime minister and other cabinet members also participated. This is what he said:

"There is the story of two Hassidim who were drinking wine after Havdalah on Saturday night. In their enthusiasm they each spoke of the greatness of their own rabbi. One said: my rabbi is inspired by Elijah and he studies with him and other holy personalities. The second one was excited and replied: who is your rabbi in comparison to my rabbi who was fortunate enough to ascend to heaven? The two Hassidim began to quarrel about whose rabbi was greater. The dispute became a fist fight and they had to be separated. Afterwards each one was asked–who is your rabbi? The first answered R. Yitzhak from

Chernobyl and the second gave the same reply. It turned out they had the same rabbi. Why did they fight, then?"

He finished by saying: "We may have differences of opinion and we sometimes fight amicably. It seems to me that have only one rabbi – our rabbi is the State of Israel."

A wonderful Jew has left us.

(Davar, 8.1.1958)

[Page 241]

Big Hearted David Wertheim
by Yosef Shapira
Translated by Ala Gamulka

David Wertheim was big hearted. This quality emanated from the love that permeated his being and everything he did.

His work was a labor of love. He loved Jews, people, his friends and his movement. He adored the Hebrew language and on top of everything he loved Eretz Israel. He loved these things with all his being.

David Wertheim was a man of the movement – not a man of the party hampered by its framework. The movement was his life. In his first years in the United States Zeirei Zion (Young of Zion) was a small movement, especially for a man who believed in a universal belief system. He worked hard to push the movement forward. His orations were inspiring and passionate. He felt this was a movement that embraced everyone and was prepared to show them his love.

His natural inclination of generosity was met with obstacles out of necessity and the reality that the few also have to struggle against the many. He earned his living by working as a teacher in a Hebrew school and was imbued with this spirit.

David Wertheim was a man of the Torah and Hassidism world, of Jewish learning and Hebrew culture in which he had deep roots. It was difficult for him to remain in the narrow confines of the Talmud Torah Jewish studies. This conflicted with his generosity of spirit.

David Wertheim's big heartedness was one of the reasons he had for unifying the Zionist Labor movement in the United States. He believed in a warm welcome, a tool more useful than just talking. Any disputes about ideas that were impractical would be helped by the unification and would strengthen the labor movement in Eretz Israel. This belief helped him to overcome the difficulties on the road to unification and the merging of separate groups. His new movement sought to include everyone. In his heart he knew that the framework was narrow, but his love of Eretz Israel overcame small problems.

David Wertheim spent a short time in Eretz Israel, but he felt it was his country, his home. He saw the difficulties involved in absorbing so many newcomers from various Diasporas, but he lived here among his own.

His generosity knew no limits, but he was not strong enough to overcome the problems of lack of opportunity.

Many aspects accompany man when he struggles to continue in his path. The struggle between the life in Eretz Israel and the pull of life outside was great, but the second won out.

His return to America made his struggle difficult. He died during his travels on behalf of Eretz Israel.

[Page 242]

Rabbi Eli the Ritual Slaughterer, Z"L
– A Scholar and a Genius
by Mordehai Sever (Tel Aviv)
Translated by Ala Gamulka

A.

In the summertime, ships on the Dniester brought tourists to busy Bendery of the past. The ships went back packed with fruit and vegetables. The streets were full of peddlers selling apricots, grapes, plums and watermelons out of carts. However, in wintertime, poverty reigned and the lack of food and the cold affected many levels of Jewish society.

In the 1920s there lived in Bendery a modest Jew called Rabbi Eli the ritual slaughterer. His family name was Chaplik.

In addition to his daily work as a ritual slaughterer and caring for his seven orphans, Rabbi Eli also found time to devote himself to the study of philosophy, astronomy and politics as well as performing good deeds, teaching Gemara and acting as a judge for the Sadigura congregation. At night he wrote his book "A Short Version of History and the Order of Generations". He began with Adam and Eve and their descendants as described in the Torah (written and oral) and ended with the beginning of the twentieth century. There were many descriptions, notes and explanations about important figures in Judaism. It was published in 1912 in Odessa.

From that time on there were many pogroms and attacks in Bendery, and the Jewish population suffered as it did in many other towns in Europe. Bendery was almost completely destroyed during WWII. Most of its Jews tried to escape the Holocaust and many of them were slaughtered by the Fascist Nazis–Germans and Romanians. This happened in the city itself and on their wanderings to Transnistria, eastern Asia and Siberia. The remainder of the refugees, about 500 families, returned after the Holocaust and they only found ruins. When the city was rebuilt, the Jews continued their miserable existence without any hope of renewing Jewish culture as in bygone days. The figure of Rabbi Eli, the ritual slaughterer, rises in my mind out of this sad past.

He was a tall Jew with fine features, sporting a long and beautiful beard. His blue eyes twinkled with wisdom and goodness. To this day, I remember clearly his voice, slightly hoarse, but pleasant and full of warmth.

B.

I recall one evening in my parents' home. It was after WWI and Uncle Eli (this is what we called him since he was an uncle of my late father) was sitting at the table with my parents drinking a hot drink. He began to speak to my father, Israel, z"l, about our dream of making Aliyah. Suddenly, Uncle Eli turned to me and asked me:

–"Tell me, Motele, do you know where Eretz Israel is located?"

–"Yes", I replied with great confidence, –I was still a small child in Heder–"It is there, far away, on the other side of the Dniester…"

–"Listen and hear!" continued Uncle Eli to speak to me and he drew a map on a white sheet of paper. "Pay attention. Here is the Dniester River flowing into the Black Sea, Further you see many countries and seas…After that you reach the Mediterranean and there, on its shores, is Eretz Israel. Jerusalem, our holy city, is not far from the Dead Sea. Here is Hebron – city of our Patriarchs where they are buried. Up above, on the Mediterranean is the city of Haifa and down here is Jaffa. Closer to Haifa is Zichron Yaakov where your grandfather, a Rabbi, resides."

That evening I received from Uncle Eli my first lesson in history when he brought his book as a gift. As stated above, he had written it himself. The book begins: "Adam was born on the sixth day of creation. He lived for 850 years." This is followed by a list of those who followed:

[Page 243]

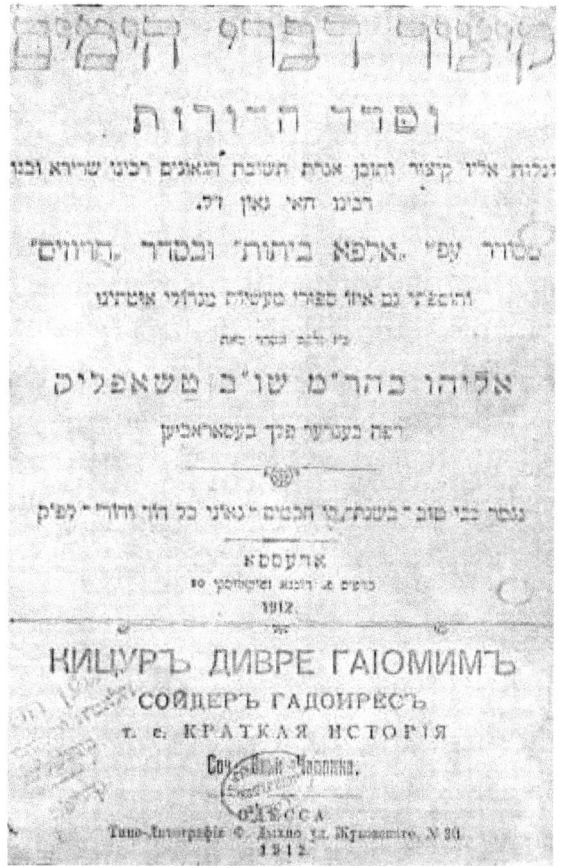

Front cover of the book

A SHORT VERSION OF HISTORY AND THE ORDER OF GENERATIONS
Also a response by our geniuses, Rabbi Sharira and his son Rabbi Hai the Genius, z"l
Arranged alphabetically in rhymes
I also added some legends from the great scholars of our people
Collected and arranged by
Eliahu, son of our Teacher and Rabbi, Ritual Slaughterer, CHAPLIK
Bendery, Bessarabia
Completed in 1910
Odessa, 1912
Printed by Dukhno and Zhukovski
1912

(Russian on bottom of page repeats some of the above.)

[Page 244]

...Seth, Enos, Keinan, Mahalel, Yered, Hanoch, Methuselah, etc. – according to the sources. The chain continues – Patriarchs, Prophets, Kings, Judges, members of the Great Knesset, Hasmoneans, Tanaites, commentators, Rabbis, leaders and so on until the beginning of this century.

Every time I came to Uncle Eli's house I would find geographic maps that he himself had drawn. On the table there were Gemara and other holy books where he made notations on the margins in his beautiful handwriting.

I received my third lesson from Uncle Eli in a round–about way. It resulted from a saying displayed near the Holy Ark at the praying stand. It was drawn in beautiful print, in the Fierman Synagogue where my uncle used to pray. This saying produced the first inspiration in me about life and ethics.

This writing, from the works of our sages, is etched in my memory to this day:

> "Man worries about shedding blood
>
> But does not worry about losing his life:
>
> Blood does not help
>
> And life does not return.*

It seems that this saying directed Uncle Eli's life daily, as well. If I am not mistaken, the drawing was done by Uncle Eli himself. I remember that to his last day we, the family in Eretz Israel, would receive from him postcards and letters decorated with drawings done by him. They had a typical traditional Jewish theme.

C.

During the times of pogroms and attacks on Jews, Uncle Eli took an active part in civic affairs. He participated in organizing self defence in our residential section in town. I remember a time when he and his son Yitzhak, in addition to other defence members, repelled an attack on their house. A soldier on horseback appeared with his sword drawn and screamed: "Go away, Jewish (derogatory term) Commissars". He was ready to burst into the courtyard. Uncle Eli, the head of his family, came out and shot his rifle at the attacker. The bullet hit the horse and the soldier ran away...

D.

In the picture below Eli the ritual slaughterer appears with his one-year-old grandson. The dedication on the back of the picture states: "To my son Yitzhak and his household, a memento –a picture of your father, Eli, Ritual slaughterer Chaplik and my grandson Aaron Averbuch.

The ritual slaughterer Eli Chaplik and his grandson Aaron Averbuch.

Uncle Eli died at a ripe old age on 11.10.1938. He had much naches and respect all his life–before the Holocaust that destroyed Europe.

The grandson Aaron Averbuch and his family were all slaughtered by the Nazi murderers, may their names be obliterated.

After several decades of living in Israel, I remembered the history book of Uncle Eli, z"l. That is A Short Version of History and the Order of Generations.

*Compare to the similar proverb (Mar'e Hamusar, 8:1

[Page 245]

One copy of the book was in my parents' home in the Diaspora in the 1920s. However, I had not seen it in all the years I have been in the country.

I approached his son Yitzhak who lived in Israel and he told me that in 1938, when he visited his father in Bendery, he took an additional copy of the book. It was a collection of single pages.

After much searching, the pages were found by Eli's granddaughter here in Israel. They were inside a school notebook cover. On it, written in Romanian was the following: "a notebook for the French language, belonging to student Aaron Averbuch…"

This is the only memorial left from the student Aaron Averbuch. May God avenge his death.

I do not know how it happened, but it seems as if by divine intervention there is one single copy of the book in the National Library of the Hebrew University in Jerusalem.

The image of Rabbi Eli, Ritual Slaughterer, a dear man and a scholar and researcher, will continue to shine among his modest congregation in Bendery. It is one of the most wonderful personages in the holy community of this city.

Children of the ritual slaughterer Eliahu Chaplik

The Influence of the Synagogues
by Moshe Sever (Sverdlik)
Ritual Slaughterer (Zichron Yaakov), z"l
Translated by Ala Gamulka

Our sages said: "I am a wall" – i.e. the Jewish community, and "my breasts are like towers"– the synagogues and houses of learning (Pessachim, 87).

The synagogue is the highest spiritual center where all the classes and the political parties become one people and one family. On Shabbat we say, during afternoon prayer: "You are one and you have one name. Your people are one nation and you have awarded them a day of rest. Avraham will rejoice, Yitzhak will sing, Yaakov and his sons will rest on that day". On this day everyone congregates and unites, grandfather and father, son and grandson–with holiness and purity. Everyone according to his rank sits apart and speaks to the maker.

The sages said about Balaam: "You know what was in the heart of evil person by the way he blessed. He told them not to have synagogues and houses of learning. God reversed the curse into a blessing and told them – How good are your tents o Jacob and your abodes, Israel" (Sanhedrin, 105). Balaam, the evil one, was described by the sages (Deuteronomy, 34) in this phrase: "No one has arisen in Israel like Moses". "Who was he? Balaam, the son of Beâ€˜or, who intended to destroy the foundation of the Jewish nation. He wanted to separate the adherents so they would not have synagogues and houses of learning, but this is what gives us strength as a nation and as a united Jewish people. Good people want to be together. If it is not permitted to congregate in synagogues and houses of learning then all public prayers, religious education would be abolished. The synagogue is the uniting force for all sectors as one nation, one that loves its people.

In olden days, all of Israel would gather when they came to Jerusalem on foot and they would exchange information on their towns and their ways. The sages thus knew what had to be corrected or changed in every town and village– for the good of the people. The houses of learning educated the next generation and directed them in the right way. The teachers were responsible for the youth as if they were young animals in a herd.

During the year, every Shabbat, the prayer leader reads the Torah portions that contain the 613 commandments. This way everyone will understand and know how to behave towards others and towards God. Our Torah is full of love and shows the proper way to act.

"Peace unto the utensil that is full of blessings". This is why the people are mentioned in the synagogues and are told: "Wise students will bring peace to the world".

This was the reason why the first Hassidim waited an hour before praying for an hour. They then waited another hour. (Brachot 32). In the synagogue each one saw his friends and relatives. "All of Israel are friends". They would chat and ask about the family and other news. This is how they became closer to each other with true love and affection, peace and friendship. They sometimes would help each other either with charity and money or by good advice and recommendation.

In the synagogue, when people saw each other, they could overcome feelings of hatred since it is not permitted. It is better to show reproof instead of hatred. It is better to openly show reproof than to love in secret. (Sifrei, Dvarim 82 and Proverbs 27:5). Reproof may be shown many times and even from a student to his rabbi, but without shaming anyone. It is more easily done within the synagogue. If the one showing reproof comes to his friend's house, the wife and other household members can ask: "Who is this person who is showing you reproof?" Or he may not be at home, or he may be busy with his work.

When people come to the synagogue on a daily basis the others are interested if one is absent at one time. They want to know if he is ill and would visit him in his home to practice the commandment of visiting the sick. This is a very important commandment since they would strengthen him and bless him to have a full recovery.

In the synagogue, each person, according to his ability could devote a specific time to study the Portion of the week, Bible, Daily Chapter, Mishna, Daily Page of Gemara, Psalms, etc. without any interruptions.

In the synagogue each person can find others like him and study with them. Our sages said that in Alexandria, in ancient times, one could see, in the synagogue various groups studying together. When a new person entered he was always able to find others similar to him so there was no need for mixing the groups.

A prize, awarded by the World Association of Former Residents of Bessarabia, distributed to Rabbi Moshe Sever The award was given for his book "A Collection of Sayings and Proverbs".A prize, awarded by the World Association of Former Residents of Bessarabia, distributed to Rabbi Moshe Sever The award was given for his book "A Collection of Sayings and Proverbs".

Among those seated, from right to left: Rabbi Moshe Sever, Yitzhak Korn, D. Zakai, MK Yitzhak Raphael. Pinhas Bendersky welcomed everyone on behalf of the Association of Former Residents of Bendery

[Page 247]

The schools were also like the synagogues since the teachers prayed with their students. It was said that there were 480 synagogues in Jerusalem and each one had a school, a house of learning, classes of Talmud and Mishna. (Gittin, 58)

We are committed to strive with all our might to return the crown to its glory and to bring peace, goodness and blessings to us and all of Israel. May God bless us in the light of the Torah, love of good deeds and complete redemption soon, in our time.

("The Synagogue", bulletins of the Tel Aviv Synagogue, booklet B)

A Proposal to Fund a Pension Fund Fifty Years Ago
by Moshe Sever (Sverdlik)
Translated by Ala Gamulka

We are in the midst of achieving the process of awarding one of the most important socialist rights in the field of pension and retirement to our members in various associations, factories and institutions. It is understood that we should now reflect upon events that occurred fifty years ago when it was but a dream. At the time only a few dreamed and fought for the realization of the optimum goal – insurance for people in their old age and in the case of disability.

It is interesting to note that not only scientists, sociologists and statisticians were involved. There were also many people, far removed from this scientific approach, but propelled by a humanitarian cause based on morality in general and on Jewish tradition in particular. Love for the individual would be shown by assisting the elderly and the weak, widows and orphans, etc.

We found a proposal in Russian of 50 years ago (1914) that advises to found a pension fund in conjunction with the Savings and Loan Bank in Bendery, on the Dniester River in Russia. We offer quotes from this proposal which was signed by M.S. Sverdlik. It is written in clear and precise language and includes statistical tables. The author shows how each person has to prepare, by himself, for old age or for disability.

The proposal is by Rabbi Moshe Sever of Zichron Yaakov. He is well-known in our country for his book "A Collection of Sayings and Proverbs", published by the Rav Kook Institute. It contains 100 000 sayings by our sages. He has earned two prizes for the book.

Proposal

Purpose: To establish a pension fund for retirement and in case of disability for the members of the Savings and Loan Bank in Bendery, Russia (1914).

1. Goal of the fund

The pension fund of the Savings and Loan Bank has the goal of paying annual pensions to its members who reach retirement age (sections 9–10) or in the case of the loss of ability to work. The amount is 100 rubles at age 65. The remainder of funds to be divided among members aged 60–65.

2. Makeup of the fund and the obligation of members

a. Members of the fund must be members of the Bendery Savings and Loan Bank.

b. Every member must pay into the fund according to the following table:

Age upon entering fund	25	30	35	40	45	50
Annual fee	2	228	266	320	4	533
No. of years to pay	40	35	30	25	20	15

c. Definition of rights of membership and its cancelation in case of non-payment on time. The proposal has 20 sections and is detailed according to them: pension payments, rights of members, administration, etc.

The author ends his proposal with the following lines:

"It is well-known that as one ages the ability to work diminishes. If one did not prepare funds for that time at an earlier age, he would have to ask for help from family or charitable institutions. It is, therefore, incumbent upon the members to seriously consider the coming days when they cannot provide for their needs. They would then be eligible for pension legally and would not have to resort to social assistance".

Member of the committee: M.S. Sverdlik

(Retirement–an article about pension funds, No. 11-12, July 1965)

[Page 248]

The Activities of ORT and OZE
Translated by Ala Gamulka

ORT, organized by the American Joint, was quite helpful to the Jews of Eastern Europe, especially to those who were poor and indigent. After WWI and the pogroms in Ukraine there were thousands of refugees that found a haven or a transition point in Bessarabia. This was also true in Bendery–the first place for their reception after crossing the border.

ORT Occupational School in Bendery (1930s)
The administration, teachers and students

The residents of Bendery were also in dire straits since it became a border town –isolated from Russia. ORT helped by providing training in an occupation. As well there was an association of cooperatives for the various occupations and for agriculture. It was thus possible to acquire machinery and work tools at reasonable prices. Loans were provided for the purchase of equipment and for the establishment of workshops. This activity was helpful to the refugees and the local residents.

In the newspaper "Our Time" from January 1936 there was a photo of the ORT school with many students standing near special machinery.

Many of our town's people who made Aliyah in the early 1920s still have their ORT certificates signed by Dr. Z. Schwartzman – the spiritual leader of this professional school. He was also a delegate to an ORT congress.

*

In 1923 there was also OZE which gave medical and social help. It had as its goal to fight epidemics and the death of babies. In Bendery, the following institutions were established:

1. Babies' clinic for nursing children and the provision of milk
2. Medical treatment by quartz lamps
3. Medical center for schools

[Page 251]

Yiddish Section

Reminiscences and Historic Reflections

Bendery – My Hometown
Avraham Hayat, Tel Giborim (Holon)
Translated by Ala Gamulka

When I begin writing my memoirs of Bendery, a heavy emotion dominates me. One does not feel like merely writing about my hometown as I remember it from childhood. It was a quiet, beautifully planned town with its long, wide and straight streets. The people I knew and the impressions I have from long ago are memorable. This feeling leads me to a time interwoven with unusual events. It brings me to a great perplexity- full of pain.

I am compelled to write about my town with lamentation. This feeling does not allow me to forget the impression made on me by Bendery in the period after WWII when I returned from Siberia.

The bloody flood which inundated the world did not miss Bendery and it was left completely destroyed. The Nazi murderers annihilated all those who did not leave town before the misfortune and stayed in their old home.

Many of us, former residents of Bendery, were fortunate to survive the bad times and to reach the State of Israel. Bendery still exists, rebuilt anew. It may even be more beautiful than before. However, it is rebuilt with cold, mute stones, bricks and sand, artistically put together. Nothing is mentioned about the people who were cut down by the Nazi murder machine.

Yizkor and Kaddish for My Town

In memory of our brothers and sisters who had lived on the banks of the Dniester, but were still annihilated even though they had lived in Bendery for generations, in ancient times and during the Turkish rule.

The town was a perpetual home.

The waters of the Dniester flowed quietly.

The gardens and orchards surrounded the town

A legend of life was woven with courage.

Now the houses are destroyed …mounds of earth…ruins

A sound of wailing can be heard

The souls are screaming

They are searching for redress

Alas and alack to them.

Yizkor should be recited by all.

The vine and fruit orchards, Acacia, nut tree, the lilacs emitting a scent far and near.

All of you must recite Yizkor.

Even the Dniester River with its velvety whisper.

This is where once youths dreamt and hoped for better times.

Yizkor is for those dear ones who lived here and for future generations so they should know there once was a destructive fire lit by people who felt no remorse.

As time passes the letters on the headstones will be erased and the souls of the innocent hover in space looking for redress.

I want my words to preserve their memory for eternity. Those times should be remembered. The gruesome memories leave stains for always.

I must remind everyone about the murder of humans and the horror, the destruction of other places, the calamity, blood and the grief.

On Heroism Day all Shoah victims must be remembered. The destruction, upheaval and the innocent souls demand revenge.

I will light memorial candles. There should be light in paradise. With so much pain is interlaced the slow death of every part of the body.

I want my words to burn in memory of the saintly victims.

There should be shaking and demanding an accounting – a penalty- no mercy to be shown to the murderers.

The victims should be remembered for many generations, never to be forgotten. The killers in the streets will always be despised.

This is for the innocent young, blameless children, the cherished, and the beautiful whose voices are still high.

This is for the destroyed elders, the sick and the weak, for those suffocated in gas chambers and for those tortured, for those hanged in pain and for those buried alive, for those strangled quietly and for all the dead in the snowy fields.

In the overview of the Shoah let my reminiscences become a silent Kaddish and Yizkor from my suffering heart and in memory of the innocent victims of Bendery.

The town

Bendery was situated on the banks of the Dniester and this added to the importance of the town.

The gardens and orchards did not only beautify the town, but they also were an important source of income and subsistence. A delicious aroma was felt in the air at the beginning of spring when the gardens and the orchards were in bloom. It was the time when the air was pure and the dust had not yet settled in.

Fruit, including grapes, were not only distributed in all parts of the Tsarist Empire, but also were exported to other countries.

Local properties attracted many tourists. This was another source of income. Bendery drew visitors who came to bathe in the Dniester River during the "fruit" and "grape" seasons. There were also vacation resorts- "Boriskova" and "Protogatlovka"- where the air was pure and filled with the scent of fruit and nut trees as well as lilacs.

Bendery was also famous for mud in the winter and dust clouds in the summer.

As soon as fall set in rivers of mud flooded the streets and only the arrival of the first frost would relieve the residents from it. If the mud was not frozen enough the wagon wheels would sink in up to the axle. Then the driver would know the wagon could neither be moved forwards nor backwards and needed help to move on.

In the summer when the driver tried to speed up he created a cloud of dust and nothing could be seen through it. However, in spite of this one would pretend the problem did not exist.

Philanthropic Institutions

In Bendery, as in other towns in the area, there were philanthropic institutions: "Help for the Sick", "Clothing for the Poor" and a Jewish hospital with a Seniors Residence attached. These institutions depended entirely on donations from the community. There was no government funding. Often there were evenings, balls to generate funds and the income was used by the institutions and to help needy people. All this help was not enough as the need was great and the efforts made were not sufficient. "Clothing for the Poor" also provided winter garments and boots for the students in the Talmud Torah.

There was also "Assistance for Poor Brides" organized by the dedicated volunteer Moshe Sverdik and "Welcoming Guests" run by Hirsh Tulchiner. A very important and separate philanthropic enterprise in those days was the kitchen in the Old Shul. It was run by volunteers- men, women, boys and girls. We must remember them with great respect. It was a beautiful volunteer effort for Shabbat and the Holidays. Large pots were placed in the courtyard of the synagogue to cook delicious food for the needy, especially Jewish soldiers stationed in the Bendery military barracks. During WWI there were a considerable number of Jewish soldiers in town. Wonderful meals were prepared and served on beautifully set tables. All the work was done by volunteers who were not looking for any special recognition. They were simply dedicated to the task. As a youngster I took an active part in this kitchen.

Cultural and Educational institutions

In Bendery there were five cinemas, the Balanov summer theatre, the auditorium- a specially large hall for lectures and theatre presentations, the municipal Pushkin library (Russian), a Jewish library with a considerable number of books in Russian, Yiddish and Hebrew and a small city museum.

There were several well-known schools: three high schools for girls- Public, Grassimenko's and Boyko's. There also three municipal schools for girls- the red uniforms, the green uniforms and the black uniforms, a public boys' school, a science high school and many elementary schools.

Jewish education consisted of Heders run by teachers and private Russian-language schools. There were Zigberman's, Reinoman's, the Russian Talmud Torah (Tiomkin) and a teachers' seminary. The Jewish Culture League ran evening classes. Its active members were Sobel, Leib Gurfeld, and Prozhansky. Postelnik was one of several private Hebrew tutors.

Obviously, these schools did not satisfy, even in those days, the liberal Jewish circles. They understood that Jewish children could not receive a good secular education in the Russian schools. Only a few students were even admitted to the Russian schools. There was a need to change the situation as circumstances demanded. It was difficult to find the correct way.

The leadership of the community was the "Committee", as it was called. It consisted of wealthy people with a small-town mentality. Cultural life was limited. It seemed that a good push from the outside was needed in order to enliven and activate. There was a need for Jewish schools which would satisfy those who wanted both Jewish and secular studies. This would become a center for Jewish activity which would bind national, Jewish and religious cultures. It would not include the Heders which should have been removed from the educational network

I must mention the advanced Heder of Yaakov Lewinsky, z"l, where I studied after I finished the strictly religious studies with Mordehai Alexander, z"l. I first learned grammar with the dear old man, Mordehai. I remember him with great thanks and fondness. I will never forget the time I spent with him. He lived across the street from Rabbi Moshele, z"l, near the newly established Jewish middle school.

In those days, I had a deep desire to attend the Jewish middle school. However, the Shulchan Aruch I received from Rabbi Mordehai as a prize for my scholarship influenced me greatly. I used to wake up early in the morning for prayers, to grieve for the destruction of the Temple, to run before dawn on snowy dark streets for Shabbat services, and to recite Psalms. I recall the eve and the day of the New Moon. It seems like a dream that old Mordehai would greet me. I wanted to know the secrets of the universe before having read Jules Verne. Life was pleasant and easy then. The deep belief in God's wondrous creation made a great impression on me. I could not even imagine the horrors of the Shoah were possible. After studying a page of Gmara I had the desire to learn more. I must mention with great thanks the dear, honest, intelligent Moshele Sverdlik. He was a scholar who taught me Mishna. When he came to the Land of Israel, and now called Moshe Sever, he did research and published three volumes on the Sayings of the Sages of the Blessed. It was a great work which required much effort and knowledge of Talmud.

The advanced Heder (directed by R. Avremel Kreitzman), R. Baruch Kolker, Haim Glass with their students

The religious education- later also partly in the Beit Midrash – came to good use for me when I used to visit my friends, the children of Shmuel Abba Sudit, Froyke, z"l, and Hannah. Shmuel Abba was a scholar who loved to discuss controversies in the Talmud. However, life intervened and slowly secular studies in the Jewish middle school began to influence me. I became a student in the school.

The Middle School

The existing educational facilities- Heders and others- did not satisfy the needs of the community. In 1912 a change occurred in the situation – a middle school was established under the direction of the amazing teacher Gregori Yakovlevitch Schwartzman (Zvi Ben Yaakov Schwartzman, z"l). His arrival in Bendery and the opening of the middle school aroused the backward thinking town. The Jewish population was in dreamland – everyone followed his own path.

We must mention the liberal-minded group of people – lovers of Zion – who immediately began to help Gregori Yakovlevitch Schwartzman, z"l. They were Velvel Weisser, Israel Blank, Moshe Haham, Zvi Holdonka, Hersh Kogan, Alexandrov, Prozhansky, Derbarmdliker and others. The Jewish community immediately understood that middle school paved the way for Jewish children to reach university and obtain a higher education. Gregori Yakovlevitch did not easily succeed during the difficult Tsarist anti-Semitic regime and later the

Romanian occupation of Bessarabia. He also had to contend with the darker elements within the Jewish community. Only thanks to his determination and dedication was he able to overcome the difficulties the powers-that-be imposed. This had to do with Jewish education in general and the middle school in particular.

The former students of the middle school have spread all over the world. They have gone on to earn academic titles- doctors, engineers, attorneys and other important professions. They would agree with me that they obtained a higher education thanks to Schwartzman. I take this opportunity to appeal to all the former students now in Israel who may not have shown the appropriate attention and thanks to him when he first arrived in the country. I will forever be grateful to him, the highly regarded Zvi Ben Yaakov Schwartzman, z"l. If anyone must be remembered with fondness and respect it is our beloved Gregori Yakovlevitch who gave the youngsters a push towards higher education.

In order to raise funds for the needy teachers, the high school used to hold cultural evenings. I was actively involved in the organization of these evenings. There were theatrical productions, musical concerts and poetry readings. These evenings were well attended. I remember the presentations, the songs, recitations and the choirs. I must mention Senya Tzehovel who had a big part in these events. When he came to Israel he became a well-known performer in the "Ohel" Theatre.

I want to include several teachers: Isaac Borisovitch Reznikov who distinguished himself with his knowledge and intelligence, Solomon Isaacovitch and Samuel Yakovlevitch Gorin-a philologer who was well-versed in the Russian language and literature as well as Latin, Motl Yosifovitch Shaikovitch- a wonderful mathematician.

Hazamir

A totally different story was the establishment of the Hazamir choir. It had great influence on the youth from a national point of view.

In Bendery there were many synagogues- some with permanent cantors and choirs such as the New Shul and the Sadigura. The New Shul was inaugurated by Mendel Kreposter who was actively involved in its construction. I saw the key to the Shul hanging in a box on his living room wall and adorned with a beautiful blue ribbon. I was good friends with Isaac Kreposter and I spent time in his house.

There were synagogues with cantors assisted by members who sang with them. Some famous cantors came out of these choirs. Arale Gelfand, z"l, worked in London. He had originally conducted one of these choirs in which I was the soloist. Cantor Yosef Schwartzman, z"l, performed in America and there were others.

Cantors who came to settle in Bendery were Cantor Gorman who had a strong tenor voice and led services in the New Shul, assisted by a choir- I was a soloist there too, Cantor Haikel and others. Even Leibel Glantz, z"l, came to perform. We knew him from his Zionist activities in Kishinev.

In our home music was prevalent. We were six boys and we all had good voices. My father, Shlomo Hayat, z"l, - referred to as Shloime-Velvel Litvak's (my grandfather came from Lithuania)- was a musician and prayed in the New Shul until his sudden death.

Bendery Hazamir Choir

The singing on Friday nights and during the Passover Seders was outstanding and drew the attention of the neighbours who used to stand by the window to listen.

I had a strong alto voice. I was considered among the best (in Bendery and outside of it) and I had quite a following. My solos of "Vemi Shenotnim Ner L'Maor", "Nahon Kisa'aha Maoz", "Umipnei Hataeinu Galinu M'Artzeinu" and others were famous and everyone would join in. I had great success at a concert in the "Blogodorny Sovornye" in Kishinev. Tkatch, z"l, the famous cantor from Budapest, arranged and participated in the concert. Kishinev had many experts and music aficionados. After the concert I was accepted in the choir of the famous cantor Kilimnik, z"l, in the synagogue on Sinopinovsky Street. I was able to read notes easily. I was taught how to read music by our neighbour, Cantor Goldstein, z"l. I also began to study the piano with Haim Shchanovsky, z"l, a renowned teacher. He was known in Bendery as the son of Tuvia Shchanovsky or as he was better known- Tuvia the Cantor. In spite of all the efforts and opportunities, love of music and cantorial chanting, I was not interested in cantorial singing as a career. I felt that the praying public would never reach the heights of the Prayer Leader as he expressed his pleadings. I thought most of those praying felt it was their "duty" to pray and not a higher calling.

I remember when Leibel Glantz, z"l, led the Selihot services in the New Shul and the audience was moved. The leader of the Labour Zionist movement in Bendery, Hersh Kogan, z"l, asked him the following question: "Leibel, tell me, when you prayed did you have the feeling that you reached heaven and G-d is responding? Did you reach a point where you forgot and were transported to a higher plane?" I think he replied, as I had felt, that the Prayer Leader is transported from reality, but the public is, on the contrary, far from that feeling. Most of them do not even understand the meaning of the prayers.

The establishment of the Hazamir choir did not produce the expected results. As I previously related, there were many singers and lovers of music. The choir needed a push. It came from the Bendersky brothers, z"l. One of them had studied in the Science High School. The choir was conducted by the well-known Pini Pertziuk, z"l. Members of the choir were male and female students and professional singers, famous bass singer Volodya Krasiltchik, tenors from the school choirs and I. Volodya taught music in the Schwartzman High School at one time. The purpose of the choir was to establish a Jewish national atmosphere by presenting evenings of Yiddish and Hebrew songs, recitations, and plays. These evenings were well-organized and well-run. The songs by Warshavsky, z"l, headed the program. One of the members of Hazamir became the famous soprano Zina Pistrova. These evenings felt comfortable in a warm atmosphere. Although many years have passed, I still remember well the singing of Zina Pistrova together with Misha Pustan, z"l.

During the Revolution the writer of these lines organized a small orchestra under the auspices of the Society for Jewish Folk Music. However, with the occupation of Bessarabia by Romania everything fell by the wayside.

There was, in Bendery, an amateur theatre group headed by Yoske Gold. Others who participated were Harushtch, Kaniverlatzky, and Alec Stein.

All the memoirs I discussed took place before 1924. This is when I married Havale Rabinovitch from Kagul (Southern Bessarabia). It was a "love affair" which developed when Havale used to spend her summers at her sister Zillah Kreposters's place (wife of Volodya Kreposter). They lived on Komandonsky Street at the end of Aleksandrovsk. Havale was a medical student in Iasi. My friends at the time were: Hamo Shtratman, Isaac Kreposter, Pini Schrybman, Moysey Shtiperlman (drowned in the Dniester), Shura Geisser, Clara Finkelstein and others. It was a group of happy young people.

In 1924, after the wedding, I moved to Kagul. Actually, I had left home in 1921 when I was invited to teach in the Torutino Hebrew High School. I taught secular subjects in Hebrew. I spent a year there and then I did my military duty in Romon at the officers' school. I completed my military service in 1923 and then I worked as an assistant bookkeeper for Shmuel Kleiner, z"l, until my wedding in 1924.

When I came to Kagul I threw myself wholeheartedly into Zionist activities until 1940. At that time Bessarabia was returned to Russia, now the Soviet Union. A new chapter began, one of a hard life, suffering, sorrows and constant moving.

When the Soviets took over I was not in town as I had been mobilized into the Romanian army. I never returned to Kagul since I would have lost my freedom. I remained in Bendery. When I was discharged from the Romanian army I discovered that all those who had been active in Zionist and other social circles were arrested and sent to Siberia and other Northern sites. Almost all of them perished. May they be remembered among the living. I do not wish to mention any names since I may omit someone. Destiny would have it that even I did not miss out on Siberia. However, my circumstances were a little easier.

In 1941, WWII broke out. People began to be on the move, my family and I among them. The war put a halt to the oppressive Soviet regime since confusion reigned. Residents were torn away from their homes and families were separated during their flight into the depths of Russia so as not to fall into the hands of the Germans. My family and I reached Northern Caucasus where I was mobilized by the Soviet army and sent to the front in Rostov. I then went to Stalingrad where I was a commander under the Red Flag. I distinguished myself with my troop and was to receive a two-week furlough and other rewards. How could I travel and where was my family? I had lost touch with them. A lucky event helped me. I entered the mail room on the Volga River and, to my great happiness; there was a postcard from my family. One can imagine my delight when I unexpectedly connected with my family. The postcard brought back the memory of my mother saying good-bye to me when I left. To this day I cannot forget her tears. How true is the saying: "There is only one mother in the world."

I will not describe my roaming until I reached Stalingrad as it would occupy too much time and space. I will only mention that I was fortunate to remain alive. On the way to Stalingrad I had to disembark many times to avoid bombings by the German Air Force.

When I reached Stalingrad I discovered a new problem. How does one bury the dead? My troop, which originally had numbered eighty men- some were Jews- was down to a third. The survivors were evacuated, most likely to Siberia. I realized I was lucky to have been on furlough and Siberia did not miss me. I also understood that it was not necessary to delve too deeply into the reasons.

After the big battle in Stalingrad a strange event happened. Many Jews, Ukrainians, Russians, White Russians and others were assembled on a freight train and dispatched to Siberia. Why? One was not permitted to question. After much suffering we arrived in Siberia where we settled into a "town" of wooden barracks. Army discipline prevailed and we were ordered to work on repairing the secondary railroad of the Trans-Siberian railway. However, there were gaps along the line where even the primary railroad was absent. It was important to repair these lines since they were essential during the war in general and on the eve of the Japanese front in particular.

After four years I was discharged. By the way, in Siberia, I found out why I had been sent there. It was actually accidental. There had been a theft of butter and potatoes and someone wanted to accuse me. The political officer had said to me: "Potatoes with butter is tasty, but adding Zionism to the mixture is even tastier." I was quite surprised because I was one of those considered to be honest. The colonel told me: "The prosecution is speaking nonsense. You are not like that. You are an honest, fine man. Do not fear. Nothing will happen to you. Although I was ordered to put you in prison until you admit to the crime."

Thank G-d it was only a scare. It turned out that the authorities changed their mind about me and nothing happened to me.

After my liberation from Siberia I made an error which could have cost me a great deal. This is what happened:

I returned to Bendery from Siberia and this was a mistake. I have already described the physical state of the town. The authorities again began to pick on me. They brought up my Zionist and Jewish activities and my candidature for parliament as a Jewish representative. To this they added the term "saboteur". Interrogations and accusations followed. I knew that I was unwanted and since I was still free I had to leave. How? Help came from a good friend, Z. Sh., z"l. He advised me to travel to Riga, the capital of Latvia. It was difficult to obtain new papers, but if one could find a job in the vineyard it was easier. I found work as a bookkeeper, rented a room and received permission to become a resident of Riga. I then brought my family.

All the suffering I had undergone made me very ill. I spent some time in hospital and Thank G-d, I survived and recuperated. My Havale and my dear mother, z"l, suffered with me. My mother made a deal with G-d to give me her remaining years.

I must repeat that my mother was not only one in a million, but she was also the best. May her memory be counted among those living.

Finally, I wish to say the following:

Bendery, Bendery: You exist and will always exist. Look around you, your residents are missing. The innocents have disappeared forever.

Orchards, gardens, acacia trees and other living plants: You will blossom in the spring and bitter tears will drip as the innocent victims who once lived there are remembered.

River Dniester: Take our dripping tears and send them to the seas and oceans. Let them be victorious and be the eternal gravestone for our innocents who were destroyed!

[Page 262]

Our Town
by David Carmel (New York)

Translated by Ala Gamulka

Our town, Bender, in Bessarabia, was situated between the cities of Kishinev and Odessa. In town, there was a large iron bridge over the Dniester River, a jailhouse, army barracks and a big fortress. The fortress had been built during the Turkish occupation and it had locks and broad canals. These could be flooded in times of need so that the enemy would not be able to conquer them.

The port of Bendery was located near the village of Varnitza. There, Turkish workers (Banibakes) would carry, on their backs, heavy sacks filled with wheat. These were to be loaded on barges (about a hundred wagons daily) and they would go down the Dniester to the border of Austria–Hungary.

The port commissioners were Hirsh Golris and Avraham Weisser. The commissioner of the passenger boats that traveled between Mogilev–Podolsk, Bendery, Mayak and Akkerman was Benny Kleiman. Several merchants imported lumber, bound with ropes, from the forests of Galicia to Austria. Then they were sawn into boards and shingles.

In the heat of summer, Bulgarian farmers from Giska, Malayesht, Farkan, Kitzkan, Ternikove, Butar, Tashlik, Speye and Varnitza brought poultry, eggs, wheat, fruit and grapes to sell.

Young farmers, working for the grape merchants, would squash the grapes with their bare feet and the juice was placed in casks. Observant Jews used to make their own wine so as not to spoil it.

The Bendery merchants who dealt in fashion and haberdashery would, on Saturday night, rent wagons from the drivers in order to load different goods that would be sent to markets in Pokorov, Bovey, Einshsikrak, Valantirovka, Artsiz, Tchimishilie and Romanovka. In addition to regular goods, there were also tarpaulins, tents, ropes and wooden planks. Some of these merchants would travel three times a year to the market in Tiraspol, the German colony of Soltes, or to Lenovo.

The Leaders of Bendery

Rabbi Aryeh-Leib Wertheim and my great grandfather, the ritual slaughterer Azriel-Moshe Eidelman, lived in Fishan in 1812. That year, when Bessarabia became part of Russia, the Bendery community, following the recommendation of the previous Rabbi, the author of the book "Lover of Israel", chose Rabbi Aryeh-Leib Wertheim to succeed him. He agreed to take the position, but he insisted that my great grandfather would be the ritual slaughterer. He also insisted that both families would be given houses next to each other. The two families moved to Bendery.

The sainted Rabbi Itzikel, grandson of Rabbi Aryeh-Leib, took over the rabbinical seat in 1875. He built a large synagogue with the help of the town leaders. On the outside, the building looked much as other houses of worship. Inside the walls were painted with oil paint and on one wall there was a picture of the Western Wall. On another wall fruit of Eretz Israel were depicted and on a third wall there were two people carrying a stick with grapes hanging from it. The latter was a reminder of what the twelve spies brought Moshe Rabenu. On the ceiling there were drawings of the symbols and names of the twelve tribes.

Rabbi Itzikel, in addition to being a Rabbi, was a really "good Jew" – a true leader with followers. He had a special room where he studied Torah, accepted notes with requests, gave blessings and distributed amulets. He was the Head of the Community and he was in charge of charitable institutions – "Help for the Sick," "Help for Women," "Help for poor Brides," and "Help for the Poor."

In 1880 the bath house burned down. Rabbi Itzikel, with the help of the community, built a new one. Since he was the head of the community the new bath house was named in his honor. However, since in the eyes of the Russian authorities there was no Jewish community, the new bath house was called "Institution of Relief Bath House."

[Page 263]

Some community leaders, headed by the generous donor Itzy Nissenboim, protested the fact that Rabbi Itzikel handled community funds. A new group took over all charitable institutions and suspended the employment of Rabbi Itzikel and his son Rabbi Shloimke for a year and a half. This caused them to live in dire straits.

Rabbi Itzikel's treasurer was Nahman Kishinevsky, a learned man and a follower of Chabad. He had brought up his grandson Leibel (orphaned at the age of 5). Leibel was related to me. He and my brother Berke studied together in the Yeshiva in Kishinev. My brother, after his marriage, became a Rabbi in Peshterov. He was also a ritual slaughterer in Odessa in Soviet times. Leibel Kishinevsky moved to Sweden where he educated a generation of learned Jews. He visited the State of Israel before he died and he was received by President Zalman Shazar with great honor.

My grandfather, Leyzer Kishinevsky, ritual slaughterer and cantor in Tiraspol and his friend, Pinhas Minkovsky – cantor at the Odessa Broder Synagogue – used to chant Hassidic melodies for their Rabbi Itzikel. My other grandfather, Haim Hirsh Eidelman, ritual slaughterer in Bendery, a follower of the Sadigura Rebbe, was a prayer leader for many years in Rabbi Itzikel's synagogue.

Itzy Nissenboim was a wealthy man with an open hand. He built the Jewish Hospital with his own money and poor Jews were cured there for free. Daily, he would check how the patients were being treated and that Kashrut was followed. On the way he would stop at the home of the widow Feiga since the teacher Aaron Nimover taught his students there. He would listen to the sounds of Gmara learning. Feiga's house was wooden with a roof made of stones and rain would seep through. Itzy built her a new house made with bricks with a metal roof, so that the students would not suffer wetness while they studied.

Nissenboim accused Itzel Goldfarb of falsifying promissory notes in the amount of 40 000 rubles by using his signature. The trial took several years, but, in the end, Itzel Goldfarb was sentenced to three years in jail. In town he was nicknamed Itzel the Arrestee. The Goldfarb family hired the greatest experts and lawyers and a new trial was announced. Goldfarb was freed after sitting in jail for 8 months and his sentence was reversed. Nissenboim had to pay 40 000 rubles in penalties. Goldfarb used the money to build a two–storey brick house. On the first floor he opened a dry goods shop while on the second there was the largest wedding hall in Bendery. The ceiling had an opening so that a Jewish marriage ceremony could be performed in plain air. After the ceremony the guests went to the hall to eat food prepared by Eli Bidnik, to see how his servers assisted in the "Golden Evening" and to listen to Yankel the Jester sing to the bride and groom. The parents would dance until dawn and the musicians would accompany them to the groom's house.

Synagogues in Bendery

In 1895 it was decided to build a new synagogue at the cost of 40 000 rubles. Yitzhak Nissenboim was among the first to donate funds and others gave according to their ability. Cantor Zaslavsky and his choir came in from Kiev and the concert brought in a considerable sum of money.

Building was started in 1900 and for three years the position of the eastern wall was changed several times. Finally, an Italian engineer was invited and the synagogue was built in Italian Renaissance style. In the center of the ceiling hung 4 large eagles surrounded by many golden stars and small blue electric lights. This created the effect of a night sky. A large chandelier nested among the eagles and it had 300 electric bulbs decorated with crystal. There were also 12 massive pillars reaching the ceiling.

[Page 264]

When the funds did not suffice for the completion of the building, the well-known wealthy woman, Mrs. Ashkenazi of Odessa, was approached. She donated 10 000 rubles. However, the two new treasurers Mendel Kreposter and David Stoliar were suspected of misusing the accounts and a large meeting was convened. The treasurers swore, on the Torah, that they were not guilty. The building was completed with a less ornate finish. The opening of the synagogue was done with speeches, prayers, Hassidic chanting and dancing.

The OLD SHUL was famous for the fact that every Friday night, after services, the town leaders would take a guest for Shabbat. It could have been a book seller who came to town to offer prayer books or cheap romance novels; an emissary from Jerusalem or simply poor people.

The Old Shul had a free kosher kitchen for Jewish soldiers who would eat there on Shabbat or Holidays. David Garfield ran the kitchen and he would bring poultry, meat and fish. We, the youngsters, used to help peel onions and potatoes and serve food at the tables. Those praying in the mornings would always recite Psalms and study "Eye of Jacob."

Sometimes lecturers would come to town and they spoke in the Alte Shul. They had special tunes for moralizing and telling fables with a moral – all with the hope that the Messiah will come and bring the Zionist dream.

Rabbi Itzikel's Shul

One time, a child became extremely ill and the despondent mother ran into the Alte Shul and put her head in the Holy Ark. She was crying and begging God to have pity on her child and cure him completely. Another time a widow, on Shabbat, would go up to the reading desk with complaints and thus she disturbed the Torah reading. She would not allow the opening of the Torah scroll for reading until the leaders agreed to give her the help she needed.

The Butchers' Shul included among its worshippers the defenders of Bendery. Right after WWI the youth organized themselves as defenders who would stop drunken Cossacks from attacking Jews. They would beat these Cossacks to teach them a lesson. The leader of these defenders was Zeidel Markman.

The Zionists Shul was full of educated people who were followers of the great authors from Odessa –Ch.N. Bialik, Achad Haam and Zeev Zhabotinsky. Every Shabbat before the reading of the Torah, there were lectures about Hebrew writers and Zionism. The speakers – Moshe Haham, Yoel Vodoboz and David Pisterov – elevated the intellectual level of the Shul.

[Page 265]

In 1937 when I was in Bender I heard arguments between the General Zionists and the Revisionists. At the time the Zionist movement had grown and the striving for Eretz Israel was bigger than in the 1920s.

The Tailors' Shul

In this Shul the worshippers were poorer than in other shuls, but they splurged and spent a lot of money on importing the best cantors from larger cities. They were experts in cantorial music and over the years they develop a musical sense. Even at work they would chant tunes sung by different cantors in all their variations.

The Reichman Shul was built by Haim and Sarah Feiga Reichman. It was actually a house of learning on one of the main streets. It was run by Haim's son Gershon and his wife Devorah. Gershon's son and his wife belong to the Bendery Society in New York.

In my time the Gabbai was a fruit commissioner, Aaron-Yossel Kramer. On Simchat Torah the worshippers would bring a Torah scroll to the Gabbai's house, accompanied by some musicians. Children would carry candles and accompanied the Gabbai back to Shul in a parade-dancing and singing.

House of Learning of Yasha (Yosef) Shaposnick

Yasha was a learned man and an important member of the Bendery Community. He was head of the Mishna group. He was married to the daughter of Rabbi Israel from Rizishin. His wife – Esther-Sima – was a leader in the "Fund for Poor Brides". She was killed in the Holocaust.

Yasha was, for many years, the host of many rabbis who visited Bendery. Among them were Rabbi Nachumtche and Rabbi Dudel from Zlotopolie, the commentator Rabbi Yehuda-Leib Friedman and Rabbi Nachumtche, the Talner Rabbi. Yasha always paid the expenses of the special tables for these rabbis.

Yasha built his House of Learning by himself and every Thursday evening the teacher Hershel Tulchiner taught young boys about life. Among the worshippers there were some fine teachers who were able to explain the most difficult passages.

My father, Ben Zion Shohet, z"l, was the prayer leader on the High Holidays.

Yasha's son, Abba, was elected at the age of 19 by the Bendery Community. In 1938–1939 he was in charge of refugees in Galatz. These people were on their way from Poland to Eretz Israel. He was active in Mizrahi and is a resident of Israel. For a long time he was head of the community in

Givat Shmuel. For over twenty years he has been a member of the Rabbinical Council of Tel Aviv where he takes care of poor families and he also performs as a cantor.

Rabbi Shloimke Wertheim, Z"L

When Rabbi Itzikel died his son, Rabbi Shloimke, succeeded him in the rabbinical seat. Rabbi Shloimke was a brilliant scholar, a questioner and a modern man. He, together with his friend, Rabbi Yehuda-Leib Fishman, published a monthly journal in Hebrew called "The Dove". Rabbi Fishman is now I.L. Maimon, the Minister for Religious Affairs in Israel.

Rabbi Shloimke's son, Israel, was my childhood friend. He was murdered by the Nazis. I used to be a steady visitor to their house. Rabbi Shloimke would receive many letters from Jews in surrounding villages with questions about laws, family matters and money disputes. There was a big division then in Tiraspol between the Talner and Sadigura Chassidim. They would not agree to have anything to do one with the other and this problem made them into enemies. Rabbi Shloimke and my grandfather, Rabbi Haim-Hirsh Shohet, became involved. The two rabbis told them off and warned them that this hatred would cause the destruction of the Tiraspol Jewish community. The conflict was resolved and a young man by the name of Israel Chaplik, a nephew of Rabbi Eli Shohet, wrote the peace agreement. Both sides accepted and signed the contract.

Rabbi Shloimke's sexton was Zalman. He used to get up at 4 a.m. in order to wake up the observant Jews to do the work of the Creator. He used to clean the building, to attend to the Rabbi and to dress the Rabbi's children. He was a God fearing man and immersed himself in the Mikvah daily. In winter or summer he used to wear high boots.

[Page 266]

On Shavuot 1908 a great fire broke out. Rabbi Itzikel's house of learning burned down. The building had been insured. However, those who suffered were the neighbors – Yerucham Beker, the book binder, Zeidel Gafman, Bendery ritual slaughterer Velvel Eidelman and the ritual slaughterer Ben Zion Berdichevsky. The community helped each one of them by giving 2 000 rubles so that they could repair their homes and put on new roofs.

Teachers in Bendery

In the years 1895–1900 it was the custom that when a three-year-old child was brought, for the first time, to Yossel Fefer's Heder, he would be put on a chair and a talit placed on him. On the table there was a tablet with printed letters of the Hebrew alphabet. The child would have to repeat, several times, "Aleph," "Beit," "Gimmel." After the child completed this task his parents would throw candies at him and they said that angels from heaven had done it.

The teacher, Moshe "the deformed one" taught his pupils Tanach and some written Hebrew and Yiddish. Shimon the teacher was more modern and he taught a few hours of Russian language. Aaron Nimover, another teacher, lived near the jailhouse and had few pupils. When he rented a large room in the house of Feiga, the widow on the Teachers Street, he had more students. He taught them Gmara and commentaries. Another teacher, Alter Shuster was an angry person. If he was unhappy with a student he would throw anything he found at him. However, he was an excellent teacher. If a child knew Bible with Rashi commentary he would give him a few coins.

My teacher, Eli Gamburd, was outstanding. He was well-versed in Talmud and Jewish knowledge. He taught us Bible, Rashi, Gmara, Yiddish and Hebrew and translations into Russian. He gave lectures on Oral and Written law, their roots and their development. Not everyone appreciated his teaching methods. It was easier to go from Gamburd's Heder to Schwartzman's Hebrew High School.

The Idea of Zion

In Bendery, prior to WWI, there was a group of young boys and girls who would meet every Shabbat afternoon in a conspiring way. They would discuss Zionist and cultural themes. Leibl Garfield was one of the leading members of this group.

At that time, the idea of Zion had deep roots in many circles of Bendery youth. There were already branches of Poalei Zion and Zeirei Zion. They would meet and dream of Zion. They read and sang many Hebrew songs. Their hymn was Hachniseni (Bring me in) by Ch. N. Bialik with its familiar melody.

Jewish Evening Courses

The Zionist movement had a strong influence on our youth due to the proximity of Odessa with its Zionist leaders and important Jewish–Russian and Hebrew writers. Anyone who knew the conditions in Bendery and its Jewish components realized the importance of organizing Jewish evening courses. The small established circle was enhanced by a wish to broaden Jewish education.

Leib Garfield fitted well into this group when he visited from America. He helped to teach youngsters Jewish knowledge and grammar without being paid. Leibel Garfield's friend David Prozhshansky, who helped him, was a wonderful educator.

The "Culture League," also founded then was, for us, the youngsters, a door to Jewish literature. We absorbed the works of our important poets and writers. We brought, from Lipcani, the writer Moshe Alterman who used to recite his poems and the fabulist Eliezer Steinberg who used to tell as his fables. All this brought warmth, happiness and much singing.

[Page 267]

David Wertheim

David Wertheim studied in Kiev in his young days.

In 1917–1918 the Russian revolution and many pogroms in Ukraine resulted in an influx of refugees into Bessarabia. Bessarabia had been conquered by Romania by then. David became one of these refugees and until he was settled he became a Hebrew teacher for the chosen. I was one of his first students – in the women's auxiliary of his grandfather's house of learning. I later got closer to him when we formed a Jewish independent defence group against pogroms. Our arsenal consisted of axes and long knives which the butchers brought, the blacksmiths – long iron sticks, and the carriers – long strings to tie the attackers. We, a group of ten boys, helped to carry the arsenal. The older defenders would spend whole nights on watch duty.

David Wertheim saw as his goal to develop the Zeirei Zion party. His modest and attractive personality immediately made him an important factor in the development of the Zionist movement. At the time Bendery was cut off from the millions of Jews in Russia, Jewish newspapers and even school texts. Our teacher, Yitzhak Reznikov, put together and printed some textbooks for the students in Schwartzman's Hebrew High School. He also brought in a newspaper in Yiddish – "the Jewish People" – which was published by Bundist writers. David Wertheim, together with Haim Grinberg, Moshe Fustan (editor of the newspaper "Jewish" Kishinev), Leybele Glantz and Shimon Schechter helped to establish three Zionist groups: "Hechalutz", "Gordonya" and "Hahaver" (the friend). The groups were under the influence of Zeirei Zion. The party had also established a Hahshara farm (preparatory) called "Masada." There the pioneers learned difficult tasks and proved that Jews could perform physical labor. They were preparing themselves for Aliyah to Eretz Israel.

When it was necessary to enforce an assistance regulation in favor of the pioneers, David Wertheim mobilized Haim Grinberg to hold a lecture in a hall. There was a holiday atmosphere in town. The wagon drivers decorated their horses and wagons with flowers and Zionist flags. Our observant parents and the clergy also came to this meeting. At the time Rabbi Tsirelson was against Zionism, but he changed his mind in 1935 and became pro Eretz Israel.

After Haim Grinberg finished his lecture the crowd of several thousand were quite enthusiastic. Men gave up golden watches, women took off their earrings and everything was thrown on tablecloths – prepared in advance. Whether it was in Bendery or in America David Wertheim was one of our beloved and popular speakers. His speeches were filled with Jewish humor and folklore. He died while on a mission on behalf of the State of Israel.

Jewish Refugees Travel to Eretz Israel

In 1918–20 there was an upheaval in Bendery. In April 1918 the Bolsheviks sent dozens of spies from Ukraine. In May 1918 several thousand "Red Guards" crossed the Dniester on fishing boats which were loaded with machine guns, guns and revolvers. They convinced the Bendery railroad workers to call a strike. There were rumors that the Romanian militia had hung a white flag on the fortress to show capitulation. There was also talk that they had arrested the Bendery Secret Service, released all political prisoners and shot the chief Popovitch.

At that time there were, in Bendery, some French citizens who stayed in town in fear of the Red Guards.

There were battles with hundreds dead and wounded. In 89 Pratigolevsky Street there was a medical clinic. The "Reds" and the railroad workers of Bendery had failed in battle, but they did capture some French and Romanian citizens. They were taken, by boat, to the Tiraspol side. When they wanted to return they no longer had any boats and the Romanians shot hundreds of "Reds" and railroad workers – without trial.

[Page 268]

Zeirei Zion in Bendery

A group of Zeirei Zion members in 1931

Yosef Shprintzak, z"l, visiting Zeirei Zion in Bendery – 23 July 1935

[Page 269] The Romanian authorities began to search for "Red Guards" and investigated every home. More than 300 Jewish refugees from Ukraine were discovered and they were pulled out of bed. This happened also in Kishinev since these Jewish refugees were considered to be spies. The Bendery community was bewildered. It was decided to speak to the representative, Rabbi Tsirelson from Kishinev. He was always ready to put his life in danger for Jewish honor in the struggle with the Romanian authorities. They also approached Shlomo Hillels, the Yiddish–Hebrew writer, a representative and director of the American Joint. The appeal in Bucharest continued for 24 hours until all the refugees were released. The proviso was that within 2 weeks they had to leave for America, Canada or Eretz Israel. In order to go to Eretz Israel there was a requirement by the British government that certificates be in hand. The Bendery community rented a printing press in Kishinev and in the evenings false documents were printed. Dozens of refugees were thus saved and they went to Eretz Israel.

Simcha Tzakhoval

Simcha Tsakhoval was a Shreibman from his father Shalom's side and his mother Kayla came from a family of ritual slaughterers in Tiraspol. These were the Kishinevsky family who were highly involved in Hassidic life.

Simcha resembled his father Shalom who was in charge of the municipal scales (the trading place). There was not really enough income for 7 people. Still, he sent his sons to the Schwartzman Hebrew High School and his daughters to the Grassimenko's Gymnasium. Simcha's brother Levi became a good artist.

I remember how Simcha used to sing his grandfather Rafael Kishinevsky's cantorial tunes. In the Schwartzman Hebrew High School he entertained us by playing various roles in our presentations.

In Eretz Israel, Moshe Halevy, the founder of Ohel Theater, invited Simcha to join his troupe of 36 actors. Simcha weighed and measured every word he spoke, but he was masterful on stage. He spent 30 years on the theater stage and he is part of the history of the theater in Israel.

Mania Tzakhoval's talented daughter, Tamar Lazar, was born in Israel. She studied at Teachers college, served in the IDF and was a fine painter, sculptor and writer. She published 55 books for children. Her books about Kofiko and Tsipopo were very successful. In her stories about monkeys and their tricks there is a great deal of information about Israel and other countries. This enriches children's knowledge and fantasy.

Tamar's oldest daughter is following in her footsteps and she shows great poetic and journalistic talent.

Prof. Zvi Orlinsky

Prof. Avi Orlinsky was not born in Bendery, but his wife Donya was a daughter of Meir Pines. He teaches Tanach at Hebrew Union College and he has earned a world-wide reputation with his interpretations of the Tanach and his original ideas. His monumental work is the translation of the Torah from our holy language into English. He is the chief editor, and along with other scholars he brings new interpretations of the Torah. Many experts agree with him, but many Orthodox rabbis disagree.

Zvi Orlinsky received many commendations for enriching Jewish American culture. He is an outstanding speaker and is extremely knowledgeable.

Honoring Prof. Yitzhak Fein

When Zionist ideology spread in Bendery, Meir Fein sent his son Yitzhak, after his Bar Mitzvah, to Palestine to study at Herzliah High School in Tel Aviv. When Yitzhak returned for his summer holidays to Bendery, WWI broke out.

[Page 270]

Later he studied in Odessa and he came to America in 1923 with his wife Haike, daughter of Rabbi Shloimke Wertheim, z"l. In America, Yitzhak became a Hebrew teacher in Jewish schools. In 1934 he obtained his doctorate from Dropsy College in Philadelphia. For 25 years he was a professor of Jewish Literature in Baltimore Hebrew College.

Prof. Fein was honored by Dropsy College for his essays, literary articles and especially for his book "The Birth of the American Jewish Community." The book describes nearly 200 years of Jewish life in American cities. It is not merely a chronological collection of facts and material, but a description of the long journey and hardships of the Jewish immigrant until they integrated religion, culture and life in America, and especially in Baltimore. The book contains descriptions of scholars, students, leaders, rabbis, businessmen, political leaders of the Baltimore Jewish community and the personality of Dr.

Herman Zeindel, head of Poalei Zion and organizer of the Jewish Legion in Baltimore in 1917.

I. Manik (Lederman) Z"l

I. Manik came from a Hassidic family. His father was a respected prayer leader and a wonderful Jew. Manik studied Bible, Rashi and Gmara with a private tutor and secular studies with two students from the Schwartzman Hebrew High School – Zelig Sofer and Simcha Tsakhoval. At a young age he showed a talent for poetry.

In America Manik studied Jewish subjects at the University of Chicago. His first poems, the series called New York Skies, were published in New York in 1930–1934. After 10 years spent in America he moved to Eretz Israel. He worked in kibbutzim, in construction and as a security guard. He took part in the War of Independence in 1948. His outstanding work was written during the war years – 1941–1942. These were the poems "One day of Winning," "What the River Tells," "After the Fire Storm" and "In the Womb of Chaos." In Eretz Israel he was famous for the publishing of his books, poems, satires and songs: "Metal Receipts," "Steps at Dawn," "In My Glass Tower," "Steps in your Wandering." His work was reviewed by Prof. Saul Liptzin, Yekhezkel Bronstein, Yosef Sheh-Lavan, Sh. Glatstein, Zrubabavel A.A. In the book "Steps in Your Wandering" he writes about the period of the Hitler catastrophe. He describes interesting personalities from our home of Bendery who were annihilated by the Nazis. In the descriptions of these personalities he brings out his own feelings and emotions, his reactions and his reflections about his grandfather, his father, his neighbor Ben Zion Shohet and Sachar Diarde who used to wake people up to recite Psalms. Manik writes songs, fables, children's stories and even philology – "The Great Dictionary of the Yiddish Language."

I. Manik died in September 1973 in Bat Yam (Israel)

Rabbi Dr. Aaron Wertheim

In his adolescence, Arale used to visit his grandfather, Rabbi Shloimke in Bendery. When he finished his studies in the Tachkemoni Yeshiva in Poland he was ordained as a rabbi by Rabbi Tsirelson in Kishinev. In 1924 when Rabbi Shloimke died, his grandson took over his position as chief rabbi in Bendery. In 1926 Arale came to America as a delegate to the Mizrahi conference in Boston.

For the past 40 years he has been the chief rabbi of the Linden Heights B'nai Israel Synagogue in Brooklyn. Rabbi Wertheim is devoted to the Rabbi Kook Yeshiva in Jerusalem. He makes sure that funds are sent annually to this important institution. He is also involved with the Jewish Teachers Seminary and the Folk University of the Judaic Sciences. His doctorate was earned at Dropsy College in Philadelphia. His topic was Hassidism.

In his book "Ways and Laws in Hassidism" it can be seen the author possesses the appropriate background for it. His deep research and his thorough analysis bring out the Halachic point of view. For his approach he is given an important place in the exploration of Hassidism. He discusses the ways of Chabad led by Rabbi Shneor–Zalman of Liadi.

[Page 271]

He tells of the time when Rabbi Shneor–Zalman had some doubts he shouted, "I do not want your Heaven. I do not want the World to Come. I only want you (God)!" In his book he analyzes the methods of establishing Hassidism: the Baal Shem Tov, his father–in–law Rabbi Avraham Gershon from Kitov, and their students. He speaks of Rabbi Levi–Yitzhak Berdichover, when he prayed he was full of wonder, in Yiddish: "Father in Heaven, dear Father." Instead of the word "Merciful God" in Hebrew he would say it in Yiddish. This is why he was nicknamed "The Merciful One."

The author also describes how in Tsarist Russia one had to pay a special penalty of 5 rubles a year for wearing a yarmulke.

Rabbi Wertheim takes the reader through a labyrinth of laws, the study of Torah, praying, customs of the Hassidim and the behavior of various rabbis – the celebratory table, the notes sent to them, different houses of learning and synagogues within Hassidism.

The book sheds light on the Hassidim and is an important contribution to the study of Hassidism.

[Page 272]

At The Dniester

by Itzik Manger

The Dniester River whispers and rumbles

It pounds the waves onto its banks,

It brings doom to us here,

And carries longing far away

Far from the black waves

The tired breaths of calm and death

Darkness quietly pokes as the

Tired water fowl's wings

Bewildered darkness sees me and asks:

"What brings you here, stranger?

Let me rest, my heart is tired,

My dream is deep and heavy".

The calm and tired Dniester whispers,

A quivering fever–dream trembles

Over the dark surface,

Its endlessly hidden dark song.

I hold the rifle, aim and fire

The darkness has a red splash

The heavy fever–dream

Dies at the gray water's edge

I fall on my knees

My eyes burn with fear

The Dniester whispers and rumbles

It carries longing far away.

At the Dniester

[Page 273]

Bendery as Seen in History
by Leon Garfield (New York)

In 1912 there were big celebrations in the Bendery summer army camp. The Russian regime was then celebrating 100 years since Bendery remained within the borders of Russia.

Bendery was on the division line between old and new Bessarabia – Old Bessarabia in the north and new Bessarabia in the south at the Black Sea. Bendery together with the rest of Bessarabia had suffered through many wars.

The history of Bessarabia starts with the beginning of Christianity. It was situated on one of the routes to the Byzantine Empire and it was part of various nations and races. In the 8th century it belonged to the "Bessa" race and thus the area was named Bessarabia.

In the mid 1300s Old Bessarabia belonged to the Galician kingdom and soon was under the rules of the Tatars. In the mid 1400s Galicia was divided between Poland, Lithuania and Hungary. In those years Lithuania pushed to spread itself over Bessarabia. In 1362 Duke Olgyard started a war with the Tatars and took away Karshov on the Dniester. Olgyard also conquered Podolia and together with the Lithuanian Dukes reached the Black Sea.

At the beginning of the 500s many new towns were built on the right side of the Dniester. Bendery belonged to the Lithuanian–Russian Duke Vitavet (L. S. Berg; Bessarabia. 1918)

In time, the Romanians took over Bessarabia. However, in the middle of the 1600s the Turks captured the fortresses of Kiliya and Akkerman and eventually Bendery (called Tighina by the Romanians). From time to time the Crimean Tatars and Cossacks attacked Bessarabia and destroyed much of it. In order to defend himself the Turkish Sultan, Suleiman II, brought over 30 000 families to Kaushany and the area. This is how the southern part of Bessarabia became larger than Moldavia.

In 1572 Moldavia again was at war with Turkey and took over Brailia, Akkerman and Bendery. Peter the Great tried to take the upper part of Bessarabia from the Turks. He even joined with Moldavia. However, the Turks repelled the Russian army –it suffered a terrible loss. Later, during the reign of Catherine II, there were plans to unite Bessarabia with Moldavia, under the Russian Empire. Catherine caused a war with the Turks and the Galician Duke conquered Iasi and Khotin. Thirteen years later Potemkin took Otchokov. (In 1768-1774) Suvorov beat the Turks and took Pashkan and Romanic and then Khadozshivi (now Odessa), Akkerman, Izmail and Bender. In a village in Small Russia near Bendery, there is a small hill which is designated as the grave of Suvorov.

Around 1910 when the street surrounding the old fortress was dug up in order to prepare it for repaving, bones a few thousand years old were found covered by earth. These were remains of soldiers who had fought in the above mentioned battles. It seems that the bodies were left where they had fallen and over the years dust covered them.

In 1897 the population of Bessarabia consisted of 47.6% Moldavians, 19.6% Russians and 11.8% Jews. The rest came from 12 other nationalities. Bendery district itself had about half of its population as Moldavians, especially in the southern section. Around the town there were mainly Russians. In 1905 the Jews in Bessarabia constituted 37.4% of the entire population.

[Page 274]

Jews had lived in Bessarabia from olden days. Beginning in the 1600s many Jews immigrated from Poland and Germany. Around 1818 there were 5,000 Jews in Bessarabia. In the 1900s many Jews came from Poland and Lithuania to find better economic conditions. Other Jews were "sent" by the Russian authorities to Bessarabia for various sins.

The fortress in Bendery

According to the Jewish Encyclopedia, the Jewish population of Bendery, in 1939, came to 12 000. The total population was 32 000.

The Jews in Bendery had a good life from the point of view of economics. Most of them dealt in commerce. There were small and large workshops and factories, two big flour mills, a beer distillery and a soap plant. In addition, all of them had Jewish employees. The Bendery train station only employed Christians.

In Bendery there was a Russian language newspaper with a Jewish publisher. There were two free Talmud Torahs; teachers with good Heders – modern and old–fashioned; a science high school for boys and a high school for girls; public elementary schools and later a Hebrew High school for boys. Many of the youth studied as external students. It is important to note that almost all the Jewish youth that attended Russian schools came to a Heder at three o'clock to continue their Jewish education. We also had a fine Jewish library.

Bendery was situated in a strategic location. Geographically – it was in the middle between Kishinev and Odessa and Old and New Bessarabia. As a result, it had the best theatrical performances from Odessa the state–theater. We also had visits from the circus and the Yiddish troupes from Odessa and Warsaw. There was also our own amateur theater group and some cinema houses. In the summers, on the boulevard and in the summer theater, there were fine orchestras from the military camp as well as private ones. There was the Dniester River with its boats and on its shores were cultivated very good grapes and other fruit. The air smelled of fruit, acacias, roses, lilacs and flowers. Vacations were spent there during the summer. On Shabbat afternoons young men and women went to the gardens and they enjoyed themselves. Bendery also had visits from world-famous cantors. There were also great musical concerts, lectures etc.

[Page 275]

The majority of the Jews were Zionists. There was a large group of territorialists (who advocated the establishment of an autonomous Jewish state other than in Palestine). Two youths – Haim Glass and David Prozhshansky – were sent to Bendery by the authorities to "organize" the community. In 1909 the Poalei Zion movement was established and it was active in social life. The Zeirei Zion movement came later after WWI. There were hardly any Bundists in Bendery, at least not as an organized group. There were some individuals who were active in the general revolutionary movement and they joined Russian workers from the railroad warehouse. There were also some Jewish Communists after the Bolsheviks appeared on the other side of the Dniester.

When life in Greater Bessarabia, including parts of Bukovina, became more orderly under the Romanian authorities, the Jewish Culture League in Bendery was founded. It offered free Jewish evening courses and arranged for concerts and lectures.

Bendery was a lively town up to WWI. The Jews were happy with their lot and they did not even dream of leaving. As in other parts of Bessarabia, very few Jews immigrated to America. After the war and under Romanian rule, Bendery began to slowly degenerate in many ways. The youth went away – many to France – and others to England, Israel and America. The murders during WW II and the pitiless treatment by the Bolsheviks of the few remaining Jews terminated the idyllic life in the town called Bendery.

The last rabbi of Bendery, Rabbi Efrati said: "a beautiful Jewish town has fallen. Jews had a great life there and every Shabbat one would see Jews coming on the street out of 20 synagogues." It was a real Jewish life in Bendery and now this is only a dream. It must be remembered.

A Bendery baggage carrier passes by Rabbi Shloimke's Shul

[Page 277]

Religious, Social and Cultural Life
Translated by Ala Gamulka

[Page 279]

A City of Belief and Conspiracies
by Prof. Yitzhak Fein (New York)
(A collection of memoirs)
Dedicated to the memory of my parents Meir and Mattie Fein, z"l

Dudele, the Rabbi's son calls me Mr. Fein

"Mr. Fein, Mr. Fein!"

I, a child of ten, became "Mr." This is what Dudele, the Rabbi's son called me. We knew each other well, Dudele and I. My late father prayed in the Rabbi's synagogue. He was a merchant, although not a very good one, and had a good seat there. This was quite an honor. The Rabbi sat at the eastern wall. Next to him was his in-law, a wealthy man, a scholar and a Chabad follower – Shepsil Berman and his three sons, Moshe, Leibel and Velvel. (All four, the father and three sons, died in Eretz Israel.) Shepsil's son-in-law, Berel Abelman, also sat there. He died tragically in Bendery. Others at the eastern wall were big merchants in town and important religious personnel. Of course, the Rabbi's son, Dudele also occupied one of the seats.

Who would have dreamed that in this town Jewish equality would rule? The social distance between the poorer areas and the main streets was as great as the economic divide. It was obvious in every facet of life and also in the synagogue. Nevertheless, Itzel Fein (that's me, the son of an ordinary merchant) played with Dudele, the Rabbi's son. After services, we would run around a bit in the yard. I was "Itzel" and he was Dudele and suddenly I was Mr. Fein.

Dudele took me to his room and slammed the door shut. I thought there would be some pranks. He presented me with a plan – he was three years older than I. He said the time had come to organize a group that would be involved in reading Hebrew books.

I was already a Hebraist and I was studying with Avremel the Tutor. I learned Tanach and grammar. Other Hebraists also liked the plan. Dudele and I brought other youngsters into the group. There were several good friends, but I especially remember Srul (Israel) Vodovetz. There must be other members of this conspiracy living in Israel. I remember Israel probably because he was the most devoted member.

From Conspiracy and Constitution to a Library

Dudele remained a good friend for many years. When Dudele became the famous leader of Poalei Zion – David Wertheim – he used to go to South America where he would see Vodovetz. David never stopped describing how Israel greeted and received him. David was like a rabbi and Israel Vodovetz was his Gabbai. It is almost like Nahman was the Gabbai for many years to his father, Rabbi Shloimke Wertheim, z"l.

A society must have a constitution. We wrote out many rules. I remember one: "If you wish to jump out the window you must pay two kopeks.

[Page 280]

The title "Mr. Fein" and the constitution were in Russian and this says much about the cultural life of the Jewish children of the middle class in Bendery. Actually, we called it Benderiruke –to emphasize its famous mud. The grapes of Bendery, and its mud, were well-known in the area.

In a town that had about 10,500 Jews, the children of the middle class spoke mainly Yiddish at home. Outside they used Russian and there were some who wanted to read books in Hebrew.

Why was it a conspiracy? What was the secret? What was the sin? Simply, we were afraid of Shepsil Berman who was influential in town in general and especially with his in–law, the Rabbi. Shepsil was not merely observant, but he also was a fanatic Jew. He was ready to chase anyone who defiled the Torah ways. Reading books in the holy language was a sin.

Forbidden Books in the Women's Auxiliary

We were quite involved in the conspiracy. On the days when new books would arrive from Odessa (Nitzanim and Prahim) a holiday atmosphere would prevail. The most important task among the conspirators was to find a safe place for their books. Who would look for forbidden books in the Women's Auxiliary in the Rabbi's synagogue?

This became the first Jewish library in town. Later, other organizations, like Hazamir, organized Jewish libraries. When I think of the later years I remember specially Misha Fustan, Baruch Kaushansky (Agadati), David Pisterov and his brother and sister Zina – a fine singer.

I do not know how it was with other people, but I can say that Dudele and I were forever affected by our organizing a Hebrew library in our childhood. We remained very close friends until David died in Havana, Cuba where he had gone on behalf of the Histadrut. David learned how to be a leader in our childhood organizing. He eventually immigrated to America where he continued his work with Poalei Zion (1930–1943). The Jewish community of America listened intently to his intelligent discourse.

As for myself, the children's library gave me the first incentive to go away to study at Herzliah (Tel Aviv). I went there immediately after my Bar Mitzvah.

Rabbi Shloimke Corresponds with Dr. Herzl

Did the Bendery Rabbi know about the secret library or did he pretend not to know? No one knows for sure. It seems to me that he knew and enjoyed quietly the fact that children were reading Hebrew books and speaking about Zionism. The topic was very close to his heart.

Rabbi Shimon Shlomo Wertheim, z"l (Rabbi Shloimke – a loving nickname) was the chief rabbi. He had succeeded his father who had held the position for fifty years – Rabbi Itzikel. He was preceded by the genius Rabbi Aryeh Leib who had founded the Bendery dynasty in 1810. Shimon Shlomo, like his father and grandfather, considered himself to be a Hassidic Rabbi. He eventually gave up the position and stopped receiving notes of inquiry. He was a great scholar and together with another famous rabbi, Yehuda Leib Fishman (later called Rabbi I.L. Hacohen Maimon, z"l) he published a Halacha journal called "The Dove" in 1907. The project did not succeed and the two friends traveled throughout the villages of Bessarabia teaching Gmara and Torah. When the Mizrahi movement was founded they were among its first members and leaders. In 1914 Rabbi Shloimke fulfilled his dream. He made Aliyah as an emissary of a substantial number of Bendery Jews. They also wanted to make Aliyah and wanted their Rabbi to be their leader there.

[Page 281]

The Jewish–Russian Library in Bendery

In preparation, he even corresponded with Dr. Herzl. Unfortunately, WWI broke out. Broken-hearted, the Rabbi left Eretz Israel and returned to Bendery after much travel and discomfort. His dream was fulfilled by some of his children. His two daughters – Pearl, z"l, a head nurse at Hadassah Hospital, and Hannah, z"l, the wife of Moshe Berman, z"l – made Aliyah. They both died in Eretz Israel. Yenta died on 11 Shevat 1973. She was married to a famous writer, Yonatan, z"l, and lived in Kibbutz Kabari. The Rabbi's two sons also died in Eretz Israel – the famous rabbi and lecturer Yosef Wertheim and the Zionist leader and head of the Jewish Agency, Avraham Wertheim. To differentiate, many of the Rabbi's grandchildren and great grandchildren live in Israel.

After Rabbi Shloimke, his son Yosef was the chief rabbi. He was succeeded by his son Aaron (now in New York) and his son-in-law Rabbi Shimon Efrati. The latter lives in Israel and holds an important position among observant Jews.

They Come to Bendery

During WWI Bendery was known to be a place where one could escape from the war. The main reason was Rabbi Shimon Shlomo. He had great influence and was able to obtain "white certificates" which would allow men not to be drafted. Many important people came to Bendery, especially from the literary world. Many stayed in the Rabbi's house. I remember some of the writers – Israel Rubin (I. Ravkai), Eliezer Steinman, z"l, (famous as the mixed-up shoes), the actor David Vardi (my classmate from Herzliah), Itzik Giterman (later became the director of the Joint in Poland and was murdered by the Nazis). There were others whose names I do not recall. They all sat all night drinking black coffee in order to lose weight. This way they would not have to serve in the army. The Rabbi's influence helped many writers, leaders and others, among them my father, to be exempt from army service.

[Page 282]

From "Down with Nikolai" to "Marx Speaks"

The Revolution of 1917 began so beautifully. It was truly a great holiday. People, Jews and Christians alike kissed each other in the streets. The great mass demonstration at the Government offices was exalting. I do not know how it happened that I greeted the crowds from the balcony of these offices. I remember, to this day, my scream: "Down with Nikolai," my tearing down the crown hanging on the wall and the cheering of the crowds.

My first teacher of "Down with Nikolai" was Yossel Shampansky, a clerk in my father's store. Yossel used to come daily to our house and repeat the phrase three times. He explained to me, in secret, what the words meant and how important they were.

That morning, at the government offices, I shouted these words with all my being. I believed implicitly that a new chapter in Jewish life in this country was beginning. I cannot explain how it happened that I became the spokesman at this mass meeting. I do not know why I earned this honor. There were more important revolutionaries in town. There was Leibel Sobel who always said: "Marx Speaks." There was also the Bundist Oshan who worked in the pharmacy belonging to the eminent Zionist Hersh Kogan. There was a group – perhaps Poalei Zion – I am not certain. I remember Zeidel Sheynkar, Leibel Gurfinkel (now in New York), the Modern Hebrew teacher Haim Glass, z"l, and David Prozhansky, z"l (he stayed in Bendery and taught Hebrew and Yiddish). I was a young kid in comparison to them.

Meetings on the Steppe and in the Synagogue

I remember attending several meetings on the steppe. There we read and were delighted by selections from Peretz. I know now that Peretz was just an excuse. Just like our Hebrew reading club, this was really a conspiracy of Poalei Zion.

There is another episode from that time that I recall. Elections for the Bendery administration had come up. David Wertheim – no longer Dudele, but this nickname remained with him the rest of his life among family and close friends – represented Poalei Zion. He lobbied for the candidates of his party. He was one of the most distinguished people in our town and was also an outstanding speaker. One day he was chairing a meeting near the Old Shul, across the street from the Rabbi's house. The Rabbi could see his child and could hear his voice. It was a stormy day and the wind was howling. Suddenly, David became excited. He was in the middle of his speech when Nahman, the Gabbai, approached him and gave him something. David was bewildered when he heard Nahman say:" Dudele, your father sent you this scarf. He is asking you to wear it so you will not, God forbid, catch a cold." David used to tell this story about the scarf his whole life. He would add: "You must never forget to offer someone a scarf. We must learn this custom from our father, z"l."

A Torah Scroll is saved from Destruction

Sometime later the Romanians took over Bendery. The Jews dispersed. Some crossed the Dniester to Ukraine and others escaped to Kaushany, Kopinka and other Jewish settlements. I no longer remember where the majority of the refugees went. Everyone was afraid. They abandoned everything and did not know what would be. They did not know if they would ever return. Most of all, the Rabbi's family was worried. I was a regular in their home – like a member of the family.

[Page 283]

I actually became a member of the family when, in 1920, I married Haya, the Rabbi's daughter. (David was also married on the same day). The family worried mostly about Dudele because he insisted on staying to protect the synagogue and the house. Nothing helped – no begging or threats. He stayed to guard the property. These were days of great fear.

I see the image as if it happened today: suddenly, on the road between Kaushany and Bendery a man appeared wearing an army coat and slippers on his feet. He was shouting from far away: "I am here, I am here." This was David. He was carrying a small Torah scroll which always lay in a cabinet at my father-in-law's house. "Everything is destroyed. The house is gone and a bomb fell into the synagogue. It is a miracle, a true miracle that the cabinet remained standing. I saved this holy object and I am bringing it to you, my dear father." We cried about the destruction of our town and we saw in this holy book a sign that not everything was lost.

It was so. In a few days, three "spies" went from Kaushany to Bendery. They were: David, Haike, David's sister and I, her future husband. The town looked like the city of the dead. The Romanian policeman whom we greeted with "We do not speak Romanian" screamed at us. He was insulted that we did not know the Romanian language. When we entered the house, there were two soldiers who arrested David. Our screams did not help. We sat frightened for some time. A day and a night went by. Suddenly, in the morning, David appeared. What happened? Two soldiers had dragged him to the station and he sat there all night.

The old Tallit Was Found

In the station, in addition to trains there were other issues in those somber days. There was a time when the Romanians added to the problems. They used to drown people in the Dniester. Finally, it was decided to send a representative to Kishinev to petition the higher authorities. Who should be sent? The most important person in town – the Rabbi. The Rabbi packed his tallit and Tfilin in a small bag (according to family tradition the Baal Shem Tov, an ancestor of the Wertheims, had used this tallit). On the way, the train stopped and everyone returned to Bendery. When the Rabbi came home he realised that, by mistake, he had taken someone else's tallit bag. He had neither his tallit nor his Tfilin. It was like Tisha B'Av in the house. A few months passed.

One day a Romanian officer brought a tallit and Tfilin to one of his Jewish friends and told him how he had taken someone else's bag when he traveled to Kishinev. In it he found "Jewish things." What happiness prevailed, not only in the Rabbi's house, but in the entire town! The old tallit was found. It had reappeared. Everyone believed it was a sign from up above.

The Bendery "artist" in 1961

Five years ago, Intourist informed me, in Odessa, that there was an epidemic in Bendery and that I would not be able to go there. There was a curious smile on the face of the person who informed me so I understood there was a "story." I knew there was a way to "forget" about the epidemic. That is what happened. I paid for a taxi and here I was, fifty years later, in the town of my birth.

I did not recognize the town at all. I did find a few people, younger and older than me. I cannot yet speak about our conversations or mention their names.

I will speak about one such meeting. It was a bearded Jew who had been my friend and my teacher. I will describe briefly our lengthy conversation. He was surviving on his army pension. He added with happiness and in a dignified manner – "I have become an "artist" in my old age."

[Page 284]

He saw the expression on my face and added with a crooked smile: "You must understand, I am a teacher again. I teach Hebrew to two young boys. One is not allowed to do it according to the law, but we figured out a way."

When I asked how he did it he told me that if he were to be caught it would not be terrible because he is doing it for the sake of sanctity. As to the two youngsters, that would be a different story. They do not only learn Hebrew, but they also feel closer to their people and Israel and they are ready to sacrifice.

What does it mean that he became an "artist"? The old man told me that since there are no Jewish books in Bendery he draws the letters, the old Jewish letters, for his pupils. No matter what happens…

****

Bendery, Bendery, the town of true belief and great conspiracy!

In Changing Times
by Leon (Yehuda–Leib) Garfield (New York)
(Autobiographical and Biographical notations)

Three Generations of a Jewish Family from Bendery
I am privileged to carry my great-grandfather's name

My great-grandfather, Yehuda-Leib Gurfel, was born in 1820. I am named after him. My father told me about his grandfather and I feel I know much about him. When I grew up I considered it to be a privilege to carry my great-grandfather's name.

Our surname GURFEL is a Russian version of HORFEL. It means trading in hair and hides of cattle. It seems my great-grandfather did that for a living. My father describes him as a strong man, very tall with a long beard and side curls – similar to other Jews in his time. He did not only deal in commerce. Great-grandfather Leib came from the Jewish colony of Galatshe, near Balta in Podolia –not far from the left bank of the Dniester. In the Russian metrical books, we were entered not as petty merchants, but as colonists. This meant we worked in agriculture.

There is one story my father remembered which left a strong impression on me. When it was time to harvest, Grandfather Leib would line up ten workers in a row, one in each area designated by the length of a scythe. He put himself in the last back row. All the workers had to cut with the scythe at the same time so as not to harm the next person. My great-grandfather used the idea of assembly line so many years ago.

Leib had two sons. Yosef, born in 1840, was my grandfather. His brother was Great-Uncle Hersh. They both looked like their father –stately and vigorous Jews from bygone days. My grandfather Yosef was married in the village. He and his wife Haya brought four sons and two daughters into the world. David, the first born, was my father. The others, according to chronological age were Yehiel, Yekhezkel, Hava, Pessia and Moshe, the youngest. Grandfather Yosef hired good tutors for his boys and they grew up knowledgeable in their religion. The girls were taught the necessities a Jewish daughter would need. He made a decent living in the village and the family did not miss anything. However, Grandfather Yosef did not want his children to remain in the village and he decided to move to a town in Bessarabia where other Jewish families were going. My father, the oldest, was the first to leave his family. He was thirteen years old when he came to Bendery.

[Page 285]

My father's move to Bendery

David, the 13–year–old boy, was not lost in the new town. Quickly he began to work in an iron business. He worked from six in the morning until eight in the evening. As was the custom, he lodged at the boss's house. After a hard day at work he still had to help the boss's wife with the housework. Grandfather Yosef had instilled in him life–wisdom and he never complained. He was quite observant and prayed in the morning and in the evening. On Shabbat and Holidays, he attended services in the Old Shul. He had a usual place there, next to Moshe Kanter.

Five years passed and David grew up. He worked in the same iron business and never missed a Shabbat or a holiday in Shul next to his friend, Moshe Kanter. The man was a hard worker like David. He worked in the mill belonging to a wealthy man by the name of Firshtenberg. Moishe's wife was known as Raize the Dish of Groats because she dealt in groats. She thus helped her husband in earning a living. They had five children –four daughters and a son. The girls were Dvora, Rosie, Haike and Gitel and Efraim–Yitzhak was the boy. Sitting in Shul, Moshe began to look at young David as a potential son–in–law. He used to invite him on Shabbat and David came to know the household. The young and beautiful girls were very friendly. The lonely young man loved the atmosphere in their home.

It did not take long for an engagement to be announced. David, son of Yosef Halevy Gurfel, was to marry Dvora, daughter of Moshe Kanter. The groom was 18 years old and the bride was 16. For those times, Dvora was well–educated as she had been sent to a modern school. There she learned Jewish subjects as well as Russian, German and arithmetic. Dvora loved to read novels and to attend Jewish theater. She loved to sing Goldfagen's songs. She was also an observant Jewish girl.

After the wedding – military service

My grandfather and the entire family came to the wedding. Grandfather, grandmother and their youngest son, Moshe, became residents of Bendery. Grandfather's other children had by then forsaken their birthplace of Galatshe. Uncle Yehiel settled in Tarutino (Antichiokrak in Yiddish), New

Bessarabia. He opened an iron-wares store with his dowry money. Tarutino was the center of several established German colonies. Uncle Yehiel dealt with them in business and over time he prospered. Uncle Yekhezkel moved to Kishinev and he dealt there in old iron-ware and other metals. He was known there as an intelligent man. He could easily calculate, without a pen in his hand, how many needle heads one would need to lay out in order to make a viorst (.6 of a mile). He had a good sense of humor and was satisfied with little. He had seven children and he used to say that he asked the Almighty to earn just one more ruble than he needed to educate them. Like their father, all my uncles were observant. Aunt Pessia also settled in Kishinev. Her husband dealt in tobacco grown in Bessarabia. There were some Jewish colonists who specialized in growing and drying tobacco. Aunt Hava married a Jew from a rural, non-Jewish area – Kutshergan in Kherson district. He later ran a grocery store. This is how Grandfather's family, descendants from a Jewish colonist in Podolia, scattered all over different parts of Bessarabia and neighboring Kherson Province.

[Page 286]

The time came for my father to be conscripted. By then he already had two children – Bassya, a little girl and Avraham, a little boy. He easily managed to get out of serving the Tsar. He devoted himself to running his iron shop and he also started to trade in old irons, metals and used rubber overshoes. These were articles that could be sold as raw material. My father also bought a house not far from Grandfather Moshe.

We were ten brothers…

Mother used to give birth with the punctuality of a clock every two and a half years. She finally "stopped" with the eleventh child. My sister Bassya remained the only daughter among ten brothers. The first three were named for the three patriarchs – Avraham, Yitzhak and Israel. The fourth son died soon after childbirth. Then came Leyzer, Aaron, Leib, Haim, Pesach and Nehemiah. Haim died in his sixth year in an accident when he received a heavy blow on his head. Nehemiah continued his studies in Belgium after high school. There he became quite ill and mother went to save him. She did not spare any work or money, but the best doctors could do nothing against a dangerous illness. The despondent mother brought her child home to die in his birthplace of Bendery. The loss of two children was a hard blow for my mother, but she got over her losses due to her belief in God. She comforted herself by believing that a Jewish woman who had brought 11 children into the world would be assured a place in the Garden of Eden.

During my childhood Bendery was not a "fanatical" town. Jewish parents worried about the future of their children and the study of secular subjects was a priority for them. My parents belonged to the category of parents for whom the teaching of Jewish subjects to their children was most important. The boys and my sister, Bassya, received a traditional Jewish education. Bassya later married in Bendery. Her husband, Mordechai–Itzel Averbuch worked in a business dealing in construction timber. Their home was more modern, but still traditional like my parents.

I Learn Bookkeeping in addition to Tanach, Grammar and Mathematics

The tine I studied with Avremel Melamed stands out in my memory. His Heder was hardly different from others, but he was scholarly and a good teacher. His style of teaching was a mix of old–fashioned methods and worldliness. His students were mostly children of middle–class and well–to–do families. In Avremel's "Reformed" Heder one studied the whole day. Aside from the regular students, at three o'clock students from the high school would come to study Jewish subjects. Avremel had assistants for some of the subjects like grammar, Modern Hebrew literature, mathematics, etc. He, as the principal, devoted himself to the teaching of Tanach and Gmara. Arithmetic included accounting, bookkeeping according to a "new method" and was taught by an old bookkeeper from Perlman's textile business.

[Page 287]

In 1909 a young man from Poland came to Avremel's school. He was a Hebrew teacher named Haim Glass. He knew Hebrew quite well and was an intelligent person. Since he also knew bookkeeping, Avremel exploited him. He used to assign him work for many long and difficult hours. Avremel demanded from Glass that he teach me extra bookkeeping. Avremel decided that this teaching should take place outside of the assigned hours and forced him to come to my home between six and seven in the morning on his way to the school. He was not to be deterred by snow and rain and winter mud for which Bendery was famous. Glass taught me bookkeeping according to the Warsaw correspondence course Naditsh. It was well–known in all Jewish shtetls. Thanks to this extra course student and teacher became close, good friends. We frequently chatted about political themes and Zionism.

We Children in the Yoke of Livelihood

When the children began to grow up they became father's helpers in his business. The oldest brother, Avraham, was taken to Tarutino by Uncle Yehiel to work in his shop. Avraham worked faithfully for his uncle, but it was not easy. He slept on the floor together with Uncle's other employees. In snow, cold and mud he used to ride along, every second week, to the market in Artsiz, a German colony about 13 miles from Tarutino. Avraham did not have a large salary from Uncle Yehiel. He worked for him for a few years until he was called up to serve in the army.

My brother Yitzhak helped out father until he, too, was conscripted.

My brother Israel was lucky because he was rejected by the army due to a small deformity. He became independent and opened an iron-wares store in Tiraspol – a town bigger than Bendery, on the other side of the Dniester.

It was my brother Leyzer's lot to become father's right-hand man and his main helper.

Father, may he rest in peace, was a hard worker all his life. He was 13 years old when he came to Bendery. He had to go to market in Bubeov (Valantirovka) every second week. The road had many uphill and downhill sections —as in the entire Dniester region. In the rainy season, he was mired in mud, and wintertime there was frost and snow. The wagon was loaded with iron-ware and it was difficult for the two harnessed horses to pull it. It was a trip of about 26.5 miles – mostly in the dark of night. When going uphill the riders had to get off the wagon to make it easier for the horses. In the dark, Leyzer had to go in front to watch that the horses would not wander off the path and fall into a trench. When father and Leyzer were away at market, mother used to become the shopkeeper and I would make myself available to help her. My brother Aaron was already working in a timber business in Tshaderlunge. The other children were still small and attending Heder. Since Yitzhak was serving in the army, Leyzer and mother were father's only helpers.

[Page 288]

My Mother – a Woman of Valor – and Mistress of the Home

Mother's work was directing the household chores, may she rest in peace. We were usually several brothers in one room. On Shabbat and holidays my brother Israel used to come from Tiraspol. At our Shabbat and holiday table there were always two Jewish soldiers who were serving in Bendery. It was a tradition in our family to befriend Jewish soldiers. Besides the soldiers, father would bring, from synagogue on Friday night, guests for Shabbat. Sometimes I was delayed in synagogue and I noticed a visitor who was left out by the leaders who were anxious to go home. I, as a small boy, would invite such a guest to our house. Thus, we always had two guests.

Sometimes there were visitors from far away – relatives of good friends. They would stay in Bendery for a few days or even longer. In our house, there was always room for these guests and they were made welcome.

I never heard my mother complain that the housework was too hard for her. She used to start the preparation for Shabbat on Thursday afternoon. She would be kept busy almost the entire night with baking of Challot and bread. While she waited for the dough to rise she used to bake a heap of potato or pumpkin knishes, moon cookies for tea and many other things. When the dough had risen she would weave the first two Challot for the blessing. She decorated the smallest breaded–loaves with little birds for the children.

On Fridays, during the day, she had little time to spare to make fish – Dniester carp, pike or flounder. The fish was fresh and was brought by the fishermen on Thursday night directly from the river. We raised chickens in the yard and it was my job to bring it to the ritual slaughterer on Thursday. My mother also prepared kugels not only for the family, but also for the rabbi. Sometimes she also prepared for relatives on the occasion of a happy event. On Fridays, when we returned from the bathhouse, she would treat us with "tzimmes." On Fridays, she would also feed poor people and provide them with a donation. She sent me around with full pots to Grandmother Reize and other poor relatives. The preparation for Shabbat would end with candle lighting in seven shining candlesticks. This would be the first time she would sit down at the beautifully set table and catch her breath. She would drink tea and wait happily for the crowd to return from services.

Mother would greet each person with "Gut Shabbes" and she looked at Father who was pacing and singing before he made Kiddush. After father, we, the sons and the guests would each make Kiddush, in turn. Mother's face shone with joy throughout the meal as if God's glory was resting on her. She was thus repaid for her hard work. She used to sing along with everyone as if part of a choir.

In his own way, father would contribute to the preparation for Shabbat. He would find out about someone who was down on his luck and who did not want to beg from others. Father would then go to the other shops to collect funds and add his own donation. He was then able to give a nice donation to a needy individual. I witnessed these transactions since childhood. Even if I knew who the needy person was, everything was done secretly.

[Page 289]

As previously mentioned, when father was away on business mother would take over. In addition to preparing for Shabbat on Thursday afternoons, there was much more work in the house during the rest of the week. In a large family such as ours there was always something that needed repair or mending. She did this by staying up half the night. As she worked, other used to sing to herself "modern" songs connected with the land and Zion. I used to love to sit next to her and sing along with her.

I remember my first trip to a big city and it is connected to my mother. She had become tubercular and had to be taken to Odessa to the Jewish Hospital. When she began to feel a little better she begged father to bring one of the children when he came to visit. She missed them so much. My father took me to Odessa in winter time and I shivered from the cold in the unheated carriage. My trip was in vain because I was not allowed to see mother as I was still too small. I remember that on the way back, at the station in Odessa I was impressed by the electric lights that hung upside down. It was not possible to do it with our kerosene lamps in Bendery.

Grandfather's Family Sets Foot in America

In the meantime, grandfather's family set foot in America. Grandmother Haya died and grandfather remarried. We now had Grandmother Miriam. Grandfather's youngest son, Moshe moved to our house.

Moshe was an active boy. He was 13 when a family of our friends took him with them to America. In New York Moshe worked in a small restaurant on the East Side. To make a future for himself he saved his salary. After five years his boss went bankrupt. He was now called Max and he did not lose hope. He began to sell cold foods which he carried in a basket. Soon Max had a stand on N Street selling hot sausages and lemonade. Little by little, a food business emerged from this little stand. It was called "Max Busy–Bee." Eventually, Max opened several such restaurants and he sold food items at low prices to many people. My uncle Max became famous even outside of New York. Several American writers mentioned him in their descriptions of immigrants living customs.

Old Age Creeps on Grandfather Yosef

My grandfather, Yosef, may he rest in peace, was a learned man and was called "Old Reb Yossi." Every Shabbat, before Mincha, he would study a chapter of Mishna with a group of men in the Old Shul. On Shabbat and holidays, at Kiddush time in our home, he loved to give a lesson from Tanach or Gmara. He was blessed with good health due to his learning and teaching.

Sometimes he would meet another scholar and he would spend time discussing important points. He would then be late for the meal that his wife had prepared.

He loved to talk to me about Jewish tradition and he spoke of following a virtuous path. He would also test me on what I had learned in my studies. It is only much later that I appreciated all the life lessons he had instilled in me.

[Page 290]

In spite of being an old man, grandfather did not stop working. He would pack old sheet–metal using a hammer to straighten it out and binding it with wire. He was a hard worker, but he was always respected by everyone in the community. He was given certain honors such as drawing the blood after a circumcision.

After Moshe went away to America, my mother would send me to my grandfather's house for the Seder so he would have someone who could ask the Four Questions. My reward for doing it was a new cap for the holidays.

I Go to America after my brother Leyzer's "escape"

My brother Avraham finished his military service and came back to help my father in the store. He married Uncle Yehiel's oldest daughter – Heidye. Uncle Yehiel provided the young couple with an iron store in Arciz. Originally the store was only open on market days, but Avraham made it into a regular business. He quickly won the trust of the Germans, the customers in the colony, and he became prosperous.

Soon my brother Yitzhak returned from his military service. It was now my brother Leyzer's turn to be drafted. He was attached to a regiment of the Kishinev garrison. It was a great relief, naturally, for Leyzer to be so close to home. In the summer, his regiment was transferred to Bendery and he spent a lot of time at home with mother and father. In spite of this, he really had no liking for life in the barracks. He had barely completed two years of service when he decided to "escape."

At Shavuot, he went away to Tiraspol with his Bendery bride. They put up a chuppa and he quickly went across the border – with the help of an agent. He arrived in America a few weeks later.

In New York, Leyzer immediately had a job with Uncle Max. Six months after Leyzer left, Uncle Max sent out two ship tickets – for Leyzer's young bride and one for me. I was already 18 by then and I was very active in Poalei Zion. Many of my comrades had already made Aliyah. My lot was to go to America. It must be said that before my brothers Avraham and Yitzhak had been conscripted, Uncle Max had sent them tickets. Mother did not want them to leave. By the time I left conditions in town had changed considerably.

My Activities in the Social–Democratic Poalei Zion

I was still a bit of a newcomer when I joined the social–democratic movement Poalei Zion in New York. It had just been organized. The addition of the term social–democratic stressed the left leaning side of the new group as against the right-leaning point of view of the Central Committee of the party.

[Page 291]

In 1915, Ber Borochov came to America. He immediately joined the social-democratic Poalei Zion. His eagerness to join reflected a protest against the leadership of the party which had moved socialism into the background and had put Zionism up front.

Shortly after Ber Borochov's arrival a number of Poalei Zion leaders came to America from Eretz Israel. They had been deported from the land by the Turkish government when Turkey joined Germany during WWI. Ben Zvi, Ben Gurion, Alexander Chasin, Yaakov Zerubbabel and others came to our meetings. They would discuss with Borochov the politics of the party. At the time, I did not appreciate what a privilege it was for me to sit next to Ben Zvi, Ben Gurion and other builders of the modern State of Israel.

On May,1916, Social–Democratic Poalei Zion marched together with other general workers in New York. Our marchers were, among others, Borochov and Kendzshersky, the theorist and founder of our party. Looking back now I feel fortunate that in my younger years I was able to work with great Jewish personalities and to breathe the air of their spirited activity. Later on, I was secretary of the organization.

Poalei Zion in Bendery, 1913

Row 1, Right to Left: Leib Gurfel, Schwartzman, Haim Glass, Booky Kaushansky, Leibel Sobol

Row 2: Jewish soldier serving in Bendery, Member of Poalei Zion, Haim Kaushansky, David Prozhansky, Zeidel Sheynkar

In order to complete this section of the chapter I must add that after WWI and my serving as a delegate to Bessarabia, I was again elected as the secretary of the organization. There followed the 1920s when the Communist ideology invaded everywhere in general, and in America in particular. Our world organization had leftist leanings. Our group, led by Comrade Kendzshersky, did not budge from its ideology and any attempts by the left and the right to unite did not succeed.

[Page 292]

The World Union of the Left Poalei Zion in Berlin sent Comrade Avraham Ravotsky to America. His mission was to lead us to a union of both sides. His task also was to shut out Kendzshersky from the party. Some members united with the left. Betzalel Sherman was chosen as the General Secretary of the United Labor Zionist Party and I became the Finance secretary.

Over the years, Poalei Zion sobered from its Communist–Bolshevik trend and came to a rapprochement between all groups. I was drawn to other community interests. I have remained, to this day, a member of Poalei Zion.

Home to Bendery after my "green years" in America

I previously referred to my memories about the Social Democratic Poalei Zion, but now I must turn back to 1917.

I had, by then, spent a few "green" years in America. I went to Syracuse from New York City. I studied diligently and prepared myself to enter the Faculty of Medicine. My plans were destroyed by the general mobilization in the United States. I was an American soldier for close to two years. I spent 14 months in France with the army. Shortly after my discharge from the army, in May 1920, I became an emissary, as were many other young people in the post–war period. We were sent to our Old Country on a mission or on our own to help the victims of the war. I went to Bendery to see how I could help. By then, there were new rulers over Bessarabia – the Romanians.

My father's custom of hospitality reached a high point with the outbreak of WWI. Bendery was a gathering place. It was a center for the Russian Army and there were many Jewish soldiers. My father realised that unless local residents took home some of these Jewish soldiers they would be lost without a proper Shabbat table. My father, together with other leading residents, built a free kitchen for Jewish soldiers. It was located in the Old Synagogue. On Friday nights and Shabbat after services each Jewish soldier was able to sit at a familiar table.

Father and the other hosts stood by the soldiers. They would only go home after the Jewish soldiers had eaten. Their wives and children waited patiently for them. The same routine was followed on holidays. During Passover, at the Seder, there was good Bessarabian wine, fresh fish from the Dniester and other delicacies.

Bendery during the War, Revolution, Pogroms and Occupation

The first few years of the war did not bring major changes in the lives of Bessarabian Jews in general and Bendery in particular. A number of young people ran away in order to avoid serving in the army as they did not want to risk their lives for the hated Russian regime.

[Page 293]

There was even some prosperity in some circles. The Russian army was a buyer of everything. Father and my brothers Avraham and Yitzhak, became providers of different goods for the military. They were, of course, not the only ones to do so. Some well-to-do businessmen moved to Odessa. My brothers bought up the largest iron business in Bendery from the Manus brothers. They ran two shops in different areas. During Kerensky's rule – under the Russian Provisional Government, the Germans extended their front to Bendery. The Jewish population had nothing to complain about these Germans.

However, these good times did not last long. General chaos soon followed. The Romanian front fell and soldiers ran home in panic. In independent Ukraine, on the left side of the Dniester, there were pogroms and Jews were attacked. My brother Israel had a large iron business in Tiraspol and he felt the menace of the Petliurists. [Petliurists "characterized the Jews as Bolshevik sympathizers and used this as a pretext to justify their destruction" http://felshtin.org/bloody-bacchanalia-the-pogroms-of-proskurov-and-felshtin/]. Israel and his family came to Bendery where they waited for the Romanians to arrive. The Jews in Bendery were afraid. Shopkeepers began to close their stores and they ran to Tiraspol. Those who remained shut themselves in their homes under many locks. Father and the family remained in Bendery. Father and my brothers kept watch over their closed shop.

When the Romanians arrived in town my father and my brothers made themselves understood in Romanian. They were left alone. Romanian soldiers robbed unwatched property and there were some Jewish victims whom the Romanians had accused of being Bolsheviks. The town looked half dead.

Under Romanian rule, all of Bessarabia, including Bendery, was impoverished. The high income was no longer available because the natural customers were now on the left side of the Dniester–Kherson and Ukraine. There could not be any contact. The entire Bessarabian population, towns and villages, Moldovans and Jews, were left without any livelihood.

Refugees from Ukraine are warmly received in Bendery

On the other side of the Dniester the situation for the Jewish population, in particular, became harder and harder. Civil War broke out in Russia. In Ukraine, bandits raged and pogroms destroyed Jewish lives and property. Jews began, under these circumstances, to escape to Romania with the hope of reaching relatives in America.

The gathering place for refugees was Kishinev. Many also stopped in Bendery. The Jews of Bendery did everything to help out these refugees by sheltering them. The women organized a free kitchen in Itzel Goldfarb's wedding hall. Jewish housewives cooked and served. Each day another group of women was on duty in the hall. The kitchen was supervised by Rabbi Shloimke Wertheim's wife.

Just then I arrived in Bendery as a "delegate" – as guests from America were called. Many former residents in America sent help to their relatives and other refugees from their home towns.

On the day when it was my mother's turn to cook and serve I had the opportunity to get to know more closely Jewish assistance at work. My mother was proud of the fact that the Rebbetzin would eat there when my mother, Dvora, worked in the kitchen. She was certain about the status of Kashrut on such a day.

[Page 294]

I attended a meeting of the Bendery leaders in the town council where they discussed aid for refugees – not only those who came to Bendery, but also the many who reached Kishinev. Jews truly helped their brethren at such times.

One day my mother was told that a son–in–law of her sister Gitel had come from Tiraspol and was arrested by the Romanian police. My parents were unable to sleep that night. The next day, my father managed to bring the young man home from prison.

Shortly afterward my brother Israel and his family came from Tiraspol. They escaped with the help of people called "transporters," and they came straight to our house. They managed to avoid the police until they obtained proper papers.

Gradually, life under the Romanians stabilized. My brother Avraham bought for Israel a large iron business in Akkerman, and he did well. In Akkerman, Israel was active in local Jewish community organizations as was the tradition of our family. The economic situation in Bessarabia, in general, and in Bendery, in particular, improved with time. Life was more or less normal. My father became the head Gabbai in the Old Synagogue. My brother Yitzhak worked on the aid–committee and in the Hevra Kaddisha. Aaron was active in the Zeirei Zion movement and mother and her daughters–in–law were on various women's committees.

There were no major events in Bessarabia in the years between the wars.

I Return to America and My Brothers Remain

I returned to America in 1922, and a new chapter in my personal life began. I am not including it in this article which is entitled "Three Generations of a Jewish Family from Bendery." I am including here the story of the members of my family who remained in the Old Country and who went through WWII and the Holocaust. One should not reduce my family's story to that of one individual, but my brother Avraham's fate is connected throughout Bessarabia. Avraham's stubbornness and perseverance are essentially characteristic of a Bessarabian Jew. I will speak about his survival and the fate of other members of the family.

As noted above, my brother Avraham settled in Arciz, one of the German colonies which existed in Bessarabia. He was known by the Germans as an honest merchant and he thrived. Avraham was also known in the Jewish community of Arciz for his generosity. When it came to charity or any general Jewish project Avraham always contributed a sum matching the total of the rest of the community. Whenever representatives from any Jewish organization came to town they always stayed in Avraham's house as befitted a wealthy Jew in the past. Avraham never missed an opportunity to finance a wedding for a poor girl. He paid all expenses including a dowry.

For the left-leaning members of the community Avraham represented the "bourgeoisie" – the exploiter. However, the truth is that Avraham was a hard worker all his life. He worked hard to earn his wealth. In order to buy old ironware he had to go to the big cities. Arciz was far from the railroad, and he used to drag himself with a horse and buggy through the night to reach a small station. He would then transfer to a larger one to go to Odessa or Kishinev. Under the Romanians it became more difficult to reach Galatz, Braila, Iasi and Bucharest. The trips took their toll on his health. Avraham would begin his work day at 6 am and he would finish at 8 pm. He did not rest in between and did all the physical work by himself. He did not have machinery for cutting and had to prepare all the orders by hand. He worked hard to earn money. I describe this in order to show what the Bolsheviks concocted against him when they came to Bessarabia as the liberators from the Romanian yoke.

[Page 295]

Take from the People and Give Back to the People

The Red Army entered Arciz and one of the leftist comrades in the village warned Avraham not to wait for them to requisition his business, but to seem to willingly give it to them. Avraham followed his advice. He was promised by the commissars that he would be repaid for everything. An inventory list was prepared and it seemed a done deal. However, time went by and not only did the revolutionary authorities not keep their word, but Avraham and his family were thrown out of the house and had to settle in a crowded apartment.

Avraham tried to prove to the representative of the authorities that everything he possessed had been obtained through hard work. Although he had been promised to be repaid he was told: "Take from the People and Give Back to the People."

Shortly afterwards, the Nazis began the war with the Soviets and the Red Army evacuated Bessarabia. Avraham had been given notice a few days earlier that he and his family were to be evacuated. They were only permitted to bring with them the bare essentials.

Avraham's wife, Heida, died on the way. One of his sons was already in Eretz Israel. He was later mobilized into the British Brigade and even reached the rank of sergeant.

The Bolsheviks mobilized Avraham's two sons who were with him and he was left alone in Central Asia. There, far, far away, Avraham was starving. Eventually, his experience as a great merchant enabled him to obtain food.

In the town where Avraham was abandoned there were also our nieces, the daughters of our sister. She had died from hunger during the evacuation. Avraham tried to help them as much as he could. However, when he went out of town to look for a way to earn a living, the girls would go to his room and search it to try to find anything he left behind – perhaps a crust of bread.

Avraham recorded his survival in a diary which I now have among my papers. In it are recorded the Soviet "realities" and the stealing among its army officers. They all stole from the State. Avraham, the foreigner, stood away from the shame and humiliation in order to at least gain a crust of bread.

Final Story of the Family

When it became clear that the war was ending, Avraham began a slow return to Bessarabia. He reached Czernowitz where his son Shmuel lived with his wife. A relative of his wife helped the three of them to "smuggle" themselves back to Romania. From Bucharest, Avraham was in touch with me and the other brothers in America. We, of course, provided them with funds and they reached Cyprus, hoping to go from there to Eretz Israel. The British did not allow them entry. The fact that Avraham's son and Shmuel's brother had served in the British Army was not enough for Bevin's [Ernest Bevin, British Foreign Secretary] underlings.

[Page 296]

Soon the State of Israel was declared and Avraham, his son and daughter-in-law were among the first arrivals to the independent new country. They quickly settled in a kibbutz.

In 1951, I came to Israel as a delegate to a world conference of Bessarabian Jews. I visited Avraham and other members of our family. I had not seen them for nearly 30 years. This is how I heard about the above-mentioned events.

My parents had the privilege of finding their eternal rest before the Red Army marched into Bendery. They would have suffered terribly otherwise. My brother Pesach came to America in 1921, after my visit to Bendery. My brothers Yitzhak and Aaron, together with their families, remained in Bendery. The Bolsheviks took everything away from them. They were thrown out of their homes and were only allotted one room per family. They were tormented cruelly and accused of being "bourgeois" and "counterrevolutionaries." One bright day, Aaron was arrested and locked up in a fruit wagon at the station. Yitzhak had hidden in the house of Rabbi Efrati. When Yitzhak heard about his brother's arrest he told the rabbi: "I cannot leave my brother all alone." He voluntarily appeared in front of the authorities. Both Yitzhak and Aaron were then sent to Siberia. They both died on their way to their deportation destination. Their families never heard anything about them.

The Communist authorities also arrested my brother Israel and held him for a long time in prison. He finally left there sick and a broken man. Later he worked for a time as an employee in an iron business in Czernowitz. He then took to his bed as an invalid. He died in 1967, and his wife Hannah followed him a year later. Their children live in the Soviet Union.

Two sisters–in–law, Yitzhak's Haike and Aaron's Haike live in Kishinev. I wrote to the latter, but she has not answered my letters. Fear of the Soviet censor probably was the reason. We have all aged by now and it may be too late to reconnect.

The fate of our family is similar to the general Jewish fate in the times of our worst disasters. However, the exterminators did not reach all of our people.

The great–grandchildren of Yehuda–Leib Gurfel, whose sons established themselves in Jewish Bessarabia, are today dispersed over several continents and many cities. After all that has happened they remain an integral part of the triumph of Israel.

[Page 297]

Poem
by Yitzhak Abramovitch (Tighina–Bendery)

About Rabbi Yosef Wertheim

The well of knowledge and of Torah –

This is what you, Rabbi, are without a doubt.

You dispel the gloom

That comes from the dark devil,

You fan the noble fire,

To build up the morale

Of dear people.

It comes from a well of Torah.

You are the ram's horn of amazing times

The horn which blows for us

It teaches us interpretations

Of all parts of the Old Testament.

You teach us with your words

About keeping the holy Shabbat,

It is a first–class Shabbat

One that Jew–haters wish to exterminate.

You plant in us the emotion

Of "Love Thy Neighbor as You Love Yourself,"

You teach us to find life's goals

Through Shabbat.

The energy and ecstasy

Which you have used

Have shown clearly, in fact,

The moral skill that you possess.

You have made me drunk

With the wine of knowledge, today,

I am thinking deeply.

I see the old Rabbi Moshe

Who is teaching his flock,

They are enthusiastic

About a lesson of remembering ancestors.

I saw the old leader

How he prays, there, at the sea.

How he enjoys Seeing the Egyptians drown on the shore.

I believe that I hear

The song "He Sings," the sweet

Singing there like a person

That does it with good intentions.

You have made us inebriated

By your lessons,

They remain deep in thought,

Not so happy as before.

My heart cries quietly,

I miss and seek Torah.

But, Rabbi, I do not hesitate to ask you –

To give us this gift of the Torah....

       May 1939

[Page 298]

Memoirs from the Bendery Rabbinate
by Rabbi Dr. Aaron Wertheim (New York)

It is not only the pen in the hand, but it is also the heart that shudders when one sits down at the table to recollect memories from this or that Jewish town or village that had undergone the Holocaust. It is even more difficult to write about it when the town is the birthplace of the author and his father, grandfather and great-grandfather – up to six generations.

"Dear and wonderful Bendery Jews!" This is the impression I received still in my childhood. This is when I began to listen to Torah lessons, stories and miracles told by my grandfather and great-grandfather. This is the custom of Hassidim in rabbinic families. This is a story found in a manuscript written by my father, z"l:

My grandfather's great-grandfather, Rabbi Aryeh-Leib, z"l, (nicknamed the "Bendery Tsaddik") was invited to become the Rabbi of Bendery in 1814. He was, at the time, a rabbi in a shtetl called Pustshan in Podolia. He traveled to Meziboz where his rabbi resided – the famous Rabbi Avraham-Joshua Heshel. He was known for his book "Lover of Israel." My ancestor asked the rabbi for advice. Rabbi Heshel told him to take the position of Bendery Rabbi. My grandfather asked him a question: Rabbi Heshel had been a rabbi in Iasi and then he moved to Meziboz. It is said that he did not like the Jews of Moldavia so why did he tell me to go to Bendery? (In those days, the whole of Bessarabia was a part of Moldavia.) Heshel replied: what I said was only about the Jews of Iasi region, but "Bendery Jews are dear and wonderful."

Grandfather was only 44 years old, and he was the Rabbi of Bendery for 40 years. He died at the old age of 84 on 3 Tammuz 1854.

The old Tsaddik was admired not only in Bendery, but also in the entire area. He even had followers in Kishinev, Odessa and other towns. His followers gave him money, but he used to distribute much to charity. When he died, he left his properties in Kishinev to charity.

At the time of his fortieth anniversary of serving as a rabbi, the intellectual life in Bender was in bloom. This can be seen in the great difference between the two rabbinic contracts given by the town. The first was given in 1814 to the old Tsaddik Aryeh Leib and the second to his son, Shimon-Shloime in 1854. The first contract was short and in primitive form. There were thirty residents who signed, without their family names, only their and their fathers' names, e.g. Yitzhak son of Avraham, Reuven son of Yaakov, etc. They merely put an X since many of these thirty people could neither read nor write. However, the second contract, 40 years later in 1854, is well-written in excellent Hebrew. It was signed by 70 people who, almost all, wrote their full names. They already had family names by then. This shows the cultural growth the town had undergone in that interval.

The old Tsaddik, Aryeh-Leib, z"l, conducted himself in the manner of the old Hassidic leaders. They did not write books nor did they give speeches. He taught Judaism to his followers by his good deeds. His motto was "I keep my words in my heart" Psalms 119.

[Page 299]

His son, Shimon, was a rabbi in Huntshest, Bessarabia before his father's death. He was brought to Bendery to take over his father's position. He was only the rabbi of Bendery for eight years and died in Kishinev on 20 Adar 1862. The Kishinev community honored him and put up a tent over his grave. Years later, it was still obvious how great and important he was to them.

Rabbi Shimon-Shlomo conducted himself like all the Hassidic rabbis of the new generation. They gave lectures every Shabbat and holiday and the followers would later write down everything that had been said. This is how an entire book is left with his speeches. It is a manuscript called Or Hashemesh (Light of the Sun).

When Rabbi Shimon-Shloime died, his son, Rabbi Yitzhak – known in Bendery as Rabbi Itzikel – was only sixteen years old. Until he turned twenty, a committee took care of the rabbinate. It consisted of several judges and important residents. He then took over the position and he became beloved and well-known in the area. He had many followers in Kishinev, Odessa, Akkerman and other towns.

Rabbi Itzikel built a big, beautiful synagogue in his yard. The construction was financed by a modern Mikveh and the bathhouse on Tregeyevsky Street. For some time, the bathhouse was called "The Rabbi's Bathhouse."

Rabbi Itzikel, z"l, wrote his own Torah scrolls which he used on Shabbat. He also wrote other books – interpretations of Psalms, Book of Esther, Passover Hagadah, etc. I have seven of his manuscripts in my possession.

Grandfather Itzikel died on 3 Sivan 1913 – one year before WWI broke out. His son, also called Rabbi Shimon-Shlomo after his grandfather, was known in Bendery by the nickname Rabbi Shloimke. He did not wish to be a Hassidic rabbi and he was simply a rabbi. He was a scholar and corresponded with the greatest rabbinic personalities of his generation. They all recognized his scholarship and greatness. He was an intelligent, modern man. Immediately after the Kishinev pogrom of 1905, a group of Jews from Bessarabia organized themselves for Aliyah in the colonies of Eretz Israel. Rabbi Shimon–Shlomo went to Paris to meet Baron Rothschild and to receive his support for this group. Unfortunately, at that time, the Turkish government issued an order not to allow the sale of land in Eretz Israel to Jews. The Baron was unable to help. He did give them land in Anatolia (Turkey). However, grandfather did not wish to have Jews settle in another country.

In May 1914, several months before the outbreak of WWI, Rabbi Shimon–Shlomo went to Eretz Israel as a tourist. He hoped to find a way to settle there. On the ship, he met a group of wealthy Polish Jews from Lodz. They liked him and they founded a group called "We Will Make Aliyah" (the well–known slogan from the Torah which Caleb Ben Yefuneh and Yehoshua Bin Nun used against the spies). The group intended to build an industrial town in Eretz Israel and Rabbi Shimon–Shlomo would become their spiritual leader. They sent him to Paris to speak to Baron Rothschild to obtain his interest and support. Unfortunately, the day grandfather arrived in Paris the war broke out and the entire plan failed. Grandfather had great difficulty finding his way home from Paris – through Eretz Israel. He arrived in time for Hanukah, travelling with a horse and buggy with other people through snow–covered Balkan rivers, through Bulgaria, Romania and home to Russia. Turkey closed the Dardanelles and it was impossible to travel by ship or by train.

[Page 300]

In spite of all these difficulties that he underwent during his journey, his love for Eretz Israel was even stronger and bigger. He instilled this love in his children and his friends. He always hoped to fulfill his dream after the war and to settle in the Holy Land. However, there was a terrible decimation of the Jews of Ukraine at the end of WWI. The Haidamaks, Petliurists and the Bolsheviks committed these crimes. He also suffered a personal loss when his son Aryeh–Leib and his grandson were killed by smugglers who were supposed to transport them across the Dniester from the Russian side. All of this made him very ill and he died at the age of 60 on 18 Shevat 1925.

The economic situation in Bendery at the time was dire. Under the Romanians the Jewish population was impoverished. The community's income was mainly from the tax on kosher meat. These funds were used to pay salaries to the rabbis, judges and ritual slaughterers and to take care of the hospital, Old People's Home and the Talmud Torah. However, when there is less income one does not eat so much meat and does not have poultry slaughtered. There was not enough money to even pay rent. The Bendery community could not afford to invite my father, Rabbi Yosef, z"l, to take over his father's position. At the time, my father held an important rabbinic seat in Hrobishov, Poland. He had an excellent reputation in rabbinic circles. He had a large family to look after and the Bendery community could not afford to pay him the necessary salary. The community accepted my father's proposal and offered my grandfather's rabbinic seat to me, the author of this article. I was the oldest grandson and his student.

Grandfather, Rabbi Shimon–Shlomo, died on a Tuesday evening, and that same time the community's important people prepared a rabbinic contract. They agreed to hire me as the town rabbi. The burial took place on Friday morning and by then 600 town residents had signed the contract offered by the community. The contract was leather-bound and the president, Mr. Alexandrov, brought it to me officially when the Shloshim (Thirty Days) were commemorated.

On Friday morning, in the old cemetery, my grandfather was buried under the tent of his great-grandfather, the old Tsaddik. His in–law, Shabtai Berman was an important leader in the community, a generous Jew, a Lubavitch Hassid and a scholar. The path to the grave where the sainted rabbi was buried was covered in black, and Berman, in a tearful voice, said:" Mazel Tov, my in–law. We have elected your grandson as our rabbi – to fill your shoes." I was only 22 years old then, and the situation scared me – the responsibility was great. This is how I became the rabbi of Bendery. My fate, however, was not to remain in Bendery and even the contract for life offered to me by the community did not stop me from going to America when I had the opportunity to do so.

The short tenure I served as rabbi in Bendery evokes two episodes. As was well known, it was not customary in Bendery and other such towns to eulogize every person who died. It was only in special circumstances that the rabbis had to eulogize. The first such eulogy that I made as the Rabbi of Bendery occurred when there was a fire in the Soborno Square shops. A young Jew – a fire brigade volunteer – was killed. He had helped to put out the fire and to save the neighboring stores and houses. The whole town came to the funeral and the ceremony took place in the New Synagogue. The date was 15 Av, a day that is considered a semi-holiday. On that day, the Tachanun (prayer of supplication) is not said. This was a day when in the Temple preparations were made for the lumber used in the burning of sacrifices. However, at the funeral, everyone cried uncontrollably when I mentioned the meaning of this date in the past. For us in Bendery, it was not a holiday because we brought to burial a victim of the fire.

The second episode happened before Pesach. Bessarabia was experiencing a terrible drought which brought much hunger to our blessed land. It was feared there would not be enough flour for the baking of Matzoth. Prices were high and poor people could not afford to buy matzoth for the entire holiday. The rabbis allowed Passover corn meal to be eaten. We koshered a mill, painted the ears of corn and prepared special flour for Pesach – according to the rules.

Immediately after Pesach, I had the opportunity to go to America. I had organized an appeal on behalf of the hospital and Old People's Home, and I hoped to receive donations from our former residents and other sources. However, not everything dreamed in Europe can be realised in America. My compatriots in New York received me warmly, but they were unable to give me as much as I thought.

Eight years after I left Bendery, the economic and social situations of many Jewish communities in Poland worsened due to anti-Semitic laws of the government. My father, Rabbi Yosef, z"l, decided to leave his post in Hrobishov and to return to Bendery. He arrived in the spring of 1935. I was visiting Bendery at the time and it was the last opportunity to see my parents in my hometown.

My father was the rabbi in Bendery for only five years. When WWII broke out in September 1939, Bendery became part of the Soviet Union since Romania gave up its territory. It was dangerous for my father to fall into the hands of the Communists due to his political activities in his previous post in Poland. He had to flee Bendery. He obtained, with great difficulty, a certificate from the British in Palestine, and he arrived in Eretz Israel on Pesach 1940.

I wish to quote from a manuscript he wrote about Bendery – it is now in my possession: "Bendery was a town famous for its charity, where the poor were always – in all generations – helped."

My father spent his last years in Jerusalem and he earned an excellent reputation among rabbis and Yeshivas. He was always given great honor and he was chosen as one of the official rabbis in the Jerusalem Religious Court.

The previously quoted description of Bendery charity was written by my late father before he died of heart ailments on 23 Adar II 1946. It is true proof that, for the past 130 years, seven generations of our Wertheim family – all felt the same way about Bendery. Dear and Wonderful Bendery Jews!

[Page 302]

Bessarabian Zionist Activists Crusade
by I.L. Yonatan (Tel Aviv)
Translated by Ala Gamulka

1910–1914

The Jewish community of Bessarabia was absorbed in a peaceful existence, like one before a storm. The Zionist movement had its best successes.

What do Zionist activities in those days mean? They involved collecting funds for Jewish National Fund, distributing "shekels," leading a campaign to have representatives in the communities, promoting the Hebrew language among the youth, establishing Hebrew schools and kindergartens and running conferences. The branches were busy with many activities.

Zionist personalities visited, from time to time, larger cities such as Kishinev, Akkerman, Bendery and Beltz. They used to come for an evening, make speeches and then attend a banquet. They would come and then leave.

In the center of all Zionist daily activities stood the Hebrew teachers – in the cities and the small towns. They were the leading spirits at Hebrew classes and in private tutoring. They would distribute the "shekels" and collect the blue and white boxes. They also provided bowls for collections for Jewish National Fund in the synagogue on the eve of Yom Kippur, at times of remembering departed members of the family, and at weddings.

I will light a memorial candle for one of these people as a symbol of all the others.

Bendery was covered, for many months of the year, with black mud. It was not only a problem for those on foot, but also for the wagons bringing guests from the train station.

The old teacher, Baruch Holodenko, seems to have grown within the Bendery vista. He wore a black hat and his feet dragged blobs of mud. This went on from morning to night.

Here is a description of a day of work for Baruch Holodenko: early in the morning he organizes pairs of collectors for Jewish National Fund at weddings planned for the evening. This is followed by two tutoring lessons (his income) and then consultations with Zionist activists – Hirsh Kogan in the Pharmacy Depot. Then again, tutoring sessions for two hours and more running around.

All day, Baruch drags himself on the streets wearing his long, mud-spattered coat. He is sneezing and coughing and shivers from the cold.

In addition to his Zionist technical help, he also gives lectures. On Hanukah, he speaks of the Hasmoneans, on Purim about gatherings, and on Succoth about the quote "Go and collect from your fields."

His home reeks of poverty, but his wife is very understanding and encourages his good deeds for the benefit of others and following his ideals.

This is how Baruch Holodenko lived in the atmosphere of Eretz Israel in his town of Bendery, steeped in mud in the winter and inhaling the dust in summer. He educated a generation who loved Zion, Hebrew, pioneering. He died in the Jewish Hospital in Bendery.

We honor his memory.

I spoke earlier about the Pharmacy Depot which was a meeting place for Zionist leaders. Hirsh Kogan was the owner of the depot. He was tall, skinny and had a pointed brown beard and clever eyes. He had a sharp tongue and during ideological discussions he was able, with his words and smart phrases, to get to the point.

[Page 303]

On a daily basis, between noon and two in the afternoon, his clean, neat store became a Zionist club for local activists and old friends. Their friendships became even stronger because of their Zionist ideals.

The Pharmacy Depot served, for many years, as the home of Zionist activities and heated discussions. If a stranger happened to come into Hirsh Kogan's store he would think that only Zionism mattered and earning a living was not so important.

Bendery did not stand out from other towns and villages in Bessarabia. Everywhere there were such "territories" where there were discussions about a Return to Zion. There was a renaissance of the Jewish people.

Ezrat Ani'im Charity
by Hanania Volovetz (Tel Aviv)

I leaf through my memories of our town and its activities and I recall the community institutions. These institutions did their utmost to help the needy. I was an active member of the Ezrat Ani'im (Help for the Poor), and I remember many facts. It is especially important to discuss 1928–1929 –called the Year of Hunger. The whole of Bessarabia was affected, especially Bendery.

It is well known that Bessarabia was always a productive part of Russia. As long as it belonged to Russia, hunger was not felt in Bessarabia. Its rich fields provided food for the rest of Russia–wheat, wine, fruit, wool. It is no wonder that Bessarabia was called the rye chamber of Russia.

All this was true until the Romanians took over in 1918. A new regime controlled Bessarabia. It was now isolated from Russia. It was as if a knife was used to sever the earning power of the Jews. A second reason was that the Romanians tried with all their might to take away commerce from the Jews. There was a terrible destruction in Jewish life. Many merchants became impoverished. Many town leaders who had always donated to good causes now were in need themselves. There was unbelievable need in that year.

That year the younger people threw out the older leaders and brought in a new regime in the institutions. The younger generation elected new leaders. Alexandrov , z"l, was the leader and he chose me and my friend Zalman, son of Haim, Kaushansky to look after the needs of the poor. We began by helping in secret – even wood for heating, matzoth and wine for Pesach. Others in the management were Shmulevitch, Pisterov, Anutov, Schmaltz, Yankel Kutchuk, I.Kh. Levitt, and others whose names I cannot remember. I ask for their forgiveness.

We were very busy that year. We had to look hard to find the former merchants who now were in need so we could bring them, secretly, what they needed in their homes. We did not want them to be shamed. We supplied poor Jewish children with warm clothing, a pair of shoes, some hot soup, a bit of meat and bread. There were also soup kitchens for poor families so they would have a hot meal.

[Page 304]

Mrs. S. Kishinevsky, the wife of David, son of Rabbi Asher Kishinevsky, was particularly active in this institution. However, as the saying goes "A little bit does not satisfy the lion."

A terrible, cruel time was felt during that year. I believe that anyone who lived through those troubling days will never forget them.

In contrast to the morose picture just described, it must be said that our young wage earners did not sit idly.

In addition to the Ezrat Ani'im institution I was chosen together with Yasha Lederman as secretary of the Jewish community.

The Jewish institutions did not cease to pulsate with activities until the Holocaust came upon us. The Germans together with the Romanians, may their names be wiped off the earth, murdered our precious Jewish members of the community. These were dear, fine people in

our Jewish, upstanding town.

The Chamber of Commerce in Bendery

[Page 305]

The Teachers Street
A Collection of Memories
by I.Manik (Lederman) z"l (Bat Yam)

This was only one block of one of the main streets in Bendery.

Why was it called the TEACHERS STREET? No one knows. It is possible that it was due to the numerous Heders found there. It was as busy as a beehive.

The Teachers Street was not part of the wealthy area of town. In that area, one could find rich people who were semi-assimilated – doctors, intelligentsia and good providers. On Teachers Street there were ordinary people, even poor ones. However, from the point of view of traditional Judaism the street stood out as special in the town. In this small area was concentrated the majority of the religious and social life of the Bendery.

In addition to the many Heders there were also four synagogues: "Rabbi Itzikel's shul," the New Shul, the Tailors' Shul and the Coopers' Shul. Next to Itzikel's Shul there was a wedding hall. On holidays and even on Shabbat, the hall was used for prayers.

The majority of the religious personnel lived on Teachers Street. They were prayer leaders, ritual slaughterers (including Pinhas Dayan), the Chief Rabbi, Rabbi Itzikel and later his son Rabbi Shloimkele. Even the comical package carrier was there – always pulling his own thin beard.

Rabbi Itzikel's Shul and the New Shul were connected to the Old Shul and the Sogeger (Sadigura?) Shul in the next block. These synagogues, and also the Butchers' Shul, were the five large synagogues in town. Except for the New Shul they were all couched in mystery and folklore. This fact played on the imagination of the children. To this day I remember the painting in Rabbi Itzikel's Shul: A figure peered from under a tree in the wilderness... The New Shul – the largest – was magnificent. It could have stood in a bigger town than Bendery. It was unique due to its architecture, its green-golden lattice which surrounded the high semi-circular windows, its four eagles with outstretched wings in the corner of the high dome. From their beaks hanging on a thin wire were crystal chandeliers. In the middle was a large bird encased in amber wreaths. It indicated the holy place. Everything was painted pure white – the walls, the ceiling, the Holy Ark with its golden decorations.

When Shabbat came, not to mention a Holiday, the street became full of people – the men going to pray dressed in special clothing together with their wives who were similarly adorned. They were on their way to synagogue. They were accompanied by their children who carried the fathers' tallit bags.

When the Torah was read, those considered more "free" used to stand outside the synagogue discussing "politics": daily events, smart remarks and jokes.

[Page 306]

Where are they now, these lovable, dear and warm–hearted people? Everything was destroyed. The synagogues remained desolate and orphaned. They stand forlorn – a remnant of the Destruction.

The story goes that when the synagogue was built a golden key was used to unlock the door at the dedication.

This key we will guard for eternity.

Diarde's Pay
by I.Manik (Lederman) z"l (Bat Yam)

I.Manik (Lederman), z"l At the end of the town lived a whole horde
"Poor people," in the courtyard of old Diarde's pay.
There was a Jew – a strong man, already in his nineties. His face
Reminded us of the Vilna Gaon, but they were not related
He was far removed from scholarship and aristocracy…
For years, in town, he would carry out
His mission:
He was dressed in Shabbat clothes, holy outfits
He went from house to house to wake "the children" to recite Psalms.
On a winter night, when outside there were snow and winds whirling,
The entire house was asleep enveloped in its warmth.
Suddenly, a knock on the window, in secret,
And a sad voice would instill in us a fear.
It aroused us from a deep slumber,
It would call: "Get up to recite Psalms, Shlomo"! *
His old age, his energy
Would bring out in us a great respect.
Perhaps there was, just a glimpse –
Of a soul searching for redemption….

*My father

[Page 307]

Poalei Zion in Bendery
by Leon (Yehuda–Leib) Garfield (New York)

I believe my memories are useful in their common interests. I must not forget to discuss the story of our movement in Bendery in the years 1909–1914.

The teacher Haim Glass, as it turned out later, found himself in Bendery as a political emissary from Bessarabia. A short time after his arrival, a second young man appeared in Bendery with a similar background – David Prozhansky. It was evident that he had greater revolutionary ties than Glass. However, he was more steeped in Judaism and in Hebrew and Yiddish literature. Prozhansky began to give private lectures and became well-known as one of the best Hebrew teachers in town. He did not have to complain about lack of income.

These two teachers, Glass and Prozhansky, had deep influence on the young Jews of Bendery of the time. They were both dedicated to awakening the national spirit of the Bendery Jewish youth. It did not take long for a Poalei Zion ["Workers of Zion"] group to be formed (around 1909). At first/ it was an open club that met on Shabbat afternoons in a member's home. Some people played chess and others discussed local issues. Eventually, new members joined and an executive committee was formed to plan lectures. There were not many lecturers from Bendery. We "exploited" David Wertheim's older brother (David was then still too young). Prozhansky was our instructor in Jewish literature. He also explained many Jewish-Nationalistic issues as well as the platforms of the various Jewish parties then active in the Jewish community. Our group was not dogmatic. We often heard speakers from other Zionist parties. We held interesting discussions with them. A young Haim Greenberg would come, from time to time, from Kishinev. It was always a great event.

Every holiday, especially at Hanukkah, we would have a party with many young participants from our town. It was a party filled with camaraderie, food, singing and a wonderful atmosphere. In this way, we showed the youth of Bendery the beliefs of Poalei Zion.

Slowly we made contact with our Zionist Poalei Zion comrades in Eretz Israel. We also collected money for the "Palestinian Workers' Fund." The general Zionists in Bendery had their own gathering place and even their special leader – Baruch Holodenko. He was a wonderful speaker. The majority of the craftsmen in town identified themselves with the general Zionists. They were also involved with the "Lovers of Hebrew" section. Many good Hebrew lecturers were imported by them. Their lectures were also attended by our members. I recall some of the best-known Zionists of the time were Hersh Kogan, Dr. Sh. Bendersky, Israel Blank, Fustan and others. Some local youths also considered themselves to be "territorialists." Their leader was a Russian teacher. He and his wife were like our modern Hippies. He had long hair, sideburns and a beard. Our jokesters nicknamed him "My Beard." The couple was also vegetarians.

[Page 308]

In addition, he was also my Russian teacher! Territorialism left me cold, but he made me into a vegetarian. In those days, this was part of the idealism. There were also debates arranged between their group and the Zionists about territorialism. They were not successful.

A Special Picture

Yosef Trumpeldor traveling back to Eretz Israel in 1913

With him: Shlomo Buchbinder (22), Zina Rabinovitch (24) – Second Aliyah

Yosef Trumpeldor (19); Next to him: Shlomo Levkovitch(Lavi) from Ein Harod

We, the Poalei Zion group, continued with our mission. Typical of those times was the fact that our main fund-raising event for the proletarian P.A.P was the traditional eve of Yom Kippur "bowl" in the synagogues, when Jews gave donations for all purposes, especially for Eretz Israel. We also collected funds at weddings, when the guests were already seated around tables. We (including me) would stand on a chair and appeal to those gathered to donate for the Palestinian Workers' Fund. An incident from 1911 well illustrates our dedication to the cause: on the eve of the Zionist Congress of that year we received a letter from our comrades in Eretz Israel asking us to dedicate our votes (for a shekel) for one of their members (I no longer remember his name). This member was a crusader for the kibbutzim movement. However, Haim Greenberg ran against him, and he was a beloved person. After a heated debate, it was decided that we would all vote for the delegate from Eretz Israel.

We were authentic adherents of Poalei Zion and we participated in secular events. At one time the "mother" of modern Jewish theatre, Esther-Rachel Kaminsky, was performing in Odessa. We heard that she was bringing her troupe to Bendery. We knew that whatever income we would have from her performance would be donated to Jewish theatre. We prepared a wonderful reception for this great Jewish artist. At the Bendery premiere, Prozhansky greeted Esther-Rachel from the stage. He presented her with an album full of dedications. He also demonstrated our deep thanks for her performance.

[Page 309]

At that time, we undertook the initiative to found in Bendery a Jewish library. The existing library was out-of-date and run-down. Definitely modern Jewish literature and translations into Yiddish of world classics were lacking. We established a new system, and we obtained several hundred necessary volumes. I was appointed the manager of the new library – located in our home. The first reader in the new library was David Wertheim.

In the winter of 1911-1912, Bendery was "fortunate" to have a local Russian-Jewish newspaper. It was in the format of a "Penny newspaper." The editor, an intelligent young man, did not come from Bendery. It happened that I met him on the train on his way to Bendery. I was traveling from Odessa where I had been sent by my parents to cure me from my "idleness." The young man told me about his plans to publish a newspaper in Bendery. Of course, I informed him about our group, and he kept it in mind. The editor of this young newspaper was interested in making connections with the Jewish community. He asked me to help organize a masked ball with proceeds going to the Odessa Committee. Our group discussed the issue and decided that we would support the event as long as income would be divided between the Odessa Committee and the Palestine Workers Fund. There was an agreement. The editor obtained the necessary permits and the newspaper generously advertised the ball. The Volunteer Fire Brigade had always sponsored an annual masked ball and the Jews attended with the rest of the citizens. It turned out that the two masked balls were scheduled for the same evening. The Volunteer Fire Brigade asked us to postpone our ball. However, our tickets were almost sold out by then. In the ensuing argument, we felt the prejudice since it was the time of the Beilis blood libel trial in Kiev [1913 – Menachem Mendel Beilis]. We did not change the date. Our ball achieved an artistic and a financial success.

During those days also took place the wedding of our friend, Haim Glass. The bride was an intelligent working girl from Odessa. I was a very close friend of Haim Glass. He would even show me the letters he and his fiancÃ©e exchanged. The young couple later became famous among us for their hospitality. Haike, Glass' wife, always received us warmly. Our colleagues always felt at home in the Glass house. Baruch Agadati (Rabinovitch) was already known as an excellent impresario, and he was a constant visitor in their home. He always entertained us. Other visitors to that house were: Rafael Shufman (lives now in Kfar Yekhezkel), Zina Rabinovitch (she became a writer), Liova Bortnik, Zeidel Shenker, Miss Lifshitz (her father was a famous teacher and one of the founder of the Zamir as well as the bookkeeper of the "Little Bank"), Prozhansky, me, students from the upper classes of the Science High School and female students from the gymnasia. Among our members were also representatives of businesses in town as well as university students who came to Bendery from larger cities. Moni Fustan once stopped me on the street and showed interest in our group. We became quite friendly. Even then he dreamed of a different world. He was not an active member of our group.

The striving to make Aliyah (to go to Palestine) affected Bendery, too.

[Page 310]

Starting in the fall of 1912 a group of young men and women left Bendery. They had to take a freight ship in Odessa. It travelled between Odessa and Jaffa. I, together with other friends, went to take leave of them. We spent several days in Odessa. To this day, I remember those days with happiness. I truly liked Odessa. I stood with Rafael Shufman in front of the bookstore, Bialik and Roznitsky. Haim Nahman Bialik stood at the entrance and was reading "Haolam" ("The World"). We were impressed with how quickly Bialik turned the pages of the journal. We also did not miss the opportunity to attend Shabbat services in the Zionist synagogue, Yavne. There, hundreds of young people stood near writers, especially Bialik. They listened raptly to their speeches. On Friday night, we went to the Broder synagogue where saw a different kind of people. For us it was a novelty.

Cultural League in Bendery

[Page 311]

The Cultural League
by Leon (Yehuda–Leib) Garfield (New York)

Leon Garfield

In Bendery, I found only a few members of our original Poalei Zion group. In 1920 they organized, with the help of some Communist Jews, a branch of the Cultural League. It was then the main organization for Jewish culture in the new Great Rumania (the old Bessarabia and Bukovina). In those days, the Communist influence was not too small in the Cultural League in the country. Prozhansky, Zeidel Sheynkar, Leibel Sobol, and a few others of my friends joined the Cultural League. We began to offer Yiddish evening classes for young people from poorer families. They never had even an elementary education. In addition to Yiddish, we also offered Hebrew, arithmetic and, of course, Rumanian. The latter was to obey the authorities.

In the summer of 1921, there was an all–Romania conference of the Cultural League in Czernowitz. I was elected as a delegate to this conference of Jewish culture. In Czernowitz, I encountered a well–organized group of left–leaning Poalei Zion. It consisted mainly of Jewish intellectuals from Czernowitz. They were people from free professions still from Austrian times. I met the Jewish writers – Yaakov Sternberg from Bessarabia, Eliezer Steinberg, Shlomo Bikel and Moshe Altman (my roommate). I had good conversations with the latter. Altman was even then a staunch follower of Lenin's beliefs. He thought Communism was the solution to the Jewish question. His tragic life shows how involved the Jewish intelligentsia were in the Russian October. In the 1950s, he was able to leave Siberia and come to Israel. He was a broken man.

The atmosphere in the Czernowitz conference was, in general, pro–Soviet. In the reports given, enthusiasm was felt for delegates from the other "side" of the Dniester. Many delegates considered themselves as Bundists. When it was my turn to give a report from Bendery, I demonstrated that we did not have any Bundists. I spoke about our cultural classes, our work among the youth. I told them that our young people are imbued with Jewish national and social ideals. I had the impression that not all the delegates were thrilled with the Communist ideas.

In general, the conference was interesting and informative. It was really a cultural meeting.

[Page 312]

Except for a few well–thought out reports, many writers simply presented their work. After Altman and Sternberg read their reports, there were reminiscences by Eliezer Steinberg and Dr. Shlomo Bikel. Among other decisions in the conference there was a resolution. Sternberg made a proposal for a theatre group that would visit all towns and villages of the three Romanian provinces. There was also a plan for a music section that would emphasize Jewish folk songs. It was also decided, with a distinct majority, that when it came to spelling in Yiddish, we would continue to use Hebrew letters, as was our tradition. I voted for this resolution and, as a result, I felt the animosity of the Communist members in our Cultural League. Still, it did not stop them from attending my going–away party before I left for America. This occurred soon after I returned from the conference in Czernowitz. A warm speech was addressed to me, presented by the members of the Cultural League of Bendery.

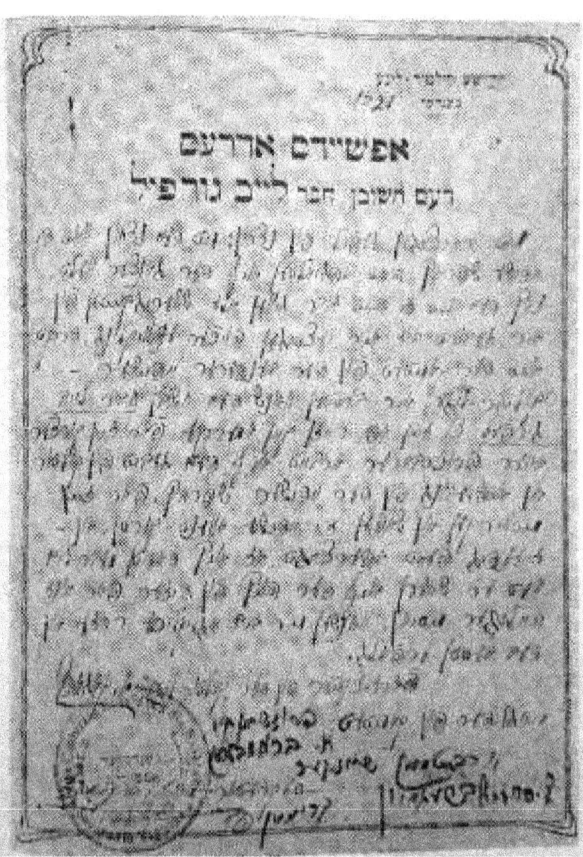

Copy of going–away address

Leon Garfield greets President Zalman Shazar, z"l in the President's House, Jerusalem

[Page 313]

We Acted In The Theatre?
by Shmaria Hrushtesh

During WWI, the Russian Revolution, and the Romanian occupation, the young Jews of Bendery, in addition to their political and social activities, also aspired to cultural fulfilment in general and the theatre in particular.

It is understood that the theatre began in a basement. Sometimes the location used was a lumber warehouse. The actual performances always took place on Shabbat or a Holy Day. This was the time when everyone was free from school and work. The actors as well as the spectators.

It was not so easy to organize an ensemble of actors, directors, prompters, costume makers, make-up specialists, scenery builders, singers and reciters. Everything had to be put together – preparing notices and programs as well as obtaining permission from the authorities.

Our troupe began its existence in the courtyard of Itale, the Rabbi's daughter. We then moved to the attic of Rabbi Arke, the son of the Dayan. It was very close to the house of Itale, the Rabbi's daughter. One Shabbat, Rabbi Arke, the son of the Dayan himself, caught us and chased us out with screams. We left house in shame and we had to do our rehearsals and presentations in the lumber warehouse – in a courtyard across from the Government Bank.

The work was divided among the first active group members: Yoske Gold and Shmerl Hrushtesh were the directors; Motel, the Dayan's son, was the decorator. We borrowed religious garments, head coverings, etc. from the homes of the clergy. The tailor used to lend us costumes and top hats in exchange for tickets for him, his wife and many children, as well as his mother-in-law. For make-up, we used water colors, and we had wigs from observant women. We also used flax and oakum in our hair.

In addition to the scandal when Arke, the Dayan's son chased us out with screams and shouts, there were other situations: for example, when Rabbi Betzalel Steiner (Tsalel the Cantor), z"l, was searching for his Shabbat head covering which had suddenly disappeared. He was a dear, shining Jew with an angelic face. His daughter (the well-known kindergarten teacher in the Schwartzman Hebrew High School), used to supply all religious garments: among them was this head covering.

There were other difficulties. For example, an actor refused to play a role that was repugnant to him, such as a figure as a caricature or a witch. G_d took care of us and a famous actor and singer –Haim Fanitch – agreed to undertake the part of the witch. He even placed a cushion on his stomach. Another one was student David Bendersky, known for his long nose, who played the part of G_d.

All income from the presentations was donated to social assistance – the poor Jews of Ezrat Holim (help for the sick), Malbish Arumim (clothes for the needy), and other organizations.

Our theatrical group was started with the arrival of the Jewish "Wonder." He used to seek capable youngsters for small parts.

[Page 314]

One time, the troupe from Kompenietz was performing in Bendery, and several actors from our group played a large part with them. Some of us even accompanied the troupe to Vilna. Doctor Hain, the editor of the Bendery Jewish newspaper (in Russian) – Yuzhnie Krai – used to praise our troupe. He wrote reviews of our plays. He signed these reviews with the name "Ados." At the same time, the poet and author Zvi Holodenko also wrote his reviews in the Odessa newspapers.

One of our first presentations was Der Talmid Huhem (The Scholar). It was performed in the auditorium opposite the jailhouse. We were once caught there by observant Jews for selling tickets on Shabbat. We also performed in the Music Theatre and the summer theatre – Belanov.

We once invited a special director – a great, though impoverished drunk. He suffered when it was cold in Bendery in the winters. When he ran out of fuel and wood for heating, each one of us brought from home left–over wood, bottles of fuel. If he did not have any food, we brought him some.

There were some visiting "stars" of all kinds. The posters had information on the parts played by them, such as "troublemaker for the parents," or "convert." The latter was written about a beloved actor from Odessa – Alec Stein. In real life, he was the son of a women's tailor from Bendery called Berel Stein. He was also known as Berel Weiss. Names would be changed often – the "helmet" – D. Dorino and the reciters – I. Gold, G. Tilis, F. Potelis and Haim Fanitch. They were famous for their poems and songs – "Mazel Tov," "Oh, little Jew." Pepi Littman's song was "We will rejoice in your reign." In order to please the audience, there were familiar encores – "Leader of the World" or "What a

Young Girl Knows." The prima donna was the well-known F. Kaniverlatski – it was a secret that she was the daughter of Moshe Beker from Bendery. The main role in Goldfaden's Shulamit was played by the beloved soprano from Bendery – Zina Fistrov. She eventually became well-known as a significant opera singer. The director and conductor of the choir of all performances, including operettas, was Volodya (Velvel) Krasiltchik.

*

When Romania occupied Bessarabia and the economic and political situations worsened, the youth began to leave Bendery.

I, myself, sneaked over the border and swam across the Dniester to Tiraspol. From there, I traveled to Odessa, and in 1920 I went on the ship Ruslan to Istanbul. In Istanbul, I met several pioneers from Bendery in the Jewish colony Messilah Hadasha (New Path). Eventually I arrived in Eretz Israel.

[Page 315]

The Writer Rivka Davidit, z"l
by David Carmel (New York)

The writer and playwright, Rivka Davidit, was the sister of the famous Israeli General Aaron Davidi. He was the commander of the parachutists who freed old Jerusalem in June 1967. They opened the road to the Western Wall.

Rivka Davidit was born in Bendery and came to Eretz Israel at the age of 12. She spoke only Russian at the time. It did not take her long to master the Hebrew language. She stood out with her outstanding style. For many years she was the theater critic at "Davaar" and an active member of the Histadrut [Israel's national trade union centre] offshoots, Am Oved (Working People), Tarbut Vekhinukh (Culture and Education), Hakibbutz Hameukhad (United Kibbutz). She also wrote plays and was very popular as an author of children's literature. Her stories were beloved by the children and they were published in additional printings.

Rivka also translated into Hebrew great Russian classics: Gogol, Turgenev, Dostoyevsky, Tolstoy, Chekhov and Maxim Gorky. Her translations were natural and it was difficult to believe that they were originally in another language.

The writer Rivka Davidit is remembered in Israel with much respect and attention.

Now It Happens*
by I.Manik (Lederman) z"l

Now it happens that I close my eyes,

I see the old, beloved likeness.

I am familiar with every movement.

His step was not loud

He did not aspire to be famous across the land.

He quietly walked along the path of the world

Like a stranger.

With every heartbeat, his soul and body were united.

It was enough for him to sustain his body

This is how a life passed with prayer to G_d

Even at night when he lay on his pillow

Even when sitting at a holiday table.

On Shabbat night he sang even louder,

During Havdalah, he would find his shadow in the wine cup.

Only once one evening did his happiness elevate him

He did not find his shadow in the wine cup.

*From the series "Shining Ways," dedicated to the blessed memory of his father, Shlomo Manik, in his book of poems, "Steps at Dawn."

[Page 316]

Hazamir
by Yosef Schwartzman z"l (New York)

Hazamir in Bendery was created by a group of actors. The first performance was "The Witch." Haim Panitch's moustache was hidden and he was dressed as an old woman. He was the Witch. He had a tin of tobacco which he would smell and chew. We used to wish him the following: "May you be well, dear grandma. We hope for your redemption." Our laughter was sky high because we really knew it was Haim Panitch.

I – Yosef Schwartzman – played the part of a Bar Mitzvah boy, and Krasiltchik also had a role. Zina Fistrov sang a few nice numbers. Then Yoske Gold came to Bendery and he played in "Yeshiva Student," "The Witch," "The Jew," "God, Man and the Devil." Freydell Goldstein (daughter of Motel the baker) – Kaniverlatski took major parts and became a famous actress. Performances were held in Bulanovs' theater.

To this day I do not know what became of Yoske Goldstein or Freydell Goldstein-Kaniverlatski.

I remember the songs we sang in Hazamir: "On the rivers of Babylon, we sat and cried," and "Let us be strong." Rehearsals were held at the home of the teacher, Israel Lifshitz. There was a large room near the entrance. However, someone had to stand outside at the door to watch for the police. The government had forbidden us our activities.

The director of Hazamir was Pinie Pertchuk, assisted by Velvel Krasiltchik. Zina Fistrov was the lead soprano. She later became an important opera singer. I was the main alto soloist and Krasiltchik – main bass soloist. In general, the members of Hazamir came from many parts of society – high school students, university students, socialists, revolutionaries, Bundists and other intellectuals.

A few years earlier, before Avraham Hayat, our alto, there was Motele Balaban, z"l. He sang with Pinie the cantor in the Sadigura Shul and stood out with his rendition of "God is Just in All His Ways." Pinie, the cantor, then tried to have me join. He used to come to our house and gave me the notes to this solo. I still remember to this day.

At the same time, maybe a few years earlier, there was another good alto – Yoske Gold. As he grew older, he became a tenor. He became an actor in Kishinev and Odessa.

The entire choir traveled to Tiraspol by boat, and we rehearsed on deck. Our voices could be heard far away. Anyone who is still alive today will remember this for the rest of his life. No one can forget our concerts which we performed in Bendery and surrounding villages. We were successful and had a great following. Unfortunately, Hazamir did not exist a long time.

How did I join Hazamir? Pinie Pertchuk was the director in the New Shul and he brought all the altos from his choir. I, Kh. A. Sternson and a few other boys joined Hazamir. We sang "Dear God We Sing Songs," written by the poet Shimon Frug.

*

When it comes to the Rabbis of Bendery, I recall the old Tzadik, Rabbi Itzikel z"l (Yitzhak Wertheim), Rabbi Yossel z"l (Rabbi Yosef, son of Sh. Sh. Wertheim),

[Page 317]

Rabbi Ahrale (Rabbi Aaron, son of Yosef, Wertheim), Rabbi Motel Yatom, z"l. Prior to WWII, there was Rabbi Yosele's son–in–law, Rabbi Shimon Efrati and after the war – Rabbi Israel Bronfman.

As far as the assistants to the rabbis, the Dayanim, I remember Rabbi Avraham Dayan, z"l, Rabbi Pinhas Dayan, z"l, Rabbi Avremel's son – Haim, and Yeshayahu, son of Rabbi Pinhas, Rabbi Azriel Schreibman's son, Meir. They went to school with me and our teacher was Rabbi Israel Talmazer.

I also remember the ritual slaughterers – Rabbi Leib Brodsky, Rabbi Eliahu Chaplik and Rabbi Moishele Sverdlik.

The Founding and the Activities of Maccabi
by Yaakov Fein (New York)

In 1919 a family arrived in Bendery from Tiraspol – Yitzhak Bitinsky. Their son Zania and his friend, Mussia Granovsky, came with them. They were both members of Maccabi in Tiraspol. They were about 16 to 17 years old. They met some young people, and the sport organization, Maccabi, was founded in Bendery.

We, the founding members of Maccabi, decided to form a football team. We began to play football in the field near the fortress. The youth of Bendery would come to watch us play. Many of them decided to establish a high school league. We went to the principal of the Hebrew High School, G. I. Schwartzman and asked him to allow us to use the school gymnasium for practices. He gave us permission and two teams were organized – one for ages 7–10 and the other for those 17–18. Soon more students came to enrol. The gymnasium now became too small and we moved to the hall owned by Itzel Goldfarb. It was normally used for weddings. Zania Bitinsky, z"l, and Granovsky were the instructors. They maintained iron discipline. The teams were disciplined and it made life easier for future instructors. Bitinsky, who organized Maccabi, soon became ill and died. Granovsky remained, but sometime later left Bendery.

A committee was established under the leadership of dentist Yaroslavsky, with A. Zigberman as secretary. There was also a group of instructors, headed by Moshe Fustan (I believe). The instructors were Sony Etlis, Benny Shaposhnik and Yasha Fein. Each instructor was in charge of a team.

In time, there were a few hundred participants in Maccabi, with some girls among them. A few years later, the President of Maccabi, Dr. Gurfinkel, became the Vice Mayor of Bendery. Maccabi became the most popular organization in town. It had its own orchestra under the direction of Liova Schwartzman. When Schwartzman left Bendery, Vida Tserliuk replaced him. He, in turn, was replaced by Yakir Kleitman.

The football team had uniforms of blue and white. From time to time we used Goldfarb's hall. Once a year we held a ball in the State Auditorium. We also traveled out of town to Kaushany, Chimeshilie, etc. We were well received everywhere. The annual Lag B'Omer celebrations of Maccabi were traditional. The entire membership went to the Borisov forest where they spent the day.

[Page 318]

Hundreds of people used to anticipate the Maccabistan when the members paraded into town in their uniforms. There was perfect marching order. When Maccabi of Kishinev brought in a gymnastics instructor from Czechoslovakia, our instructors went there to learn from him. The gymnastics instructor was invited to Bendery, and he trained all groups in preparation for an interesting program. Many people from Kishinev came for that special evening. They were headed by their instructor, Manny Feldman and joined by their orchestra.

When Jagodzinski came in 1925 to Bendery, Maccabi organized a large reception for him. He came to Maccabi for a demonstration of gymnastics. He praised the organization and greeted his listeners.

In the last years, the leader of Maccabi was lawyer Rubashevsky. Maccabi moved to a hall owned by Khatzkelevich where there was a movie theater – "Science and Life." Names to be mentioned are Mrs. Manus, Shalom Hayat, Misha Fustan. They helped Maccabi tremendously. Cultural events were led by A. Zigberman and Hersh Kogan.

In addition to the physical benefits for the youth there was also a fostering of national spirit. Many Bendery youth were part of the nationalistic movement. It is thanks to Maccabi that many Bendery youth made Aliyah.

There were more special friends, members of Maccabi of Bendery. Whether they are mentioned here or not they contributed a great deal to the success of Maccabi in Bendery.

To all these old friends I send our traditional Maccabi salute: Hazak Ve'Ematz! (Get strong!)

[Page 319]

The Poet Yehoshua Manik (Lederman)
by Yekhezkel Bronstein (Jerusalem)

Yehoshua Manik (Lederman) z"l.

He died in September 1973 in Bat Yam (State of Israel)

Yehoshua Manik (Lederman) was born in 1909 in Bendery (Bessarabia). He studied in cheder, but soon he became immersed in world studies, especially Russian literature.

He went to America as a young man. There he went to work and soon began to study in the University of Chicago.

In New York he published his first poem in the "Free Workers' Voice." In 1925, he made Aliya as a pioneer. He tried many pioneering jobs.

Y. Manik was active as a Yiddish poet all the time. He shared his creations everywhere, here in Israel and outside it – wherever there was a Yiddish audience. He wrote poems, fables and children's stories. His works were also translated into Hebrew and English.

Y. Manik also occupied himself with philology. He was also a correspondent for "Great Dictionary of the Yiddish Language."

His book "Wherever One Wanders" is his fourth collection of poetry.

***

The poems in "Wherever One Wanders" are full of original content. There are many rich ideas and the language is truly beautiful with additional slants and daring. There is a new genre in his poetry.

The new genre that Y. Manik uses is quite complicated and difficult to understand due to its unusual content. Even his language, in the style of cosmic poems, e.g. "Scenery of the Stars" and "Poems for my Earth Planet" is special. In the poems, the poet hopes to live in "a far away space." Soon the poet turns around and veers to the natural clarity of his poem, "It is my home and my shield and my weapon."

An outstanding illustration of his home, shield and weapon is the series of poems "Ashes and Dust." It is full of the pathos of his suffering and its connection to our worst destruction.

His first poem "Autumn" is full of laments of a mourner who is agonizing over the fate of his Bessarabian village. There are

[Page 319]

"No more synagogues nor the old house of learning

Where there were once Jews

(Reciting Psalms)

~~~~~~~~~~~~~~~~~~~~

I do not know how day can be day

And night be night without any Jews."

He brings down the creator from his mystic and lofty perch, after the firestorm, with his power of a poet in mourning. He directs the creator over the destroyed villages and instructs him to look there where dead bodies lie in the fields...

"And God, desperate, will wring his hands,

He will ask a haphazard question,

For whom did I create? Who will now call my name?

I have lost my people."

Here appears the sorrow, the bitterness, the pain and some irony – in the second poem:

"God will tear his clothes in mourning

He will cover is head with a sack of ashes,

He will sit Shiva in his palace,

But he will be informed by those buried,

That this time we forgive you, we forgive you!"

In "Day of Victory," slaughtered children come to him in a dream and ask:

"Why did all this happen?

Where did we sin?

Why?"

He, himself, notices, like a poet, an orphan, who: "Instead of singing joyous, sparkling

And radiant ballads,

I, forever, will only recite Kaddish."

The beauty of art, as is the beauty of life in general, always grows in the game of contrasts. It is like the playing of light and shadow. Anger is the contrast with the colorful life of the world and man. For that reason, it is worth reflecting on the lighter moments of Y. Manik's series of poems, e.g., "Green Miracle." In it, our pioneer–poet identifies himself with the dynamics of our new State of Israel. Right after the second discussion of our destruction, on a basis of mystic–symbolic pictures, there is anger and order in Safed. E.g.,

"Sorrow mixed with a Psalm

Psalm is recited by itself."

Haifa seems like a shining temple. In general, his wonder at the land of our fathers make him more decisive.

"I accept the position...

Of judge and prayer leader."

The idea of becoming a judge and prayer leader came to the Yiddish poet, Y. Manik, from his father. The latter said: "I carry on my countenance." Tel Aviv seems like a symphony to him. This is characteristic of his pioneering spirit which always guides him. It is like a pillar of fire that illuminates his way in the orchard of Yiddish poetry. This is how our poet treads in the dark alleys of our present–day Israel. He is overwhelmed by what the future will bring:

"I worked hard all day

Spent hours in the field

I will sleep well."

He is thrilled with his own poem –

"What have the city and the villages put in order

And road after road, built and paved,

And produce brought for those who require it

On hill and valley, it was planted and tended."

[Page 321]

"Songs" reads like a mystic scroll of love of the sounds of life. It struggles between being and non–being. It is a cosmic love that

"Stands guard over me

And caresses me,

Even when you are no longer here."

Songs" is:

Earth

Its forests and wind

Man, and his walking.

This is the song

That once was sung by "Songs" ...

The poem "From Father's Chalice," serves as a key to Y. Malik's psychic biography. It was rooted in the tunes of his father who sang:

"Leading the prayers with

Beautiful ballads, I

Was cleansed for the fast."

All this, while –

"Father believes

That with a tune

As with wisdom,

As with thought,

Man reaches

Every minute

From rung

To rung."

We can see from this that as his father came to the prayer stand, the son-poet Y. Manik – reached, in our present-day – holy Yiddish. He demonstrates this in his volume of poetry "In the Footsteps of Our Wandering." It is, without doubt, an addition to the treasure of our literature. Each step was a price he paid for it to be his home, his shield and his weapon. He operates like an experienced, well-traveled and complete poet. Even his boldness and daring literary language and his using less words show his ability. He allows himself to retreat from the usual method. Our philologists will have to explain the son's development and character.

(News of the Organization of Former Residents of Bessarabia in Israel–
August 1965).

Ben Zion Shochat
by I.Manik (Lederman) z"l

It is good when the moment comes: from the dust of the grave

The long-forgotten figures stand!

Ben Zion Shochat was a Jew – a quiet man,

He kept himself far away

From daily tumult.

A shining soul with a loving heart,

Always searching to help,

Seeking to do good.

There was no lack of needy people

He was a devoted person – even

To a distant relative.

He even helped a once wealthy person

Now starving.

Ben Zion gave help to all people.

Quietly and carefully.

So as not to shame or insult them.

Where did he spend his days and nights?

Where did hunger catch up to him?

Where was he dishonored

When Hitler's bats spread their brown wings

On many lands?

[Page 322]

Father Sings a Folk Tune
by I.Manik (Lederman) z"l

When father

Sings a folk tune,

You may think that

An angel is singing.

He lifts his head

Towards heaven,

And with closed eyes.

He does not pay attention

To the table,

As he is deeply immersed

In his tune.

Every wrinkle,

His cleanliness –

Until he evokes

The beauty.

He is extremely

Charming.

It seems as if

Nations are sobbing.

Lonely tears

Remind us of dreams

And endless suffering

Caused by the Romans...

Father believes

That with music,

With wisdom,

With intelligence,

Man climbs

Every minute

From rung to rung

To higher

Stages

That the righteous

Will earn...

When father

Sings a folk tune,

You think, that

An angel is singing.

Thoughts For the Fifteenth of Shvat
by Israel Rabinovitch

"My people will be like the lifetime of a tree" (Isaiah, 65:22)

There is no other nation on earth that has cared for its memoirs, its past, like the Jewish people.

The Jewish nation had to abandon, in its exile, the Hebrew language. However, it only did so for everyday affairs and it kept the holy language for prayers and sanctified subjects.

When the Jews, for several reasons, changed their clothing for daily living, they still did not forget to dress up for Shabbat and holidays. It was kept for Jewish religious occasions.

[Page 323]

There were also several reasons for changing names, but they used their Jewish names when called to the Torah and other religious occasions. Our ancestors always kept their Jewish names, language and clothing. This is why they have survived.

It is one thousand eight hundred and sixty years since the Jewish people were exiled from their land, but they have not forgotten it. Even in the diaspora we pray for rain in our land. It happens during winter when there is a lot of snow and the trees are dressed in white. Everyone feels very cold, but that day we still remember our Jewish past. We celebrate the holiday of trees – fifteenth day of Shvat. In Israel, it is the beginning of spring and the trees are beginning to bloom. Winter is gone and spring is coming in Eretz Israel. Everyone remembers the past when Jews sat under their fig trees and vines. We remember the fruit of the land and special prayers are recited. We even recite "Shehecheyanu" in our happiness for the arrival of spring. The Jew is like a tree because "my people will be like the lifetime of a tree," as spoken by the prophet Isaiah, son of Amotz. He found the tree and the people of Israel.

The tree suffers many changes, afflictions, and windstorms. These try to uproot him. The small creatures that grew on the tree, the worms and other living beings which were nourished by it – they all now devour the tree. It is almost destroyed. The tree is under fire, but it holds firm in place and manages to overcome all the evil difficulties that want to destroy it.

The Jewish people are like this tree. Even when it is pulled out, it still grows again in a different place. The seeds and branches come out and the tree is reborn. On the fifteenth day of Shvat, the holiday of the trees, when every Jew eats the fruit of Eretz Israel, we remember the old, sweet times of the tree and we bless it. In it we see our hope to return to the homeland, the land of our ancestors, soon, in our time, Amen.

Mother
by Abraham Hayat (Holon)

On the eve of Sukkot, a hill was formed

In a field in Riga.

Mutely, without a headstone,

I placed a marker on the fresh mound.

I etched your beloved name on it

With deep pain in my heart –

Under it lies my mother

She was the best in the world.

Holy angels will sing for you

They will float recalling your dedication,

Your deep love,

The warm tears you shed

When blessing the New Moon,

When lighting candles,

When praying "Unetaneh Tokef"

With deep faith...

When you begged for your children to be blessed

With good health and luck.

Your eldest is sad –

Your children were left alone at a young age.

Your prayers were not answered.

Your children only have a memory of you.

Although the steps to your grave are

Overgrown with grass,

I cleared the last step on your mound

It remained in my heart.

May Her Soul be Bound in the Bundle of Life

[Page 324]

Rabbi Moshe Sever
by I.Manik (Lederman) z"l

In my younger years, pioneering days, I came once at harvest time to Zichron Yaakov. As I was walking the streets of the village early in the morning, on my way to the vineyard, I see a familiar figure…

"This is, I believe, Rabbi Moshe Sverdlik. How do you come to be here? Is it a mistake?"

He looks at me and my not so–nice "Good Morning" and replies with a smile. It is a sign that he recognized me.

On the last day I spent in Zichron, I visited my dignified countryman. I had the honor of being received by him and his wife.

I only found out about his famous "Collection of Sayings" much later.

It is not rare in our literature that someone would publish a work that would be the basis for an institute. We can recall Dr. Zinberg and his "Story of Literature Among the Jews," Yehoash and his translation of the Bible into Yiddish, Dr. Simcha Petrushka and his translation into Yiddish of the Mishna, Nahum Stutchkov and his "Treasury of the Yiddish Language." Also, more recently the translation into Yiddish of the Baba Metzia and the Baba Batra by the Rabbi Shmuel Hibner. There were also many translations into Hebrew.

Rabbi Moshe Sever collected in a space of fifty years one hundred thousand items! Every saying is more than a word that the lexicographer amasses for his dictionary. There is cataloguing, separating, finding the correct expression. In addition, the huge task of editing looms. Thanks to his outstanding devotion, his amazing memory, and his deep knowledge, Rabbi Moshe Sever accomplished a volume others needed a larger staff to complete, as stated above.

His name is a jewel in the crown of the intellectual face of the Jews of Bessarabia.

Literary Prize Given to Rabbi Sever

"It is with a feeling of great enthusiasm that I share with you the decision of the Presidium of the World Association of Bessarabian Jews to award the

Literary Prize for the year 1962, to the outstanding Rabbi Moshe Sever from Zichron Yaakov. A Jew from Bessarabia, he wrote an important volume "A Collection of Sayings." It was published by the Harav Kook Institute." These words were spoken by MK Yitzhak Korn as he opened the festivities at the impressive meeting. The elderly Rabbi Moshe Sever of Zichron Yaakov, received the Literary Prize for the year 1962 on Sunday, 26.11.1961 in Beit Sokolov in Tel Aviv.

The prize was modest – 500 Il, but it honored the great dedication of over 40 years to collect the best pearls of Jewish wisdom and that it was finally published.

[Page 325]

"One person," says Korn – "collected in a classic work 100,000 Jewish sayings. They were scattered in hundreds of religious texts, Midrash and Halacha. Rabbi Sever was imbued with Zionist spirit from his youth and he made Aliyah in 1923. He settled in Zichron Yaakov where he worked as a ritual slaughterer and spent his free time in studying and collecting sayings. He was influenced by Rabbi Aaron Hyman, z"l, who had also done some collecting of these sayings. Rabbi Sever's work has a forceful scope and it has no equal in Rabbinic literature. At the end of his speech, to thunderous applause, Korn presents the prize to Rabbi Sever.

David Zakai, editor of Davaar, announces, in his speech, that "this is a special meeting in honor of man who deserves the respect of many." Zakai says that he had seen the tiny narrow room of Rabbi Sever, his desk piled with books, and he was surprised. He saw that the work being done there was unequalled. The book does not only contain sayings of our sages, but it is divided according to topic: Shabbat, Torah, redemption, death, life, etc. Such a book has never been done so far. It is difficult to believe that one person could accomplish such a philological project.

Zakai discusses the exemplary order and the way in which the sayings are analyzed and are surrounded by a treasury of the wisdom of many generations, Torah, love of Israel and the Land of Israel, all brief and yet detailed.

MK Yitzhak Raphael, Assistant Minister of Health, welcome Rabbi Sever in the name of Rabbi I.L. Maimon from the Harav Kook Institute. He speaks about the uniqueness of the book, its qualities and the special significance it has for those who will use it.

The author, says MK Raphael, analyzed and broke into sections every saying. The parts are mirrored in the work, not only as sayings, but, also the use of dialects is stressed.

The author was also greeted by Yaakov Levy, president of the executive committee of the town of Zichron Yaakov and by Pinhas Bendersky, also from Bendery.

Rabbi Sever replies in a short speech. He thanks everyone for the honor bestowed on him. The meeting was arranged in my honor and my book "Collection of Sayings." It is really an honor to the Torah which our sages studied and taught from generation to generation. I was only the organizer and there were many before me. I collected the sayings – pearls of wisdom of our sages – and I assembled them for the Jews in the world to know.

The elderly Rabbi was visibly moved and showed his happiness that he achieved a blessing in his old age. His book was beautifully printed by the Harav Kook Institute. He recited the "Shehecheyanu" blessing.

Rabbi Sever ended his speech by recalling the destruction of the holy Jewish communities in general and Bessarabia in particular. He emphasised that he was very fortunate to have made Aliyah with his family, 40 years ago. He saw, with his own eyes, the "beginning of the Redemption."

Rabbi Sever thanked the World Association of Former Jewish Residents of Bessarabia for the beautiful ceremony in his honor, Rabbi Maimon and MK Yitzhak Raphael for their help in publishing the book, and the presidium and managing committee of the Harav Kook Institute, the editor, A. Darom, print setter Greenberg – who helped to publish the book. He also thanked his wife, Rachel, for creating the appropriate atmosphere to allow him to do his work. Also, everyone who came to the meeting was given blessings to continue celebrating cultural works.

[Page 326]

The atmosphere was hearty and elevated and Korn adjourned the meeting. Many of our friends went closer to Rabbi Sever to congratulate him and to shake the skinny, weak hand of a genius...

(News of Bessarabian Jews)

Hear, Brother, Hear...
by Mordechai Sever (Tel Aviv)

Hear,

My brother, hear...

Voices from Bendery pursue us –

Fathers, mothers, brothers, sisters,

Near the fortress on the Dniester,

The last shouts of desire –

Homesick for this place...

Hear...

Hear,

My brother, hear...

Our town Bendery is gone and exiled –

There is nothing left...

Now, Bendery

Is transformed into tears...

Hear...

Hear,

My brother, hear...

A new Bendery has risen – – –

Like flames in a barn

It is gone up in fire and smoke

Jewish Bendery,

Jewish Bendery,

Hear...

[Page 327]

Two Generations in Public Life

A group of businessmen

"Hechalutz Hatsair" youths leave for preparatory kibbutz

Young people are taught by "Hechalutz Hatsair" to do productive work

[Page 328]

Front page and one side from the book "Kitzur Divrei Hayamim"
(A Shortened History) by Rabbi Eliyahu Chaplik, published in Odessa,
1912.

[Page 329]

From the Jewish Press
Translated by Ala Gamulka

[Page 331]

News From Bendery
(From local Jewish Press)
A Frightening Murder in Bendery

Yoel Kogan, from Kishinev, disappeared suddenly while he was under arrest. He had been suspected of Bolshevism, and he was found dead in an open field near Bendery. There were two other corpses next to his – two men and a young woman. The victims of white terror in Bessarabia were: Dwoskin, Shechsman and Tamara. The latter had been detained some time ago. After a short "investigation," following the lines of the Inquisition, she was freed. In other words, she was found not guilty. A few days later she was arrested again – to continue the interrogation.

Yoel Kogan, Dwoskin, Shechtman and Tamara were taken from Kishinev to Bendery. The reason for this was to compare them to other accused people. However, in the same night, when they were brought to Bendery, agents of the Secret Service placed the four in chains and took them to the Dniester. As they were being transported, the four threw themselves on the ground and refused to move. Their screams were heard in town. The agents pushed them with their revolvers. An agent then killed all four on the bank of the Dniester by shooting them in the head. Their chains were then removed and they were left lying there, to give the impression that they were smugglers who were caught crossing the border.

Passersby found the four bodies the next day. One of them was still alive, but he died on the way to the hospital.

"The New Life" 10.2.22

The "Shekel" Campaign

Bendery

The work of our branch was recently reorganized. Every member had to reregister and a new Committee was chosen: D. Fistrov – President; Z. Drobetsky – Vice President; M. Noikhovitch – Treasurer; Rachel Shotman – Secretary; members – A. Finehertz, Goldenberg, I. Soltanovich, Sarah Slepoy and Krutiansky.

We opened a reading room where all Zionist and general Jewish newspapers are available.

Four members were designated to collect funds for "Land and Labor."

We are also intent on planning the Shekel Campaign.

A. Finehertz

Land and Labor 10.5.1929

"Help for the Poor" in Bendery

On Sunday, May 3, a general meeting of the Help for the Poor was held in the assembly room of the City Hall. It spanned the time between Jan. 1, 1931 and April 16 of that year. The meeting drew many residents. The President was chosen by a secret ballot and he received a clear majority. He is Asher Nutov. Secretaries are Sh. Weiser and A. Krasnov.

The Treasurer, Z. Kaushansky gave a financial report. After a short debate and after the President, A. Nutov read the report of the Revision Commission, the sum of 229,806 lei was accepted. The committee was thanked for its enthusiastic work.

[Page 332]

"Help for the Sick" – Flower Day, Bendery, May 1, 1925

The children's colony of Help for the Sick in Borisovko

[Page 333]

Member Kahana tried to interrupt the proceedings, but he did not succeed. We began the election of eight members of the committee to replace those who lost out by lot. A. Derbaremdiker, Zvi Schmaltz, Shlomo Shmulevitch, G. Krasnov replaced the outgoing A. Alexandrov, H. Volovetz, A. Abramovitch and Z. Kaushansky. Those had willingly given up their positions.

Official opening of the Children's Colony in Borisovko (1934/35)

A motion was made by chairman of "Help for the Poor," Avraham Alexandrov, that members Derbaremdiker, B. Abramovitch, B. Bendersky and Z. Schmaltz be elected unanimously. He was leaving due to his old age, and he wanted his work to continue. He was certain that these four men would act for the good of the institution. Once more, Kahana tried to disturb the proceedings, but again, he was silenced. However, when A. Kogan wanted to say a few words about outgoing chairman Alexandrov, he was interrupted by Kahana, again. The patience of the assembled exploded and they began to shout "Enough, terrorist!" When the audience calmed down a motion was made to exclude Kahana from Jewish Bendery societies. The motion was passed unanimously. After that they immediately turned to the agenda. Alexandrov's motion was also accepted unanimously. In addition, the following joined the committee: M. Shaposhnik, M. Fishov, Shlomo Krasik and B. Kaushansky. The Revision Committee members were: Shlomo Koplevatsky, Abramovitch, Frantz, Fistrov and Krasnov. The chairman, H. Nutov, thanked, in the name of those assembled, members Alexandrov, Abramovitch, Volovetz and Z. Kaushansky for their energetic and devoted years of work for the good of "Help for the Poor." They were all now retiring of their own accord. He also suggested that Alexandrov would be the Honorary President forever. This motion was also accepted unanimously and with long lasting applause and everyone left happy.

Ben–Yshai
"Our Time" 7.5.1931

Sanitorium and Children's Colony

The "Help for the Poor" in Bendery has, this year, accepted more than 40 people into the Sanitorium in Borisovko. They all come, understandably, from the poorer section of society. These people need a new atmosphere and fresh air. It is hoped that the sanitorium will, this year also, provide the patients with new strength and a chance to go back to their daily lives. This, in spite of the big crisis.

It was not expected to organize the Children's Colony as in previous years, but thanks to the "Joint" it did open in Borisovko. There are 60 children from poor families in the Jewish community. The committee secured funds from AZA and cooperating members and the children are provided with all their needs.

Our recently opened AZA is functioning well. The Jewish community understands better the needs of AZA. It is hoped that, in time, it will be even more successful.

Ben-Yshai
"Our Time" 7.5.1931

Fires in Bendery

(Details about the great fire in the center of town – a second fire in Borisovko)

In addition to the telegraphic report about yesterday's fire, I can add the following details:

The fire was noticed at 5:45 am from the roof of bakery owned by Yitzhak Gelfenbein on Gogol Street. It was in the house of Moshe Resnik, in the center of the marketplace. The fire had very quickly spread to the right and to the left. In a short time, it engulfed the entire block between Lermontov and Sovorne Streets. Burned down were the dress manufacturing of Shinkar, Mordekovitch, Groisman, Rashkovsky,

[Page 334]

Taxir and Sudit and Chaplik; grocery store of Chasin; paint store of M. Resnik; harness maker Balabaner; pharmacy of Ferdman and the bakery of

Gelfenbein. Also, the apartments of Bilenkis, Kiner, Rashkovsky, B. Wertheim, L. Wertheim, M. Resnik, Chasin and Gelfenbein.

Thanks to the fact that the fire broke out in the morning, all the store owners were in their shops, and they were able to begin to save the goods. The owners did not escape without any damage. Many goods – textiles, paints and groceries were flooded, dirtied and spoiled. Those who suffered the most were: Ben Zion Rashkovsky, Chasin, Ferdman's pharmacy, Moshe Resnik, Bilenkis and the Wertheims.

Only Resnik and Rashkovsky had insurance for their apartments for 100,000 lei each. All the others were not insured. Total damage came to about 3 million lei.

As soon as the fire started, the prefect Stamatov, the prosecutor and several commissioners and military officers arrived. They guarded the goods that had been rescued.

About 8 of the 30 firefighters had to go to another fire burning in Borisovko.

It was thanks to fire chief Kolesnichenko that by 10 am the fire was tamed. By 1 pm the fire was localized.

The fire created great panic in the community since it had been a long time since something like this had happened.

Ben-Yshai

Grandiose Election Rally in Bendery

(A fight is provoked by Zifshtein's agent – the complete failure of the Zifshtein "drink" – success of the meeting)

On Wednesday at 7 o'clock in the evening, the representatives of the Jewish elections in Bendery called for a large meeting in the Old Shul. The meeting was chaired by Israel Blank, the candidate on the Jewish List.* There were about 800 people at the meeting and order was exemplary.

The first step was taken by Israel Blank who presented the audience with the candidates on the Jewish List.* He explained the importance of the list and asked that no Jewish vote should be lost. As he was ending his speech, in came Moshe Zifshtein with his drunken followers and he began to disrupt the meeting. The audience demanded quiet and Moshe had to acquiesce.

The next speaker was Yosef Lerner. He brilliantly described the Romanian Jewry and the success of the Jewish National party. Everyone listened intently to Yosef Lerner. Moshe Zifshtein did not like the speech and began again to disturb the meeting. His followers and Blackists with whom he had an understanding started their work. Their noise did not succeed. The entire audience was so enthusiastic about the Jewish List that "Drink" Zifshtein had to stop. When Lerner began to speak about Warsaw, Zifshtein clutched his heart and stopped Lerner by hitting him. This left a bad impression on the audience who had almost all decided to vote for the Jewish List. Blank and Lerner adjourned the meeting and the police kept the scandal quiet. When Zifshtein felt his solitude, he went on stage and asked those assembled to not make him miserable. He wanted them to vote for the Tsarist List for parliament. If not, the Tsarists, Moldovans and Gagazis will not vote for him for the Senate. He will then, be penniless, without an income. When the crowd heard this, they knew that Zifshtein was not

* There is a chapter in the Yizkor Book The Jews in Bessarabia: Between the World Wars 1914–1940 on Jewishgen.org: "The first elections in 1920 and the success of the Jewish list."

[Page 335]

to be trusted. This is how Moshe became a failure and the Jewish votes went to the Jewish List.

Ben–Yshai
"Our Time" 1.9.1931

In the Predicament of Need …

Bendery

Outside it is dreary. There is a damp mist. It is a cold wetness. The snow is dirty, wet and over abundant, mixed with dirt, on all the streets. It is a real, frightening mud. Rivulets of dirty water are running down.

I am striding together with the chairman of the Hunger Committee in the Jewish street to check the needs of the desolate. We have so many of them in the last few years.

Familiar pictures of home. Tiny houses looking like graves. Small holes filled with rags to replace windows. Tiny, hunchbacked walls are covered with pipe-like icicles. There are no closets, no tables, no beds, not a stick of furniture. There is only a broken chair and nothing else. No bedding!

Why did a Jewish family live in such poverty? Not even bedding.

What kind of Jew does not even have pillows?

Their life is so terrible and bitter that they even sold their last pillow.

How can I describe what my eyes have seen? One should write a whole book about the great needs in which some Jews found themselves in the last few years. We are the poorest nation in the world. We never stood out in our good health in the diaspora. We were always sickly, wheezing, asthmatic, afflicted with lung disease, heart ailments, etc. It is easy to see what a destruction this needy hunger has fraught on the Jewish nation. One can see the misery. Everywhere I go I see the hunger in the cellars. In these houses like graves I find sick men, sick women and sick children. Instead of beds they lie on the bare floor on some straw and rags. They lie and moan, feverish and cold. They have a special request from those still alive: have pity on them and send death their way.

Suddenly my eyes see in these grave-like houses in Bendery:

A miracle!

An old lady is lying sick. She is skin and bones – a skeleton. What is left of a person! She is lying on a few rags. Her eyes are vacant and she moans and begs for the Angel of Death to come. He is always on time, but not now, when she wants him. He is dawdling to liberate her from her hell.

Also sick are her daughter and son-in-law. They wear torn shoes, without soles. They do not have warm clothes – only rags. Five little children are crying, one smaller than the other – wearing torn clothes or completely naked. All full of pus and sores. They are eaten up by parasites and their complexions are waxy. They are ill with jaundice, are feverish and have the flu and tuberculosis.

The door to the grave-like house is open and there is no heating. It is cold and slippery in the darkness of the cemetery, in the tomblike dwelling. They are alive? It seems like it, but according to these conditions, they should have been dead.

[Page 336]

Actually, another woman, in a similar dwelling, told me, almost casually, that three weeks earlier, her five-year-old daughter had died of Typhus. A week ago, another child died of Scarlet Fever.

A seller of bagels

I remember that she had not told me her story directly, but in a round-about way. She confirmed a rumor, in a calm way, as she was praying "that God made me according to his will." She said that she had had three children, and two were taken away by God. The third child is naked and shoeless and falls frequently. She does not have shoes for the child, and it is very, very cold in this hovel.

An acquaintance told me about another village in the starvation area. There, he found a Jew who, only a few years before, had been wealthy and had a beautiful home. He was poverty stricken. God gave him another "gift" – crabs. My acquaintance found this Jew shivering from the cold. The Jew suffering with crabs apologized saying: "I know that I will die. I am not so ignorant that I would live much longer with this cancer, but I would prefer to die from cancer than from cold."

The need and the hunger destroyed Jewish health. Epidemics of Typhus and other diseases did not happen by chance when there is hunger, no clothing and shoes or washing, living miserably in a broken, low, wet unheated home.

In the chairman's house, there is a hard–working young man. He is still very young. The need and the troubles have made him old, before his time. The young man is crying and begging for compassion:

I do not want to be a shnorer. I do not need riches. My horse has died. Give me, no, lend me, 1,000 lei so I can buy a new horse. I pray to God" – the poor, prematurely gray, young man clapped his heart – "I pray to God that I will return the money to you myself."

Again, the subject arises: why do people shy away from begging and are prepared to die of hunger and thirst?

A Jewish woman whose husband is not earning anything, a so–called broken kopek, has six children at home. The oldest girl, a dressmaker, has no work. The oldest boy was, until recently, a clerk, but the store was closed. The others are young children with the youngest, a nursing baby, only five months old. What do you do? There is not even a crust of bread in the house. To the committee the man says he will not live another hour if he asks them for help. They are hungry, but the mother's heart cannot stand to see her children suffer. They have sold everything possible from their house and there is nothing left. The mother has become, secretly, a wet nurse for another baby four times a day. For that she receives 200 lei. She has to walk on several streets and she must do it in such a way that her husband and children do not find out. If they do they "would be terribly ashamed."

[Page 337]

What can a starving woman give a child, never mind two of them?

This starving woman goes, four times a day, on schedule, for two hundred leis a month to nurse a child, in addition to hers.

One needs nerves of steel to listen to these tales of woe.

I must not say that I saw only sad cases. I did have some good news.

My heart was so happy when I saw these starving children from these hovels receive a breakfast or a hot meal.

Here are the children with torn shoes, almost barefoot, in their pants full of holes, sitting at long tables. The women of the committee are serving them. Every chid receives a piece of bread, a bowl of soup and a bit of meat. Their faces are blazing and their eyes are shining with happiness. Every bite adds color to their faces. The children from the Talmud Torah, from the Religious School, children of those who are hurting, sit at the table and eat. They are of all ages–twelve, ten, eight...even three. The little three-year-old, with his ragged pants, climbs up to the bench and Mrs. Kishinevsky shows me: see, look at the beautiful black eyes. How I love him. How adorable he is.

I look at this little guest – his eyes are shining because he is sitting in front of a bowl of soup. What does he need? Only a bit of soup.

–Little boy, what is your father's name? – I ask his older brother, a young man of seven.

The boy stutters:

–I do not have a father. I am an orphan.

–Nu? and your mother?

–My mother's name is Sara-Riva.

–What does your mother do?

–My mother works in the daytime. My brother and I – he points at the three-year-old – stay at home.

I can imagine what a fancy apartment they have. No mother looking after them, no food or drink and wearing ragged clothing. Who can appreciate the words of a child?

The starving children sit – orphans, street children, lonely, poor, displaced, but a new skin is appearing on them. A bowl of hot soup and a piece of bread. Blessed must be those who are doing this work.

Such cleanliness here, but I would not want to give ordinary praise from us, the correspondents in the province. I do not wish to abuse this power, but, surely, the women who give such care have earned special praise.

Allow me to describe a great celebration which my own eyes saw.

What celebration?

The principal of the Romanian elementary school – a Christian – came to the Hunger Committee with tears in her eyes and begged us to buy shoes for the Jewish children. She could not stand the sadness when she saw them come to school shoeless. The entire Hunger Committee unanimously decided to buy shoes for the children. They even got a bargain – 75 lei for a pair.

I saw, with my own eyes, when shoes were distributed in the community hall, how it was besieged by children and parents. Dozens of children wearing large, donated, twisted large shoes with holes, sloshed through the mud and were fortunate to receive a new pair of shoes. One can see a poor little girl, her feet wet, being washed and cleaned up. She now receives socks and is being measured for shoes. I look at the twinkling eyes, the shiny faces, the overpowering bliss in these children. Who is now equal to them? Who?

A pair of whole shoes, later placed back in the box, held near the heart and taken home to the hovel, while the feet are still with the torn shoes sloshing in the mud...

Zalman Rosenthal
"Our Time" 3.3.1936

[Page 338]

Memorial Service for the Riot Victims in Eretz Israel

A few days ago, the Jewish Community of Tighina held a memorial service, in the New Shul, for the victims of the latest riot in Eretz Israel. All representatives of the national groups were invited to the memorial service. The shul was packed, and Cantor M. Cohen recited El Maale for the fallen. The speakers in the name of the Zionist organizations, were: Rabbi Yosef Wertheim (Mizrachi), A. Derbaremdiker (General Zionists), D. Fistrov (Poalei Zion–Zeirei Zion) and H. Yakhinson (N.Z.A.). The latter came with a speech with a conscientious slant – pointing out that Jabotinsky [Odessa–born Ze'ev

Jabotinsky, Jewish Zionist and founder of the Jewish Self–Defense Organization] had predicted the riots. On the other hand, all other Zionist representatives called on the audience to stand strong and to not be afraid of the provocation by the Arab extremists. They also spoke of the need to strengthen Zionist work with more energy and also to increase the income from the Jewish National Fund. This would enable a larger Aliyah and a quicker rebuilding of the land and the people. The large audience showed solidarity with this calling and left the hall with sadness.

Ben–Yshai
"Our Time" 6.5.1936

A Memorial Service After the Death of Nahum Sokolov in Bendery

A few days ago, a memorial service was held in the New Shul for Nahum Sokolov. The large shul, including the women's section, was packed with people. Cantor Kh. Cohen recited the "Maale" and the large audience listened quietly.

The first to eulogize the deceased was Rabbi Yosef Wertheim.

Mr. Derbaremdiker spoke in the name of the General Zionists and D. Fistrov represented the united Poalei Zion–Zeirei Zion.

The speakers described the great achievements of the deceased leader. They urged those assembled to continue in the way of the "brains of the generation" – Nahum Sokolov [Zionist leader from Poland to London, author, translator, and a pioneer of Hebrew journalism – Wikipedia]. In this way, they would show their appreciation and loyalty to him.

The assembly was in deep mourning.

Ben–Yshai
"Our Time" 2.6.1936

Keren Hayesod in Tighina

In the last few days we were occupied with happenings at Keren Hayesod [United Israel Appeal]. A large meeting was held in the big New Shul. It was opened by the chairman, Israel Blank. He introduced to those assembled the important guest, director of Keren Hayesod in Bessarabia, Sh. Pinsky. After him, Pinsky was also greeted by Rabbi Yosef Wertheim, Community Chairman Asher Nutov, Chairman of the General Zionists – A. Derbaremdiker, the United Party – D. Fistrov and Mizrachi – S. Finkel.

After these greetings, Sh. Pinsky gave his interesting presentation – "The Present Situation in Eretz Israel." The audience listened with great interest and showed their appreciation by applauding for a long time.

After the scheduled meeting, Pinsky met with the leaders: I. Blank, A. Derbaremdiker, Mrs. S. Blank, F. Finke., D. Fistrov, etc. They discussed, with great success, practical matters. In spite of the late hour,

[Page 339]

We must thank Sh. Pinsky and his ability to conclude matters.

Lecture by Poet Sh. Pinsky

Some days ago, the famous poet Sh. Pinsky, introduced a literary presentation in the hall of the I.L. Peretz auditorium (The Dead City, The Village, Bontche Shveig). The large hall was packed with people who listened to every word with great satisfaction and attention. The two-hour presentation highly pleased the audience and it gave them a good picture of issues in the Jewish world at that time. It also illustrated important world problems. They warmly thanked Sh. Pinsky. It is to be hoped that, in a short while, Pinsky will read again for us in Tighina and we are impatient to hear it.

Ben-Yshai
"Our Time" 2.9.1936

Spelling changed in the articles.

Memorial for Bendery martyrs in "Martyrs' Forest" near Jerusalem

(From right to left): Z. Drobetsky, Chana Berman, D. Fistrov)

(10/8/1959)

[Page 340]

The Leon Shpor Fund
(The Jewish "Little Bank"), 1925

General meeting of the members

The clerks and the clients

[Page 341]

Occupation and the Holocaust
Translated by Ala Gamulka

David Wertheim, Z"L
He was taken from us suddenly on 25 Nisan 5713 – April 1953

*

David Wertheim, z" l, began his intensive activities at a young age in Bendery. His eminent father and famous grandfathers came from a dynasty originating with the Baal Shem Tov, z" l. They instilled in him a love of Zion and his people. His great-grandfather, the genius Rabbi Shimon-Shlomo, a most liberal man, used to say "When a Jew loves other Jews and Eretz Israel, God will forgive all his sins…"

In his Bendery youth, he immediately joined Zeirei Zion [Zionist Socialist Party] in Bessarabia. He quickly started to draw young Jewish people with his fiery oratory and warm treatment of others.

His revolutionary boldness gave him the strength to oppose not only the Tsarist rule, but also, later, the Soviet police. He also stood against his own fanatic background which did not understand, then, that the pioneers were not against the Messiah, but were helping him to delay the "end."

Bendery was a true Jewish town and people always described details about this young man from town who was able, under the nose of the police, to speak in front of large groups, from a balcony, in the middle of the street. Among his listeners were not only young men and women, but also their fathers. These were followers of his own father. They would gaze at him and wonder how a child of the Rabbi would dare go against his own dynasty, his own flesh and blood.

After David Wertheim came to America, he played an important role in his Poalei Zion and in the united party of Poalei Zion. He served the party for 13 years as the General Secretary and he represented it in various conventions and congresses. He was always fired up, but his honesty and heart were visible. Not everyone agreed with Wertheim and some criticized him. However, he always promoted our ideals in a dynamic way. No one could ever oppose him for his willingness to sacrifice for these ideals.

Lately, Wertheim carried a heavy burden in the Histadrut campaign in the United States and South America. He attracted thousands of new friends by his appealing personality and our ideals.

His tragic end came while he was actually at work.

David Wertheim had fulfilled his duty in Miami and was on his way by taxi from the airport in Havana, Cuba, when he was stricken. He had worked diligently at his duties and was doing his utmost to promote the party ideals. He had done so all his life, until the end.

We mourn the loss and we will never forget him.

Avraham Wertheim, Z"L

Our dear member and chairman of the National Board, Avraham Wertheim, died at the age of 66, after a long illness.

This is a loss not only for our association, but also for other institutions where the deceased was active.

Avraham Wertheim, z" l, was born in Bendery into a famous rabbinic family. The family had the Ba'al Shem Tov as an ancestor. He was active in many cultural, social and community affairs. Prior to his Aliyah in 1919, he spent a long time in Warsaw as a "Joint" leader. In Eretz Israel he was active in the Jewish Agency and he also headed the workers' section. There he dealt in arbitration.

[Page 342]

After the founding of the State of Israel he switched to the Ministry of Labor. His heart condition prevented him from doing more activities as a volunteer. At the end, he was chairman of the Association of Residents from Bessarabia in Israel.

At his funeral, there were many representatives of the Ministry of Labor, national institutions and many friends.

L. Kupershteyn, spoke, representing the Association of Residents from Bessarabia in Israel, Rabbi Efrati spoke for the family and Cantor Leib Glantz recited the "Maale."

There was a special memorial assembly for Avraham Wertheim, z"l, at the end of the thirty days. It was held in the Jewish National Fund Hall in Tel Aviv. The following gave eulogies: Yitzhak Greenbaum, Prof. Fishel Shneyerson, Cantor Leib Glantz, Y. Korn and D. Fistrov, representing his fellow compatriots. Cantor L. Glantz recited the "Maale."

We mourn, and we will never forget.

("News of Bessarabia in Yiddish," March 1958 – Adar 5718)

[Page 343]

Women's Organizations in Bendery

WIZO in Bendery

Unknown names designated with —— Fania Chaplik, Schwartz, Bendersky, ——, ——, ——, Yatom.

(first on top: Bettye Sverdlik) ——, Pagis, Bendersky, ——, Berman, Rosa Fein, Veizgendler, Fania Resnik, ——, Shprintzak,

Rachel Kogan, Krasnopolsky, Ida Kishinevsky, Sonia Slepoy, ——, Chana Averbuch

A group of WIZO members

[Page 344]

"Women's Association" Bendery (Tighina) – 1931

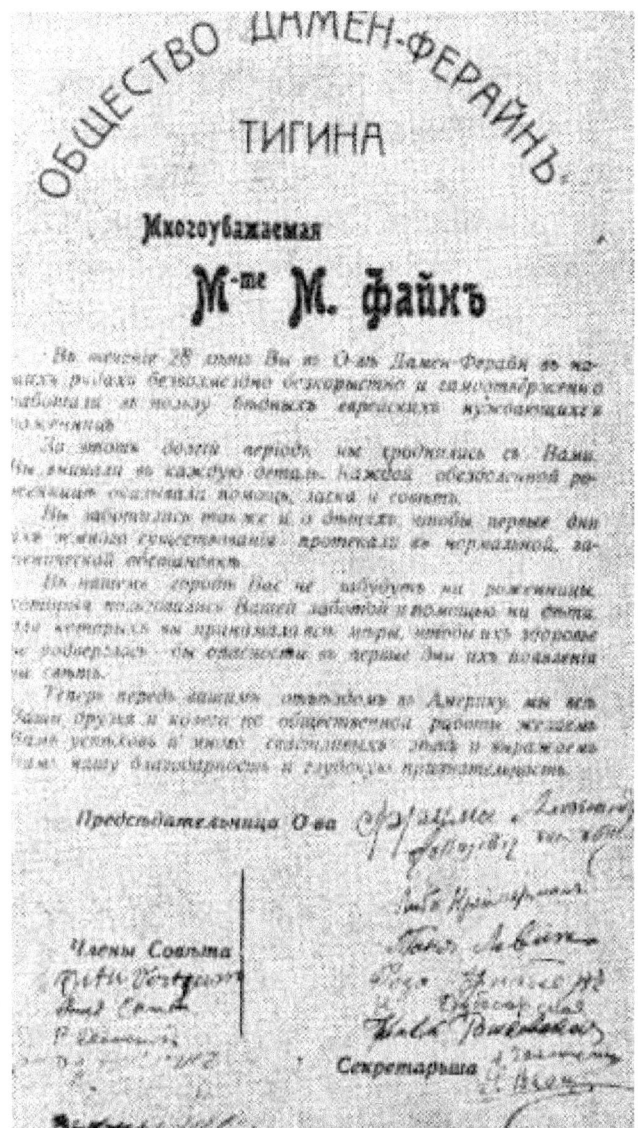

Appreciation from Women's Association
to Mrs. M. Fein upon her going to America

[Page 347]

Bendery After the Shoah
Rabbi Israel Bronfman (Jerusalem)

On the banks of the Dniester, in Bessarabia, lies Bendery – or as it was called in Romania – Tighina. Before WWII there were about 5,000 Jewish families living there. We had 18 synagogues, a Jewish hospital, a Seniors' Residence, a Jewish high school, Talmud Torahs, etc.

The life of local Jews was much the same as in other villages and towns in Tsarist Russia. In 1918, the Romanians annexed Bessarabia. Jewish occupations were as merchants, clerks and craftsmen, free professions and even ten idlers. The Jews were always busy and worried about their livelihood: how do we buy food for Shabbat? It was difficult to overcome the constant stress and fear of the Romanian authorities. They always looked for ways to lay their dirty murderous hands on Jewish earnings.

I was born in 1915, and I do not remember, at all, how life was under the Tsarist regime in Bessarabia. I was attached to the House of Learning almost until the arrival of the Soviets. However, I often heard that honorable people had prayed for the Soviets (the Reds) to come. God listened and the Soviets occupied Bessarabia. Actually, the Jewish masses rested a little from the Romanian terror. It was bad in the last few years before they left Bessarabia. Sadly, it did not take long for the population in general, and the Jews in particular, to feel Stalin's might.

At the beginning of the war, in 1941, many Jews escaped from the Nazis and were evacuated deep into Russia. The Soviets helped those who wished to be evacuated, at the beginning – Jews and non-Jews. Many Jews were thus saved. The Jews of Bender had better opportunities to escape because the town was on the banks of the Dniester. I heard from many sources that there was a smaller number of Bendery Jews killed by the Germans.

The war ended and the Jewish families that remained alive returned to their former homes. I did not know Bendery before the war as I had never been there. In November 1945, I was liberated from the Work Army and I returned to my village. I had lived in Kalarash before the war. The village was 95% destroyed and I had nowhere to live. Rabbi Yosef Applebaum of Kishinev offered me a position in Bendery as a religious leader.

What I then find in Bendery?

After the end of the war, in May 1945, Jews slowly began to return to their former homes. They no longer believed in the "Red Messiah." They saw the lies, suffering and terror. They began to return to God and to visit the cemetery with their tears flowing. They organized a Minyan for Shabbat and even during the week, as well as a Hevra Kaddisha. The Sadigura Shul had remained standing because the Germans used it as a barn for their horses. The Jews took it over and held services there on Rosh Hashana. Those involved in organizing the Jewish community were Yaakov Kutchuk, Haim-Moshe

[Page 348]

Fishov, Yosef Moshe Goldmacht, Meir Hochman, Leib Alter, Alter Itzkovitch, Efraim Sudit, Avraham Finkelstein, Tzirelis and many other young people who returned from the war as invalids. The shul was cleaned up, arranged for a women's section, hired a cantor – Shuster, a war invalid. This is how we were able to pray on the High Holidays after the war, in 1945. At that time, a leader emerged for all Jewish matters. He was Yaakov Kutchuk, z" l.

Rabbi Israel Bronfman with Cantor Cooperman in the Sadigura Shul in 1954/55

Yaakov Kutchuk always worked as a bookkeeper at the business of Zeidel Katzap. He was a fine and noble person and a Jewish nationalist. It is thanks to the dedication of Yaakov Kutchuk and the faithfulness of many local Jews that there was such a strong Jewish community. After Sukkot, Yaakov Kutchuk was called to City Hall. There, he was told that he was obliged to register the Jewish Community in the Soviet Ministry in Kishinev. The office of religious affairs required a rabbinic leader – as the law required at that time. On November 15, 1945, I became the religious leader of the Bendery community.

At the head of the community then was Yaakov Kutchuk as President. He died in 1949. Others were Yosef–Moshe Goldmacher, first Treasurer, who made Aliyah in 1956 (he died in 1967); Shlomo Burstein, may he live and prosper, and Yehuda–Leib Alter who moved to Riga in 1958 and passed away there. The Search Committee had Alter Itzkovitch – who later left Bendery, Avraham–David Giterman (Ish Tov) – still in Bendery, and Noikhovitch.

After we cleaned up the synagogue we began to organize the two cemeteries – the Old Cemetery located in the lower part of town, near the Dniester, and the New Cemetery, in the upper section. The Germans and the Romanians had started to destroy the Old Cemetery and the Russians completed the task. Since I was the Chairman of the Jewish community from 1947 to 1957, I was often approached by the Soviet regime asking me to sign away our right to the Old Cemetery so they could liquidate it. I refused every time and I told them to get permission from those lying buried there… Of course, they took it anyway, without our knowledge, and they put a few hundred pigs on the premises. We saw that the Old Cemetery was almost completely ruined. We announced, in the synagogue, that anyone who had relatives buried there could transfer them to the New Cemetery. We moved the graves of the four sainted members of the Wertheim family, and we built a built a new little house. It is still standing. The Christians living nearby used many headstones to renovate their homes. The regime built a stone fence around the stadium. They pretended that it had been the Romanians who had done it in January 1943.

[Page 349]

During the hard times of Stalin, the leaders of the Jewish Community were treated very badly and they suffered greatly. For instance, they were called in to the Town Committee many times and given new orders about the synagogue, the cemeteries, baking of matzoth and even about the hiring of cantors. In 1948, after the founding of the State of Israel, there was a "visit" in the synagogue. They probed and searched and, I, as the chairman of the community, did not know what was happening. Of course, they did not find anything wrong. Later, I discovered, that at the same time exactly, there were such searches in all Jewish communities that had administrative offices. It was all connected to the arrival of Mrs. Golda Meir, Israeli ambassador to the Soviet Union. Many Jews requested permission to make Aliyah and the NKVD thought that the Jewish communities were connected to this event. This was followed by the Doctors' Trial, known to every Jew. It created great fear among the Jews who thought they would all be sent to Siberia. During Stalin's time, the NKVD did not interfere in the inner affairs of the Jewish Community. We could elect people to the synagogue leadership, but there were secret service agents watching us. They reported everything, even "how many times the rabbi cried during prayers." On the High Holidays we noticed, among the audience, some Christians – secret service agents dressed like Jews. There was no pressure on Jews when it came to circumcision, weddings, ritual slaughter. Except that I, as Rabbi, ritual slaughterer and circumciser, had to pay high taxes. Other Jews always came to my aid and the leaders took care of me. I, too, looked after myself and God took care of all of us.

It was different after Stalin's death. In Khrushchev's time, the NKVD – now called the KGB – there were no secret service agents in the synagogue. However, anyone elected to the leadership had to be approved by the authorities and, it turned out, they were all followers of the KGB.

In 1957, I was ordered to resign from my position of chairman of the community. In 1960, I was forbidden from serving as the Rabbi. I then left Bendery and moved to Odessa

[Page 350]

In Those Dark Days...
B. Levi

Usually, when we speak of the destruction of European Jewry, we think of the victims of the war. As to the Jews of Bessarabia, it is not entirely true. The destruction of Bessarabian Jewry began in 1940 when Stalin, the Cruel One, broke up all Jewish institutions and organizations. Many "undesirables" were evacuated to Siberia where they were placed in prisons, forced-labor camps. These people were mostly leading Jewish personalities, businessmen and intelligentsia.

These tortures took place in Bessarabia in 1940–1941, and the Jews were petrified. Many Jews, a high percentage of them, ran from town to town to disappear from the horizon. They wanted to avoid having Paragraph 39 inscribed in their passports. Paragraph 39 indicated people to be non-productive or socially unacceptable, and they would become candidates for evacuation from their homes to Siberia. The Jews were running from Kishinev, Bendery, Soroca, Beltz, Khotin, etc. to Czernowitz, Lvov (Lemberg), Ternopol and Stanislav. They went from villages to towns and vice versa. The unavoidable happened. The terrible days of June 13 and 14, 1941 will never be forgotten. In those days "Comrade" Stalin managed to produce the "cleansing" of Bessarabia of all socially unacceptable and undesirables because they did not suit the purpose of the revolution...

Hundreds of thousands of citizens of Bessarabia were evacuated. Among them – due to their social and commercial standing – the majority were Jews. Jewish Bessarabia was inundated with a flood of tears. It was Tisha B'Av in all homes. People sat on their suitcases, fearful, and waited. They listened to every rumor – they are coming to get us, they are knocking on our doors... The "Father and Leader of all people", Genghis Khan the Second, was raging like a madman. "Moscow does not believe in tears." Nothing helped. "Why?" He, "Joseph the Terrible" had decided on cleansing the area, and his orders were followed blindly, without pity, stubbornly.

Thousands of Bessarabia Jews, entire families, were evacuated. No one knows the exact numbers. It was kept secret. The Gulag was also not published.

Some of these evacuated people were allowed to return to their homes after Stalin's death. Their rights were restored to them. A few even recovered their belongings in Khrushchev's time.

The majority, however, perhaps 80% of those evacuated, never returned. They were victims of the brutal regime of Stalin and they died. Their souls found their final rest, far away from family and friends – in cold far–away places – in snow covered hills…

[Page 351]

Testimony of a Witness
(Archives of Yad Vashem, Jerusalem)
Miller David (Tirat HaKarmel, Amidar 88)

I was born in 1913 in Bendery, Bessarabia. Our town was on the right side of the Dniester. During the 20 years of Romanian occupation, Bendery was a border town, and the Dniester was a natural division between Russia and Romania. In Bessarabia, there were many Jewish towns and villages where Moldavian was the language used. However, Bendery was always a Russian town with a fine and intelligent young Jewish population.

The town is also famous for its ancient Turkish fortress which occupies almost half the area.

My father was a tinsmith. There was a large train station in Bendery with a big depot. My father, even before the revolution, worked there even though Jews were not usually hired for this work.

Our town had a thriving Zionist movement. The approximately 20,000 Jews maintained a Hebrew High School, under the direction of Zvi Schwartzman. In 1934 he made Aliyah.

My father gave me a religious education – I attended a Heder until I turned 13.

In time, our neighborhood changed completely. In 1918, Bessarabia was occupied by the Romanians, and Bendery was considered a town with Russian leanings. The Romanians did not allow the town to develop because most commerce was handled by Jews. Thus, the Jews suffered from this new occupation.

It must be said that in comparison with the status of the Jews on the other side of the Dniester, Bessarabia was like Garden of Eden. Still, life was difficult.

My father allowed me to learn a trade, but I saw that, in Bendery, there was no future for a young man. In 1933, I left for Galatz (Romania) and I worked in a big factory called "Fernik."

I stayed in Galatz for one year and then I moved to Bucharest. In 1938, I married a woman from Bucharest – Hinda, daughter of Shmuel Segal.

I had not even managed to organize my family life and WWII broke out.

We immediately understood that the Russians will retake Bessarabia from Romania. They were only waiting for an excuse.

Indeed, in 1940, the Russians, "without a drop of blood", took Bessarabia back. All of us who were born in Bessarabia were given permission to return home.

Although I was quite young, eight years old, when the Romanians occupied Bessarabia, I spoke Russian well. I could also read and write. All young people from Bendery were attached to Russian culture, literature, music – even those who were Zionists and remote from Communism.

In 1940, I returned to Bendery with my wife. I settled in a house and I was given a job in the railroad station. This is where my father had worked for many years.

I was content. We thought the Molotov–Ribbentrop Pact would last. However, we were wrong.

[Page 352]

The day came – 21 June, 1941 – the Germans entered Russia. Two other countries – Romania and Hungary – joined Germany.

Bessarabia was especially singled out for suffering by the Romanians. They began again to anticipate becoming the owners of Bessarabia again.

Swarms of German airplanes filled the skies on the Russian border from the White to the Black Sea.

Millions of citizens, me, women, children and old people filled the roads as they were fleeing from the border deep into Russia.

My home town of Bendery played an important part in saving and helping hundreds of thousands of refugees in the years of WWI and the Russian Revolution. Thousands of families in Eretz Israel, America and other countries remember with thanks the wonderful hospitality. In Bessarabia, in Kishinev, Bendery, Beltz, Soroka, Akkerman and other places, they found the residents happy to share, with them, to the last piece of bread. There were many refugees, especially from the Russian Revolution.

Now, 25 years later, this wonderful town fell into a muddy war. Hundreds of thousands of refugees left their homes and searched for havens. They left their belongings behind – belongings they had worked years to obtain. It must be said that Russia did its best to organize an orderly evacuation.

I was an employee of the state and I was evacuated with other personnel. My wife and my mother came with me.

My father was no longer alive and other members of the family had escaped wherever they could.

After much travel, we arrived at Rostov on the Don River. This was in the first few months of the war. Everywhere in southern Russia there was not a place to be found that would be safe and restful.

Rostov was full of refugees and it had already evacuated children and women who worked in the government. It was not the last place to stay when escaping.

My friends and I were mobilized to work. My mother and my wife were registered as refugees. They were given a place to sleep and they lived on a "refugee" ration. This lasted only a short time.

The front chased us and the cruel blitzkrieg did more harm to civilians than to the military.

One day, I came home for a few hours to see my dear ones, but I did not find them. I was told by neighbors that they had been further evacuated. Where to? I did not know and neither did anyone else. There were no lists available to see who had been evacuated.

I found my wife six months later and my mother only in after four years. She was sent to Turkestan. The front lines changed and reached Rostov. When the first sounds of war were heard, we were sent away.

I was sent to the railroad line Batiusk–Aksiov in November 1941. There was cold rain and winds from the Black Sea and from the North it was difficult to be at the front. We did not have warm enough clothing.

On such a cold, wet day, the Germans sent a barrage of artillery.

I was lying in a ditch and near me a large bomb exploded. I was flung and I lost consciousness.

To this day, I do not know how long I was lying there, but I was taken to the hospital in Krasnodar. Either my friends, or the nurses, told me that I was unconscious for 2–3 weeks. I could not remember.

[Page 353]

For several months, I could not recall anything. Slowly, I began to speak, but I had a hearing loss – to this day. It took me about 6 months to regain my memory.

A piece of shrapnel had pierced my skull. I lost part of my ear and I had a concussion.

I "travelled" from hospital to hospital: Krasnodar, Minvada and others. My last stay was at the military hospital #5 in Kagan, Uzbekistan.

In the summer of 1942, I was brought in front of a military commission. It recognized me as an Invalid of the War, second group. I was liberated from the army.

My wife had been evacuated from Rostov. I was astonished to discover that she was alive. She came to me, to Kagan, after my liberation. We remained there until 1943.

In Kagan, I was obliged to live on the small pension and rations given to War Invalids.

Naturally, the pension did not supply us with food. Like other Jews, I had to do some business in order to earn enough to pay for food.

However, I was not a good businessman. I had always worked before, but it was difficult to live as an invalid – so far away from home. I decided to ask to be mobilized again. The military did not want me anymore. I had previously worked for many years on the railroad and had technical experience. I was then sent to complete a special technical course in Omsk, Siberia.

I completed the course as a lieutenant of an operating military group. I specialized in setting up benches for the railroad.

The Russian military was, by then, in full offensive state. Every day, news came of dozens of liberated towns and villages. The Russian front became broader from the center and from both sides – north and south.

In July 1944, my town of birth, Bendery, was liberated. I immediately asked to be sent there in order to rebuild the railroad depot. I was delighted to go back home.

Unfortunately, just at that time I received some bad news. My brother, Berel (Boris), had been killed on the front, near Konigsberg. My mother, wife and I stayed in Bendery until the end of 1945. In the beginning of 1946 we crossed the border into Romania. We did not imagine what kind of a regime would be coming to Romania.

In Romania, I was again recognized as a War Invalid. I found work in a casting plant in Bucharest. I worked there until 1950. The agreement between Russia and Romania dictated that all former residents of Bessarabia would be sent back. I did not wish to go to Russia,

I managed, with great difficulty, to obtain permission to go to Israel.

My mother died in Czernowitz, and my wife and I arrived in Israel in 1950.

We were sent to Tira North where we stayed in a small shack. There was no work. There was very little food. Soon after we arrived "rations" were instituted. People were complaining and moaning, but I could not understand how quickly they forgot that we had suffered "there." I realized that the difficult war with the Russian "Garden of Eden" was now but a dream. I was very hopeful and knew life would be good. I was not wrong. In 1953, I found a steady job in the Alliance factory (rubber products). We moved, from the shack, to a nice apartment in a new development. I was recognized as a War Invalid – 50% disability. I now live a normal, quiet life. May it be to a 120! Amen

[Page 354]

Deep in the Autumn Night
Y. Manik (Lederman)

Deep in the autumn night

I wander in destroyed villages.

A muddy street, hit by fire,

I follow quickly; the roads are disappearing.

How long has it been since this place was full of life?

A long tune was heard,

In the forest and the valley,

One could hear the warm sounds of my language.

How long has it been since my youth blossomed here?

And now – the owl hoots on the ruins

And the windmill is like a phantom

With broken wings...

I think that God is wandering

In the forlorn streets,

Lonely voices stop him

And he cries...

A synagogue is here – a reminder of the destruction,

Where once the voice of the Prayer Leader was heard

The Torah is orphaned.

There is no reason to rejoice here.

An old menorah,

That was lit here

Every Shabbat...

In Your Blood Shall You Live
Yehuda–Leib Garfield (New York)

"And when I passed by thee, and saw thee polluted in thine own blood, I said unto thee when thou wast in thy blood. Live; yea" (Ezekiel 16, 6)

The extermination and humiliation of the Jews of Bessarabia by the Romanian police together with the Nazi murderers in the summer of 1941 is described in the Archives of YIVO, New York:

The Romanians had previously tolerated the Jews in Romania proper. The towns of Iasi and Galatz, bordering on Bessarabia, were not spared. There were many Jews killed there.

Our town of Bendery, on the Dniester, suffered greatly. Of over,15 000 Jews, only 58 remained after the war. This according to a tabulation at the time. It seems that in Bendery, itself, there were no concentration camps. Most people were killed in place. Others were taken to Transnistria.

In October 1941, when the Germans and the Romanians marched to Odessa, they killed thousands of Jews on the way. At the time, the Jews of Bendery were marching and many lives were lost.

The remaining Jews of Bendery were to be sent to Transnistria, but the order was postponed for a little while. It was either due to a lack of communication from Berlin or an official decree.

"In accordance with discussions with the Board Envoy Khodomeier and S.S. officer Eichmann (May his name be erased), on August 30, 1942 I share with you the situation and the relation towards Tighina (Bendery). In addition, I wrote about it on March 5, 1942. I have obediently taken the following stance...

[Page 355]

In order to strengthen transportation and due to the need to get along with the Romanian authorities in the interest of conducting the war, the Romanian commanders want us to stop, for now, evacuating Jews across the Bug River. Temporarily, the Jews of Tighina (Bendery) are to be kept in local centers before it becomes possible to send them East.

This was signed for the Romanians by General Shtob and Major General Tataramu, for the Germans Ubercommander, Major–General Haufefe.

There is no doubt that many Jews of Bendery had already been sent to various camps throughout northern Bessarabia. The following official decree shows how inhumane and gruesome was the treatment of the Jews, in the concentration camps, by the Germans:

In Edinets, many Jews were killed and other Jews had to dig common graves for them There were 300 bodies in each common grave. Those who dug the graves were also then shot.

10,000 Jews were evacuated from Lipcany and Khotin. They were tormented and forced to hard labor. In addition, they were not allowed to buy food in the marketplace (Order of July, 1941).

On July 17, 1941, the Gestapo, together with the Romanian army, arrived in Kishinev. More than 10,000 Jews were transported to a camp in the forest.

The first 300 Jews brought by a Romanian Corporal to the Dniester in order to transport them to Transnistria, were forbidden by the Germans from crossing the Dniester. The soldiers shot and killed them. The Romanians told the survivors that if they would hand over money and jewelry, they would be allowed to cross the river. The murderers were immediately given a few hundred rings and other jewelry as well as cash. When the Jews went into the water, they were shot. 60 people survived and were able to give testimony of this horror.

Those Jews who survived the camps had to do hard labor. They were humiliated, oppressed, starved and made ill. Young girls and women were shamed by the Romanian officers and soldiers. On the other side of the Dniester, the Germans sent the Jews from Transnistria Camp to Ataki. From Novoselitza, there were also Jews sent to Ataki, to a camp on the riverbank. Romanian patrols accompanied the Jews there and back. They shot those who were tired and sick. Many of those shot were thrown into the Dniester. The events were described, in a laconic manner, to the authorities in Kishinev. The authorities reacted by putting aside all these reports.

On October 9, 1941, Dr. Fielderman, president of the Federation of Jewish Communities, appeared before Marshall Antonescu as a representative of the Federation. He requested that a stop be put to the evacuation of Jews from Bessarabia to Bucovina – where they would surely die.

On October 12, 1941, there was an order to evacuate all Jews from Bessarabia to Bucovina and to confiscate their belongings. They were allowed to take food and clothing, only what they could carry.

On October 14, Professor Antonescu promised Dr. Fielderman to stop the deportation of professionals, businessmen and partisans. However, Dr. Fielderman asked also for all others to be returned home.

On October 19, Dr. Fielderman received a reply from Marshall Antonescu. He accused the Jews of the two provinces of collaborating with the Communists against Romania. They are now being punished for their behavior.

In the meantime, Jews in Kishinev were treated with cruelty. Only converts to Christianity and capable craftsmen were spared. The situation in the concentration camps worsened.

October 16, 1941. Hans Raguer, a camp administrator, came to Camp Petchero and ordered all girls 14 to 20 to be used as nurses in the military hospital near Vinnitsa.

[Page 356]

Around 150 young women were assembled and they were placed in special cars that were waiting for them. The girls were driven to a nearby forest, where they were shamed, beaten and then shot. Only one girl, Frida Kofler, survived with the help of a German soldier. He had previously worked in Dachau.

On May 26 – previously mentioned that Dr. Fielderman was asked to pay 4 billion lei. Dr. Fielderman did not have the money, and he was sent to Transnistria on July 30, 1941.

On January 1, 1944 – Marshall Antonescu announces the following: "We handled the residents of the occupied areas with gentleness and humanity. No one was beaten or looted in these places. Wherever we went, no one was deported and no one was hurt in our camps. We did not uproot any families or people because of national or political interests."

I only chose some examples of the Nazi horrors, together with Romanian collaborators.

This is a table indicating the extermination plan of the Romanian authorities in September 1941 – in the locations shown:

Beltz	2,923
Kohul	47
Akkerman	55
Kiliya	130
Ismail	1,259
Lopushne	215
Orgeyev	360
Soroka	1,279
Bendery	58
Czernowitz	49,497
Staradjhinetz	4,311
Khotin	559

And the camps:

Securin–Edinetz	20,909
Markulesht	10,737
Vertujhen	24 000
Ghetto Kishinev	10,096

The Jews of Transnistria do not belong to this table.

The pre-war statistics indicate these provinces had 274,036 Jews. This number grew higher when Jews from the Soviet Union arrived in 1940. It is estimated that more than 150,000 Jews were murdered by the Nazis and the Romanians.

**

"My ancestors belong to the present House of Israel. I come from these martyrs who gave the world God and morals. They suffered through the battles of memory."

[Page 357]

The Bendery Society
Yehuda–Leib, son of David, Halevi (New York)

The Bendery Society of New York at a memorial assembly for the Jews of Bendery who were murdered in the Holocaust

Bendery was a town with a colorful setting. It sat in the middle, between old and new Bessarabia. It was an important summer resort on the Dniester. There were fruit orchards on one side and vineyards on the other side. The most important actors from Peterburg (St. Petersburg), Moscow and Odessa used to perform in Bendery, using their vacation time. There was good income for all, and very few Jews had immigrated to America. Some young people went to study in Paris and remained there. Others made Aliyah. After WWI, there were young working people who moved to America.

The Bendery Society was founded in 1920, and it was always, and still is, a lively and mobile organization in America. It strives to cooperate with all Jewish institutions. When Bessarabia absorbed many refugees from the Soviet Union and the economic situation was critical, the Bendery Society sent financial help. It also sent help, with a full heart, to other groups. All this until WWII broke out.

When the Association of Bessarabian Jews was established, the Jews of Bendery were an important part of it. They helped considerably in the work of the association and later in the Council of Bessarabia.

Those from Bender remain in contact with their compatriots in Israel.

[Page 358]

In Israel, they established a loan fund to help those who are in need.

Many compatriots from Bendery are quite enthusiastic and interested in the "Center of the Jews of Bessarabia" in Tel Aviv. They decided that it was their duty to uphold the good name of the Jews of Bendery by giving larger financial support and building the Center of the Jews of Bessarabia.

Bendery was, for many generations, a beautiful Jewish town with its cherished Bessarabian Jews and Jewish institutions. It can also be proud of the beautiful and important monuments in the society here, in America.

"Bessarabian Jews" bulletin, 21.10.1967

Bessarabian Jews Intensively
Construct a Building in Israel

The Association of Bessarabian Jews, established at the beginning of WWII, did much to help the remainder of the community. The author of these words held all important positions in this association, and he faithfully served the Jews of Bessarabia during all that time.

When the Cold War brought a cooling in our midst, those who were nationalistic Jews left the Association. The Council of Bessarabia was then established with the help of MK Yitzhak Korn, the dynamic Jew from Kishinev. He is the President of the World Association of Jews from Bessarabia.

Throughout the years, we built dwellings for newcomers, as well as absorption centers, residences for seniors, and other projects. However, the most important project of Yitzhak Korn was the construction of the Center for Jews from Bessarabia. It will be a grand building with a lot of sections and great historic perspective.

It is essential to note that the more notable Jews from Bessarabia, all over the free world, have enthusiastically participated in this project. The building is almost completed, and we are now waiting only for the official opening in May, or beginning of July, this year.

My intention is to draw the attention of the locals, mainly the New York members from Bessarabia, especially those who have not yet committed themselves to this building. The time is short and they must be involved now. If not, they will be late in becoming partners, with others from Bessarabia, in this historic project. It will be the Center of the Jews of Bessarabia.

This building is a monument for Bessarabia and all Jews from there must be involved.

There is still space for these people to contribute their portion in the building of this monument. History will note this fact.

Several organizations have pledged large sums. In front is the Bessarabian Society of Baltimore. In second place is the Bessarabian Society of Pittsburgh. Among the individuals there are many important personalities such as President Moshe Libman, z" l and, to differentiate, the present president, Morris Ginsburg. The Bendery Society of New York has pledged to pay for the Bendery Room in the Center for the Jews of Bessarabia.

If you want to sponsor a room in your name or you wish to give a lesser amount, there is still time to do so. This is the last opportunity. There will not be a second chance for you.

With warm regards and with great respect,

Leon Garfield

National Secretary

"Day–Morning–Journal," New York

[Page 359]

The Progressive Bendery Benevolent Society

The organization was established in 1920 by 18 members, headed by Yosef Tabachnik, z" l. When the Association of Bessarabian Jews was founded five years later, the society was among the first to join in relief–work. In the last few years, they lost three of their active members: Yosef Tabachnik, z" l, Zelig Broitman, z" l, and Eliezer Sverdlik, z" l. They had done much for the Bendery and the Bessarabian Associations.

The President, Yosef Gorenstein, Rabbi Moshe Z. Berman, Avraham Forman and Leon Garfield were the only ones who helped to create the Association of Jews of Bessarabia. Leon Garfield is one of the most active leaders and Vice–President of the Association. An important role is played by Max Broitman as the Chairman of the Relief Committee. The Relief Committee was established by H. Bidnik, L. Kliatz, Leon Garfield, Paul Garfield, I. Gorenstein, S. Roth and A. Forman.

David Carmeli

"The Jews of Bessarabia," January 1946

A meeting of former residents of Bendery, Tel Aviv, 1969,

where it was decided to publish the Bendery Yizkor Book

[Page 361]

Afterword
P. Bendersky

Jews have a nice custom – going to the cemetery – to remember and honor their ancestors. This custom is connected to the forging of the "golden chain" which entwines the Jewish past with the present. There should not be, God forbid, a break in the chain.

The Yizkor books are written by those who survived the Holocaust. It is a miracle that they were not annihilated by the murderous dogs during the terrible times of WWII. They remember well the life of the Jews – in spite of the evil decrees and confinements. They did not have a country, and they were strangers in all the foreign lands in which they found themselves. How great was their spirit!

The present generation and the future one, when they will come to discuss Eastern Europe, will learn about the spirit of the once vibrant Jewish life in towns and villages, everywhere in the diaspora.

Our longing, we Bendery Jews, will never stop. We have undertaken a difficult task – to eternalize our beloved town, with its fine Jews – religious and secular – and its institutions and societies.

Bendery was a cherished community, and it is truly important to eternalize it.

It is possible that we began this large and important task too late. Many smaller communities in Bessarabia have already done it some time ago. However, in spite of all difficulties, we have not stopped, and we will complete our task. As it said – better late than never.

In Bendery, thanks to its topographic location, there was a colorful community life. There were Hassidim, Zionists and their branches, Bundists and Revolutionaries who vociferously opposed the Tsar.

The generation that had the luck to be born at the end of the 19th century and the dawn of the 20th was one that was imbued with high moral ideals. This is why our Zionist ideas were followed. To our great sorrow all of this disappeared. This is why our memories of those days must not be forgotten. Our parents have earned it, and the memories will truly honor them.

This Yizkor Book has as its base not the individual memories of every family, but those that are true of the entire Jewish community of Bendery.

In our Yizkor Book there are descriptions of Jewish life until the last stroke. There are wonderful pictures of nature in Bendery and surroundings, its river and fields. All seasons of the year, memories of Shabbat and Holidays, and Jewish customs are included. All of this together with the horrors of the Holocaust. This why our Yizkor Book is our memorial to the generation that no longer exists. All those who were cut down and did not manage to make Aliyah to our great Jewish homeland– the STATE OF ISRAEL.

[Pages III to XVIII]

English Section

Yizkor Book of Our Birth-Place

BENDERY
&
HER HOLY CONGREGATION

Editor: Dina Ginton

The Committee of the Inmortalization* at New-York are:
President: A. Furman, L. Garfield, D. Carmel J.Y. Fain
Tel-Aviv 1975

Bendery
An invitation to view our city before World War II

IN MEMORY OF MY GRANDSON GIL CARMEL
WHO DIED AS A SOLDIER IN THE ISRAELI ARMY

By David Carmel

The sign at our railroad-station read Bendery II, the "y" at the end indicating the plural form of the name of our city. We had one more railroad-station, on the outskirts of our city, which had been the original and only station when the city was still small (probably still under the Turks). Not far from this old station the Turks had built a fortress surrounded by canals and hills. When the canals were filled with water, no enemy could penetrate the fortress.

The entrance to the fortress at Bendery

In 1812, after the Russians drove the Turks out, the city started to develop and expand, and quickly became prosperous. It had then become an important railroad-center, with a depot employing many workers in its shops, and it was then that a new station was built and named Bendery II.

Chaim-Leib Gorenstein (father of Joe), was the man who did the contracting work for the depot. In 1918, during the uprising of the Russian railroad-workers against the Rumanian occupation of Besarabia, Chaim-Leib nursed the wounded workers.

The trains were running from a northern town called Ungeni, close to the Rumanian border and the city of Yassi, through the Bessarabian capital city Kishinev on to Bendery, and further on, over a long iron bridge on the Dniestre River, to the city of Odessa. Those desiring to travel to the Southern part of Bessarabia had to take the train running from Bendery to the town of Reni, close to the Rumanian city of Galatz.

To the east, south and west of the railroad lay vast stretches of wheat and farmland, reachable only by horse and oxen-drawn vehicles.

The city was surrounded by Moldavian and German settlements in the north; Moldavian and Mallo-Russian in the south and west. To the east run the Dniestre River, which has its source in the Carpathian Mountains and flows downstream to the Black Sea.

All along the Dniestre River, on both of its banks, spread vineyards and orchards, whose fruit and produce used to be brought into our city as early as three o'clock in the morning. The entire marketplace and its surrounding streets would then become jammed with the farmers' vehicles, filled with seasonal fruits and other produce. Some farmers used to bring in lambs, pigs, chickens, ducks, geese and pigeons. Jewish merchants would be there to meet them and bargains would be quickly reached, at prices prevailing from year to year, and varying only according to quality. The fruits would be packed in large straw baskets by professional packers and shipped to many distant cities in the country by freight trains.

Among the fruit merchants were Kornfeld (the father of Jean Bidnick), Levi Davidovich (the father of Zvi, Chabiba, the writer Rivka Davidit, and Aaron Davidi, Professor at the University of Tel-Aviv and former Commander of the Israeli Paratroopers), Chaim Capusta, Joseph Goldman (the father of Naum, Assistant Chief of the Police of Tel Aviv, killed by a bomb by subversives,

Abram, Lily, Aniuta, Rivka and Mania), and Tevya (the cantor) Schachnovsky, the grandfather of Lia Gendelman-Segal.

The Dneistre River

The favourable natural conditions: the climate, the black earth, the seasonal rains, the warm sunshine in daytime combined with cool nights, in addition to the love and care that the local farmer and his entire family put into their labors, produced fruits and vegetables with a taste unmatched elsewhere in the world.

The grain would be packed and then shipped, sometimes by freight trains, but mostly in deep barges on the Dniestre, and up the river all the way to the Austrian border. The longshormen carrying the 200 lb-sacks on their shoulders, were known as the "Banibakes", the descendants of the Turks. The agents expediting at the Varnitza Port were Hersh Goldins and Avremel Weisser, who also had a lumber yard. His manager in the lumber business was Mordechai-Itzil Averbuch, the father of Clara Steinmetz.

Beside the grain-filled barges, Bendery also had passenger and freight steamboats, owned by the Yassky Brothers. These steamers, sailing the Dniestre from Mogilev Fodolsk, through Bendery to Ackerman at the Black Sea, used to stop also at other cities. Expediting agent for these boats was Benny Klayman, the father of Harry, Clara and Dora. Twice a week we used to have special markets for hay and other cattle-food, on a square outside the city where also horses were bought and sold, and where huge city scales had been provided to weigh all the farm-produce and cattle. An official city ticket had to be issued as to the net weight of every product. The concessionaire for these scales was Shulom Tzechoval, father of Senka the actor, Levi the art-painter, Nechemia, and Mania Bronstein.

The passenger and freight steamboats owned by Yassky Brothers at Bendery

Bendery had two large flour-mills and several smaller ones, the latter patronized by the local farmers for grinding flour for their home-consumption. Situated by the river was also a beer-brewery, and many town-people would come there either walking or by rowing a boat, in order to enjoy the beer while watching the beautiful scenery of the river and the fruit orchards on the opposite bank. There were also several factories: a soap factory, a tile-factory, several redbrick factories, and beside these-numerous blacksmiths, machinists, (like Abe Lerman), wineries, cabinet makers. The town possessed a number of ready-made men's clothing-stores and stores for farmers' wear, employing tailors for the elite as well as for the poor and the peasants.

To expand their sales and improve their incomes, some of the storekeepers used to pack up wagonloads of seasonal merchandise and travel to various farm centers, on their "market days". This was known as a "Yarid" or a market gathering, and the merchants supplied the farmers' needs while cashing in some extra income.

The Jewish population was orthodox, but not fanatically so. We had a Chief Rabbi, two Dayonim (assistant Rabbis) and twelve Shochtim, all of them learned and pious Jews. On Shabbath, and holidays, all the business establishments would be closed and only the drugstores would stay open.

The prominent synagogue of the Rabbi and family Wetheim

Our twenty two synagogues would then be packed with parishioners. The more prominent among our synagogues was that of our official Rabbi Wertheim. It had been build by David Wertheim's grandfather, Reb Itzikel, a scion of a Rabbinic family descended from the Baal-Shem-Tov, the 18th century founder of the Hassidism. It was traditional in style; its ceiling and walls were covered by oil-colors depicting the twelve Jewish Tribes and various fruits that grew in the ancient land of Israel. The Western Wall was painted as a replica of the Western Wall of the Holy Temple in Jerusalem that remains standing to this day, a reminder of the glory of ancient Israel. Besides his official function as the Chief Rabbi, Reb Itzikel acted, first and foremost, as a Hassidic Rabbi, receiving people in distress and praying for them to the Almighty to ease their lot. The needy would then leave a donation for the synagogue. The Gabbai, or the President of the synagogue, was Reb Meir Fein, the father of Isaak Fein, Katia, Jack Fine, the secretary of the Benderer Society, and Donia Orlinsky.

Rab Itzikel the father of Shloime Wertheim of Rabbinic family descended from the Baal Shem-Tov

Rabbi Shimon Shloime Wertheim

Other synagogues served every class and layer of our population, whether rich, poor, artisan, laborer, merchant, etc. Most young men used to come with their parents to pray in the synagogues, keeping thus up the tradition of the Jewish ethics and learning.

Upon leaving the synagogue, a parishioner would take with him along a stranger, who would be standing quietly near the door, indicating that he wants to be invited for a kosher Sabbath-meal. Beside the stranger, we would also have at our tables Jewish soldiers from the local regiment. These soldiers, who came from distant cities, were glad to find themselves in a warm Jewish home whenever off duty. Our Sabath meal would last a good two hours. Between courses we would sing the prescribed songs, as well as songs from the cantorial liturgy, Hassidic songs, and even the Jewish theatre songs. The Sabbath used to be a day of joy and relaxation.

During the first World War Bendery received an additional influx of soldiers. The newly arrived could not be adopted by the Jewish families, who were already "overloaded". But before long there was formed a committee, headed by Reb David Gurfel (the father of the Garfield brothers, Louis, Leon and Paul), which provided for the establishment of a free kitchen in the vestry of the old Beis-Medrash (synagogue). The kitchen was there to feed all the Jewish soldiers on Friday-nights, Sabbath-noons and all the Jewish holidays. Some of the food and chalas were donated, the rest was bought. The womenfolk cooked the fish, the soup and the chickens and kugel, condiments and wine were also served. The tables were usually covered with clean white cloths, tableware was provided and the members of the committee themselves were the waiters and also helped along with the rituals. The soldiers, away from home, were happy. So was the committee and all who helped.

The name David Gurfel stood for love and kindness in our city. He worked hard, managing entirely voluntarily the free kitchen. Very often we kids used to help Reb David carry kosher food for the Jewish political prisoners to the 'Ostrog' prison.

The "Nye Shil", our newest synagogue which took a long time building, used to attract many people from other cities thanks to its interior, decorated in the style of the Italian Rennaissance. Its President (Gabbai), was Reb Chaim-Moishe Fishov, father of Rose Fine.

Naturally, we pride ourselves upon the scholars, the renowned musicians, painters and other artists of our city, but we also remember the homage we owe to yet another group of our Benderer Jews, namely, to the drivers of the horse-drawn vehicles, who stoutly protected their Jewish honor. To illustrate: when a group of antisemitic truck-drivers would start a fight with our Jewish boys, our boys would grab an oak pole used for rolling up barrels of wine or oil and swing it as if it were merely a whip. Those hit by it would be either dead or have their bones crushed. Those boys were so strong that with one stroke they could kill a man. Even the police would be frightened and in order to prevent any further disturbances, they would exact from those truck-drivers a written promise to abstain from any further fights. Here is also the place to mention that during the World War I new contingents of Kossacs were brought into the military baracks of our town. These Kossacks used to get drunk at night and beat up the defenseless Jews in the streets. And it was the butchers, (whose President-Gabbai was Zeidel Markman, the father of Betty Lerman and the Markman brothers), which formed a group of vigilants to take care of them.

In the times of the Bolshevist Revolution (1917-1920), there appeared in Bendery Sholom Shwarzbard (born in Izmail, Bessarabia), who came from Ukraina and started to organize the butchers and other boys into a self-defence group by training them in combat. This same Shwarzbard had also been active in the defence of the Ukrainian Jews during the Ukrainian pogroms led by the Atamans Machno and Petliura. 50 thousands Jews were killed in those pogroms. The list of the Ukrainian atrocities is long and inexhaustible. On May 26th, 1926, Shwarzbard recognized the General Petliura on a street in Paris, and killed him on the spot. Shwarzbard had been tried in a Paris court, but was found innocent.

There existed several Grammar and High Schools in our city. Shwartzman's Hebrew High School was perhaps the most prominent among them all. Gregor Yackovich Shwartzman had devoted all his life to his students, rich and poor alike. An exacting and demanding scholar and pedagogue, he dedicated himself to Hebrew studies, and, beside his educational activities, he also edited a Hebrew Geography book. Another of our teachers, Isaak Borisovich Reznikov, devoted himself to Yiddish and became the editor of the Bundist weekly newspaper "Dos Yiddishe Folk". Isaak Borisovich had also published a Hebrew Mathematics book. Still another of our teachers, Samuel Gorin, published a Hebrew History book, which many Hebrew Schools were making use of.

Shwarzbard's self-defence group

Students of the first Hebrew high school established by Dr. G.Y. Shwartzmann

Some of our students were active in the underground work, creating illegal Zionist cells, from which there later developed the groups of "Hecholutz", "Hashomer-Hatzair" and "Gordonia". We had also established several athletic groups, such as "Hatikva" and "Maccabi". Yasha Fein was our star in the socker football. In our school we also had a mandolin-orchstra and a drama-group, who used to perform for our department, our students and our parents.

Welvele Rabinovich donated a building for the Talmud-Tore. The students there came from poor families and were given regular free warm lunches and some new clothing before the high holidays. A part of this came from the donations of the Benderer Society of New York.

The Maccabi group at Bendery

The mandolin orchestra

In the Chedorim (private Jewish parochial schools), we were taught the traditional Jewish subjects.

Our Jewish hospital had been built, subsidized and maintained by the philanthropist Reb Itzie Nissenbaum. Attached to the hospital was an old age home. We had other regular social services, like: Ezras Cholim, a committee to aid the sick and provide them with free drugs; Malbish Arumim, a committee to clothe the poor school children; Hachnosas Orchim, a free hostel for wayfarers; Hachnosas Caloh, a women's committee to aid the poor brides; a ladies' organization to aid women in childbirth and in distress.

The Bendery philanthropist
Reb Itzie Nissenbaum

The Benderer Jews were charitable and supported all Jewish causes. When Jewish refugees came streaming in from across the river, having escaped from the Ukrainian pogroms and Bolshevick revolution, the Benderer gave them shelter, food and services to ease their burden.

Politically, we had our share of Socialists, Zionists, Labor-Zionists, and also a few Bundists, Territorialists and Revisionists. We also had our Jewish amateur theatre-group from which several fine artists emerged. To name but a few: Shmerl Chrush, Rose Kaniberlatzkaya, Panish, Rose Celnik, Liza Klotz-Gorenstein, Yoske Gorenstein, Bendersky, Krasilchik, Motke and Yosi Gold.

The first group of Zionists at Bendery under the leadership of N. Lifshitz

In addition to our own cantors: Tevya Schachanovsky, Kolochnick, Moishe Chazkelevich, Reb Pini from the Sadigerer Shil, Balaban, Banish and Yosele Shwartzman, we used to enjoy the performances of the finest opera-troupes from the bigger cities and the most famous cantors from Russia.

Head Hazan Reb Pini Mesonsnic at the Sadigure Synagogue

Summertime, our city would become a vacation center and the greatest actors with their companies would then appear in our summer theatre.

We must devote at least a little space to the unusual honesty of our artisans. Here is an illustration: dressing up in her fineries to attend a wedding, my Mother notices that her diamond ring is missing, and she gives it up for lost. After some time, before another wedding, she takes her good dress to the best tailor in town, Reb Itzchok Furman (father of Abe), for a slight alteration. A few days later, Reb Itzchok brings my mother's dress back with the missing diamond ring, which he found hidden in the hem of the dress. And since we mentioned a wedding, let us now and here describe one. It usually started late in the afternoon and lasted till dawn. After the Chupa ceremony, the caterer and head waiter, Reb Elia Bidnick, (father of Henry), would announce that all the guests of the groom's side were to be served bouillon with mondlen. The bride's guests would simply sit and watch. The main dinner for all would take place about midnight. Before the last course, the sexton would announce that wedding gifts were then in order. Some would give a rubble, some half rubble, a few would bring gifts. The obvious reson for this procedure was that the money had to be used to pay the cooks, the waiters and the musicians.

The prosperous families would arrange more modern weddings. It is worth noting that the building where these weddings were held, was built and owned by Reb Itzil Goldfarb, (grandfather of Label Goldfarb from Montreal, Canada). The Chupa ceremony would take place on a huge outside balcony, which could hold more than 50 guests, and hundreds of people would be watching the ceremony, usually conducted by the Chief Rabbi Reb Shliomke Wertheim. Reb Itzil Goldfarb had been a President of the old Synagogue for a long time. During his term in office he rebuilt, renovated and redecorated the old Beis-Medrash, but kept its interior in the old tradition and spirit. After him Reb David Gurfel became the President.

Reb Itzil Goldfarb's wedding Hall was also used as the Zionist Synagogue on the Sabbath and holidays. Its spiritual leaders were: Baruch Cholodenko, Hersh Kogan, Israel Blank, M. Chacham, Yoel Vodovoz (Dora Furman's uncle) and David Wertheim. The guest lecturers who came to this Zionist Synagogue were Chaim Greenberg and Leibele Glanz and a number of Yiddish Poets who nourished our souls and minds with the true meaning of Jewish education, Jewish bravery and the hope of reviving the Jewish homeland in Eretz-Israel.

During the refugee years (1918-1921) Goldfarb placed the Hall at the disposal of the women's committee

Left: Hersh Kogan, The Zionist leader at Bendery
Right: Israel Blank one of the leaders of the Algemeine Zionisten

The first group POALE ZION at Bendery
(1) L. Gurfild*, (2) Pruzhansky, (3) Glass *Garfield?

When in 1920 Leon Garfield came on a visit from America, he met in Bendery his old Poalei-Zion friends: D. Pruzhan-sky, Dr. Bregman, Z. Shenker, A. Kogan, Z. Bromberg, L. Shneerson, Miss Dubosarsky, Sperling, Arbitman, Rabinovich, Mrs. Kremon, Mrs. Yasky and Chaim Glass. Together they organized a branch of the "Yiddish Cultural League", with a nursery for little children and an institute for Yiddish literature evening courses for boys and girls. All the above leaders of the league were acting as instructors without any pay. The same league was also responsible for the organization of a choir group under the direction of Zina Pistrow, the sister of David Zina, a talented singer and musician, became later a member of the Bucharest Opera House and also gave individual recitals in various cities.

I believe that our young American generation should know about our parents' enormous struggle in their efforts to make living. Antisemitism and persecutions forced us to leave Bendery and emigrate to the United States of America and to Israel. Those of us who came here had to struggle and work hard to raise our families.

The members of the Benderer Progressive Benevolent Society

And now let us glance at the achievements of the members of the Benderer Progressive Benevolent Society and the Ladies Auxiliary of New York. Its President, Abe Furman, has been active in the society for many years. Under the leadership of Leon Garfield, Irving Faerman, Louis Garfield, Abe Furman,

Max Broitman, Joe Gorenstein, Henry Bidnick, Harry Winsaft, Moishe Sudit, Paul Garfield, Abe Lerman and Yasha Fein, the society helped to organize the "Council of Bessarabian Jews", affiliated to the "American Histadrut Geverkshaften Campaign". Leon Garfield, as the council's National Secretary, and David Carmel, as its Publicity Secretary, had helped to provide for more than 300 housing apartments for the Bessarabian refugees in Kiriat Israel near Tel-Aviv. The Benderer Society established a free loan fund for the Benderer newcomers in Israel, donated over $9,000 (with the most help of Leon Garfield) for the new large building of "Beth Yehudey Bessarabia", which with its library, conference, and recreation halls serves the Tel-Aviv University students in their research work. This building serves as a center for various social activities, including dances for the Israeli soldiers on furlough and for the neighborhood youth, and conferences and lectures for the Jewish newcomers from the Soviet Union. The society is also helping the "Benderer Izkor Book", which is devoted to the history of the Benderer Jewish Community liquidated by the Nazis.

Reb Elie (Shoichet) Chaplick

We derive great satisfaction from the fact that some of our Benderer Landsleit's creative effort have been recognized and esteemed. Especially deserving in this respect is **Reb Elie (Shoichet) Chaplick,** father of Yasha, Lana, Isaac, Chaika and Moishe. A famous Talmud scholar, he used to give Talmud lessons to 25-30 middle-aged Jews every night after the prayers in the Sadigerer School in Bendery. In 1912 he published in Hebrew "Kitzur Divrei Hayamim Veiseder Hadoroth", in which he included commentaries on our Prophets, Kings, the Macabees, and sages of the great Yeshivas, and some research about the deported from Eretz Israel to Babylonia 2500 years ago. His works had been praised by all the critics as an invaluable source for studying Hebrew literature.

Reb Moishe Seiver (Sverdlick), also a Shoichet, devoted his time to the studies of the Talmud, searching out the epigrams of wisdom and collecting them as he went along for a period of 40 years. After having settled in Eretz Israel, and after long years of hard work, he published his collected works in three large Encyclopedic volumes containing over a hundred thousand quotations and his own commentaries on them. In his works he recorded the deepest wisdom of the Jewish masters. His works can be found in the librairies of the universities throughout the world.

Dr. Isaak M. Fine is another outstanding personality. From 1943 until his retirement in 1967 a Professor of Jewish History at the Baltimore Jewish College, he also served for many years as Curator in the Baltimore and Boston Jewish Historical Society, and had been honored by many fellowships and grants, has published a great number of research articles dealing with Jewish History. In his new book, "The Making of an American Jewish Community: The History of the Baltimore Jewish Community in the years 1773-1920", he goes beyond the chronological review of that -period and describes the persecution of the Jews and their struggles before they came to this country. The book includes the stories of the lives of a great number of historical figures, and is written in a vivid and clear style

Professor Harry M. Orlinsky, Dunia Fein's husband, the Professor of Bible at the Hebrew Union College-Jewish Institute of Religion in New York City, is an outstanding Bible scholar. In his book "Ancient Israel", he gives a brief narrative account of the history of the people who created the Hebrew Bible and an outline of the integral relationship between the development of their societies and the growth of the Biblical tradition. His other contribution in the field of Biblical research is the editing of a new translation of the Torah. The text had been put into English directly from the traditional source as preserved throughout the centuries by the Masoretic scribes. Dr. Orlinsky has been a Gugenheim fellow and has lectured at Oxford, Jerusalem, Moscow and Rome Universities. He is considered one of the world's leading Bible scholars. He was also consulted by the archeologist General Yigael Yadin about the authenticity of the famous Dead Sea Scrolls bought from Jordanian Arabs for the sum of $250.00 donated by Samuel Gottesman. The Scrolls are now in the possession of the National Museum in Jerusalem.

David Wertheim, the son of the very cultured Talmid-Chochom Rabbi Shliome, had elevated .himself by his thorough knowledge of Judaism as well as by his extraordinary regard for the general humanitarian ideals. As a Poalei-Zion leader he proved not only a gifted orator, but also a person striving constantly to improve prove his mind, and a man able to endear himself upon all who came in contact with him, leading writers and thinkers as well as a wide following of appreciative friends from all walks of life. one of the most popular and beloved Yiddish and Hebrew speakers, he knew how to turn each of his speaches into a holiday for the Jewish community whenever he appeared, starting from Bendery, and later in any town in Bessarabia, the United States and South America.

Rabbi Dr. Aaron Wertheim had been the chief Rabbi of Bendery for a few years before he came to New York, where he was appointed the Rabbi of the Congregation Bnei-Israel of Linden Height in Brooklyn, N. Y. After a few years of studying he presented to the Dropsy College in Philadelphia, Pa. a thesis on Hassidism. His educational work entitled him to the degree of Ph. D. He published in Hebrew a study in the historical background of the teachings of the Hassidic Movement and its leaders from its beginning in the life of the Jewish people, devoting much space to Rabbi Israel Baal Shem Tov, the founder, Rabbi Levi Yitzhak of Berdichev, the well-known spokesman and defender of our people, Rabbi Shneur Zalmon of Liadi (Liubavicher) the builder of Hassidic thought, Rabbi Pinchas of Koretz, the champion of the ethical principles of life, and Rabbi Nachman of Bratzlav, the master of the message of and for Eretz Israel. Thanks to this study Dr. Aaron Wertheim has come to be considered a distinguished scholar, particularly in the area of Hassidism.

Rivka Davidit (Davidovich) was born in Bendery and at the age of 12 (not knowing one word of Hebrew) she came with her parents to Israel. When she grew up, she established for herself a fine reputation as a theater critic (in the newspaper "Davar"), a playwright and a children's writer. She has been a co-worker of the Histadrut educational publishing houses: "Am Oved", "Tarbut Vechinuch" and "Hakibutz Hameuchad". Apart from all these, she has also translated into Hebrew a number of short stories by Russian classics: Gogol, Turgeniev, Dostoevsky, Tolstoy, Chekhov and Gorki. Rivka Davidit's reviews are highly respected in the literary world and her writings have been described as natural, simple and sincere.

Mordechai Seiver, the editor of many educational Hebrew booklets, is a fine translator of poems and articles from Russian and Yiddish into Hebrew. He translated short stories and poems of Shimon Frug, Nathan Alterman, Kadia Molodovsky, Shika Manik and others. The struggle for Israel's independence has inspired his script for a movie show. He has also published a biography of the deceased speaker of the Israeli Knesset (Parliament), Kadish Looz.

The poet Shika Manik

The poet **Shika Manik** is another distinguished Benderer. Professor Sol **Lip**tzin gave an interesting review about Shika Manik's (Leiderman) Yiddish book "Along Your Wandering" (Trit Fun Dain Vander), where he says: "This fourth book of lyrics by a poet who left Bendery for America, and then for Israel over three decades ago, contains a few poems of New York, reflecting his American experience and a few recalling his Bessarabian childhood, but more lyrics are based on his experiences as a chalutz. He catches the spirit of Safad, Tel-Aviv and Sodom. He sings about the blue Mediterrenean, about the beautiful nights when the whole land appears like a temple. Sharply contrasted to these joyous lyrics of Israel are the poems devoted to the Holocaust".

The actor **Simcha (Senka) Tzechoval** started his career while still a student at the Benderer Shwarzman's High School where he used to appear at the concerts in numerous sketches, and Hassidic and Hebrew folk songs and monologues. After having settled in Eretz Israel and joining the Ha-Ohei Theatre, he has won instant acclaim from the audience and press for his performance in "Uncle Vania" (Chekhov).

Memorial Candles

Translated by Ala Gamulka

[Page 365]

Eli Abramovich   Yehoshua Otzkovsky

Eli Abramovich was born in 1881. He was one of the most important members of our community. He and his brother Bouya were great supporters of the Jewish community. Eli was always ready to listen to individual needs. If a horse belonging to the water carrier or the wagon driver or the cow of the milk maiden fell, they knew to come to R. Eli for help.

Eli also financed the pioneers so they could prepare themselves in the Hahshara.

On June 13, 1941, before the Nazis came to our town, his family was transferred to Russia by the Soviets. He himself was exiled to Siberia. There, he died of hunger on the 19th of November, 1942 in the Ibadel concentration camp in Sverdlovsk.

His burial place is unknown by his family.

May his soul be bound among the living together with other victims of the Holocaust.

Written by his son,

P.B.

He was born in 1915 in Bendery. In his youth he was active in the youth movement "Gordonia".

He made Aliyah in 1936 and immediately joined the Haganah. He served for five years in the British police. Upon leaving, he received a high commendation for his services. (Haganah order #173)

When the War of Independence broke out Yehoshua joined the Israel Defense Forces and served in the Galil and the Jezreel Valley. He attained the rank of sergeant major and was described by his commanding officer as "a devoted and true combatant for many years".

This is an accurate description of Yehoshua's character. He was always ready to help others. His commanders saw these aspects of his character.

In the same manner that he fulfilled his public obligations, he was also a loving and loyal husband. Unfortunately, he was stricken with a mortal disease and he was unable to overcome it. He died at the age of 54.

May his memory be blessed!

[Page 366]

Yitzhak Otzkovsky

The son of Yaffa and Avraham, he was born in Bendery in 1909. He was a member of "Hechalutz" in his town.

He made Aliyah in 1929.

He died on July 11, 1970.

May his Memory be blessed.

His wife Tzilla and his daughters Neta and Aviva

Left: Avraham and Yaffa Otzkovsky

Right– Y.M. Eidelman, his wife Liba, their daughter Mindel and her bridegroom

A Cup of Sorrows

In memory of my unforgettable parents my father Yosef Mendel and my mother Liba Eidelman, z"l, who were killed during the war at the beginning of 1940. They were bombed by the Germans while they were wandering in the Caucasus.

May their souls be among the souls of the living.

Yehiel Efrati

[PAGE 367]

Yitzhak Bauh, Efraim Bauh, Zina Bauh   **Mordehai Atlis, Massya Atlis**

A Memorial to my dear Family members

My father and teacher Mordehai, son of Israel, was born in 1875. He died on 8 Tammuz 1936.

My mother and teacher Massya, daughter of Efraim, was born in 1878 and died on 19 Elul 1969.

My sister, Zina Bauh, her husband, Yitzhak Bauh, born in 1906, fell in the battle of Stalingrad in World War II. He was an officer in the Red Army.

Israel (Sonya) Atlis, Tel Aviv

Hersh Weisser and his wife Haya-Baila

They lived on Haruzina Street in Bendery in the house of Kardonsky.

Hersh was born in Peshtzan in 1864. He was one of the scholars in town. In his youth he studied in Yeshiva and was certified to become a Dayan (judge). However, he never abused his status. After he married Haya-Baila, the daughter of Samuel Bronfman, he settled in Bendery and earned his living running a flour store on Haruzina Street (near Rachman's store). He had two sons and three daughters who were all well educated.

He died in 1932 at the age of 68. May his soul be among the souls of the living.

His wife, HAYA-BAILA, his daughter Vera Shagansky, his young son Shmuel (Moussia), his daughter Sarah (Sonya) Marmis, her husband David Marmis and two sons were all killed by the Nazis.

[Page 368]

Hersh Weisser, his wife, Haya-Baila and their family

They lived on Komandtskaya Street, corner Pushkin in Bender.

Shoel-Leib was one of most respected leaders in town. He was a merchant of wheat and wines. He was pious and a follower of the Rabbi from Sadigura. He attended services in the Sadigura synagogue. He was a generous donor to all Jewish institutions in town.

He died in 1927 at the age of 63.

His wife, Hanna-Ethel was a good housekeeper. She helped in the business and was active in Jewish institutions, such as the Jewish Hospital, Ezrat Nashim, and others.

She died in 1937 at the age of 75.

They had six sons and two daughters and all received a good Jewish education. They were fortunate to see all of their children settled.

May their souls be among the souls of the living!

Shaul-Leib Burris, his wife Hanna-Ethel and their family.

[Page 369]

Hanna Broun – Haim Broun

This is what I remember from the depth of my being:

My mother and teacher **Miriam Broun** died in 1929 at the age of 49.

My father and mentor, **Haim Broun,** died during his wanderings in 1948 at the age of 64.

My beloved sister, **Hanna Broun**, died in 1955 at the age of 46.

My dear brother-in-law, **A. Prakansky**, died in 1946 at the age of 50.

May their souls be among the souls of the living!

Moshe Baron

Misha Betlzer

"When my time comes, wrap me in a blue and white", requested Misha Betlzer of his parents. The parents were distant from Judaism, but the son had a strong love for Zion in his heart.

Misha was a talented young man and had a poetic soul. He wrote poetry in Russian and they were published as well. His life was full of poetry, mathematics, music and Zionism.

He used to lecture to the youth groups about different topics: Nietzsche's philosophy, Borochov's beliefs, literary subjects, etc.

Unfortunately, due to ill health, he was unable to fulfill the dream of Aliyah in which he believed whole-heartedly. He was grieved over this event.

He went to study at the University of Lieges in Belgium in the hope that he would be useful to his homeland and his people after graduation. He hoped to make Aliyah, but that day never came...

His disease weakened him and ended his hopes and aspirations. He died of Tuberculosis before his 19th birthday.

Dear Misha, may your name be forever inscribed in the annals of our town.

Your childhood friend,

L. Sh.

A Candle in Memory of the Bromberg Family of Bendery

The father, AVRAHAM (Zeidel), son of Haim-Yaakov Bromberg, arrived in Eretz Israel in 1955.

He died on 1.12.1964.

The mother, SHEVA, daughter of Asher, died in Russia during the evacuation (when the Germans were advancing to the Caspian Sea). It was on 13.2.1942.

The daughter, MANYA, was born in 1921. She died in Russia, close to the time of her mother's death, on 3.3.1942.

The oldest son, Asher, was born in 1917. He was killed while serving as a soldier in the Red Army on the Finnish front, on 28.1.1942.

May their souls be among the souls of the living!

The son and brother who is in mourning,

Zeev Bromberg

[Page 370]

Brothers Eliezer and Moshe Buchbinder

In the annals of Aliyah from Bendery, a special spot should be kept for the Buchbinder brothers. They were among the first pioneers. Shlomo Buchbinder was the first. He came in 1913, with the Second Aliyah, with two friends from Bendery. These were Raphael Shufman (later a resident of Kfar Yehezkel) and the author Zina Rabinovitch. They made Aliyah with Joseph Trumpeldor and Shlomo Levkovitch (Lavi) who was one of the founders of Ein Harod. Eliezer Buchbinder came with the Third Aliyah.

The two brothers grew up in a traditional home in Bendery. Their parents were the tailor Haim-Yehuda and his wife Sosia. Shlomo planned to make Aliyah before the First World War, but his parents opposed him claiming that it will be the Messiah who will bring the Jews to Eretz Israel. Shlomo went through many trials and tribulations. He worked in security In Kolandia (Atarot), Jerusalem, Kineret, Rosh Pina, Ayelet Hashachar, Tel Hai, Ein Harod, Tel Aviv and others. He was also involved in guarding the Eitz Haim Yeshiva in Jerusalem in 1920. In those days he was invited, with others, by Chief Rabbi Kook to the Third Meal. The Rabbi received them warmly and congratulated encouraged them on the good deed of protecting man and Torah with all their might.

His only son Yitzhak (Buchy) Buchbinder followed in his father's ways. He was a member of Ramat Hanegev kibbutz and was killed, during the War of Independence, while fighting over a road in Hulikat. He died on 18.7.1948 at the age of 19.

Shlomo Buchbinder is especially remembered for his impressive visit to the Hashomer Hatzair in Bendery in 1922. He spoke about the lives of the pioneers in Eretz Israel and the defense of Tel Hai. Our young people heard, from him, for the first time the song Hava Nagila. When we made Aliyah we remembered him fondly and stayed in touch for many years. He truly was a pleasant and gentle man.

He wrote the following lines to his friend P. I. on the picture with his brother Eliezer in Jerusalem in 1922: "... A day will come when each one of us will be in his special corner, but we will still remember the good and the bad days we spent together..." This shows his generosity and fine character.

I last visited Shlomo Buchbinder in 1973and he showed me Joseph Trumpeldor's belt. He had exchanged it with him to have a memento and as a sign of their friendship.

I met his brother Eliezer in Haifa during a difficult period of unemployment and real hunger. He worked as a tailor at that time. He was a kind and good man and he shared his tiny apartment with me. It was a small tent near fig trees on the hill of Hadar Hacarmel.

Over the years, in difficult times, Eliezer began to work on a ship. He left the country and we lost track of him. There are many versions of the story of his disappearance. It is not clear whether he drowned in a sunken ship or during World War II and the Holocaust. We only know he is no longer among us.

May their souls be bound among the souls of the living!

Mordehai Sever

[Page 371]

R. Haim Berman

Yehudit, daughter of Mordehai, Berman
Died on 12th of Av

R. Haim Berman and his wife Yehudit

R. Haim Berman had a grey beard and dark skin. He was a scholar, very intelligent and pleasant. He lived a long life and was a quiet man. It seemed as if he was having a silent conversation with the world around him.

During World War I and the disturbing times afterwards any wanderer could find a haven in his home. Such people could rest there from their turbulent times.

R. Haim played the violin. When he was inspired he would play the sad song "Cry Israel" which was popular then among the Jews of Russia. His children received a Hebrew education and the home was infused with Zionism.

An interesting story about him, not known to many people should be related. R. Haim arrived with the Second Aliyah. While in Eretz Israel he built a flour mill in the then Arab town of Ramle. He was lonely in the Arab settlement and he could not participate in the building of the country. Sadly, he returned to the exile of Bendery. He brought some things, notably two dogs, with him as mementos. One dog was called Lifendzi (perhaps based on the Arabic word Effendi).

M.S.

[Page 372]

Yitzhak Balaban   **David, son of Yitzhak, Buckstein**

We lovingly called him 'Davidka' because he was beloved by everyone. From early childhood he stood out as person of strong character and a lover of his people. He had a sharp sense of humor and had a gentle soul. He liked to help others and to defend the weak. He was still a high school student in Bendery and a member of Maccabi when he participated in defending young Jews.

Another time, David was ready to defend his honor again, when a Christian student insulted the Jews. Events reached a point where Davidka and that Christian student were prepared to hold a duel on the outskirts of town. However, when friends and relatives found out, they prevented him from having the duel so as to avoid the spilling of blood and a catastrophe. Another time he taught a lesson to two anti-Semitic "badmouthers" – he met them in private and he banged their heads together. He wished to prove that there were consequences to insulting the honor of the Jews.

Davidka was courageous and brave, but he was also gentle and kind-hearted. He is well-remembered by all his friends, to this day.

He died at the age of 20 while studying in Belgium. May his memory be blessed!

His family and his friends

Yitzhak Balaban

He was born in 1907 and he was killed in 1942.

In memory of my brother Yitzhak who was a victim of the Holocaust. His grave is unknown.

Yitzhak was more than a brother. Due to circumstances he was also our father and our teacher.

In 1920 a Typhus epidemic swept our town and our father, Pinhas, z"l, died. He left a family of ten souls without any means of income. Yitzhak was only 16 at the time and a high school student and he undertook the job of looking after the family. His mother, Ziporah, was unable to earn a living since she was sickly.

Yitzhak and his oldest sister, Odell, opened a bakery together with a professional baker. He used to walk with two large baskets distributing his wares. When he met a former classmate he would lower his eyes in shame because he had to quit school and stay away from his friends. However, he faithfully fulfilled his duty to his family – the youngest was only 4 years old – until he was drafted by the army.

[Page 373]

Feiga Balaban

In the meantime, we, the younger brothers and sisters grew up. We studied and acquired trades so that each one of us could be independent and help the family. We are all grateful to Yitzhak for giving us the chance to do it and for guiding us in many ways.

Yitzhak was married in Russia and had a son and a daughter.

In our family, only my sister and I made Aliyah. All the others, including our brother Yitzhak and our sister Odell, were slaughtered in the Holocaust.

May their memories be among those of the living!

Yonah Balaban,

Hulda

I remember the following:
Members of the family of Pinhas Balaban from Bendery

The father, Pinhas Balaban, was born in 1862 and died in 1920.

The mother, Feiga Balaban, was born in 1866 and died in 1936.

Odell Balaban (Mozgovsky)

The sister, Rachel Balaban-Shuster was born in 1898 and died in 1970.

The sister, Sima Balaban, was born in 1904 and died in 1927.

Slaughtered in the Holocaust:

My brother, Yitzhak Balaban, was born in 1907 and died in 1942.

My brother, Shlomo Balaban, was born in 1909 and died in 1942.

My sister, Odell Balaban-Mozgovsky, was born in 1900 and died in 1941.

Her husband, Idel Mozgovsky, was born in 1892 and died in 1945.

Their son, Pinhas Mozgovsky, was born in 1925 and died in 1944.

Their daughter, Sonia Mozgovsky, was born in 1927 and died in 1942.

Their daughter, Sima Mozgovsky, was born in 1929 and died in 1942.

Their youngest child, whose name was unknown to us, was the last to die in this family that was gone completely.

May their souls be among the souls of the living among the people of Israel!

Yonah Balaban

Hulda

[Page 374]

Abram Borsotzky

Abram was born in 1899 in Bendery. His parents dealt in commerce and agriculture and were wealthy. He made Aliyah in 1920 with a group of the first pioneers of the Third Aliyah.

In Eretz Israel he did hard labor. He participated in the taming of the Jezreel Valley and was among the founders of Kibbutz Tel-Yosef. He worked in paving roads and the drying of marshes. He became ill with malaria as a result.

After he left the kibbutz he settled in Afula and was one of the first postal workers during the British Mandate. He took part in the laying of the telephone line connecting Haifa and Afula and reached the level of inspector – one of the first Jews to do so.

During the battle for Haifa he was one of the defenders of the telephone exchange in Burj, in the lower town.

He remained an employee of the post office to the end of his days and was noted for his dedication to his job and for his gentleness and honesty. He was a member of the Labor Party and was a follower of its tenets.

May his memory be blessed!

His daughter,
Sara

In memory of our brother-in-law Arieh, son of Pinhas, Bendersky

Arieh Bendersky was born on 13.5.1908. He had a pleasant disposition and was always happy. He was well-liked and everyone called him "Leib".

His large family was true to the Zionist dream and he absorbed a great love of Israel and Zion. Leib was a proud Jew and could not accept the attacks on the Jews by the Christians. This belief brought him to join Maccabi and he became a counsellor in the movement.

He was a devout Zionist and he believed that only if the Jewish people would return to physical labor would they be able to build a homeland.

He studied in ORT School in order to be able to be useful in Eretz Israel.

In 1935 he made Aliyah as part of the first Maccabia where he represented his town. Here he started a family and built a hospitable home. He was a nice person and this fact brought him many friends and acquaintances. He was a modest man all his life. He joined the Haganah and fulfilled his tasks properly.

He died at work on 19.4.71 and left behind his wife Dossia and his orphaned daughters to mourn him.

Told by his brother-in-law **Eliezer** and **Fira Kishon**

And written by **P. Bendersky**

Members of the Bendersky Family

Very few have remained from my large family in Bendery- only those who managed to make Aliyah. The others died in the Nazi Holocaust or by the Soviets when accused of being bourgeois.

My family was one of the leading followers of the Zionist movement – one of them was Dr. Shlomo Bendersky.

My late father, Zeev Bendersky, always wished to make Aliyah and he succeeded in the late 1920s. He first sent my oldest brother as a pioneer with the Third Aliyah. My father died in Eretz Israel on the 22nd day of Sivan 1954 and my mother died on the 29th day of Kislev 1962. They were both buried in the cemetery in Haifa. My father`s parents, Rabbi Yehiel-Moshe Bendersky and my grandmother Manya died in old age in Bendery. My mother`s father died in Safed in 1915.

Zeev and Leah Bendersky

My grandfather Yehiel-Moshe, my grandmother Manya and my aunt Nessya Bendersky

[Page 376]

Bendersky Family

**Top line (right to left): Fishel, Simcha, Nehama, Pinny, Nessya
Second line (from the right) seated Booky**

Right - Booky Bendersky on the right

Left - Haim Bendersky (Second from left)

My uncle, Fishel Bendersky, was exiled by the Soviets to Siberia and he died there after great difficulties. His son Haim made Aliyah with the first Maccabia. He died here after a serious illness and was buried in Netanya. My father's second brother, David Pinny, was exiled to Central Asia. There, he and his wife contracted a disease and they died in great pain and hunger. My father's sister, Nessya,, was unable to flee and was slaughtered by the Nazis together with other Jews of Bendery. Her burial place is unknown.

Pinny Bendersky's son, known as Leib, also came to Eretz Israel with the first Maccabia. He died here.

My mother's family – the Butzlnis- were killed in the Holocaust. They were Mordehai Butzlin (the son of one brother), Yitzhak and Yaakov Butzlin (the sons of another brother).

May this article be a memorial to all those I mentioned.

Shmuel Ben David, Haifa

Picture collage on Pg 377 - Ben-Zion Berdichevsky and his family, May they rest in Peace
Row one: Haya-Rivka, Ben-Zion; His son Nahum-Dov was a rabbi in Pshetrova and a ritual slaughterer in Odessa.
Row two: Ziporah, Ben-Zion`s daughter, Nahum-Dov Gerstein, son-in-law of Ben-Zion
Larger picture left: Gil Carmel, soldier in IDF, great-grandson of Ben-Zion, grandson of David Carmel.

The Family of Ben-Zion Shohet (Berdichevsky)

Ben-Zion was the son of Haim-Hirsh, a cantor in Bendery. He was known as a young genius and everyone expected much from him. He was married at the age of 18 to Haya-Rivka, the daughter of the ritual slaughterer and cantor Eliezer Kishinovsky from Tiraspol.

Ben Zion was a Hassid and a pious man. During the times of the Tsar he was able to obtain the release from the army of several young Jews.

During World War I many members of his family lost their fortune and he had to help them.

He led services in the synagogue of Rabbi Yossy Shaposnick in the Citadel of the Hassidim. He also was a member of the Way of Life (Orach Haim). They remained covered in their prayer shawls after morning services and studied Gmara together.

During World War II, before the Nazis came, he was able to flee to Tashkent where he died of hunger.

We, his son, his daughter, his grandchildren and great-grandchildren remember our parent who shone the way for us.

May their souls be bound among the souls of the living.

In Memory of My Dear Parents

My mother, Pessia, was born in Lithuania and my father, Israel-Shmuel, was born in Ukraine. After their marriage they came to Bendery and set up a household. They did honest work and raised their sons and daughters to be honest and hard-working. They were always involved in bringing up their children and to prepare them for life.

World War II hurt them badly. They wandered from one place to another, through Stalingrad and Caucasus. After the war, they returned to destroyed Bendery where there were no Jews left. They were broken in body and spirit and tried hard to restart their lives. They died a few years later.

Shabtai Blei

[Page 378]

Zeev (Volodya) Berman

He was the third son of Shebt'l Berman. In his youth he was sent to study in a Chabad yeshiva in Gizhin, but he interrupted his studies and returned to Bendery. He learned mechanics and driving, unacceptable in his family. He moved to Hotin and worked there as a chauffeur in a sugar factory.

In 1923 he made Aliyah and worked as a stone mason in a work unit in Jerusalem. He then moved to the Galilee to work on farms in Melhamia. From there he went to Petah Tikva where he worked in agriculture and packing. He built a house in Kfar Maas and planted a vineyard and a citrus grove. He worked independently with his wife and children.

He was active in Haganah and was in charge of guarding his village and their ammunition. During World War II he enlisted in the British army and served under difficult circumstances in Egypt.

He was an honest and loyal man and he worked hard to his last day. He died in 1955 while working in the citrus grove. He left behind his wife, two married daughters and a son – Yitzhak. Although he is employed by the electric company he still runs his father's farm. (This son was injured in the three wars of our country).

Officer Nahum Goldman

In his youth Nahum studied in Bendery and made Aliyah at the age of 18 with his father, Yosef and his brother Yaakov. They reached Eretz Israel on foot walking from Beirut and they settled in Petach Tikva. At first, Nahum worked in agriculture and later he was part of the border patrol. In 1921 he was promoted. He served everywhere; from Metula to Nitzana (it was called Oudja el Hafir during the mandate).

In 1925 he transferred to the police force and served as an officer in Petach Tikva. In 1928, during a labor demonstration demanding work for the Jews in Petach Tikva citrus groves, he defended them. He was then punished by being transferred, with his family, to Beer Sheva. In those days Beer Sheva was an Arab town without a single Jew. He served there for two years and was again transferred to Jaffa and from there to Rehovot and Ramle. Finally, he was appointed assistant to the late officer Schiff in Tel Aviv. He was by his side in the action in which, tragically, they both lost their lives.

A group of police officers, Jewish and English, headed by officers Schiff and Goldman, were searching a roof storage area in Tel Aviv. They had received a telephone tip about it. The group, including the two Jewish officers, went to the roof of the building. A mine was hidden on the roof. It exploded and many were injured. Among them were the two Jewish officers who were killed.

Eventually, it was discovered that this was an action of revenge by one of the underground groups. The two officers had investigated a case of bank robbery (Bank Hapoalim).

In his lifetime, Officer Goldman helped the Jewish policemen who had to work with Arabs and the British. He did all he could to defend the Jewish population and his superiors were always suspicious of him.

He left behind a wife and three daughters.

Those I Mourn

During my lengthy wanderings in Russia after the Holocaust, I reached my hometown- Bendery. I had left there a part of my family – my father and a brother. I was hoping to find them among the living. This was my dream. My pain was great! Not only were they no longer alive, but I could not even find their graves. I began to question those who remained in town and those who returned after the evacuation. This is what I discovered:

My father, Motti Greenberg, had always resided in Bendery. He worked as a cashier in the flour mill owned by L. Blank. He was well known as a loyal and honest man. He was quite observant. He refused to leave town after it was evacuated by the Russians who had been the first to enter. In 1941, the Romanian-Nazis, may their names be erased, returned to town. My late father and my little brother, who stuck to him, were taken to the citadel. There they were shot to death together with all the other Jews who stayed in town. They were buried in a communal grave, but its place is unknown. There is no list of those who were killed. The story was told to me by the non-Jews who lived near the citadel.

This is how my saintly, honorable, pious father died together with his Jewish brothers whose fate was bound together with his. He loved his people and their fate hurt him, too.

God of revenge, revenge them!

This was written by the son who remained and made Aliyah from Russia.

His sons Yitzhak and David

Left - Haya Rachel Greenberg   R. Mordehai Greenberg and his son who fell in the Holocaust

[Page 380]

Haim Leib   **Etel Gornshtein**

Our father, Haim-Leib Gornshtein, was born to his father, Hersh-Zvi Gornshtein in Safed, Eretz Israel in 1875. Our grandfather, an observant man, a keeper of Mitzvoth, brought up his son according to Jewish tradition and with love for his people. When our father was seven years old the family returned to Russia and settled in Bendery. My father studied in a Heder there – as was the custom. When he grew up he succeeded in obtaining, due to his good character, the good will of the Railroad Company. He was appointed the painting contractor of the line from Bendery to Reni. Our father continued his work even after the Romanian rule, up to the Holocaust.

He did not only work to feed his family, but he also volunteered in the community. He was one of the first supporters of the founding of the Schwartzman Hebrew High School. Our brother, Yosef, was one of its first students.

Our mother, Etel, was born in Tiraspol, near Bendery. She excelled as a homemaker and a devoted mother. She instructed her children in the proper way. When the Holocaust began, my parents went, with others from Bendery, to Central Asia. They lived there until the Soviet authorities decided to return everyone to their previous homes.

My mother died in 1944 on the way back. She was buried in Alexandrovka, District of Kirovgrodesk. Our father continued alone. He lived in Bendery, but he missed his homeland, Eretz Israel. In 1953 he was among the first to be allowed by the Soviets to immigrate. Our father arrived in Israel and found there his daughter Ida, married to D. Drobetsky. She had made Aliyah many years earlier.

Our father lived to a ripe old age. He died in 1961.

May the souls of our dear parents be among the souls of the living!

Their daughter Ida and their son Yosef (and Fuma)

[Page 381]

Haim Glass

Avraham Dimant

Hannah Dimant

Haim Glass

Haim was born in 1888 in Bendin, Poland. He was active in the Zionist movement from an early age and he made Aliyah with the Second Aliyah in 1909. He worked in Ein-Ganim and in Jaffa and he contracted Yellow Fever and had to leave the country to recuperate. Haim became a Hebrew teacher in the Hebrew high school in Bendery and educated generations of young people. He instilled in them love of their people and a desire to make Aliyah.

Haim became active in the social-Zionist movement and was one of the organizers of Hechalutz in Bessarabia.

In 1925 he made Aliyah again and joined his family in Ein Harod.

In 1930 he fell ill once more and went to France to convalesce.

He was 43 when he died. On the kibbutz he left his wife, Haya, and two sons: Zrubavel (Gilead) and Yuval (Gal).

[Page 382]

Avraham and Hannah Dimant

Our father, Avraham Dimant, was born in Poland in 1878. In 1908 he came to Bessarabia and settled in Bendery. There, together with H. Volovetz, he opened a factory to produce oil. It continued to exist until World War II when the Soviets conquered Bendery.

Our mother, Hannah, was born in 1888 in Odessa. Her whole life she was a homemaker and helpmate to her husband.

Our father was a gentle, pleasant man. His honesty served as a model for his children and brought them up in that spirit. He was always ready to help those in need. He was also an important donor in the community.

Zana

In 1941, when the Soviets reached our town and as the war closed in on us, Avraham advised the Jewish residents to leave for the Asian Republics of Russia. On the way, a terrible catastrophe hit our family. Our brother Arieh's only daughter, Zana, fell ill with measles. The sanitary conditions on the freight trains were frightful and the cold was extreme. There was no medical help and medication was not available. The little three-year- old died in great pain. It was not possible to keep the body on the train until we would reach a permanent place. The train was stopped on the way and the body was handed over to a Russian peasant woman for burial. The death really hit her parents and grandparents and left them deeply wounded.

Our parents, together with other Jews, arrived in Dombol. It had been settled by the Tatars. There was hunger, filth and despair to deal with and as a result many infectious diseases were upon us. Our father, already physically weakened, could not overcome all the difficulties. He died on 7 Tevet 1941. His funeral was attended by several people from our town, including H.Volovetz, our mother, our brother Arieh and our sister Raya. His grave, like his granddaughter's, is far away. We will probably never visit it.

Our mother and brother Arieh with his wife arrived in Eretz Israel in 1948. Our brother Moshe had arrived four years earlier and our sister, Raya, came a few years later. Our mother was fortunate to live surrounded by her family and reached a ripe old age. She died on 23 Tammuz 1971 at the age of 82.

May the souls of our dear ones who left us be bound with the souls of those who are living.

Yocheved Veinman

The daughter of Shlomo and Charna Levitt of Bendery, she was born in September 1902 and died on 10.2.1969.

Yocheved, my wife, our mother, was a beautiful, special person. She was a woman of valor and an excellent housewife. In 1921 she established a good traditional Jewish home with her husband Mordehai Veinman. They had two sons – Shlomo and Yaakov. They brought them up to work hard and to be good people, just like their mother Yocheved. May she rest in peace.

After the Balfour declaration, the longing to make Aliyah was awakened in Yocheved and Mordehai Veinman. In 1925 they fulfilled their dreams. The head of the family worked in his trade as a baker and the sons attended Herzliah and Balfour High Schools in Tel Aviv. The family later moved to a kibbutz.

When Moshe Shertock (Sharett) called on young people to enlist in order to help the Allied forces fighting against the evil Nazis, the older son joined the Brigade and the younger one was in the Palmach.

This was a result of the teachings and influence of the parents. They had always lived together in mutual admiration.

Yocheved was not a fancy lady and did not put herself forward. There are many anecdotes about her charitable spirit. One story is about a young poor woman who was getting married. She bought cloth for her wedding gown, but she did not have enough money to pay for the sewing. When Yocheved found out, she told the bride: "What is the problem? Give me the cloth and I will sew you your gown..."

This charitable act and many others illustrate her generous aristocratic soul.

Her memory will forever remain within her family, among her friends and admirers.

May her soul be bound with the souls of the living!

Yosef Darbrimediker

Yosef, son of Rabbi Ephraim and Ita, was born on 4.2.1919. He fell on the Russian front fighting the Nazis (he was 25 years old) on 21.8.1944.

He studied at the university in Bucharest. When the Soviets entered Bessarabia, he interrupted his studies and enlisted in the "Service of the People" as the Comsomol called it. He also wanted to help his parents. Most of his work was to lecture in the villages and to teach.

When World War II broke out, he was injured twice at the front and was commended by his superiors. When he recuperated he was sent to take leadership courses. His superior officer invited his parents for an interview because he wanted to meet them and to find out who they were. "Who are these people who brought up such an amazing son?"

Thanks to his knowledge of the local language – Romanian – he was sent again behind enemy lines near Kitzakny, District of Bendery. There he handled propaganda with the peasants and the Romanian army. His message was: "Do not fight the Soviets. Put down your arms."

In his first letter home he wrote to his mother: "Mother, you ask me to be careful, but who will avenge the innocent blood of our people being spilled by the Fascists? It is my moral and patriotic obligation to fight!" He even added "I am going to execute an important undertaking. If I am fortunate to stay alive, I will be decorated for it..."

He did not achieve the decoration. After the news of his death came, his fellow soldiers wrote to his family telling them that Yosef had a special task behind enemy lines. He was perched on a tree scouting and he was discovered by the enemy. They threw a grenade at him. When everything had calmed down, his friend found his binoculars on the ground. When he climbed the tree he discovered Yosef's body.

He was buried in Zoloteyvka, not far from Bendery, the town of his birth. He died a hero, but as an unknown soldier of the Jewish people in the Diaspora. He died fighting the German-Nazi enemy.

May his soul be bound among the souls of the living and may the Jewish people be revived in the State of Israel.

[Page 384]

R. Yekutiel, son of Aaron, Hochman

R. Yekutiel, son of the honorable Hassid R. Aaron Hochman, z"l, served as a judge and a ritual slaughterer for 30 years in the village of Vishnigovsky in Bessarabia.

He was an observant Hassid who studied daily – Zohar, Gmara and Interpreters. He was up before dawn and stayed up past midnight. He wept and devoted his spirit to study. He was respectful and respected. There was never any dirt on his clothing. At first, he travelled to Rabbi David, z"l, of Liova and later he followed the famous Rabbi Yitzhak, z"l, of Bahush. He would sit at the feet of his Rabbi.

His wife, Milka Baila, may she rest in peace, was the daughter of the famous Hassid R. Yossy Hazan of Hoshi. She was a woman of valor, modest and full of life. She had an aristocratic soul and a good heart.

In their old age they lived in Bendery for ten years. She died there on 13 Tammuz 1928 at the age of 77. She was buried in Bendery.

R. Yekutiel moved to Bahush and lived with his son, R. Levi. He spent five years with the Hassidic Rabbi of Bahush. However, he missed the rest of his children and returned to Bendery where he stayed for another four years. R. Yekutiel died at the age of 84 on 21 Adar 1935. He was buried in the cemetery in Bendery.

May his memory be blessed!

Rabbi Shlomo Zalman Hochman

[Page 385]

R. Levi, son of R. Yekutiel and his wife Sara-Feiga

R. Levi Hochman

R. Levi Hochman, z"l, was born on 1 Nissan, 1870 in Hoshy, Romania. He was the oldest son of the judge and ritual slaughterer, R. Yekutiel, z"l. He was the eighth generation – son after son- in the dynasty of Rabbi Zeev Wolf Kitzis, z"l. This was the Rabbi of Tulchin who had been a student of the Baal Shem Tov.

Levi was a well-known and loyal Hassid of the Rabbi of Bahush. He was especially devoted, with his whole being, to Rabbi Israel Shalom Yosef, z"l. Every year he would travel to Bahush, even during the dangerous years of the war. He was a Hassid, a generous man and very pious. He was quite exacting about all religious laws and regulations. Levi was very active in the Hassidic world and always helped others. He worked hard for the elderly of Eretz Israel and donated and collected donations for the Ramban Fund.

His wife, the late Sara-Feiga, was also a pious and honest person. She was a woman of valor and very gentle. She and her husband were fortunate to produce descendants who followed in their footsteps and loved Torah, Jewish people and Eretz Israel.

They lived in Bendery for 30 years. From there they moved to Moyeneshti and then to Bahush where they stayed for 20 years. Before making Aliyah they lived in Galati and Bucharest. In Kislev1950 they were able to make Aliyah. They lived in Kfar Shalom, near Tel Aviv. In his last years, R. Levi devoted himself to the study of Torah, to prayers, and a deeper study of the Zohar. During the Holocaust they lost their children: Sheyna-Rachel Hochman (22 years old), Brucha and her husband, Moshe Orentlicher from Romanovka, Yaakov Hochman (their 24 year-old talented son). They all died in Siberia.

It was a miracle that their daughter Esther, her husband David Sheinberg, and their family remained alive in Kishinev. In Eretz Israel they were lucky to be with two sons - R. Meshulam Zissia Hochman, his wife and their children and Rabbi Shlomo Zalman Hochman, his wife and children. They also had two daughters: Shlomit, her husband R. Yehoshua Karuk and their family, and Pessia and her husband Yosef Sigler. The two elderly people were fortunate to have grandchildren and great-grandchildren around them. About ten of them served in the Israel Defense Forces.

R. Levi Hochman died on Thursday night, Parashat Hayei Sarah, 20 Heshvan 1957 at the age of 87 in Tel Aviv. He was buried in the old cemetery in Tiberias in a plot he had bought earlier. He was a Hassid of the Rabbi of Ossiatin.

May his memory be blessed!

His wife, Sara-Feiga, daughter of R. Israel David, died on 3 Sivan 1964 in Bnei Brak. She was buried in a plot she had previously bought in Kiryat Shaul cemetery, Tel Aviv.

May her memory be blessed!

Rabbi Shlomo Zalman Hochman

[Page 386]

Lussia Darbrimediker

The daughter of Ephraim and Ita, she was born on 24.7.1915 and died on 29.3.1957. She was a lovely, talented woman. In 1940 she graduated from the law faculty in Iasi. She was so outstanding as a lawyer appearing in court that she was commended by judges and even by prosecutors. During the evacuation she studied nursing and worked in the hospital. She later worked in the legal section of a laboratory in the Institute of Anatomy and Pathology in Chernovtsy. She was greatly appreciated by her co-workers and supervisors. She was deeply loved by her family, friends and acquaintances. Her death from an illness shocked everyone and spread sadness on all those around her.

May her memory be blessed!

Nurse Pnina Wertheim

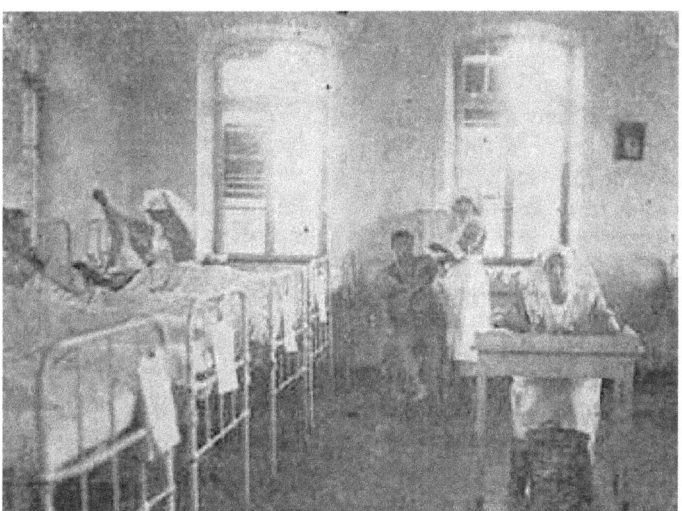

Nurse Pnina Wertheim (near table) in Hadassah Hospital in Safed 1924

[Page387]

Nurse Pnina Wertheim

It is a blessing for every person to have outstanding ancestors. However, Perele – as we lovingly called her – was outstanding on her own. Her character and special attributes directed her way of life.

She came from a special family. Her father was the chief Rabbi of Bendery, Rabbi Shloimenu (or as we lovingly called him Rav Shloimke). Pnina grew up in a brilliant family where Torah and greatness co-existed. There was always an atmosphere of love of Zion and of the people of Israel. This atmosphere was imbued in all the sons and daughters of the family. Although they resembled each other on many levels, they were individuals in their own right.

Perele inherited from her father special attributes – aristocratic bearing, goodness, calmness and serious deliberation. No wonder that she was loved by anyone who got to know her.

She was fortunate to be part of the first group of seven pioneers organized in Bessarabia. This was at the start of the Third Aliyah in 1920. They made their way to Eretz Israel through the settlement "New Tracks" in Turkey, headed by Rabbi Shapiro. From there we continued by boat to Eretz Israel. It took three weeks and we arrived in Petach Tikva where we worked in Mr. Yanovsky's nursery.

My sister-in-law, Rosa Tiomkin, z"l, worked as a dentist in the settlements of the Upper Galilee and she recommended Pnina and talked her into working as a nurse in Hadassah Hospital in Safed.

In her new position, Pnina showed her aristocratic spirit by being always ready to help others; this was the true calling of a nurse. She used the best in herself and cast her personality around her. She looked after the sick people in her care. At the time there were four people from Bendery in Safed. These were Pnina, my sister-in-law, my wife and I. We became a close-knit family.

Later, Pnina worked in Hadassah in Jerusalem and became a supervising nurse. Her circle of friends and admirers widened within the Hadassah family in the capital. Her reputation as a model to others especially influenced the trainees who were just beginning their careers.

She left us too early and it created emptiness in the hearts of all who knew her.

Her bright aura will accompany us forever.

P. Bendersky

Pinhas Wertheim
A man of accomplishment

Pinhas left us too early and our hearts are inconsolable. He was a wonderful friend from his young days. We studied together in Bendery in the Talne Yeshiva and in the study house of "Mishna Learners" during World War I. Even then he excelled in his studies with R. Leibush who was brought from Poland to teach him.

Pinhas was the son of R. Yossele and Hannah Wertheim. He was born in Bendery on 10 Elul 1904 and died on 7 Kislev 1968 in Tel Aviv. He had worked for 43 years as a pioneer in different settlements and cooperatives.

During World War I he lived in his father's, the Rabbi, house in Ostilo and then in Ostrara. In 1921 he studied in a rabbinical seminary for teachers "Tachkemoni" in Warsaw. It was headed by Prof. Balaban. He received a teaching certificate and made Aliyah in 1925. He planned to study at the Hebrew University, but he changed his *(continued on* mind and decided to become a pioneer. He went to Kfar Hassidim with some Yablona Hassidim. However, malaria struck the family and he had to move to Haifa. During the unemployment and terrorist attacks of 1929-1931 he and his family suffered horribly, but quietly. After Haifa he went to work in the Tnuva dairy in Pardes Hannah. When the management recognized his qualities he was appointed branch manager. Later he was invited to work in Hamashbir Hamerkazi in Tel Aviv and finally as director of Shiluv, a subsidiary of Hamashbir.

He was a devoted family man and radiated warmth and humor around him. On occasion he would recite poetry and rhymes and his family enjoyed the cultural atmosphere.

His shining memory will never leave us.

His friend Mordehai

Sara Volovetz

Sara Volovetz was born on 14 Iyar 1892 and died on 23 Adar 1971. She was a woman of fine character. She was married to Hanania Volovetz, may he live a long life, and was the daughter of Yehoshua-Leib Burris. Her father's home was one where Jewish tradition and general Russian culture were integrated.

Sara was one of the first students in the government-run girls' high school. Thus, she absorbed Jewish tradition and love of her people from childhood, as well as the Russian culture of those times.

She had an aristocratic soul and was always interested in learning. She admired all cultural matters, written and oral. She loved to read and somehow managed to do it daily while not neglecting her duties as a homemaker and head of the family. She loved to share her thoughts about every book she read, music she heard, ballet performance she saw or an interesting lecture she heard. She loved good intellectual stimulation.

Everything about Eretz Israel and its issues interested her. She especially reacted to all those who hated Zion and Jewophobes and what they did to the Jews only because they were Jews.

Everyone who knew her well was saddened by her passing. Let us hope these lines will depict her as a dear woman who influenced her surroundings with her warmth.

May her memory always be with us!

P. Bendersky

[Page 389]

Yeva Zinger

Yeva was born on 22 July 1902 in Odessa. After her father's death she moved with her mother (Immes family) to her grandfather's House – Shlomo Boomajny in Balti. She then came to Bendery.

In Bendery she graduated from high school and worked in Mulman's pharmacy. She visited the university in Iasi and then moved to Galati. There, too, she worked in a pharmacy. She met her husband there. He was the manager of the Eretz Israel office. All Aliyah from Romania was under his jurisdiction. Women from Bendery who were on their way to Eretz Israel would meet in her home.

In 1933 she made Aliyah with her family and her parents, Haya and Issachar Shlein. She lived in Haifa. She fell ill suddenly and died after a few days on 30.7.1968.

May her memory be blessed!

Written by those who mourn her bitterly,

Her husband Yosef Zinger

Her sons: David, Natan, Gideon and their families

Moshe Tulchinsky

A memorial candle is lit in memory of my dear, unforgettable, brother Moshe, son of Avraham, Tulchinsky.

He was born in Bendery in 1912. He graduated from the Schwartzman Hebrew High school in Bendery. He was slaughtered during the Holocaust in 1942.

May his memory be blessed!

Nahman Tulchinsky, Tel Aviv

Avraham Zigberman

Avraham was born in 1901 in Bendery. He received a general and Jewish education in the Schwartzman Hebrew high school in Bendery. He always loved books and literature and excelled in writing. He was educated in the tradition of the best minds of the Russian-Jewish intelligentsia and he was thus influenced to follow humanist and cultural values. He was a dedicated Zionist from his youth and he loved nationalistic ideals and Jewish culture. He was a regular correspondent for two Russian newspapers in Bessarabia and he published articles about Jewish life and its public and national institutions. He wrote about Maccabi, Jewish schools, local issues and general problems in Bessarabia. All this was written from a nationalistic Zionist point of view.

He was active in the leadership of Maccabi in Bendery. Before he made Aliyah he was involved with the Jewish Agency in Bucharest.

In later years, he belonged to the Revisionist movement. He was polite, easy-going and loved by his Zionist friends. He lived in modest material circumstances and was always happy with his lot. He made Aliyah in 1944. His wife`s lengthy illness and his own heart condition brought his demise in 1960.

May his memory be blessed!

Avraham Zigberman   **Anya (Hannah) Roit (nee Zigberman)**

Anya (Hannah) Roit

Anya (Hannah) Roit was born in Bendery to her father Zelig Zigberman, a teacher, and her mother, Haya. She studied in the Hebrew High school and was active in Zionist youth movements. Her father died when she was young and she had to earn a living to take care of herself and her mother who was ill with asthma. She then worked in Galati and later in Czernowitz in a textile-weaving factory `Hercules`. There she met her husband Yehoshua Roit.

When war began her husband, Yehoshua, was drafted into the Red Army. She, with her daughter Tanichka, wandered to Russia. On the way they suffered from bombings until they finally reached Astrakhan on the Volga.

They lived in different public establishments together with other refugees. There was a measles outbreak and her daughter fell with it. She was 3 years old when she died.

Anya was left completely alone and far from her husband, who had been drafted, and the rest of her family. She worked in a fish cannery to earn her keep. She encountered her husband by accident and they reached Central Asia together.

In 1948 they made Aliyah. At first they lived in Petach Tikva and then they moved to Ramat Gan.

She suffered greatly from an early age and her difficult life influenced her health. She died of a heart attack at the age of 62 on 9.10.1971. She was survived by her husband and sisters.

[Page 391]

Daniel, son of Meir, Hamlis

Daniel was born in 1865 and died on 6.9.1919. He was a community leader and a modest, honest man. He conducted a traditional home – open to everyone. He insisted on giving a good education to his children. They were also involved in the life of the Jewish community in general and Zionism in particular.

May his memory be blessed!

Leah Hazin-Kutcher

Kindergarten teacher Leah Hazin-Kutcher
(wife of the poet Yaakov Kutcher)

Leah died in a nursing home for aged, sick, single women. She just fell asleep and did not wake up again. She left no relatives behind. Leah had earned many honors, especially in the field of education and culture in the Diaspora over a period of 50 years.

When she was still a young girl, a daughter of pious parents and a granddaughter of the town Rabbi, she dared to rebel against tradition. She studied the Hebrew language and became a teacher of other young girls who were keen on learning Hebrew. She did not take any payment for these lessons, most of the time. Leah and her students were the first ones in Bendery to speak Hebrew at home and on the street. Many of them eventually became teachers.

Leah`s dream was to study education and to become a kindergarten teacher. The best place to do it was in the Prebl Academy in Warsaw which was headed by the late Yitzhak Alterman. How does a young woman from a Godforsaken place in Russia at that time and without funds reach a metropolitan distant Polish Center? Leah`s will and energy paved the way. When she finished her studies in Warsaw she returned home and opened the first Hebrew Kindergarten in Bessarabia. The Kindergarten was very successful. She was a talented teacher and was beloved by her students and their parents alike. She was also admired by Zionist circles who appreciated her work. A few years later she moved to Kishinev where she opened Yavne Kindergarten. It, too, was successful.

She continued her work for nearly 40 years. She taught Kindergarten and other grades in other towns in Romania and Bessarabia. The network of schools in the Diaspora grew and expanded in the meantime. There were more institutions and teachers. Hebrew became the official language in Jewish schools, recognized by the authorities. Many students attended these schools and many graduates made Aliyah. They fulfilled Leah`s dream. I was among them. She continued her work until the Holocaust.

She reached Eretz Israel later in her life, after much suffering and with no material goods. She was all alone, as were many others who came from those countries. She was elderly and life as a newcomer was not easy. However, she managed to establish herself by giving private lessons.

She lived for some years in her simple home in an immigrant section. She was old and alone. She received all visitors with warmth and without any complaints about her lot. She never spoke about her rich past. She only talked about her students with love, like a mother discussing her own children who are now far away.

During the time she was ill, when fear and despair were reflected in her eyes, I wanted to encourage her and I began to bring up memories. Among other stories, I recalled a fancy Hanukah party in Gan Yavne with all the details. I even began to sing the Hanukah song she taught us: "Children take the candles, walk two-by-two on Hanukah..." "The children's eyes sparkled and the happy parents watched with love and awe" "You – the miracle worker," I added. She wiped her tears and her pupils expanded and grew brighter as she tried to absorb the special feeling brought on by her memories. "Sing it again!" she asked me in a weak voice.

Her students, male and female, loved her and she loved them. She is the one who put the first Hebrew word in their mouths and she lit the fire of love of homeland. This is the dream that brought us here. We will always remember her in our hearts.

Leah A.

Nahman (Neshke) Hazin

Nahman was the son of Malka and Avraham-Eli, our parents who were slaughtered in the Holocaust.

My brother, Neshke, came to Eretz Israel as a pioneer in 1935 after graduation from the Schwartzman Hebrew High School.

In Eretz Israel he worked most of his life in the Ata factory in Kfar Ata. He was modest, aristocratic in character, honest and loved by his family, his friends and acquaintances.

In memory of my family members who are no longer alive: Rabbi Nahman (judge) and his wife, Rebbetzin Hannah, their daughter Rebbetzin Babke, wife of Rabbi Sh.Sh. Wertheim, their sons Aaron and Motel (Mordehai) Hazin.

In memory of Dr. Sara Hazin

She was my relative, born in Bendery. I was very close to her in my childhood. When World War I broke out she volunteered to serve on the front as a nurse. She even earned a commendation for her dedicated work. When the Revolution began, she did not join the Communists; by doing that she remained loyal to her tradition. However, she still offered her services as a nurse to the Soviet regime.

When Hitler's army, may their memory be erased, invaded Bessarabia, she went with all the other refugees to Uzbekistan. She lost her whole family on the way, but the catastrophe did not break her spirit. She gave medical help to suffering Uzbeks.

After the war, before the Iron Curtain came down, she was permitted to leave the country for three months on a tourist visa. She arrived in Eretz Israel and remained there. She was absorbed in Tel Hashomer hospital under the auspices of the women's organization Yael. She was popular with her co-workers and the patients nicknamed her "Mother Sara". She was totally tied to her country and everything in it. She only had a few years to be with us before she became ill. Even when she was lying on her death bed in the hospital she was full of humor. It was pleasant to have a conversation with her. On my last visit with her she pointed to the word "State of Israel" stamped on her sheet. This gave her great satisfaction.

She was childless and there was no one with her when her soul returned to her creator. Perhaps that "State of Israel" stamp was her only and last consolation. She was, for a short time, a partner with that small state she loved so much.

May her memory be blessed!

L. Sh.

Hayat Family

Shimon-Shlomo, son of **Zeev, Hayat**
He was born in Bendery in 1872 and died there in 1913.

Shalom, son of **Shimon-Shlomo, Hayat**
Born in Bendery in 1897 and died in 1941

Heny Hayat, daughter of **Alter Litvin**   **Marcus (Motel) Hayat**
Heny: Born in Tatarovna in 1872 and died in Riga in 1952

Marcus: Born in Bendery in 1895 and slaughtered in Baku (Caucasus) 1922

[Page 394]

Left: Israel, son of **Shimon-Shlomo Hayat**
Born in 1904 and died in 1928

Right: Yosef, son of **Shimon-Shlomo Hayat**
Born in 1907 and died in 1929

The Family of Yehoshua, son of Issar, Tiomkin

Our father, Rabbi Yehoshua, son of Issar-Dov, Tiomkin was a descendant of the Tiomkin dynasty. Others were the appointed rabbi Yonah Tiomkin in Yelisovetgrad and his brother Dr. Vladimir Tiomkin from Odessa. Yehoshua was born in Minsk in 1866. His father died when he was a young child and he moved, with his mother, to live with his uncle, R. Arieh Tiomkin. He brought up our father.

He began his studies in Volozhin Yeshiva and continued in a government-run teacher's seminary during the Tsar's times. He received a certificate as a general teacher. This certificate allowed him to live anywhere in Russia. This right was unavailable to other Jews. He then studied dentistry and graduated, but he really wanted to teach. He found great satisfaction in teaching and he was able to integrate his vast Jewish knowledge with Russian culture.

Our father's first steps in teaching were in the opening of a Hebrew middle school in Priluki together with the linguist Avraham Avronin. There he married Malka Bershtein, our mother. Due to our father's profession they moved from to town to town whenever they were invited by the Jewish community. Their members wanted to give their children a Jewish and a secular education. This is how they reached Bendery where he was appointed principal of the Russian Talmud Torah. (The building was donated by Mr. Velvel Rabinovitch.)

Our father ran the Talmud Torah to the end of his days, assisted by the Hebrew teachers. He was a proud Jew and entered into many arguments with the Tsarist authorities. Sometimes he clashed with them about the percentage of Jewish students allowed to enter the school. He never feared the authorities and he knew how to stand his ground. He knew his students and their abilities well. He influenced them to complete their studies. His personal attributes earned him respect and recognition by the government functionaries. He even won a medal for his service in the field of education.

In 1929 he went to Galati in Romania to visit a dental clinic. He died suddenly and was buried there.

[Page 395]

Left: R. Yehoshua, son of **Issar-Dov, Tiomkin**
Right: Malka Tiomkin

Left: Malka Tiomkin, Sonia and **Bat Sheva**
Right: Rosa (Tiomkin) Immanuel

[Page 396]

Malka Tiomkin

Our mother, Malka, was born in Priluki, District of Poltava. She received a Jewish education and was also comfortable in Russian culture. We spoke Russian at home, but since both of our parents felt strongly about the Jewish people, they brought us, the children, up in that spirit. Thanks to the education and guidance our father gave us we were accepted at the government Russian high school. Upon graduation we applied to the university. Due to the 1917 revolution we had to interrupt our studies. Only our oldest sister, Rosa, had managed to complete her dental studies in Odessa.

During World War II, when the Russians entered Bendery, our mother and sisters were exiled to Central Asia. Our mother, as well as our sister Sonia, died there. Their burial place is unknown. Sonia was a teacher, beloved by her students. She excelled in science and she taught it to her students. The youngest sister, Bat Sheva, died young and was buried in Bendery.

May their souls be bound among the souls of the living!

P.B their daughters

Shoshanna (Rosa) Immanuel
Daughter of Yehoshua Tiomkin

The oldest daughter of the teacher Y. Tiomkin was a dentist. When she arrived in Eretz Israel in 1920 she was referred by Menahem Sheinkin to Safed. She worked there and also in the entire Galilee as a dentist. She had Jewish, Arab and English patients (government employees). She performed her tasks with loyalty and devotion. She was recognized for her good work. Among her patients was the Mufti of Safed who treated her with respect. Her reputation even reached Kuwait and its Sultan came to Safed to be treated. Afterwards he gave her a gift as a thank you.

Shoshanna was not a member of a Zionist movement in Bendery, but when she came to Eretz Israel she fell in love with it.

She died on 8.10.1974 after a lengthy illness. She left behind an only son, an engineer.

May her soul be bound with the souls of the living!

Batia Kimayev (nee Tiomkin)

She was a member of the Third Aliyah group. From the early 1920s she worked on her farm in Hadera. She died on 20.1.1975.

May her soul be bound with the souls of the living!

[Page 397]

Right - R. Zeidel (shohet) Yatom

Left - Rabbi Mordehai (R. Motel) Yatom

My father, R. Motel, son of R. Zeidel, the shohet, was the first ritual slaughterer in Bendery. My mother (nee Slipo) was also born there.

There were four sons and one daughter in the family.

After World War I the family of R. Motel moved to Peschenka (Ukraine) where he was the chief rabbi. The Rabbi and his family went through many trials and tribulations there. The town had changed hands during the civil war in Russia and the Rabbi had to greet warmly the representatives of each new regime. In the days of Petlura he almost died. Petlura's officers had sentenced him to death and sent two soldiers to escort him back. On the way to carry out the verdict they met a priest who asked him where he was being led. R. Motel told him his story. The priest said: "I will go with you. Whatever will happen to you will be my destiny, too." The Rabbi was saved from death. Whenever he prayed and reached the words "Redeemer and Savior" he would cry and bless the good-hearted priest.

In 1917, the family returned to Bendery. R. Shloimke appointed R. Motel as his assistant. When R. Shloimke died, R. Motel became head of the Beth Din. He remained the Rabbi in Bendery until 1934. He died young at the age of 57.

One of R. Motel's sons, R. Yosef Yatom, became a Rabbi in Kaushany when he returned from Russia. The regulations in Romania stipulated that in order to graduate from high school one had to pass final examinations in Romanian. Rabbi Yosef studied at the Schwartzman High School for one year. According to Yosef Rabinovitch there were several adults at that time that had returned from Russia and had to study in Romanian. R. Yosef Yatom was an outstanding orator and spoke on behalf of Mizrahi.

Another son was a ritual slaughterer after his grandfather's death.

The sister married a rabbi from Transylvania (Ashkenazy). After R. Motel's death her husband took his position in Bendery.

Brother Moshe, a teacher in Maneshti, died young.

All the Rabbi's children studied in yeshivas and served as rabbis in Russia and Bessarabia. The family was dispersed in different places

[Page 398]

I made Aliyah with Hapoel Hamizrahi in 1934.

In 1935 B'Nai Akiva was founded in Bendery. My brother Baruch was a counselor in that movement and their meetings were held in his house. All members of my family belonged to Mizrahi, except for Moshe who was a Revisionist.

Except for me, all my siblings remained in the Diaspora.

When I came to Eretz Israel I settled in Rehovot where I established my home.

Right - Moshe Yatom, son of Eliahu and Sara
(Grandson of **R. Mordehai Yatom**)

Eliahu Yatom

He was born 11.1.1938 in Rehovot.

Moshe graduated from Tachkemoni High School where he distinguished himself as a counselor in the Scouts movement.

He fell fulfilling his duty on 7.4.1956 when he fell in battle. He was buried in the Army section of the Rehovot cemetery.

R. Mordehai-Dov Katz (brother in-law of Rabbi Mordehai (Motel) Yatom)
His wife **Etel-Shifra Katz** (daughter of R. Zeidel the Shohet)

[Page 399]

Shmuel Katz
(Son of Mordehai-Dov and Etel-Shifra)

Shmuel was born on 1.5.1909 and died on 27.4.1971. His love of his people and his country was developed while he was still a member of Zionist youth movements in his hometown –Bendery. His personality was colourful and he knew how to treat other people well. He was honest and correct in his daily life. He was a deep thinker and a cultured man. All these characteristics were evident in his work as a bookkeeper at Tnuva.

Shmuel was a dedicated family man and worked hard at bringing up his children. He served as a model for them.

He was always careful not to hurt anyone. He was responsible and diligent, and he was well-liked by everyone. In spite of his heart condition he continued to work hard at home and at his job.

He died at the age of 72. His family, friends and admirers will remember him forever.

His wife **Buzia** and his sons **Dov** and **Haim**

Zeev Carmi

Zeev died at a demonstration against the closing of the borders to Aliyah, in 1946.

"One must not dodge responsibility, even a child like me." This is what he said as he left his parents at home in Haifa when he went to join the demonstration. They were protesting the expulsion of illegal immigrants from the shores of Eretz Israel.

He was only 14 ½ when he died.

This is what his fellow movement members wrote in his memory:

"Zeev joined our group about one year ago. We worked together to build and shape it into a united community. Zeev lived our life and together we overcame obstacles we found on the way. He was often the first in line in any activity. His memory will remain with us in the many drawings he prepared for our yearbook.

Certain events created difficult times for our kibbutz and some of our members were taken to Rafiah. Zeev tried to do the work of those who were absent.

He showed his great loyalty to the kibbutz and its members in the message he sent just before his death.

Even now Zeev showed his readiness to demonstrate with many others because he felt great harm had been done by the authorities. The remnants from the Nazi Holocaust, who had suffered so much, had been denied entry to Eretz Israel. He fell during the struggle of our people.

A cruel destiny has separated us, but his memory will always be in our hearts."

Offer Group
Kibbutz Mizra
Hashomer Hatzair

[Page 400]

Meir Levy (Monia Lev)

Meir was born in 1902 to his parents Israel and Dina Levy. He was a brother to David and Simcha, Manya and Rivka. He began his studies at the age of 3 in the Heder of Avraham Lavonsky. He continued his studies with Alter Shuster, Shmuel Krassilover and Yankel Lonievsky. When he was 9, he and his brothers were accepted at the Railroad Workers School. They were the only Jewish children. Their father was a government clerk in the railroad company and that is why they were able to attend this school. . At the age of 12 he passed entrance exams to the Schwartzman Hebrew High School. His teacher was Feinish who had been a student at Herzliah High School in Tel Aviv. He had returned to Bendery before World War I.

When he was 15 he traveled to visit his brother David who was a director of a fruit export company in Samarkand. When he returned a year later, Bendery was already under Romanian rule. His brothers David and Simcha and his sister Manya remained in Russia. He saw them again many years later. In 1965, he went with his sister Rivka to the Soviet Union. He was able to see those relatives still alive.

In 1920, Monia joined Zeirei Zion. This was a youth group planning Aliyah. Others in the group were Avraham Sirkis, L. Chubruncher, David Weisser, Pnina Wertheim, Pinhas Bendersky and his wife Hava and Mrs. Tiomkin. They left for Galatz with the help of Shmuel Pinless. They received, from the British consul, a visa to Constantinople. There they met Dr. Tiomkin who was the one responsible for Aliyah. He sent them to a transit camp – Mesilla Hadasha (new path). It had been deserted since the war between Jamal Pasha and the Greeks.

Six weeks later, a large group arrived from Russia. It was led by Berel Raptor. Everyone boarded an Egyptian freighter- Mahmudya. After a difficult voyage of 14 days they docked in Jaffa. They first went to Petach Tikva where they stayed together and looked for work. It was only in 1921, after the riots when the Arabs left their jobs, that these pioneers took their place for a short time,

In 1923, Monia and David Hayat went to visit the family in Bendery. There he was drafted into the Romanian army. He was able to free himself after a short while. He returned to Petach Tikva where his girlfriend Bronia was waiting to marry him.

Monia served in the Petach Tikva police as well as in the British police. Later, he was a foreman in Mehadrin, a company that planted orange groves. He retired from there.

It must be noted that he was able to bring his parents to Eretz Israel. They lived to a ripe old age in Tel Aviv.

Monia died on 16.12.1971, a month before his 70th birthday. He left a wife, three sons and four grandchildren.

May his memory be blessed!

[Page 401]

R. Yaakov Lonievsky
Teacher and Educator

He was born in 1863 and he died in Bendery in 1937.

Yaakov Lonievsky was an outstanding educator who stood out due to his greatness of spirit, deep knowledge, honesty and unusual politeness to young and old alike. He was a beloved person in our town and especially so by his students. They remember him so many years later for his gentleness.

He was highly knowledgeable in history and Hebrew language and he had unique methods in teaching these subjects to his students.

He had ten children. They all achieved in their chosen fields and served their community with dignity.

His noble spirit was evident in his exterior appearance as well and in his bright eyes which were full of life experiences. His image is cherished and will always be remembered by his acquaintances and his admirers.

May his memory be blessed!

M. Sever

[Page 402]

Mrs. Rivka Lifshin
Died in 1943 at the age of 68

and

R. Yeshayahu Lifshin
Died in 1934 at the age of 62

Our Honored Parents

You always showed interest in our aspirations and in all our activities in public life. You paid attention to our dedication, heart and soul, to the Zionist movement in general and the youth movement in particular.

For all this we show our gratitude and we fondly remember the blessed memory of our parents.

We light a candle in your memory and we also honor the memory of our dear family members who are no longer with us:

In memory of our brother **HAIM** and our sisters **HAIKE** and **HANNA** who were killed together with our mother in Transnistria in 1943.

In memory of our brother **SENDER** who fell in the Soviet Union during World War II.

Your children, sister and brother
ZVI & MORDEHAI LIFSHIN - Tel Aviv
LEON & RAHEL LIFSHIN - Soviet Union

[Page 403]

A Memorial Candle to Our Unforgettable Dear Family Members

RIGHT Our mother, **Rahel Levonsky** (nee Rotberg), was born in Proskarov, Ukraine in 1874. She made Aliyah with her husband and died in 1952 at the age of 74. [sic]

LEFT **R. Avrahm Llevonsky** was born in Alt-Constantine, Ukraine in 1872. He resided in Bendery for many years and earned his living by teaching generations of children to read and write. He made Aliyah in 1933 and died in 1942 at the age of 68. [sic]

Moshe Levanon

Our brother, **MOSHE LEVANON**, was the son of **AVRAHAM** and **RAHEL LEVONSKY**. He was born in Bendery in 1903 and graduated from the Schwartzman Hebrew High School. After he left school he learned a trade and made Aliyah in 1923. He was among the first settlers in Beit Oved. Unfortunately he fell ill and never recovered. He died in 1963 at the age of 58. [sic]

[Page 404]

Left - Reuven Miller

Right - Sioma (Shlomo), son of **Aryeh, Mironiarsky**, was born in 1909.

Sioma (Shlomo) Mironiarsky was a man of culture and had a beautiful soul. He dreamed of and fought for a better world. Sioma was killed by terrorists while on guard duty on 7.7.1941.

David (son of **Moshe) Miller** and **Tzipora (**daughter of **Manus) Miller**

David (son of **Moshe) Miller** from Bendery died in Romania in 1936.

Tzipora (daughter of **Manus) Miller** died in Russia in 1944.

Reuven Miller (son of David and Tzipora) died in Eretz Israel at age 50.

As soon as Reuven came to Eretz Israel he did all types of pioneering work. However, he fell ill and he was forced to do clerical jobs.

Reuven was the treasurer of the Workers Committee in Rehovot. Anyone who requested assistance from the committee was well looked after by him. Thanks to his loyal and dedicated work he was well-liked by all workers in the city, especially agricultural laborers. They saw him as a true and loyal friend who always supported their cause.

May his soul be included bound the souls of the living.

[Page 405]

Right - R. Mordehai Malamud

Left - His wife **Shaindl Malamud**

R. Mordehai Malamud

R. Mordehai Malamud was the supervisor of the meat Kashrut under the auspices of the Bendery Rabbinate. He organized a Society for Anonymous Donations, helped the Rabbis and was really the guiding spirit behind the Rabbinate. He often used his own money to help the needy and he also arranged for loans guaranteed by members of the Society.

He died in Bendery.

May his memory be blessed!

Shaindl Malamud

Shaindl lived in Bendery all her life until 1934. She was active in the Society for Anonymous Donations and she considered it holy work. She was fortunate to make Aliyah.

May her soul be bound among the souls of the living!

[Page 406]

In eternal memory of our dear parents **ZAIDL and FRIDA MARKMAN**, our brother **YOSEF**, his wife **DORA**, their children **YAAKOV** and **HAIA** and our brother **LEIBL**, his wife and daughter. They were all murdered by the Nazi killers.

The children: Betty and Avraham **LERMAN**, Sam **MAX**, Moshe and Sol **MARKMAN**

(Avraham Lerman is the son of Sonia and Eliezer Lerman)

Rozalia Schwartzman Merlin

Rozalia Yaakovna Schwartzman Merlin was born in Balta. Her father was a ritual slaughterer and her grandfather was a teacher.

Her father died when she was four years old.

Rozalia studied Russian and attended university in Peterburg.

When her brother Zvi, son of Yaakov, founded the Hebrew High School in Bendery she joined his staff. She was active in the "Bund", as well as being a member of the Yiddish school directed by Tiomkin.

In 1924 Rozalia Yaakovna married Shabtai Merlin, a teacher at the Schwartzman Hebrew High School. She later became active in the Zionist movement. To her great sorrow she did not achieve her dream of Aliyah and she died at the age of 86.

May her soul be bound among the souls of the living!

Shabtai Merlin

Shabtai Merlin was born in Zugivka, Ukraine. During World War I he was imprisoned by the Hungarians and learned to speak Hungarian. Shabtai was a Hebrew teacher in Arciz. In 1924 he was invited by Zvi, son of Yaakov, Schwartzman to join his teaching staff. He was knowledgeable in Hebrew literature and the Bible.

After Bessarabia was conquered by the Soviets Merlin escaped to south Asia. After the war he returned to Kishinev and worked there as a teacher. The Soviets recognized his teaching experience in the Hebrew schools. He was sent to study at the university. After he completed his studies he continued to teach until his last days,

Shabtai Merlin died at the age of 62 and did not achieve his dream of Aliyah.

May his soul be bound among the souls of the living!

[Page 407]

R. Israel, son of **R. Yitzhak, Sverdlik**

R. Israel was a ritual slaughterer and respected public personality in Bendery. He made Aliyah in 1907.

He lived in Zichron Yaakov for 25 years where he worked as a ritual slaughterer. He was also a Justice of the Peace in Sumeria under the auspices of the local authorities. He was well-known as an intelligent and learned person. He was aware of world events, listened to anyone who came to him and helped everyone in need.

He died at the age of 70 on 26 Iyar, 1930.

May his soul be bound among the souls of the living!

I Never Met Anyone As Noble As This Person

This is an excerpt from memoirs of the veteran laborer Aaron Kaminker to a friend in his hometown of Akkerman – Noah Zukerman. Zukerman was one of the founders of Kfar Hess. He writes about his days of making Aliyah in 1920 and how he ended up in Zichron Yaakov with his friends. They were looking for work and found there an open house and a helping hand. R. Israel, the ritual slaughterer, z"l received them with an open heart.

"...It seems to me that I will not exaggerate if I praise him. I have not met many noble people like him: a true scholar, a God-fearing man, true to himself and to his faith. He was an original, gentle man who was well-loved and who loved others.

He was a highly moral and noble man.

I will never forget his generosity and kindness to us and the warm reception and loving welcome he showed us.

We spent three days in his home. He satisfied our hunger and encouraged us in difficult times. He recommended us to the directorship of the Jewish Colonization Association in Zichron Yaakov as good workers in the Gazla citrus grove. It was hard labor for one month.

I knew then that we must have faith in the future of man."

May we remember him forever!

Aaron Kaminker
Haifa, 1957

These I Remember...

My father and distinguished teacher **MOSHE**, son of **ISRAEL, SEVER**. He was the author of the book *"Encyclopedia of Sayings and Proverbs."*

He was born on 3.3.1881 and died on 17.6.1967.

Rahel Sever

My mother, my teacher, a noble woman, **RAHEL SEVER** (daughter of R. Matityahu Morgenstern) was born on 4.10.1886 and died on 2.9.1971.

My beloved sister, **DINA,** died before we made Aliyah. She was born on 27.11.1915 and died on 15.9.1921.

My darling brother **MEIR** was a pure and loving man. He only wished for a beautiful world and a good life for all humanity. He died a martyr in the cellars of the G.P.O in the Soviet Union. He was born on 27.11.1908 and was killed on 3.6.1938.

My brilliant **UNCLE MEIR** whose artwork adorned the walls of the Sadigura Synagogue in Bendery for many years died at the young age of 20 on 23.12,1906.

My aunt **RIVKA**, my first teacher, died during the times of starvation in Eretz Israel. She was only 25 when she expired in Zichron Yaakov on 18.10.1919.

I also remember all my other relatives who graced our home with their presence and from whom I learned Torah and proper behavior when I was so young.

May their souls be bound among the souls of the living!

Mordehai Sever

Right to left: Meir, son of Moshe, **SVERDLIK-** killed in the cellars of the GPO in 1938; Shifra **GILIK (CHAPLIK),** Yaakov **GILIK** – both killed in Odessa during the Holocaust.

[Page 409]

R. Mordehai (Motel) Sverdlik, son of **Asher Sverdlik**

R. Mordehai was born in Bendery in 1875 and was killed there during the Holocaust together with other sainted residents. He grew up in an observant family and always lived a religious life. He had a traditional Jewish education as well as a proper grounding in the Russian language.

During the Tsar's days he provided food to the Russian army in Bendery. He was also a member of city council until the Tsarist government fell. After Bendery was conquered by the Romanians he was a member of the town board of trustees and represented it before the federal authorities. He was a well-known public figure and he was active in many institutions- general and Jewish. He was responsible for the management of the Jewish Hospital founded by Y. Nissenboim. He did the same for the Jewish and Christian Old People's Homes. He was the Gabbai of the Butchers Synagogue and was one of the founders of the Savings and Loan Bank. He was deeply involved in all phases of the Jewish community in Bendery.

He was always ready to help the needy and he stood out for his generosity. He and his late wife, Liuba, raised four children: two daughters- Clara and Liza and two sons – Asher and Yitzhak. Yitzhak followed in his father's footsteps and was active in Maccabi in Bendery. He made Aliyah in 1934.

This is written in memory of our dear parents, sister and brother who are no longer among us: our father, **MORDEHAI**, son of ASHER, **SVERDLIK**, our mother, **LIUBA** (nee Veisgendler), our sister **CLARA**. All three were murdered in the killing fields in Bendery in the early 1940s. Our brother **ASHER** died in the United States in the 1960s.

May their souls be bound among the souls of the living!

The mourners,

Liza and **Yitzhak**

Dr. Yaakov Sofer

Yaakov, son of **SHAUL** and **HENYA SOFER,** was born in Bendery on 15 October 1908. When he completed his studies at the Schwartzman Hebrew High School he went to Iasi to study pharmacy. He continued his studies in Bucharest and graduated in 1934.

When World War II broke out he was in Kishinev and he managed to get out of town before it fell to the Germans. He wandered in Russian Asia dreaming of going to Eretz Israel where he could raise his children. He achieved his dream in 1945 when he made Aliyah. He was well-integrated in life there.

He died of a heart ailment on 26.10.1957.

Dr. Ida Sofer

My late mother, **GENIA (YENTA) SOLOMON** (nee **Steinbeck**) was born in Bendery in 1891.

My late father, **REUVEN SOLOMON** was born in 1876 in Ukraine. He settled in Bendery in 1899.

They left Bendery in 1941, before the German conquest. The last news from them came in 1942 from Voroshilovgrad where they had found refuge in a collective settlement. When Voroshilovgrad was taken by the Germans they were murdered together with other Jews.

My sister **ROZA** and the girls were murdered in the Holocaust.

Pinhas Solomon

[Page 410]

In memory of our dear parents:

Our father **YONA** and our mother **HANNAH SOLOMONOVICH**.

They were honest and straightforward people who raised six children. Four of them are no longer alive:

MEIR was killed in 1944 while escaping from the cursed Germans.

YOSEF was taken with 10 000 other Jews to work for the Germans, but he never returned.

ISRAEL hid in a Christian home during the Holocaust. The owner sent him, his wife and child away and they were killed.

HASSIA died in Odessa.

May their souls be bound among the souls of the living!

The Sudit Family

They were beloved and gentle people in their lifetime and they remain together in death.

Name	Date of Death	Burial Place
R.**SHMUEL ABBA**, son of **DAVID SUDIT**	26 Av 1932	Kishinev
My mother, **MIREL**, daughter of **AVRAHAM ITZHAK**, **SUDIT**	2 Nisan 1939	Bendery
My brother, **LEVI MEIR**, son of **SHMUEL ABBA**, **SUDIT**	14 Tevet 1949	Paris
My brother, **MENAHEM-MENDEL**, son of **SHMUEL ABBA, SUDIT**	9 Heshvan 1969	Bendery
My brother, **YOSEF**, son of **SHMUEL ABBA, SUDIT**	10 Tevet	Bendery
My brother, **EFRAIM**, son of **SHMUEL ABBA, SUDIT**	29 Kislev 1962	Bendery
My brother **MOSHE NAHUM**, son of **SHMUEL ABBA, SUDIT**	6 Iyar 1970	New York
My sister **GNESSIA**, daughter of **SHMUEL ABBA, SUDIT**	I do not remember when	Bolgrod
My sister, **Gitel**, daughter of **SHMUEL ABBA, SUDIT**	killed in 1941 on way to Caucasus	Bendery

[Page 411]

Shmuel Abba Sudit

Shmuel Abba was born in Bendery and was considered a wealthy and respected businessman. He was a scholar and a follower of the Rabbi from Pashkan. He had a large and well-educated family. In his youth he was a treasurer of an army unit and he served in Caucasus. He was also Gabbai of the Sadigura Synagogue. His store was in the center of town and in it there was a special room where the followers of the Rabbi would congregate.

He was a member of the executive board of the Jewish community and a recognized leader. He was also well-known as a generous and honest man. He opened his home to groups of people who studied Mishna and Torah.

On special Holidays he and his wife travelled to the Rabbi to study with him. When the Rabbi from Pashkan came to Bendery he and his entourage stayed in his home for the entire visit. They even received their guests in that home.

His son, Mendel Sudit, was exiled to Siberia for 15 years by the Soviets. He was accused of being a bourgeois. The rest of his sons immigrated to the United States.

Yeshayahu Sudit

Yeshayahu, son of David-Menahem, Sudit

A descendant of the SUDIT and IMAS families, he was born in Bendery in July 1885. His father died when he was a young child. He studied in Talmud Torah and in a public school in Bendery. When he turned 13 he began to work in the business belonging to the late R. MOSHE TAXIR.

In 1909 he married **SARA**, daughter of **R. MOSHE TAXIR**. They raised two daughters and a son. He was an honest and straight businessman, a modest man totally devoted to his family. He was involved in the life of the Jewish community in Bendery and was a well-known Zionist.

Yeshayahu made Aliyah in 1935 together with his family. After some absorption difficulties he was able to purchase a herring factory in Petach Tikva. He worked hard for 27 years. He ran his business as he had run the previous one in Bendery and he was well-liked by his customers and acquaintances.

His love of family was great and his devotion to them was outstanding. He was content and enjoyed life.

He was fortunate to live to see his grandchildren married and to be blessed with great-grandchildren.

He fell ill suddenly in 1963 and was taken home from the store. He died soon afterwards.

His good name, dedication to the love of his family and all people, his modesty and goodness will never be forgotten.

His friends often think of him and speak about his kindness and devotion.

May his soul be bound among the souls of the living!

His wife, **Sara Sudit**
Son, **Menahem Sudit**
Daughters, **Massia Grinholtz, Ziporah (Benzvi) Azmon**

[Page 412]

Pessia, Moshe, and Aryeh Saifer

A Memorial Candle Lit for Our Dear Family from the Home of Pessia and Aryeh Saifer

Pessia and Aryeh Saifer made Aliyah in 1924.

Moshe Saifer and his family were murdered by the Nazis during the Holocaust in Galatz, Romania. May their souls go up to heaven!

Itzhak Sofer

Yitzhak died in 1964. He was highly involved in all aspects of life in Eretz Israel, especially in public organizations. He was a veteran of the Haganah and a member of the cultural committee.

[Page 413]

We will never forget those we lost

R. Shmelke Sirkis

My father, my teacher, **R. Shmelke (Shmuel**, son of **Yehudah Zeev) Sirkis**, Z"L, was a scholar and a generous man. He served as a Gabbai in the Talne synagogue and was also an active member of the Jewish community.

He was born in 1872 and he died on 29.1.1919.

My mother, my teacher, **DOBA** (daughter of Binyamin **Geker)**, was an active woman of valor.

She was born in 1879 and died on 22.10.1943.

My sister, **BILHA ROSENSHEIN**, was born in 1907 and was killed in the Holocaust in 1941.

My brother, **ITZHAK SIRKIS**, was born in 1909 and was killed in the Holocaust in 1941.

[Itzhak Sirkas? – picture not identified in book]

[Page 414]

Yehiel Sirkis

My brother **Yehiel Sirkis** was born in 1911 and was killed in Transnistria in 1941.

Shmuel Bortnik (Sirkis Family)

My sister's son, **Shmuel Bortnik**, was born in 1920. He died at the front in Sevastopol, Crimea, Russia in 1941.

May their souls be bound among the souls of the living!

Dr. Haim Sirkis

Our Parents Freyada and Shaul Frank

Our parents were born in Bessarabia. Their home was imbued with Zionism and, at the same time, with Russian culture. Mother loved to read in her spare time. Father used to recite poetry by Lermontov and Nikrassov to his children. They both worked hard at earning a living and taking care of their home. They endeavored to give their children a proper education. The parents left their imprint on all their children. Most of them joined Hashomer Hatzair and the parents followed their progress.

Our home was the center of our family life and was open to all emissaries of the movement. Our mother welcomed everyone and was nicknamed "mother of the shomrim."

We owed much to our parents and we are fortunate to have been able to bring them to Eretz Israel before the Holocaust. They found comfort here and they were surrounded by their loving children and grandchildren.

Every year our family meets to visit their graves in the cemetery of Kibbutz Maabarot. We remember them with love.

The girls

[Page 415]

Right - Shaul Frank **Left - Freyda Frank**
28,04,1872 – 7.09.1965   15.03.1872 – 28.03.1956

Raphael Pardis

Raphael was born in Bendery in 1875 and he died there in 1934. He was an honest man in his relations with God and with his fellow man.

He always helped the needy quietly and in secret.

He raised his sons to love Eretz Israel.

Our mother, his helpmate, was born in Akkerman and was killed in the Holocaust in Bendery.

May their memory be blessed!

The sons,

MOSHE, ISRAEL, AVRAHAM
(as told to P.B.)

[Page 416]

Pinhas Feuer – The Dayan of Bendery

My parents were both born in Putshayev, Volyn, near Krementz. The tradition of our family, according to our father, tells us that he was a descendant of a student of the Baal Shem Tov, R. David Likes, z"l. My father used to travel to the Maggid of Trisk, z"l, and was his follower all his life.

When he arrived in Bendery he was tested by R. Itzikel Wertheim (grandfather of Rabbi Yosef Wertheim). He was then chosen by R. Itzikel to teach his grandchildren.

R. Itzikel recommended my late father to be the Dayan (judge) of Bendery. My father managed the rabbinate in a respectful way and earned the trust of the Jews of Bendery. Even non-Jews would choose to be judged by him. They always respected his decisions.

An event which occurred exemplifies his honesty and his love of peace. A young wealthy couple from Kishinev came to him to be granted a divorce. They had a child of ten. As rabbis usually do he tried to mediate and to establish peace. However, nothing worked and he still continued to investigate and to ask. He spoke to the man and my mother had a conversation with the wife. He discovered that the reason for the request for a divorce was a meddling mother-in-law. The divorce was denied and peace was restored.

May their souls be bound among the souls of the living!

Their son,
Y. Feuer

Zvi, son of Yosef, Paschan

He was born in 1891 and made Aliyah in 1925.

Zvi was raised in a traditional home and was instructed in religious subjects by local teachers. He also attended a public school.

He was one of the first importers in Eretz Israel. After he made Aliyah he opened a tile factory and later a plant for refrigeration and smoked fish.

He was active in public life and was well-liked by everyone.

His two daughters studied in Balfour High School in Tel Aviv.

He died in 1962 at the age of 71.

May his memory be blessed!

[Page 417]

Yocheved, Daughter of Yaakov, Paschan

Yocheved was born in 1895. She was a wonderful mother and a beautiful soul, modest and charitable.

She died in 1968 at the age of 73.

May her memory be with us forever!

The girls

Batya Tselnik

Our father Gershon died at the age of 32. Our mother was only 30 and her children were young orphans without any support. Our mother undertook to earn a living and to raise her children. She was courageous and had a pleasant disposition. Everyone around her reacted to her warmth. She always encouraged others.

When we grew up we made Aliyah and she joined us. Her love of life helped her to overcome many difficulties. Unfortunately, illness overcame her and she died at a ripe old age on 22.12.1966. Her children and grandchildren were by her bedside.

Her memory will last forever.

Leah Tselnik

[Page 418]

Eliahu Chaplik

In Eternal Memory of Our Beloved Father

We will never forget:

Our father, a scholar, a writer and a ritual slaughterer in Bendery, who died on 17 Tishrei 1928, our beloved mother **DINA-RAHEL**, daughter of R. **MORDEHAI ITZHAK**, died on 9 Adar 1909, our sister **SHIFRA**, her husband **YAAKOV GILIK** and their children and our sister **MIRIAM**, her husband **MORDEHAI AUERBACH** and their children. They were slaughtered by the Nazi murderers.

Children, brothers and sisters:

Yaakov and Zina **Chaplik**, Toronto

Lena **Auerbach**, Philadelphia

Yitzhak and Rahel **Chaplik**, Tel Aviv

Haike and David **Gilik, Toronto**

Moshe and Katya **Chaplik**, Toronto

And their grandchildren

Note the above is written in Hebrew on the right and in Yiddish on the left. It is exactly the same!

[Page 419]

R. Israel Zvi Chalik   **Mrs. Esther-Leah Chalik**

Israel Zvi died in Argentina in 1946. He was a respected merchant in Bendery and served as Gabbai in Rabbi Sh. Sh. Wertheim's synagogue. He stood out in his philanthropic activities, especially in Talmud Torah and the hospital.

He also represented the Jewish community on the municipal council in 1925-28.

In Buenos Aires, Argentina, he continued to be a respected and active member of the Jewish community and in religious circles

Esther-Leah died in Argentina in 1958.

May their souls be bound among the souls of the living!

Rahel Chaplik

Rahel became the only daughter of Nahum and Etel Sverdlik when her brother Reuven was killed in World War and her sister Fraidel died young.

After her father's death she went to work at a young age. In 1921 she made Aliyah with her husband and young daughter. She worked hard, ran her household and raised her children. She worked at TNUVA for 27 years. Not only was she an excellent worker, but she was always ready to help everyone, even if they did not ask for it. Her colleagues appreciated her and chose her to be their representative in many aspects of the workers union.

[Page 420]

Rahel Chaplik

She was born on Simchat Torah – 26.9.1899 and died in Tel Aviv on 1.2.1964.

Rahel encouraged her children – Dina, Rivka, Nahum and Ruthie – to attend general and professional schools. They were all involved in serving their homeland and became members of the British army and later the Haganah and the Israel Defense Forces.

She was fortunate to be alive when they were all married and she had great enjoyment from them.

The image of Rahel is that of a homemaker, a woman of valor and a nurturing mother. She fulfilled all her tasks with love and loyalty and her memory is etched in the hearts of all who knew her.

May her memory be blessed!

Niunia Zukerman
He was born in Kishinev in 1897 and died in Tel Aviv in 1949.

Eliezer Zukerman
He was born in Bendery in 1919 and he died in Tel Aviv in 1951.

[Page 421]

A Memorial Candle is Lit in Memory of My Slaughtered Family Members

My father, **Pinhas-Yosef**, son of **R. Mordehai, Krajevsky.**
He was born in 1880 and was killed by the Bolsheviks in 1920.

Left: Bluma Krajevsky

Right: My mother, **Riva (Rivka) Krajevsky**, daughter of **Aaron Hazin**.

She was born in 1882 and was killed during the Holocaust in a communal settlement on the road to Leningrad in 1942.

My sister, **BLUMA**, was born in 1910 and was killed in 1942.

My sister's son, **PINHAS**, was born in 1932 and was killed in 1942.

They were all shot during the times of the Red terror and the invasion by the Fascist Nazis.

Their memory is always in our hearts.

[Page 422]

Moshe Kaushansky
(A member of Beitar in Bendery)

Moshe was the son of Israel and Batya, and he was born in Bendery on 12.07.1917. He received a public education and he wished to make Aliyah as an agricultural worker. His wish came true when he arrived in Eretz Israel on 10.03.1939 on the ship "Katina". In 1939-40 he worked in the citrus groves in Hadar near Ramatyim. He was given a piece of land where he grew vegetables. In 1940-41 he studied diamond polishing in Netanya. In 1941 he joined the Jewish Brigade and was sent first to Egypt and then to Europe. He returned in 1946 and continued to work as a diamond polisher. He still wanted to join an agricultural settlement. In February 1948 he joined the defense forces in the struggle for independence. He served in Harel and later Moria in the Israel Defense Forces. He fought in the battle for Jerusalem and participated in the conquest of Hirbat Al Lehem near Latrun. He was a brave soldier and was careful in protecting military secrets.

Moshe was killed during a dangerous mission in Beit Tul near Jerusalem on 18.07.1948. He was reburied on Mount Herzl on 28.02.1950.

(Yizkor, Ministry of Defense, 1957)

A Memorial Candle Dedicated To My Dear Late Parents,

My Sister and Her Daughter

My father, **MENAHEM-MENDEL KIRSHNER**, 1875- 14.03.1926

My mother, **ELKA**, daughter of **SHMAYA**, 1876-6.11.1949

My sister, **YAFFA (SHEIND**L), 1912- 1.9.1941

My late father was a hard-working, honest man. His father died when he was young and he had to help support the family. He learned to be a locksmith and a machinist. This is how he always earned his living. He was a traditional man and he educated his children in Jewish values. He was always ready to help the needy.

Although I was the only son, my father understood that I would be making Aliyah. He, himself, also planned to do so, but he fell ill at work and died of pneumonia. He was buried in Bendery.

My mother was a gentle woman who taught her children good values. In those years she was the designated reader of prayers for other women on Shabbat and Holidays. After my father's death, my mother and my sister, Yaffa, made Aliyah in the 1930s. Here, too, she stood out for her generosity and good deeds. She donated a Torah scroll to the synagogue on Bookie Ben Yagli Street in Tel Aviv. She also paid the expenses incurred in managing a bed in the old people's home on Avoda Street in Tel Aviv.

My sister, Yaffa, was one of the first female workers in the Lodzia factory. She died after a lengthy illness brought about after her only child, Menahem, died. He was killed during the Italian bombing in Tel Aviv in the 1940s.

May their souls be bound among the souls of the living!

Zvi Kirshner

[Page 423]

Asher Kishinovsky

R. Asher Kishinovsky was well-known in our town as a wealthy merchant who had extended business dealings. He was a director of the Moldova Bank and was later succeeded by his son, David. In addition to his business involvement he was also active in public affairs. Everyone came to him for help. It could be a wagon driver whose horse died or a poor Jew whose wife was ill or a father who was marrying off his daughter and had no money for a dowry.

R. Asher Kishinovsky assisted in the construction of the Great Synagogue in Bendery and he exerted much effort in looking after the congregants. He was also drawn to Zionism. He was one of the first to donate to Jewish National Fund and Keren Hayesod. He also brought in other donors.

His memory will be with us forever!

P. Bendersky

David (Kishon) Kishinovsky

David Kishon – known as Kishinovsky in Bendery – was born in 1893. He was a well-known personality in our town. He was active in many aspects of public life. David was a director of the Moldova Bank and many Jews would come to him asking for help. This was especially so during difficult economic times. David Kishon was also the president of the Chamber of Commerce. It was an important position during Romanian times.

David was especially involved with our youth. He helped to found a commercial school. Needy students were given free textbooks. He believed in a `Healthy soul in a healthy body`. He was chairman of Maccabi youth movement. He also tried to obtain Aliyah permits for young people. Many young Jews endangered their lives by crossing the Dniester on their way to Eretz Israel. They stopped in Bendery and David helped and encouraged them.

David Kishinovsky was commended for all his efforts and his good deeds.

He made Aliyah and died on 28 Elul 1972.

His memory will be with us forever!

P. Bendersky

Engineer Bubby (son of David) Kishon (Kishinovsky)

R. Shmuel Krassilover

Shmuel was born in Katriliva where he grew up, was married and had two daughters and one son. His wife died in 1890 and he moved to Bendery with his children. He remarried and had five more children – two sons and three daughters.

In both Katriliva and Bendery he earned his living by teaching. His Heder was on Benderskaya Street. He later taught in the Talmud Torah and some of his students moved with him.

He was known to his students, especially on the bone of their thumb- which he lacked. The students were afraid to complain to their parents because he threatened to hit them even harder on the next day. Still, they actually liked him.

When he was six years old, Russian soldiers came to the village to kidnap Jewish children to serve Tsar Nikolai. When his father heard this he told Shmuel to place his thumb on the anvil and he chopped it off with his ax. This is how he was exempt from military service.

He was good-natured and all the children in the family loved him.

R. Shmuel Krassilover was a Cohen and he officiated at Pidyion Haben ceremonies. His students came from wealthy homes. He also taught Gmara to other students. He worked in the Talmud Torah until his last day. He died in 1928 at the age of 88. He left a large family. Some of them live in Israel.

Told by his grandson Shoel Zilberman, Rehovot to interviewer Y. Raviv

(Special article on page 231-page number in original Yizkor Book)

[Page 425]

Haim Kaushansky **Zalman Kaushansky**

Rahel Kaushansky

My grandfather, **R. Haim Kaushansky**, was a well-known and highly respected personality in Bendery. He was clever and his opinions were well received by the public. He was a leader in the Jewish Community as well as an experienced and honest merchant. He headed the Chamber of Commerce and was commended by King Ferdinand of Romania.

My grandfather was raised in a traditional Jewish home and this is how he brought up his sons and daughters. When they became adults they, too, contributed to the Jewish and general communities.

He had an open hand and he was always ready to donate to different causes.

He died in Bendery on 23 Tammuz 1931 and was beautifully eulogized.

May his soul be bound among the souls of the living!

His grandson,
Attorney Eliezer Kishon

[Page 426]

Zalman Kaushansky

Zalman Kaushansky, son of Haim, was one of the most highly respected personalities in Bendery. He was born on 12.2.1887. He was educated in the Jewish tradition and remained true to it all his life.

R. Zalman was an important merchant in our town. He was well-liked and trusted by all who knew him. He was quite active in public life and was always prepared to work on behalf of Jewish institutions, to help the needy and to encourage others to donate to Eretz Israel. No one ever refused him.

In 1950 he and his wife arrived in Israel. His son, Eliezer Kishon, a lawyer, was there already. Even in Israel he was recognized as a leader and he was elected Gabbai in his synagogue.

R. Zalman died on 9.4.1972 at the age of 85. His wife, Rahel, daughter of Moshe, was born in Kishinev in 1888. She was active in public life in Bendery.

She died on 2.5.1974.

May their souls be bound with the souls of the living!

His friend, Hanania Volovetz

R. Shmuel-Yosef Klibansky

He was born in Vilna in 1855 and he died in Bendery in 1909.

R. Shmuel-Yosef Klibansky, z"l, was a Jewish scholar and a teacher of the Bible. He studied in a yeshiva and was ordained a Rabbi. He always loved to study and to develop. He moved to Bendery where he married my mother, Batsheva, and he raised a large family.

In addition to teaching he was also active in public life. He was one of the founders of two synagogues in Bendery: Mishnayos Shul and the Carpenters Shul.

My father taught at the Talmud Torah and also at the day school in Bendery. He was modest and always ready to help the needy.

May his memory be blessed!

unnamed – see article following.

Batsheva (Peretz) Klibansky

She was born in 1860 and she died in Eretz Israel in 1935. My mother, Batsheva, was my father's trusted helpmate. They created a blessed home and raised a large family.

Their son,

Shlomo Levni (Klibansky)

[Page 427]

Left: Zev (Volodya) Kraposter

He was born in 1886 and he made Aliyah in 1956. He died in Ramat Gan in 1965.

Right: Yitzhak (Isak), son of Mendel Kraposter

He was born in 1900 and he died in 1921.

Mordehai Kraposter

Mordehai, the son of Sossel and Mendel, was born in Bendery on 24.8.1902. He studied in the Schwartzman Hebrew High School. When he was quite young, his father died and Mordehai had to manage the family business. In spite of his poor health, he served in the Romanian army.

In 1931 he came to Eretz Israel with a group of tourists to see if conditions there were suitable for him. Someone had denounced the group to the British authorities accusing them of planning to remain in the country. The ship's passengers were arrested. They went on a hunger strike and eventually they were promised certificates to enter the country.

In 1933 the certificates were received. Since family members were included, he, his wife and oldest son made Aliyah.

On his first day in Haifa he began to look for work. He waited and waited until he did obtain a job.

In 1934 he began to work in Solel Bone as a construction worker. During the upheavals, there was much less work and he could only get a few days a month. He even went to dangerous places like Nablus and Jenin.

After many years he switched to work in the warehouse of Solel Bone. He retired in 1967 after 33 years.

He died suddenly on 20.4.1971. He left a wife, a son, a daughter and 6 grandchildren.

[Page 428]

Tsipa Kogan

Aaron (Arel) Kogan (Cohen) and His Family

My father, Arel (Aaron) Kogan was the son of Leibush, the cantor of the Great synagogue in Bendery. He was born in 1881.

He was a public figure who worked for the good of the citizens of his town. He was totally dedicated and was active in many institutions: "Help for the Sick", "Clothes for the Needy", Ort school, charitable organizations and summer camps for poor children. His main goal was always to teach the younger generation to be productive and to learn a trade. Most of his life he worked in the Savings and Loan Bank in Bendery (the Jewish Bank).

Aaron Kogan   Genia Hochman (Kogan)– Sister

He was a scholarly man, well educated in Jewish culture in general and in Yiddish literature in particular. He was well-versed in world affairs and he was an outstanding orator. He had leanings to the left and admired the "Bund". However, he was a dedicated Jew, heart and soul. His home was traditional, but not observant. He was the Gabbai of the Rahman synagogue. He directed his children towards Zionist youth movements. In fact, I, his son, belonged to Hashomer Hatzair. My late sister, Genia, was a member of Zeirei Zion. My younger brother, Avraham Kogan, who remained in Bendery, taught his children to follow the saying: "Be a human being on the outside and a Jew in your own home."

My mother, Tsipa (Tzipora) Kogan was born in Tiraspol in 1885. She was a gentle person and an outstanding homemaker. She taught her children to perform good deeds.

World War II uprooted my parents from their home and their town. They both died of starvation and illness on the way to Uzbekistan.

My sister, Genia Kogan (Hochman), was born in 1915. She was widowed during WWII. After much wandering she reached a communal settlement in Saratov where she was killed in 1943. She was only 29 years old.

She was a high school graduate and had a beautiful singing voice. She had planned to make Aliyah in 1941, but she was unsuccessful because the Russians invaded Bessarabia.

May their souls be bound among the souls of the living!   Arieh Cohen

[Page 430]

Haim Kapusta   and   his wife Batsheva

Our father was born in 1889 in Kopinka, a village in the District of Bendery. His father was the ritual slaughterer of the village. He received a Jewish education and he was imbued with love of his people. His door was always open and he was always ready to help needy Jews, especially in the years 1919-1922.

In 1919, during the battles between the Romanians and the Bolsheviks on the other side of the Dniester, many Jews fled Bendery. They wandered in the direction of Kaushany and Kopinka. The refugees who arrived in the village were warmly received by my parents.

Soon, pioneers from Russia, on their way to Eretz Israel, crossed the Dniester into Bessarabia. They were endangering their lives and needed a refuge. Again, my parents opened their home to these young people and protected them from the Romanians. They were quite courageous. In addition, my father employed these pioneers in his fruit groves. He was a fruit merchant and an exporter. In this way, the pioneers were able to earn their keep and to prepare themselves for their agricultural work in Eretz Israel.

Our mother was born in Uman in 1889. Her father was the town Rabbi. She, too, was imbued with love for her people and her Jewish tradition. She was always ready to help the less fortunate.

My parents made Aliyah in 1939. We, their sons and daughter, soon followed. Our father was a merchant in Eretz Israel.

Our mother died on 9.7.1952 while our father left us in 1956.

May their souls be bound among the souls of the living!

As told by his sons to P.B.

[Page 431]

IN MEMORY OF OUR DEAR ONES WHO LEFT US TOO EARLY

Moshe Reznik

In memory of our dear ones who left us too early

Our father, MOSHE REZNIK, was born in 1882 and died in the Asian Republics in 1946 at the age of 64.

My husband, MUSSIA (MOSHE) BELL, was born on 22.10.1908 and died on 4.4.1968 at the age of 60.

Our son, AVRAHAM-YAKOV (ABRASHA), died in the Asian Republics in 1941 at the age of four and a half.

Mussia (Moshe) Bell

Our father, the late Moshe Reznik, was a traditional Jew – a quiet and modest man. He dealt in paints in Bendery. He brought up his children to learn Torah and to do good deeds and he served as a model to us.

When WWII broke we fled from the Nazis. My parents, my child and I went to the Asian Republics where we suffered greatly. My child died, followed by my father.

My husband, Mussia Bell, was a graduate of the Science High School in Bendery and a member of Beitar. In 1938 he moved to Trinidad (British West Indies) where he was a businessman. I had planned to join him, but the war intervened. He helped us by sending parcels to Asia. We corresponded, intermittently, through my sister and brother-in-law in Eretz Israel. It was only on 27.7.1955 that my mother and I were permitted by the Soviet authorities to leave and to go to Israel. In the meantime, my husband had moved to Venezuela and I joined him there after a separation of 17 years.

In 1964 we came to Israel together. Mussia prepared himself to begin a new life. We settled in Givatayim and hoped for a better future. Unfortunately, my husband fell ill and a week later he was taken from us.

Hava Bell

[Page 432]

In Memory of our Beloved Mother

Feiga Ziporah (Reznik)

Our mother, Feiga (Ziporah) Reznik was born in 1885 in Kishinev. She was raised in a traditional Jewish home imbued with love for her people.

She graduated from a public school and continued, on her own, to study the Russian language and its classic literature.

She married our father, Moshe Reznik, in 1905 and moved to Bender. There she was active in charitable institutions and helped the poor. She was highly involved in all activities of Zionist women.

During WWII, my parents, their oldest daughter, Hava, and Hava's only son, were evacuated by the Soviets to the Asian Republics. Our father and Hava's son, after much suffering, died there. Our mother made Aliyah in 1964

AHARON LIPA, son of YOSEF, RABINOVICH

Died in Rehovot in 1940 at age 75

and

HAIA, daughter of ARIEH-LEIB, RABINOVICH
Died in Rehovot in 1956 at 74

[Page 433]

Zev Reznik amd his wife Golda Reznik

Zev, son of Yitzhak, Reznik was born in Dubossary, Ukraine in 1863. He died in Bendery in 1919. His wife Golda, daughter of Dov, was from Bendery.

Zev, Son of Yitzhak, Reznik

My father, Zev, son of Yitzhak, Reznik was born in 1863 in Dubossary, Ukraine. Prior to WWI, our family moved across the Dniester to Bendery.

At first, we lived with relatives who helped us with the local language. Eventually, we moved to our own apartment on Michaelovskaya Street (The Street of the teachers).

At that time the economic situation of the Jews of Bendery was difficult. Many heads of families were forced to immigrate to the United States. Their families were left behind and had nothing. My late father helped these families. He also looked after refugees from Poland and Lithuania by feeding them in our home. For many years he hid in his home and in his vineyards the son of a friend who did not want to join the army. In 1917, when the Revolution broke, this young man's life was saved.

In 1919 my father contracted Typhus that was then rampant in the area. He died at the young age of 56.

We, together with friends and relatives, still mourn him. He was a good and honest man.

Our mother and all her daughters made Aliyah in 1929. Our oldest sister had come in 1922.

Henya (Reznik) Veintraub

[Page 434]

Israel Rozlovsky

In Memory of our Parents whose Image is still in our minds.

Our father, Israel Rozlovsky, z"l, was considered as one of the wealthiest merchants in our town. All other merchants respected him.

He was well taught by his father to love his people. He came to Israel where he settled happily and where he died.

Our mother, FRIDA, was born in Kishinev where she also attended school. She was quite knowledgeable in Russian culture and she taught us about it.

She, too, like our father, is buried in Israel.

May their souls be bound among the souls of the living!

The mourners: MOSHE PARDIS
His wife - ZILA (ROZLOVSKY)
Her sister - MARY in Israel
And our sister   IDA   in the United States
As told by the daughters to P.B.

Yeshaya Reznik

Reznik Family From Bendery

In memory of our father and grandfather YESHAYA, son of ARIEH, REZNIK. He made Aliyah in 1921 and he died in Eretz Israel on 12 Iyar 1938.

[Page 435]

Zvi Reznik

Rahel Reznik

Israel Reznik

In memory of my husband, my father, our grandfather and our dear brother:

ZVI (son of Yeshayahu and Rahel) REZNIK
He made Aliyah in 1933 and died on 17 Heshvan 1963.

In memory of our dear mother and grandmother:

RAHEL, daughter of Shimshon, REZNIK
She died in Bendery on 4 Iyar, 1918

In memory of my husband, our father, grandfather and dear brother:

ISRAEL (son of Yeshayahu and Rahel) REZNIK
He made Aliyah in 1921. He was an officer in the Haganah in the Dan area. He died of a serious illness on 15 Tevet 1969.

[Page 436]

THESE PEOPLE I REMEMBER:

My parents, my brother and my unforgettable dear ones who left us too early.

My father, MORDEHAI REDER, was born in 1883 and died on 18.5.1918.
My mother, SARA REDER, was born in 1883 and died on 30.8.1961.
My brother, ZVI REDER, was born in 1914 and died in 1920 at the age of 6.
My brother, YOSEF REDER, was born in 1909 and died on 25.10.1962.
My uncle, YEHIEL REDER, was born in 1901 and drowned on the Struma in February 1942.
May their souls be bound among the souls of the living!

Efraim Reder

Avraham Shwartz and his wife Batya

We mourn our parents.

Our father, AVRAHAM, son of AVIGDOR, SHWARTZ, z"l, was born in Kiev in 1882. He began his Zionist activities there and he remained with the movement till the day he died. He arrived in Bendery in 1924 with his family.

In Bendery he continued his Zionist activities and was elected head of the Tel Hai Fund.

Our father was a scholar and a member of the Jewish intelligentsia. He followed his own personal philosophy. He was kind, reserved and made friends easily. He brought us up with gentleness and taught us to look for justice and truth.

My parents made Aliyah in 1947 and they settled well in their new home.

Our father died on 5.3.1961 and he was buried in Tel Aviv.

Our mother, BATYA, (daughter of M. Levinstein), came from a well respected family in Bendery. She was born in 1884. Her home was traditional, but she also received a good secular education.

My mother was always a loyal helpmate to our father. She died in 1972 and was buried in Tel Aviv.

Told by their daughter, FIRA and her husband, ELIEZER KISHON, to P.B.

Zvi, son of Shlomo, Schmaltz

He was called Gregori Solomonovich in Bendery where he was born in 1876. His father was a mechanic in town. His wife TATIANA, daughter of NAHUM EDELSHTEIN, was born in 1884. Her father was a Notary Public.

Their house stood at 37 Pavlovskaya Street and G.S. Schmaltz had his business- mechanic and locksmith- on the ground floor. He also had a lumber yard on Pushkinskaya Street.

G.S. Schmaltz was the vice-mayor of Bendery. He also assumed other responsible positions in the Jewish community with Rabbi Wertheim and others. After his wife's death he established a Matzo bakery for the community, on Alexandrovskaya Street, in her memory.

He used to rise early and went to visit the homes of the needy where he provided them with food and money.

Hirsh-Zvi, son of Shlomo, Schmaltz

When the Soviets entered Bendery in June 1940, He was invited by the Communist authorities to continue his charitable work and to represent the Jewish community. In October 1940 he died while attending to his city hall activities. Rabbi Wertheim held him in his arms as he was dying. His daughter Nadia, her husband Yosef and their son Vitia were exterminated by the Germans.

His son VOLODYA (ZEV) lived in Israel until his death. The late Volodya and his wife, BELA KAPUSTA, had two sons. Arieh lives in Canada and Gideon Sharon resides in Tel Aviv.

Dr. Alexander Schmaltz is another son of Hirsh-Zvi and he is still in the Soviet Union.

We light a candle in memory of my husband and our unforgettable father – VOLODYA (ZEV) SCHMALTZ

His wife, Bella Schmaltz
His son Arieh Schmaltz, Montreal
His son, Gideon Sharon, Tel Aviv

Volodya (Zev) Schmaltz

Tova Shaposhnik – born in 1875

Aharon Shaposhnik – born in 1873

Our late mother was a great homemaker and a woman of valor. She concentrated on our welfare and on raising us properly. Our late father worked hard and took care of our education. He was involved in public life in the community. He was a modest man and never looked for honors. He always helped those in need in the Jewish community of Bendery.

We fondly remember our father as a building contractor. One of his projects was constructing a floating bridge on the Dniester. He had good relations with the authorities. In addition, we remember a few episodes that describe our father's work for those in need. We will mention only two of them:

My father always approached the army commander before major holidays to arrange for furloughs for the Jewish soldiers. He and other Jews invited these soldiers to their homes after services. They wanted to make certain these soldiers would celebrate the holidays as if they were still at home. Once, when permission was not given to the soldiers to leave, my father, the ritual slaughterer R. Moshe Sverdlik and a few others arranged meals for the soldiers which they brought to the army camps. In this way the soldiers could celebrate the holidays.

Our father was a wealthy man and he always contributed to charitable organizations in the community e.g. Fund for Poor Brides, Jewish Hospital, Help for orphans. In addition, he also helped on a private basis anyone who came his way. He looked after an elderly man and his orphaned granddaughter.

He assured her education and when she was ready to marry he helped the young couple to establish a home.

When my wife, RAYA, and I made Aliyah in 1925, we left our mother, father, 3 sisters and 2 brothers in Bendery. The political and economic situations were getting worse at the time.

Before we parted, this is what my father said to me: "Who knows if we will ever meet again. Always remember to be a good human being!"

My 2 sisters and one brother eventually made Aliyah. We did not hear from the others when WWII began.

After the Holocaust, we discovered the following: our father, already a widower, escaped from Bendery with two daughters, a son-in-law and a grandson. They went towards the Soviet Union, having placed their belongings on a cart when the Nazis came. After a difficult journey they reached Caucasus.

Although they managed to escape the Nazis, my brother-in-law fell ill and died at a young age. His death dealt a blow to my father and he, too, died.

We, the members of the family, light a memorial candle to those who were so cruelly taken from us. We will never forget them.

May their souls be bound among the souls of the living!

YITZHAK SHEFI

[Page 439]

I mourn the following:

The SHLIOMOV family:

My father, my teacher, YAKOV, z"l, who was born in 1891,

My mother, my teacher, HAIA, z"l, who was born in 1893,

My sister, RISSA, z"l, who was born in 1916, and

My sister, SIMA, z"l, who was born in 1919

My parents, YAKOV and HAIA SHLIOMOV, were born in Bendery and lived on Sovoronaya Street. My father was a locksmith. Our home was full of Zionist youth activities. My father hoped that after his Aliyah in 1935 the rest of the family would follow.

The war interrupted these plans. Our relatives, together with other townspeople, were evacuated by the Soviets and wandered to the Asian Republics. Contact with members of the family was sporadic since everyone was scattered.

I found out through relatives who managed to return after the war that my family was not seen after 1941. Their burial place is unknown.

May their souls be bound among the souls of the living!

ROZA FANER

Pinhas Shteiner

He was born in 1909 and he died on 12.8.1970.

Our unforgettable brother, you left us so quietly without bothering us – just as did in your lifetime. I think constantly about you and our childhood. We grew up like twins. Our home was full of love for everyone and you represented that love.

Piniele was a sweet and gentle child. He was pale and had sad Jewish eyes. Under his yarmulke there were curly blond forelocks. He always recited the Shema before he went to sleep. He woke up repeating the Mode Ani and kissing his tzitzit like his father. My mother hoped her youngest child would become a rabbi, like her own father.

I remember the first day he attended Heder- run by R. Mordehai-Shmuel. Mother dressed him in a long coat with a warm scarf. The assistant teacher, Simcha, lifted him on his shoulders and took him to Heder. Piniele kissed the mezuzah and looked at me silently as if to say "I have no choice, my sister. I am a Jewish child and I have to learn Torah". I watched out of the window as the assistant trudged through mud with snowflakes falling around him.

Years went by. My brother was a student at the Schwartzman Hebrew High School. He was physically weak, but he studied hard. In winter he learned Gmara by candlelight. He rose at dawn to pray. In contrast, he eventually joined Hashomer Hatzair.

At the age of 16 he was forced to help the family. Full of heartache, he gave up his dreams of Aliyah and left for distant Canada. In 1927 he finally made Aliyah and settled in Jerusalem. He saved money which he sent to his parents. In this way he saved them from the Nazis as they were able to come to Eretz Israel. They arrived with empty hands. It was a difficult time as there was no work and very little help. One time, we returned home to find the door locked and our belongings outside.

Pinhas refused to accept social assistance and said:"You have to search for work until you find something." He went out with his tools and returned triumphant – he found work. My delicate brother, a former Talmud Torah teacher in Canada had become a sought-after laborer. He worked in construction, in cleaning sewers. He accepted any type of work and he even was a guard in dangerous locations. After the recession he became a stone worker. He would place his tool next to his heart to show its importance. He eventually became an expert in tile work and he trained other pioneers in the field. He worked in the Rotenberg plant in Naharayim and was one of the first to build a home on the sands in Kiryat Haim. His pioneering spirit pushed him to continue working and serving his country. He was a modest and introverted man. He was cultured and a deep thinker.

This is what I remember: early one rainy winter morning, my brother arose with the alarm as always. I knew his health had worsened and I wanted to say to him: "My brother, go back to bed. You have worked enough!" However, I knew he would not listen. He wrapped himself in a raincoat and a scarf and left the house. I watched him through a sheet of rain as he went to work. He did this for 42 years.

Rest in peace, my beloved brother, in the land you loved so much and which you served with deep loyalty.

Your sister LEAH

My Sister Hanna-Shteiner Margolit

(One of the first members of Zeirei Zion in Bendery)

...I remember her from my childhood: an earnest, alert, good-hearted and pretty young woman. She took care of us and of the house with great devotion. She studied and read books at night. Even then she dreamed of Zion.

At the age of 16 she joined Zeirei Zion in our town. She studied Hebrew and learned to speak it well. This was unusual in our town.

On Saturdays members of the movement gathered in our home. She was the youngest and liveliest. They read classic books in Yiddish and discussed conferences and Herzl. They sang Zionist songs with great enthusiasm: "On the Road," "Where the Cedars Grow," "Carry the Flag to Zion," etc.

The family was in dire straits and she undertook to immigrate to Canada to help us. She dreamed of making Aliyah from there, but she was not successful.

She helped us, the younger ones, and our parents to make Aliyah. She taught her two sons to love our people and our land. When the War of Independence broke, her son was one of the first to volunteer to fight for our people. He and his brother and their children live in Israel. She was fortunate to visit the land.

In Canada she taught in a Talmud Torah and was a member of Poalei Zion. She was one of the founders of Pioneer Women in 1925. Her colleagues always appreciated her devotion and her hard work on behalf of our people. Pioneer Women is still a going concern in the cold northern city of Winnipeg. It links this city in Canada with Israel.

★

My dear sister! You were buried in a distant Diaspora under ice and snow. Your soul will always be attached to our homeland. You longed to be there, but you were never fortunate enough to live in it.

Your sister

LEAH

[Page 441]

R. Eli – The Ritual Slaughterer and a Scholar

A.

An important Jewish scholar, a ritual slaughterer, lived in the noisy town of Bendery. He was a widower and the father of seven. He found time to study philosophy, astronomy, politics and he still performed good deeds. He also learned Gmara in the Sadigura synagogue. Nights he wrote a text on the history of man – from Adam to the 20th century. Included were commentaries by important personalities. The book was printed in Odessa in 1912.

From day one, troubles, disturbances and disasters which touched other communities did not skip our town. Many deaths occurred at the hands of the German and Romanian murderers. The murders took place in town as well as on the way to Transnistria, Siberia and the Asian Republics. Those who survived – 1200 families – returned to town and found it in ruins.

B.

I remember an evening in our home after WWI when Uncle Eli (this is what we, the children, called him even though he was our father's uncle) sat with my parents at the long table drinking a hot drink. He was talking about my grandfather, Israel, z"l. By then, my grandfather was already a resident of Eretz Israel. Suddenly, he asked me the following: "Tell me, Motele, do you know where in the world is Eretz Israel?"

"Yes," I replied with certainty. I was skinny Heder student. "It is far on the other side of the Dniester."

"Listen," he said and immediately drew a map on a piece of paper. "Here is where the Dniester flows into the Black Sea. Further on there are other countries and seas. Then the Mediterranean Sea follows. On the banks of the Mediterranean is Eretz Israel. In the middle of the country, near the Dead Sea, is the holy city of Jerusalem. On the northern shore lies Haifa and south of that is Jaffa. In between is Zichron Yaakov where your grandfather Israel lives."

Sometime later he brought us a gift- a copy of his book "The First Man." In it we read that Adam was created on the sixth day. It is followed by a series of names describing when and where they were born: Seth, Enos, Canaan, Mahalel, Yered, Hanoch, Methuselah, Lemech, etc. Also listed were our patriarchs, prophets, kings, members of the Big Assembly, Hasmoneans, Tanaim, Scholars, Rabbis and leaders up to our times. There were many details about all of them.

I learned so much from Uncle Eli in the synagogue where he prayed (Fireman's). The Holy Ark had an important lesson etched on its front:

> *"Man worries about mundane belongings,*
> *but he should worry about the passage of time.*
> *The elapsed days will not come back*
> *and belongings will not help."*

I understood it to mean that man worries about money instead of remembering that time moves on and cannot be recaptured. These words were always his motto. I believe that he even etched them himself.

C.

In the difficult days of the Russian revolution, Uncle Eli continued his activities in Jewish organizations. He, his son Itzik, and other people saved his house. A soldier, riding a horse with a sword drawn in his hand yelled: "Down with the Jewish Commissars!" Uncle Eli held a gun in his hand and shot at the soldier, but he hit the horse and the soldier ran away.

Uncle Eli died at a ripe old age, highly respected and loved, before the bloody events that touched Europe. However, his grandson Aaron Auerbach was slaughtered with his entire family by the Nazi murderers.

Many years later I recalled Uncle Eli's history book. My parents had once owned a copy in their home in the 1920s. However, here in our country I could not find any copies. I asked his son, Itzik and he told me that in 1938 when he was in Bendery he found a remnant of the book – a list of the names.

After much searching, a copy was found here. His grandson also had a notebook in which the following was written, in Romanian:"This French notebook belongs to the student Aaron Auerbach." This was the only remnant of the student Aaron Auerbach. May God avenge his soul!

There is also one copy of this book in the National Library of Israel located in the Hebrew University in Jerusalem.

The memory of R. Eli the ritual slaughterer and brilliant scholar will always live on among the important personalities of the holy Jewish community of the town of Bendery.

Mordehai Sever

Aaron Helfand – Famous Cantor

Aaron Helfand

When he was still a child, Aaron had a phenomenal soprano voice. He sang with other cantors: Aaron Humenik (U.S.) – from whom he was taken by the choir of the famous cantor Avraham Kalechnik Bercovitch in Kishinev. From there he went to the Cantor David Moshe Steinberg (Odessa). His voice changed to an amazing lyric–dramatic tenor. He sang with Cantor Yehuda Leib Kilimnik and Cantor Yonah Dinovitzer.

He was also a cantor in Odessa, Kremenchug, Grodno, and Warsaw (Tlometzky). In 1931 he moved to Manchester and then spent most of his life as the head cantor in London (see page 228).

He died in 1965.

May his soul be bound among the souls of the living!

Moshe Bik

[Page 443]

Errata

Page 216 should read Aaron David is the brother of Rivka David, not her son.

Page 263- right side – there are two Itziks. One is the sainted Rabbi Wertheim and the other is the philanthropist Itzy Nissenboim who built the hospital.

Page 380 – left column, 5th line from top should read Ida, wife of D. Drobetsky, not Dvoretsky.

INDEX

A

Abelman, 216, 217, 224, 227, 244, 252, 433
Abramovich, 167, 242, 570
Abramovitch, 27, 40, 43, 44, 145, 147, 458, 509, 510
Abramson, 131
Adir, 294, 295
Adler, 13, 283
Agadati, 285, 435, 476
Alexander, 404
Alexandrov, 40, 86, 280, 290, 405, 463, 468, 509, 510
Alter, 146, 247, 248, 529, 530
Alterman, 420, 568, 603
Altman, 479
Amiel, 192
Ansky, 166
Anutov, 468
Apelboim, 247
Applebaum, 528
Arbitman, 564
Aronson, 270
Arye, 62, 71
Ashkenazi, 99, 415
Ashkenazy, 13, 233, 610
Assaf, 192
Atchkover, 62, 63
Atlis, 572
Auerbach, 153, 642, 677
AUERBACH, 642
Averbuch, 203, 391, 392, 444, 525, 552
Avergun, 234
Avineri, 192
Avronin, 8, 607
Azmon, 632

B

Balaban, 43, 114, 115, 160, 486, 561, 578, 579, 597
Balabaner, 511
Balaban-Mozgovsky, 579
Balaban-Shuster, 579
Balatzianu, 244
Barshadski, 142
Batzman, 327
Bauch, 358, 360, 361
Bauh, 572
Beilis, 476
Beker, 14, 418, 483
Belkovsky, 272
Bell, 660, 661
Ben Ami, 37
Ben Gurion, 449
ben Shaul, 154, 155, 157
Ben Tzvi, 327, 339
Ben Yefuneh, 266, 462
Ben Yehiel, 348
Ben Zion, 89
Ben Zvi, 449
Bendersky, 4, 37, 50, 51, 54, 62, 65, 101, 144, 147, 151, 153, 157, 201, 206, 242, 272, 273, 274, 275, 306, 308, 309, 310, 330, 395, 408,

474, 482, 503, 510, 525, 547, 561, 581, 582, 583, 596, 598, 615, 649, 650

Benedict, 65

Ben-Shaul, 151, 153

Ben–Yshai, 510, 511, 512, 513, 519, 520

Bercovitch, 106

Berdichevsky, 22, 418, 584

Berdichover, 426

Berger, 292

Berman, 28, 40, 53, 145, 170, 200, 202, 290, 291, 433, 434, 436, 463, 521, 525, 546, 577, 585

Bernstein, 45, 50, 56, 68, 92, 152, 301, 308

Bertensky, 144

Betlzer, 575

Betzer, 129

Bialik, 127, 152, 188, 192, 280, 292, 416, 419, 476

Bidnick, 551, 562, 565

Bidnik, 414, 546

Bierbrier, 314

Bik, 185, 678

Bikel, 479

Bilenkis, 512

Bin Nun, 462

Bitensky, 145, 149

Bitinsky, 488

Blank, 37, 40, 49, 51, 53, 58, 59, 66, 86, 92, 165, 200, 203, 204, 228, 234, 305, 307, 321, 405, 474, 512, 513, 519, 520, 562, 563, 587

Blei, 86, 584

Bley, 152

Bloomenfeld, 68

Bock, 81

Boger, 86

Bondarov, 25, 203

Bon-Miller, 16

Boomajny, 599

Boratnik, 48

Boris, 43

Borochov, 277, 449, 575

Borovsky, 45

Borsotzky, 166, 580

Bortnik, 476, 635

Bregman, 564

Brodsky, 22, 166, 260, 487

Broitman, 546, 565

Bromberg, 564, 575

Bronfman, 147, 167, 246, 250, 251, 252, 487, 528, 529, 573

Bronstein, 57, 425, 490, 553

Broun, 574

Brust, 237, 238

Buchbinder, 47, 50, 474, 576

Buckstein, 147, 578

Burris, 574, 598

Burs, 200

Burstein, 248, 530

Butzlin, 583

Butzlnis, 583

C

Capusta, 551

Carmel, 338, 363, 412, 484, 549, 550, 565, 584

CARMEL, 550

Carmi, 153, 614

Celnik, 561

Chacham, 562

Chalik, 643

Chaplick, 565, 566

Chaplik, 22, 43, 387, 391, 392, 418, 487, 506, 511, 525, 642, 644

CHAPLIK, 389, 625

Chasin, 449, 511, 512

Chazkelevich, 561

Chirelis, 247
Cholodenko, 562
Chrush, 561
Chubruncher, 615
Chulak, 27, 355
Cohen, 29, 50, 92, 290, 301, 308, 518, 519, 657, 658
Cooperman, 529

D

Daniel, 298
Darbrimediker, 25, 55, 179, 252, 592, 595
Darom, 193, 346, 503
Davideyev, 12
Davidi, 345, 484, 551
Davidit, 341, 345, 484, 551, 567
Davidovich, 341, 551, 567
Dayan, 22, 33, 55, 82, 306, 345, 470, 481, 487
Delmetzky, 254
Derbaremdiker, 509, 510, 518, 519, 520
Derbarmdliker, 405
Diarde, 367, 425, 472
Dikler, 353
Dimant, 589, 590
Dinovitzer, 678
Dizengoff, 272, 307, 308, 312, 328
Dobserer, 32
Doliner, 200, 203
Dorfman, 165
Dorino, 482
Dory, 276
Dostrovsky, 276
Drabmridiker, 153
Drahelis, 200
Drebrimdiker, 278
Drobetsky, 371, 374, 508, 521, 588, 679
Duborsky, 145

Dubosarsky, 564
Dubossarsky, 14, 200, 202
Dukler, 166
Dushman, 313
Dvoretsky, 679
Dwoskin, 507

E

EDELSHTEIN, 669
Efrati, 3, 153, 204, 216, 233, 253, 431, 436, 456, 487, 525, 571
Efroni, 151
Eidelman, 153, 168, 204, 413, 414, 418, 571
Elkayam, 345
Epstein, 321
Etlis, 144, 145, 152, 153, 358, 488

F

Faerman, 564
Fain, 549
FANER, 672
Fanish, 64
Fanitch, 482
Farkonsky, 48
Feffer, 200
Fein, 37, 57, 144, 200, 202, 288, 293, 328, 424, 433, 434, 488, 525, 527, 554, 559, 565, 566
Feldman, 201, 489
Fenitch, 42, 57
Ferdman, 511, 512
Feuer, 638
Fichman, 89, 185, 351
Fielderman, 540, 541
Figler, 200
Fine, 554, 556, 566
Finehertz, 508

Finke, 520

Finkel, 520

Finkelshtein, 103, 216, 217, 247

Finkelstein, 409, 529

Firshtenberg, 64, 204, 442

Fishbein, 200

Fisher, 146

Fishezon, 13

Fishman, 21, 81, 82, 192, 265, 418, 435

Fishov, 247, 510, 529, 556

Fistrov, 483, 486, 508, 510, 518, 519, 520, 521, 525

Flavish, 147, 166

Flexer, 103

Forman, 546

Frank, 151, 153, 165, 166, 636

Friedgidler, 168

Friedman, 166, 417

Frug, 487, 568

Furman, 549, 562, 564

Fustan, 91, 92, 146, 165, 203, 290, 421, 435, 474, 476, 488, 489

Fustman, 40, 52, 59, 147, 200

G

Galperin, 241

Gamburd, 320, 419

Gamburger, 32

Gamulka, 1, 4, 61, 62, 72, 74, 77, 80, 86, 89, 93, 96, 111, 114, 116, 136, 139, 143, 144, 146, 149, 151, 157, 160, 165, 170, 179, 182, 195, 197, 200, 203, 204, 207, 209, 211, 214, 216, 234, 236, 237, 241, 246, 254, 257, 269, 272, 274, 276, 278, 280, 281, 284, 287, 290, 292, 295, 299, 301, 303, 305, 307, 311, 314, 317, 319, 320, 326, 332, 335, 338, 341, 345, 347, 348, 351, 352, 360, 371, 375, 377, 379, 381, 385, 387, 393, 396, 398, 400, 412, 433, 466, 507, 523, 570

Garfield, 415, 419, 420, 428, 441, 473, 478, 480, 539, 545, 546, 549, 556, 563, 564

Geisser, 409

Geker, 634

Gelfand, 363, 407

Gelfenbein, 511, 512

Gendelman, 142, 242

Gendelman-Segal, 552

Gershkovitz, 82

Gershom, 67

Gerstein, 584

Gilead, 293, 589

GILIK, 625, 642

Gingis, 245

Ginsburg, 545

Ginton, 549

Giterman, 248, 437, 530

Glantz, 177, 255, 321, 363, 407, 408, 421, 525

Glanz, 562

Glass, 34, 143, 314, 315, 316, 405, 425, 431, 437, 444, 450, 473, 476, 563, 564, 589

Gödel, 168

Gogol, 6, 7, 51, 52, 484, 511, 568

Gold, 409, 481, 482, 486, 487, 561

Goldberg, 200

Goldenberg, 508

Goldenfeld, 49

Goldfaden, 13, 363, 483

Goldfarb, 200, 321, 414, 453, 488, 562

Goldins, 552

Goldis, 232

Goldmacher, 167, 247, 248, 530

Goldmacht, 529

Goldman, 339, 551, 586

Goldstein, 408, 486

Goldstein–Kaniverlatski, 486

Goligorsky, 46
Golris, 412
Gordon, 105, 106
Gorenstein, 546, 551, 561, 565
Gorin, 142, 293, 406, 557
Gorman, 407
Gornshtein, 588
Gorodensky, 63
Gorodetzky, 67
Gottesman, 203, 567
Granovsky, 145, 488
Gratzenberg, 327
Grebet, 166, 167, 168
Greenbaum, 525
Greenberg, 44, 51, 52, 96, 143, 201, 303, 473, 475, 503, 562, 587
Grinberg, 241, 242, 245, 421
Grinboim, 292, 301
Grinholtz, 632
Groisman, 511
Gur, 267, 377
Gurfel, 29, 142, 441, 442, 450, 457, 556, 562
Gurfeld, 404
Gurfild, 563
Gurfinkel, 145, 437, 488
Gurman, 362
Gutov, 144, 200
Gutskozek, 168

H

Haam, 33, 318, 416
Haber, 345
Haham, 37, 46, 51, 327, 405, 416
Haikel, 407
Hain, 482
Halevy, 185, 423
Halperin, 136, 242

Hameiri, 296, 298
Hamlis, 602
Haness, 27, 172, 260
Hanger, 172
Harizi, 17
Harushtch, 409
Hatzkelevitch, 16, 24
Hatzkelevitz, 152
Hayat, 142, 165, 400, 407, 486, 489, 500, 606, 607, 615
Hayman, 192
Hazan, 593
Hazanovich, 121, 125
Hazin, 82, 605, 646
Hazin-Kutcher, 603
Hein, 40
Helfand, 678
Herzl, 33, 74, 75, 76, 211, 212, 362, 435, 436, 675
Herzog, 192
Heshel, 460
Hibner, 501
Hochberg, 27
Hochman, 168, 247, 529, 593, 594, 657, 658
Holdonka, 33, 34, 50, 51, 405
Holodenko, 62, 66, 67, 69, 70, 73, 116, 117, 121, 281, 282, 283, 290, 321, 323, 466, 467, 474, 482
HORFEL, 441
Horodetzky, 151, 154, 155
Horovitz, 165
Horvitz, 166, 167, 188
Hrushtesh, 481
Huberman, 111, 112
Humenik, 678

I

IMAS, 632
Immanuel, 608, 609
Immes, 26, 40, 42, 43, 46, 51, 60, 65, 70, 71, 200, 203, 236, 599
Itzkovich, 247, 248
Itzkovitch, 529, 530

J

Jabotinsky, 290, 518
Jagodzinski, 489

K

Kahana, 509, 510
Kahanovitch, 45
Kaiser, 24, 111
Kalechnik Bercovitch, 678
Kamelis, 167, 168, 200
Kaminker, 623
Kaminska, 288
Kaminsky, 475
Kaniberlatzkaya, 561
Kaniverlatski, 483, 486
Kaniverlatzky, 409
Kanter, 442
Kapusta, 165, 659
KAPUSTA, 669
Kardonsky, 573
Karp, 1, 3, 240
Karuk, 594
Kasp, 50, 309, 310
Katz, 193, 612, 613
Katzap, 247, 530
Katzenleson, 168
Kaushansky, 88, 102, 149, 154, 155, 168, 285, 435, 450, 468, 508, 509, 510, 647, 652, 653
Kaushensky, 144
Kendzshersky, 449, 450
Kersel, 192
Kesselman, 56
Khain, 203, 284, 285
Kharker, 171
Khatzkelevich, 489
Kilimnik, 408, 678
Kimayev, 609
Kiner, 512
Kipnis, 200, 363
KIRSHNER, 648
Kishinevsky, 146, 413, 414, 423, 469, 517, 525
Kishinovsky, 46, 48, 166, 242, 584, 649, 650, 651
Kishon, 581, 650, 651, 652, 653
KISHON, 668
Kitzis, 594
Klarman, 168
Klatchkin, 298
Klavenski, 152, 201
Klayman, 552
Kleiman, 142, 412
Klein, 168
Kleiner, 409
Kleinman, 105
Kleitman, 145, 147, 200, 488
Kleyman, 374
Kliatz, 546
Klibansky, 653, 654
Klotz-Gorenstein, 561
Kochuk, 247, 248
Kofler, 541
Kofman, 241
Kogan, 37, 50, 51, 53, 88, 145, 166, 200, 203, 236, 283, 290, 291, 292, 321, 405, 408, 437, 467, 474, 489, 507, 510, 525, 562, 563, 564, 657, 658

Kolker, 32, 34, 203, 405
Kolochnick, 561
Kolpekoshi, 25
Kook, 23, 192, 396, 426, 502, 503, 576
Koonstein, 56
Koplevatsky, 510
Korn, 395, 502, 503, 525, 544
Kornfeld, 551
Koussevitzky, 363
Krachevsky, 311, 312
Kradonsky, 329
Krajevsky, 646
Kramer, 417
Kraposter, 655
Krasik, 510
Krasilchik, 561
Krasiltchik, 56, 408, 483, 486
Krasiltzik, 43
Krasnopolsky, 525
Krasnov, 200, 508, 509, 510
Krassik, 153
Krassilover, 31, 365, 368, 369, 370, 615, 651
Krassnolov, 62, 200
Kratchevsky, 49, 51, 57
Kreimerman, 200
Kreisin, 151
Kreitzman, 34, 57, 405
Kremon, 564
Kreposter, 406, 409, 415
Kritzman, 54
Kroscon, 242
Kruk, 381
Krutiansky, 508
Kunitzer, 177, 203
Kupershteyn, 525
Kushner, 43, 53, 55, 201
Kushnir, 328
Kutcher, 603

Kutchuk, 468, 529, 530

L

Landman, 28, 114
Landris, 8
Laski, 48
Laskin, 46
Latman, 47, 55
Lavi, 1, 3, 237, 474, 576
Lavi-Levinstein, 1, 3, 237
Lavonsky, 80, 84, 143, 200, 615
Leandres, 327, 353, 356
Lederman, 145, 379, 425, 469, 470, 472, 485, 490, 495, 496, 501, 538
Lederman–Yardor, 166, 168
Leiderman, 569
Leiman, 257
Lerman, 553, 557, 565, 621
Lerner, 202, 513
Lev, 8, 54, 615
Levi, 532
Levin, 193, 304
Levinsky, 192
Levinson, 245
Levinstein, 3, 43, 47, 668
Levitt, 244, 468, 591
Levkovitch, 474, 576
Levni, 152, 654
Levonsky, 618
Levontin, 76
Levy, 503, 615
Lewinsky, 404
Libman, 545
Lieder, 213
Liev, 45
Lifshin, 617

Lifshitz, 8, 34, 37, 51, 55, 307, 308, 309, 310, 476, 486, 561
Lifshitz-Kasp, 51
Likes, 638
Linevsky, 32
Liptzin, 425, 569
Litman, 13
Littman, 482
Litvin, 606
Lonievsky, 100, 142, 320, 615, 616
Looz, 568
Luboshitzky, 185, 187
Lvovsky, 88, 102, 200

M

Machneimy, 116, 117, 283
Maherson, 66
Maimon, 192, 418, 435, 502, 503
Makhelis, 200
Malamud, 160, 620
Mandel, 43
Mandelstam, 65
Manger, 427
Manic, 379
Manik, 425, 470, 472, 485, 490, 491, 492, 494, 495, 496, 501, 538, 568, 569
Manus, 146, 452, 489, 619
Marculescu, 239
Markman, 416, 557
MARKMAN, 621
Marmis, 573
Maslyansky, 304
Meder, 318
Meir, 250, 531
Meizel, 120, 123
Melamed, 444
Melech, 59

Merisis, 242
Merlin, 621, 622
Mesonsnic, 561
Miller, 62, 70, 533, 619
Minkovsky, 414
MIntz, 237
Mironiarsky, 619
Mironinsky, 84
Misonzshnik, 43, 200, 362, 364
Mitelman, 168
Mocher Seforim, 170, 377
Molodovsky, 568
Mordekovitch, 511
Morgenstern, 184, 624
Moss, 317
Mozgovsky, 579
Mulman, 47, 48, 56, 200, 203, 599

N

Nafah, 82
Natani, 328
Natanzon, 40, 51, 52, 86, 200, 214, 215, 274, 275, 328
Nimover, 414, 419
Nisanov, 134
Nissenbaum, 560
Nissenboim, 9, 10, 42, 45, 64, 66, 67, 68, 69, 183, 200, 276, 277, 280, 413, 414, 415, 626, 679
Noichovitz, 248
Noikhovitch, 508, 530
Nordau, 21, 265, 266
Nutov, 508, 510, 520

O

Olaf, 363

Orentlicher, 594
Orlinsky, 202, 424, 554, 566
Oshan, 56, 166, 437
Otoshansky, 234
Otzkovsky, 570, 571

P

Pagis, 43, 46, 525
Panish, 561
Panitch, 486
Pardis, 637
PARDIS, 665
Paschan, 639, 640
Pastelnikov, 201
Pasternak, 43, 48, 165
Peretz, 35, 140, 166, 190, 437, 520, 654
Perla, 192
Perlman, 42, 444
Perlmutter, 307
Persis, 168
Pertchuk, 486, 487
Pertziuk, 408
Petrov, 12, 45, 200
Petrushka, 501
Piker, 105
Pinko, 154, 155, 157
Pinless, 615
Pinsker, 287, 308
Pinsky, 520
Pisterov, 142, 201, 321, 416, 435, 468
Pistrova, 100, 285, 408
Pistrow, 564
Polsky, 165, 168
Poronchik, 151, 200
Postelnik, 35, 143, 404
Postman, 53, 86
Potelis, 482

Prakansky, 9, 574
Pravis, 147
Projensky, 35, 143
Prokopetz, 234
Promishlianer, 44
Prozhansky, 16, 287, 288, 289, 404, 405, 437, 450, 473, 475, 476, 478
Prozhshansky, 420, 431
Pruzhansky, 563
Pruzhan-sky, 564
Pustan, 12, 321, 408

R

Rabalsky, 303
Rabinovich, 559, 564
RABINOVICH, 663
Rabinovitch, 8, 34, 37, 46, 51, 66, 70, 200, 409, 474, 476, 498, 576, 607, 610
Raday, 170
Radi, 202, 302
Radiboim, 241
Raines, 74, 75
Rampel, 55
Ranoman, 203
Raphael, 193, 395, 502, 503
Raptor, 615
Rashkovsky, 511, 512
Raviv, 245, 320, 651
Ravkai, 437
Ravotsky, 6, 450
Rebnitzky, 188, 192
REDER, 668
Reichman, 417
Reifman, 168
Reinoman, 403
Remez, 192
Resnik, 511, 512, 525

Reznik, 43, 153, 166, 168, 660, 662, 664, 666, 667
Reznikov, 293, 317, 328, 366, 406, 420, 557
Rivkin, 366, 367
Rivlin, 51, 200, 290, 295
Rodnitsky, 294
Roey, 193
Roit, 601
Roitman, 45, 80, 255, 363
ROSENSHEIN, 634
Rosenthal, 518
Rotberg, 618
Rotenberg, 673
Rotfarb, 84
Roth, 546
Rothschild, 76, 171, 462
Rotman, 142
Rovner, 311
Rovshavsky, 165, 241
Rozenboim, 272
Rozenhaft, 228
Rozlovsky, 665
Rubashevsky, 92, 489
Rubashky, 147, 242
Rubin, 437
Rudshavsky, 244
Ruvinsky, 145
Rynewman, 35, 45

S

Saifer, 633
Saltonovitch, 47, 173
Sapir, 203
Sautzky, 166, 167
Schachanovsky, 561
Schachnovsky, 552
Schechter, 160, 421
Schiff, 586
Schmaltz, 219, 220, 226, 468, 509, 510, 669, 670
Schreibman, 487
Schrybman, 202, 352, 409
Schultz, 168
Schwartz, 147, 525
Schwartzman, 6, 38, 43, 44, 47, 85, 92, 93, 98, 104, 106, 136, 137, 139, 141, 142, 145, 182, 200, 234, 243, 279, 280, 292, 293, 294, 295, 296, 317, 320, 321, 322, 327, 328, 331, 332, 362, 363, 364, 366, 367, 399, 405, 406, 407, 408, 419, 420, 423, 425, 450, 481, 486, 488, 533, 588, 610, 622
Schwartzman Merlin, 621
Segal, 136, 534
Seiver, 566, 568
Seltzer, 200
Sever, 22, 23, 40, 151, 152, 153, 182, 185, 193, 255, 294, 297, 318, 347, 352, 360, 380, 387, 393, 395, 396, 404, 501, 502, 503, 504, 576, 616, 624, 677
SEVER, 624
Shagansky, 573
Shaikovitch, 406
Shakhnovski, 16
Shalom Aleichem, 19, 35, 140, 156, 166, 198, 370
Shampansky, 437
Shapira, 385
Shapiro, 596
Shaposhnik, 328, 488, 510, 670
Shaposnick, 9, 26, 142, 147, 152, 153, 166, 200, 203, 252, 417, 584
Sharett, 591
Sharira, 389
Shariv, 202
Shatzky, 185

Shazar, 182, 192, 344, 414, 480
Shchanovsky, 44, 68, 408
Shechtman, 507
Shefi, 152, 153
SHEFI, 671
Sheinberg, 594
Sheinfeld, 242
Sheinkin, 609
Shenker, 476, 564
Sherman, 450
Shertock, 591
Sheynkar, 437, 450, 478
Shinkar, 511
Shitman, 200
Shivel, 64
Shkhanovsky, 311
SHLIOMOV, 672
Shmishelevitz, 203
Shmulevitch, 468, 509
Shneerson, 564
Shneirson, 28, 49, 200
Shneyerson, 525
Shochat, 495
Shohet, 417, 418, 425, 584
Shotman, 508
Shousterman, 58
Shpigel, 221
Shpor, 522
Shprintzak, 422, 525
Shreibman, 24, 43, 46, 48, 55, 77, 79, 93, 423
Shrybman, 335, 336
Shteinberg, 363
Shteiner, 98, 202, 332, 335, 673
Shteiner Margolit, 675
Shtiperlman, 409
Shtopelmn, 245
Shtratman, 409
Shufman, 316, 476, 576

Shumer, 35
Shuster, 143, 247, 419, 529, 615
Shvidkey, 151, 153, 154, 155, 156
Shwartz, 668
Shwartzman, 557, 561
Shwartzmann, 558
Shwarzbard, 557, 558
Sigler, 594
Sirkas, 634
Sirkis, 43, 46, 54, 615, 634, 635
Sirota, 200
Skorepedsky, 6
Skvirsky, 321
Slatnovitz, 168
Slepoy, 508, 525
Slipo, 610
Smirnov, 57
Sobel, 47, 48, 58, 404, 437
Sobol, 234, 450, 478
Sofer, 140, 295, 297, 298, 330, 374, 425, 627, 633
Sokolov, 33, 57, 519
SOLOMON, 628
SOLOMONOVICH, 629
Soltanovich, 508
Sperling, 564
Spiegel, 147
Spivak, 241
Spooner, 165
Stein, 409, 482
Steinbeck, 628
Steinberg, 34, 37, 89, 420, 479, 678
Steiner, 43, 44, 139, 179, 207, 209, 211, 481
Steiner-Faigenbaum, 136
Steinman, 437
Steinmetz, 552
Stern, 49
Sternberg, 228, 479

Sternson, 487

Stoliar, 46, 48, 101, 415

Stutchkov, 501

Sudit, 26, 27, 43, 46, 55, 203, 247, 405, 511, 529, 565, 630, 631, 632

Sultan, 42

Sunis, 33

Sverdik, 22, 49, 403

Sverdlick, 566

Sverdlik, 144, 146, 147, 151, 152, 165, 166, 191, 193, 200, 321, 393, 396, 397, 404, 487, 501, 525, 546, 623, 626, 644, 670

SVERDLIK, 625, 626

Svredik, 40

T

Tabachnik, 546

Talmazer, 487

Tamari, 1

Taxir, 511

TAXIR, 632

Tchernikhovsky, 152

Tepper, 84

Terer–Drobetsky, 371, 372

Tilis, 153, 200, 482

Tinkelman, 142

Tiomkin, 6, 8, 9, 10, 54, 310, 330, 403, 596, 607, 608, 609, 615, 621

Tiomkina, 330

Titiner, 241

Tkatch, 407

Toibman, 257, 269

Tomshopolsky, 166, 168

Tomshpolsky, 245

Trinchka, 145

Trumpeldor, 151, 152, 165, 474, 576

Tsakhoval, 293, 296, 423, 425

Tsap, 186

Tselnik, 641

Tserliuk, 488

Tsirelson, 230, 421, 423, 425

Tulchiner, 82, 203, 403, 417

Tulchinsky, 600

Tzahoval, 328

Tzantziper, 272

Tzechoval, 569

Tzechoval, 553

Tzehoval, 374

Tzehovel, 140, 375, 376, 377, 406

Tzirelis, 529

U

Umansky, 162

V

Vanderberg, 45

Vardi, 142, 437

Vasiatzky, 144

Veinman, 153, 591

Veinshteyn, 326

Veintraub, 664

Veisgendler, 626

Veizgendler, 525

Vilensky, 201

Vineshneker, 9, 40, 47, 306

Vinitsky, 11, 228

Visliv, 165, 168

Vodoboz, 37, 166, 203, 416

Vodovetz, 434

Vodovoz, 562

Volovetz, 27, 48, 468, 509, 510, 590, 598, 653

Vunderbar, 203

W

Warshavsky, 408

Weiser, 43, 46, 140, 326, 327, 508

Weiser-Boris, 46

Weisman, 41

Weiss, 482

Weisser, 54, 292, 296, 405, 412, 552, 573, 615

Weissman, 55, 245

Wertheim, 19, 20, 21, 22, 37, 41, 52, 53, 54, 59, 61, 70, 74, 75, 82, 111, 112, 113, 143, 170, 171, 175, 176, 201, 203, 249, 252, 257, 262, 263, 264, 268, 269, 270, 293, 301, 303, 321, 328, 330, 365, 381, 382, 383, 385, 386, 413, 418, 420, 421, 424, 425, 426, 434, 435, 436, 438, 453, 458, 460, 465, 473, 475, 487, 512, 518, 519, 520, 523, 524, 525, 530, 554, 555, 562, 567, 595, 596, 597, 605, 615, 638, 643, 669, 679

Winsaft, 565

Y

Yaakovitz, 320

Yadin, 567

Yakhinson, 518

Yanishevsky, 200

Yankelevich, 140

Yanovsky, 596

Yaroslavsky, 145, 319, 488

Yasky, 564

Yassky, 552, 553

Yatom, 165, 203, 487, 525, 610, 611, 612

Yehoash, 501

Yoeli, 28

Yonatan, 257, 269, 283, 291, 436, 466

Yotam, 22

Z

Zahoval, 202

Zaidman, 47, 56

Zaik, 153, 154, 155

Zakai, 192, 395, 502

Zaslavsky, 415

Zerubbabel, 449

Zhabotinsky, 146, 200, 416

Zhakovskaya, 40

Zifshtein, 512, 513

Zifshteyn, 245

Zigberman, 144, 146, 168, 200, 403, 488, 489, 600, 601

Zigelboim, 321, 328

Zilberman, 651

Zinberg, 501

Zinger, 599

Zingerman, 165

Zipstein, 49, 147, 148

Zmora, 241

Zoberman, 374

Zufshteyn, 242

Zukerman, 623, 645

Zweit, 142

www.ingramcontent.com/pod-product-compliance
Lightning Source LLC
Chambersburg PA
CBHW081421160426
42814CB00039B/269